UNIVERSITY TREATISE SERIES

AN INTRODUCTION TO TAX LAW AND POLICY

Yoseph M. Edrey
Dean and Professor of Law (Emeritus)
Haifa University

Reuven S. Avi-Yonah
Irwin I. Cohn Professor of Law
University of Michigan

FOUNDATION PRESS

The publisher is not engaged in rendering legal or other professional advice, and this publication is not a substitute for the advice of an attorney. If you require legal or other expert advice, you should seek the services of a competent attorney or other professional.

860 Blue Gentian Road, Suite 350
Eagan, MN 55121
1-877-888-1330

Printed in the United States of America

ISBN: 978-1-63659-517-7

To Bella, who walks with me in the wilderness,
Yael, Eliav, Tamar, and Yuval.

Acknowledgments

In 1979, I first arrived to the USA as a post-doctorate fellow at Penn Law school. That was the beginning of a long and most fruitful exchange of ideas and research with colleagues in the USA. Since then, I have visited American law schools, almost every year, as a Scholar in Residence and a visiting professor of law.

Honestly, I am thrilled by the wonderful welcome I have enjoyed from the many colleagues and friends who introduced me to the intricate and fascinating labyrinth of the American tax system. The encouragement, deep friendships and enthusiastic desire to help me, both professionally and personally move me to this day. Each visit expanded the circle of personal friends and supportive colleagues. There is no doubt in my mind that a large part of the knowledge and insights I have accumulated and developed over almost fifty years in the fascinating fields of tax law, tax policy, and public finance originates from the amazing human capital I have met. I am deeply and sincerely indebted and grateful to a long list of all those wonderful friends and colleagues, some of whom are no longer with us, and to them, and many others, I owe this gratitude:

Howard Abrams, Norman Abrams, Larry Alexander, Bill Andrews, Reuven Avi-Yonah, Lucian A. Bebchuk, Ruth Bader-Ginsburg, Sheril Bloch, Keren Brown, Tom Buergenthal, Burt Cain, Guido Calabresi, Evan H. Caminker, Richard Doernberg, Allen Dershowitz, David Epstein, Richard Friedman, Steve Goldstien, Frank Goodman, Claudio Grossman, Charles Gustafson, Henry Hansmann, Dan Halprin, Al Johnson, Doug Kahn, Bill Klein, Sheldon Krantz, Burt Lazarow, Peter Liacouras, Kyle Logue, Reimann Mathias, Christopher McCrudden, Elliot Milstein, Frances Olson, Jeff Pennell, Bob Peroni, Andy Pike, Richard Pugh , H. David Rosenbloom, John Sexton, Dan Shaviro, Maimon Shwartzschild, Herman Shwartz, Bruno Simma, Joel Slemord, Rodney Smith, Lester Snyder, Janet Spragens, Roger Trangsrud, Al Warren, Mike Young.

Yoseph M. Edrey, 2022

I thank Mr. Guy Halberthal for his excellence research assistance.

Prof. Avi-Yonah would like to thank Anastasia Bruss, Patrick Fraser and Madeline Landau for excellent editing and Adam Girts for outstanding research assistance.

Foreword

What brought one of the leading figures of the American Revolution to compare death and taxes"? (Both are defiantly certain). Why are taxes a vital tool in any country, whether a democracy or a non-democratic political entity? Is a tax in a democracy distinguishable from the harsh description given by Samuel the prophet during the biblical era?:

> *This will be the manner of the king that shall reign over you: he will take your sons, and appoint them unto him, ... And he will take your daughters to be perfumers, and to be cooks, and to be bakers. And he will take your fields, and your vineyards, and your olive-yards, even the best of them, and give them to his servants. And he will take the tenth of your seed, and of your vineyards, ... And he will take your menservants, and your maid-servants, and your goodliest young men, and your asses, and put them to his work. He will take the tenth of your flocks; and ye shall be his servants. And ye shall cry out in that day because of your king whom ye shall have chosen over you.*

To what extent is such a description of taxation rooted in general public perceptions of any tax, even during the modern era, as a punishment or fine and not as a noble expression of living together and financing our common social, economic, national and even international goals?

Indeed, we have gone quite a long way since the biblical era. In modern times, where the sovereign—the people—elects the rulers, and human rights are recognized, respected and protected by democratic governments, taxes (117) should be regarded in a different way, i.e. as the economic expression of the Social Contract. And yet, the Western democracies are still looking for the most appropriate tax system that complies with the basic concept of a liberal democratic system.

Hence, we shall ask some basic questions: What is a "tax", [p. 21] and what are other mandatory payments [p. 36] in a modern democratic state? Why do we have to pay taxes to our government? When will a tax be regarded as a confiscatory measure? When should a mandatory payment to the government be treated as an economic measure aimed to correct market failures caused by negative externalities by shifting their cost to the wrongdoers [pp. 13, 36, 53–54]? Moreover, when should those payments to the government be treated as taxes, which should be seen as a fair and reasonable price for public goods and services (101) that we consent to pay to the elected government? What functions does taxation serve? Is Tax an accepted profit-sharing-mechanism between all the parties who invest social, human and financial capital in the income producing process? Or it is also a redistributive tool? Are there any limitations on the power to tax? Is it an acceptable assumption that the tax reduces our personal or aggregate welfare? Can we assure that the tax is levied by the Congress "to pay the Debts and provide for the common Defense and general Welfare of the United States", as the Constitution orders? Are there any accepted requirements for a good tax system? What are the criteria for fairness in taxation? When can we agree that the tax is levied in accordance with the principle of equality? Efficiency? Does the legislature have the power to lay a discriminatory tax? Is tax legislation subject to constitutional judicial review (70)? Is there a trade-off between equality and efficiency? If so, does the tax system reach the optimal balance between equality and efficiency? Or, as some theoretical and empirical research indicates lately, there is no contradiction between a certain degree of equality and efficiency, since equality increases efficiency? What are the sources of the tax law? Is economic ability a sensible measurement of the benefit that the taxpayers receive from the government? Why is the most common personal tax levied on income? What is income (58)? What are capital gains (18)? What is value added (145)? What is consumption (26)? What are property and net wealth (86)? What turns a transaction into a business activity versus a passive investment, or even a personal, nontaxable behavior? Why does our understanding of the meaning of interest (64) help us to analyze complicated tax problems? Why do governments use tax reliefs and incentives? Do they achieve their goals? How bad is tax avoidance and aggressive tax planning? Who really gains and what is the social loss from such measures? Who are the forces that are pushing for tax reductions? Are the policymakers, the courts and the lawyers equipped with the necessary knowledge when asked to interpret tax provisions?

All these questions are examples of issues that should be discussed in any public, social, political or legal debate, which deals with national budgets, public finance, social policy, or tax legislation. On the one hand, tax is the most concrete economic expression of the social contract—it is the price for the public goods and services (101) we receive under the social contract, which we entered into in order to enhance our aggregate and personal wellbeing. On the other hand, some may argue that taxes, almost by definition, confiscate our property, distort our optimal behavior, and decrease our welfare.

Tax Avoidance and even Tax Evasion entail significant consequences for the domestic and global social-economic structures. As has become quite clear lately, unfair tax systems—de jure or de facto—enhance social gaps, harm the economic efficiency, erode social solidarity, and undermine the structure of society. International tax planning raises its own problems as long as its purpose is to produce double non-taxation, which undermines Avi-Yonah's "single tax" principle, up to the level that "radically undermine[s] the meritocratic values on which democratic societies are based" (T. Piketty, 2014). Indeed, until recently, most Western governments demonstrated either indifference or helplessness while dealing with aggressive tax planning. Not any longer. The U.S. government initiated some new measures (e.g. "**Foreign Account Tax Compliance Act**—"FATCA"). The OECD has published its reports regarding the battle against "**Base Erosion Profits Shifting**—BEPS", offering some measures that should be taken by governments and international organizations in order to cope with tax avoidance and evasion in traditional and digital business activities. The communication and internet revolution has led to aggressive tax planning by multinational corporations—mostly American ones—that have managed to manipulate their place of residence and the location that they generate income. These companies are able to re-route their profits through low tax jurisdictions. The immediate result of international tax evasion is a significant drop in government tax revenues. Such a loss of revenue is leading to the undermining of democratic regimes around the world. It prevents governments from investing in welfare, health, education, and educational programs. The inevitable result is an increase in social gaps and poverty.

The international response to the phenomenon of international tax planning and avoidance was delayed until the end of the first decade of the 21th century [pp. 232, 60]. The OECD, encouraged by the American administration, initiated an international cooperation. Hence a hundred and thirty-six countries agreed to enforce a corporate tax rate of at least 15% and a fairer system of tax regime. Time will tell whether this initiative will materialize or if capital owners and interest groups will succeed to block it.

One of the main reasons for the international effort to cope with tax avoidance through international agreements stems from economic findings that were published at the beginning of the current century. As discussed below [p. 95], some leading economists (such as Atkinson, Stiglitz, Sachs, Piketty, Ostry, and others) have published some **empirical data**, indicating the inefficiency of social gaps, poverty and inequality. No doubt, these are fascinating developments in what we consider to be the first chapter of the first scene of the social-economic revolution that the Western world is facing in the near future.

The purpose of this book is to offer an accurate, concentrated, and yet integrated, interdisciplinary, and comprehensive discussion of the modern theory of taxation; and to provide the readers an analytical and systematical discussion of the above questions. It is designed for a diverse audience: lawyers and judges; the legislature and policymakers; economists, accountants, and financiers; political scientists; academics and students of these disciplines, and for any member of our community who is interested in learning about the decision-making processes of our society, especially in matters of fiscal policy (48), the annual national budget and tax laws. In addition, the book seeks to reveal to the public the true, sometimes ugly or even nasty, meaning of the current tax system and its contribution to hurting the common citizen and increasing the social gaps that ultimately also undermine sustainable economic growth; and to increase public recognition/awareness that some elected politicians often hide their true intentions—to help their donors—through populist and misleading rhetoric, and tax legislation—which is unnecessarily and probably intentionally complicated—is an effective means for this deception.

The book is based on our teaching and research activity for the last forty years, in the U.S., Europe and Israel in various areas of the legal systems, including welfare law, tax (individual, corporate, international) law, transnational taxation, fiscal legislation, public finance, tax policy, and the economic aspects of constitutional law (22). We owe all our students a debt for their patience and the inspiration they provided during all these years.

Introduction

1. OBJECTIVES

The book has a dual purpose: the social one mentioned above [p. ix], and a professional purpose, to present to the readers, in a simple and comprehensible manner, the general principles and theories of tax system and to introduce the current U.S. income tax system in an inclusive and comprehensive study and critical analysis. This presentation is based on the following goals:

A. To provide readers with basic insights and knowledge of the essence of taxation (117), its justification, and its role in a democratic society. Once we agreed to live together, taxation has become an inevitable part of our public and social lives. Taxation plays a central role in social, political, economic, and philosophical issues. Taxation, as Justice Oliver Wendell Holmes indicated, is the price we pay for living in a civilized society. Taxation reflects the economic aspects of the Social Contract. It should cause our private and national welfare to increase only.

B. To present the relationship between tax law and the legal system; the connections of the tax system with public law—both constitutional and administrative law. This topic has been woefully neglected in the U.S., for reasons discussed below.

C. To offer a comprehensive observation of the theory of taxation by discussing its various sources. Indeed, the term tax law represents a tip of an iceberg. It signifies what we refer to as an "integration of disciplines". Hence, one of the central goals is to reveal its multiple sources: legal (public and private law) and non-legal as well, including social philosophy, social behavior, economics, public finance, accounting, and finance, just to mention a few.

D. We find that the two major sources of the theory of taxation are legal analysis and insights that have been developed in a special and unique branch of economics, known as "Public Finance". We have also found that there is a significant gap of insights and communication between both scholars and practitioners of these fields. Accordingly, another purpose is to bridge the gaps of knowledge and vocabulary between these two major fields, i.e. to expose some of the tax law's analyses to those economists who are dealing with public finance and are interested in taxation, and to introduce the basic concepts of public finance to lawyers, judges and other jurists who are interested in this field. A byproduct of such bridging may serve accountants, business managers and of course policymakers and political scientists as well.

E. To raise the readers' awareness of the personal price that each member of society has to pay through the tax system in order to enjoy the benefits of the Social Contract.

F. To provide a solid foundation of fiscal, accounting and public finance (39, 48) vocabulary, which will enable interested readers to further their studies into more advanced literature in those fields.

G. To draw a distinction between a free market economy, which is an important component of a meritocratic and democratic system, and the capitalist system, which provides political, economic, and social privileges (mostly through tax incentives) to the financial sector and its owners.

H. To reemphasize the idea that in modern times it is quite evident that there are three factors of production (45): Real/financial capital: Human Capital and Social capital; and that no significant economic activity is possible without all three.

I. To offer an analytical way of thinking about fiscal legislation and taxation. At the national-collective level, the book discusses the decision-making process behind tax legislation. At the personal level, the book offers an understanding of our economic and social decisions as individuals, firms (47), and as members of our communities.

J. To re-introduce the basic idea that from an economic point of view we all actually "suffer" from schizophrenia; As Households we make decisions regarding the level of our desired consumption (26)—current and future through saving. In order to finance the consumption, we act through firms—owners and members including investors and employees. The concept of the Firm helps us to see more clearly the way it operates and functions, who its members are, and to realize how those insights help us in understanding the income producing process, and why, how and who should be taxed.

K. To reach professionals who are engaged with tax law: Policymakers, Judges, lawyers, financiers, accountants, financial managers, businesspersons, and students. The book is supposed to provide them not only with a superficial and mechanical knowledge, but rather with a comprehensive framework, and a professional way of thinking ("tax mind"), which will enable them to substantially understand the current tax system and to follow and predict future trends and developments.

L. Another prominent goal is to foster readers' understanding of the rule of law; that any law intents to promote our welfare through the optimal balance between various social needs and interests; and that the principal meaning and purpose of living together in a community is to enhance our personal and common wellbeing and utility, to enrich and cultivate our awareness of mutual aid, support and solidarity, and the importance of human rights (22). This conclusion is not due to ethical and moral biases, but rather as a utilitarian concept that leads to a more efficient societies with a greater well-being.

M. To study how sincere and loyal the governments are to the public and if they are really committed to their only mission—to enhance the public wellbeing; To examine whether the elected government and its administration owe fidelity to an un-democratic Coalition of politicians, wealthy donors, media, and powerful groups that use subtle tactics and are responsible for the complicated and sophisticated tax legislation, which enables certain segments of the society to avoid paying their taxes according to their economic ability and the real benefit they enjoy from using social/ public capital.

2. METHODOLOGY

The book begins with basic assumptions and starting points. Then it moves onto some theoretical background and analysis of the major issues related to taxation. This part is intended to reveal the rationales, the goals of and the justifications for the modern tax system and its various sources and connection with related academic fields, which include *inter alia,* social philosophy, and a variety of economic insights and legal disciplines. The following parts, which are more practical, present the basic attributes, rules and provision ***of the domestic U.S. tax*** system. The emphasis is on individual taxation. The book does not deal directly with advanced problems of corporate and partnerships taxation. Yet through the study of the basic questions, the book provides a solid foundation to enable the readers to deal with more advanced issues. The purpose of such a methodology is to provide a holistic and comprehensive perspective, which also helps the reader solve specific and isolated problems.

In order to provide a broad knowledge of the various sources of the tax system and its structure, the book is based on an interdisciplinary approach and offers, in a friendly way, complicated analyses/problems in various disciplines.

The interdisciplinary discussion of tax law raises an almost natural assumption: that there is a built-in tension between moral and philosophical concepts on the one hand and economic analysis on the other hand. Such tension is expressed, for example, in the title of Arthur Okun's book: "Equality and Efficiency—the Big Trade-off". Hence, we should emphasize at the outset that the basic assumption that underlies the book is that there is one basic ethical principle, expressed some two thousand years ago by Hillel the Elder: "That which is despicable to you, do not do to your fellow"[1]. Once you accept this command, which we refer to as the "canon of reciprocity", all other values, ethical behaviors and even constitutional principles are analyzed according to it and based on utilitarian enquiries. Indeed, most of the arguments offered here are based on economic-utilitarian analysis rather than on mere ethical-philosophical ones, and on the "benefit principle" for tax justification. As is discussed below [pp. 90–95], utilitarian analysis that is subject to the canon of reciprocity supports both efficient and ethical outcomes.

A central question in the theory of taxation is Tax Justification. One practical approach would be to say that there is no need to justify taxation. Reality dictates that taxes are a need, a must for any organized society. They are an integral and inseparable part of any regime; they are here and they'll always stay with us. We find such an approach very much unsatisfactory in the modern democratic era. Taxes should be justified, whether they are a confiscatory measure, mandatory payment or based on consent. A careful discussion should identify several sub-questions. First, do the members of an organized society **consent** to pay taxes, or is it really a mandatory payment that we have almost no discretion, or even a choice, to pay?

We argue that the taxpayers consent to pay taxes because we all receive a full consideration from the government. Such an approach raises two separable questions. Do we agree to pay the taxes, in return for the public goods and services (101), and do we approve the amount and the quality of the consideration we receive. The latter question is basically a political one, and we hardly discuss it here. It is suffice to mention

---

1 This statement was given by Hillel the Elder as a response to an odd request of a foreigner who wanted Hillel to convert him to Judaism demanding that the whole Torah be taught to him quickly "while standing on one foot". Babylonian Talmud, Tractate Shabbat 31a. Such an approach is embedded within most of the known faiths. E.g. "In everything, do to others as you would have them to you; for this is the law and the prophets"—Jesus, Mathews 7:12; "Not one of you truly believers until you wish for others what you wish for yourself", The prophet Muhammad, Hadith. On what is termed the Golden Rule in the Religions of the World, see:

https://www.bard.edu/news/releases/pr/fstory.php?id=1447.

that the elected government's fiscal policy (48) has to be approved by the public's agents annually via the deliberations over the budget.

Under both assumptions (tax is either based on consent or is a confiscatory measure) the justification issue should be discussed for political, legal and constitutional reasons. In a democratic society the elected government owes accountability to the public, and the legislature is confined to the Constitution, its values and principles.

When dealing with tax justification, one has to realize that the overall question is of course what kind of tax are we dealing with? What is its base (Property? Net wealth? Consumption? Income? Wealth transfer?) What are its rates? Is it a proportional (99), Progressive (98), or Regressive (106) one? It is quite obvious that some taxes meet the justifications' tests/standards and some do not. The methodology we use here is that we introduce a proposed modern/contemporary model for Adam Smith's four canons of a "good tax". According to that model we examine the major known tax systems. The major examination focuses on the Federal Income tax system.

3. TWO FINAL COMMENTS ABOUT THE SUGGESTED METHOD OF READING THE BOOK

The multidisciplinary approach requires the use of a significant amount of professional terms-of-art and expressions derived from the multiple sources. Hence, a detailed alphabetical lexicon for most of the terms and expressions that are used in the book is offered at the book's appendix. Whenever a term of art is mentioned in the text, a numbered reference (in round parentheses) refers the reader to its definition or explanation within the lexicon. However, some readers will find it better to read the lexicon first, before diving into the book itself.

Since we tried to present a condensed discussion and avoid repetitions, the text contains referrals to the book pages [the page number within square brackets], that deal with or elaborate on similar issues.

Finally, a caveat: The book's structure, its methodology and conclusions are not always traditional or conventional, and not necessarily accepted by the IRS and other branches of the government that deal with tax law or by other scholars or colleagues.

Summary of Contents

Page

ACKNOWLEDGMENTS V

FOREWORD VII

INTRODUCTION XI

PART ONE. THE GENERAL THEORY OF TAXATION

CHAPTER ONE. THE COMPLEXITY OF TAX LAW, ITS SOURCES AND MEANING 3
1. The Need for Comprehensive Observation 3
2. The Constitution and Tax Laws 6

CHAPTER TWO. THE POWER TO LEVY TAXES 7
1. No Taxation Without Representation: The Public Consent 7
2. The Quality of Tax Laws and Their Adjustment to Constitutional Principles 8
3. The Requirements of a Good Tax 9
4. A Tax Should Be Certain and Not Arbitrary 9
5. Convenience of the Contributor 11
6. Efficient 12
7. Fair and Equitable 14
8. Equality and Efficiency 15
9. The Road Map 15

PART TWO. THE DEFINITION OF TAX, ITS SOURCES AND OBJECTIVES

CHAPTER THREE. WHY TAXES? 21
1. Definitions of Pure Taxes and Regulatory Mandatory Payments 21
2. Taxes as Price for Public Goods and Services 24
3. The Legal Definition 26
4. The Goals of the Tax System 27
5. TRI—Tax Incentives and Other Reliefs 31
6. Phase-Out of Tax Reliefs 35
7. Negative Tax Reliefs: Pigovian Tax Payments (PMPs) 36
8. The Importance of the Distinction Between Tax, TRIs and PMPs 36

CHAPTER FOUR. LEGAL SOURCES 39
1. Tax Legislation, Constitutional Law and the Threats to Human Rights 39
2. Administrative Law 56
3. International Law 58
4. Criminal Law 61
5. Other Branches of Law 61
6. Tax Law 61

CHAPTER FIVE. NON-LEGAL SOURCES **63**
Introduction: Tax Law and Other Disciplines 63
1. Philosophy 63
2. Economics 73
3. Conclusion of the Second Part 108

PART THREE. MAJOR TAX BASES: GENERAL VIEW

CHAPTER SIX. TAXES, AND OTHER MANDATORY PAYMENTS **113**
1. The Variety of Taxes and Mandatory Payments 113
2. One Tax Base v. Multiple Bases: Optimal Taxation and Equity 115

CHAPTER SEVEN. VALUE ADDED TAX **117**
1. Basic Principles 117
2. Operation and Illustrations 120
3. VAT—Cancelled Transaction and Refund Taxes 122
4. VAT on NPOs and Financial Institutions 123

CHAPTER EIGHT. PROPERTY AND REAL ESTATE TAX **125**

CHAPTER NINE. CONTRIBUTIONS TO NATIONAL SOCIAL SECURITY AND HEALTH INSURANCE **127**
1. The Need for Mandatory Programs: Adverse Selection 127
2. Social Security in the U.S. 128

CHAPTER TEN. TAXATION OF WEALTH TRANSFER—ESTATE, GIFT AND GENERATION SKIPPING TRANSFER TAXES **135**
1. Should Transfer Payments Be Taxed? 135
2. Should Wealth Transfer Be Taxed? 136
3. The Preferred Way to Tax Wealth Transfers 137
4. The Taxation of Wealth Transfer in the U.S. 138
5. Transfer Tax or Tax-Free Wealth Transfer? 143

CHAPTER ELEVEN. FEDERAL EXCISE AND DUTIES **145**

CHAPTER TWELVE. INCOME TAX **147**
1. Why Income Tax 147
2. Methodology: On the Appropriate Way to Discuss the General Principles of the Income Tax Code 147

PART FOUR. CHOOSING THE APPROPRIATE PERSONAL TAX BASE, ITS DEFINITION, AND ITS ATTRIBUTES
Introduction 153

CHAPTER THIRTEEN. NET WEALTH = FUTURE INCOME **155**
1. The Theoretical Merits 155
2. The Uncertainty 155
3. The Taxpayer's Convenience and Efficiency 156
4. Tax Rates 156
5. Net Wealth—Conclusion 156

AN INTRODUCTION TO TAX LAW AND POLICY

Part One

THE GENERAL THEORY OF TAXATION

Chapter One

THE COMPLEXITY OF TAX LAW, ITS SOURCES AND MEANING

The first hurdle for those who approach tax law stems from the wide and diversified range of the sources that compose the field of "Tax Law." Hence, the first part of the book discusses those legal and non-legal sources, and describes the various components of tax law, which helps us untangle the myth and, in some way, ease "tax law phobia".

In an era where courts prefer substance over form; where many support the purposive approach to statutory interpretation; and where the purpose of the legislation is constantly updated in accordance with social, geopolitical and individual conditions, values, insights and needs, it is crucial to understand the goals of tax legislation in the most comprehensive way. This is important not only for the interpretation of tax laws, but also to assist the tax legislature in reaching optimal legislation.

1. THE NEED FOR COMPREHENSIVE OBSERVATION

A. The (Risky) Use of Tax Reliefs and Incentives

One of the major reasons that the tax system tends to become complex is the fact that it is quite difficult to discover the purpose of a tax provision. Even when we identify the stated purpose, we may find that it is almost impossible to conclude whether the provision actually achieves its stated goal or if it creates an unintended outcome. Modern tax systems contain a long series of tax relieves and incentives (Hereinafter: ***TRI***) (131). At this stage, suffice to say that theoretically there should be a general tax system applied equally to all taxpayers. Once a progressive tax system (98) is accepted, all the taxpayers situated in the same position (e.g. economic ability or amount of benefit derived from public goods and services [p. 71]), are supposed to pay the same amount of taxes. As far as we know, under all the tax systems this does not happen. Politicians, decision-makers and legislators cannot resist pressure from interest groups and introduce into the tax system a significant amount of provisions that ease the tax burden on certain taxpayers or activities (and eventually add an extra burden on the rest). As is discussed below [pp. 31, 36], not all tax reliefs/tax breaks are of the same nature and justifications, yet for the sake of the discussion here, we use the general term Tax Reliefs and Incentives"—TRI (131).

The most significant problem with TRI is that they lack transparency. As opposed to the government's direct spending, which appears each year in the annual budget's deliberation and must get the approval of the public agents at the Congress every year, it is almost impossible for the public to estimate the TRI's full cost. That happens despite the introduction of the concept of Tax Expenditure Budget to the national annual budget (42); [pp. 31, 33], which requires the administration to include its estimation regarding the national cost of tax incentives within the annual budget. In addition, TRI (84, 127, 131) [pp. 3, 31] are enacted only once and they stay until the legislature finds the time and the interest to reevaluate their aims and justification. Experience teaches us that tax relieves stay within the tax code long after the need for them has expired. They create unjustified spending/wasting of the taxpayers' money and create a most significant economic distortion, inefficiency, and a problematic wealth distribution. All that happens without the public's full awareness and understanding [p. 240]. The arguments against TRI may be demonstrated with several simple examples.

1. There is a common belief that for social reasons, certain tax reliefs should be granted to lower-income families. Under Code Secs. 24 and 151, taxpayers are allowed to take tax credits (43, 125) and personal exemptions (38) for their dependents. Simple examination reveals that such exemptions and non-refundable tax credits provide the highest economic benefit to the wealthier families, and no benefit at all to those families whose income is low enough that it is subject to a zero tax rate. This is because the taxpayer's ***Tax Saving(s)*** (133) [p. 240] is equal to the amount of the exemption/deduction, multiplied by the taxpayer's marginal tax rate (74). For example, if a person's marginal tax rate is 40% and they receive an income of $2,000, this income leaves them with a tax of $800 and a net income (after-tax) of $1,200. If they are entitled to a personal exemption of $2,000, this exemption/deduction nullifies the $2,000 income; they do not owe any tax and their after-tax income goes up to $2,000 i.e. their tax saving is equal to (2,000*0.4=)$800. The same amount of $2,000 exemption/deduction produces (2,000*0=)zero benefit for a taxpayer whose marginal tax rate is zero. A similar result occurs with non-refundable tax credits (125). A careful scrutiny reveals [pp. 240–241] that tax credits should be regarded/viewed as a net/after tax amount received from the government. When a 10% marginal taxpayer is granted $150 tax credit (125), it represents a grossed-up (83) amount of (150/0.9=)$166; the same credit for a 50% marginal taxpayer, represents a gross income of (150/0.5=)$300, which is significantly higher. The point here is not whether such an outcome is desired or justified, but rather to expose the significance of the phenomenon: poor families do not enjoy those reliefs; wealthy families enjoy them very much, regardless whether the relives are granted as exemption, deduction or even tax credit. One may argue that such an outcome promotes efficiency (at the expense of equality) since any TRI (131) may serve as an incentive for poor families, who would be interested in enjoying the TRI, to increase their work supply, earn more, be able to enjoy the relief, and eventually exit the poverty circle. Such policy considerations should be revealed to the public and its agents in order to make the optimal decision, based on full information and insights. Note though, that some of the TRIs are phased-out (94) once the taxpayers' incomes reach a certain amount [p. 35].

2. To reemphasize the point that, due to their complexity, the TRI (84, 127, 131) [pp. 3, 31] can be counterproductive or defeat their purposes, we use another example: Code Sec. 163(h)(3) provides that interest payments on personal mortgages (or more precisely, payment of "qualified resident interest"), that meet the statutory requirements, are fully deductible against taxable income, despite the fact that the interest payments finance personal consumption that is part of the taxpayer's taxable income [p. 157]. We are told that the reason for this is to help poor and middle class families become homeowners. Yet a close examination reveals, once again, that this tax incentive promotes the building of expensive housing, reducing their price for those who can afford them without the government incentive, and causing the price of small apartments to rise, thereby pushing away the ability of poor families to realize the American dream. In addition such a deduction reduces the actual tax rates of the wealthy, creates a revenue loss and, as indicated long ago by Joseph Stiglitz, distorts the designated role of the banking industry: instead of

financing the business sector, the banking industry has turned to financing personal consumption.

Furthermore, the deductibility of mortgage interest brings some more undesirable results at the macro level: expansion of suburbs at the expense of the inner city; an increase of travel expenses, and more pollution on the one hand, and widening social gaps by providing more profits to contractors, their wealthier customers and lawyers. Moreover, there is no direct empirical finding that encouraging the building industry entails economic growth. On the contrary, some commentators suggest that such interest deductions created a distortion and market failure—an artificial demand—which eventually contributed significantly to the subprime economic crisis.

B. Tax Incidence—Who Bears the Tax Burden and Who Enjoys TRI

One more reason for the complexity of the tax system and the difficulties in designing it, is that there is no clear answer to the question "who bears the tax burden" (129). In the middle of the previous century, Hugh Dalton introduced his "theorem of the invariance of tax incidence". He considered tax incidence as the direct economic burden (money or money's worth) of tax on the person who ultimately pays it from an economic, rather than a legal point of view (i.e. incidence rests on the person who cannot shift the burden of the tax to any other person). As a rule, it is almost impossible to know in advance, who the unfortunate persons are who are unable to shift the tax since it depends on the price and income elasticity (41), which are calculated on too many variables. According to the theorem, the legal/statutory obligation to remit the tax payment is irrelevant from an economic point of view. Assume the government levies (or increases) a tax on corporations. X corporation might have the power/ability to shift the tax to another entity, e.g. the stockholders—by giving up some dividends; its top management—who lose some raises and bonuses; the corporate workforce—by being fired or getting salary cuts; the corporation's customers—by paying higher prices. In such a case, the corporation collects the amount of the tax from that entity and remits the tax to the government. If that entity is unable to shift the tax to another entity (customers, employees, competitors or shareholders), it actually pays the tax, though X corporation is the statutory taxpayer. Indeed, tax incidence depends on the elasticity of the income of these entities and the demand and supply (41) of the various industries' goods and services.

Furthermore, it is also difficult to know whom actually benefits from the TRI. Suppose the government decides to provide a tax relief for young mothers' earned income (e.g. an exemption of $5,000 a year). Employers are very much aware of that relief. Will they be able to shift (129) the relief to themselves by reducing the young mothers' wages, while maintaining their after tax income? The problem might be even worse. Suppose Mom and Dad are very much alike in terms of work skills. An employer hires them and is willing to pay both of them the same salary. When the new exemption has been granted only to Mom, it might be that the employer will be able to shift the relief (partially or all of it) by paying Mom a lower before-tax salary, since most of the employees are interested in "how much money gets into my bank account". As a result, both Mom and Dad bring home the same net income for a certain time. However, Dad's income before-tax is higher for severance payments, pension plans, bonuses etc. Furthermore, once the kids are grown and Mom is no longer entitled to the relief, she realizes that her net income has become lower than Dad's. One may wonder if it is possible that the good intentions of some legislatures in Western democracies to encourage mothers to increase their work supply, has contributed to the severe problem of the gender wage gap?

A similar argument applies to the right to file a joint return available for married couples [p. 305]. At first glance, this seems to benefit couples and women. Yet there is a strong argument that it encourages women to stay home and give up the desire to develop their own careers and personal ambitions.

In addition, we hardly know how much, if it all, any tax—income, consumption or property—affects our behavior. What impact does any tax have on our work supply? On current consumption or saving? Do higher tax rates reduce or increase the economic growth? These questions are discussed below [pp. 13, 83–85].

All these issues present serious challenges to the legislature and to policymakers, especially in Western democracies where tax legislation may face constitutional judicial review (70). Courts are no longer reluctant to intervene and scrutinize tax laws by constitutional standards. Accordingly, we begin our journey with a discussion about the connection between constitutional principles, general fiscal legislation, and especially, tax legislation.

2. THE CONSTITUTION AND TAX LAWS

The U.S. legal system has led most modern democracies to accept the idea that every legal discussion should begin with a constitutional framework. The government is authorized to do only what the constitution allows it to do. Limitations on the government's power have two dimensions: one formal and the other substantial. The first deals with mere authorization: Has the government been granted power to act? The latter deals with the question "how": What are the right and appropriate ways in which the government should exercise its powers according to constitutional rights, principles and interests? The government, including the Congress, has to follow some constitutional guidelines and to respect constitutional rights and interests such as human dignity, equal treatment, property rights and so on. The following chapter examines whether such constitutional principles and limitations also apply in tax legislation. Yet a caveat: in this book we draw a very definite distinction between the term TAX, and other Mandatory Payment, mainly for purposes of constitutional analysis. The meaning and the consequence of this distinction is discussed below [pp. 8, 39–55].

Chapter Two

THE POWER TO LEVY TAXES

1. NO TAXATION WITHOUT REPRESENTATION: THE PUBLIC CONSENT

The famous catchphrase "no taxation without representation," which probably symbolizes the beginning of U.S. independence, has substantial legal, constitutional and even economic significance in modern times. In a liberal society, no person is required to make any payment without consent. The fact that any tax in a democracy may be levied only by an act of the legislature—which is elected by the people to serve as the public's agent—means that the tax is the product of a collective consent to pay the price for public goods and services offered by the elected government. The original idea came from the Massachusetts legislature that proposed calling the General [colonial] Congress, which was composed of delegates from each of the colonies, to remonstrate and protest against the British Stamp Act of 1765. On October 19, 1765 that Congress announced its DECLARATION OF RIGHTS OF THE STAMP ACT CONGRESS:

> *The members of this congress, sincerely devoted. . . to His Majesty's person and government, inviolably attached to the present happy establishment of the Protestant succession, and with minds deeply impressed by a sense of the present and impending misfortunes of the British colonies on this continent. . . esteem it our indispensable duty to make the following declarations, of our humble opinions, respecting the most essential rights and liberties of the colonists, and of the grievances under which they labor, by reason of several late acts of Parliament.*
>
> *1st. That His Majesty's subjects in these colonies owe the same allegiance to the crown of Great Britain that is owing from his subjects born within the realm, and all due subordination to that august body, the Parliament of Great Britain.*
>
> *2d. That His Majesty's liege subjects in these colonies are entitled to all the inherent rights and privileges of his natural born subjects within the kingdom of Great Britain.*
>
> *3d. That it is inseparably essential to the freedom of a people, and the undoubted rights of Englishmen, that no taxes should be imposed on them, but with their own consent, given personally, or by their representatives.*
>
> *4th. That the people of these colonies are not, and from their local circumstances cannot be, represented in the House of Commons in Great Britain.*
>
> *5th. That the only representatives of the people of these colonies are persons chosen therein, by themselves; and that no taxes ever have been or can be constitutionally imposed on them but by their respective legislatures.*

This idea is integrated within the U.S. Constitution [p. 39]. In order to allow our representatives to levy taxes, the Constitution has to include a specific provision that empowers them to do so. Yet mere empowerment is not enough.

The contents of the tax (in its Constitutional meaning) ought to be accepted by the public. Based on the concept of the Social Contract, we assume that we are willing to enter into the social contract and obey the elected government only if its actions provide security (protecting our lives and property), improve our lives and enhance our welfare.

This assumption is also required in tax law. Behind each tax law lies the underlying assumption that all taxpayers accept the tax and consent to pay it to the elected government in exchange for the public goods and services it provides. Of course, this is only an assumption, or if you will, only a tacit consent. One may defy the assumption if they can demonstrate that no sensible member of our society would agree to pay the challenged tax. In other words, the tax has to contain certain attributes in order to be considered a "good tax", that any reasonable member would be willing to pay. Hence, we should study the quality of a tax, its merits, and its purpose in order to substantiate the assumption that the tax is "good". Otherwise, the challenged tax might not withstand judicial review (70). Thus, in the modern constitutional era, "no taxation without representation" means no taxation without public consent. Public consent is granted only if the tax maintains the qualities of a "good tax," which will be discussed later on [p. 39].

2. THE QUALITY OF TAX LAWS AND THEIR ADJUSTMENT TO CONSTITUTIONAL PRINCIPLES

Under a common constitutional law (22), every law should be in accordance to the principles, interests, and values embodied within the Constitution. Once a certain law is challenged for violating these standards, the courts are called upon to examine whether the violation is valid. If the court concludes that the challenged law does violate Constitutional principles, and cannot find sufficient justifications, such law cannot survive the court's judicial review (70) and is declared void. Indeed, the Constitution devotes special attention to the Congress' power to lay and collect taxes. As noted we refer to the term Tax as a very strict and limited term, which is distinguished from other mandatory payment [pp. 39–55].

The same rules apply to fiscal legislation. The U.S. Supreme Court has commented some eighty years ago [*U.S. v. Butler*, 297 U.S. 1 (1936)]: "While, therefore, the power to tax is not unlimited, its confines are set in the clause which confers it, and not in those of section 8 which bestow and define the legislative powers of the Congress."

Tax laws are a constant threat to human rights, constitutional interests, principles and vital values. (Some) tax laws may violate the constitutional right to property, the freedom of occupation and contracts, principles of equal rights, human dignity, and the right to dignified survival.

As will be elaborated below, a "good tax" is not a hollow phrase. It follows certain criteria that ensure that it does not violate principles of equality, liberty, freedom of contract, and occupation and the right of personal property. A good tax is not a confiscatory or arbitrary measure. As is discussed below, [pp. 9–15, 70] the tax, which is required from a firm (an economic body intended to generate profits (47)) is a "profit sharing mechanism" between the owners of the factors of production, i.e. financial capital, human capital and social capital. In the case of households, the tax is their payment for their consumption of the public goods and services provided by the government, while taking into consideration the taxpayers' circumstances. [pp. 21, 70]. A good tax is an efficient tool that enhances the public's wellbeing [p. 12]. For firms, it does this through increasing social capital, which contributes to their production; for households, by increasing the quality and the quantity of public goods and services that they consume.

3. THE REQUIREMENTS OF A GOOD TAX

During the biblical era, the tax embodied one of the toughest expressions of the rulers' arbitrariness and the subjects' defenselessness. According to our concept of modern democracy, based, inter alia, on the concept of the Social Contract and the principle of consent [pp. 7, 48–50, 100, 102], tax no longer represents despotism. The public is sovereign and the state's purpose is to enhance our individual and collective welfare and happiness. The tax, under this concept, is the amount we are willing to pay to live in a civilized society—a political organization charged with meeting our needs according to our choices and priorities. Through the election process and the Congressional annual approval of the administration's proposed budget, we—both as households and firms—choose to buy public goods and services from our elected government. Those public goods and services have an economic price, which we are ready to pay.

In "The Wealth of Nations," Adam Smith sets forth the need to consider the price of a tax and its attributes. According to Smith, taxes should follow four basic attributes—the "canons or maxims of good tax". A good tax should be in accordance with the following requirements:

1. Certain and not arbitrary;
2. As convenient as possible for the contributor to pay;
3. Efficient;
4. Fair and Equitable.

Modern economists suggest some additional criteria, like neutrality (though one may argue that neutrality and efficiency are basically the same) and flexibility, meaning that the tax system can be easily adapted according to the economic system and the elected government's fiscal policy (48).

The abundance of modern economic and philosophical literature, together with comparative legal studies, enables us to add a modern dimension to the above canons.

4. A TAX SHOULD BE CERTAIN AND NOT ARBITRARY

The certainty requirement has several dimensions, meanings and expressions.

A. Retroactive Taxes

The practical meaning of the certainty requirement is almost obvious. If taxation is indeed based on consent, it is inconceivable/quite difficult to assume retroactive consent. The concept of rational economic behavior and decision-making is based on information. It would be inconceivable for a democratic government to observe any type of economic activity, (either income production, its accumulation or consumption) free of tax or at a low tax rate, and then, after the action is over, to change the rules and charge a different amount than what was previously agreed. A consent to pay a tax and retroactive change do not go hand in hand. The reasonable assumption, that the taxpayers agreed to pay a tax, prevails only when the taxpayers know the price in advance, have the chance to consider it, use a cost-benefit analysis and appreciate whether the price is fair and stipulated in an acceptable way. No reasonable person agrees to purchase any item—whether private or public, goods or services—before knowing its price and value. In our time, the application of such a rule is embodied within the statutory requirement under which the administration has to present its proposed budget to the public and get its congressional approval every year. As indicated below, The U.S. Constitution adopted this notion. [p. 52]

B. Certainty and the Realization Requirement

As we will discuss later on [p. 198], the certainty requirement leads us, in most cases, to prefer the taxation of **realized income** over **potential/future/non-realized income**. This is because the evaluation of the former is quite easy and certain while the evaluation of the latter is based entirely on ***estimates*** rather than facts. Furthermore/ Nevertheless, we will examine the way the realization requirement was interpreted by the courts, which led William Andrews to dub it as the "Achilles' heel" of the income tax system [pp. 163, 198].

C. Non-Arbitrary

There are several dimensions to arbitrariness when it comes to tax laws. We mention two: The constitutional legal level, which is aimed mainly at the legislature, and the administrative dimension, which deals mainly with the authorities and powers vested to the tax administration, its agents and officers. We do not intend to go into the myriad means available to the government to prevent, or at least curb, these phenomena.

Once we agree that in a democratic system the government's only purpose is to serve the public and improve its wellbeing, the administration's arbitrariness threatens citizens' right to know what obligations apply to them and affect the course of their lives, and to plan their producing income and consumption accordingly. The government's activity in the absence of transparency constitutes a barrier to criticism and supervision by the public, and as a result thwarts the possibility of improvement of the government's actions.

In addition, the certainty requirement leads to an extremely important prerequisite: In a democratic system, where the tax administration is granted a significant power to asses taxpayers, to conduct civil and criminal inquiries and collect tax payments, there is a real danger, or even a constant threat, that the tax administrators might abuse their power in a discriminatory way and grant some concession to preferred taxpayers while providing unfavorable treatment to others. Furthermore, such situations might invite public corruption. Hence in most of the tax systems, in addition to the clear prohibition to tax people beyond the amounts provided in the tax code, there is an express provision prohibiting the tax authorities to grant ex gratia tax-reliefs.

D. Simplicity

The certainty requirement raises yet another insight: No consent can be presumed with regard to any complex issue whose principles and basic rules are not understood or not available to the general public. Since the tax is a very significant part of the relationship between government and citizens, the relationship must be clear and understandable. Unfortunately the actual reality is different. Simplicity in tax law is a relative and elusive matter that is not easily achieved. Simple scrutiny may expose that the complexity of the tax laws is not bound by reality. The lack of transparency and clarity of tax laws often serves the interests of politicians supported by wealthy and influential groups and contributors. The complication of tax laws creates loopholes in the tax system, which provide "opportunities" for tax planners who offer their services to influential and powerful "free riders", who then manage to reduce their fair share of the total price they would have had to pay for enjoying the public goods and services provided by the government.

5. CONVENIENCE OF THE CONTRIBUTOR

The meaning of the convenience requirement is quite straightforward: the tax system must consider the personal circumstances of the taxpayer and should not put them in a worse position in comparison to the conditions that existed before the taxable transaction took place. Here we focus on two aspects. The first one refers to a matter of timing and the availability of funds to pay the taxes. The second concerns the constitutional concept of Human Dignity [p. 50].

A. Timing and Tax Payments

The practical meaning is that no person should be put in a situation where they are required to pay taxes without having a liquid means. It has a dual aspect: one has to do with the realization requirement (103), which is a substantive rule also derived from the certainty requirement [p. 198]. The other is a matter of the availability of means to make tax payments.

One basic rule that emerges from this dual aspect is that a mere appreciation of non-liquid property before its disposition should not be taxed. Otherwise, the taxpayer may be forced to sell the appreciated property unwillingly, or under pressure, or at a high transaction costs. (143). In addition to the simple inconvenience, such a forced sale of non-liquid property may also be considered a violation of the taxpayer's right to property or freedom of contract/occupation. If the tax system is indeed based on consent, it is inconceivable to assume that a taxpayer would be willing to enter a situation where his condition worsens.

In some cases, although the wealth increase has been realized, the taxpayer receives income in some form other than (62) cash. A sensible tax system should allow the taxpayer in some cases to defer the tax payment plus a reasonable interest (64) until they sell the asset received as a consideration to the transaction. For example, when an employee receives options or stocks in return for their labor, their income is realized just when they provide their services—and yet they might have some difficulties paying the tax. Again, if they have to sell a non-liquid asset received, they might lose a significant amount by selling it under pressure and unwillingly. One sensible solution is to allow them to defer the timing of the tax payment until they sell or exercise the asset, and the total gain should be subject to the ordinary tax rates (18) plus interest on the tax owed during the time they received the option until they sell the stocks.

In *Turner v. Commissioner*, 13 T.C.M. 462 (1954) a taxpayer (a married couple) won two nonrefundable, nontransferable first class steamship tickets from New York City to Buenos Aires on a radio call-in show. The taxpayer claimed that the cruise's market was significantly high and that it is quite obvious that "the winning of the ticket did not provide them with something. . . for which they would have made an expenditure in any event" and that they would not buy such a cruise in the free market. The court decided to reevaluate the tickets for income tax purposes and took into consideration the taxpayers' subjective position.

The same sensitive approach should lead us to use property taxes with caution. The convenience requirement regarding property tax, (which is a tax on the future unrealized income—as discussed below—pp. 105, 154, 125) leads to a conclusion that it should not force the owner to dispose of the property in order to finance the tax. On the other hand, one may argue that if the taxpayer does not have enough resources and the property does not produce the needed sums, economic efficiency requires that the property should reach another person who can use it more proficiently. Note that property taxes also violate the certainty requirement since the evaluation process of each property involves some significant uncertain assumptions [pp. 101, 154]. (97)

B. Human Dignity, Discretionary Power to Consume and Personal Exemptions

Human dignity features as a core principle in many modern constitutions. The International Covenant on Civil and Political Rights provides in its Preamble, "recognition of the inherent dignity and of the equal and inalienable rights of all members of the human family is the foundation of freedom, justice and peace in the world . . . [and] these rights derive from the inherent dignity of the human person". The idea has found its way also to the American Courts (e.g. *Furman v. Georgia*; *Cohen v. California*, 403 U.S. 15, 24 (1971)). There is no need to elaborate on this concept here. It is understood that a tax that drives a person into poverty violates this constitutional concept. Contributing to this principle, the Carter Commission in Canada defined the tax base as the "discretionary economic power" (25); meaning that the government should not tax all the taxpayer's wealth, but should exclude the portion needed for non-discretionary consumption, i.e. a minimum standard of living. This includes funds needed for dwelling, food, medical insurance or services, basic education, etc. Indeed, most income tax systems around the globe allow a minimum amount of income to be free of tax. In the U.S. such provisions have been established in the personal exemption and the standard deduction granted to every individual taxpayer and their dependents. [pp. 12, 287]. [Note that The Tax Cuts and Jobs Act of 2017 eliminated the Personal and Dependent exemptions while the rates for the standard deduction were nearly doubled] The Earned Income Refundable Tax Credit (82), [the refundable part the <u>child tax credit</u>], [p. 325] and the allowable offset of non-business casualty losses (22) are other notable examples of this qualification.

6. EFFICIENT

The efficiency requirement has several traditional as well as modern dimensions.

A. Efficiency of Tax Administration

The basic meaning of the efficiency criterion is very simple: the costs of administering and collecting a pure tax should be as low as possible so that a large portion of the amount taken from taxpayers is not used to finance bureaucratic costs. In other words, if the administration costs are equal to or higher than the revenues, society will be better off eliminating the tax and firing the administration, unless it is a regulatory tax, meant to achieve certain social and economic goals.

B. Optimal Taxation

Economic efficiency should achieve optimum welfare (92). As discussed below [p. 82], public finance theory concludes that every tax—excluding poll taxes (95)—creates some economic distortion and therefore leads to deadweight loss/excess burden (90), i.e. the loss of welfare caused by the tax (either by extra expenses that the taxpayers spend on tax planning measures, or due to the distortion caused by the tax that changes their original priorities) is greater than government revenues. If this is the case, in order for the tax to meet the efficiency requirement, the government has to assure that the benefit the public derives from the public goods and services, which are financed by the collected tax, is higher than—or at least equal to—the welfare loss it creates. Regrettably, public economic literature has not yet been able to provide measurable tools to satisfy this requirement. Still, the efficiency requirement serves as an analytical criterion and as a practical tool for evaluating what good and acceptable taxes are [p. 85], at least in extreme situations [p. 49].

Another way to present the efficiency requirement is through the **tax neutrality** concept. The origin of the concept is that in a free market economy, free human beings choose their actions and behavior according to their own priorities, thus promoting and enhancing their welfare—their own happiness. Government intervention, which forces people to change their priorities, creates distortion and consequently reduces welfare. Hence, a tax that is not neutral, but instead changes our priorities, activities and behavior, is not efficient—it decreases our welfare. The common way to evaluate tax neutrality is to first assume a "world without tax" and evaluate our behavior and priorities. Then we levy the tax and measure how much, if at all, we change our behavior and priorities. If we change, then the tax is not neutral.

Yet a pure free market economy (48) hardly exists. There are significant forces and powers that prevent the existence of an efficient free market and full competition. Market failures (75), such as asymmetric information (75), rent seeking (107), free riders (50)) and monopolies (75), do exist in modern democracy, and the government is called upon to intervene.

One notable way of intervention is a "Pigovian tax" (93), [pp. 36, 255] named after the British economist Arthur C. Pigou. As explained below, we do not consider Pigovian tax as a tax at all, but rather a mandatory price, levied to correct the price of goods and services that cause non-internalized behavior, i.e. negative externalities (44) to affect the community or its members. The revenue raised by this measure should be allocated to fix the damages caused to the public by the negative outcomes. Hence, we refer to these payments as Pigovian Mandatory Payment (hereinafter: PMP).

To offer a contemporary example: No reasonable and responsible person can deny nowadays that we, humans, cause huge damage to our earth, mainly due to uncontrolled and irresponsible air pollution. The difficulty in treating and preventing the problem lies in the fact that those who cause the damage do not pay its economic price, since the created damage is not included in the production cost of the damaging products, and therefore neither the producers nor their consumers are required to compensate those who suffer. Hence, in the best-case scenario most of the cost is shifted onto the public's shoulders. In the worst and most frightening case, the damage may turn out to be irreversible, endangering our very existence. A significant example is the meat industry. Scientific studies [*inter alia,* Xu, X., Sharma, P., Shu, S. *et al.* Global greenhouse gas emissions from animal-based foods are twice those of plant-based foods. *Nat Food* 2, 724–732 (2021), Hannah Ritchie, *et al*, "CO_2 and Greenhouse Gas Emissions". OurWorldIn Data.org.] indicate that the beef industry's contribution to worsening the emissions problem is huge. In such a case, a Pigovian Mandatory Payment might be a most effective way to minimize the externality. It would raise the beef price and as result reduce its demand. The revenues from this mandatory payment could be routed to R&D funds for the development of non-polluting substitutes, or for developing other measures aimed to reduce hazardous emission. No doubt that the imposition of such mandatory payment only on the U.S. meat industry would cause difficult problems of competing imports. However, since such a mandatory payment is not a tax or a customs duty, but a means of reestablishing the real economic price of those products, no legal or constitutional problems will arise if it would also be imposed on imported products.

The British-American economist and law professor, Ronald Coase, offered a different approach by arguing that Pigovian taxes are redundant. As long as trade in an externality (44) is possible (i.e. the polluting producers are able to buy the right to pollute the environment from the neighboring population) without transaction costs (143), and property rights are clearly defined, then the free market economy can take care of such problems without government regulation and intervention. Under such conditions, bargaining between the parties involved will lead to an efficient result and eliminate the negative externalities, regardless of the initial allocation of property rights. The problem with Coase's theorem is evident when there are a large number of victims, each of whom has suffered small damages. They face serious practical difficulties in trying to organize and to conduct an efficient negotiation with the "offender." In such a case, it is probably more efficient to allow the public to legislate a law that shifts the economic cost from the victims to the offenders by PMP. PMP may prevent the creation of a negative externality in the first place. Alternatively, it is possible to compensate the public's agents via efficient procedural measurements such as punitive damages or class actions.

7. FAIR AND EQUITABLE

Fairness and equality are probably the most basic, common and obvious requirements for a good tax system, especially if we accept the concept of collective consent.

In theory, we might be tempted to accept that ***justice*** is the best and most appropriate criterion for fairness. Yet justice suffers from two notable deficiencies: first, it is a multidimensional and subjective concept; second, it is a very difficult concept to measure and quantify. Therefore, it is hard, if not impossible, to use justice as a practical and acceptable criterion for fairness if certainty and collective consent are to be assumed.

Equity, on the other hand, may be regarded as a unidimensional, measurable and even objective criterion. It can be used to determine **economic fairness**. The basic and intuitive criteria for economic fairness are economic **equality** and economic **difference**. Put them together and we face two forms of equity: **Horizontal equity**, which means equal taxpayers contribute equal shares and **Vertical equity**, which means different taxpayers contribute different shares. By defining Vertical and Horizontal equity (42), we indeed diminish the ambiguity surrounding concepts of fairness and equity. However, this is not enough. We should now consider what criteria are most suited for deciding which taxpayers are equal and which are different. As discussed below [p. 71], the "ability to pay" and the "benefit principle" **are important deciding factors**.

8. EQUALITY AND EFFICIENCY

For a long period the leading thought has been that there is a "big trade off" between equality and efficiency. A common theory suggests that from an ethical and moral perspective, equality is the ultimate goal of any democratic society. On the other hand, a popular argument is that equality undermines efficiency. Such a conclusion seems a bit shortsighted. It is quite conceivable that if the government takes some resources from the rich and spends it on—say—education of poor children, the immediate result is a drop in the wellbeing of the rich without a corresponding increase of the children's welfare, which is the definition of inefficiency. Nevertheless, a more accurate analysis—economic and utilitarian—will examine the results of such a transfer in the longer run. The increase in the educational level of children means that they will become productive citizens who will add a significant contribution to our society—obviously greater than the social and economic contribution (probably negative) they would have added without getting such education. Furthermore, a more accurate and thorough analysis reveals that the rich also benefit from transferring/shifting some of their money to the poor; as a result of the increase in the educational level of children, a better and more qualified workforce is available, as well as increasing demand for their goods and services due to the expansion of the circle of potential buyers. Therefore, we may argue that the tension between equality and efficiency is—if at all—only in the short run. As we will discuss below [p. 90], latest empirical research show that equality, up to a certain level, and redistribution policy, enhance long last economic growth, i.e. promote efficiency.

9. THE ROAD MAP

Here, in order to follow the detailed, yet condensed, discussion above, we offer a road map as a friendly tool that enables us to see the whole picture. This guideline outlines the fascinating steps involved in solving the many puzzles inherent in modern democratic tax systems. The flow chart below illustrates that the design of any tax—either pure or regulatory—has several stages and indicates the steps involved in analyzing a tax system's rationale. The first stage begins with the Constitution, leading to questions of human rights and the Congress' powers (and limitations) to lay/levy taxes. It deals also with the quality and contents of a tax, which is an important step in creating a good tax that will meet constitutional, economic, legal, political, and moral standards and requirements. The following chart concentrates mainly on pure tax, but it could be applied to other mandatory payments.

Figure 2.1:

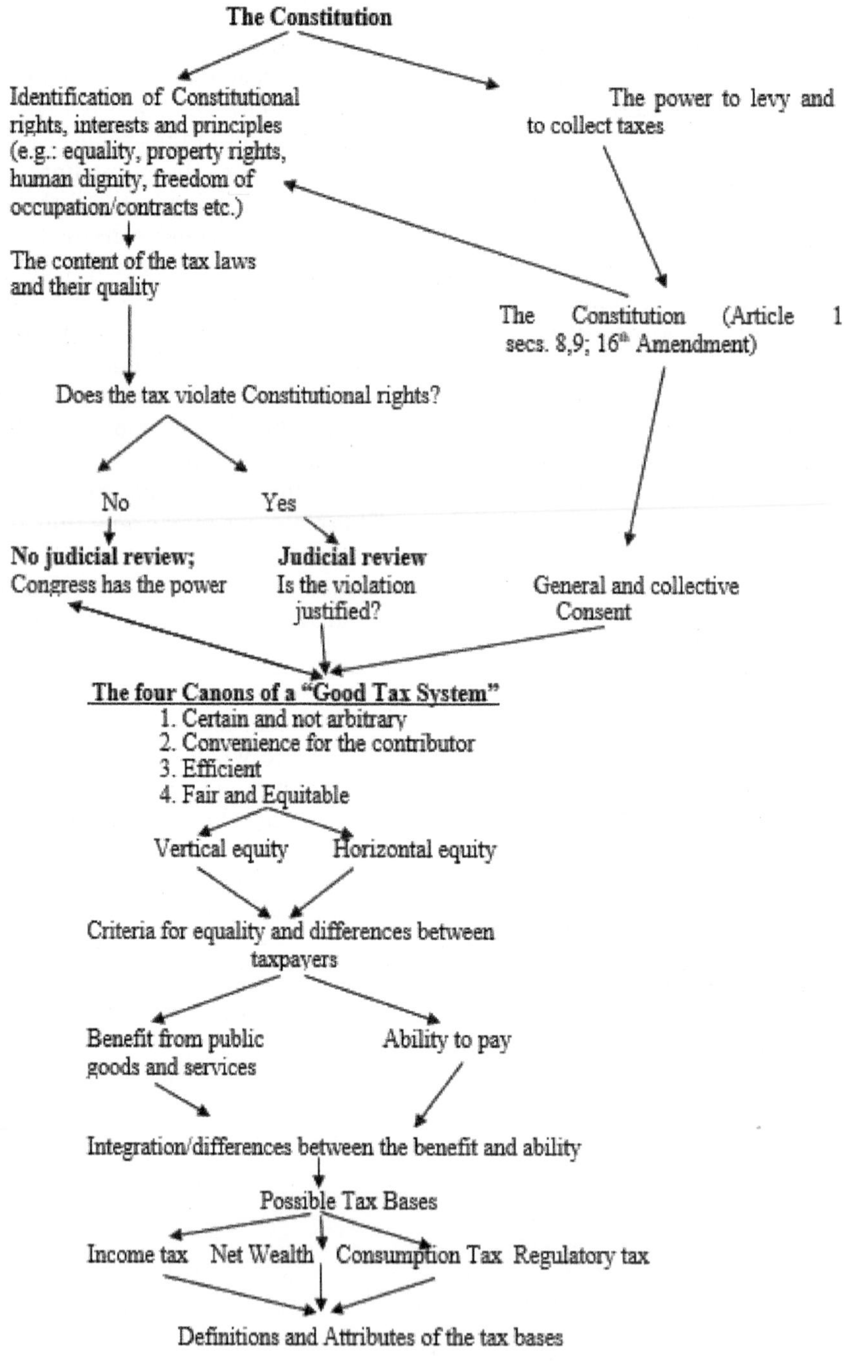

As can be seen above, the four canons of a good tax are at the center of this flowchart. These canons help us decide if a tax law violates constitutional rights, and, if so, if the violation is justified. From the policymakers' point of view, as well as the public's, the four canons serve as useful tools in determining whether the tax bill or proposal is sensible and acceptable. Does it reflect a possible and reasonable public consent? Will it increase the social welfare? A similar examination should be used while reviewing other mandatory payments. In those cases, special weight should be given to the questions of whether the payment's purpose meets constitutional criteria, and whether it has achieved its purpose i.e. whether it has successfully shifted the real price of negative or positive externalities onto the shoulders of the taxpayers that created them?

The study of this roadmap also reveals the diverse disciplines that make up what is known as "Tax Law." Among these fields are Public Law (Constitutional and Administrative), Private and Business Law; Social and Political Philosophy; Macro-Economics, Labor and Welfare Economics, Public Finance, Finance and Accounting. All are discussed below.

Part Two

THE DEFINITION OF TAX, ITS SOURCES AND OBJECTIVES

Chapter Three

WHY TAXES?

1. DEFINITIONS OF PURE TAXES AND REGULATORY MANDATORY PAYMENTS

The question of what a tax is and how it should be defined has several dimensions. We concentrate here on two: the legal-constitutional and the social-philosophical. For the first dimension we propose an accurate, exact, and narrow definition of the term ***pure tax***, which is distinguished from other mandatory payments. For the second dimension we will try to show that socially and philosophically, a tax is nothing but the price of the goods and services we receive from the elected government. It further appears that there is in fact no difference between the two dimensions and that a careful and thorough analysis ultimately leads to the same definition.

A "tax" for purposes of the Taxing Clause is a ***pure tax***: A tax, which is a mean/ measure designated "*to pay the Debts and provide for the common Defence and general Welfare of the United States.*" [U.S. CONST. art. I, § 8, clause. 1.] Accordingly, a pure tax's sole goal for the constitutional dimension is raising revenue to finance the elected government's policy and its implementation.

Compared to pure taxes the purpose of *regulatory taxes* is different. They are not meant to raise revenue but instead to restore free market principles and rearrange the right economic price of a product in two different, yet similar, cases, which occur due to market failures and generate two types of economic externalities.

A *negative* externality is created by a producer or its customers and causes damage to a certain group or to the general public (e.g. a manufacturer of tobacco products and smokers; Swelling or flatulence of animals raised and maintained by the meat and dairy industry and its consumers). Without the public representatives' intervention, the products' prices are set regardless of the amount of damage caused. As a result, the actual prices of the products are too low. These low prices increase—due to moral hazard—the sales of the damaging products. It is the government's role to ensure that the prices of products are set in accordance with the rules of the free-market economy and basic concepts of responsibility and accountability, and should reflect the overall economic price of the products. This can be done by taking into account compensation for the damage caused to the public. In other words, the aim is to restore the products' prices to their proper real economic level, or to reduce the overall demand for the damaging products. As is discussed below [p. 36] the most efficient measures for such government action are Pigovian taxes (93).

Positive externalities occur when firms create an economic advantage through their economic activities, by spending—directly or indirectly—extra expenses. The market does not compensate such efforts but the public has a special interest in ensuring that such rewarding activities continue. Once again, the government is called in order to compensate the firms who create the positive activities. This can be done by either a direct grant or by charging those firms lower tax payments using special tax reliefs. Hence, Pigovian taxes and certain *tax reliefs* [p. 31] both have a common goal: to restore basic principles of free market economy by using *regulatory* taxes or tax reliefs. The government is authorized to legislate those mandatory regulatory payments by the "Commerce Clause" of Article 1 Sec. 8 clause 3.

The distinction we offer between pure tax and mandatory regulatory payments raises the following question: Why bother with such a distinction? For what purpose? This question is somewhat theoretical for now, and has been discussed in depth on other occasions. In short, the judicial review of pure taxes is limited. This is because pure taxes are aimed at funding the policies of the elected government, and, generally speaking, courts are inclined to refrain from judicial review of elected government's policies (as long as they or their implementation do not violate constitutional principles).

In contrast, judicial review of regulatory taxes must be broader. The regulatory mandatory payments' goals are specific, identified, clear and known; the means/measures taken to achieve these goals are measurable. In addition, one can easily examine the correlation between the goal and the means and weigh whether the means actually achieve their goal, i.e. restore the proper economic price of private goods and services when their production processes create positive or negative externalities. If the measures are excessive, the result is that some taxpayers are penalized without due process (a Pigovian tax that raises revenue beyond the damage incurred); or that other taxpayers who are not entitled to tax reliefs are discriminated against (tax reliefs in amounts above the benefit incurred). In other words, in such cases there is a call to inquire whether violation of the principles of equality, freedom of contract and occupation occurred.

An interesting problem arises. How should the main tax system, which is levied on income, be classified? Is it a pure tax or a regulatory tax? Regardless of whether such a question is a theoretical one or has some practical aspects or implementation, we present the following approaches.

First, we should distinct between *lex ferenda* and *lex lata*, there is no doubt that income tax and corporate tax in the U.S. today contain, in practice, components of both pure and regulatory taxes. However, the question is whether this situation is desirable.

We are dealing here with definitions, and are not inquiring whether the income tax currently contains regulatory elements in practice, but rather whether the constitutional-legal definition of income tax also includes a regulatory nature. To be more precise, is distributive justice part of the definition of income tax? Does the purpose of any income tax include, by definition, a social goal of distributive justice? Put differently, if the purpose of the income tax is not only to raise revenue but also to promote social or distributive justice, is it still considered a pure tax?

Professor Avi-Yonah has long argued that taxation has three goals—revenue, redistribution and regulation. There is no dispute that some taxes (e.g. taxes on alcohol on tobacco) are designed primarily to change taxpayer behavior and therefore fall outside the definition of a pure tax. There is also no dispute that the primary goal of other taxes, such as the VAT, is to raise revenue for the government, and therefore these are pure taxes.

The question is what about taxes whose primary goal is to reduce inequality, i.e. redistributive taxes. In Avi-Yonah's opinion, the personal income tax, and in particular its progressive rate structure, is primarily designed to reduce inequality. That is the reason why the United States adopted the Sixteenth Amendment to the Constitution in 1913, allowing Congress to levy an income tax, because an income tax could be progressive in a way that consumption taxes (the main source of revenue for the federal government before 1913) could not be. Moreover, Avi-Yonah does not believe that the progressivity of the income tax can be defended on economic grounds like the greater benefit the rich receive from government services or the declining marginal utility of income (i.e. that an extra $1,000 are worth more to the poor than to the rich). In his opinion, the decision to use an income tax for redistribution is a political decision, which is subject to the will of the majority in every election, and which depends on the degree of inequality that is considered tolerable. He would therefore include redistribution as a legitimate goal of a pure tax.

Professor Edrey's approach is a bit different.

My basic approach is that pure tax should be defined by a "clean" neutral definition: "mandatory payment paid to the central/Federal government "*to pay the Debts and provide for the common Defence and general Welfare of the United States*." U.S. CONST. art. I, § 8, cl. 1.

Such a neutral definition fits the democratic concept [pp. 7, 48–50, 54, 100, 102]. A concept that allows any party or government to implement its socio-economic policy in accordance with the decision of the voters—as long as the implementation does not violate constitutional rights. Thus, a conservative administration is allowed to avoid social policies designed to reduce social gaps and poverty, and if the voters prefer a different policy, they will democratically replace the administration with one which will take care of achieving a different socio-economic policy. The two administrations will not be considered as violating constitutional rights, and the competition between the two perceptions will strengthen the nation and improve our collective decisions.

A regressive consumption tax is not a neutral tax. It undermines the consent-to-pay assumption [pp. 7, 48–50, 100, 102]. A tax that forces taxpayers to pay for undesired public goods and services, at a price which is too high in relation to their economic ability is not a tax that is imposed by consent but rather by coercion. On the other hand, a progressive income tax follows the basic concept of consent. Those whose economic ability is low, and who benefit less from public goods and services, are required to pay less for them. In my view, this is the theoretical explanation for replacing the consumption tax by a progressive income tax after 1913.

General taxes, including income tax, are not intended/earmarked for specific purposes. When the administration decides to spend money for certain security purposes, purchase modern fighter jets, or launch a spacecraft into outer space, the needed funding for such programs comes from the general coffer. The national coffer is built up by the aggregate/accumulated tax payments. The fact that part of the income tax was used for these programs does not make the income tax a regulatory tax that contains security purposes. The tax is a pure tax because its purpose is to raise money for financing the expenses of the elected government, in accordance with its policies and priorities, whether those are national security, enhancing national pride or fighting poverty or significant social gaps.

Hence the above conclusion should apply if the government decides on a social policy of distributive justice and allocates funds for the implementation of this policy. The question of whether it is appropriate for the government to fill "Okun's leaking bucket" [p. 28] with the money of the rich and transfer it to the poor cannot be determined on the side of a state's revenues, but rather on the side of its expenditures. A government that has decided to adopt a redistribution policy needs to set goals, means, and programs for achieving redistribution. Such policies and their implementation require money. The money comes from the public through the pure tax system. In other words, there must be a clear line that draws a distinction between the "revenue side" and of the "spending side" of the government's activity.

Moreover a strict and straightforward definition for Tax, and its precise and limited goals should limit the opportunities of the **Coalition** of interested groups [pp. 32, 75], composed of politicians, officials, tax lawyers, accounting firms, lobbyists, media, and other powerful wealthy and influential groups (hereinafter: the Coalition). and prevent its members from introducing into the tax system sophisticated provisions whose real aims are hidden from the public, [pp. 32, 75].

Such a distinct and a narrow definition for the term tax raises the hottest question: is a progressive tax rate a **pure tax** or **any other mandatory payment**? If it is the former, is there a possibility that the Supreme Court might regard the progressive income tax as unconstitutional? I don't think so.

An analysis of the justifications for progressive taxation, which are elaborated below, [pp. 55, 100, 101] shows that progressive taxation is not an expression of social policy arising from principles of distributive or social justice, but instead is required/derived by the two principles on which the book is based—the **consent** to pay and the **benefit** the taxpayer receives from the elected government. Accordingly, taxpayers with low economic ability will not agree to purchase goods and services that are beyond their abilities or interests. They won't be able to afford some expensive public services (e.g. recognition of private property, freedom of occupation or expression; national pride, taking care of the climate crisis, or sending American troops to protects national economic interests of the American oil industry's interests) since they hardly use them and could not care less about national pride or sending people to the moon. On the other hand, taxpayers with a high economic ability are willing to purchase more public good and services, which are very valuable for them, and are willing to pay for expensive goods and services at an appropriately high price. In other words, the free-market economy integrated with the consent and the benefit principles, justifies a progressive tax system.

In conclusion, progressive taxation does not result from a policy of distributive justice or social justice but rather from the basic principles of tax theory. Hence, the definition of a pure tax does not also to distributive justice. It is indeed limited to a sole purpose—raising revenue "*to pay the Debts and provide for the common Defence and general Welfare of the United States.*"

Any other component of the mandatory payment should be reviewed not as a tax levied by Art. I, § 8, clause 1 but under a different article, such as the "Commerce Clause" of Article 1 Sec. 8 clause 3.

2. TAXES AS PRICE FOR PUBLIC GOODS AND SERVICES

As mentioned, in this book we draw a very definite distinction between the term TAX and other types of mandatory payment, mainly for constitutional analysis. The meaning and the consequence of this distinction is discussed below [p. 8] and later on [pp. 39–55]. Most of the definitions of the term (pure) "tax" share the following basic characteristics: "unrequited/not reciprocated mandatory payments collected primarily by the central government for raising funds to finance the government's expenses"

Lawyers tend to emphasize the fact that the taxpayer does not receive ***direct*** and ***equal*** consideration in return for their payments. This insight reflects a slight confusion between the substance/fundamental role of taxes and the "technical" aspect of tax collection. From the substantial point of view, as previously indicated, taxes are justified by the benefit principle [pp. 51, 71] and based on consent [pp. 7, 48–50, 100, 102]. The theoretical assumption must be, then, that taxpayers **do** receive full ***quid pro quo*** consideration through the public goods and services (101) the elected government provides, such as law and order, national defense, a stable economic system, physical and social infrastructure, a civilized and organized society, and a workable and enforceable legal system. Hence, taxes (from the Latin *taxare* = *estimate* (are supposed to serve as the estimated price of such public goods and services consumed by taxpayers. The fact that tax is an enforced contribution exacted pursuant to legislative authority, is a reflection of the need to collect taxes efficiently, due to an unfortunate human phenomenon known as ***free riders*** (50) i.e. those members of the community who try to take advantage of the fact that they can enjoy public goods and services without sharing their cost. As in the private market, any purchase of goods or services entails a legal obligation to pay their price. This basic rule should be applied to both private and public goods and services, bought either in the private market or from the elected government. In other words, taxes are based on the benefit principle (14). Firms, who produce income, as well as households who use the income and consume public goods and services are all able to enjoy the benefit of their taxes. As firms—i.e. income producers, public goods and services enable us to produce income and wealth. Without the government, which provides goods, services and enables social capital [pp. 64–66] we would not be able to function, operate or produce our income. In other words, our economic production is a joint activity of the ***firm*** (47) together with the public. The public invests in physical and social infrastructure and, through the government, enables and maintains the domestic social capital which provides the economic conditions that allow the firm to function, operate successfully, and achieve its economic goals. We refer to this concept as the "***Joint project approach***" [p. 64].

The other aspect of the benefit justification focuses on us as households, and the consumption side (26, 61), which has two aspects. First, the current or future consumption of private goods and services is possible only in an organized and civilized society, that recognizes our human rights and protects them, with functional markets and regulated and efficient financial institutions. In addition, we also directly consume public goods and services, such as national and domestic defense, recognition of private property and its protection, social and legal order, national pride, etc. Those goods and services cost money and we have to pay for them. When the provider is the public government, the payment goes to the public coffers through the tax system in order to cover the provider's costs. In addition, as is discussed below [p. 73], the pricing process in a free market of private goods and services is not substantially different from the way public goods' prices are set in a democratic society.

Hence, from a philosophical, economic, and social point of view we define tax, in a democratic society as, ***a mandatory payment collected by law in exchange for goods and services the elected government provides to the public, directed to the general budget without pre-apportionment for a particular or specific purpose***.

Note that the "mandatory" aspect is part of the definition only for two reasons: the "free rider" phenomenon (50), and the fact that public goods and services (101) are not bought by the taxpayers through individual decisions and choices [p. 27].

Such a definition insists that a tax's purpose **only** for financing the elected government's general budget in order to execute its stated policy. This means that no tax revenue would be designated in advance for any specific goal. Other mandatory payments, such as user fees, duties and PMP, are not within such definition. As was mentioned above [p. 21] and further below [p. 36], the distinction between taxes and other mandatory payments has a significant meaning regarding constitutional judicial review (70) and the public participation in the democratic deliberation.

3. THE LEGAL DEFINITION

For practical reasons, the legal definition of taxation in a democratic society has a small but necessary addition: ***a mandatory payment collected by law, <u>which is assumed</u> that it is in exchange for goods and services the elected government provides to the public, directed to the general budget without pre-apportionment for a particular or specific purpose***. The rationale for this addition—the assumption—derives from the concept that the taxes are based on consent [pp. 7, 48–51, 7, 100, 102]. Yet, it is quite difficult for the government to provide solid legal evidence that it provides a full consideration for each and every member of the society [p. 75]. Hence, we need the assumption that the consideration is fulfilled/provided by the government. The burden of proof is shifted to the taxpayers. If taxpayers argue that they do not receive a quid pro quo for their tax payments and therefore do not consent to pay the tax, they bear a very heavy burden of proof. In rare cases, however, this burden is not impossible to bear [p. 49].

In 1938 the Supreme Court offered the following concept:

"Taxation is neither a penalty imposed on the taxpayer nor a liability which he assumes by contract. It is but a way of apportioning the cost of government among those who in some measure are privileged to enjoy its benefits and must bear its burdens" (*Welch v. Henry et al.*, 305 U.S. 134 at pp. 146–7). A careful analysis reveals three components. First, the purpose of a tax is to finance the elected government's expenses according to the benefit principle. Second, the obligation to pay the tax is not based on contractual relationship. Third, tax should not be used as a punishment [p. 53].

The first and the third components go hand in hand with the definition of the term tax, which is offered throughout the book [pp. 21–27, 51, 71]. The second one might be considered contradictory to our approach, which bases tax on consent [pp. 7, 48–50, 100, 102].

Note though, that our narrow, precise and accurate definition of the term 'tax' and its goals might be in conflict with some statements made by the Supreme Court. In *National Federation of Independent Business v. Sebelius*, (2012): (hereinafter *Sebelius*) [pp. 41, 53], Chief Justice Roberts states: *"taxes that seek to influence conduct are nothing new"* referring to Justice Story for the proposition that "*the taxing power is often, very often, applied for other purposes, than revenue*"; (*United States v. Sanchez* (1950)). In the *Sanchez* case the Supreme Court went further, concluding: "*A tax is not invalid merely because it regulates, discourages, or deters the activities taxed, nor because the revenue obtained is negligible, or the revenue purpose is secondary. . . . A tax is not invalid merely because it affects activities which Congress might not otherwise regulate.*"

On the other hand, Justice Ginsburg's opinion in the *Sebelius* case may be construed as closer to the proposed approach here regarding the distinction between pure tax and regulatory tax. As is discussed below [pp. 41, 53] Justice Ginsburg tends to reject the conclusion that the payments under discussion should be classified as penalties or as tax. Her analysis indicates that such payments are in fact Pigovian Mandatory Payments [pp. 13, 36], which are levied according to the "Commerce Clause" of Article 1 Sec. 8 clause 3 and not according to the taxing power of Article 1 Sec. 8 clause 1.

4. THE GOALS OF THE TAX SYSTEM

A. The Size of the Government, Free Market and Capitalism

As is discussed above [pp. 21–26, 21], our definition of the term 'tax' is based on the idea that the power to levy taxes in a democratic regime is limited to a narrow objective: to finance the elected government's provision of "public goods and services" aimed *to pay the debts and provide* ***for the common defense and general welfare of the United States***; (101). The major public goods and services include, *inter alia*, national security, economic stability, a legal system, law enforcement, physical infrastructure and, due to market failure caused by adverse selection (8) [p. 127], social and health insurances, which the private sector is unable to provide efficiently. The most prominent attributes of public goods and services are that they are non-rival, (i.e. their consumption by one does not significantly affect the total amount available for others, such as the warning signals of a lighthouse), and non-excludable (i.e. no one can be effectively excluded from using them, such as recognition and protection of human rights).

Levying taxes raises two major issues: How much should the government collect from the public? And how should the tax burden be distributed among the members of a given society? The first issue, which has a political connotation, is discussed below very briefly. The second issue is discussed and elaborated throughout this book.

The first issue refers to the volume of the government activity, i.e. how big the government should be. Do we want a small government that refrains as much as possible from intervening in market activities and leaves the bulk of goods and services provision to the private sector? Or would we rather have a big government that provides a wide range of goods and services? These questions are indeed political ones—unless the government is trying to deny its basic responsibilities or violate the core of the social contract embodied within the constitution. A common and accepted economic approach, in a very general term, is that the best and most efficient means of promoting a society's well-being is through the free activities of the private sector. A free market economy (49) provides—via the invisible hand—the greatest amount of wellbeing to the largest number of the community's members. Yet one must acknowledge that the private sector is unable to provide **all** the goods and services that the society and its members require in effective and efficient ways, either because of **market failures** (75) and the unfortunate phenomenon of **Free Riders** (50), or because the private market is not sensitive enough to preserve and honor the principles of democracy, such as human dignity, the right to survive and equality. Under the "minimal/small government approach", the government should intervene in the market as little as possible.

Yet, a caveat should be added. Some economists (and conservative politicians) tend to confuse a free market economy and the capitalistic system. Careful scrutiny reveals that these are two different concepts. The free market economy is part of a democratic and ethical system that strives to enhance and promote the individual, and eventually the aggregate well-being of the whole community. As long as certain conditions exist, the invisible hand leads us to increase our welfare and wellbeing. Where and when the required conditions are missing—due to **market failures** (75) and powerful economic forces, which take advantage of their position to undermine free competition and tilt the rules of the game in favor of their own selfish interests—the government should be called upon to intervene. It is noteworthy that the great thinkers of classical economic literature, who introduced the invisible hand, dealt chiefly with ethics and equity as attributes of the principles of a free market [p. 72].

A capitalistic system, on the other hand, has turned out to be a system that prevents free competition, and that provides financial capital and its owners with certain privileges and benefits. As the American economist John Kenneth Galbraith has indicated (among others) half a century ago, the new capitalistic system has prevented the public's agents and the government from supervising free economic activities and from assuring the functioning of the free market economy and free competition. Powerful producers tend to undermine consumer sovereignty, increase the production of their goods beyond an efficient amount, reduce the provision of public goods and services and over-provide private ones due to the process of modern advertising that has created an artificial demand beyond the individual's real needs and true desires. Furthermore, as the economist Joseph Stigliz indicates, those powerful groups are able to persuade the government to significantly reduce its regulations. Thus, we note that an aggressive capitalistic system sanctifies infringement on the basic human rights of weak populations (e.g.—human dignity, property, freedom of contract), violates ethical principles and allows individuals and big corporations to covet public property and confiscate it for their own use and satisfaction. The striking phenomenon is that, due to what we mention below [p. 24], modern and Western-democratic governments tend to support the capital owners [pp. 81, 90]. The governments' provisioning of special privileges to capital owners through the lower tax rates on capital gains and capital (passive) income may be seen, under a careful scrutiny, as an expression of the capitalistic system that violates the free market economy and infringes upon the principles of equality and equity and as a result of this capitalist system, sustainable economic growth is also being undermined [pp. 51, 90–95].

Contrary to the above "minimal" approach, there are those who believe that the role of the government should be broader and that the government is supposed to promote social causes, assure a just distribution of the national wealth (since market economic wealth distribution is not necessarily efficient, just or ethical) and play an active role in the economic life of the nation, including efforts to restrain huge companies who focus on profits maximization, undermine free competition, and ignore social and national goals. In that case, the government's role is to regulate some activities and certain industries and institutions (e.g. banking, insurance, environment), and to make sure that free competition is restored. In addition, there are some good arguments, based not only on ethical and normative claims but also on economic analysis and empirical data [p. 90], which support the claim that governments should guarantee some basic human needs, such as a dignified standard of living to all its subjects [p. 12], and that the government should make sure that significant social gaps are not endangering the social and economic structure [p. 90]. Democratic governments may adopt the basic principles of the free market, and yet not necessarily follow the capitalist system. Also, not every government's intervention in national economic activity undermines the concept of free market. The American economist Arthur Okun has warned that scientists—including economic technicians [p. 90]—should not determine the size of the hole in the leaky bucket, which transfers wealth from the wealthy to the neediest. Instead, the decision should be made by the public's moral, social, and political perceptions as well as by "worldly philosophers". As we can see below [pp. 72, 90] a broad utilitarian analysis is not detached at all from social values such as equality and redistribution.

B. The Rationales and the Reasons for the Narrow Approach for the Goals of Taxation

As stated above, the proposed definition of 'tax' is based on the concept that the objectives and goals of taxation are clear, simple, and limited; its role is to finance the elected government's expenses according to its fiscal policy (48) through the annual budget. This is indeed quite a narrow approach, compared to a very popular and common insight that taxes are an efficient vehicle for redistributing the national income. Taxes, according to this approach, have a significant role in promoting and improving social and distributive justice. A similar approach is that taxes have a regulatory purpose (e.g. through TRI) [pp. 3, 5, 31, 36] which aims to induce firms and households to act or behave in one way rather than another. The underlying rationale for these approaches is that using the tax system as a vehicle promotes a just and efficient society. Alas, experience teaches us, at least within the last decades in the U.S., that a broad definition for the term tax and wide-ranging goals lead to the opposite—an unjust and regressive tax system, which leads eventually to increasing poverty, social gaps and slow economic growth.

Therefore, our approach toward the definition of "tax" and determining its goals is indeed different. The purpose of such a narrow approach is to ensure an accurate analysis of tax law, which strives to prevent any deviation from the clean model of the role and purposes of tax. The underlying rationale of such approach is a dual one: to make sure that the government does not impose any other kind of mandatory payments in disguise of a tax, and to prevent the government from enacting tax provisions that provide significant privileges to small yet powerful groups in a subtle and hidden way without the public's supervision and awareness.

As a series of economists (such as George Stigler and Jean Tirole among others) have suggested, the public stands a very small chance against big and dominant firms, which have a wicked tendency to integrate vertically and to increase their power. Moreover, there is a constant danger that government officials, including legislators who rely heavily on fundraising, are "captured" by the same businesses they are supposed to regulate and supervise. In the area of tax legislation, any complicated and complex tax system without a clear definitions and limited goals, ultimately serves the interests of the aforementioned **Coalition** [pp. 24, 32, 75] of powerful interest group Hence, a strict and straightforward definition for Tax, and its precise and limited goals should limit the opportunities of the Coalition and prevent its members from introducing sophisticated provisions, whose real aim is hidden from the public, into the tax system. In other words, once policymakers agree to harness the tax system to various and different purposes other than raising revenue, we get an opaque tax system which primarily serves, in a concealed way, what the economist Joseph Stigliz coined in 2011: "*Of the 1%, by the 1%, for the 1%*".

Experience teaches us that most tax reforms in recent decades, carried out primarily in the U.S., have served the interests of big firm and capital owners, led to a constant increase in social inequalities and made the U.S. income tax system a regressive one [p. 90]. The suggested approach, i.e. a narrow definition of the term tax with limited goals, which in our minds is rooted within the U.S. Constitution, enables a careful review and supervision both by the public and the judiciary. It is noteworthy that we do not express here any argument for or against any policy adopted by a political party and approved by the public through the election process. The claim is that promoting socioeconomic goals requires/entails serious distortions of economic decisions. The government's adopted policy should be executed through the spending side of the government's activities, by direct grants and other expenses, detailed within the annual budget and approved annually, which is much more transparent and accessible to the public than TRI.

As long as the government uses direct expenses and grants in order to achieve its fiscal policy (48), the public is able to track annual spending through the national budget's deliberation and allocations, and can thereby control and criticize the government's policy and spending. Conversely, using the revenue side—through the tax system—has some notable deficiencies. TRI are not transparent; it is almost impossible to evaluate the benefits they create and who really enjoys them. Furthermore, per constitutional requirement, the House of Representative must approve any spending and allocation the government intends to make. whereas TRI (84, 127, 131) [pp. 3, 31] are enacted only once and remain forever as part of tax law until new legislation removes them.

Reality also suggests that TRI might serve as tools created by politicians to deceive the public and hide governmental spending. As indicated [p. 4], under a progressive tax system (98) they provide the greatest benefit—in the form of tax savings (133) [pp. 4, 240]—to wealthy taxpayers [p. 4]. Assume Taxpayers A (with marginal tax rate of 40%) and B (with no taxable income i.e. zero tax rate) spend $2,000 on solar energy systems in their homes. Since such spending is part of their private consumption, it is not deductible. Suppose the government decides to encourage use of solar energy in order to reduce global warming and pollution, and allows the taxpayers to deduct the above cost. This means that said deduction provides Taxpayer A with a tax savings of (2,000*0.4=) $800. Taxpayer B does not have any tax saving (2,000*0). The significance of this example is simple: as the income of a taxpayer increases and the taxpayer is charged a higher marginal tax rate, he reaps a greater benefit from the deductible amount. Such a result distorts the principle of horizontal equity and undermines the progressivity of the income tax system, and at the same time distorts economic efficiency by changing the price of such a system to different households. Note that, in order to ease the equity problem, some of the TRI are phased-out (94) once the taxpayer's taxable income reaches a certain level [p. 35]. Such a "counter measure" enhances economic efficiency.

On the other hand, one may argue that providing a greater incentive to higher income taxpayers might be a good or sensible policy—to ease and encourage the most efficient taxpayers and to penalize the poor, lazy and untalented ones. This possible argument could be considered as long as the public realizes and approves its consequences.

The suggested narrow approach enables us to draw a distinction between the term tax and other types of mandatory payments. The prominent reasons for the need for such a distinction derive from legal and constitutional analysis. Any type of legislation has to comply with known constitutional guidelines and legal methodology. The suggested approach offers the thesis that constitutional judicial review (70) (as well as that of the public) of the legislation of taxes—according to the above narrow definition—is different from the review of other mandatory payments—TRI (127, 131) and PMP (93). The logic behind this is that the latter should be based on accurate calculations and estimates, which provides the public and judiciary with a better understanding and analytical and measurable tools in order to consider the government's decisions and actions. In other words, if the government levies a tax, the burden of proof that it does not provide quid pro quo consideration to the taxpayer, who argues that the tax is not based on consent hence there is no obligation to pay it, is upon the challenger. If, on the other hand, the government imposes any other mandatory payments, such as duties for specific and designated public goods or services, PMP (93), or TRI, which might infringe upon constitutional rights or values, (e.g. property rights, equal rights, freedom of contrast or occupation), then the burden of proof shifts to the government to justify such a violation. In the legal field, this is not a small matter. However, one has to acknowledge that, for the time being, U.S. Courts have demonstrated a significant reluctance to apply their judicial review on tax legislation as is discussed below [p. 40].

5. TRI—TAX INCENTIVES AND OTHER RELIEFS

Once we have adopted a tax system based on a clear model with a sensible base and tax rates, we should assume that the system should apply to all taxpayers equally and consistently in accordance with clear criteria. Alas, it turns out that the aforementioned Coalition [pp. 24, 75] of legislators, politicians and pressure groups have some difficulties accepting this idea. Indeed, every tax system known to us contains various tax breaks (122), which represent legal concessions aimed at easing the tax burden from different groups or certain activities (122). Note that the term we use in this book, Tax Reliefs and Incentives—TRI (84, 127, 131) [pp. 3, 31]—is quite similar to the general expression "tax break". The first category of tax breaks is hardly a relief. It stems from the constitution right for human dignity, the right to survive [p. 50] and from the benefit principle as well. The category is composed of several Code provisions aimed to leave enough resources out of the tax base to provide the taxpayer with a dignified minimum standard of living. These provisions draw a line of minimum income below which the government should not charge taxpayers for the public goods and services it provides. The common and general measures for this category are personal exemption and standard deductions [pp. 12, 287].

The reasons and justifications for this are as follows: First, taxes should not infringe upon the basic constitutional right to survive. Taxes are not supposed to drive any person below the poverty line. It seems a bit redundant to elaborate on that [p. 50]. Second, a person who is below the minimum standard of living gets very little benefit, if any, from the provision of public goods and services [p. 71].

The major problem with these provisions is that they are available to all taxpayers, even to the wealthier. Hence, they provide a greater tax saving (133) to those who earn more [pp. 4, 240]. This problem is moderated by phase-out (94) provisions [p. 35].

The next category deals with special reliefs for special personal needs and circumstances. We mention briefly the deductibility of the following costs and expenses: high medical expenses; special expenses for schooling including tuition or tutoring by someone especially trained to meet a child's specific needs; typical preschool education for children who suffer from developmental delays; the cost of aides required for a child to benefit from regular or special education; the cost of special instruction, training or therapy such as OT, speech, remedial reading, etc.; expenses for diagnostic evaluations by qualified personnel, and for exercise programs if recommended and monitored by qualified medical personnel to treat a specific condition; the cost of transportation to and from specially-equipped schools or therapy sessions, including airfare and lodging for parents and children to obtain treatment or testing; the cost of equipment or devices used primarily for the alleviation of a person's illness; and limited costs of home alternation or adaptation to the medical condition of a member of the household. Parents' attendance at disability-related conferences and related books and materials are deductible as well, as are expenses for special diets and legal expenses incident to medical care. In addition, there are some tax credits which aim to encourage special social causes and activities [p. 324].

One may justify these reliefs by considering them as providing positive externalities to the whole society. As explained above [p. 21], a better-educated society with healthier members is a better society. Yet using tax incentives for these causes entails a significant price. First, in some ways these reliefs are a substitute for an efficient and workable welfare, and national educational and health programs. Those reliefs should be considered as an indication that the government fails to provide those programs directly. Instead, the government privatizes those goods and services [which the private market is unable to provide due to a market failure caused by adverse selection (8)] and indirectly provides private programs that benefit the better-situated members of the U.S. society. It serves much better the Coalition [pp. 24, 75]: the physicians' organizations and interests, the pharmacological industries and the politicians, who are funded by those organizations and industries. Second, we mentioned the higher tax saving (133) [pp. 4, 240] to taxpayers with higher ability, and the partial solution of phase-out, which makes the tax system much complicated than is needed.

Since there is no certain way to determine who enjoys these tax incentives—e.g. the patient or the physician who provide the medical service [pp. 3–5]—the role of those incentives regarding the growing social gaps in the U.S. should be studied thoroughly.

The third category of tax breaks stems from the government's failure to provide other types of public goods and services to a specific population group. The rationale for granting these tax reliefs can be explained by the fact that the taxpayers entitled to these reliefs do not enjoy the full range of public services provided to the general public. In the absence of full benefit, it is likely that these taxpayers would not agree to pay the full tax payable by other taxpayers who do benefit from the full range of public services. As is discussed [pp. 7, 48–50], without real, direct or constructive consent to pay the tax, the tax might not withstand a judicial review (70). Code Sec. 165(i) might serve as an interesting and innovative example. The traditional explanation for the deductibility of casualty and theft losses (22) [p. 50] is the concept of discretionary economic power, i.e. the tax base should be the taxpayer's discretionary power to consume or the taxpayer's accretion of wealth [p. 159]. When there is an unexpected decrease of wealth, the taxpayer is entitled to a deduction. Yet, there might be an additional explanation. Losses caused by disasters, larceny, theft and robbery happen, in fact, due to the government's failure to provide public goods and services, prevention measures, good education to the offenders, or reliable protection to the victims. Ponzi schemes are possible probably due to the lack of government regulation. In such cases, the government fails to provide the expected goods and services to the victims. As a result, the victims do not receive a quid pro quo consideration for their tax payments. A fair and sensible legislature has to reach a balanced situation—a reduction of the tax payments to match the unsatisfactory goods and services. Such a reduction is embodied in the casualty loss deduction. [pp. 50, 51].

Code Sec. 139, which exempts disaster relief payments from income tax, or the *Katrina Emergency Tax Relief* Act of 2005, which was extended later on to other disaster areas, may serve as examples for such an argument.

Another type of tax relief is granted to certain taxpayers who directly execute and promote government goals at a considerable expense. Such activities by the private sector entail significant positive externalities (44) and enable the government to reduce its spending as well as its revenue. If these taxpayers were also required to pay the general taxes, which supposedly finance the same government goals, they would end up paying the tax twice. Hence, special expenses may be deductible by such taxpayers. For example, there are several provisions in the Code that can be explained in light of the above analysis. The immediate deduction for oil and gas exploration [or the immediate deduction for R&D expenses (108)], might be viewed as a transaction that represents the government's interest in achieving energy independence and economic growth, and therefore it decides to invest in such activity. On the other hand, a free market economy rejects the idea that the government would be involved directly in such business activity. Hence, governments enter into a partnership with the private sector wherein the private partner invests the labor and some of the capital, and the silent partner, i.e. the government, invests the additional capital. Yet instead of allocating the needed capital through direct grants, the government provides it through allowing the private partner the immediate deduction of its capital investment. As will be shown below [p. 256] immediate deduction of capital expenses provides a significant tax saving (133). Such an observation leads to the conclusion that those tax reliefs should be regarded as part of (negative) PMP (93): they are granted to the taxpayers as a return to their contribution to the positive externalities they provide.

Note though, that these types of tax reliefs, although they might be justified, actually embody several controversial issues. As mentioned, the major problem is lack of transparency. Despite the publication of the tax expenditure budget (127), which is explained below, it is almost impossible to evaluate in advance how much money the government spends in such a "partnership", as opposed to a transaction where the government and the private investors agree ahead of time how much each of them will invest, or what the maximum amount spent will be. Hence, such relief allows the private investor to spend as much money as it pleases, and the government has to fulfill its part of the deal and keep giving up revenue, even if the amount exceeds what the government would have agreed to spend by a direct investment. Consequently, due to the moral hazard phenomenon (79) the private investor might spend much more money than needed and the structure of such a transaction might lead to significant inefficiency. In addition, these tax relief indicate, once again, a certain degree of privatization, which the Coalition [pp. 24, 75] is very much anxious to promote.

The fifth category of tax reliefs consists of those provisions that are meant to encourage taxpayers to perform certain activities or behaviors. For example, tax credits for building affordable houses for the needy, or for new home ownership; Qualified Bonds Credits; credit for purchasing New Clean Renewable Energy Bonds, or qualified energy conservation bonds; qualified school construction bonds; and other social purposes [p. 324].

The sixth category of tax reliefs consists of tax provisions intended—as argued above [p. 21]—to compensate those taxpayers whose economic activity creates significant positive externalities that benefit the public.

The legislation of tax reliefs involves a fair amount of problems. Toward the late 1960s, law professor Stanley Surrey developed the concept and coined the term of Tax Expenditure (127); [p. 3]. The idea is simple and sensible. Any kind of a deviation from the comprehensive income tax base and the "net income concept", which lowers the taxpayers' tax payments, should be considered as a government grant or spending, and should be reported to the public through the annual budget in the Tax Expenditure Budget. In 1974 the Congress adopted the idea, and enacted the Congressional Budget and Impoundment Control Act of 1974. Since then, the Office of Management and Budget and the Congressional Joint Committee on Taxation has published lists of tax expenditures annually. The Tax Expenditure Budget elaborates the estimated revenue losses from special exclusions, exemptions, deductions, credits, deferrals, and preferential tax rates provided by Federal income tax law. Yet, it is difficult to follow the full significance of the benefits and to estimate the true amounts that certain taxpayers or activities receive indirectly from the government.

Even with the tax expenditure budget, there are serious problems with TRI (127, 131). Most tax scholars agree that using the tax system to encourage or stimulate certain activities or behavior, or to compensate taxpayers for providing positive externalities, is wrong. There are several arguments for that claim.

The first argument is indeed the lack of transparency. Despite the tax expenditure budget (127), [p. 3] TRI give a lot of power to the government to disperse public money without proper supervision. When the government provides direct grants, expenses must be elaborated and detailed in the annual budget and the allocation deliberation every year. Those processes face direct public scrutiny and criticism. On the other hand, TRI provide hidden advantages to a certain part of the public (mostly the members of the Coalition) [pp. 24, 75]. The public is hardly able to evaluate the magnitude of the total revenue losses for the government due to its waiving of the taxes.

Furthermore, as opposed to the government's direct spending, which appears each year in the annual budget's deliberation and must get the approval of the public agents—the government—every year, TRI (84, 127, 131) [pp. 3, 31] are enacted only once and they stay until the legislature finds the time and the interest to reevaluate their aims and justification. Therefore, TRI stay within the tax code long after their justification has expired.

In addition, the actual meaning of the TRI is that they enable a hidden process of privatization by transferring part of the government's responsibilities (the provision of public goods and services including effective supervision and regulation, and taking care of market failures) to the private sector. The problem with privatization is that in some cases it contradicts the major goal and mission of any government, which is to provide public goods and services that the private sector is unable to provide in an efficient way. Adverse selection (8) [p. 127] and moral hazard (79), which cause market failures in the areas of health, social and educational insurances should lead a reliable and accountable government to make sure these kinds of services are provided to the public in a direct, universal and efficient way. Refraining from doing so, and encouraging private entities to offer these good and services in return for tax reliefs, might create a situation where private entities—usually with economic and political power and self-interests—may dominate some economic components of the regime in a non-democratic process, and without public awareness or attention. And, once again, the impact of such situations on the growing social gaps seems quite obvious. Moreover, and above all, there is no certainty that TRI achieve their stated goals.

In addition, direct grants that are provided in a discriminatory way may face constitutional judicial review whereas selective discriminatory TRI might escape such review due to the fact that U.S. courts are quite reluctant to scrutinize tax legislation [p. 40]. Additionally, it seems almost impossible for the public to estimate the TRI's full cost. Experience teaches that most of the Congressional deliberation and the public debate focuses on direct spending and hardly on TRI.

As for efficiency considerations, using TRI is regarded a wasteful measure, since part of the tax benefits "leak", to taxpayers and activities that there is no need or intention to encourage. Moreover, the incentives create economic distortion by changing the goods and services' prices for different taxpayers. Another significant problem is that TRI, almost by definition, increase social gaps and socio-economic inequality, and consequently create economic distortion and inefficiency. Another special and significant economic problem has arisen as a result of the use of TRI. Taxpayers who are eligible for TRI achieve a higher rate of return due to the relief they enjoy. The result is that these taxpayers tend to make unnecessary and inefficient financial decisions just because of the tax reliefs, instead of diverting or channeling their economic activity to more efficient investments, which are not eligible for these reliefs.

Another argument is the issue of higher tax saving (133) [pp. 4, 240] for high income taxpayers. As the income of a taxpayer increases and the taxpayer is charged a higher marginal tax rate, they reap a greater benefit from the TRI amount. Such a result distorts the principle of might horizontal equity and undermines the progressivity of the income tax rates presented to the public. Note that in order to ease the equity problem, some of the TRI are phased-out (94) once the taxpayer's taxable income reach a certain level [p. 35].

The magnitude of the TRI in the U.S. is almost unbelievable. The President's Office of Management and Budget (OMB)'s projection is that the total cost of tax expenditures in 2015 is $1.339 trillion, with $131 billion in corporate tax expenditures and $1.208 trillion in individuals. The largest individual tax expenditures are aimed at health, housing, and various ways of personal saving, mainly for retirement. The largest corporate tax expenditure is tax deferral. Law professor Calvin Johnson launched an exciting endeavor—"The Shelf Project: Revenue-Raising Projects That Defend the Tax Base". His conclusion and proposal, which was sent to leading Senators, Congressmen, and other government officials and organizations, lists 50 ways to raise a total of $1 trillion in revenue per year (without the introduction of a VAT or income tax rate hike) by eliminating most of the TRI provisions (84, 127, 131) [pp. 3, 31] over a decade beginning in 2009–2010.

6. PHASE-OUT OF TAX RELIEFS

In order to cope with the regressive impact of the tax breaks—deduction, exemption and tax credits, the Congress has introduced a phase-out mechanism (82, 94) to those provisions that aim to ease the tax burden of the lower income earners, or to eliminate the benefit of the tax reliefs from higher income taxpayers. During the last decades, phase-out provisions were introduced for the following TRI: Personal exemptions [pp. 12, 287]; Itemized deduction [p. 288]; EITC (37), [p. 325]; Child Care credit, Child and dependent tax credit, and tax credit for adoption cost [p. 320]; American opportunity credit for eligible educational expenses [p. 323]; Lifetime learning tax credit of eligible expenses [p. 323]; Deduction of education tuition and fees [pp. 149, 289]; Coverdell educational savings account; Student loan interest deduction; Exemption of interest on education saving bond program [p. 295]; Saver's Tax credit; Tax credit for Roth IRA contributions [p. 324]; Deduction for IRA contribution; quasi exemption for Taxation of Social security benefits; and Exemption from liability of the Alternative minimum tax [p. 328].

7. NEGATIVE TAX RELIEFS: PIGOVIAN TAX PAYMENTS (PMPs)

In accordance with the distinction we have offered above between a pure tax and a regulatory tax, [p. 21] Pigovian taxes are indeed not actually taxes. Their purpose is not to raise revenue but rather to restore basic principles of a free market economy [p. 13]. It is levied because the taxpayer, who enjoys the benefit of goods or services—usually provided by the private market—avoids paying their real cost. In order to correct such a situation, the government might levy PMP [p. 13] which are indeed "negative tax expenditures"; i.e. ***mandatory payments*** whose purpose is to correct market failures (75).

Experience teaches us that in some cases the free-market mechanism cannot allocate the right price of certain goods and services that entail negative externalities. Thus, the optimal way (not according to Coase—[p. 13]) is to shift the real economic cost to the one who creates the externalities. This is also known as "internalizing" a tax. For example, there may be a mandatory payment on cigarettes or alcohol ("sin tax"), or on goods whose production involves pollution. Such a payment aims to shift the economic cost of damages against public health and safety to the producers, consumers, or both. One may also consider a PMP on "junk food", designated to shift the additional national health expenses caused by unhealthy nutrition to the consumers/producers, and to finance the extra medical outlay. In other words, PMP serve as a **pricing process,** which is supposed to determine the real economic cost of goods and services that come with negative externalities and shift it onto those who produce the externalities or enjoy/benefit from them.

Pigovian mandatory payments are not penalties either; according to our legal and constitutional values, there is no way to punish anybody without due process (33), i.e. trial, evidence and a judicial verdict. They are not intended to deter the public from using those harmful products, although they can certainly cause a reduction in their aggregate demand due to the increase in price, and ultimately reduce the amount of the negative externality. They are just a tool aiming to fix those market failures that harm free market economy; a means designated to shift un-internalized social costs.

Such an analysis suggests also that PMP are the economic (though compulsory) price, which does not undermine tax neutrality nor distort economic and social behavior, but rather improves the free market and enhances the common welfare.

8. THE IMPORTANCE OF THE DISTINCTION BETWEEN TAX, TRIs AND PMPs

As we mentioned already, and is discussed further below, the U.S. courts are very much reluctant to review almost anything that is labeled as tax. Such labeling provides almost instant immunity from constitutional review and enables the government, which is constantly under the pressure of the other members of the Powerful Group Coalition [pp. 24, 75], to legislate "tax" provisions—TRI (127, 131) [pp. 3, 31]—that eventually do not necessarily enhance the wellbeing of the general public.

Since TRI and PMP bills are based on assumptions, estimations and calculations, and their goals are usually stated openly to the public, they could be evaluated and reviewed quite easily. The following simple examples may serve the argument.

1) Under the U.S. income tax system the personal exemption was a given amount of money ($4,050 per individual in 2016) regardless the taxpayer's personal circumstances (besides the phased out (82, 94) which begins with a high amount of taxable income) [p. 287]. In addition, the Code allows another fixed amount as a standard deduction [p. 287].

   The Tax Foundation adjusted the Bureau of Economic Analysis, which compared the cost of living in all U.S. states in 2013. It shows how much $100 can buy in each state in 2015. The difference between the state where $100 is worth the most ($115.21) and the least ($84.96) is a little more than $30! One may wonder whether, due to constitutional principle of equality (either of the Fourteenth Amendment or the Due Process Clause (33) of the Fifth Amendment), these differences should be taken into consideration while the federal legislature calculates the proper amounts of the personal exemption & the standard deductions.

2) Suppose the government decided to deal with the negative externalities caused by smoking products. Good econometric research can produce the estimate of the monetary aggregate damages smoking produces, directly and indirectly, to the public and to the annual national health expenses. That should produce the total amount the PMP should raise. Another research can produce the estimate of how this amount should be distributed on every smoker. Suppose these studies arrive to the conclusion that a smoker has to pay the amount of $3.40 per cigarette pack. If the PMP is higher, the smoker has a good claim that he is penalized. If the amount is lower, the public has a good argument that it shares—without consent—the price that the smoker is supposed to pay. In both cases, an active court should decide either to lower the PMP on cigarettes, or raise it.

3) The government has arrived at the conclusion that it should be responsible for public health. In order to encourage the purchase of health insurance it offers a tax incentive: a special exemption that an employee receives for their employer's contribution to medical insurance. Such an exemption violates several constitutional concepts such as equal treatment (between employees who do not buy health insurance and those who do), freedom of contract and occupation, and indirectly the right of property of the rest of the taxpayers who have to pay higher tax payments for an exemption they do not enjoy. An active court would require the government to provide solid justification for such violations. The court could probably accept the notion that health insurance is a positive goal (with positive externalities) but would insist on some proofs that the tax exemption is the most efficient solution. A good economic study can evaluate two factors: the loss of revenue the government suffers from this exemption and what the aggregate cost will be of a mandatory national health insurance [p. 127]. In addition, we have to consider whether the mandatory health insurance will add to the national budget and how the new burden should be distributed among the public. Furthermore, optimal taxation's insight [pp. 13, 85] should inquire if the additional burden that

the extra tax causes is lower or higher than the additional welfare caused by the new program.

Chapter Four

LEGAL SOURCES

The purpose of the above discussion is to demonstrate that under any tax system lies a wide array of concepts, principles, insights and rules from numerous disciplines [p. 17]. The only way to levy taxes is through the legislative process. Tax laws have to comply with known legal and constitutional concepts and methodologies. Furthermore, a purposive interpretation of tax laws requires familiarity with wide and multiple sources and disciplines—constitutional, legal, economic, social and philosophical. We refer to tax law as "an integration of disciplines".

1. TAX LEGISLATION, CONSTITUTIONAL LAW AND THE THREATS TO HUMAN RIGHTS

Tax legislation raises two major constitutional issues: 1) The power/authority to levy taxes; and 2) The substance and quality of the tax laws, their compliance with constitutional principles and the degree of possible infringement on such principles.

A. The Power to Lay Taxes

Article 1, Section 8 of the U.S. Constitution describes the general power of the Congress in terms of tax laws as follow:

> *The Congress shall have power to lay and collect taxes, duties, imposts and excises, to pay the debts and provide* ***for the common defense and general welfare*** *of the United States;*

(emphasis added)

The traditional approach, expressed by the Supreme Court is that "the public funds may be appropriated 'to provide for the general welfare of the United States . . .While, therefore, the power to tax is not unlimited, its confines are set in the clause which confers it," [*United States v. Butler*]. A broad interpretation is that in practice, the power to tax is indeed unlimited; one may argue that it is impossible to provide evidence that a tax's revenue, which is spent by the government, does not provide for the general welfare of the United States. Based on some insights and doctrines developed in the last half century in the field of public finance—known as "optimal taxation" (90 below)—welfare and its decline due to taxes can be estimated. As discussed below, [p. 85] any tax has a deadweight loss, meaning that the amount of the loss of the general welfare is greater than the tax's revenue that the government collects. Hence, the government has to be efficient enough to provide a greater amount of welfare than the deadweight loss, or the assumption regarding the public consent to pay taxes [pp. 7, 48–50, 100, 102], the benefit principle and the constitutional requirement of the ***general welfare*** *of the United States* do not hold (Who consents to pay any price just to receive a smaller amount of welfare in return? How can a court justify a tax that does not align with one out of the two goals set by the Constitution?). In other words, an inefficient government may levy un-constitutional taxes.

Section 9 of Article 1 of the U.S. Constitution states:

"No Capitation, or other direct, Tax shall be laid, unless in Proportion to the Census or Enumeration herein before directed to be taken".

Consequently, when Congress legislated the first income tax in the United States, it was held invalid by the Supreme Court (*Pollock v. Farmers' Loan & Trust Company*, 1895). The Court ruled that a particular type of income tax (a tax on income derived from property) was actually a direct tax and had to be levied in proportion to each state's population. The response was the Sixteenth Amendment to the United States Constitution, approved by Congress in 1909 and ratified in 1913, which removed the requirement that taxes on income have to be apportioned by population and provided that:

"The Congress shall have power to lay and collect taxes on incomes, from whatever source derived, without apportionment among the several States, and without regard to any census or enumeration."

Note that some scholars argued that the power of the Congress to tax income derives from Article I, Section 8, Clause 1 and not from the Sixteenth Amendment, which only removed the apportionment requirement from income tax (if it is a direct tax at all). Anyway, the traditional belief is that the specific wording of the Amendment left the apportionment to apply to other direct taxes (including capitation and real-estate taxes, and maybe a direct-consumption tax). Such belief ignores economic analyses, which indicate that Income, Wealth, Property and Consumption have much more in common than envisioned in 1909 [pp. 111, 145, 153].

B. The Quality and the Substance of Tax Legislation: A Case of Judicial Reluctance

In 1920 the Supreme Court demonstrated, in one of the most famous, fundamental and significant cases in the history of the U.S. tax law, a high degree of judicial review regarding tax legislation. Ms. Macomber had received a significant amount of stock dividends (28). Since the Congress specifically declared in the Revenue Act of 1916 that a "stock dividend shall be considered income, to the amount of its cash value," the IRS thought to tax her. The Supreme Court disapproved. The majority concluded that a stock dividend is not within the ordinary meaning of the term "income", which contains two major attributes. One is a gain or profit. The other according the majority's view:

" 'the gain—derived—from—capital,' etc. Here we have the essential matter: not a gain accruing to capital, not a growth or increment of value in the investment; but a gain, a profit, something of exchangeable value proceeding from the property, severed from the capital however invested or employed, and coming in, being "derived," that is, received or drawn by the recipient (the taxpayer) for his separate use, benefit and disposal;—that is income derived from property. Nothing else answers the description."

In other words, Income means **realized** gain or profit.

Since stock dividends are not separated from the issuing corporation, i.e. do not distribute money to its shareholders but provide them with additional "papers", and since "enrichment through increase in value of capital investment is not income in any proper meaning of the term".

The majority concluded:

"Thus, from every point of view, we are brought irresistibly to the conclusion that neither under the Sixteenth Amendment nor otherwise has Congress power to tax without apportionment a true stock dividend made lawfully and in good faith, or the accumulated profits behind it, as income of the stockholder. The Revenue Act of 1916, in so far as it imposes a tax upon the stockholder because of such dividend, contravenes the provisions of Article I, § 2, cl. 3, and Article I, § 9, cl. 4, of the Constitution, and to this extent is invalid notwithstanding the Sixteenth Amendment."

This decision raises several issues, including the full meaning of realization and its impact on the development of income tax in the U.S. [pp. 163, 198], and retroactive tax legislation [p. 52]. The essential point here is that the Supreme Court had signaled to the Congress that it is not free to change the meaning of words or terms by twisting their accepted meaning; that the Congress does not have the power to redefine the term income as it appeared in the Constitution.

Some 90 years later the United States Court of Appeals for the District of Columbia Circuit had a different view. In the controversial *Murphy v. IRS* case [pp. 190, 245], the court originally held that the federal income taxation of emotional distress awards is unconstitutional. That decision was revised by the same Court a few months later. The later decision of the Court was that the taxpayer's recovery could be taxed under Article I, Section 8 of the Constitution even if the recovery was not classified as "income" under the Sixteenth Amendment. The court ruled that gross income under section 61 of the Internal Revenue Code includes compensatory damages for non-physical injuries, even if the award is not an "accession to wealth." Furthermore, the court decided that the income tax imposed on such an award is an indirect tax, regardless of whether or not the recovery is restoration of "human capital." The Court stated:

"[a]lthough the 'Congress cannot make a thing income which is not so in fact,' [. . .] it can label a thing income and tax it, so long as it acts within its constitutional authority, which includes not only the Sixteenth Amendment but also Article I, Sections 8 and 9.

The personal injury award was 'within the reach of the congressional power to tax under Article I, Section 8 of the Constitution. . . [even if the award was] not income within the meaning of the Sixteenth Amendment.' "

On April 21, 2008, the Supreme Court declined to review the *Murphy* decision.

We find the court's argumentation quite surprising—maybe disappointing—and we'll get back to it later [p. 245].

A few years later the Supreme Court had to cope with another type of "labeling"—the *Sebelius* case that deals, *inter alia,* with the question of whether the Congress has the power to require all citizens to obtain health insurance or penalize individuals who refrain from buying medical insurance offered by the Patient Protection and Affordable Care Act ("Obamacare"). One of this act's major purposes was to increase the number of Americans covered by health insurance and decrease the cost of health care. The case focused on 26 U.S. Code § 5000A, of which the title of Subsection (a) states: **Requirement to maintain minimum essential coverage.** The title of Subsection (b) is: **Shared responsibility payment.** Yet paragraph (1) states "If a taxpayer . . . . fails to meet the requirement of subsection (a) . . . . there is hereby imposed on the taxpayer a **penalty** with respect to such failures. . . .". The Congress labeled the mandatory payment as a "penalty" eighteen times throughout the Act. The amount of the penalty was to be determined with reference to the individual's income and the size of their family, and would be paid to the IRS with the individual's income tax. In addition, the Act provided that the penalty should be assessed and collected in the same manner as tax penalties, such as the penalty for claiming too large an income tax refund. One of the questions presented to the Court was the constitutionality of the payment levied by the Act.

The Court was divided. The minority (composed of four Justices: Scalia, Kennedy, Thomas, and Alito) concluded that the payment was unconstitutional since it is indeed a penalty, not a tax and that such economic activity regulation is beyond the powers granted to the Congress under the Commerce Clause. The majority (Chief Justice Roberts, Justices Ginsburg, Breyer, Sotomayor and Kagan) who upheld the law were divided as well. Chief Justice Roberts argued that the payment was not really a penalty, but rather an indirect tax not specified under the apportionment requirement: "A tax on going without health insurance does not fall within any recognized category of direct tax". In some way Chief Justice Roberts' opinion implies that the payment is under the umbrella of income tax: "Congress has done as increasing taxes on those who have a certain amount of income, but choose to go without health insurance. Such legislation is within Congress's power to tax." This is consistent with the regulatory function of the tax system, which seeks to influence conduct.

Justice Ginsburg, joined by Justices Breyer, Sotomayor and Kagan, concluded that the payment is within Congress's power under the Commerce Clause of Article 1 Sec. 8 cl. 3 of the Constitution.

Justice Ginsburg elaborated on the issue of adverse selection (8) [p. 127], and the free rider phenomenon (50), and she concluded:

> *"It is well established by decisions of this Court that the power to regulate commerce includes the power to regulate the prices at which commodities in that commerce are dealt in and practices affecting such prices. . . . the Commerce Clause authorizes Congress to enact the minimum coverage provision."*

As discussed below [p. 54], it seems to us that Justice Ginsburg's approach is addressing and implementing (though not in so many words) the accurate definition of the term (pure) "tax"—i.e. payment, which is levied on the general public, intended **only** to finance the costs of the elected government [pp. 21–26] and its limited goals. Indeed, the way both Chief Justice Roberts and Justice Ginsburg describe the challenged payments is that they are a regulatory measure. The (significant in our mind) difference is that Chief Justice Roberts' approach relates to the power of the Congress to lay such payment in the Taxing Power of Article 1, Section 8, Clause 1, while Justice Ginsburg's approach relies on the Commerce Clause in Article 1. Section 8, Clause 3. In other words, according to Justice Ginsburg's approach, the payment in question is in fact not a tax nor a penalty [p. 36], but rather a Pigovian Mandatory Payment [pp. 13, 36, 54], which the Congress has a power to levy, under some limitations.

The *Murphy* decision and Chief Justice Roberts' opinion in *Sebelius* embody a constant tendency. For about the last eighty years, the U.S. courts have demonstrated a significant reluctance when facing constitutional challenges regarding tax legislation. It seems that the general trend is quite simple—perhaps simplistic. The courts confine their review to the issue of the Congress' power/authority to levy taxes, and refrain from a substantive judicial review of fiscal legislation, and from examining the quality of the tax laws, their purposes, whether the goals are achieved and the possible violations of constitutional rights and interests.

One explanation for this reluctance is based on the conclusion that, once the Congress had been granted the power to lay and collect taxes, and the Sixteenth Amendment removed the apportionment requirement from income tax, the Congressional limits have been greatly narrowed and their discretion has been vastly broadened.

Another explanation for the courts' tendency not to intervene probably relies on the Fifth and the Fourteenth Amendments, which grant the government the power of eminent domain, i.e. the power to take private property for "public use." Under this approach, whether a tax is indeed a "taking"/confiscatory measure is no longer relevant since it is for "public use." The underlying rationale for such an explanation is that taxes, by definition, are confiscatory measurements. As indicated throughout this book, such a rationale is unacceptable in a modern democratic society; taxes are not "taking" or confiscatory measures. They are meant to be the right price, that we consent to pay, for the public goods and services.

A factor that has probably contributed to such reluctance is the "Lochner era"—or trauma—roughly spanning the period between 1890 to 1937. During this era the United States Supreme Court tended to strike down economic regulations mandating certain working conditions or wages, or limiting working hours. In 1937 this tendency was changed by the *West Coast Hotel Co. v. Parrish* Supreme Court decision, and the Lochner era has since been considered as an unfortunate period in U.S. jurisprudence. As a result, it might be that the courts have adopted an "anti-Lochner" approach and refrain from undermining or questioning issues of economic and social policy, even if the application of such policies entails infringement of constitutional principles and rights. Another possible explanation, which is very much connected to the ones above, is the courts' tendency (or excuse) of offering a very conservative interpretation to the standing requirement (114), [p. 45]. In 2014, the U.S. Supreme Court dealt with a challenge to strike down a discriminatory statutory provision that provided special tax privileges to religious institutes and their employees [*Arizona Christian School Tuition Organization v. WINN et al.* (2011)]. The Court repeated its persistent approach:

> *"To obtain a determination on the merits in federal court, parties seeking relief must show that they have standing under Article III of the Constitution. . . . . .* ***This Court has rejected the general proposition that an individual who has paid taxes has a "continuing, legally cognizable interest in ensuring that those funds are not* used *by the Government in a way that violates the Constitution"*** (emphasis added).

The Court of Appeals of the 7th Circuit (Chicago) took the same approach. A few months later, in the *Freedom From Religion Foundation v. Lew* case ("the *FFRF v. Lew* case") it stated similarly:

> *"As a general rule, standing to challenge the legality of a government expenditure 'cannot be based on a plaintiff's mere status as a taxpayer'. Winn,* 131 S. Ct. at 1442".

We find these traditional arguments hard to swallow at the beginning of the 21st century. Basic constitutional questions were swept away. As is discussed below [p. 46], it is very bothersome that the petitioners in both cases (as with other previous cases), had assumed that they had a better chance if they relied on the cozy, comfortable and more favored ground of the Establishment Clause, instead of general Constitutional arguments such as principles of equality, freedom of contract and occupation and private property. Yet they were refused by the courts due to the Standing requirement (114). In practice, the Standing requirement, especially in economic matters, mainly serves the interest of those small but influential groups and leaves the public indefensible. In the area of private law, the American legal system has found ways to offer legal defenses and remedies to individuals who serve the public's interests, such as punitive damages and class actions. Thus, one may wonder whether it is about time to eliminate the Standing requirement in petitions and lawsuits challenging discriminatory tax laws.

C. Substantive Judicial Review of Tax Legislation

1) The Limitations on the Power to Tax

Our approach suggests that merely labeling an act as "tax", or a receipt as "income", or a payment as a "penalty", should not change the standards of constitutional judicial review. Furthermore, if labeling a regulatory act as a "tax", which under the umbrella of the Sixteenth Amendment provides a quasi-immunity from judicial review, then policymakers who prefer to avoid judicial review would rather promote their policy by using Tax Reliefs and Incentives (TRI) as a regulatory tool instead of using other—more direct and appropriate—means. Thus, the courts' reluctance to perform judicial review of tax legislation may produce two undesired consequences. First, discriminatory laws, which probably won't survive judicial review if enacted as non-fiscal legislation, enjoy the "quasi-immunity" reserved for "tax law". Second, such legislation causes the tax code to become complicated, and obscures and detracts it from its true and designated goal—to finance the expenses of the elected governments. As is discussed below, in most cases, such a situation serves the interests of the powerful groups and sectors and as a result the tax system becomes regressive; TRI (84, 127, 131) [pp. 3, 31] create economic distortions, lack of public supervision on the government, a hidden process of privatization of the government chores, increased social gaps and eventually inefficiency [pp. 29–36].

Thus, our claim is that the term 'tax' should be very clear and narrow [p. 30] and, like any other legislation, taxes have to comply with the limitations imposed upon the legislature by the U.S. Constitution. Tax legislation (both primary and secondary) may be declared void if it is used exclusively to punish or to ban an activity, if it is too harsh and oppressive, or if it violates the Equal Protection Clause and the Establishment Clause [p. 43]. Furthermore, if the tax deprives property without due process (33), it should be reviewed. The aggregate private property is the common-collective property of the community's members. Reality teaches us that today, the real threat to private property is the small but influential groups that covet the collective private property more than the government might violate this constitutional right.

Furthermore, providing benefits to one group but not to the general public violates the principles of equality, free competition, and freedom of contract and occupation. A penny is a penny, and if a person loses one penny because his fellow gets a direct subsidy, this is a violation of constitutional principles. Arguing a "lack of standing" in order to government intends to provide, and specifies their price—the cost to the public. If we do not approve the budget—through our representative agents in the Congress—then the elected government is not allowed to function—a government shutdown. This is the constitutional reflection of the basic rule "No Taxation Without Representation". Since representation is not a mere formal concept but rather expresses the voters' approval, then the substantive rule means: "No Taxation Without Consent".

The conclusion that the tax is based on the taxpayers' consent to pay is a significant one. It brings in an important factor to the legal and constitutional discussion. When the legislature imposes duties and limitations there is an assumption that, under the terms of the Social Contract, we have agreed to those duties and limitations. Yet, it may be, in rare and unusual circumstances, that the legislature deviates from the "terms of agency" and legislates a law that a reasonable person cannot be assumed to have agreed and accepted. In cases where the enacted tax law is so unreasonable, the assumption of consent has no merit nor basis. For example, the tax law may be extremely unfair, decrease the taxpayer's welfare without due consideration/compensation, or create unjust discrimination. If the taxpayer is indeed able to satisfy the burden of providing hard evidence that he or she does not receive a fair return for her tax payments, the consent assumption is no longer valid. In such circumstances she may have a constitutional right not to pay the unjustified tax. [p. 7]

Code § 1402(e) and (g) may give us a unique and insightful example of how tax legislature perhaps accepts this reasoning and provides a relief when a taxpayer can prove that the assumption of consent has no merit. These sections provide an exemption from Social Security taxes to religious persons who have a religious objection to receiving public insurance and belong to a religion that will provide the assistance that others ordinarily would receive under Social Security, i.e. they will not receive any consideration in return for the mandatory payments. In several cases the court held that these sections are permissible accommodations of religion. E.g. *Hatcher v. Com. of Internal Revenue* (1930); *Templeton v. Com. of Internal Revenue* (1983); *Droz v. Commissioner of Internal Revenue* (1995).

We dare to argue that in some other unusual cases, when the government fails to provide its public goods and services to a certain area, the population of this area should not bear the same tax burden as the rest of the nation's taxpayers. Assume there is a remote border town. Due to its hostile neighbors, the town suffers occasionally from its enemy attacks. The enemy constantly shells the town, hence the daily life is totally ruined: the educational system does not function, trade and business activity is significantly down, free movement is restricted, and the property and the life of the town's residents are in jeopardy. In such a situation, is it still sensible to assume that the town's residents agree to pay taxes, even though they do not enjoy the basic goods and services? Do they have to pay the same amount of tax as the other safe towns' residents? Don't they have the constitutional right to pay less since they get less, or at least they should not be obligated to pay the full amount of tax until the government takes the necessary steps to restore peace? Note that such argument is quite similar to the justification for progressive tax rate we offer [pp. 24, 99–102]

Another example, which is discussed above [p. 32], is the deduction for casual loses. Such losses occur, most of the time, due to the government's failure to provide satisfactory public services. Suppose an innocent bystander is affected by a hostile, terrorist, or criminal action or natural disaster and suffers significant damage. The chance he can collect damages through civil suit are actually none. Is he entitled to tax reliefs or government compensation? After all, the government failed to provide the most important public services: preventing criminal or hostile activity and protecting personal security and private property. The deductibility [p. 291] of the casualty losses (22) in such cases, might be a reasonable means to ease or answer these questions.

Another example relates to the inhabitants of some parts of Louisiana who suffered from Hurricane Katrina and from the inefficiency of the government that failed to provide sufficient assistance. They paid their taxes in order for the government to provide them with reasonable protection in any circumstance. Since they did not enjoy this protection, should they be granted some tax reliefs? Note that under the current system those taxpayers who suffer economic casualty indeed pay a lesser amount of tax due to the deductibility of causal and theft losses (22) under Code Section 165(c)(3). [p. 32] The question of whether such deductions are sufficient enough or if the taxpayers should receive additional tax reliefs is beyond our point.

The above examples demonstrate the basic requirement of taxation: no taxpayer is expected to pay taxes without consent. The consent is assumed as long as the taxpayer receives quid pro quo consideration—the benefit derived from the public good and services. If the benefit is missing, the taxpayer is entitled to a tax relief that should reflect the absence of the benefit.

4) Tax and the Right to a Dignified Minimum Standard of Living

As mentioned above, [p. 12], any tax system that does not leave the taxpayer with a dignified minimum standard of living probably violates the constitutional right to human dignity. Some scholars draw a line between negative-passive rights and positive-active rights. The former mean that the government should not violate the right by driving humans below a certain level of poverty. The latter means that the government is obligated to ensure that any member of society has the dignified minimum standard of living and, when needed, is obligated to **actively provide** the minimum standard of living [the "second generation human rights" (96)]. Note though, that the line between those types is much thinner than it seems. Anyhow, since we deal here with tax law, we confine our major discussion to a passive-negative human right, i.e. the government should not violate this right by taxing a person and leaving him or her without enough means that guarantee a minimum standard of living. After all, human rights include by definition the right to survive. The economist Arthur Okun expressed this idea in a simple yet clear and precise way:

> *While I am not persuaded by the arguments for many proposed new rights, the case for a right to survival is compelling. The assurance of dignity for every member of the society requires a right to a decent existence—to some minimum standard of nutrition, health care and other essentials of life. Starvation and dignity do not mix well. . . . I do not know anyone today who would disagree, in principle, that every person, regardless of merit or ability to pay, should receive medical care and food in the face of serious illness or malnutrition.*

Indeed, most personal income taxation systems around the world have their own version of leaving the individual with an amount suitable enough to enable him or her and their family to maintain a basic standard of living. The American system reaches this goal by various measures. The major ones are the personal exemptions [§ 151] (of the amount of $4,050 in 2016) for a taxpayer and for each dependent. The child tax credit

[§ 24], (which is worth in 2016 up to $1,000 per child under the age of 17), [§ 32]. The standard deduction [§ 63(c)], which amounts in 2016 for single taxpayer and married couple filing separately the amount of $6,300; for married couple filing joint returns the total amount of $12,600 (69) Tax credit for the elderly and the permanent and totally disabled [§ 22], up to $1,125. For a married couple filling jointly in 2015; deductibility of medical expenses [§ 213(a)]; and the deductibility of casualty losses (22), Code Sec. 165(c)(3).

In addition, the earned income tax credit (37), which is a refundable "negative income tax" [p. 325] signals that the right for a minimum standard of living has turned in the U.S. to a positive-active right (96). As is discussed below, some of the deductions, exemptions and tax credits are phased-out (82) for taxpayers with higher income [pp. 240, 255, 287, 320].

5) The Constitutional Right to Equality

As previously discussed [p. 14], fairness is the most fundamental requirement for a good tax system. Horizontal and Vertical Equity (42) express the principles of fairness in taxation: Mandating that equal taxpayers have to pay equal tax payments and different taxpayers ought to pay different tax payments. The next step is determining the most suitable criteria for equality and differences between taxpayers.

The most prominent trait of taxation is money, the means that we use for paying our taxes. Money represents economic value, an economic ability. Hence, one may argue that the taxpayers' economic ability is the right criterion for equality and differences between taxpayers; taxpayers with equal economic ability (***"ability to pay"***) (1) should pay the same tax payments, and taxpayers with different economic abilities should pay different tax payments.

On the other hand, a very strong argument undermines this conclusion: if the purpose of the tax system is financing public goods and services, then the price each member of the community ought to pay should be in accordance with the taxpayer's benefit derived from those goods and services. Accordingly, equal taxpayers are those who derive/enjoy equal benefit from the government while different taxpayers are those who enjoy different benefits from the government. As we argue below [p. 71], these two criteria (the ability to pay and the benefit principle) are not in conflict, but rather coexist and may be integrated into one synergetic concept.

It should be mentioned though, that in some European countries, the principles of Horizontal and Vertical equity (42) are no longer theoretical or philosophical concepts, but rather constitutional principles mentioned in the written constitutions. Furthermore, some foreign constitutional courts have expressed the notion that the ability to pay is the leading criterion for measuring equality and difference among taxpayers. According to this approach, different tax rates levied on the same amount of income from different sources (e.g. labor, capital income such as interest (36) and capital gain (18)), may be considered a violation of the constitutional principle of equality. Hence, a good constitutional review would ask whether the preferred tax rates for passive income, such as capital gains and interest are justified. As will be discussed below [p. 90], lower tax rates for capital income and capital gain not only contradict principles of equality but also harm efficiency, decrease economic growth and widen the social gaps.

Furthermore, as is discussed below [p. 232], the international community is bothered by international tax planning and tax competition (124). Using the proposed constitutional review on discriminatory tax legislation might solve some of these problems.

6) The Constitution and Retroactive Taxes

Clause 3 of Article I, Section 9 of the United States Constitution prohibits Congress from passing any bill of attainder or ex post facto law. While the term "ex post facto laws" might be construed to embrace all retrospective laws, in the early case of *Calder v. Bull* (1798), the Supreme Court decided that the phrase, as used in the Constitution, applies only to penal and criminal statutes, and eventually not to tax legislation [pp. 53–54].

Retroactive application of a statute may violate substantive due process rights under the Fifth Amendment. In 1938, the Supreme Court acknowledged that applications of new laws to preceding taxable years, might be regarded as an unconstitutional deprivation of property without due process of law. Yet the Court put a proviso to that rule: "the nature of the tax and the circumstances in which it is laid [are] so harsh and oppressive as to transgress the constitutional limitation" (*Welch v. Henry*, 305 U.S. 134, 147 (1938)).

In 1981, the Supreme Court (*U.S. v. Darusmont*) demonstrated, once again, its reluctance to review tax legislation. It concluded that "Current year retroactivity" (the application of income tax statutes to the entire calendar year in which enactment took place), is not a per se violation of the Due Process Clause. That is in spite of the fact that the taxpayer might have relied on the old rules and cannot alter pre-enactment transactions in the light of the new rules.

Furthermore, when the new I.R.C. of 1986 was enacted, taxpayers realized that there was a loophole in one of the Code's provision and took advantage of it. Once the government found out about it, it announced its intention to amend the provision in order to prevent the abuse. The legislation process ended only in 1987 but applied retroactively to 1986. Based on the government's announcement (warning) and due to the fact that the period of retroactivity was slightly over one year, the Supreme Court upheld the amendment.

Only in a rare case with unusual facts, the Supreme Court invalidated a retroactive application of a Federal estate tax provision transaction which took place 12 years (!) earlier. [*Nichols v. Coolidge*, 274 U.S. 531 (1927)].

It seems that the underlying rationale to the courts' general tendency was laid down in *Welch v. Henry*'s statement (1938): "[t]ax legislation is not a promise, and a taxpayer has no vested right in the Internal Revenue Code." This statement is twofold. As for the first part—tax legislation is not a promise—our approach is indeed different. As indicated a few times already [pp. xi, 48] tax legislation is indeed part of the social contract and is based on a presumed consent to pay quid pro quo for the public good and services. As with the private market, one party is not allowed to change the term of a contract unilaterally, so is the case with tax legislation. Each year taxpayers learn (out the deliberation and the approval of the national budget) what kind of public goods and services they will get from the elected government and how much they are going to pay for them. They make serious decisions based on that price, e.g. whether to work harder or spend more time on leisure; to make an investment and postpone current consumption; to take higher risks, etc. Hence, only in very rare cases, where the government can argue seriously and sincerely that without a retroactive legislation the structure of the social contract is in danger, such retroactive tax legislation should be upheld. Another exception to the general rule would be when it is very clear that the tax law's drafter made a clear mistake which leaves the law ineffective, and the tax authority acknowledges the mistake and announces its intention to fix the problem. In such a case, the amending legislation should be upheld even if the process takes longer than one taxable year.

In case the tax legislation is done during the taxable year, it should not be effective before the end of the legislation process. All the transactions that were concluded prior to that date are subject to the old rule and those that take place after that date will be subject to the new rule. There are not too many practical problems in having two different sets of rules during one taxable year.

The second part of the above statement—that a taxpayer has no vested right in the Internal Revenue Code—has two meanings. No doubt, taxpayers have a vested right in the Internal Revenue Code against any retroactive legislation. Yet no taxpayer has the right to act with the belief that the Code will remain unchanged in the future. Suppose a taxpayer made an economic decision (e.g. business, investment) on year 1, based on the Code's provisions in that year. The investment did not materialize/conclude it in that year. If in the beginning of year 2 the law changed, and afterwards she concluded the transaction, then such legislation is not retroactive. It applies to the entire transaction, which was concluded after the date of the legal change. Tax legislation is like any other variable that any person should consider might change in the future during the process of contemplating a deal up to its conclusion.

One may argue though, that our approach is inconsistent. If the tax is based on consent, and if the Congress decided to change it retroactively, then the public consents to the retroactive change. Such an argument is wrong. The consent to pay taxes is just assumed. The assumption is valid as long as the tax is based on accepted principles and ideas—the four canons of a good tax [pp. 9–14]. Changing the rules of the games after the game is over (i.e. the transaction is concluded), definitely contradicts the above canons—the tax should be certain and not arbitrary and consider the convenience of the taxpayer. Furthermore, economic stability is a significant factor of efficiency. Hence, disallowing retroactive tax legislation promotes, in ordinary times, economic efficiency as well.

7) The Constitution and Punitive Taxes

There is no clear line that distinguishes taxation from regulation accompanied by a penalty. Yet, it has been widely accepted that the legislatures cannot use tax law as a punishment. As noted above [p. 26], the Supreme Court stated in *Welch v. Henry* (1938) that taxation is not a penalty imposed upon the taxpayer. One may suspect that in light of the Court of Appeals of D.C.'s approach in the *Murphy* case [pp. 41, 245], if it is taken to the extreme, the Congress might have the power to label a penalty as a tax and legislate it as a tax law in order to bypass the Fifth and Fourteenth amendments' Due Process requirement. However the chances for such an occurrence are probably slim.

The *Sebelius* case [p. 41] deals with the opposite scenario. The case, decided in 2012 by a slim majority, might serve as an example for the confusion in this area. Both Chief Justice Roberts and Justice Ginsburg concluded that the mandatory payment imposed in Code § 5000A(b) is not a penalty, even though the drafter used the term "penalty" some 18 times in the "Obamacare" legislation.

A more accurate analysis, similar to Justice Ginsburg's approach in the *Sebelius* case [pp. 41–42], would lead to the conclusion that the payments are neither tax nor penalties but instead they are "Pigovian Mandatory Payments". (93) As mentioned above [p. 36], PMP are nothing but a regulatory measure designated to correct the price of goods or services that the free market fails to achieve in an efficient way. In fact, the PMP concepts underlies Chief Justice Roberts's approach in the *Sebelius* case:

> *First, for most Americans the amount due will be far less than the price of insurance, and, by statute, it can never be more. It may often be a reasonable financial decision to make the payment rather than purchase insurance.*

Indeed, Code Sec. 5000A does not command taxpayers to buy medical insurance, nor to pay the payment either. It is a tool aimed to improve the free market economy. It is supposed to take care of a market failure (44) and adverse selection (2) and promote efficiency. It requires the market's participants to bear the economic price and the social cost of their actions and decisions. Justice Ginsburg reminds us that, in the medical insurance industry, there is a built-in market failure due to the adverse selection (8) phenomenon, which prevents the free market from reaching the efficient market price. Hence, the government is called upon to fulfill its obligation to what Okun refers to as the "assurance of dignity for every member of the society [which] requires a right for a decent existence—to some minimum standard of nutrition, health care and other essential of life" [p. 50]. I.e. to make sure that the industry operates efficiently. In other words, those who refrain from joining the national medical insurance plan are not penalized by the law, but are required to pay the public the right economic price that is supposed to compensate the public for the damage they create by avoiding the plan.

The amount of the mandatory payment must be estimated and calculated. Accordingly, there is room for judicial review (70). The government carries the burden to convince the Court that it made all the efforts to calculate the payment, so it is not over- or under-charging: that it is not "taking revenge" against (or persuading) those who do not cooperate with the government on the one hand, and that it does not accept that those who joined the program pay a higher price due to those who did not.

8) Tax Legislation and Freedom of Occupation

Tax law may violate the constitutional right to freedom of occupation and freedom of contract if it prevents the taxpayer from exercising their free will in trade, business, professional or occupational choices or even jeopardizes free competition and the profitability of the taxpayers' economic activities. A government subsidy to one or to a group of taxpayers discriminates against other taxpayers who have to pay higher tax payments in order to meet the government's designated budget. Hence, any kind of a discriminatory tax system jeopardizes free competition and may be considered a violation of freedom of contract/occupation. Note the progressive tax rates are not considered as a discriminatory measure but rather a reflection of the benefit and the consent principles [pp. 24, 55, 100, 101].

Indeed, the Congress is aware of such concept and reasoning. For example, Non-Profit Organizations (87) enjoy a wide range of tax reliefs as long as they engage only with ***non-business*** activities and their revenue is ***not derived from trade or business***. The reason is free competition. Non-Profit-Organizations are supposed to deal with the activities allocated to the "third sector," not to the business sector. Any tax reliefs provided to NPOs in their business activities jeopardizes free competition and infringes on the concept of freedom of contract and occupation.

D. Is Tax a Confiscatory Payment? Taxes and the Property Right

The "Taking Clause" of the Fifth Amendment instructs: "private property shall not be taken without just compensation". A popular, yet a bit superficial observation, may lead to the conclusion that any tax, by definition, infringes upon property rights, since it transfers wealth from the taxpayer to the government "without just compensation." This issue has been answered already by the Supreme Court. As a rule, the Court exempted taxes from a substantial review under the Takings Clause, and supported the constitutionality of progressive taxation (e.g. *Brushaber v. Union Pacific Railroad Co.* (1916)). Yet not everybody agrees. A notable and assertive voice of opponents is law professor Richard Epstein.

Epstein—then, in Chicago—expressed fiercely in "Takings—Private Property and the Power of Eminent Domain", (and in some earlier articles) his claim that government actions, actually all the government redistribution programs, undermine/infringe on the Taking Clause. Under his sweeping and one-sided/short-sighted approach, any government action, or even plans that cause apparent/observable reduction in the value of a person's asset might be considered as taking; what might be called "regulatory takings". Accordingly, any kind of taxes are forms of taking and should be examined under principles applicable to all other taking, i.e. to ask if the tax provides just compensation to those taxpayers who are subject to high marginal tax rates. According to Epstein's approach, progressive taxation is a clear example of taking without a just compensation, since it takes wealth from those who have and transfers it to those who do not have.

There are two major problems/flaws with Epstein's approach. One is the sweeping definition of the term property. As we argue below [pp. 9–15], good taxes do not take any private property, neither from firms (47) nor from households (56). As for firms, i.e. income producers, Epstein relies quite significantly on John Locke's labor justification of private property. Alas, even if we ignore Locke's own famous "provisos" and concentrate on the core of the justification, a clear conclusion emerges. In modern life no person can sincerely argue that they operated alone and produced their wealth without using a critical means/factor of production, namely ***social capital*** (45). Hence the fruits of the "joint project" [pp. 64–66] go to all the participants, i.e. the taxpayers and the public as well. Indeed, as is argued below, a good tax is a "profit sharing mechanism" between those who contribute their means of production, including the public and its agent—the government [pp. 64–66]. In other words, taxes, which follow the good tax's four cannons [p. 9] are not taking. They distribute the proceeds of the joint project to its members—the owners of financial, human and social/public capital—who are ***entitled*** to their return on investment.

As for households, good taxes are the quid pro quo for the benefit of the public goods and services we, the consumers, enjoy [p. 70].

The second problem with Epstein's approach stems from his implied assumption that taxes, especially progressive ones, do not provide just compensation to the taxpayers who are subject to higher tax rates. Such assumption ignores Adam Smith's subtle argument that the ability and benefit principles do not contradict each other but are actually complementary. As we argue later on [p. 71], firms which have higher economic ability—wealth and income production—enjoy much better the major public goods and services e.g. recognition of private property and its protection, freedom of contract, the existence of functioning economic markets and sustainable law and order. Those who don't have economic ability barely enjoy those public goods and services. The same applies to households. The more we have—wealth and consumption—the greater benefit we enjoy from public goods and services, i.e. security, law and order, recognition of property rights and their protection, regulation on financial institutes, and economic stability. Hence, those who have more receive a just compensation for their higher consumption of public goods and services, and rightly pay a higher amount of taxes than those who have less [p. 72].

The conclusion, which we suggested already above, is that good taxes do provide full compensation to the taxpayer. Nevertheless, when sufficient arguments and evidence are provided to support that the taxpayer does not enjoy the same public goods and services as the rest of the community's members, such a tax might not sustain/prevail Constitutional Judiciary review (70) [pp. 7–9, 26–27].

It's noteworthy that Epstein attacked recently "Obamacare" and the majority's opinion of the Supreme Court's decision in the *Sebelius* case [pp. 41–42, 53]. The problem with this is probably that Epstein regards Pigovian Mandatory Payments [PMP, pp. 13, 36, 54] as taxes and not as a means/mechanism aiming to fix the right economic price of public goods and services that suffer from market failures (75), [p. 54]. A careful analysis would lead to the opposite direction of Epstein's. Due to the market failure, the market economy takes private property from those citizens who cannot afford to buy medical insurance in the free market, due to the adverse selection phenomenon (8). In order to prevent such taking, the government has to impose a certain type of PMP, otherwise its omission takes the chance to buy medical insurance from certain populations and deprives them the right to human dignity and the right to survive [pp. 12, 50].

Since most of the arguments that support the above deliberations are based, mainly, not on legal analyses but on philosophical and public finance insights, we discuss them further in the following chapters [p. 61].

2. ADMINISTRATIVE LAW

Some interesting questions that are within the interface of ***constitutional law*** (22) and ***administrative law*** (4) arise due to the possible violations of human rights by the tax administration, i.e. gathering information about the taxpayers; invasion and violation of the taxpayer's privacy and intimacy; infringement of principle of equal treatment; etc.

Administrative Law (4) deals mainly with two questions: the public administration's power and jurisdictions ("What") and its discretion ("How") while exercising them. A basic rule states that the administration is authorized to act only where it is granted a specific authority by a law with accordance to the constitution. The tax administration's powers and authorities are the power to legislate tax regulations, to adjudicate tax matters, and enforce tax laws according to its specific areas of delegated power.

Tax laws establish executive mechanisms which empower tax officials with a significant amount of authority to collect far-reaching and sensitive information about the taxpayers.

Under **§ 6011,** any person—meaning U.S. citizens, residents and even nonresidents—who has tax liability to the U.S. government must make a return or statement according to the forms and regulations prescribed by the Secretary. The return or the statement must include the information required by such forms or regulations.

With regard to income tax, Code § 6012 requires every individual having, for the taxable year, a gross income that equals or exceeds the exemption amount according to the U.S.A. tax jurisdiction to submit such a return, even if no tax is owed. Individuals (who are not dependent on another taxpayer) are exempted of this duty if their total income for the year doesn't exceed the standard deduction plus one exemption. Other individuals may also be exempted, depending on the amount of income, the individual's age and filing status.

§ 7603 authorizes the tax administration—the Internal Revenue Service (IRS) to examine books and records, issues summonses and take testimony under oath for the purpose of ascertaining the correctness of any tax return, determining any person's tax liability or collecting any debt. In addition, the IRS has the authority to conduct searches and make seizures, provided that a warrant is issued, based upon probable cause and supported by oath or affirmation, in accordance with the requirements of the Fourth Amendment of the Constitution. The tax administration also has a considerable amount of adjudicative power: It can issue tax assessments ("audit"); deal with the taxpayers' protests; impose administrative penalties and issue rulings.

In addition, the tax administration has an important legislative power to issue both "interpretative" and "legislative" tax regulations. Interpretative regulations purport only to interpret, explain, and apply the rules prescribed by Congress (Code § 7805(a)). The tax administration (the Secretary) can also issue legislative regulations, which are often said to have the force of law because they entail an exercise of power delegated by Congress to the agency as though it were a deputy legislature, and they can create new binding rules. Regulations set forth under particular code sections are usually considered legislative tax regulations. Note that such secondary legislative cannot change or undermine the Code nor contradict any code provision.

The standard of review that should be applied by a court to government regulations was articulated generally in *Chevron U.S.A. Inc. v. Natural Resources Defense Council, Inc.*, (1984) where the Supreme Court held that "a court may not substitute its own construction of statutory provision for a *reasonable interpretation* made by the administrator of an agency." This approach has been approved and applied to tax regulations (whether "interpretative" or "legislative") in *Mayo Found. for Med. Educ. & Research v. U.S.*, (2011).

In addition, the tax administration has a significant role in the development of the tax law, either through presenting tax bills to the legislature or by arguing court cases.

An interesting question is whether a tax official also has the power or the authority to grant an ex-gratia tax ruling or decision. The fact that the IRS was required by the Supreme Court to publish its rulings publicly indicates that discriminatory decisions are supposed to be under the public review. Yet, since the negotiations and the final decisions made by tax officials with taxpayers are confidential, it is hard to answer or even to estimate if such power is exercised or abused by the tax administration. Note that the line between granting an unjustified ex-gratia concession and reasonable compromise based on cost-benefit analysis is quite slim. Yet under the concept of the rule of law, it seems that such concession should be minimal, if at all.

Due to the broad discretion the tax administration has regarding its adjudicative power, a taxpayer has the right for judicial review in three different options: filling a petition for review with the Tax Court (this option is available only if the taxpayer had declined to pay the tax as of the date of the petition); sue for a refund in the federal District Court where the taxpayer resides (jury trial is available) or sue for a refund in the U.S. Court of the Federal Claims.

The IRS has adopted a Taxpayer Bill of Rights. It groups the dozens of existing rights in the Internal Revenue Code into ten fundamental rights, and makes these rights more clear, more understandable, and more quickly available to taxpayers. The IRS published the following 10 rights: 1. The Right to Be Informed; 2. The Right to Quality Service; 3. The Right to Pay No More than the Correct Amount of Tax; 4. The Right to Challenge the IRS's Position and Be Heard; 5. The Right to Appeal an IRS Decision in an Independent Forum; 6. The Right to Finality; 7. The Right to Privacy; 8. The Right to Confidentiality; 9. The Right to Retain Representation; 10. The Right to a Fair and Just Tax System.

The IRS is subject to a special Statute of Limitations when dealing with the IRS's powers to audit, collecting tax payments and provides refund. The IRS has three years to audit a tax return or to assess any additional tax liabilities, from the day the tax return was actually submitted (but not before the deadline of April 15th). There are some exceptions: if the taxpayer omits income that amounts to more than 25% of the income that was reported on the tax return, or in the case of income related to undisclosed foreign financial assets if the omitted income is more than $5,000, the length of time is extended to 6 years. The statute of limitations on audits and assessing additional tax remains open indefinitely if the taxpayer files a false or fraudulent tax return.

The IRS has 10 years to collect outstanding tax liabilities, measured from the day a tax liability has been finalized.

Taxpayers have up to three years from the date of the original deadline of the tax return or two years from the date the tax was actually paid to claim a refund of overpaid taxes from the IRS in case the refund derives from deductions for bad debt or worthless securities. There is no statute of limitation for claiming a refund in case that the taxpayers are unable to manage their financial affairs due to physical or mental impairments.

3. INTERNATIONAL LAW

Economic activities are not confined to domestic arenas. People and corporations are free, in most of the western democracies, to invest their money around the world by either direct or indirect investments, or earn their income by working abroad. Transnational activities raise some significant tax issues, such as tax jurisdiction, the prevention of double taxation and double non-taxation as well, which will be introduced and discussed briefly later on [p. 226]. Here, it is sufficient to mention only some of the institutions related to the matters of taxation of international activity.

The prominent one is a bilateral tax treaty, negotiated and concluded between two countries. Tax treaties play a significant role in the context of international cooperation in tax matters. Their aim is twofold. One is to encourage international trade and investment in order to promote global economic growth, which is accomplished by reducing or eliminating international double taxation over transnational income and allocating the tax owed between the two contracting countries. The other is to enhance cooperation among governments by providing means for exchange of information between their tax authorities.

Two international organizations and the U.S. Government have drafted model bilateral treaties: The United Nations Model Double Taxation Convention between Developed and Developing Countries (United Nations Model Convention); the Organization for Economic Co-operation and Development Model Tax Convention on Income and on Capital (OECD Model Convention), and the U.S. Model Income Tax Convention.

These documents, which are regularly updated, provide models for countries to use in negotiating the terms of their bi-lateral treaties. In addition, these bodies issue guidelines and suggested interpretations such as the United Nations Handbook on Selected Issues in Administration of Double Tax Treaties for Developing Countries; the official commentary for the OECDs and the Technical Explanation for the U.S.A. model.

In case of the OECD, its members have, from time to time, agreed on various provisions of the model treaty and the official commentary, and member comments serve as a guidance as to interpretation by each member country.

As a result, we have recently witnessed efforts, mainly by the U.S.A. and the OECD, to put an end to these phenomena of tax evasion and the lack of sufficient information. In 2010, the United States passed a law designed to identify meaningful information about American taxpayers holding foreign money. The **Foreign Account Tax Compliance Act (FATCA)**, obligates U.S. taxpayers to report their financial accounts held outside of the United States, and requires foreign financial institutions to report to the IRS about their U.S. customers. The major purpose of FATCA is to improve tax compliances. So far, the U.S. government has been able to convince a significant number of foreign governments to join an Intergovernmental Agreement (IGA) that implements FATCA, so their financial institutions deliver the required information to the IRS.

In addition, the OECD Global Forum on Transparency and Exchange of Information for Tax Purposes is another novel initiative that aims to address the risks of tax compliance posed by tax havens. The OECD released its latest report on this matter in 2020.

Another project that strives to increase the international cooperation in tax matters is the OECD's Action Plan on Base Erosion and Profit Shifting (BEPS). The OECD is very much determined to pursue this project. Hundreds of senior tax officials from more than 100 countries and international organizations met in Paris on late September 2014 to discuss solutions to unintended double non-taxation caused by BEPS. The participants examined the first set of tax treaty-related recommendations developed under the OECD/G20 BEPS Project and discussed the main tax treaty issues and options.

On September 2014, the OECD published its "BEPS 2014 Deliverables". It elaborates on some actions that should be taken in order to help ensure the following goals: coherence of corporate income taxation at the international level, to restore the intended effects and benefits of international standards, to ensure better transparency, and to promote increased certainty and predictability.

A key focus is to eliminate double non-taxation. However, in doing so, new rules should not result in double taxation, unwarranted compliance burdens or restrictions to legitimate cross-border activity. The goal is to provide recommendations ("actions") for a coordinated international approach to combat tax avoidance by multinational enterprises. In October 2015 the OECD published 15 actions set out below in order to equip governments with domestic and international instruments to address tax avoidance, ensuring that profits are taxed where economic activities generating the profits are performed and where value is created [p. 232].

These are the recommended actions:

Action 1: Addressing the Tax Challenges of the **Digital Economy**

Action 2: Neutralizing the Effects of **Hybrid Mismatch Arrangements**

Action 3: Designing Effective **Controlled Foreign Company Rules**

Action 4: Limiting Base Erosion Involving **Interest Deductions** and Other Financial Payments

Action 5: Countering **Harmful Tax Practices** More Effectively, Taking into Account Transparency and Substance

Action 6: Preventing the Granting of **Treaty Benefits** in Inappropriate Circumstances

Action 7: Preventing the Artificial Avoidance of **Permanent Establishment** Status

Actions 8–10: Aligning **Transfer Pricing** Outcomes with Value Creation

Action 11: **Measuring** and Monitoring BEPS

Action 12: Mandatory **Disclosure Rules**

Action 13: Guidance on **Transfer Pricing** (142) **Documentation** and Country-by-Country Reporting

Action 14: Making **Dispute Resolution** Mechanisms More Effective

Action 15: Developing a **Multilateral Instrument** to Modify Bilateral Tax Treaties.

A recent and novel step to enhance international cooperation to minimize tax evasion is the *Global Agreement on Corporate Taxation*. In 2020, members of the OECD/G20 Inclusive framework initiated a global consensus-based solution to reform the international corporate tax framework. The reform is based on two major issues: "Pillar One", the partial re-allocation of taxing rights, and "Pillar Two", the minimum effective taxation of profits of Multinational Enterprises (MNEs).

Pillar One aims to modify the international rules on how the taxation of corporate profits of the largest and most profitable MNEs, who engage mainly but not exclusively with intangible trade and production without a material physical presence in any country, should be allocated amongst tax jurisdictions.

Pillar Two will set a floor to excessive tax competition. It aims to ensure that multinational businesses will be subject to an annual minimum effective tax rate on all their profits. The global minimum effective tax rate will be at least 15%.

4. CRIMINAL LAW

As we mentioned already, due to the ***free riders'*** phenomenon, (50) taxes are enforced and collected as a mandatory/compulsory payment. That aspect is embodied mainly in the criminal provisions of the tax laws.

Tax laws define certain behaviors as criminal offences. Some are technical, some are minor, some are major and severe. In this book we do not deal with these aspects of tax law. Yet it is noteworthy that the line between legitimate tax planning, illegitimate sham and artificial transactions and illegal criminal tax evasion (13) is not clear at all. Hence, we will provide later [p. 107] some basic guideline to the issue of the Economic Substance Doctrine or "substance over form" principle, and the judicial doctrine of Artificial or Sham Transaction (13).

5. OTHER BRANCHES OF LAW

There is no point in elaborating the fact that in order to deal with the questions of the taxpayer's tax liability a significant amount of legal issues and problems arise. Tax is usually levied on economic activities and their outcomes. The meaning of those activities is determined according to legal norms in various legal fields, such as contract, torts, property, agency, trust, antitrust, corporate, etc. The legal classification might determine the tax liability of a certain activity. For example: if we classify an amount of money received by one person from her friend as a personal gift, the amount is usually free from income tax [pp. 135, 143]; if a contract between two taxpayers is classified as a partnership contract, the proceeds are considered income from a business, whereas if it is considered as a rent, the income is passive/capital income (36) and sometimes subject to different tax rules and rates. The same is with regard to heritage versus compensation for previous services, i.e. mere heritage is free from income tax but a bequest granted as compensation for professional services is subject to income tax; prizes and awards according to commercial contracts versus lottery and immature gambling, and so forth. In sum, legal knowledge is a must while dealing with tax issues.

6. TAX LAW

The term "Tax Law" is the general expression that encompasses all the sources underlying the fascinating field that deals with tax legislation, interpretation, liabilities, disputes and payments. It is the very intersection where different disciplines meet with legal norms—statutory, such as the Internal Revenue Code (I.R.C.) and its regulations; International Tax Treaties; courts' decisions, Tax Administration Rulings ("Revenue Ruling"), legal interpretation, rules and conventions, and legal doctrines offered by scholars. All these compose the interdisciplinary field named Tax Law.

Chapter Five

NON-LEGAL SOURCES

INTRODUCTION: TAX LAW AND OTHER DISCIPLINES

The constitutional era together with the modern way of legal interpretation—where the original intent is no longer the primary test, but rather the text's purpose updated to the current time, allows/drives/forces us to discuss and consider the normative aspects of the law—"What should be the best/most suitable/appropriate interpretation within the linguistic possibilities?". The most notable normative aspects in the area of tax law are equality/fairness/equity and efficiency [pp. 9–14].

A traditional observation—alas, not necessarily accurate—claims that fairness and justice are dealt mainly by philosophers, while efficiency is dealt with by economists. Eventually, both schools deal with almost the same issues, yet eventually from different points of view, although, as is discussed later [p. 90] those two requirements (equality and efficiency) have much more in common than it seems at first glance.

1. PHILOSOPHY

A. Tax Justification: Forced Labor, Confiscation, Consent and Entitlement

As noted, [pp. xiii, 7], a major concern in the theory of taxation is the tax justification issue. "Tax justification" is too broad a term/concept. Mostly it depends on the type of the tax under review and its attributes. Yet, as is shown below [p. 111], the difference between the various tax systems—income, consumption, property, or net wealth—are smaller than seems; actually, the differences stem from matters of timing. Hence, we focus our discussion here on the major tax system in the U.S.A.—the Federal income tax and its progressive rates.

The connection between taxes and philosophy is almost obvious. Some leading modern philosophers (Thomas Hobbes, John Locke, Adam Smith, Jeremy Bentham, John S. Mill, John Rawls, Robert Nozick, Murphy and Nagel, just to mention a few), are constantly engaged with the issue of the optimal conception of the role of taxes in modern democracies. Tax justification and issues of redistribution and distributive justice have been dealt with by philosophers for hundreds of centuries. Some even ignore the independent rule of tax policy, since justice is the goal, and the tax system is only a vehicle that is supposed to promote social and political justice, moral, ethical values, social solidarity, and redistribution of wealth.

B. Property Rights, Laws, and Taxes

An obvious inquiry of the tax justification looks into the relationship between private property and taxes. A very basic and intuitive assumption would be that any mandatory payment to a government undermines private property. It is indeed quite a superficial observation. Partly because the initial question is whether the right for private property is a "natural right" or rather a creation of law. According to a notable/leading British philosopher, Jeremy Bentham, "Property and law are born together and die together," meaning that law recognizes property. Hence, tax law does not violate property rights, but only redefines private property as the residual of the property minus the tax, as long as the tax is levied by law.

A different reference point with a similar conclusion offered by Jean-Jacques Rousseau and Thomas Hobbes is that, although on a personal-private level people are entitled to own private property, by accepting the Social Contract the parties waive their property rights and surrender them to the sovereign. In relationships with the government, it is as if the state possessed all property. Whatever the state needs, it keeps for public purposes and only the remainder/residual is "given"/"returned" to the members of the community/state. Once again, taxation is what the government keeps for the public's use and therefore cannot be considered a violation of private property.

A totally different perspective is offered by the American philosopher Robert Nozick's provocative iteration: Taxation is equivalent to forced labor. If a person works 8 hours a day, for $20 per hour, receives $160, and pays $40 in taxes, the government takes 2 hours a day from the taxpayer. Hence, this is almost a confiscation even if it is based on consent; the tax takes some property from one person, making that person spend a proportion of his working time for another's purposes. According to Nozick, there is no inherited justification in forcing one person to work for another's benefit. Due to tax-financed social welfare programs, eligible members living in poverty have a claim on the actions and products of others, whether or not those others freely entered into relationships that might give rise to such claims and whether or not they voluntarily take these claims upon themselves.

As we can see, two extreme approaches emerge. One is that no tax law is an infringement of private property (e.g. Bentham, Rousseau and Hobbes). The other is that any tax by definition is a confiscatory means. The gap between these extremes can be bridged by two other/additional attitudes.

The first attitude relates to firms (47)—the economic units that produce income—and concentrates on the taxpayer's income/wealth production process (the ***sources side***, 60). We refer to this attitude as the "Profit Sharing Mechanism" of the "Joint Project" [pp. 55, 66]. Its roots are within John Locke's "labor justification" for private property.

The second attitude relates to households (56). It focuses on their **use** of their income (the ***uses side***—61), i.e. current consumption and saving for future consumption. It concentrates mainly on the concept we refer to as "the Purchase Price for Public Goods and Services [pp. 70–78]."

C. The Process of Income/Wealth Production, Property Rights, the Joint Project, and the Profit-Sharing Mechanism

1) John Locke and the Labor Justification for Property

The first approach—the "Joint Project"—begins, surprisingly, with John Locke's "labor justification" of private property: Humans have a natural exclusive right of proprietorship over things in which they have invested their labor; thus, property is a natural right in the sense that it is created even in the absence of a government and a legal system. Consequently, humans have the right to keep to themselves the asset/product produced by their own work, or to trade it for assets produced by others. Upon careful analysis, Locke's qualification of the right to property as a natural right is not as absolute as it might seem (even if we overlook the two famous ethical provisos Locke added, i.e. (a) An individual's property is contingent upon not excluding or denying the necessities required by others, and (b) Man acquires property only according to his needs). Indeed, under Locke's approach, man acquires a right to the asset through adding to its value by the means of labor. However, even if we assume that this was the original intent, and even if we ignore the above two moral or ethical provisos and use only economic and utilitarian analysis, the ultimate conclusion derived from the inner logic of Locke's approach is considerably different in modern times, due to modern insights, economic analysis and knowledge. The labor justification, under a modern and careful scrutiny, leads to the conclusion that government is **entitled** to receive its fair share from the income/wealth production process as a return on its investment.

The argument is as follows: where one individual produce or improves her own asset by herself, she is the sole owner. When someone works with another, the asset belongs to both. When a couple share their chores—one at home and the other at work—and only the latter is paid, the law assumes that the payments belong to both of them. Moreover, when a group works together to produce or improve an asset, each member has a right to a pro rata part of the asset. Thus, an individual's right to property is limited only to the component they add through their own labor. In other words, the natural right of private property is restricted to the "added value" that an individual augments to the original asset. Essentially, this means that an individual has an exclusive right only to the components of the property that can be attributed **solely** and exclusively to that individual's investment in labor. Consequently, one can only conclude that there is a natural right to property insofar as it represents only the individual's return on his invested human capital. The individual does not have a natural right to all the property if it is produced by several members; if a group of people combines their factors of production to produce wealth, assets, or property, they all have a common right to it. Today's economic insights of knowledge and reality allow us to advance a step further. Property is not limited only to the value added by labor—i.e. human capital—alone, but also through the investment of the fruits of that labor, i.e. financial capital. The basic example is when two individuals unite to form a joint venture in which one partner contributes work and labor while the other makes a financial investment. The firm (47), which is a nexus of contracts, is an example of this joint venture and embodies the "Joint Project" concept. Labor itself, in modern life, is not enough. The proceeds from labor turn to be a factor of production as well, i.e. real/monetary capital. Yet, there is one more investor who brings in its factor of production—the public!

2) The Labor Justification and the Joint Project Concept: Towards Public Property and Social Capital

In order to transform labor and its fruits into wealth production, basic preconditions must exist. In order to facilitate the transformation of labor and real capital into other goods and services we need to have both physical and institutionalized infrastructure, such as law and order, safe and functioning markets, security, education and an educated workforce, stability and effective regulation, which enable production and efficient and reliable trade. The income or wealth production process requires the use of factors/means of production (45). Traditionally, two factors of production were identified: Real Capital (money, real property-land and assets bought by money and money worth); and Human Capital (labor, time, private knowledge, skills and abilities). Gradually, we witnessed the emergence of an additional factor of production. Leading economists such as Gary Becker and Robert Sollow introduced, in the modern era, the argument that in addition to the two kinds of capital mentioned, the third factor of production is Social

Capital, which refers to the institutions, relationships, and norms that shape the quality and quantity of a society's social interactions. The prominent components of Social Capital, as a factor of production, are national physical infrastructure, social cohesion and solidarity, supervised educational systems, level of research, good health systems, effective rule of law, safety, efficient and functioning markets, a skilled labor force, national security, political stability, recognition of private property and freedom of contract and their protection, stable markets and effective regulation, regulated the banking system and the insurance industry, just to mention a few.

These insights provide a greater understanding of the income production process, which in turn allows for a more accurate identification of each party's contribution to the production process. For example, suppose a book is sold in the bookstore for a market price of $100. Certainly, no one can seriously argue that the entire $100 belongs to the author. Rather, part of this sum must be used to pay all the members of the firm (47)—the nexus of contract—that invested their own factors of production in the process: wages to printers, editors, proof-readers, interest on loans granted to facilitate the publishing process, rent to the owner of the building used by the publisher, compensation to the truck driver who moves the books, the bookstore owner, and the salesperson's salary. Marketing and advertising agencies must also be paid, as well as the designers and producers of the paper on which the book is published, and finally—the author.

Furthermore, there is an additional step involving the author. The economic value of the book is determined by the economic process of **selling** the book (and having a realized income instead of a potential or future income [pp. 163, 198]), or developing its potential to sell in the future. In economic terms, the existence of demand for the book is a crucial factor in determining its economic value. Had the author lived and written the book in an illiterate community, there is little chance it would have sold. Indeed, the value of such a book will increase proportionally to the development and progression of the educational system, the community's literacy and education rates, and even the potential buyers' amount and quality of leisure time.

In addition, without an educational system and a stable and secure environment, the author would presumably not have been able to write. Furthermore, the ability to write stems, at least in part, from the social environment and community in which the author resides and professional active.

Likewise, a publisher will not be able to distribute and market the book unless there is a physical infrastructure that allows for both the shipment of merchandise and the establishment of a venue where shoppers may purchase the book.

Thus, the creation of the book and its sale to the costumers might be possible due to the surrounding conditions supported, maintained and developed by the government, which provides, inter alia, physical infrastructure (roads, airports, sewers system etc.), a safe, civilized and secure economic, cultural and educational environment together with a solid rule of law and stable markets.

In a modern society, people do not live and work in their own secluded environments. For instance, a law professor produces income through teaching and research only because the community in which the professor acts and lives makes it economically possible to earn a living in such fashion. A law professor can make a living only if there is a demand for her professional services. A state where there is no legal system does not need judges and lawyers; there will be law students and legal researchers only in a state that provides, maintains, and develops a legal system. In order to publish her research and give her lectures, the professor needs an audience of students who come from a society that has invested in educational programs that have taught them to be able to read, write and learn, from nursery school through to the university level. Furthermore, the professor would be unable to teach classes without the provisions of roads, buildings, public transportation, safety, security, and other public services provided by the state. Thus, the income production process of our professor depends not only or her performance, skills, and abilities, but also on a partner that enables the production by making the social investments. Without such investments, our law professor is out of a job. In other words, she invests her labor and human capital, and the government invests the social, economic, physical and social infrastructure, i.e. the third kind of factor of production—the social capital. When the professor provides her services she represents a partnership—a joint project—between herself and the government. When she receives compensation, she has to share it with her partner. And indeed she does. She pays income tax. As long as the tax follows the four canons of a good tax [p. 9] then it is not a mandatory payment, let alone the taking of private property, but simply a profit sharing means/mechanism. She gets her return for her human capital, and the public, via the government, receives its return on its investments in institutional and physical infrastructure—the social capital.

The same logic/concept applies to professional athletes (according to law professor Richard Posner's eye-catching example of two identical "Michael Jordans" one of whom lives in Chicago and the other in an under-developed country); with a computer engineer who is able to generate income only in a country that has an educational and technological infrastructure, R&D, potential customers who can use his products, an efficient and safe electrical system and internet access. Bill Gates could not have developed his products without the existence of training institutions, public research and development centers, universities and research institutions, an educated work force and an educated and skilled population capable of using the products he produces.

Arthur Okun provides a brilliant and most convincing example:

> *"Henry Ford's mass-produced automobile was a great success in a country with a high average income, three thousand miles for unimpeded driving, an alert and ambitious work force, and a government that could protect travelers* and enforce the rules of the road. It would be a loser in Libya."

Returning to the Lockean approach, the fruits of labor that stem from a worker's products are actually the fruits of a few sources that represent three factors of production: public investments (social capital), private labor (human capital) and financial/real capital, which all contribute to the income production process. As such, each of these three factors has a property right in the final product: the private human capital, the private real capital and the public as the owner of the social capital. Locke's labor justification leads to a very clear conclusion: the owners of the three factors of production have a right to the produced property. Hence, a good tax is far from being semi-slavery. A good tax is actually a profit-sharing mechanism between the three investors.

3) The Role of Tax Under the Joint Project Approach and the Benefit Principle

As indicated earlier, based on the concept of a Social Contract, the benefit principle is the common justification to tax: Each taxpayer extracts benefits from the public goods and services (101) provided by the government. Those goods and services have a price tag. Every member who enjoys them has to pay their price.

The benefit justification from public goods and services has a dual meaning. First, it enables both firms (47) to produce income and wealth ("the source side"), and households (56) to consume or save them for future consumption ("the uses side"). Without government, which provides the social capital (45) we wouldn't be able to function, operate, produce our income or enjoy it by current or future private consumption.

The other aspect of the benefit justification focuses on the consumption side (26, 61) of the public goods and services. As consumers, we enjoy security, public roads, human rights, law and order, a stable economic system, and regulation that aims to allow a normal way of living. The provision of such commodities costs money and we pay their price to their provider. As Justice Holmes put it: "Taxes are the price we pay for a civilized society".

4) Modern Synergies of Human, Real and Social Capitals

A modern analysis of the causes of wealth and its production provides yet another source of support for our argument. Modern economic insights (from economists such as Edwin R. A. Seligman, Arthur Okun, and Richard Posner) describe the ways wealth and property are produced in modern society. They use Hegel, stressing that economic rights are "luxuries enabled by social organization." This analysis further leads to the conclusion that the property of an average person is not exclusively the result of own human capital (i.e. his or her own work, deeds, and personal contributions). Rather, the opportunities produced and created by the society and community in which an individual lives and works are extremely influential factors in the acquisition of property. As Arthur Okun explains:

> *"The productive contribution of the service I could sell in a hypothetical competitive market depends on four sets of elements: (1) the skills and assets that I have acquired through my lifetime; (2) the abilities and talents with which I was born; (3) the effort I am willing to expend; and (4) the supply and demand situation for other services related to the ones I can offer".*

As Okun's example [p. 67] demonstrates, a person's skills, talents, and opportunities to use them significantly are available only in a community with strong and substantial social capital.

A similar point was offered by law professor Richard Posner, in comparing two basketball players who share identical talents and qualities but live in two different societies with huge economic and social gaps between them. Indeed, although they have identical personal and physical skills, they will not earn the same income, property and other economic achievements, since an individual living in an advanced and wealthy community will most likely profit much more than an individual living in a poor, underdeveloped one.

Thus, an individual's wealth primarily depends not on their skills and abilities alone, but on the abilities of other individuals in the community—personally and aggregated—and the economic strength of the community itself. The more advanced and developed the social capital is in a given society, the greater the opportunity each member has to use their human and financial capitals to increase their wealth.

As a result, a modern synergy concludes that property rights are not only basic and natural rights, but also the result of communal life and social interaction.

5) The Concept of Economic Allegiance

In 1923, a special professional committee composed of four world-renowned tax experts submitted a report to the League of Nations in order to make its recommendation with regard to the taxation of international activity. A significant part of the report was based on a book written by one of the committee's members, Professor Edwin R. A. Seligman. In his own book, Professor Seligman developed the doctrine of economic allegiance, which is based on four primary theories: (1) the faculty theory, or the ability to pay, is the base of a modern income tax system; (2) the ability to pay is determined according to a person's wealth, income and consumption; (3) a taxpayer owes economic allegiance to those states or countries that provide the conditions to create the taxpayer's wealth; and (4) the production process is composed of the following three stages:

a) The actual physical production process;

b) The materialization of the physical production, resulting in products with economic value;

c) The use of wealth for saving/investment or consumption.

It is quite evident that the second stage of the production process, where the product receives its economic value, is significant. Without it, all human efforts to produce goods and services would be essentially futile. Indeed, this process depends not only on the existence of a legal system that recognizes property and protects it, but also on the presence of an economic market that maintains economic demand, efficient trade, the availability of suitable consumers and a skillful workforce, and an enforceable legal system. Without those factors, the physical/material production process is worthless (at least from an economic point of view), except for the purpose of self-sufficiency. In sum, no real wealth can be produced without the existence of a well-organized society.

The differences between the above insights (Locke's labor justification, the modern synergy and the economic allegiance) are indeed subtle and they all serve as the basis for the doctrine of the ***joint project***, the concept of public property, and the tax as a profit-sharing mechanism.

6) The Joint Project Doctrine and the Concept of Public Property

As already argued, economic, productive, and efficient activity is possible where risks to businesses are minimized due to the existence of good Social Capital. New developments and inventions, as well as technological improvements, are most often made in countries where a solid base for scientific research exists, primarily through academic institutions and secure investments. As Okun indicated, automobiles or other hi-tech industries can be initiated, survive and flourish only in well-developed, efficient and secure societies. [pp. 28, 50, 67, 90]

These analyses call for a revised observation about the distribution of a community's aggregate wealth, not as a matter of distributive justice, morals or ethical principles, but rather from an ***entitlement*** perspective: each individual, business and social entity, and the public as well, are all **entitled** to a yield on their investment.

There is a joint endeavor within a modern community in which the private sector—individuals and legal entities—works as part of a partnership with the community. The former brings in their human and real capital, and the latter brings in, maintains, and develops the social capital. On the production side, the private sector operates, produces, or invests using human and real capital. The community, through the government, invests in the needed physical and intangible infrastructure—the social capital. At the end of the production process, when wealth or income is yielded, it belongs to all of those who invested human capital, real capital, and social capital into the project. This is the doctrine of the ***joint project*** between individuals, firms, and the community. This doctrine represents a social contract between the private sector (i.e. workers, managers and monetary investors), and the community's government. Such a social contract calls for a reasonable division of the wealth created by both parties. The remaining question is how much of the wealth created by the parties should each party be entitled to receive. This question should be answered by the theory of taxation, tax policy and legislation, which are based on the guidelines of a good tax [pp. 9–14].

As we see below [pp. 73–78], a similar approach should guide us with regards to tax as the purchase price of public goods and services.

7) Tax as a Profit-Sharing Mechanism

Taxes in modern society are based on the formal concept of "[n]o taxation without representation." Representation in democratic societies is provided by the elected public agents at the legislative and administrative branches who serve as the societies' members' consent. Hence the substantial concept essentially means "no taxation without consent." [pp. 48–50]. Indeed, consent is achieved through legislation. As long as we can reasonably assume that the process of determining the price of public goods and services is in accordance with principles which any reasonable person would accept, then the tax, which is levied by the elected agents of the public, is the agreed-upon price of public goods and services. Thus, a good tax should not be construed as a violation of the right to property, but rather as a profit-sharing mechanism used to distribute income and wealth created by the ***joint project***.

Clearly, the power to legislate tax laws is limited like any other area of law. Tax laws should not violate constitutional rights. They cannot be used as penal or deterrence measures [p. 53], nor as a means for confiscation [p. 55]. Their goal should be very clear, precise, and limited: to finance the public goods and services offered by the elected government, which get the public's approval every year through the deliberation and approval of the national budget.

Another tax justification focuses on households and individuals as consumers. When turning our focus from the sources side (60, 61)—the creation/production of wealth and income—to the uses side—how the wealth or income are used [pp. 157, 188], the same conclusion emerges. A "good tax" does not violate the right to property. Such a tax is the fair price households (56) are willing to pay for purchasing public goods and services. This argument—tax as the purchase price for public goods and services—relies on some economic literature and is discussed further below [p. 73].

D. Distributive Justice

The American Philosopher John Rawls is probably the most prominent supporter of distributive justice in the 20th century. Rawls defies the assumption that the market economy pre-intervention of wealth distribution is justified. Using his attractive metaphor of the veil of ignorance, he is able to offer several basic guidelines of justice. Under his "maximin" formulation of *social equality* (stands for maximizing the minimum), he suggests the alternative that produces the highest portion for the least advantaged positioned. The representatives beyond the veil of ignorance would select two principles of justice in the organized society/community: the principles of Equal Liberty and Difference. The first principle means that each member is guaranteed a fully adequate scheme of basic liberties, which is compatible with the same scheme of liberties for all others. The second means that social and economic **inequalities** are acceptable only if they satisfy two conditions: equal liberty (all positions and offices are open to all); and the maximin rule (the maximum/greatest benefit for the minimum/least advantaged). Note that economists tend to simplify the veil of ignorance metaphor by describing a situation where two people have a pie to share. They agree upon the process: one cuts the pie and the other has the first pick.

According to these principles, the tax has a most significant role: it is supposed to assure the interests of the least advantaged group within the society. In addition to other redistribution programs, tax is supposed to collect higher rates from the rich and lower or no rates from the poor, i.e. a progressive tax system. Note though that our argument that justifies progressive taxation is different. It is not a reflection of philosophical and moral values but instead is a by-product of the consent and benefit principles [p. 101].

E. The Benefit Principle and Ability to Pay

The Romantic Era of the 19th century—which emphasized social unity instead of the individualistic social contract—produced the equal sacrifice doctrine ascribed to J. S. Mill: taxation should be made to bear as nearly as possible with the same pressure upon all. During the 20th century, the equal sacrifice doctrine was developed into the theory of ability to pay (1, 98). The concept that was developed is simple. The sacrifice of tax payments should be assessed according to the impact of the tax on the taxpayer's ability to pay, which is in turn measured by the taxpayer's economic ability. But here we have a problem: if the purpose of the tax is to pay for the public goods and services (101), it should be levied on each taxpayer according to his or her ***benefit*** derived from those goods and services, i.e.—the benefit principle.

Intuitively, the benefit principle and the ability to pay theory are contradictive: the more money you have (i.e. greater ability to pay), the less you need public goods and services; you can buy most of the goods and services by yourself. On the other hand, the less you have, the more you rely on the government, welfare system, free education, subsidized health services, etc. Hence, the taxpayer with the greatest ability to pay enjoys the least amount of government goods and services while the taxpayer with the least ability receives the greatest benefit from the government. We beg to differ.

Like others before us we believe that these two principles (the benefit principle and the ability to pay) lead to the same conclusion: the greater ability a taxpayer has, the greater benefit she or he derives from the government's provision of public goods and services, both on the source/productive side and the uses/consumption one.

From the productive side, the high-income/ability/wealthier taxpayers benefit from the major public goods and services provided by the government more than the low-income taxpayers. The former benefit from law and order, defence, security, recognition of property, freedom of contract and occupation, educational systems that produces both skilled workforces and capable consumers, and the existence of efficient markets which enable prosperous economic activity and allow them to produce their income, to keep their wealth or consume it. The latter, who don't use all the above services in order to produce income and keep it as their own property do not enjoy these public services and liberties as much as the former.

From the consumption side: those who have more, enjoy more benefits deriving from the major public goods and services: their wealth is recognized, protected and secured by governmental law enforcement measures. The greater the wealth, the higher the economic value of those benefits. Those who have, say, ten million dollars enjoy much better the government's recognition of their wealth and the protection the government provides—including domestic and national defence—than those who have a property worth of only fifty thousand dollars. This is like the private market, where those who buy insurance for a property worth $50,000 pay lower premiums than those who buy insurance for a property worth $10,000,000.

The argument is quite straightforward: Poverty and social gaps lead to social instability and criminal activities. Those with little or no property may find it undesirable to agree to a property rights system with no redistribution. To keep their wealth and social position, the wealthy are very interested in social order, which can be achieved either by buying a social-industrial peace—by giving up part of their wealth—instead of losing a greater portion or conducting an endless war against the poor. Experience teaches us that the former option is a better deal than the latter. [Piven, & Cloward, *Regulating the Poor: the Functions of Public Welfare,* 1971]. Under such analysis, the benefit and ability principles complement each other.

This equation is not new. Adam Smith proposed it already in his book, *An Inquiry into the Nature and Causes of the Wealth of Nations.* While arguing for the benefit principle, Adam Smith connected it to the ability as well:

> *The subjects of every state ought to contribute towards the support of the government, as nearly as possible, in proportion to their respective abilities; that is, in proportion to the revenue which they respectively enjoy under the protection of the state. The expense of government to the individuals of a great nation, is like the expense of a great estate, who are all obliged in proportion to respective interests to the estate.*

As we can see below, this equation serves as another justification for the basic rules of international tax justification [p. 228].

F. Social Justice, Worldly Philosophers, Welfare Economics

Not everyone is aware of the relationship between philosophy and economics. In "Worldly Philosophers", Robert Heilbroner illustrates how the science of economics has changed during the last two and a half centuries. Some neoliberal economists and scholars tend to forget that those who created the science of economics—like John Locke, Adam Smith, John S. Mill and others—were, above all, philosophers. They dealt with philosophical issues such as ethics, values, general welfare and social justice. Gradually, the gaps between economists and philosophers began to grow. Instead of dealing with welfare and wellbeing, the common economists turned towards a technical/mathematical science that focused on mechanical measurements of short-run economic growth, profits and business' success. Such tendency became prevalent during the 20th century and has been adopted by the "neoclassical" economics movement, which concentrates mainly on shortsighted earnings. Consideration of long-lasting efficiency and social welfare were replaced by profit maximization and business success. Market economy became confused with "business economy".

However, prominent economists have expressed a great deal of concern regarding the new trend of business economy. Alfred Marshall, Arthur Pigou, Thorstein Veblen, Mancur L. Olson Jr., Garry Becker, Kenneth Arrow, John Galbraith, Robert Heilbroner, Robert Sollow, Arthur Okun, Amartya Sen, William Vickrey, Joseph Stiglitz, Paul Krugman, Thomas Piketty, Jean Tirole, George Akerlof, Robert Shiller, Jeffery Sachs, Jason Hickle, and even Luigi Zingales, among many others, are concerned with social gaps, general welfare, economic inequality, income distribution, free market and economic efficiency in its broader sense, and the constant threat to democracy caused by small and cohesive groups, who manage to gain privileges from the policymakers. The discontent from the new tendency is very well expressed by the Nobel laureate Joseph Stigliz, who notes that: "creating market value had become entirely separated from creating employment." We discuss some of the "worldly philosophers' " ideas, especially those related to taxation, below [p. 90].

2. ECONOMICS

Economics is a social science that studies the optimal behavior of individuals, firms, households, and governments, in allocating scarce resources to satisfy their desires and goals. Its ultimate (or at least original) goal is to promote the general welfare of both individuals and society by studying the production, distribution, and consumption of goods and services. Economics aims to explain how markets work and how producers and consumers interact. Economic analysis is applied throughout society, in households, businesses, finance, organizations and governments.

A. Microeconomics and the Pricing Process

Under a traditional classification (maybe redundant, archaic, and obsolete these days) the two major branches of economic studies are Microeconomics and Macroeconomics. In general terms, the former studies the behavior of the market players while they have to decide how to allocate their own limited resources. This branch examines how these decisions affect the supply and demand for goods and services, which determines prices, and how prices, in turn, determine the quantity supplied and quantity demanded of goods and services.

1) Tax Justification and Pricing—the Purchase Price of Public Goods and Services

As indicated above, [p. 64] one aspect of tax justification refers to the wealth and income producing process (the "source side"). The other aspect refers to households and the way they use their wealth (the "uses side") [pp. 157, 188]. The former was discussed above [p. 64]. Here we turn our focus to the uses side in order to provide another argument in support of our conclusion, i.e. that taxes are based on the public's consent and the benefit principle; that a "good tax" does not violate the right for property. Instead, it is the fair price households (56) are willing to pay for purchasing public goods and services. The public elects the government according to the political parties' platform and promises, and afterwards asks the elected government to provide us a basket of public goods and services. Furthermore, the public expresses annually—via its agents in the House of Representatives—its consent to pay for that "basket".

A basic observation concludes that the process of purchasing goods or services ("products") involves several stages:

(1) the mere decision to purchase the product according to the degree of discretion the purchaser exercises;

(2) agreement on the price and on the quality of the product;

(3) the possession/usage of the product and the obligation to pay the price;

(4) the price collecting measures.

A careful comparison of the process of acquiring products in the private sector ("private products"), with the purchase of public goods and services ("public products") shows that the differences between them are not as significant as they first appear. On the contrary, the common ground shared by these two kinds of transactions is indeed quite broad.

A) The Decision to Purchase Products

(1) **Private Products**: This decision consists of two dimensions: 1) the general interest in a certain type of product; and 2) the specific product and the others available on the market. Generally, we assume that the decision to purchase a particular product is affected by the level of the discretion the purchaser has. Such discretion is influenced mainly by the elasticity of the demand for the products. Elasticity (41) varies among products because some products may be more essential to the consumers. Essential products that are needed to maintain a minimum standard of living ("basic products"), are, *inter alia*: basic foods and food-related products (refrigerators, cooking facilities etc.); health services; basic dwellings; education; media tools/facilities needed in modern times to live in an organized society; etc. When considering to purchase "basic products" we possess a certain degree of discretion, though it is quite limited. Although we must acquire the basic products, the purchasers have the option to decide where to buy them, and from whom, as long as the supplier is not a monopoly (78).

When it comes to purchasing non-basic private products, the general assumption is that the level of the purchaser's discretion is broad. However, it is noteworthy to mention the sound doubts raised mainly by economists such as Thorstein Weblen and John Kenneth Galbraith (as well as the Canadian scholar Marshall McLuhan) regarding whether the consumers are indeed free to make their own purchasing decisions. According to them, and others, the control of the production process flows from consumers to the organized producers and firms that have significant influence over consumers through aggressive advertising and sophisticated marketing techniques. As a result, we tend to buy various products, not because we really need them or even want them, but because we are manipulated by producers and vendors to believe that we have to have them. According to McLuhan's coined phrase "the medium is the message", and due to advanced electronic mass communication (then, radio and television, and now the new era of the internet and social networks developed after his death), mankind in the "global village" will move from individualism to a collective identity with a "tribal base". Though people tend to believe that they make their own decisions on an individualistic basis as consumers of private products, a realistic observation indicates that the tribe's will and pressure is much more significant than they admit. Suffice to mention that according to the rules of the free market the price of a good or service is determined according to the supply and **aggregate** demand, i.e. the ability/power of an individual to influence the price of a product is certainly extremely limited.

In sum, the level of discretion of whether to buy products in the private market is not based necessarily on the consumers' real and meaningful free will or independent choice. It is indeed much closer to a collective decision.

(2) **Public Market**: It is quite certain that an individual citizen does not possess meaningful power to influence the collective decision regarding the variety of the public products the government should provide. No one is asked personally whether they want to purchase a particular component critical to national defense (A F-35 Jet? A particular missile?); to foster the national pride (by sending a delegation to the Olympics games or participating in the race to the moon); to narrow social gaps or to promote distributive justice (whether as an ethical concept or a matter of economic efficiency) [p. 90].

However, in a democratic regime, the public makes these collective decisions through our agents whom we select through the election process. We vote for a certain party or candidate according to their platform, promises, records and obligations, and we acknowledge the ways our elected government charges us by legislating tax laws, and how it spends our money through the annual approval of the national budget ("collective agreement"). Furthermore, in February 2014, the **U.S. House of Representatives** (which has the exclusive power to initiate revenue bills) passed the Taxpayers Right-To-Know Act, which would require government agencies to identify and describe each program they administer, the cost to administer those programs, expenditures for services, the number of program beneficiaries, and the number of federal employees and contract staff involved. It would also require information on how the program gets evaluated.

In addition, it can be easily assumed that most public products are important to every member of the society. Every member agrees to enjoy, up to a certain level, depending on personal circumstances, and to pay for the rule of law, property rights and their protection, personal and national security, the provision of physical and economic infrastructures that enables collective existence, social and economic activities, the recognition of human rights, etc. In that sense, public products are quite similar in nature to the basic private products with one prominent exception: there is only one supplier of public products—the government. On the other hand, in a democratic regime, the government represents the public. Its only goal ought to be the promotion and enhancement of the public wellbeing and happiness. The private suppliers, on the other hand, are interested mainly in their own welfare and profits. We should mention the "capture" concept, offered first by George Stigler and further developed by Jean Tirole—both are professors of Economics and Nobel Laureates. The argument, if we may be blunt again, is that the Coalition [p. 24], i.e. interest groups, mainly big producers and other political participants, use their regulatory and coercive powers in government to shape laws and regulations in a way that is beneficial to them, not the common person. In other words, under the "capture" concept the differences between the private market and the public one are less significant; the powerful and the influential groups play a significant role in setting the prices in both markets.

In addition, there is seemingly a significant difference between purchasing a bottle of water—or any other private products—and public products. The former is decided individually. The amount of the discretion regarding the latter is much more limited. Once a collective decision is made, we, the individuals are forced to buy and consume the public goods and services. We may decide not to buy the bottle of water if we do not like its price (though, as indicated below, the individual's ability to set the prices in the private market is also quite limited), but we cannot refuse to buy national security if we consider that the price is too high.

There are several possible remedies for the public's and the individuals' dissatisfaction with their government's performance, and with the basket of public good and services it offers.

One is to improve the information the public receives regarding the basket of the public goods and services offered by the government. The Taxpayers Right-To-Know Act is a significant step toward this goal.

Another democratic remedy might be getting rid of the elected government, although this is quite a long and tedious process.

A third remedy is the **Tiebout Model**, (named after the American economist and geographer Charles M. Tiebout), which assumes that governments compete with one another. If we don't like the public services provided by our government, we can "vote with our feet", i.e. move to another jurisdiction that provides another, more favorable basket of public goods and services that comes with a different tax structure; a package more suitable to our tastes and priorities. Though Tiebout offered his analysis regarding local municipalities and state governments, in our shrinking world and the globalization era it is seems that sovereign nations may too be forced to compete more aggressively for their residents' support. The flood of refugees from developing countries who are rushing into the developed countries, mainly in Europe, Australia and the United States is a vivid yet sad proof/reminder of this model.

B) The Price

(1) **The Private Market**: Supposedly, the price of a product is determined by a private individual's decision through free negotiations. A careful observation reveals that this is not an accurate description. The pricing process in the free market is based on the common assumption that no individual has the ability or the power to affect the price, which is set according to the point where the **aggregate** demand by consumers equals the **aggregate** supply by producers. The fact that such a process creates a producer's and a consumer's surplus (115) implies/indicates that the market price does not reflect the price that an individual consumer is willing to pay. In general, a person cannot walk into a store and try to bargain for a price, which had been determined in advance without their personal and specific consent. This is the case with basic products, and usually with non-basic as well. The difference between these two types of private products is that the purchaser must purchase the basic products, but has some degree of discretion whether to buy the non-basic ones. If the price of the latter product does not seem right, the consumer won't buy it, or in some cases will be able to negotiate and get their desired price.

(2) **The Public Market**: The public, through its agents, collectively determines the price of public products provided by the government or by government agencies. The main difference between the prices in the private market and the public market is that the former is determined collectively but not in an informed and planned decision, while the latter is determined (subject to the deficiencies and difficulties indicated by Sitigler, Tirole [p. 75] and Zingales [p. 73]) through tight control by the public's elected bodies, free press and public involvement, pressure and protests and soon by the requirement of the Taxpayers Right-To-Know Act, once it is eventually approved by the legislature.

When comparing the price determination process of private and public products, one may conclude that the ability of the individual purchaser to influence the price is extremely low in both cases.

C) Reporting, Payment, and Collection

(1) **Private Market**: Once a buyer decides to purchase a product and is obligated to conclude the transaction, under private law she must report to the seller what she takes. Accordingly, the final obligation ("how much") is determined, regardless of what their economic ability is. Fraudulent reports provide the seller with the right to use legal proceedings—private lawsuits and criminal charges as well. Due to the direct, close, and immediate relationship between the seller and the purchaser in the private market, the seller is able to supervise the fulfillment of the parties' obligations at small cost, including verifying the buyer's identity and determining whether he possesses the product and has failed to pay in due time. In addition, the free rider (50) phenomenon is not exclusive to public goods and services offered by the government. Shoplifters, common thieves, and violators of intellectual property are quite common in the private sector as well.

(2) **Public Market**: One may assume that all citizens consume the same amount of non-rival and non-excludable public goods and services (101). If this is the case, consumers apparently are not required to report the amount of public goods they consume. However, according to our analysis and conclusion [p. 71], the degree of a person's economic ability also indicates the amount of benefit she derives from the public products the government provides. Hence, if the purchasers/consumers are required to report to the "seller" the amount of the "products" they acquire/consume, they fulfil this duty by submitting an accurate and sincere annual income tax return. Failure to fulfill this duty in an honest way is similar to any other fraudulent behavior of a private purchaser, which entails legal consequences. Based on the personal annual tax return, and the agreed price set by the public within the Internal Revenue Code, the taxpayer is expected to pay their debt. If the taxpayer fails to do so, the seller is entitled to proceed with collecting measures.

Since the government "sells" its public products to a very large number of "customers", and does not maintain a close and direct relationship with each and every one of them, its ability to supervise, control and manage the collecting methods, which are based usually on private law, is very limited. The practical difficulties of supervising and controlling the reporting, payments and collecting measures invite "free riders" (50) who might take advantage of these difficulties in order to avoid paying their debts. The free rider phenomenon, which is more common in the public market, leads to the possible conclusion that the enforcement measures available in the private market are not sufficient in the public marketplace. Consequently, the need to use more severe measures for tax avoiders is greater with public products. The degree of criminal enforcement measures have to be higher in the public market than in the private one. In other words, the differences between the collecting and enforcing methods in the private and public markets are, once again, not substantial and essential but only a matter of degree. However, as indicated above, the free rider phenomenon is not exclusive to public goods and services, but is also quite common in the IP industry, and it might be that it is no less common than tax evasion.

In conclusion: our starting point is that "good tax" is based on consent. The above discussion is intended to show that although there are differences between buying private products and purchasing public goods and services from the government in a democracy, they are not significant and substantial. The common ground between the two types of products is much more significant than it appears at first glance. The term "mandatory/compulsory payment" assigned to taxes is inaccurate and misleading. There is always an obligation to pay for all type of purchases, whether from private or public providers. Failure to comply with this obligation grants the sellers, in both markets, the right to use civil law measures against the purchaser, and in certain circumstances might lead to criminal proceedings. The significant difference is that the free rider phenomenon is probably more prevalent/widespread when it comes to purchasing public products. Without free riders, we would live in an ideal society of angels where every member pays their fair share in order to finance the cost of the public products. Free riders with their selfish tendencies—like thieves in a store—are driving us to use expensive collection enforcement mechanisms in order to make sure that everybody pays their shares.

Hence, a simple conclusion every healthy society has to reach is that tax offenders are not cultural heroes. They damage our welfare and hurt all of us. The ***negative externalities*** (44) of their actions are enormous. Due to their actions, we either pay more than we should, or enjoy less of the public goods and services that we would like the government to provide. Without free riders, tax offenders, robbers and thieves, the price of private and public goods and services would be lower and society's aggregate welfare would be higher.

2) Tax Justification—a Summary

Both doctrines, i.e. the ***Joint project*** [p. 64] and the ***purchase price of public goods and services*** attitudes lead to the same conclusions: (good) tax is the price we **consent** to pay (either as producers-firms or consumers-households) for the public goods and services we order from the government that we elect. Hence, the provider of those products—the elected government—is fully **entitled** to get its fair share. As for the compliance and enforcement processes, they are needed in both private and public purchases, though due to the prevalence of free riders, those measurement have to be more severe and deterrent in the public market.

B. Public Economics and Macroeconomics

Public economics deals with the government's policy, mainly in terms of efficiency. It provides a framework for evaluating the level of the government's involvement—if any—in economics markets and to what extent.

One may argue that from a purely economic point of view, the government does not have to finance its expenses through taxes. Careful planning may produce a calculated set of fees (46) and loans that could provide the necessary resources needed for the provision of the public goods and services. Yet no government, to the best of our knowledge, has replaced its general tax system with such a mechanism. One reason is that such a system might create a national debt that endangers the current economic system and shifts a heavy burden from the current generation to the future generations.

Two major tools are available for the government to achieve its economic goals: Monetary Policy (77) and Fiscal Policy (48). The former is used by the government to achieve its goals by controlling the domestic interest rate and the money supply. The latter deals with the government's spending and revenues and is more relevant to our discussion.

As is explain throughout of this book, the ideal concept is that the major tax system serves only for one clear and transparent purpose, i.e. to finance the government's spending. Its fiscal policy should be manifested in the government spending. Yet, in most countries, general tax systems use Tax Reliefs and Incentives [p. 44] as a tool by the government to regulate the national economic activities, such as private and public consumption, spending, and investments. Governments may use the tax system to supervise the level of consumption in order to, among other purposes, control the rate (aside of monetary measures) of inflation (63) or to stimulate economic activity.

A different approach is reflected in the principles of the monetary policy (77): the government minimizes its involvement and regulations and strives to use the principles of tax neutrality as much as possible, i.e. a tax whose impact on economic decisions is as small as possible.

Macroeconomics is a branch of economics that deals mainly with the performance, structure, and behavior of the national economy. It studies the impact of economic activities over the collective welfare of the society. In order to understand how the whole domestic/national economy functions and how we can improve it, macroeconomics deals with some economic indicators such as GDP (53), unemployment, price indices, interest rate and inflation (63), national income (81), consumption (26), and savings (111).

1) Gross Domestic Product and Other Alternative Indicators

One of the most important goals of economic policy is to enhance the individual and the aggregate wellbeing of the community. A common indictor that is used is ***Gross Domestic Product***, or ***GDP*** (53) (which is a new variation of the original Gross National Product—55). GDP is a simple indicator that measures the national economic performance—final goods and services produced and sold—within the state's borders during a year. It serves as a tool to appreciate the national income (81) and the growth of the state's economy. If the current year's GDP is higher than the previous year by 5%, it only means that the national economy grew by 5%.

An increase in GDP indicates economic growth, but it should be emphasized that temporary economic growth does not necessarily bode well. Instead, sustainable economic growth means **a rate of growth which can be maintained without creating other significant economic problems, especially for future generations**. Experience teaches us that there is a significant trade-off between rapid but temporary economic growth in the present, and sustainable growth in the future.

However, some economists (and shortsighted politicians) may conclude that under economic growth of 5%, the aggregate and individual welfare went up by 5% as well. Yet there is growing discontent from such a simplistic approach. Some notable economists, including the American Nobel Laureate Simon Kuznets, who developed the concept of measuring the Gross National Product during the 1930s for the U.S. administrations national accounting purposes, consider GDP and its current uses as a very much overrated tool, simply because it fails to measure welfare and wellbeing.

The measurement and reliance on GDP (even when divided by the national population—GDP Per Capita) and "economic growth" is a result of the practical difficulties of measuring or even defining ***welfare/wellbeing*** (Happiness? Wealth? Physical, emotional, or intellectual satisfaction?). Hence, the tendency to confuse mere economic performance with individual welfare has become quite popular. One has to admit that GDP does not distinguish between positive economic activities and negative ones; it does not deal with normative aspects of economic growth and its distribution among the members of the society. The GNP ignores the deficiencies that economic activity creates; e.g. pollution, depletion of natural resources, less social activities, leisure, "quality time", etc.

Evidently, there are some political and social movements that are trying to provide some alternatives. ***Redefining Progress*** fustigates the current indicators: "By the curious standard of the GDP, the nation's economic hero is a terminal cancer patient who is going through a costly divorce. The happiest event is an earthquake or a hurricane. The most desirable habitat is a multibillion-dollar Superfund site. All these add to the GDP, because they cause money to change hands. It is as if a business kept a balance sheet by merely adding up all 'transactions', without distinguishing between income and expenses, or between assets and liabilities".

Even the United Nations has begun, starting some twenty-five years ago, to use an alternative index: the Human Development Index (HDI), which aims to put people at the center of development. It is about people realizing their potential, increasing their choices and enjoying the freedom to live lives they value. Since 1990, annual Human Development Reports (http://hdr.undp.org/en/global-reports) have explored challenges including poverty, gender, democracy, human rights, cultural liberty, globalization, water scarcity, climate change, and mobility. The HDI is a summary measure of a country's human development. It measures the average achievements in a country in three basic dimensions: a long and healthy life, as measured by life expectancy at birth; access to knowledge, as measured by the adult literacy rate and the combined gross enrolment ratio in education; and a decent standard of living, as measured by GDP per capita in purchasing power parity in U.S. dollars. Countries are ranked on the basis of these values with a rank of 1 representing the highest HDI value.

An interesting approach is the **Centre for Bhutan Studies'** idea to use an alternative indicator: "**Gross National Happiness**", which is comprised of nine dimensions that were selected on normative grounds, and are equally weighted: Psychological Well-being; Time Use; Community Vitality; Culture; Health; Education; Environmental Diversity; Living Standard; and Governance.

It is not surprising that the ecological destruction and the climate crisis, which many believe that they endanger our health, our future, and the prospect of the planet, intensified the criticism of the blind worship of economic growth. We will mention here the economic anthropologist from the Autonomous University of Barcelona, Jason

Hickle's approach who argues that high-income nations need to scale down and stopping waste the use of unnecessary energy and resources ("degrowth") in order to eliminate those crises s and replace them with renewable energy together with significant changes of social and economic traditional concepts. Hickle argues that high-income nations do not need economic growth in order to achieve social goals; instead, they can reduce excess resource and energy use while at the same time improving human well-being, by distributing income more fairly, reduce the working hours' amount, while full employment must be guaranteed. Accordingly, Haykel proposes a Sustainable Development Index, which adjusts the Human Development Index by accounting for nations' ecological impact, in terms of per capita emissions and resource.

Another, similar approach is advanced by Kohei Saito, a philosopher from the University of Tokyo. In his book, Capital in the Anthropocene, Saito argues, in simple terms that capitalism's demand for unlimited profits is destroying the planet and only "degrowth" can repair the damage by slowing down social production and sharing wealth. Hence Saito proposes that mass production and the mass consumption of wasteful goods such as fast fashion should be restricted. He also advocates decarbonization through cutting working hours and focus on essential "labor-intensive" work such as caregiving.

Still, one may argue that from a purely economic point of view, economic growth is a significant and relevant factor. It provides essential data about the nation's economic activity. In other words, though we have to increase the size of the national pie, but taking into account the danger that uncontrolled, unrestricted, mere greed, and abusive growth may create both dangerous social gaps and risk the very existence of our planet. That is to say we have to consider also the normative and efficiency aspects of the wealth creation and its distribution [pp. 92–93], whether the growth "trickles down" or "trickles up" (144) [pp. 92–93].

Hence, we continue with the more conventional economic indicators, considering the relationship between the national economic growth and the tax system, and refer to some other factors as well.

2) Economic Growth and Taxes

A popular argument is that there is a negative correlation between tax rates and sustainable economic growth: the higher the former, the lower the latter, and vice versa. The problem with this argument is that there is hardly any empirical evidence that supports it. If anything, the evidence indicates, at least in the U.S., that the rate of economic growth was high during those years when tax rates were also high! One explanation is based on the **Keynesian Theory** (named after the ideas of 20th century Nobel laureate British economist John Maynard Keynes). One aspect of this theory is that in order to stimulate a shrinking economy, there is a need for increased aggregate demand. Aggregate demand is composed of private demand, demand for investment, and public demand. Though tax cuts increase the net income of the taxpayers, the marginal propensity to consume is lower than 1, hence tax-cuts do not increase the domestic private demand and demand for investment by the same amount that the net income is increased. On the other hand, if the government is efficient, a tax increase raises the public demand by the full amount of the government revenue. Hence, in times of recession or even a slow economy, economic growth could better be achieved with higher tax rates and an efficient government that provides public goods and services whose value is higher than the deadweight loss [p. 85] caused by the tax.

Furthermore: income and wealth production derive from using ***factors of production*** (45). As discussed above [p. 66], taxes and efficient government provide the third factor of production—the social capital—and its contribution to economic activity, production and economic growth [p. 68] is undeniable and no less important than real and human capital. In other words, a good tax system and an efficient government play a significant role in sustainable economic growth.

We note, however, that if we do come to the conclusion that excess production does create ecological problems and increases the climate crisis, it is quite possible that in order to reduce the negative externalities, the tax system will use regulatory-Pigovian taxes (93) in order to shift the costs of dealing with these problems to the shoulders of the producers and the consumers, [pp. 13–14, 53] even at the cost of reducing production.

3) Taxes as Automatic Stabilizers

Governments may use taxes—especially progressive income tax—as automatic measures that influences the economy.

Income tax (especially a progressive one) rises more than proportionately when income increases (98). During times of recession or a slow economy, the amount of progressive taxes (98) drops faster than income; such a decrease in taxes has a multiplier effect, partly offsetting the drop in private consumption, so that the equilibrium income doesn't drop as far or as fast as it might otherwise. In other words, higher disposable income increases aggregate demand, which increases productivity, which in turn eases recession and stimulates economic growth. Although, such a revenue decrease might cause a decrease in social capital which might decrease the aggregate demand. Yet governments have the privilege to maintain, or even increase their activity by increasing the national deficit until the recession is over.

Taxes have a similar, yet opposite stabilizing effect during times of economic boom that might lead to inflation (which is usually created by higher supply of money) (63). During such periods, both households and firms end up paying higher proportions of their income in taxes. Hence, the government absorbs a greater amount of money, which reduces the amount of disposable income, which leads to a restrained aggregate demand and eases the inflationary pressure. If needed, the government may limit the "excessive" revenue from enhancing the public demand by reducing its aggregate annual deficit.

Note that the same phenomenon exists with regard to transfer payments. Welfare allowances, transfer payments (including negative income tax (37, 82)), and direct services for poor people grow during a recession or slow economy, thus increasing private and public demand; and vice versa.

C. Public Finance

The theory of public finance is a relatively young branch of economics. It began to develop after the second World War, influenced by J.M. Keynes, whose work initiated Western governments to increase their involvement it the national economy. Public finance (government finance) deals mainly with fiscal policy (48): both government spending (through the national budget) and its revenues (mostly from taxes and fees). Public finance deals with the following questions, among others: What are the optimal tax systems (36)? Cost-benefit analysis of government activity; Who bears the tax burden (i.e. Tax incidence (129))? What are the goods and services that the government ought to provide (Security? National health system? Education? National pride?), and how it should charge the public? Should the government interfere with the free-market mechanism and redistribute national income? If so, how far should it go? What activities should be left to the private sector? Should the government use national social insurance and public health systems, and what kind? How efficient is the government at pursuing its objectives? Do taxes, and the services they finance, increase the aggregate welfare, or maybe, by creating a deadweight loss (90) [p. 85] leave society worse off? How do taxes affect the labor supply? Do we need one comprehensive tax system with high tax rates, or should we prefer several taxes levied on different tax bases (120) with lower rates? What is the "most preferred" tax base: net wealth (86) or income (58, 60, 61) or maybe consumption (26) or a flexible hybrid base?

Obviously, we will not deal with all these issues but rather confine our discussion to those that are most relevant to the theory of taxation.

D. Public Finance and Optimal Taxation

As mentioned [p. 13], a fascinating field in public finance theory is Optimal Taxation, (90) [p. 85] which is actually a set of normative prescriptions for tax policy that seeks to maximize social welfare for given required revenue. Optimal Taxation also considers how progressive (98), if at all, the tax should be [p. 89]; how much economic distortion, if any, does a given tax system have on the general welfare; which of these tax systems is least distorting; and what might the best combination of tax systems look like.

1) Optimal Taxation and Work Supply

Good economic analysis allows us today to see reality clearer, to better appreciate our personal and collective decisions, and to get rid of some prejudices. For example: our "natural" inclination is to accept the popular assumption that income tax drives us to cut work supply and to spend less time on working hours. Yet a more calculated approach and careful analysis reveals a different conclusion. This is because in terms of work supply, tax creates two contradicting effects. On the one hand, the ***substitution effect*** states that income tax drives us to reduce the amount of work we are willing to offer. On the other hand, the income tax's ***income effect*** pushes us to increase it. The explanation is quite basic.

Since the total amount of hours in each day is given (and limited), we may spend them on working or on its alternative—leisure. The more hours we spend on work, the less leisure hours we have. The more we consume leisure time, the less hours we can use for work. Hence, the value of a working hour is equal to the value of one hour of leisure (e.g. "If I work one additional hour for $50, it means that I 'sold' one hour of leisure for that price. If I gave up working an additional one hour for $50, I buy one hour of leisure for $50"). The higher our income per hour is, the higher the cost of one leisure hour is, and vice versa: the lower our compensation per hour, the lower the value of one hour of leisure is. As a rule, a higher wage yields a ***substitution effect*** by which there are incentives for more hours of work, and reduced leisure time: it becomes more costly to consume expensive leisure. Therefore, higher wages impose pressure to work more hours and spend less on leisure. Since income tax reduces net income, the ***substitution effect*** of the tax is in the opposite direction: lower net income produces incentives for fewer hours of work and increase leisure time—it becomes less costly to consume leisure. (A popular presentation of the substitution effects is "it is not worth it to work for that lower net income. I would rather stay at home").

Income effects on leisure consumption may be positive, (as they are for normal goods, i.e. a larger income entails greater consumption), negative (in cases of inferior goods), or zero. People tend to consume more normal goods as their income goes up, and reduce their consumption of normal goods when their income goes down. Since leisure is considered a normal good, and income tax decreases net income, such tax reduces the consumption of leisure, and necessarily increases its alternative—labor. (A popular presentation of the income effect is: "I need to earn a certain amount of income in order to maintain my and my family's standard of living; due to income tax my disposable income is lower, and 8 hours of work is no longer enough; I have to increase my working hours in order to maintain my financial goals").

It is quite difficult to conclude which of these two tax effects is more dominant. People have different tastes, motivations, ambitions, and priorities. Empirical findings have not yet provided a conclusive, unequivocal, and sweeping answer either. There is some evidence that taxes do not have an aggregate effect on men at their working age (before their retirement age). For those taxpayers, it seems that on the aggregate, the two contradicting effects offset each other. Some men are affected by the substitution effect, some by the income effect. Yet there are some indications that the substitution effect is more common among higher income taxpayers, whereas the income effect is dominant among lower income taxpayers.

Different findings were collected regarding women between the age of 20–45 (possibly mothers to young children). With them, the substitution effects are stronger. They tend, generally, to reduce their working hours as income tax rates go up.

A 2004 study by American economist and Nobel laureate Edward C. Prescott, has suggested that the reason American workers now work 50 percent more than German, French, and Italian workers is due to the differences between the top marginal overall tax burden between these countries. When comparing statistical data between industrial countries (the G-7) during two periods—1970–74 and 1993–96—he found that labor supply (hours per person) in the second period was much higher in Japan and the United States than it was in Germany, France, and Italy, and Canada and the United Kingdom were in the intermediate range. Another finding was that U.S. output per person is about 40 percent higher than in the European countries, with most of the differences in output accounted for by differences in hours worked per person and not by differences in productivity, which is measured in output per hour worked. Prescott determined that the importance of the *effective marginal tax rate* on labor income is accountable for these differences in labor supply for those countries. Hence, he suggested that the tax rates alone (lower—40% top marginal in the U.S. and higher—over 60% top marginal—in Europe) account for most of the differences, though he mentions strong evidence that other factors were important as well. Prescott concluded that the welfare (in terms of lifetime consumption) gains from reducing the effective marginal tax rates on labor income in **the high tax rate** countries would be significant. Note though that Prescott deals only with income tax on labor; not with low tax rate on capital income or with inequality and social gaps. These issues are discussed below [p. 90].

2) Optimal Taxation and Deadweight Loss

Optimal taxation (90) offers some tools that enable us to determine whether a tax is efficient, or whether the total amount of the loss of welfare due to the taxes versus the benefits provided by the tax revenue leads to an aggregate increase or decrease in the society's welfare. A common argument provided by public finance economists is that every tax—besides poll tax (95)—creates economic distortion and leads to deadweight/ excess-burden. The distortion created by income tax is real, even if its aggregate impact on the work supply is nil. The fact that there is no decline of the **total national** work supply after the imposition of income tax can only indicate that some of the taxpayers were affected by the ***substitution effect*** and the others by the ***income effect***. Hence, both groups' behavior was distorted, and some welfare was reduced: the former reduces their desired level of work supply and their income and increased their leisure time, and the latter reduced their optimal leisure time and had to increase their time at work. Furthermore, according to this argument, even if the taxpayer does not change their work supply at all, they suffer a loss; they have less disposable money, and hence have to reduce their current or future consumption (i.e. current savings).

A slightly different way to present this concept is as follows: in a world without taxes, the free-market economy provides the equilibrium quantity of goods and services according to the free demand by buyers and the supply offered by sellers. Once we introduce tax into the market, it affects the price paid by the buyers, and the price received by sellers. It does not matter whether a tax on a good is levied formally on buyers or sellers; the price paid by buyers rises, and the price received by sellers falls. The tax creates a gap between the price buyers pay and the price sellers receive. The gap, called a "tax wedge", also reduces the amount of the goods sold below the amount that would have been sold in a world without tax. Both the consumers and supplier' surplus decreases. The decrease in surplus of consumers and producers exceeds the revenue raised by the government. Furthermore, the reduction in the total surplus and the tax revenue is equal to what has been termed *deadweight loss* or *excess burden* [p. 13]. Those basic principles apply to all kinds of goods and services, including labor. In the labor market, industries/employers create the demand, and employees provide the supply.

The size of the deadweight loss depends on the price elasticity (41) of the supply and demand of the goods and services involved: when the supply is inelastic, the tax's deadweight loss is small, and vice versa: elastic supply entails larger deadweight loss. The same is with the demand: when it is inelastic, deadweight loss is small; when demand is elastic, the deadweight loss is larger. Hence, if the labor supply is elastic, the deadweight loss is large. Such insights produce some unusual, impractical, and insensible conclusions, such as the tax design known as "Ramsey tax" [p. 88] and even Mirrlees' zero tax rate on high income [p. 100].

Some basic causes of labor elasticity are, *inter alia,* flexible hours of work; multiple earners (couples, elders who have pension funds); illegal activity; a strong temptation to enjoy leisure (e.g. parents of young children).

A common representation of the validity of the deadweight loss may be found in the following demonstration (*figure 5.1*). The government levies a new income tax. According to the taxpayer's preferences and priorities, her reaction to the new tax is a reduction in her work supply ("the substitution effect"). Yet the employer's cost per hour stays the same. The process can be illustrated by the following ***figure 5.1***:

Figure 5.1:

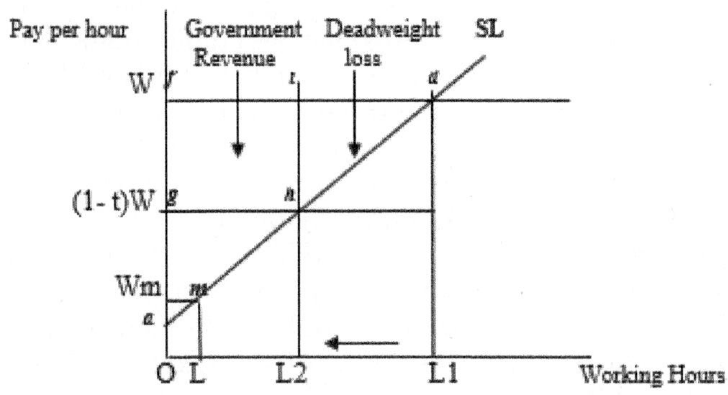

Under a common assumption, the work supply offered by workers increases as compensation grows. We can see that the slope SL increases from left to right. In a world without taxes, for W income, a worker is willing to work L1 hours. Her total income is W multiplied by L1, represented with the rectangle OL1*df*. The worker "gains" what economists call "producers' surplus" (here "workers surplus"), which is represented in triangle *adf*. *Triangle adf* is the amount that the producers (workers) benefit by selling their services at a market price that is higher than they would be willing to sell for; as can be seen, the worker was ready to work Lm hours for Wm income, but their income is much higher and equal to W for all their work, including Lm.

Once an income tax (t) is levied, the after-net income (83) goes down to (1−t)W and the employee's net income goes down from point *f* to point *g*. The before0-tax compensation per hour paid by the employer is still W, yet due to the lower after-tax income, the employee's work supply goes down to L2. The employee's total surplus is down, represented by the new triangle *agh*. Hence, the total reduction of the employee's welfare is the difference between the original *adf* and the new *agh,* which is the trapezoid *ghdf*. On the other hand, the total tax raised by the government is represented by rectangular *hgif,* which is the tax on working hours L2 multiplied by *tW*. The difference between trapezoid *ghdf* and rectangular *hgif* (rectangular *idh*) is the loss of the aggregate/total welfare; the deadweight loss/excess burden.

Note that even though the above illustration assumes that the employee's reaction to the tax is due to the *substitute effect,* the same deadweight loss occurs also if the taxpayer responds to the *income effect*, i.e. he increases his work supply; regarding the above figure 1, instead of working hours, we place "leisure hours" on the lower horizontal axis. Furthermore, deadweight loss may result even if there is no visible change in the taxpayers' behavior, since what matters is the compensated response to the tax, i.e. lowering either consumption, savings, or leisure.

Such a demonstration of the concept of deadweight loss is too narrow and one-sided. It ignores the benefits and the welfare that is connected to the public goods and services provided by the government when using its tax revenue. Hence, we should refrain from hasty conclusions, and not assume that the tax system's overall impact is a reduction of the aggregate welfare of our society. Such an assumption is valid only when the total welfare or the public's benefit from the goods or services provided by the government in return for the tax is lower than the deadweight loss created by the tax.

The assumption that the tax reduces the taxpayers' welfare is quite remote in a democratic regime. After all, why does anybody agree to pay any amount of money if what is received in return is worth less than the amount paid? We are ready to pay any price, fee, tax, or loss of leisure only when we benefit. We consent to pay the government only if the value of the government's goods and services are **higher** than the value of the same services produced by ourselves or bought in the free market from the private sector. The government has an advantage regarding the production and provisions of public goods and services. Without such an advantage, we would not need the government and its services, and we would not have entered the Social Contract to begin with.

To illustrate, assume a "before-tax world" without an organized government; there is no recognition of property or any other rights, nor any law enforcement services. Accordingly, the taxpayer has to spend their leisure time guarding/watching their family and belongings. Suppose, in a world without a government, a person divides their 24 hours a day in the following fashion: 8 hours on working, 8 hours on sleeping and eating, and 8 hours on guarding their property and securing the safety of their family. They contemplate entering into a social contract with the government. The government provides them with legal recognition of their property and security services. In return, the government charges them a tax equal to their compensation for 4 working hours. In this naïve assumption, they are about to have a great deal: in return for 4 hours they gain 6 hours, since due to the government's public goods and services they only spend 2 hours (instead of 8) on guarding their property and securing their family (the government is not 100% efficient). They might increase their working hours by 4 hours—in order to finance their new tax bill. Hence, their total gain is an increase of 2 hours that they may spend either on leisure or on profitable work. Either way, their welfare goes up by these two extra hours.

In addition, the provision of public goods and services entails positive externalities (44) as well. It provides social capital and promotes economic growth, which further increases the community's and individuals' general welfare. Hence, an additional prerequisite emerges, as was expressed some one hundred and fifty years ago by German scholar L. von Stein: "It is the most essential goal of each tax to be capable, through its administration, to return as an element of capital formation to the individual who paid it. A Tax, in this respect, is more correct and justified to the extent it can accomplish this goal, and that it becomes wrong where, through inefficient administration, it loses this capacity".

In other words, for the taxpayer to agree to pay the tax, it has to meet the efficiency requirement. The tax has to provide us with a return that is equal to or larger than the deadweight loss (in the above illustration—triangle ***idh***), i.e. the total value of the public goods and services is equal to the government's revenue plus the deadweight loss (the trapezoid *ghdf*). If it does not, it is doubtful if it has economic, political or even constitutional justification. After all, the Congress is authorized to "*lay and collect taxes, duties, imposts and excises, to pay the debts and provide* ***for the common defense and general welfare of the United States***"; [Article 1, Section 8 of the U.S. Constitution] *(emphasis added)* [p. 39]. Hence, it seems that an inefficient tax should not stand public and judicial review.

Alas, the practical road to present a solid **legal** and **constitutional** argument based on the above inefficiency against any tax is quite long. The major obstacle is the appraisal/evaluation/quantification of the market value of the government's services (What is the value of a military fighter jet during time of peace? During wartime? What is the value of the services provided by policeman on the beach? Streets? Roads? How much do we appreciate the property and freedom of contract rights that are recognized and enforced by the government? The national pride (or the far future prospects) gained by space research? Academic studies and research?

One possible conclusion might be that tax theory cannot and should not enter to the complicated labyrinth of defining the scope and the meaning of the public goods and services. Nor should the law control the process of determining the collective-political decisions about what kind of services we expect the government to provide.

Such an approach does not seem right. It might grant the government unlimited power or far-reaching immunity from judicial review of tax legislation. These practical hurdles should not prevent us from presenting a theoretical structure, a broad framework of analysis that can improve our understanding of possible constitutional judicial or political review on tax laws. Furthermore, as mentioned above [p. 49], in the rare cases when taxpayers are able to provide a clear and persuasive claim that they do not receive a reasonable return for their tax bills, they may have a constitutional justification for tax reduction.

3) Is a Multi-Bases Tax System More Efficient than a Single Tax?

Public finance literature demonstrates a most significant phenomenon. Based on mathematical calculations and empirical surveys, public financiers argue that as the tax rate increases, its deadweight loss goes up by its square. Doubling a tax quadruples its deadweight loss. As a result, the marginal deadweight loss from raising one more dollar of revenue exceeds the average deadweight loss. Assume that the average deadweight loss per dollar of tax revenue is $0.18 while the marginal deadweight loss per additional dollar of tax revenue is around $0.36 (or even a bit higher). The social cost of each dollar raised for a given public project is the dollar plus the incremental deadweight loss of 36 cents (and **not** 18 cents). This means that the public goods and services provided by such a tax must produce a marginal benefit of more than $1.36 if they are to improve welfare.

Two meaningful conclusions may be drawn from this. One is that the measuring of the deadweight loss of any given tax is possible. The other is that when the government needs a certain amount of revenue, it should consider multi-bases taxes (120) with lower tax rates instead of one tax base with high tax rates. Note though that under Dalton's "theorem of the invariance of tax incidence" [p. 5], any type of tax, whether on income, profit, property, or consumption, has an independent effect on the market, regardless of who has the statutory obligation to remit it. Therefore, the tax is shifted and born according to the market forces rather than the formal and legal path.

4) Ramsey's Optimal Tax Rule

An example of an efficiency analysis that led to an unexpected conclusion was provided by the British philosopher, mathematician, and economist Frank Ramsey. Ramsey showed that excise taxes should be levied in inverse proportion to the representative consumer's elasticity of demand for the good. Accordingly, the goods with an inelastic demand should be taxed at higher tax rates. The Ramsey optimal tax rule aims to minimize deadweight loss: deadweight loss is related to the elasticity (41) of supply and demand for goods and services. Hence, it follows that putting the highest tax rates on the goods and services for which there is most inelastic supply and demand will result in the least overall deadweight loss, and vice versa. One possible result would be a higher tax rate on basic and necessary goods and services—including for low earning individuals—and very low tax rates on luxuries and movable financial capital.

There are two major problems with the Ramsey rule. First, it seems to be in conflict with the principle of equity and a basic sense of social justice. Second, there are some serious doubts about its actual capability of promoting efficiency. If implemented, such a rule will probably increase inequality, widen social gaps, and eventually undermine efficiency, at least in the long run [p. 90].

5) Optimal Tax Rate—the Laffer Curve

Another interesting aspect of tax efficiency is an idea attributed to Washingtonian economist Arthur Laffer, who argued that raising the tax rate not only does not always entail higher government revenue but might actually decrease it. The basic argument is quite simple: tax revenues would be zero if tax rates were either 0% or 100%, Somewhere in between 0% and 100% is a tax rate that maximizes total revenue. The underlying rationale is quite clear. If the tax rates were too high, taxpayers—who use basic cost benefit-analysis—would either reduce their economic activities or shift part of this activity to the underground unreported economy ("a hidden tax revolt"). The key is to locate the optimal point—not too high not too low—which provides the maximum amount of revenue for the government.

The following (and naïve) illustration demonstrates the Laffer's theory: Point O is the optimal point where the tax rate (t*) brings the maximum tax revenue:

Figure 5.2:

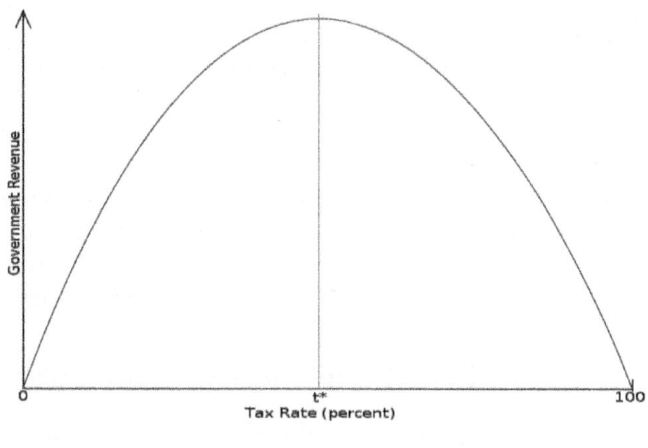

There are two major problems with the desire to locate the magic point O. First, there are some serious doubts as to whether tax revenue will be indeed zero if the tax rate is 100%. Volunteers, scientists, blog publishers and most players of the third sector (87) provide vivid proof that such an assumption is not always valid. The other problem is more significant: unfortunately, there are very few conclusive empirical studies that support such curve and can locate the magic point in a real economy. According to the American mathematician Martin Gardner (1996), the real life curve matches Laffer's original curve only near the two extremes of 0% and 100%, but rapidly collapses into a chaotic shape at the middle, and looks like the following figure 3:

Figure 5.3:

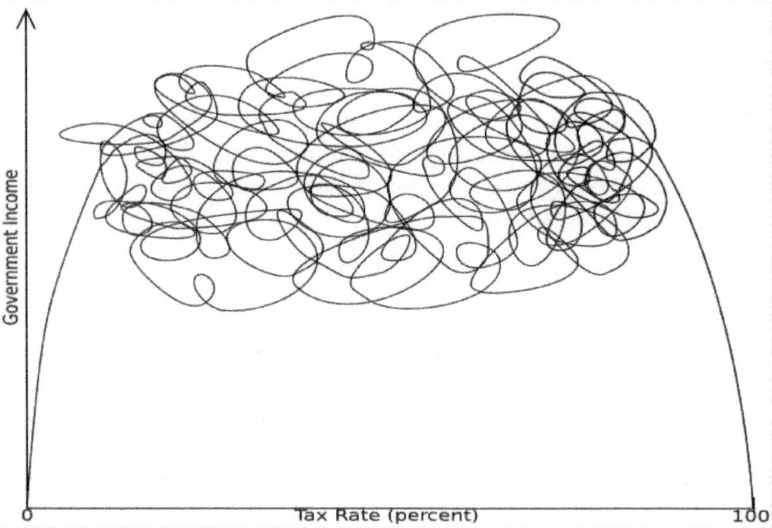

In conclusion, due to Gardner's argument and later insights from economists like Piketty, Stiglitz, Krugman, Atkinson, and Ostry, which are discussed below [pp. 90–95], it seems that the Laffer curve has gone out of fashion.

6) Economic Growth, Social Gaps, Redistribution, and Taxes

We mentioned earlier [p. 72] that a growing number of economists ("worldly philosophers") are very concerned with poverty and social gaps. Some express ethical and normative considerations; others use utilitarian claims to defy the assumption that efficiency and equality are conflicting or contradictory ideas. The common ground throughout their writings and research is a sharp criticism of the neoclassical interpretation of the free market economy. Such an interpretation confuses the free market and the invisible hand, and the capitalistic concept concerned mainly with one factor of production—financial capital; a concept that strives to provide financial capital and its owners certain privileges, even when no market failures exist, and in some awkward yet sophisticated ways prevent real competition. Furthermore, it rejects the government's attempts to intervene where there are market failures that reduce the aggregate efficiency and welfare [p. 28].

A) Equality and Efficiency—the Big Trade-Off?

Evidently, after experiencing the horrible effects of communism, no reasonable person would support the extreme claim for pursuing total and complete economic equality through the elimination of private property. Yet, inequality bothers us. Among those schools of thought that acknowledge the claim that sharp inequalities and social gaps are undesirable and a negative phenomenon, two types of arguments emerge. The first is based on normative and ethical considerations. The second relies on utilitarian and economic analyses that lead to the conclusion that mitigating inequality and minimizing social gaps brings significant economic growth and benefits.

Some forty years ago, in his lecture *Equality and Efficiency: the Big Tradeoff* (which was later published as a book), the American economist Arthur Okun drew a distinction between ethical, normative and constitutional principles on the one hand, and economic efficiency on the other hand. Okun argues that the concept of Human Dignity is at the center of the Social Contract and forms the core of all Human rights. Hence,

> *"[T]he assurance of dignity for every member of the society requires the right for a decent existence—to some minimum standard of nutrition, health care and other essentials of life. Starvation and dignity do not mix well. . . . ."* [p. 50].

In order to enable a decent existence to all members of the society, sharp social gaps and inequalities should be lowered. Therefore, a certain degree of economic efficiency must be sacrificed to achieve a certain degree of social equality. As an eye-catching demonstration, Okun introduced the "leaky bucket" metaphor: "The money must be carried from the rich to the poor in a leaky bucket. Some of it will simply disappear in transit, so the poor will not receive all the money that is taken from the rich". Such leakage is attributed to the administrative costs of taxing and transferring, and to the incentive effects, i.e. the recipients have less incentive to work since their basic needs are provided by the transfer payments and, if they earn from their labor, the transfer payments are reduced. On the other hand, so goes the argument, the rich also have less incentive to work due to the "Substitute effect" because high marginal tax rates would take a large fraction of their additional income [p. 83]. Hence, there is a clear trade-off between equality/redistribution and efficiency/economic growth.

B) Inequality and Economic Efficiency—the Theory

Even if we ignore ethical and constitutional considerations and concentrate only on economic analysis, we can realize why broad social gaps are considered market failures that require government intervention. The inequalities of opportunity, poverty, ignorance, bad education, and lack of medical services decrease the major factors of production in both developing and developed countries, i.e. human and social capital. Neglecting a poor child who is unable to get a good education, reasonable medical treatment, sufficient nutrition, and equal opportunity could potentially cause the society to lose a brilliant scientist, an innovative inventor, or a skillful and productive worker in the near future. Furthermore, a neglected/deprived child might become an offender who causes negative externalities, mostly by delinquent activities, which add to the government's expenditures on law enforcement and public health. Due to adverse selection (80) [p. 127], the free market is unable to provide poor families with a suitable education, an efficient health system, social insurance and similar goods and services. This is the government's role. This is the main reason for humans to enter the Social Contract. That is, we assume and expect that living together in a democratic state, under an elected government that serves us in the most efficient way, will increase our wellbeing. The public, through the elected government, seeks to invest in and improve on the social capital, and decides upon the level, quality, types and methods of those services that aim to assure a decent existence for every member of the state. These services require funds. Thus, we pay taxes to ensure that our agents, the elected government, to fulfill our needs that the free market fails to, due to a matter of values and ethical norms as well as a matter of economic efficiency. Those public services enhance human and social capital as factors of production and eventually lead to sustainable economic growth and higher productivity. The arithmetic is quite simple. With an efficient and sincere government, the higher the government's revenue, the better the public goods and services it can provide. Such provision of services enhances human and social capital (45); better human and social capital contributes more to the nation's income, economic activity, production, growth and employment which eventually add income and wealth to both the poor and rich members of the society.

Alas, for many years the supporters of neoclassical capitalism have argued that any reduction in taxes produces greater economic growth. The capital owners and their political supporters (and donors) cherish this argument, adopt it, and further claim that, due to deadweight loss (90) [p. 85], any increase in tax rates decreases economic growth. As indicated above [p. 87], such a one-sided and shortsighted claim ignores the benefits that the government provides by using tax revenue. As for the general welfare of the whole society, their popular argument is mainly based on "trickle-down economics" (144), i.e. privileges for the rich lead to economic growth, and wealth will eventually leak down to the poor.

Professor and Nobel laureate in Economics Simon Kuznets offered, some 60 years ago, another semi-comforting theory, which is known as the "Kuznets curve". It suggests that as an economy develops, a natural cycle of economic inequality driven by market forces occurs, which at first increases inequality, and then decreases it after a certain average income is attained. Alas, there are some serious doubts about whether this optimistic curve actually works. Newer empirical studies challenge and even contradict it [p. 91].

One explanation for the fact that high taxes may increase economic growth and low taxes may decrease it was mentioned already: efficient governments use tax revenue in order to enhance sources of social capital including infrastructure, public knowledge and education, technological progress, health, and welfare systems, which all contribute to human capital as well. These are measures that maintain and enhance factors of production that contribute to the economic activities that lead to economic growth, higher employment rates and greater collective and individual wellbeing. A similar aspect of this theoretical explanation refers to **Keynesian Theory** and the need to increase aggregate demand [p. 81], which is composed not only of private consumption but also of public demand and investments, which are usually financed by taxes [p. 81]. Likewise, providing equal opportunity to the poor also increases private demand, which increases efficiency and productivity.

The underlying explanation for the above claim is purely utilitarian, both on the personal/individual level and on the national level. On the personal level, poverty and lack of education go hand in hand with viciousness, hostility, and criminal activity. Wealthy members of society have much more to lose economically as victims of violence and offences. Hence, by giving a little wealth to the poor, the rich actually buy insurance that enables them to live their own good lives and to continue earning more wealth (both by having more customers and being able to hire a better work force) and reduces their costs for protecting their lives and property [p. 72]. As for the national level, eliminating poverty by providing satisfactory public goods (education, health care etc.) enhances two factors of production—Human and Social capital, as mentioned earlier. In addition, as Bernard Shaw (a Nobel laureate in Literature and a co-founder of the London School of Economics) indicated a century and a half ago, eliminating poverty, crimes, and ignorance significantly reduces the national spending on law enforcement costs.

In sum, there are some convincing arguments that, at least in theory, there is no need to balance between equality and efficiency. Reducing social gaps does not harm efficiency and that redistribution improves economic activities. Taxation and efficient governing increase the amount and the quality of human and social capital, which lead to long and sustainable economic growth and greater general welfare. There is no need to sacrifice efficiency in order to promote equality. Equality and efficiency go hand in hand up to a certain level.

Interestingly, this conclusion is supported by empirical evidence.

C) Inequality and Economic Efficiency—Empirical Findings

In 1996, Joel Slemrod and Jon Bakija argued in *Taxing Ourselves*, that if anything, empirical evidence indicates that, at least in the U.S., the rate of economic growth was higher during those years when tax rates were also high.

Professor Joseph Stiglitz, American economist and Nobel laureate, states: "It is no accident that the periods in which the broadest cross sections of Americans have reported higher net incomes—when inequality has been reduced, partly as a result of progressive taxation—have been the periods in which the U.S. economy has grown the fastest. It is likewise no accident that the current recession, like the Great Depression, was preceded by large increases in inequality".

The 21st century and the digital era have enabled economists, once again, to greatly advantage from using multistate and historical empirical databases to re-examine, modify and even defy the alleged trade-off between equality and efficiency argument, and to remove the discrepancy between efficiency and social normative values.

In 2011, Stiglitz in an article titled "Of the 1%, by the 1%, for the 1%", once again presented his arguments regarding the economic price we pay for allowing huge social gaps and inequality. A year later, the expanded argument was published in his book *The Price of Inequality: How Today's Divided Society Endangers Our Future*. The argument is clear and straightforward: social gaps, inequality, and lack of equal opportunity make growth more volatile and create the unstable conditions for a sudden slowdown in GDP growth. Stiglitz argues that inequality in America has been widening for decades. The gap between the 1 percent and the 99 percent is vast when looked at in terms of annual income, and even vaster when looked at in terms of wealth—that is, in terms of accumulated capital and other assets. Stiglitz argues that trickle-down economics (144) does not work: "While the rich have been growing richer, most Americans (and not just those at the bottom) have been unable to maintain their standard of living, let alone to keep pace. A typical full-time male worker receives the same income today he did a third of a century ago". On the other hand, trickle-up economics probably works: "All—even those at the top—could benefit by giving more to those at the bottom". Stiglitz concludes that "an economy like America's, in which most citizens' wealth has fallen, median income has stagnated, and many of the poorest citizens have been doing worse year after years, is not likely to do well over the long haul".

American economists are not alone. In his book *Capital in the Twenty First Century,* French economist Thomas Piketty bases his research and conclusions on large and extensive historical and comparative data covering three centuries and more than twenty countries, which were unavailable for previous researchers, as well as on a new theoretical framework that affords a deeper understanding of the underlying mechanism of the distribution of wealth. Piketty notes that modern economic growth and the diffusion of knowledge have made it possible to avoid the Marxist apocalypse but have not modified the deep structure of capital and inequality. As with others, Piketty is very much concerned about the widening of social gaps, which, according to his findings, will continue unless the government takes some drastic measures.

The underlying rationale for Piketty's argument is direct, rational, and convincing. "When the rate of return on [financial] capital exceeds the rate of growth of output and income [i.e. the average rate of return of the combined return on human capital and financial capital], capitalism automatically generates arbitrary and unsustainable inequality that radically undermine the meritocratic values on which democratic societies are based". In a simple formula: when returns on capital (r) grow faster than the economy (g), i.e. "r>g", the return to financial capital is obviously greater than the return to labor. In other words, income from capital and wealth, and not earnings from labor, dominates the income distribution in our society. Furthermore, under the current tax systems, the (very few) owners of capital enjoy a significant rate of return on their investments with minimal taxation; meanwhile, economic growth is only around 1 percent. The conclusion of this argument is clear and inevitable: wealthy individuals could easily reinvest enough of their income to ensure that their wealth grows much faster than the wealth of those who earn their income from labor, reinforcing their economic dominance and possibly political influence. Note, however, that in our mind it is irrelevant whether the individual members of this wealthy minority group remain constant over time or if their individual identity changes.

In addition to wealth accumulation, Piketty (and some other scholars) also refers to the huge salaries paid by big firms to their CEOs and other managers. Piketty claims that this new phenomenon (which the Nobel laureate Paul Krugman calls "super-salaries") is a direct result of the sharp reduction of the marginal tax brackets from 80–90 percent tax rate to around 40 percent. This sharp and dramatic reduction has dramatically transformed the way executive salaries are determined. It is one thing to ask for a significant raise when only 10–20 percent of the amount goes to the individual executive while the rest goes to the government, and another thing entirely to insist on the same raise when only 40 percent goes to the government and the other 60 percent stays (the "retention rate", as Atkinson terms it) in the individual executive's pockets.

This new phenomenon is not detached from wealth and capital. As Krugman describes it: "real wages for most U.S. workers have increased little if at all since the early 1970s, but wages for the top one percent of earners have risen 165 percent, and wages for the top 0.1 percent have risen 362 percent". CEOs and other "super-salary" earners are inseparable from the capital owners; they are their agents and servants. The huge salaries—which usually come at the public's expense (from other workers, the firms' customers or the companies' common shareholders) are not a real return on work and labor, but rather the CEO's own share of the capital they produce for the capital owners.

Indeed, the data regarding social gaps and inequality is staggering and alarming. As Stiglitz describes it: "In America the share of the national income going to the top .01% (some 16,000 families) has risen from just over 1% in 1980 to almost 5% in 2014. . . .the 400 wealthiest Americans took home an **hourly** 'wage' of $97,000 in 2009 and, as mentioned, their average income tax rate was 8.4% [p. 183]. On the other hand, median wealth fell by almost 40 percent. All of the wealth accumulation in this country has gone to the top. If the bottom has shared equally in America's increase in wealth, its wealth over the past two decades would have gone up by some 75 percent".

Stiglitz, Krugman and Piketty are not alone. Another empirical study supporting the claim that redistribution and efficiency go hand in hand was published in February 2014 by a group of researchers (Jonathan Ostry, Andrew Berg, and Charalambos Tsangarides) from the International Monetary Fund (IMF), an organization which has gained a conservative reputation. Their "**Staff Discussion Note**" contains fascinating findings based on empirical evidence mainly from the World Income Inequality Database. The Note concludes that social gaps are significant factors for lower economic growth: inequality can undermine progress in health and education, cause investment-reducing political and economic instability, and undercut the social consensus required to adjust in the face of economic and social shocks. Thus, it tends to reduce the pace and durability of growth.

The Note defies the possible claim that inequality may impede growth, at least in part *because* it calls forth efforts to redistribute, which undercut growth themselves. It found enough data to support a different conclusion, that equality enhancing interventions could actually help growth, e.g. taxes on activities with negative externalities (44) paid mostly by the rich or cash transfers aimed at encouraging better attendance at primary schools in developing countries. Based on a compiled cross-country dataset that distinguishes **market** inequality (before taxes and transfers) from **net** inequality (after taxes and transfers), the researchers calculated redistributive transfers for a large number of country-year observations. The IMF note's main findings are as follows. First, more unequal societies tend to redistribute more. Second, lower net inequality is robustly correlated with faster and more durable growth, for a given level of redistribution. Third, redistribution appears generally benign in terms of its impact on growth; only in extreme cases is there some evidence that it may have direct negative effects on growth. Thus, the combined direct and indirect effects of redistribution—including the growth effects of the resulting lower inequality—are on average pro-growth.

The Note further indicates that the common conclusion of a big tradeoff between redistribution and growth is probably unfounded. "The best available macroeconomic data does not support that conclusion. . . . What we find is that we should not assume that there is a big trade-off between redistribution and growth.

An additional note titled "Causes and Consequences of Income Inequality", which was published in June 2015 by another IMF team (Era Dabla-Norris, Kalpana Kochhar, Frantisek Ricka) reached similar conclusions:

> *Our analysis suggests that the income distribution itself matters for growth as well. Specifically, if the income share of the top 20 percent (the rich) increases, then GDP growth actually declines over the medium term, suggesting that the benefits do not trickle down. In contrast, an increase in the income share of the bottom 20 percent (the poor) is associated with higher GDP growth. The poor and the middle class matter the most for growth via a number of interrelated economic, social, and political channels.*

D) The Causes of the Growing Inequality

Stiglitz, like Piketty, identifies two major reasons for the drastically widening inequality of our era. In addition to increasingly deregulated financial sector, the reduction in the progressivity of the tax system is one of the most significant factors. According to Stiglitz "The irony is that just as markets started delivering more unequal outcomes, tax policy asked less of the top. The top marginal tax rate was lowered from 70 percent under Carter to 28 percent under Reagan; it went up to 39.6 percent under Clinton and down finally to 35 percent under George W. Bush." ". . .first the top rate was lowered from 70 percent to 28 percent, had been raised to 39.6 percent . . .then back to 35 Percent . . . But then the taxes on forms of income received disproportionately by the rich (capital gains, more than half of which are earned by the top 0.1 percent) were lowered further . . .to 20 and then further to 15 percent. Furthermore, according to the OMB (Executive Office of the President of the United States) and CEA (Council of Economic Advisers, an agency within the Executive Office of the President), the 400 wealthiest billionaire families in America paid an average tax of just 8.2 percent of their income—a lower rate than many ordinary Americans pay [p. 183]. These incredible figures certainly contribute to the widening of social gaps in the U.S. [p. 90] and decrease efficiency as well [p. 93].

Piketty also puts blame on the elimination of what he labels "the confiscatory taxation of excessive incomes". He refers to the year 1944, when the tax rate for top earners went up to 94 percent due to various surtaxes. The top rate then stabilized at around 90 percent until mid-1960 but fell to 70 percent after that.

There is ample evidence to suggest that a significant factor in the increasing social gaps is a gap in the quality of education and its outcomes. Many studies show that highly educated taxpayers have high incomes. This trend intensified with the occurrence of the technological revolution. Prof. Jeffrey Zacks believes that the technological revolution will bring about a real revolution in the current social structure and change it completely. The demand for "classic" professions—including lawyers and accountants—will decrease, while high-tech workers will become in demand when the free-market rewards them accordingly. As a result, society will eventually be divided into two classes.

If indeed, Prof. Jeffrey Sachs is right in his prediction regarding social gaps growing due to the technological revolution, then the solution might be a new **fiscal policy** (48).

One growing idea might be what is called the Universal/unconditional Basic Income, (UBI) which has emerged lately as a realistic policy, not only in Northern Europe but also in the Netherlands, Scotland, and India. The idea, which was conceived in the 16th century by Thomas More in his book "Utopia", is quite simple: the government grants every citizen/resident an unconditional monthly fixed amount of money' which is aimed to ensure every member of the society/state/community sufficient income to meet basic needs and to provide human dignity. The grant should be taxed. Those who would rely on the grant for their only income would not exemptions. The others would pay a progressive income tax.

Some experiments were conducted (in most cases by private organizations) in 1968 and in various jurisdictions (Alaska, North Carolina, New Jersey, Pennsylvania, Iowa, Seattle, Denver, and Gary, Indiana, Stockton, California, and Oakland, California) and some foreign countries (Canada, Brazil, Finland, Germany Spain, The Netherlands, Iran, Kenya, Kenya, India, Hong Kong, Macao, and Japan). In general terms the findings are not conclusive, yet not discouraging. There was an increase of the recipients standard of living, almost no reduction of their work supply, and even a small increase in employment [Tera Allas, Jukka Maksimainen, James Manyika, and Navjot Singh An experiment to inform universal basic income **Mckinsey&Company** (2020); Rebecca Hasdell, What We Know About Universal Basic Income—a Cross-Synthesis of Reviews **Stanford Basic Income Lab** (July 2020)].

E) Taxation and Inequality

In order to cope with these **economic** problems of social gaps and inequality, some economists support the use of progressive income tax (98) [p. 98]. British economist Anthony Atkinson supports the idea of reinstating Britain's top marginal tax rate to 65 percent (it is currently 45 percent) and broadening the tax base by eliminating most tax expenditures/concessions. Piketty suggests two possible remedies. First, a global wealth tax. Second, for the United States, a top income tax rate of 80 percent on income above $5 or $10 million, in addition to 50 or 60 percent on income above about $200,000.

Piketty's first idea, a global wealth tax, contains two aspects: international cooperation that provides enough data for enforcing the global tax, and the concept of net wealth.

As for the first aspect, we are unfortunately quite far from such optimistic international cooperation for tax purposes. However, as indicated above [p. 58] some significant measures aimed to strengthen international cooperation on tax matters have been introduced lately, and the idea is already with us. Yet, as Piketty himself acknowledges, this idea is in a very early stage.

The second aspect of the global wealth tax is a net wealth tax that, as explained below [p. 154], has some significant problems. Any property tax, whether limited to real estate or one that includes any type of wealth, can be replaced by realized income tax [p. 125] which follows the "convenience of the taxpayer" and the "certainty and not arbitrary" requirements of good tax systems [pp. 7–14]. As demonstrated below [p. 125], a property—or net wealth—tax, alongside income tax, may lead to double taxation and even to tax rates above 100 percent. Alternatively, an income tax on the annual imputed income (57) may reach the same result [p. 197], i.e. broadening the tax base by increasing taxes of the high ability taxpayers without giving up the realization requirement.

As for the second idea: a top marginal tax rate of 80% for annual income above $5 or $10 million in addition to a 50% or 60% tax rate on income above $200,000 is extreme. Piketty acknowledges that these high tax rates are not measures that aim to raise revenue in order to finance the government's activities, but instead ought to attenuate the explosive dynamic of wealth accumulation and social inequality. In other words, the 80% rate is not a tax, at least not according to the concept we offer in our book (***quid pro quo payments for public goods and services provided by the elected government that are enforced by law.***—[p. 25]), but rather a kind of Pigovian Mandatory Payment (93) that aims to cope with the negative externalities (44) caused by super-earnings.

Such a high tax rate is a very drastic measure. In order to fight social gaps, we suggest beginning with a more modest and restrained phase, i.e. applying the comprehensive tax base through the following steps.

First, eliminating the special tax incentives and lower tax rates that are currently being provided to financial capital and its owners.

Second, reverting to a unified, effective and real "progressive tax rates" system [p. 98] to be applied to all kinds of income, regardless of their sources.

Third, including within the income tax base all kinds of imputed income (58) [p. 160], i.e. the goods and services that the property produces and the owners consume while using their owned assets.

Fourth, including all aspects of transferred wealth within the income tax [pp. 135–144]. This should be done by eliminating the exclusions for the value of properties acquired by gift, bequest, devise, or inheritance from Gross Income, as well as the "carry over basis". The special taxes on Estates, Gifts and Generation-Skipping Transfers, which have generous exemptions and are only minimally effective after innovative tax planning, should also be eliminated. As a result, any accretion to wealth—still subject to a modified requirement of realization—whether earned, consumed, or received as a gift or inherited, will be subject to income tax. In addition, the donor realizes the gain, which derives from the disposition of the appreciated asset, and should include it within their income.

It seems that these four measures, which are integrated and correlate with the principles of the current income tax system, would make redundant the need for the two remedies offered by Piketty, i.e. taxing net wealth and raising the top marginal tax bracket to an extreme rate. Only in very rare cases, where a certain activity or income-producing process creates negative externalities (44), could Pigovian Mandatory Payments (93) be used [pp. 13–14, 36, 54].

Note however that in the discussion of tax, inequality, and efficiency, once we combine Prescott's claims [p. 84] with the above analyses offered by Ostry, Piketty, Stiglitz, Atkinson and others, a clear conclusion emerges: lower taxes on capital and higher taxes on labor widen social gaps and reduce both economic growth and the general welfare.

E. Welfare Economics and Progressive Taxation

Welfare economics is a branch of economics—somewhere between microeconomics and macroeconomics—that concerns the optimal allocation or distribution of resources, mainly income and goods. It studies how the optimal allocation can be achieved and how this affects social welfare in order to promote the highest overall level of social welfare.

1) Progressive Tax System

The idea of a progressive income tax is quite simple: progressive tax (98) is a system that levies higher taxes as the taxpayers' income increases. Note that, under such definition, even a flat tax rate produces higher taxes on taxpayers with larger incomes. A 20% income tax on $50,000 produces a higher amount of tax ($10,000) than 20% on $10,000 ($2,000). Hence, the more common definition for progressive taxation does not refer to the tax **amount** but rather to the tax **rate** in terms of percentage of income, which increases as the taxable income increases. As a result, the marginal tax rate is always higher than the average tax rate, except of course when the marginal rate is zero.

2) Why Progressive Taxation

The debate about progressive tax systems is quite old. We already discussed—briefly—Richard Epstein's (shaky) legal argument that considers progressive income tax as a violation of the taking clause of the Fifth Amendment [p. 55]. Here we discuss some of the economic arguments for and against the progressive tax system.

Although J. S. Mill introduced the basic argument of equal sacrifice, and that "equality of taxation" meant "equality of sacrifice", it seems that efficiency considerations were his major concern: "To tax the larger incomes at a higher percentage than the smaller is to lay a tax on industry and economy; to impose a penalty on people for having worked harder and saved more than their neighbors". According to Mill, in the first edition of his *Principles of Political Economy with some of their Applications to Social Philosophy,* a system where capital-passive income and capital gains are fully taxed "[I]s partial taxation, which is a mild form of robbery". Nevertheless, Mill acknowledged the idea that the marginal utility of money declines: "[T]o take a thousand a year from the possessor of ten thousand, would not deprive him of anything really conducive either to the support or to the comfort of existence; and if such *would* be the effect of taking five pounds from one whose income is fifty, the sacrifice required from the last is not only greater than, but entirely incommensurable with, that imposed upon the first". Yet even though equality ought to be the rule in matters of taxation, his proposed remedy was to grant a basic exemption to all taxpayers (which, as shown below, maintains a certain degree of progressivity): "[T]he mode of adjusting these inequalities of pressure, which seems to be the most equitable, is that recommended by Bentham, of leaving a certain minimum of income, sufficient to provide the necessaries of life, untaxed". Mills went on and argued that even the benefit principle does not justify progressivity since most of the taxpayers enjoy the same amount of benefits from the government's major services [p. 71]. On the other hand, Mill realized the need to broaden the tax base and favored the taxation of heritance on the basis of the need for equal opportunity.

The traditional justification for progressive taxation (98) is based on the assumption, which Mill acknowledged, that the marginal utility of money diminishes inversely to the amount of income. The higher the income, the lower the marginal utility (simply imagine how much utility and welfare someone with $10,000 annual income derives from a salary raise of a $1,000, compared to the indifference that another person, with an annual income of $1,000,000, demonstrates when receiving the same raise of $1,000). Hence the argument—which is not undisputable—that if the goal is to achieve equal sacrifice from different taxpayers, then a progressive tax rate should be used. Taxpayers with higher income should be subject to higher tax rates than those with lower income.

The problem with this argument is that it totally depends on assumptions, which are almost impossible to empirically support. For example, as Arthur Pigu put it (1951) in his *A Study in Public Finance*:

> *All that the law of diminishing utility asserts is that the last £1 of a £1000 income carries less satisfaction than the last £1 of a £100 income does. . . . . In order to prove that the principle of equal sacrifice necessarily involves progression we should need to know that the last £10 of a £1000 income carries less satisfaction than the last £1 of a £100 income; and this the law of diminishing utility does not assert.*

In 1952, Blum and Kalven published their comprehensive and analytical work on "*the Uneasy Case for Progressive Taxation*", an article that was published shortly afterwards as a book. They acknowledged Pigu's comment and agreed that there is no scientific justification for progressive taxation. As long as we do not know exactly how steep the curve of the diminishing/declining marginal utility of income is—assuming it really does decline—then there is no scientific way of structuring tax rates that provide equal sacrifice to different taxpayers. In addition, they have shown that progressivity can be achieved with a flat tax rate and a basic exemption. For example: under a flat tax rate of, say, 20% with a basic exemption for $50,000, taxpayer A, with an annual income of $50,000, pays 0%; Taxpayer B with $100,000 annual income, pays (0*50,000+0.2*

50,000=)$10,000, which is 10% of their income; Taxpayer C with annual an income of $250,000, pays (0*50,000+0.2*200,000=)$40,000 which is 16% of their total income.

3) The Consent to Pay Taxes, the Benefit Principle, and the Progressive Rate Justification

As is discussed below [p. 101] the straightforward justification for a progressive tax system is derived from the two premises we use throughout of the book—the consent to pay and the benefit principles. Before we introduce the argument we present some other ideas against the progressive tax rate.

4) Mirrlees's Zero Tax Rate on High Income

The major economic opposition to progressive taxation is based, as Mill emphasized, on economic efficiency. The Scottish economist James Mirrlees tried to integrate optimal taxation theory [pp. 13, 83] with the function of social welfare, assuming that the marginal utility of income does indeed diminish. Mirrlees' contribution to this field is quite complex, but it allowed him to offer what he regarded as the optimal balance between equality and efficiency. On the one hand, equality calls for a progressive system. On the other hand, high marginal tax rates reduce the incentive for the most productive people to keep producing income.

Mirrlees used a most sophisticated and complex analysis, which is beyond our discussion. The major feature of his analysis is that the best income tax structure should be an almost flat tax rate with a basic exemption for poor households. The reliance on efficiency led him to a surprising conclusion (which is quite similar to the "Ramsey tax" [p. 88]): the marginal tax rate on the highest-income person should be zero. The logic is interesting: Assume that the top-earning person makes an extremely large annual amount of money (X)before tax. If the government reduces the marginal tax rate to zero for all income over X, it will not lose any revenue because no one was earning more than X. Under this new rate (0%), those who earn X might, due to the increased incentive to earn, decide to work more. They would be better off because they voluntarily chose to do something they did not do before, and the government would be no worse off. The net result is that society, which includes those high-income earners, would be better off. The GDP (53) and the national income (81) would increase.

There are two major problems with this idea. First, it relies too much on some radical assumptions regarding people's utility function, as if it is the same for everybody. Second, it basically concentrates solely on the specific taxpayer and ignores other taxpayers who have a business relationship with them.

The impact of income tax on work supply is not clear at all [p. 83], as Mirrlees acknowledged while trying to draw a distinction between taxpayers according to their skills. It depends mainly on the work elasticity, which is very difficult, or even impossible, to estimate. Ever since Daniel Kahneman, Amos Tversky, and Richard Thaler, scholars have acknowledged (what ancient Greeks like Aristotle, and also Adam Smith in his *Theory of Moral Sentiments* pointed out much earlier), that though we may be considered "rational creatures" who are looking to maximize our wellbeing and happiness, wealth and income are not necessarily the right and only means and measures of doing so. Individuals are different from each other not only by skill but by tastes and priorities. They have different desires and motivations. Some enjoy staying at home, playing with and educating their kids. Other prefer reading books and listening to free lectures. Some prefer power, control, and prestige, whereas some spend a significant number of hours on voluntary work or publishing their ideas over the internet with no monetary compensation. In other words, some taxpayers are sensitive to the substitution effect of income and taxes, and some to the income effect [p. 83]. In addition, as is discussed above, economic growth and the conventional measure of GDP do not necessarily promote welfare and happiness [p. 79].

5) Zero Tax Rate and Employees' Compensation

The second major problem with Mirrlees' idea is that a tax rate of zero on the taxpayers who earn a very large amount of X income might entail some very inefficient outcomes to the national economy. If indeed the taxpayer—obviously a profit maximizer [p. 240]—is encouraged by the zero-tax rate to increase their income above X, they may do it in various ways, not necessarily by increasing their production. They may raise the price of the goods or services they sell and cause their customers to pay higher prices (and give up other goods and services). They may cut their employees' salaries or fire some [pp. 240, 285]; They may be more aggressive with their suppliers and cut those suppliers' profits. The explanation for why a tax rate of zero serves as an incentive for cutting expenses is quite simple. As shown [pp. 4, 240], any business deductible expenses produce tax saving (133) to the taxpayer. A salary of $3,000 paid **by** a taxpayer who is subject to marginal tax rate of 45% produces tax saving of (3,000*0.45=)$1,350 and their out-of-pocket cost is $1,650. This means that if the employee provides services that produce $2,000, the employer's profit is (2,000−1,650=)$450. On the other hand, if the employer/payer is subject to a 0% tax rate, the salary does not provide them with any tax saving. The out-of-pocket cost is $3,000 and the employer is losing ($2,000−$3,000=)-$1,000, which causes a rational employer to either fire the employee or cut the salary to below $2,000. Any reduction of their expenses provides the employer a 100% tax saving (133) [pp. 4, 240], which is an extremely high incentive to either lower their employees' salary, or to reduce their workforce.

Such analysis might explain that the constant tax cuts during the last decades contributed indirectly to the growing social gaps, and why the ordinary employees' real incomes are in decline. Since the employer's tax saving (133) [pp. 4, 240] reduces as their tax rate lowers, they would be more hesitant to spend more on business expenses and would rather increase their after-tax income. Thus, applying a low tax rate on big firms will eventually lead to unemployment, to an intensive concentration of wealth, and to the expansion of social gaps.

If the taxpayer who earns the magic income of X is an employee, the 0% tax rate may cause them and their employer to increase their supersalary at other taxpayers' expense, such as other employees, suppliers, or shareholders.

In short, the zero-tax rate is not a win-win situation in terms of economic efficiency. Most probably, the taxpayer's employees, customers, and the small suppliers would pay the price.

In any case, such an income increase above the X level, which comes at the expense of someone else's income, might turn out to be a zero sum game. It will not increase GDP, and might even reduce it, and probably, as Picketty, Stiglitz, Atkinson, Ostry and others claim [p. 90], would increase social gaps which in turn might harm the national economic growth [p. 81].

6) Hall and Rabushka's Low Tax, Simple Tax, Flat Tax

In 1983 Robert Hall and Alvin Rabushka, from the Hoover institute, published the first edition of their book, *Low Tax, Simple Tax, Flat Tax.* A second and updated edition was published in 2007. They proposed a mixture of income and consumption tax where the major point was a flat tax rate of 19% on all types of income (but not on capital gains or investments) with a basic standard deduction and personal exemption, which would achieve a certain degree of progressivity, exempt poor households and provide lower income earners a lower average tax rate. Any other households and businesses would pay the flat tax rate. The idea caught the attention of some politicians. Parts of the idea were integrated into the Tax Reform Act of 1986, which set the basic tax rate for low annual income to 15% and the designated flat tax rate for income above the low bracket to 28%, though the top rate for large income was set higher—to 33%—in order to offset the 15% tax brackets.

7) The Justification for Progressive Tax System—Consent to Pay and the Benefit Principle

The direct and almost self-evident justification for progressive taxation lies in the two related and paramount premises that we use throughout the book: the benefit principle and the constructive consent-to-pay principle. These two principles, which are related to each other, support and justify progressive taxation as well.

Suppose the elected government offers the public a "basket" full of countless public goods and services, including the right to a dignified standard of living, recognition of property rights and their protection, freedom of occupation, freedom of contract, various liberties, rule of law and order, a free but supervised/regulated economy that prevents monopolies, cartels, and market failures, and significant activities aimed to glorify national pride and solidarity.

The government turns to its first "buyer": Citizen 1, whose economic ability is very low, and offers him the above basket. Citizen 1 examines it and its contents, and concludes that out of the variety of services, he hardly enjoys the right to a dignified standard of living and protection of his and his family's security. Due to his low economic ability, he subjectively estimates that he does not enjoy the rest of the public services: he has no real property, freedom of occupation is not beneficial to him, and neither is freedom of movement, freedom of expression or the public's right to know. National pride is a luxury that does not interest him either. Moreover, even the right to dignified life is not that important since he does not have much to lose anyway. Furthermore, the government estimates that it will not be able to tax him because such taxation would infringe on his constitutional right to a dignified standard of living. [pp. 12, 50] The government further estimates that it is worth encouraging Citizen 1 to get out of poverty and giving him a chance to lift his standard of living, which enables him to become a productive and law-abiding citizen [p. 67]. The government concludes that since the degree of Citizen 1's benefit of public goods and services is extremely low he can neither pay nor is willing to pay. As a result, both the government and Citizen 1 agrees that his tax rate will be zero.

Next, the government addresses Citizen 2, a taxpayer whose economic ability is extremely high. She owns a lot of property, makes a great deal of income by extensive use of freedom of occupation, freedom of contract, the existence of a thriving and regulated economic market, and the existence of social capital that provides her, inter alia, with both an educated and skilled workforce and a crowd of buyers and customers who are able to purchase her products. Citizen 2 also realizes that her personal, financial, and social well-being may be jeopardized if Citizen 1's dignified life is in danger, since living with dignity prevents Citizen 1 from delinquent behavior/activities. Of course, national pride is very important to her—she is extremely "proud to be an American". In addition, Citizen 2 realizes that if she fails to pay to the government, the chances for a functioning government go down, and she might lose her property; she might lose her business and her personal and public security will be in danger. Thus, she agrees that the public goods and services are very valuable for her. As a result of all these assumptions, estimates and calculations she is willing to pay large amounts for the consideration she receives.

Note that in the cases of both Citizens 1 and 2, the government uses a subjective evaluation, rather than an objective one—fair market price value. Such evaluation is supported by the tax court's decision in *Turner v. Commissioner*, (13 TCM (CCH) 462, 1954 TC Memo 38—Tax Court, 1954), where the court upheld the taxpayers' argument that the value of an income in kind they received—cruise tickets—should be estimated based on the taxpayers' personal circumstances—low economic status—and not according to the tickets' fair market value, which was significantly higher.

Quite certainly, between Citizens 1 Citizen 2 there are a variety of intermediate degree of taxpayers with different economic abilities, which leads to multiple progressive tax rates.

In other words, taxpayers with low economic ability agree and are required to pay tax at a lower tax rate while higher-ability taxpayers are required and consent to pay higher tax rates. How much? Since Blum and Kalven, we know that there is no scientific answer to the question. The proper answer—as Slemrod and Jon Bakija argued in *Taxing Ourselves*—seems to depend on the public's sense of fairness and equity.

In light of these arguments, Ramsey, Epstein, Mirrlees and Hall & Rabushka's ideas and suggestions seem narrow, short-sighted and unconvincing.

8) Tax Rates and Sustainable Economic Growth—Conclusions

There is a tendency among some economists to assume that any tax decreases work supply and sustainable economic growth, and that progressive high rates enhance this effect. Hence the most efficient tax system, according to their concept, is a flat tax rate with a basic exemption, which maintains a certain degree of progressivity, where the tax base is broad with no Tax Relieves and Incentives (TRI). However, the major claim for progressivity is based on the assumption that the marginal utility of income declines as income increases, and that the equal sacrifice requirement, the assumed consent to pay tax, and the benefit principle justify a progressive tax system. In addition, we see that lower tax rates on high income earners, especially those who buy services from their own employees and from small suppliers, lead to growing social gaps and poverty, which undermine economic growth, social solidarity and the basic core of human rights, i.e. Human dignity and a minimum and dignified standard of living. Furthermore, concentration of wealth leads to a situation where too many factors of production are funneled into a limited number of people, which may lead to conditions of monopoly or oligopolies. Such high concentration reduces free competition and consumers' choice and promotes cartel-like behavior, which reduces competition and prevents small firms from entering the market due to deliberate barriers. Such measures can lead to higher prices and reduced output. All of these factors create a real and significant loss of economic welfare. In other words, a high concentration of wealth creates a real potential for market failure, at which point the government ought to intervene to promote the aggregate wellbeing.

While examining the current income tax system, where, on the one hand, there are seven progressive tax rates, but on the other hand a regressive tax system is produced due to too many Tax Relieves and Incentives (TRI) (84, 127, 131) [pp. 3, 31] and lower tax rates for capital gains and capital income, one may wonder which out of these two approaches is more preferable.

However, the common beliefs and justifications for a progressive tax system rest not necessarily on the normative and ethical concepts and beliefs of a given society but on a utilitarian approach, and an accurate free market economic analysis. Indeed, a utilitarian analysis may promote normative objects of social justice as well. A just society maintains a sense of solidarity: crime rate tends to decrease, as well as public spending on domestic security (police, jails, legal courts etc.). Personal and aggregate welfare and happiness increase, alongside with domestic human and social capital, which attracts local and foreign capital and investments that contribute to sustainable economic growth, increase the general welfare and so on. As discussed above [p. 90], such analysis is shared not only by philosophers and humanists but also by leading economist in the 20th and 21st centuries.

Although there is no way to scientifically measure the shape of the marginal utility of income, it seems that it does decrease as income increases and a therefore a certain degree of a progressive tax rate is justified (just imagine what an extra $500 a month can do for a family with a monthly income of $1,000, or for a family with an income of $20,000 a month; or a family with $100,000 a month: what kind and how much of public goods and services each family agree to buy and at what price). Furthermore, we find that the most convincing justifications for progressive tax rates are reflection of the benefit and the consent principles [pp. 24, 55, 100, 101]. On the other hand, the justification for an extreme marginal tax rate (as suggested by Piketty—80% on very high income and "super-salaries" [p. 95]) might serve as a Pigovian Mandatory Payment [p. 13] and should face stricter judiciary review.

F. Finance Theories

Finance theories are the doctrines, concepts and studies used to better understand finance and its role in markets, firms (and their management), business activities, and investors' considerations and calculations: measuring investment values, risk and return, markets' behavior and fluctuations. For the purpose of our book, we concentrate only on two important insights that are very much relevant to tax theory, namely the concept of a firm (47), and the meaning and role of interest (64).

1) Firms and Households

Human economic activities are aimed at and driven by one purpose: to provide ourselves (and our close relatives) with the standard of living we wish for by to financing our desired consumption to fulfill our satisfaction and needs—including spiritual and intellectual needs. Accordingly, regardless of legal definitions and terminology, the study of economics and finance divides the market's players into two major categories: those who create/produce the wealth, namely the firms (47), and those who currently spend/consume it or save it for future consumption, namely the households (56).

A firm [p. 249] is a nexus of contracts that aims to set the relationships among individuals and entities for producing income in the most efficient way.[Ronald Coase, Franco Modigliani & Merton Miller] A firm consists of all of those who have invested in the process of income production and expect a return on their investment. The parties of these contracts comprise of all the individuals that take part in the various factors of production. This includes the investors in the firm's equity, who are its (legal) owners and receive dividends; the lenders who make loans (or invest in the firm's debentures) and receive interest in return; Mutual Funds (80) who collect money from interested people and invest it on the investors' behalf; property owners (real, tangible and intellectual) who rent, lease or license their properties and receive rent, royalties and commissions; and employees who provide their own human capital and get their wages. All of them have an interest in the success of the firm's economic activities. All of them prosper if it succeeds, and they all lose if it fails. The most important aspect for our book is that the firm produces income and distributes it to its members. Hence dividends, rent, royalties, license fees, salaries, and wages are sourced from within the firm. They are the returns the firm pays out for using its members' factors of production. Whenever we have to identify the source of income and its location, we have to look for the core of the firm's economic activity and its location.

As we see throughout the book, a better understanding of the concept of a firm helps us to analyze complicated tax problems, such as the taxation of trade and business and their taxable income; the complex problems of employees and their "dual capacity" as taxpayers and the special limitations on the deductibility of their expenses [pp. 224, 293]; the sources of rules on taxation of international activity and other interesting questions.

2) Interest and Timing

It is indeed quite difficult to comprehend some of the basic rules of the tax system without a solid and basic understanding of the phenomenon called interest (64) and the central role it plays in business and economics. Interest serves, inter alia, as an efficient and accurate tool for the evaluation of profitability of investments; for calculations of present and future value (51, 97) and for estimation of assets' value; and to direct and even regulate national economic activity through monetary policy (77). A better understanding of the nature of interest and the logic behind it provides a broad and deep ability to perceive and analyze complicated tax problems, such as the definition of Income; the distinction between current income and capital gains; the classification of income to different categories (sources/schedules); the quantification of income and capital assets; and the deduction of business expenses and depreciation.

According to a famous epigram popularized by Benjamin Franklin, nothing is certain except death and taxes. Tax theorists would probably agree to add another dimension: timing is another common ground. Since both death and taxes are certain, the only thing left for us to do is to try to postpone them as much as we can. Indeed, timing has a most significant role in tax law and tax planning. A rule of thumb is "A tax deferred is a tax saved". The idea is very simple. Tax deferral works when the taxpayer is able to pay a fixed amount of money (say $500) next year instead of paying it in the current year, since that deferral decreases the real economic payment to the "present value" PV (97) of $500 for the current year. As long as the interest rate is higher than zero, the present value is always smaller than the discounted amount. If the interest rate is 5% the present value of $500 paid next year is (500/1.05)=$476. Put it differently, the taxpayer can invest $476 for one year and receive 5% interest, around $24 [pp. 343, 347]. Suppose the taxpayer's tax rate is 20% and they are able to include taxable income of $2,500 next year instead of the current year. They save around $24 (20% tax on $2,500 is $500 and its PV is 500/1.05=$467) by doing so.

Interest represents the mutual relationship between time and money. The concept of "time value of money" contains two functions: one is the "actual function", i.e. the price for using other people's money. Interest paid by a firm is the cost of borrowed funds. A firm takes a loan—in any legal form—when it expects that the borrowed fund will produce a higher rate of return than the interest paid to the lenders. Interest paid by a household represents the price for advancing consumption, whereas interest received represents the compensation for delayed consumption.

The other function of the "time value of money" is the "potential function", i.e. interest as the quantifier of potential profits, which serves to estimate an investment's value/worth relative to the alternatives. It indicates the rate of return that capital is expected to earn in an alternative investment with a similar risk. The potential function provides the monetary value of time. The interest is the measurement of the value of the amounts of money we receive in a certain time (current/present or future). The calculation of the ***present value*** (97) of a given amount of money that we will receive in the future is called ***capitalization***.

Interest also enables us to calculate an asset's value by capitalization of its future stream of income; to accurately compare between a few streams of incomes in different times; and to set the monetary value of deferring (or advancing) income producing activities. Interest also helps us comprehend the concept of current income and capital gain; what the financial costs are that are deductible from taxable income; what the difference is between real financial income and expenses and imaginary (inflationary) ones; what the gains of annuity payments (11) are and what the capital recovery components are (20). Furthermore, accurate analysis based on the interest rate helps us to see the full meaning of immediate deduction of capital investment (17) and why such a deduction is equivalent—under certain conditions—to an exemption of the income that the investment produces [p. 256]. Understanding the meaning of interest also helps us to fully comprehend the real difference between ***net wealth, income, and consumption*** as tax bases (120). All these issues are discussed below [p. 154].

G. Accounting

1) General

Accounting is the discipline of measuring, communicating and interpreting financial and business activity. It is a professional language that aims to report a firm's business activities and financial events to its owners, the authorities and to the interested public. Accounting deals with various issues in reporting current activities in monetary terms including income and expenses, selling and purchasing, pricing and budgeting. The two most important financial reports are a firm's balance sheet and "profit and loss statement".

Financial accounting is one branch of accounting that involves processes by which financial information about a business is recorded, classified, summarized, interpreted, and communicated to the firm's internal and external parties. The purpose of financial accounting is the preparation of periodical (annual or quarterly) financial statements such as a balance sheet, income report and cash flow. These statements are intended to provide a firm's financial position and performance to external parties, such as shareholders, potential investors, creditors, and the authorities. In the case of public companies, this information is generally publicly accessible.

These statements serve as a professional language aimed to communicate with various addressees. They must follow the accepted accounting standards issued by the domestic regulator in each country. In the United States, these statements are composed according to the Generally Accepted Accounting Principles (GAAP). Recently, International Financial Reporting Standards (***IFRS***) were adopted by the International Accounting Standards Board (IASB) and most Western countries have adopted them, but not yet the United States.

The implications of financial accounting on tax laws are significant. For example, bookkeeping methods, tax reporting such as cash or accrual basis (132) and inventory accounting (67), doubtful and bad debts, accounts payable, accounts receivable and cancellation of indebtedness are some basic financial accounting conventions that are very relevant to tax laws. We mention a few additional accounting conventions that have some income tax implications below:

Disclosure requires that all material facts must be disclosed in financial statements. Full disclosure does not mean disclosure of each and every item of information, but only those that are of significance to owners, investors & creditors.

Consistency requires that transactions and valuation methods are treated the same way from year to year, or period to period, so meaningful comparisons of financial performance over time can be made and provide valuable information regarding a firm's business/investment results. When a firm changes its accounting policies it is required to disclose this fact and explain the impact of any change.

Matching: Income should be properly "matched" with the expenses of a given accounting period and with the activity that produced it.

Conservatism means that when choosing between two solutions, the one that will be least likely to overstate assets and income should be selected.

Historical cost means that each entry of assets or liability should be in the original cost. In times of inflation (64), such a requirement faces some serious problems and different methods of adjustments are used.

Substance over form is an accounting principle used to ensure that a firm's business statements give a meaningful, real and accurate report of the firm's activities. The principle requires that the statements indicate or expose the real economic aspects of the firm's activities, rather than the formal-legal form.

Note that the last two conventions are still (arguably) relevant for U.S. GAAP, but have lost some of their impact under the new IFRS standards. Furthermore, the adoption of the IFRS standards (if they are adopted and approved in the U.S.A.) does not mean that they would apply automatically for tax accounting purposes.

In order to assure the integrity and effectiveness of the firm's activities and the accuracy of the financial entries, firms/companies are required to conduct a financial audit, which is an independent assessment that acknowledges the accuracy of the firm's financial reports/statements presented by its management. Financial audits are performed by qualified, independent and objective auditors or accountants, who then issue an Auditor's report.

Management accounting provides information that is used within the firm. It aims to provide information to the management so they can assure the best possible course of action, and is usually confidential and accessible only to a small group, usually the firm's decision-makers.

2) Tax Accounting

One should remember that the purposes of financial accounting and taxation are different. With financial accounting, firms seek to impress the public, potential investors and institutions, and tend to report higher earnings. On the other hand, when it comes to tax authorities, firms try to reduce their amount of "taxable income" (137). Hence, there is a need for adjustments and modification between financial accounting and the tax accounting. In some countries, national tax systems follow their general financial accounting standards and, only when there is a specific need, they develop and prescribe—through case law or by statutory provisions—the necessary adjustments for tax purposes. In other countries, the financial accounting rules are just the starting point, and numerous and significant modifications are added by the tax authorities, the courts and the legislature. Generally speaking, the United States' tax adjustments are numerous and significant.

As a general rule, financial accounting rules, standards, and principles are found within tax systems. They are followed and enforced by tax laws, regulations and the tax administration's instructions and rulings, as long as they do not negate or contradict the tax laws' essence and purpose. Furthermore, tax accounting rules are considered secondary to the substantial tax law.

3. CONCLUSION OF THE SECOND PART

We conclude our review of the various sources and disciplines that comprise the magnificent field of tax law. It is magnificent since it touches every field and doctrine of human behavior, including human rights, social science and philosophy. Taxes, which we refer to in the book as "pure taxes", are specific mandatory payments to the central government that are meant to raise money for the government to finance its expenses according to it policy. They should be distinguished from regulatory tax, including Pigovian taxes whose purposes is to restore the real economic price of goods and services that create negative externalities.

Taxes must comply with the attributes of "good tax". They have to be based on principles of respect, human dignity, fairness, and efficiency. To achieve the optimal balance is not so difficult, which we have seen above, since in most of the cases and under an accurate utilitarian analysis, supported by new empirical data, redistribution and efficiency go hand in hand up to a certain level. Undoubtedly, policymakers have to be sensitive to human needs and desires in order to design a satisfactory and sensible tax system that provides the elected government only the necessary amount needed to perform its duties and commitments while offering its public goods and services. In order to achieve the right system, the tax designers have to use insights from every possible discipline and sub-discipline known to us: ethics, philosophy, economics, finance, accounting, and various fields of law.

The same applies to the taxpayers. In order to be an obedient citizen on the one hand, and to pay only one's fair share for the public goods and services' price on the other. We have to understand the logic and the justification for levying and paying taxes, and be familiar with court decisions. We should master the rules' logic, their underlying rationales, their purpose, their scoped, and to be familiar with statutory articles, sections, provisions, regulations and the Revenue Service's approach and interpretation, as well as case law. As tax professionals we also must be equipped with a good understanding of business activity, knowledge of public, business, private and international law, the ability to interpret statutory provisions and to provide the tax authorities and the courts a reasonable interpretation based on the modern purposeful/ substantive interpretation and on the multidisciplinary approach toward legal studies.

Part Three

MAJOR TAX BASES: GENERAL VIEW

Chapter Six

TAXES, AND OTHER MANDATORY PAYMENTS

1. THE VARIETY OF TAXES AND MANDATORY PAYMENTS

Tax systems all over the world are composed of taxes and other types of mandatory payments paid to governments (Federal, state and localities). While comparing the U.S. Federal tax system with other developed countries, the most significant difference is that the former relies mainly on individual and corporate income taxes, which include capital gains currently subject to lower tax rates. In most of the other OECD countries, a major source of revenue is Value Added Tax (VAT), which is considered a consumption tax, alongside with National/social insurance, individual income tax, corporate tax and in some cases national property taxes. In addition, governments charge fees for specific public goods and services, and use their revenue system to regulate economic and social goals by introducing either Tax Relieves and Incentives (131) [pp. 3–5] or Mandatory Pigovian Payments [pp. 13, 36].

The underlying concept of our book is that taxes have only one direct purpose and justification, i.e. to finance the cost of the government's public goods and services. Any other types of levies imposed by statutory provisions are termed in this book as other mandatory payments. Careful scrutiny reveals that other mandatory payments are either aimed to serve as fees—a fair price for certain and specific goods and services (e.g. toll roads, water supply), or as regulatory taxes that express an honest and sincere efforts to use a Pigovian tax (93), which deals with negative externalities (44). As mentioned already, a Pigovian tax is not a real tax, and is not meant to finance the government budget [pp. 13, 36, 54], but rather to shift the real economic cost of negative externalities to the producers or consumers of goods that cause damages or harms to the general public [pp. 13, 36, 54]. A PMP's revenue is supposed to finance the compensation for victims or to cover the expenses needed to reduce the harm.

In addition, there are direct fees on specific public goods and services, such court fees, water consumption fees, etc.

As explained earlier [p. 36], the reason for the distinction between "real" taxes and PMP and other fees is that the latter should be calculated carefully and accurately in order to withstand judicial review (70).

The introduction of the concept of the welfare state, and the adverse selection phenomenon (8), which leads to market failure, brought the modern world to recognize the need for compulsory social insurance—known in the United States as the Social Security system. [p. 127]. In addition, other OECD countries have adopted various national health insurance systems. As discussed above, such a concept has been adopted recently in the U.S. and has sustained the Supreme Court's review [pp. 41, 53] but was drastically curtailed in 2017.

A special tax system, whose aim is not necessarily to raise revenue but rather to promote equal opportunity and ease social gaps, taxes wealth transfer—in the U.S., there are special taxes on estates, gifts and generation skipping transfers. As is discussed below [pp. 126–135, 143], there are troubling indications that the current system does not achieve its stated goal, and probably undermines its own efforts to mitigate social gaps.

Since our book intends to present a holistic and comprehensive observation of the common tax systems in democratic states during the globalization era, we briefly present the rationale of these taxes, including VAT, even though some of them are not part of the U.S. Federal income tax system.

The VAT (145) is a very efficient tax system, which has some serious regressive components.

The first country that levied the VAT was France in 1954, which simultaneously reduced its top marginal income tax rates. Since then, VAT has become a common tax system in Western countries. It was a prerequisite for joining the European Common Market, which developed into the European Community and then into the European Union. Each EU member state is required to adopt VAT and it has to comply with the EU VAT code. Different rates of VAT apply in different EU member states, and in most states there are some reduced rates for special goods and services (e.g. foodstuff, water supply, pharmaceutical products, medical equipment for disabled persons, transportation of people, books, newspapers, admission to cultural services and so on).

In 2006, the EU released its VAT directive. Its purpose was to harmonize VAT within the EU VAT area, and the directive specifies that VAT rates must be within a certain range. (*Council Directive 2006/112/EC of 28 November 2006 on the common system of value added tax*). Another reason for the introduction of the VAT was the increasing number of ***free trade*** treaties, which prohibit using customs, tariffs, discriminatory excises and other import and export duties. Hence, VAT was meant to replace those old selections of mandatory payments.

The most significant trait of the VAT is tax neutrality on international trade. Accordingly, VAT is based on the designation principle, i.e. that all the goods and services sold in a domestic market are subject to the same VAT rates applied in that market by the local government.

Some American scholars argue that because of the U.S.' hesitancy to legislate a Federal VAT, the Federal tax system suffers from a lack of diversification of tax bases. This leads the U.S. to rely heavily on income and corporate taxes. Hence, the deadweight loss of U.S. Federal tax system is quite high [pp. 88, 113], which puts the U.S. in an inferior position in terms of international trade and increases the deficit of the national balance of payments

It might be that one reason for the U.S.' hesitancy to follow the rest of the Western countries and levy VATs and property taxes at the Federal level, is the common belief that the Constitution allows the Federal Congress to levy taxes, which are not apportioned among the states, only on income. Such a belief is doubtful, both because indirect taxes are not subject to the apportionment requirement, and because those tax bases (consumption and property) have much more common ground with income tax now than centuries ago. Although VAT is not part of the U.S. tax system, we present below [pp. 115–125] the basic attributes of this tax system.

Even though the most popular personal tax is called income tax, in most countries it is a hybrid system that is composed of several components of income (58) and consumption (26) as well. As is discussed below [pp. 153–183], the three possible personal tax bases (113)—property/net-wealth, consumption and income—are basically identical in the long run, and the only (yet meaningful) difference between them is timing, whose significance depends on the interest rate [p. 105].

2. ONE TAX BASE V. MULTIPLE BASES: OPTIMAL TAXATION AND EQUITY

Suppose a person earns $100,000 and pays a 5% state income tax ($5,000) and then a 20% federal income tax, (95,000*0.2=$19,000) and spent $50,000 (tax included) on buying consumer products, which are subject to a 7% state sales tax/VAT ($3,270). In addition, the taxpayer owns a small house, which has a value of $300,000 and is subject to a 5% state property tax ($15,000) and a county tax of $2,000. The total amount of tax payments for enjoying public goods and services is $44,270. Is there any logic behind such a multi-bases system? Why do we need this variety of tax bases, tax administrations and collecting expenses? Can't we simply charge the above taxpayer with one single tax—e.g. an income tax with an average rate of 44.2%—and distribute the revenue between the above government branches and agencies? One formal answer is that the U.S. the constitution does not allow it. Yet, the substantial question is: what is wrong with such a system? Why did the Founding Fathers decide against it? The main answer involves efficiency and the desire to decrease deadweight loss (89), [p. 85] on the one hand, and to base the tax systems on principles of fairness on the other hand.

As has already been indicated, most economists believe that deadweight loss increases with the square of the tax rate [p. 88]. Since the purpose of good tax legislation is to levy an efficient tax with the smallest distortion relative to the tax revenue, it is better to levy several low-rate taxes on different tax bases than one higher tax on a single tax base.

Another aspect of the above efficiency argument is that diversification of tax bases lessens economic distortion by distributing the tax burden between individuals who make different economic decisions (income production, consumption and saving) according to different personal tastes, priorities, and abilities.

One may argue that the introduction of VAT in European countries together with the reduction of income tax rates has been the result of the governments' goal to balance efficiency and equity: flat rate VAT is considered a very efficient, simple, yet regressive tax system (106), whereas income tax is more complicated, mainly due to the legislature's tendency to integrate regulatory provisions into it.

Chapter Seven

VALUE ADDED TAX

As mentioned already [pp. 13, 85, 115], ***optimal taxation*** analysis (90) indicates that it is more efficient—i.e. creates a smaller amount of ***deadweight loss*** (90)—to have several tax bases with lower tax rates rather than one tax base with high rates even if they raise the same amount of aggregate revenue. This has been one of the major reasons for the worldwide introduction of VAT. Another reason is that bilateral and multilateral Free Trade agreements minimize the use of customs and duties by contracting states and drive them to use VAT, which is based on the tax neutrality principle. As mentioned previously [p. 114], VAT has been adopted in most of the Western world. Note, though, that in some countries a very similar system has been adopted instead, which is called GST (Goods and Services Tax). However, we refer in this chapter only to VAT.

In the U.S., most States impose general sales taxes that applies to the sale or lease of most goods and some services, but Federal government does not. However, in light of the fact that VAT is a major source of tax revenue in almost every industrialized country in the Western world [p. 114], it seems to us that the U.S. government is under pressure to introduce a certain type of VAT in order to improve the U.S.' position in terms of international trade. Additionally, in order to deal with international trade, there is a need to be familiar with this common tax system. Hence, it is worth introducing the basic concepts and methods of the VAT, which was first adopted in Europe, and later on in most of the rest of the world.

1. BASIC PRINCIPLES

A. The Final Tax Burden Is on Consumers

The VAT's goal is to tax domestic households' consumption through a sophisticated mechanism that is very simple to operate: the VAT is levied on firms (47) and they are allowed to shift (129) it onto their own clients—whether other firms or final consumers. If levied onto other firms, those firms are allowed to shift the tax to their clients until the products reach the final domestic consumer.

B. Tax Base: Consumption—Cash Flow

Value-added tax (VAT) is imposed and collected on the "value added" at each stage in the production process (145). The tax base is a "Consumption—Cash Flow" type. That means that all receipts/revenue generated by a firm and all the payments it makes are taken into account without any distinction between the purchases and sales of Capital assets (17) or the purchases or sales of "current" goods and services. Every item is taken into consideration; no depreciation (20, 31, 76) or matching (88) calculations are d.

C. Tax Unit—the Firm

Value Added (145) is a tool for measuring national income (55, 53, 81) in an efficient way: instead of measuring all the national aggregate income, only the firms' value added is considered: their its profits, plus their employees' income, plus its passive payments (mainly interest) to households. Thus, Value Added Tax, applied only to ***firms*** (47), while disregarding ***households*** (56) (as opposed to a Personal Income tax system that taxes any income, business and non-business, from both firms and households).

D. Self-Administration

From an administrative point of view, any firm conducting any trade of business must register at the VAT district office. It receives an official VAT number, which should be printed on the firm's invoices. The firm is required to fill and submit a very simple periodic return (usually once a month). If sales are higher than purchases, the firm pays its VAT. If purchases are higher than sales, the firms receive a refund from the VAT authority.

E. Method of Calculation—Invoice-Tax Credit

There are several ways to compute the taxable base for a VAT. The amount of value added can be calculated as the difference between the value of the firm's sales and its purchases. This can be done in several ways. The Credit Invoice method is the one that is currently used in all the countries that have adopted a VAT.

Under the VAT-Invoice-tax credit method, each firm determines the VAT on every sale transaction it makes by multiplying the sale's amount by the VAT tax rate. The firm ("Firm 1") then charges the VAT to its customer and provides them with a certified invoice, indicating the sale price, the VAT (which is called ***invoice tax***) and the total amount charged. If the customer is a household, the tax reaches to its final destination—the consumers. A household cannot use the invoice tax received from the selling firm. On the other hand, if the customer is another firm ("Firm 2") that uses the purchased good or service in its business, Firm 1's VAT is shifted to Firm 2 who gets an invoice. At the end of the taxable period, Firm 2 adds up all its sales during this period and calculates its "tentative" tax by multiplying that amount by the VAT rate. Then, Firm 2 uses the invoice taxes shifted on it by all its own suppliers, including Firm 1, as credit against the "tentative tax" it is supposed to pay. The remaining balance is Firm 2's final VAT that is sent alongside its periodic tax return to the VAT authorities. Note that only firms that are subject to VAT are allowed to receive the Invoice credit. Furthermore, according to the matching rule (76) no invoice tax is allowed as a credit against the firm's VAT on its exempted transactions.

The VAT credit provided for all VAT paid on purchases of taxable goods and services purchased by the firm from its suppliers prevents the imposition of multiple layers of tax. As a result, the total VAT paid at every business stage is based on the value added only by that taxpayer at that stage. As illustrated below [pp. 121–122] the total/aggregate amount of tax paid with respect to a good or service from all levels of production should equal the sales price of the good or service to the final (domestic) consumer multiplied by the VAT rate.

F. Tax Neutrality and Prevention of Double Taxation

The common VAT system is designed to achieve two additional goals: First is "import tax neutrality", which would allow free competition between all producers—local and foreign—bringing their goods to the domestic markets. The second is to prevent double taxation on international trade. Hence, the basic principle here is the "destination principle".

G. The Destination Principle: Taxing Imports and Exempting Exports

In order to achieve the two goals mentioned above, the VAT system is based on the "destination principle", i.e. the tax is paid only where the goods or services are sold to the final consumers. In other words: when international transactions take place, they are taxed only at the country of destination and not at the country of origin. Hence, domestic VAT exempts all exported goods and services and charges the imported ones. The exemption of exported goods and services is done through charging the export transaction with a ***zero percent tax rate***.

If the goods or services are exported to a country that does not have VAT, they reach that country's markets free of any VAT and compete with domestic and imported goods and services. The same free/equal competition is achieved when the exported goods are shipped to a country that has a local VAT: all goods and services sold in this market, whether domestic or imported, are subject to the same local VAT rate. No double taxation occurs. Hence, the tax jurisdiction principle of VAT is purely territorial.

H. Tax Exemption and Zero Tax Rate

There is a very distinct line between **exempted transactions** and **zero percent tax rate transactions**. The former is simply a transaction that for some reason is exempted from VAT. Yet, since the VAT is a **multi-stage tax,** if the last transaction is exempted, only the exempted transaction is not taxable, meaning that all the previous local transactions were subject and paid VAT. Furthermore, the firm who performs/provides the exempted transaction is not allowed to issue an invoice-tax, which means that its customers, including other firm are not entitled to get the invoice-tax credit. On the other hand, if the final transaction is a ***zero percent tax rate*** transaction, all of the previous stages of the transaction are also exempted. This is because the firm is "charged" with a zero percent rate and is therefore still entitled to get refunded for all the invoice taxes its suppliers charged it at its previous purchases.

I. Value Added Tax on E-Commerce Transactions

E-commerce presents some new challenges to the application of VAT. Yet, since the tax is on consumption, the current underlying concept provides satisfactory answers to these challenges with a few modifications.

If the e-transaction is a sale of a tangible good, it is subject to the domestic VAT whether the goods are provided by domestic or foreign suppliers. Theoretically, the same idea also applies to e-transactions of intangible goods.

Since the VAT is eventually a consumption tax and is based on the destination principle, it should be levied on the consumers regardless of the identity of the firm that provides the intangible good or service. In other words, the firm's major role is to be a collection agency on behalf of the destination's governments. The collection process is supposed to be simple, and in our era of computers the conventional system requires the firm to directly charge the domestic consumers. The firm, whether domestic or foreign, can identify the consumer's residence by the IP number of the computer used in the transaction and by the means of payment—usually a credit card, or any other electronic payment devices.

The same concept applies to the provision of services over the internet. As long as the provider is a domestic resident, it is charged by the local VAT and shifts the charges to its customers in the same country. If the firm is foreign—such as Google, which is an Irish company, or Facebook etc.—selling advertisement packages to customers residing in country X (identified by their IP or other payment devices), they are requested by the government of country X to charge VAT to their customers and submit the tax to country X's tax collection agency.

Such a system requires a significant cooperation between governments. Accordingly, the EU established new rules based on a destination-based tax principle. Starting in January 2015, VAT rates became based on the customer residences, regardless of the location of the selling firms and consistent with directive 2008/8/EC issued on January 12th, 2008. In order to facilitate compliance, particularly for small/micro companies, a MOSS (Mini One Stop Shop) system was created, which allows businesses to identify themselves in one of the EU states and consistently charge VAT with the applicable state law (and rates) in force.

The OECD 2015 BEPS guidelines [p. 232] follow this path, and focus on identifying and developing implementation mechanisms to **facilitate VAT collection** based on the country where the consumer is located, which is particularly relevant for online ordering and delivery of goods and services. However, as electronic devices of payment become more sophisticated, the difficulty of identifying the location of the payer-buyer increases. One of the suggestions for solving this problem is that if the selling firm fails to identify the place of residence of the buyer, the transaction will be taxed by the selling firm's country and such a transaction will be not entitled to a zero tax rate.

2. OPERATION AND ILLUSTRATIONS

The VAT calculation and tax returns are quite simple and are based on three stages. In the first stage, the firm calculates its **tentative tax**. In the second, the firm calculates the **invoice-tax it paid** to its suppliers. In the third stage, the firm subtracts the invoice-taxes from its tentative tax ("tax credit"). If the balance is positive, the firm must pay it. If the balance is negative the firm receives a refund from the government. If the firm provided goods or services that are exempted from VAT, all the invoice taxes paid to its suppliers allocated to those exempted goods and services are not allowed as credit against the firm's other taxable transactions.

A. The First Stage: Calculating the Tentative Tax

The taxable firm has to add up all its proceeds for all of its sales. Then it multiplies the amount by the VAT rate. Suppose the total sales during the taxable period (either a month or two months) are $25,000 and the VAT rate is 15%. The **Tentative tax**, then, is (25,000*0.15=)$3,750.

B. The Second Stage: Summing-Up the Total Invoice-Tax

The taxable firm has to keep records—VAT invoices—on all its taxable purchases from other VAT taxable firms. It is in the firm's best interest to make sure it gets a VAT invoice indicating the VAT amount the other firms have shifted onto it. Without such invoice, the firm is unable to credit the VAT it paid on its purchases. This is a crucial attribute of the VAT: it has a built-in self-regulating mechanism that ensures that all the firms in the producing process will pay their share. As we see below, if one or more of the intermediary firms does not pay the VAT and does not provide a VAT invoice, the government's revenue goes up! Suppose the firm's total purchases from other suppliers that provide VAT invoices sum up to $18,000 during the taxable period—then, its creditable ***invoice-tax*** is equal to (18,000*0.15=)$2,700.

C. The Third Stage: Tax Payments or Tax Refunds

If the tentative tax is higher than the total invoice-tax, the firm pays the remaining balance (the tentative tax minus the total invoice-tax) to the VAT authorities (in the above example: $3,750−$2700=$1,050). However, if the total invoice-tax is greater than the tentative tax—let's say the total sales are instead $15,000 and tentative tax becomes $2,250—the firm is entitled to receive a refund of (2,250−2,700=)-$450 from the VAT authorities. This might happen if the firm is losing money, or more typically when, during the taxable period, the firm purchases a significant amounts of capital assets (17), or the firm exports some of its goods or services that are subject to the **Zero Tax Rate**.

D. Illustration

For the sake of simplicity, we assume that the VAT rate is 10%.

Firm A is a writer. She does not make any purchases, hence no cost, and she does not have any VAT invoices.

She sells her manuscript to B, a professional agent, for $100. Her total sales are $100. The tentative tax (10%) is $10. Her total invoice tax is $0. Her VAT liability, therefore, is $10. She shifts the tax on B and charges him the total amount of $110: $100 for the book and $10 for VAT. B pays her the full amount and receives an invoice from her, which indicates the VAT payment of $10. A then pays $10 to the VAT authority, but since she charged B, no VAT comes out of her pocket!

B sells the manuscript to C—a publisher—for $350, shifts the VAT of $35 (=$350*0.1) to the publisher, collects the full amount of $385 and provides an invoice. Note that B's value added is $250. Therefore, B's tax liability is $25 (which is 10% of his value added): his tentative tax of $35 (10% on sales) minus the invoice tax of $10 he already paid to A. B pays $25 to the government. Once again, since B charged C with the $35 VAT, no VAT goes out of B's pocket.

C sells 100 books to D, a bookstore, for $850, charges D the 10% VAT tax of $85, and collects the total of $935 (850+85). C sends the government a total VAT of $50; his $85 tentative tax minus $35, the amount of his invoice tax already paid to B. As a result, C also does not pay any VAT out of his pocket.

D sells the books to 100 customers for $13.75 each ($12.50 per book plus $1.25 VAT per book) for a total of $1,375 ($1,250+$125 VAT). Assuming these are the only transactions D has during the taxable period, its tax payment to the government is $40 (tentative tax of $125 minus the $85 invoice tax paid already to C). Note that D charges her customers the full amount of the tax but does not keep it to itself. Part of it is paid to the government, and the other part had been paid previously to its suppliers. And yet, D does not pay VAT out of its pocket either.

However, suppose that during the taxable period D sells only one book for a total of $13.75 (=$12.50+$1.25). D's tentative tax is $1.25 and since its invoice tax paid to C was $85, the negative balance of $83.75 is refunded to D by the government.

Now suppose that D exports the 100 books overseas for $1,250. This transaction is charged a **zero percent tax rate**, so the tentative tax is $0. Yet D's invoice tax is still

$85, and therefore D receives a full refund of that amount. This means that all the stages of production for the exported books are totally exempted. Although the government collected VAT from A, B, and C, none of them paid the tax out of their own pockets but shifted it to the next stage up ending at D. Since D got a refund from the government, none of the firms paid VAT. The government pays back the total VAT ($85) collected in the all of the previous stages: $10 paid by A, $25 paid by B, and $50 paid by C.

Assume now that for some reason B does not participate in the process; he is not a "Registered VAT Taxpayer". A pays the $10 VAT, but since B is not a registered VAT taxpayer, he does not/cannot use A's invoice and does not get any credit or refund. B sells the books to C and collects $350, but does not provide a VAT invoice to C, who is a "Registered VAT Taxpayer". When C sells the books to D for $850+85, his tentative tax is $85 but since he does not have an invoice from his supplier B, his final VAT payment is $85. The total amount the government collects is $135 ($10 more than the amount it would have collected had B participated: D's $40+C's $85+A's $10. Assuming that B was able to shift part of the $10 VAT paid to A, and he sells the books for, say, $1,000, then we can see that C has a very strong incentive not to cooperate with B but instead with a "registered VAT supplier".

Needless to say that if B's reluctance caused A to also not pay the tax, the government is even; it still collects the designated amount of $125. On the other hand, if D is a tax offender and does not pay its VAT, the government (and of course the public) lose revenue.

The following table demonstrates the VAT tax credit system based on the above example: ***purchase***.

Firms ***Transactions, Final VAT Computation Tax credit system***	***Firm A Writer***	***Firm B Agent***	***Firm C Publisher***	***Firm D Bookstore***	***Total***
Purchase price + Invoice Tax	0	$100+10	$350+35	$850+85	$1,300+130
Sales	$100	$350	$850	$1250	$2,550
Firm's Value added	$100	$250	$500	$400	$1250
Tentative Tax on Sale (10%)	$10	$35	$85	$125	$255
Invoice tax	0	($10)	($35)	($85)	($130)
10% VAT* (Tax on sales minus invoice taxes)	$10	$25	$50	$40	$125**

* The firm collects the VAT from the client, provides him an invoice and forwards the net tax (tentative tax minus invoice tax) to the government.

** The amount of $125 is the sum of the aggregate VAT paid by all of the firms; it is also equal to a 10% VAT on all the firms' total value added ($1,250), and also to the total VAT ($225) on the total amount of the transaction ($2,550) minus the total amount of invoice tax ($130) that was credited by all the firms.

3. VAT—CANCELLED TRANSACTION AND REFUND TAXES

The fact that a firm, "X", can sell goods or services to another firm, "Y", charge firm Y with VAT and provide it with a valuable invoice, from which Firm Y is then entitled to receive credit or a cash refund, has caused tax authorities to take a tough approach with taxpayers who cancelled their taxable transactions. Assume Firm X entered into a transaction with firm Y and commits to provide merchandise worth $100,000. It charges

Firm Y with that amount plus the 10% VAT, provides Y with an invoice indicating the total of $100,000+invoice tax of $10,000, and pays the VAT on this transaction. Both parties agree that the payment will take place one year after the agreement is signed. Y uses the invoice tax it received in its first VAT tax return and receives either credit or a cash refund. Now assume that when the payment is due, Y disappears and does not pay any amount to X. X is in a strange situation: it already paid the tax on the transaction to the VAT authority but never got the payment. Under any other tax systems, the solution is simple: firm X cancels the transaction and does not pay any tax. Yet under VAT, such a solution leaves the government with a loss, since Y already used the invoice tax. The statutory solution is simple: a canceled transaction requires a "Canceled Transaction Invoice" indicating that none of the firms used the invoice tax for credit or refund purposes. The problem is, of course, if the purchasing firm Y already used the invoice tax and vanished without issuing a "Canceled Transaction Invoice".

4. VAT ON NPOs AND FINANCIAL INSTITUTIONS

As mentioned, a firm's value added is equal to its profits plus two of its payments: wages paid to its employees and interest payments to its creditors. This poses some problems with regards to VAT on non-profit organizations (NPOs—87) and financial institutions.

Since a NPO does not make any profit, its value added is only the labor it uses in its activities and its interest payments. Hence, a simple and practical way to tax a NPO with VAT is to charge a smaller rate of tax on its total payments to its employees and creditors and disallow it from issuing invoices to its clients. Assuming that NPOs do not pay interest to households, a more efficient way of taxing a NPO is to charge it only on its payments to its employee. Such a system, which is called a ***wage tax*** on NPOs provides an extra advantage: it encourages NPOs to use volunteers instead of fully-paid employees, which much better serves the basic idea of the third sector (87). Note that a NPO is not eligible to provide VAT invoices, nor to receive any credit or refund for its purchases from registered VAT suppliers.

Charging VAT on financial institutions is much more complicated. On the one hand they do have profits, but on the other hand they pay out a significant amount of interest to households (consumers) which cannot issue a VAT invoice. In some countries, the VAT applies to such institutions the same way it applies to any other firm. In others, however, financial institutions are only charged with a "profit and wage" tax. In those cases, financial institutions are not allowed to get credit or refund from any VAT invoice received from their suppliers and cannot provide VAT invoices to their clients.

Chapter Eight

PROPERTY AND REAL ESTATE TAX

The **Sixteenth Amendment** to the United States Constitution allows Congress to levy (only) an income tax without apportioning it among the states. Other taxes are subject to Article I, Section 9, Clause 4 which states: "No Capitation, or other direct, Tax shall be laid, unless in proportion to the Census or Enumeration herein before directed to be taken". Since property tax is considered a direct tax and is not included within the Sixteenth Amendment, the common understanding is that Congress has no power to lay any kind of property tax. Note however, that based on the following analysis, one may argue that since property tax is levied on the present value of the future income a property produces then such a tax might be within the boundaries' requirements of the Sixteenth Amendment.

Property taxes—a variation of the net wealth tax [p. 154]—are levied as a percent of a property's Fair Market Value. The most common way to calculate FMV is to capitalize the property's future stream of income to its present value (97) [p. 105]. In other words, a property tax taxes the future income a property produces during its lifetime. Hence, in a system that taxes property in addition to income, the annual stream of income is taxed twice. For a simple and basic illustration, assume that an apartment's monthly rent is \$750 and the annual rent is \$9,000. Under an income tax rate of 25%, the annual income tax owed for the rental income is \$2,250. Further assuming that the apartment lasts 25 years (for the sake of simplicity we ignore its salvage value (110)—vacated lot—at the end of this period and the annual depreciation, though we may assume that the annual income is calculated after the depreciation deduction), and the market interest rate is 5%. As noted, the apartment's estimated value equals to the present value of the future stream of income it produces during the next 25 years. Under these assumptions, the apartment's current value is equal to $\frac{9.000\times25}{1.04^{25}}=84,401$

Now assume that the property tax rate is 2.66%, 66,443×0.0266=\$1,727. The total tax—income and property—is (\$2,250+\$1,767)=\$4,017, which is almost 47% of the annual income. If the income tax rate is 50%, the annual income tax payments go up to \$4,500 (9,000×0.5=) and if the property tax rate is 7% the annual property tax payments increase to \$4,651 (\$66,443×0.07), and the taxpayer's total annual tax payments would increase to \$9,151 (\$4,500+\$4,651), which is higher than the annual income and would leave the taxpayer with a negative return (of \$151).

The right way to avoid this double taxation is to allow the property tax as a credit against the income tax. In that case, in this example no income tax is paid. In the previous assumption the income tax is only (\$2,250−\$1,767=)\$483. In the latter example the federal tax payment is 0, unless the credit for the property tax is refundable and the taxpayer receives the amount of \$151.

Though this book does not discuss any type of state or local taxes, it is noteworthy that most local governments (state, counties, and school districts) impose **property taxes**, usually on real estate, as an important source of their revenue. In order to avoid the issue of double taxation on the property's stream of income, local property taxes are deductible as itemized deductions (65, 68, 113), [pp. 288, 295] against Federal taxable income. This deduction creates some asymmetry: on the one hand, if the owner is using the property for their own use, they do not pay income tax on the imputed income (57) [pp. 160, 292] they enjoy from it, and therefore the deduction is against an exempted income, i.e. its violates a basic matching rule (76), [pp. 197, 252, 279]. On the other hand, if the property is rented out then the rent is taxable and, as explained above, the total result is over-taxation.

Chapter Nine

CONTRIBUTIONS TO NATIONAL SOCIAL SECURITY AND HEALTH INSURANCE

1. THE NEED FOR MANDATORY PROGRAMS: ADVERSE SELECTION

The modern welfare state has two major general social programs: first, a national Social Security system (sometimes called "National Insurance"), which is mandatory insurance aimed to prevent people from dropping below the poverty line due to certain events. The second program is national Health Insurance, which aims to provide the whole population with a minimum level of inexpensive, efficient, and comprehensive health services. The funding needed for both programs is raised through mandatory premiums on the public, usually administered as additional mandatory payments taken from a low percentage of earned income—including from employees and those who are self-employed.

The question is why do we need these programs to be mandatory? Why not wait for the private market to offer them on the private insurance industry? The answer is due to market failure caused by the ***adverse selection*** (8) phenomenon.

The basic principle underlying the private insurance industry (whether a mutual non-profit group or a business-oriented insurance company) is one of mutual support. The insurer calculates the policy prices: the premium that is supposed to fund claims to be paid, the administrative costs, and—in the case of private insurance companies—profit. The cost of insurance is determined by calculations made by professional actuaries using actuarial methods (primarily probability, statistics, sociology, finance, and business knowledge). The whole group of the insured persons is asked to pay the premium amount to cover the risks that the group's members face. Such a calculation cannot work with social and health insurance, due to the reluctance of certain potentially insured individuals who made their own calculation and conclude that due to their own personal circumstances—usually unknown to the insurer—the premium is too high—and they decide not to buy the proposed insurance. This reluctance, which is caused by adverse selection and asymmetric information, leads to a market failure (75). The explanation for this is simple. The potential purchasers of social and health insurance are individuals who possess valuable and intimate personal information. They know better than anybody else what their expected lifespan is, their family's medical and genetic history, their emotional and psychological well-being, their ambitions, their skills, their own expectations regarding standard of living, the number of children they plan to have, etc. They can better appreciate how much they need, and what value social and health insurance has to them. The insurer does not have this information. In order to overcome the adverse selection issue, the insurer has to either raise the premium or reduce the level of insurance coverage. As a result, the healthier, more educated (with a higher earning potential), and stronger individuals are more reluctant to pay the new premium, and they refrain from joining the insured group. Therefore, the group get smaller than expected. This in return requires additional increases in premiums and creates a vicious circle of potential candidates constantly dropping out of and the premiums further increasing. Consequently, too many individuals find the insurance too costly and they give up the coverage. Furthermore, the people who are interested in buying insurance—many of them socially vulnerable and unhealthy—cannot afford the new increases. Fewer members lead to yet another raise of the premium and the new price drives away even more potentially insured individuals, which leads to another raise and on goes the vicious circle. Evidently, no efficient equilibrium can be achieved, which means that the free market fails to provide efficient health and social insurances. Put more simply: those who are most likely to need these insurances won't be able to purchase them.

As mentioned above, it is quite an acceptable idea that, though not mentioned within the Constitution or its Amendments, the rights to human dignity and of survival are constitutional rights in the U.S. [p. 50] Moreover, under international law the right to social security is considered a human right. This is expressed in Articles 22 and 25(1) of The Universal Declaration of Human Rights adopted by the United Nations in 1948, which states the following: "Everyone, as a member of society, has the right to **social security** and is entitled to realization, through national effort and international cooperation and in accordance with the organization and resources of each State, of the economic, social and cultural rights indispensable for his dignity and the free development of his personality." (See also Article 25(1) of the Universal Declaration and Article 9 of the International Covenant on Economic, Social and Cultural Rights of 1966).

The emerging conclusion is almost obvious. To ensure basic human dignity and a satisfactory standard of living, governments must offer affordable social and health insurance. In order to overcome the aforementioned market failure, those insurances must be mandatory. This drives every individual member of the community into a big insured group, thus enabling the insurance provider to drop the premium price to a sensible rate so everybody can pay it and enjoy insurance coverage. Note that Obamacare adopted the general idea, but instead of forcing all the U.S. individuals to buy medical insurance, it levied an interesting Pigovian tax meant to internalize the damage that those who refrain from buying health insurance create by compensating the community through the "penalty" levied on them [pp. 13, 36, 41, 46, 53, 58, 133].

2. SOCIAL SECURITY IN THE U.S.

The first meaningful federal legislation to introduce the concept of mandatory national insurance came in 1935, half a decade after the economic crisis known as the "Great Depression", which literally eliminated the retirement and general savings of millions of Americans. The enactment, the Social Security Act, was part of a group of legislation known as the "Second New Deal", and faced significant opposition, including severe constitutional judicial review. Eventually, the Supreme Court upheld the Act's constitutionality with a slim majority of 5–4 (*Steward Machine Company v. Davis*). The Act provided benefits to retirees and the unemployed, and a small grant at death. Thirty years later, Congress added another two programs to it, which are discussed briefly below [p. 130]. One is Medicare, a federal program that provides medical insurance mainly for elderly individuals who have earned income and paid the mandatory fees. The second is Medicaid, which is a joint program between Federal and State governments that aims to provide medical insurance for American citizens and permanent residents of all ages who cannot afford sufficient health care.

A. Old-Age, Survivors, and Disability Insurance (OASDI)

The OASDI program offers limited social insurance for workers, employees and self-employed individuals on their earned income. As with any other insurance program, the insured person pays premiums for purchasing the insurance. The premium for Social Security is mandatory and is called a "payroll tax". When an insured event occurs, the program pays the insured the benefits agreed upon according to the policy's terms and conditions. The payroll tax is calculated as a percent of the insured person's income, which is limited to a ceiling, i.e., any income above a certain limit, and capital income, is not subject to the payroll tax. The same annual limit also applies for the benefits computation. This limit changes each year according to the changes in the national "average wage index". The limit for 2021 is annual earnings of $142,800. The monthly Social Security benefit amount to which the insured is entitled depends upon the payroll tax paid and upon the age at which the retiree chooses to begin receiving benefits, after reaching the age of 62.

For OASDI, the total statutory payroll tax rate is 12.4%. In the case of employees, their employers pay half (6.2%) and the other half must be withheld from the employees' pretax salaries.

The collection agency for the program is the IRS; employees pay the payroll tax according to the Federal Insurance Contributions Act tax (FICA). Self-employed individuals pay tax according to the Self Employed Contributions Act (SECA). The IRS allocates the revenue raised by these taxes to the Social Security Trust Fund, the Federal Old-Age and Survivors Insurance Trust Fund, and the Federal Disability Insurance Trust Fund.

The OASDI program's benefits include monthly payment of retirement benefits, disability insurance, and retirement benefits for widows and widowers.

As a general rule, if these taxpayers have any additional income, part of their Social Security benefits—up to 85% of the benefits—are subject to Federal income tax.

B. Unemployment Insurance Program

The current unemployment insurance program (UI) is a joint project of the Federal government and those States that have decided to join it. The program aims to provide partial income replacement to individuals who become involuntarily unemployed for a limited period (usually six months). The program is state administered with Federal involvement and participation. It is funded with both State and Federal unemployment taxes paid only by employers (no withholding (136) from their employees' salaries) under the Federal Unemployment Tax Act (FUTA) and State laws.

Each state is free to decide whether to join this UI program, provided the state meets some threshold requirements, such as the total amount of wages paid by the state's employers and the number of their employees in each period.

The current FUTA tax rate is 6.0 percent of the total taxable wages paid to all an employers' employees, who meet the aforementioned requirements regarding total amount paid and number of employees. The taxable wage's base is only the first $7,000 paid in wages to each employee during a calendar year. Employers who also pay state UI tax are entitled to a credit of up to 5.4 percent regardless of the tax rate they pay in their own state. As a result, at the Federal level, the net FUTA tax rate after the credit is 0.6% (6%−5.4%), and the maximum annual amount is usually $42.00 (7,000*0.006) per employee per year. Without credit for states UI tax, the maximum Federal amount is $420 (7,000*0.06) per employee per year.

The states are free to set their own UI tax rates. Each participating state runs its own program and pays benefits to qualifying unemployed individuals out of the state's UI fund raised by the state's UI taxes. The Federal government sets broad guidelines for coverage and eligibility, but states vary in how they determine benefits and eligibility, as long they comply with the Federal guidelines. For most states, the maximum period for receiving benefits is 26 weeks, though there is an extended benefits program authorized through the Social Security Act. The unemployment allowance for qualified employees is between 40–50% of their previous salary.

The state's unemployment insurance agency handles unemployment claims and pays the benefits. The role of the Federal government in terms of the benefits paid to the qualified unemployed individuals is indirect and quite limited. It does not directly pay the insured. Instead, the Federal fund mainly lends money (and charges interest on the loans) to the states when states' UI funds cannot cover the cost of the outstanding claims for UI benefits. The states are required to pay back the federal loans on time. If a state fails to do so, it is labeled as a "credit reduction state." In that case, the rate of the credit that employers receive against the Federal UI tax is reduced, according to the credit reduction rate for that "credit reduction state". This means that that the Federal UI tax is increased.

C. Supplemental Security Income (SSI)

Although this program is not financed directly by a special tax or any other mandatory payment, it is part of the Social Security system and should be mentioned here. SSI provides cash assistance to the aged, blind and/or disabled. The program is funded and administered by the Federal government out of the Federal government's general revenue. There is no minimum age limit for establishing eligibility on the basis of blindness or disability. Applicants for SSI do not have to have any insured status, but their incomes and resources must be below a specified amount. Any state can join this program and provide additional benefits with its own funds.

D. Federal Medical Insurance

For decades, foreign scholars who studied the U.S. system were puzzled by the fact that, in the most powerful and wealthy democracy, tens of millions of American citizens were without any kind of medical insurance. Such a situation is inconceivable in the rest of the OECD countries. As mentioned, market failure (75) caused by adverse selection (8) prevents the provision of an efficient free market medical/health insurance. The income tax system provides some significant subsidies to health insurance, mainly by allowing taxpayers to deduct the premiums they paid against their taxable income, and by exempting employees' fringe benefits provided by their employers' contribution to the insurer from tax, which is significantly larger than the employees' portion. Nevertheless, until lately the health insurance industry has been dominated by the private market.

In 1965, the American government addressed this problem with a limited solution by enacting an amendment to the Social Security Act. The amendment introduced two new programs aimed to provide Federal health insurance: Medicare for elderly (ages 65 and older) and disabled individuals, and Medicaid for poor families.

1) Medicare

Medicare utilizes private health insurance providers and offers health insurance to eligible insured Americans (U.S. citizens or non-citizens legally residing in the U.S. for at least five consecutive years) who have paid Medicare taxes for at least 10 years. The program has four components: Hospital Insurance; Medical Insurance; Prescription drugs; and a Supplement option, which has some benefits to the insured on the one hand, but some disadvantages on the other hand. Medicare benefits are subject to medical necessity tests.

Medicare has several sources of financing. The major one is the payroll tax. Originally, the statutory rate was a total of 2.9%; in the case of employees, half is paid by the employer and the other half is withheld from the employee's salary. During the last few years, though, the calculation for the Medicare tax base and its rates has been modified. Since 2013, in addition to earned income, investment income (capital gains, dividends and nonexempt interest) is included within the tax base. Furthermore, some progressivity has been introduced. The Medicare tax rate for taxpayers with large incomes (earned and investment income above $200,000 for individuals and $250,000 for married couples filing jointly) is 3.8%. In the case of employees with the large incomes, the employee's portion is 2.35% and the employer's is 1.45%. Self-employed individuals pay the full premium and can deduct half of it against their taxable income subject to income tax.

As for the Hospital Insurance (HI) program, there is no limit to maximum earning for the payroll tax, and of course not to the amount of benefits paid/reimbursed by the program, though there are some reasonable ceilings on the reimbursable costs.

2) Medicaid

Medicaid is a government program that provides health insurance for poor individual U.S. citizens and legal residents whose incomes and resources are insufficient to pay for health care. The program is funded both by the federal and states' governments but is run and managed by each participating state, at its own discretion. Yet, each participating state has to comply with some basic statutory Federal guidelines (e.g. "medically necessary services", ceilings for charged premiums and co-payments by Medicaid participants). The Federal matching funds and designated Federal grants are funded by the Federal general revenue.

The federal matching/participation rate is determined by a special formula (Federal Medical Assistance Percentages). Accordingly, the rates vary depending on each state's own per capita income. The richest states receive a federal match of 50% while poorer states receive a larger rate.

There is no special tax or fee as a prerequisite to becoming an eligible participant.

E. The Patient Protection and Affordable Care Act (PPACA)

As mentioned, [pp. 36, 41, 53, 128] this Act, legislated in 2010 together with the Health Care and Education Reconciliation Act amendment, represents the Federal government's acknowledgement of the market failure regarding health insurance. The Act's aim is to increase the quality and affordability of health care by encouraging individuals to buy health insurance, requiring large employers to provide their employees with such insurance, and consequently lowering the uninsured rate, increasing the size of the insured groups which eventually expands both public and private coverage and at the same time reduces both public and private healthcare costs.

The Act requires insurance companies to accept all applicants with a minimum premium rate, regardless of pre-existing health conditions or gender. In addition, economically poor individuals are exempted from paying the premium, and are eligible for government assistance. Furthermore, a phased-out refundable income tax credit is granted for low- and middle-income individuals and families in order to make the health insurance more affordable.

Only employers with more than 200 full-time employees are required to purchase health insurance for their employees that complies with the standards set by the Act. As mentioned, the payment is deductible for income tax purposes, and no income tax is charged on the employee's benefit.

Other taxpayers, employers as well as individuals, are only encouraged to purchase qualified health insurance by charging them if they refrain from buying the health insurance, a **Shared Responsibility Payment** which is a Pigovian Mandatory Payment (93). Some individuals (such as those suffering financial hardship, members of special communities or those covered by government health programs) are exempted from the payment. As discussed above, the Supreme Court has upheld the constitutionality of the mandatory payment, although it has been labeled a "penalty" [pp. 41, 53].

The penalty for adults is a set amount—$95 in 2014, $350 in 2015, $750 in 2016 and thereafter, and half that amount for individuals younger than 18 years.

The penalty for employers who have more than fifty full-time employees but do not offer coverage is $750 per full-time employee. An employer with more than 50 employees that offers a form of coverage that does not comply with the required standards is also subject to financial penalties. On the other hand, an income tax credit is provided to assist small businesses with less than 25 employees for up to 50 percent of the total health insurance premium cost for those employees.

The Act established the concept of a special organization known as the 'Health Insurance Marketplace" ("Health Exchange"), which aimed to enable and simplify the purchase of health insurance that complies with the Act's requirements. The exchange provides a set of government-regulated and standardized health care plans available to individuals and small businesses who are interested in purchasing qualified health insurance. In addition, the Act provided some subsidies to low- and middle-income individuals through a phase-out refundable tax credit (37, 93, 94).

F. Summary

The way national health insurance has been introduced in the U.S. is an interesting example of the social and economic tensions that have existed in the American society for centuries. It is clear that a built-in market failure prevents efficient medical insurance. The most obvious solution is to create mandatory national insurance and obligate every member of the society to purchase such insurance, which guarantees an adequate health service that ensures the constitutional right for human dignity. On the other hand, there is a tradition under which the government should avoid the imposition of obligatory measures on personal matters. Such a tradition is not free from economic considerations, mainly of the health services and the pharmacological industries. A regulated health insurance, which increases the number of people insured, might lead to a certain degree of reduction in the status and income of those who dominate these industries.

The Obamacare program seems to be the optimal solution for the time being. The American people have been brainwashed for centuries regarding the opposition to the government “forcing” free men and women to purchase medical insurance. The above analysis [pp. 41–42, 41, 53, 128] shows that those who refuse to purchase mandatory health insurance create negative externalities for the whole American society by pushing the health care prices much higher than acceptable, and as a result too many poor families have been left without health care coverage and services. Hence, this program avoids mandating a purchase but shifts the cost of the negative externality to those who create it, i.e. those who refuse to participate. Time, experience, and education will eventually enable the American people to appreciate such programs and to realize that such a mandatory program has nothing to do with eroding the basic principles of free economy or undermining the concept of human liberty. On the contrary, a citizen with a dignified standard of living, including good health care services is a freer human being.

Note that the political, perhaps ideological or commercial, struggles and deliberation have not stop. The Tax Cuts and Jobs of 2017 cancel the “penalty” starting in 2019.

Chapter Ten

TAXATION OF WEALTH TRANSFER—ESTATE, GIFT AND GENERATION SKIPPING TRANSFER TAXES

1. SHOULD TRANSFER PAYMENTS BE TAXED?

An interesting question is whether transfer payments (141) should be subject to tax. On the one hand, the principle of equal opportunity should lead to the conclusion that every person should enjoy the chance to compete on an equal basis and receive a fresh start. On the other hand, the traditional argument against such taxation is that the source of transfer payments is income that has already been taxed once by the donor. Since donee do not pay for the transferred wealth the donors are not allowed to deduct those payments against their own taxable income. If the donee is subject to income tax on the amount received, so goes the argument, then it is taxed twice: once by the donor, once by the donee.

The British income tax system, which is based on the source doctrine [p. 158], has followed the latter idea. Any income amounts that have no source that produces a constant stream of income are not included in the British income tax base. Accordingly, since accretion to wealth originating from transferred payments do not have such a source, they are not included in the British income tax base. The underlying rationale, according to the American economist Henry Simon's analysis [p. 159], is that the British concluded that the income tax system is supposed to tax the national income (81). Since transfer payments are not included in the national income, they should not be taxed. Therefore, gifts, which are made in good faith and not in return for goods and services, and inheritances received by a taxpayer, are not included in the income tax base. Needless to say that, once such an idea was installed in the British kingdom, the upper classes were free from worries about a real and meaningful redistribution of income.

The U.S. income tax system has gradually departed from this concept. It started a tendency to implement a broad definition of the income tax base. As the Supreme Court put it some sixty years ago (*C.I.R. v. Glenshaw Glass Co.*), income for income tax purposes is: "undeniable accessions to wealth, clearly realized, and over which the taxpayers have complete dominion". The logic—which is based on the writings of two American economists, Murray Haig and Henry Simon—is quite straightforward: if the purpose of income tax is to levy it according the taxpayer's benefit from the public good and services) including recognition of property and the right of a person to bequeath and give gifts) that is measured by their economic ability [pp. 51, 71], it does not matter where and how the ability is made or comes from. Any realized accretion to wealth—either saved or consumed—whether it has a source or not, whether it was granted in exchange of goods or services, out of pure generosity, or from a family tradition or obligation—should be included within the income tax base.

Theoretically, this broad definition includes transfer payments, such findings, inheritances, and gifts, unless a special statutory provision exempts them from the definition of the taxable income.

2. SHOULD WEALTH TRANSFER BE TAXED?

One of the most significant social-economic troubles of the Western democratic world is a constant growing of social gaps and poverty indices. Such increase threatens both democratic regimes and sustainable economic growth [pp. 90–95]. Taxation of wealth transfer has a dual purpose: first, to prevent the increase in social gaps by slowing the rate of wealth transfer between generations. Second, to strengthen the concept of meritocracy (a philosophical-political-social concept in which important functionaries—economic or political—are appointed to their position based on merit; neither according to their economic, social or family ties, nor status inherited from previous generations. Both goals are indeed about economic efficiency. Both social gaps and the destructive undermining of the principle of meritocracy, lead—in accordance with theoretical as well as empirical studies—to harming sustainable economic growth and the general welfare. [pp. 90–95].

The justification for taxing wealth transfers is two-fold. One is the traditional reason for taxing the taxpayer's ability to pay as a measurement of their benefits received from the government [p. 71]. The other is based on the basic idea of equal opportunity and the claim that there is no inherent moral, ethical or efficiency justification for specific members of the next generation to receive the wealth created by the old generation, and to enjoy the fruits of the skill, efforts, and diligence of other people, at least not tax-free. In order to offer equal opportunity to all the members of the new generation, it seems both ethical and economically efficient to distribute the wealth accumulated in the hands of a few members of the past generation to many members of the new generation. It is noteworthy that even J. S. Mill, who expressed some serious reservations regarding a progressive tax system, still thought that a utilitarian society would agree that everyone should be equal one way or another. Receiving inheritance would put one person ahead of society unless they are taxed on the inheritance.

A transfer of wealth, dictated by the decedents or donors, leads to the perpetuation/preservation of social gaps and eventually to economic inefficiency [pp. 90–95]. Capital, as a factor of production, produces the highest rate of return to the most skillful, industrious, and assiduous producers. Heirs and donee do not necessarily have these qualifications. Furthermore, the less-wealthy younger generation, who get some share of the older generation's wealth—through the tax system that finances better public education, good health systems and even monetary subsidies to start a business—receives a better opportunity to become productive members of the society. Such an incentive may allow the young members of the society to become the new generation's economic success. This aspect of equal opportunity is supposedly the American dream. It is the basis/foundation of meritocracy, which is a most significant component of modern democracies [p. 94]. The idea is attractive and appealing, yet its implementation in the U.S.A. is complicated and symbolizes a compromise in a divided society and a combination of ideas. Instead of using the income tax system to promote the idea of equal opportunity and the efficient principle of meritocracy, Congress gave up the principles of a comprehensive tax base and created instead an inefficient separated unique estate and gift tax system. This tax system has a large basic exemption and contains significant loopholes, which enable innovative tax planning. The Gift and Estate tax system has a good rhetoric of equal opportunity and redistribution, but the system is far from prompting/implementing these ideas.

Taxation of wealth transfer can be done in two ways. One, which does not require peppercorns and legislative efforts, is through Income Tax. The other possibility is more convoluted, complicated, specific tax of one is through the laws of estates or inheritances plus gift tax.

The experience in the Western world is neither successful nor encouraging. In the United States inheritance tax and gift tax laws are not effectively enforced and there is even a claim that they were created to allow capital owners, lawyers and accountants to devise sophisticated measures whose "real" purpose is to prevent the reduction of the transfer of wealth between generations.

3. THE PREFERRED WAY TO TAX WEALTH TRANSFERS

When a wealth transfer takes place, there are two parties involved in the transaction: the donor/transferor and the donee/recipient. Gift and estate tax deals with the former. On the surface, income tax concentrates on the latter. In order to avoid what seems to be double taxation, the legislature has to decide whether to tax the former or the latter. In a deeper inquiry, if the transaction is done through transfer of an asset—including monetary means—or service in kind, such transaction produces two tax events, not one.

Yet before we proceed, the concept of double taxation should be analyzed quite carefully, with some basic examples. First, suppose Mom works very hard and earns $50,000. She pays her income tax bills (including from other resources) and deposits the $50,000 in her bank account. After a few weeks, she decides to fulfill her dream and buys a round-the-world luxury trip for $50,000. She withdraws the money from her account, pays it to her travel agent, and enjoys the trip. One may argue that if the tax base is measured by economic ability and since the balance in her bank account after the withdrawal is zero, her ability is zero and no income tax on the previous earnings should be paid. We know already that this is wrong conclusion. Mom exchanges her money for another asset, which is a consumption, i.e. her satisfaction from the trip. [p. 148] Her "balance sheet" before the trip was $50,000 cash, and zero satisfaction. After the trip, it shows zero cash and consumption of $50,000 worth of satisfaction. As is discussed below, income (in the source side) is equal to consumption) in the usage side, whether current or future = saving). [p. 154]

Assume instead that Mom bought a stock of shares for $50,000. She holds it for a few years. Each year the asset's value increases by $5,000. Each year her ability increases by $5,000, but due to the realization requirement (103), [p. 163] she does not pay any income tax as long as she holds the stock. After five years, she sells it for its Fair Market Value of $75,000. Since she paid $50,000 (her **basis** in the stock), she realizes a gain of (75,000−50,000=)$25,000. Since Mom has other resources, she pays the tax on the $25,000, and gives her Son a gift of $75,000. Once again, one may argue that by transferring the $75,000 to Son, her balance sheet (and her ability) after the transaction is zero. Yet the right way to describe the above events is to consider the gift to Son not as a financial loss, but rather exchanged for other assets—the love, sympathy, respect, and devotion she receives from Son in return. She also derives comfort and satisfaction from knowing that Son's economic position has been improved. All those intangible assets are worth $75,000. Hence her balance sheet after the transaction still has an asset worth $75,000 (Stock = $0; Son's affection and Mom's satisfaction = $75,000) and no reduction in her tax bills should take place. When Son receives the $75,000 gift, there is a tax event, and his ability—as his benefit from the legal system that recognizes and protect his right to receive the gift increases by the same amount and should be taxed.

Now assume that instead of selling the stock, Mom gives it to Son. The above analysis is still the same. Instead of having a cash transaction we have an "in-kind" transaction [p. 193]. Mom disposes the stock for its FMV of $75,000 (otherwise, she would not give the money to Son, but would sell the stock and give Son whatever amount she considers as a reasonable consideration for those intangibles) and her realized gain is $25,000. Son's accretion to wealth is still $75,000 and should be included in a comprehensive income tax base.

The picture is now clearer. When an appreciated asset is given as a gift or an inheritance, there are two tax events, not one. One is the gain (or loss) the donor realizes. The second is the accretion to wealth, which occurs to the donee. If Mom pays income tax on her $25,000 realized gain, and Son pays income tax on his accretion to wealth of $75,000, no double taxation takes place. Mom and Son are two separate tax units. Mom is supposed to pay taxes on her own ability and satisfaction/consumption, and so is Son. Note, that when Son sells the stock, say for $80,000, his basis is $75,000 and his gain is $5,000. If he sells the stock for $70,000, he has a loss of $5,000.

The conclusion is quite evident. In order to tax a wealth transfer correctly, there is no need for a separate estate and gifts tax system. A comprehensive income tax system that taxes all the realized accretion to wealth/economic ability can achieve this goal in an accurate and efficient way.

Hence, one may suspect that giving up the comprehensive tax base alternative, and creating a separate and unique estate and gift tax system, which has a large basic exemption and contains significant loopholes enables innovative tax planning, which detracts from the accomplishment of its rhetorical goals. One may wonder if maybe the special legislation behind the separate estate and gift tax is a calculated and subtle way to avoid the taxation of the wealthiest.

4. THE TAXATION OF WEALTH TRANSFER IN THE U.S.

Although the U.S. income tax system moved away from the British source system, one of the major attributes of the old-fashioned British tax system has been reinstalled in the U.S.A., and eventually has contributed a great deal to the growing social gaps. Although the Supreme Court adopted any realized accretion to wealth as the comprehensive definition of income [pp. 135, 159] for income tax purposes, the legislature did not approve such a broad tax base, and introduced a long list of exemptions and deductions that narrowed it [p. 205]. A prominent institution is Code § 102, which states that Gross income does not include the value of property acquired by gift, bequest, devise, or inheritance.

On the other hand, special legislation initiated during wartimes levies three special taxes on wealth transfers: The Federal Estate Tax, the Federal Gift Tax and the Generation-Skipping Transfer Tax. According to a general estimate, those taxes apply to less than two percent of the American taxpayers, i.e. in terms of revenue they raise an insignificant amount.

There are many descriptions of the developments of transfer taxes in the U.S.A., how they began during wartime in order to finance defense expenses and have turned into a semi-redistributive measure, and how capital owners were able to organize a most aggressive and sophisticated lobby that managed to persuade the legislature, in 2001, to phase-out those taxes gradually by dropping their rates until they were supposed to vanish in 2010. Yet, President Obama's administration and the Congress reversed this process and revived the taxes.

Chronologically, the Federal Estate tax was first enacted in 1916. The *gift tax* was first *enacted* in 1924, repealed in 1926, and was overhauled and reintroduced in 1932.

The purpose of the gift tax is to prevent taxpayers from evading the estate tax by giving their property as gifts to their loved ones. Currently both taxes are very similar and connected as is seen below.

The tax planning industry is creative in this area of wealth transfer taxes. Unique and very innovative devices were invented to avoid the estate and gift taxes, or at least to defer them. In 1976 Congress enacted the Generation Skipping Transfer Tax (GSTT) in order to minimize tax planning with legal trusts, such as a transfer from a grandparent to a grandchild. In this case, the transfer escapes one generation (the child) of estate and gift taxes, so the family is tempted to make transfers that skip as many generations as possible as each skipped generation would escape those taxes. The GSTT attempts to eliminate or at least minimize such tax deferral. There are two basic forms of generation-skipping transfers. One is the indirect skip, where the Dad or Mom's generation (# 2), which is one level below the deceased Grandpa (generation #1), receives some beneficial interest in the property before the property passes to the third generation (Grandchild) or beyond. The other form is the direct skip, where the property passes directly to the Grandchild's generation or more levels below the decedent. One simple way to do this was for Grandpa to create a special trust to transfer his property into, which was usually managed by Mom or Dad, while the ultimate beneficiary was the Grandchild. The idea was that when the trust transfers the property to Grandchild, no estate or gift taxes could be charged. The GSTT's purpose is to prevent such an arrangement. It levies tax on both outright gifts and transfers in trust to or for the benefit of unrelated persons who are more than 37.5 years younger than the donor; or to related persons more than one generation younger than the donor, such as grandchildren, but only if the transfer avoids both gift and estate taxes at each generational level.

Still, the most significant provisions of these three wealth transfer taxes are the exemption and the tax rate. Currently, due to the Tax Cuts and Jobs Act, the exemptions both for the estate tax and gift tax in 2022 is the aggregated amount of $12.06 million; a married couple has a combined exemption of 24.12 million, which is indexed to annual inflation, per a descendent or a donor. As for the gift tax exemption, these amounts are for each of the donees regardless of their number. In January 2026 the estate tax and the gift tax exemptions are set to drop back to what they were before 2018, i.e. $5 million adjusted to inflation. Note that only 0.1% of estates filed an estate tax return in 2020, with only about 0.04% paying tax.

The current ***federal estate tax*** is levied "on the transfer of the *taxable estate* of every decedent who is a citizen or resident of the United States." In order to arrive at the taxable estate, the descendant's "gross estate" is calculated.

The gross estate includes the fair market value—usually at the date of death, though the executor may choose an alternate date defined in the code—of any real or personal property, whether tangible or intangible, in which the decedent owned an interest at time of death. That includes, under certain conditions, the proceeds from a life insurance policy on the life of the deceased. In addition, gross estate also includes certain interests in property, which were transferred to another person prior to the decedent's death, such as the value of lifetime gifts over which the decedent retained a life's interest ("revocable transfers"). The location of the property is irrelevant.

The estate tax is levied on the transfer of property at death, which is measured by the size of the decedent's estate. The tax is computed through a series of adjustments and modifications for the gross estate. Certain allowable deductions reduce the gross estate to the "taxable estate," which is then added to the total of all lifetime taxable gifts made by the decedent. The tax rates are applied and, after reduction for certain allowable credits, the amount of tax owed by the estate is reached.

The most significant deductions are property left to the surviving spouse, under certain conditions. In that case, the tax on the entire estate is deferred, provided that the surviving spouse is an American citizen. Other prominent allowable deductions are the estate administration expenses, certain debts and losses, including any uncompensated casualty or theft losses sustained by the estate during the settlement of the estate, and charitable bequests. In addition, any estate, inheritance, legacy, or succession taxes actually paid to any State, in respect to property included in the gross estate are also deductible from the gross estate.

In order to avoid double taxation or double non-taxation on transfer of wealth, such as the tax on gifts given during the decedent's life as well as tax on the decedent's estate, the computation of the latter tax should take into consideration the payments made for the former.

The computation of a decedent's estate tax liability requires a combination of the decedent's lifetime taxable gifts and the decedent's taxable estate, to which the tax rate schedule is then applied. The tax rate is applied to the tentative taxable estate. Any allowable credits are subtracted in determining the decedent's estate tax obligation. Note that due to the "applicable exclusion amount," the first $5,340,000 is excluded.

The estate tax is quasi-progressive (98). The lowest rate is 18% on the first $10,000 and the top marginal rate is 40% on any amount above $1,000,000 of the taxable estate (i.e. above the exemptions and the deductions). The tax brackets are as follows:

Table 10.1:

Taxable Estate	**Tentative Tax**		
(above the exemption)		Tax Rate	Accumulated Amount
The first $10,000	18%	$1,800	
$10,000–$20,000	20%	$3,800	
$20,000–$40,000	22%	$8,200	
$40,000–$60,000	24%	$13,000	
$60,000–$80,000	26%	$18,200	
$80,000–$100,000	28%	$23,800	
$100,000–$150,000	30%	$38,800	
$150,000–$250,000	32%	$70,800	

\$250,000–\$500,000	34%	\$155,800
\$500,000–\$750,000	37%	\$248,300
\$750,000–\$1,000,000	39%	\$345,800
Over \$1,000,000	40%	\$345,800+40% of the amount above \$1,000,000

As mentioned, credits should be subtracted from the above amounts. The three major estate tax credits are as follows. The first is the credit for foreign estate or inheritance taxes paid by the estate or by an heir. The second is a phase out credit (94) for federal estate taxes paid by previous estates on property transferred to the decedent within the last ten years; 100% credit for estate tax paid for property inherited during the last two years before the decedent's death and 20% for property received during the ninth or tenth years. The third credit is the most significant one: the unified transfer tax credit, referred to as an "applicable exclusion amount," is the amount of taxable gifts or estate that the credit would cover.

The Federal Gift Tax is imposed annually on all gratuitous transfers of property made by the donor during his or her lifetime that could otherwise reduce the estate tax at death. It is an integral part of the "unified" federal gift and estate tax. Gift tax applies to lifetime gifts; estate tax applies to assets left at death. The idea is that whether the taxpayer gives assets while alive, or leaves them at death, they should be taxed the same way, at the same rate.

The gift tax is levied on the value of the "taxable gift", which is the gross value of the gift reduced by allowable deductions and exclusions. Its liability is determined on the basis of the donor's taxable gifts, minus the available unified transfer tax credit.

The Gross Gift is the fair market value of the gift at the time it was made. There is no clear definition for the term "gift" for the gift tax purposes, yet the Code mentions that the amount of a gift is ascertained when "property is transferred for less than an adequate and full consideration in money or money's worth." (§ 2512(b)). According to the regulations, a gift is made when there is a transfer for inadequate consideration and the transaction does not take place in a business context.

The calculation of Taxable Gift is as follow: Once the gross gift is determined, certain exclusions and deductions are allowed for the computation of the gift tax base. The major deductions and exclusions are as follows: any gift made by the donor to their U.S. spouse, or a limited amount (\$164,000 in 2022) for gifts made to a noncitizen spouse. Division of property due to a divorce decree or separation agreement that takes place during a given period of time (one year before to two years after the decree of divorce or the separation agreement) is also excluded from the taxable gifts. This exclusion is subject to certain conditions, mainly to assure the marital rights of the spouses and the provision of a reasonable allowance for the support of minor children.

The annual per-donee exclusion in 2022 is \$16,000 or \$32,000 if married couples grant the gift. The exclusion refers to any gifts, which may be given to any number of different donees, each year. There is an unlimited exclusion for gifts that are direct payments to the donee's educational institution for tuition expenses or to the donee's medical provider for health care expenses.

Also excluded from the gift tax base are gifts to a political organization and gifts to certain charities.

In addition, there is a special rule that allows, under certain conditions, the exclusion of the value of a gift of a life insurance policy made in trust, or a gift to a minor.

Due to the "unified" system of the Federal gift and estate taxes, the calculation of the gift tax is integrated with the computation of the estate tax. A simple example can demonstrate this concept.

Assume that in 2022, Mother makes a one-time gift of $200,000 to her Son. The first $16,000 is tax-free and the remaining $184,000 is a taxable gift. However, instead of paying a gift tax, Mother reduces her lifetime gift tax exemption by the amount of $184,000. Hence, in 2022 she is allowed to give another (11,060,000−16,000=) $11,044,000 free of federal gift tax. In the case that she gives this amount to relatives or friends, then any other gift above the annual exemption ($16,000 per each donee) will not be eligible for the "applicable exclusion amount," both for gift tax and for estate tax. This means that her estate will be also subject to the estate tax rates on any amount she leaves. If she gives another gift in later year, it will be taxed according to the same tax rates applied to estate tax mentioned above. If she gives $160,000 to ten of her relatives or friends and each receives $16,000, there will be no gift tax on this amount.

The Generation-Skipping Transfer Tax (GSTT) is levied at a flat rate, equal to the top marginal estate and gift taxes (currently 40%) and is in addition to any estate and gift tax imposed on the transfer. The combined tax paid on a generation-skipping transfer is typically higher than the estate and gift tax that would be paid if the property were transferred through each successive generation. The GSTT enjoys the same amount of exemption as the estate and gift taxes ($11,060,000 in 2022) provided the taxpayer has not used the full amount on the gift tax. In addition to the exemption, the GSTT tax is not applied to gifts excluded by the annual gift tax exclusion or qualified transfers for medical and tuition payments.

The GSTT is paid on either "taxable distribution" or "taxable termination". The former means a distribution from a trust to a skip person (Child). The latter is a termination by death, lapse of time, release of power, or otherwise of an interest in property held in trust. A taxable termination does not occur if, immediately after the termination, a non-skip person has an interest in the property or if the trust makes a distribution to a skip person after the termination.

For direct skips (all the interests in the trust are held by skip persons, e.g. Child), the taxable amount is the value of the property received by the transferee and the tax is levied in proportion to the value of the transferred property before the imposition of the tax. In other cases, the taxable amount for taxable terminations and distributions is tax-inclusive, meaning the taxable amount for this property is included in its value.

An indirect skip occurs when the generation one level below the decedent (Child) receives some beneficial interest in the property before the property passes to the generation two or more levels below (e.g. Grandchild).

With a direct skip, where the estate is left directly to Grandchild or other younger recipients, the donor or the donor's estate pays the GSTT. Taxable distribution applies if a donor establishes a trust, which is subject to the GSTT, paid by the recipient of trust distributions. This only applies if a trustee receives distributions; if the trust does not make any distribution, there is no tax event. Taxable termination applies when a trust is terminated and pays out the remainder of its funds. Under taxable termination, the trustee is responsible for paying the GSTT.

The GST tax is a flat-rate tax. The rate is set at the highest estate tax rate (currently 40%).

The calculation of the final GSTT obligation, and even the determination of the tax payee is quite complicated and is not elaborated on in this book.

5. TRANSFER TAX OR TAX-FREE WEALTH TRANSFER?

The impression that one can get from the above description is that Congress was sincere regarding the concepts of equal opportunity and of a meaningful redistribution of wealth between generations. Still, the overall picture is a bit different. As mentioned already, the general estimation is that less than 0.4 percent of American citizens pay the estate, gift and generation skipping taxes. There are few reasons for that. The first one is the generous life-time exemption (of the cumulative amount of $5,340,000 in 2014) per a descendent or a donor, and an annual exemption of for gifts up to $14,000 a year for each donee. The second reason is the aggressive tax planning industry that constantly finds some loopholes in the system. The third reason is the questionable system adopted in the U.S.A. regarding the exemption of wealth transfer from income tax and the treatment of appreciated inherited assets.

As explained above, when a taxpayer buys an asset, and after a certain period sells it for a gain—the difference between the price paid for the asset subject to some modifications (the "adjusted basis") and the amount it was sold—the gain is subject to income or capital gain tax. Suppose Mom bought an asset for $1,000,000, and made no modification and took no deductions so the asset's adjusted basis is $1,000,000. When she sell it for its fair market value (FMV) of $5,340,000, the $4,430,000 gain is taxable. Now suppose that instead of selling the asset, Mom leaves it to her son in her will. Not only does the heir's accretion to wealth escape taxation, but the whole gain the family made is tax free. This is because the tax Code allows a **step-up basis** [p. 214] for the heir, meaning that the Son's basis of the asset is the FMV at the day of the decedent's death. As we saw above, if the only property in Mom's estate is the asset with a FMV of $5,340,000, Son receives it free of estate tax. If Son disposes of the asset for $5,340,000, due to the step-up basis, Son has no gain (the basis of $5,340,000 minus the selling price of $5,340,000 equals $0) and does not have to pay tax. If he sells it for, say, $6,000,000, then Son realizes a taxable gain of $660,000. The result is quite clear and astonishing: the gain of $4,340,000 the family made during its holding escapes taxation.

If the estate is higher than the exemption and is subject to estate tax, the amount of the estate tax paid by the estate is added to Son's basis of the asset.

Note that the FMV basis of the inherited assets applies only when it is higher than the decedent's adjusted basis. If it is lower, meaning the asset accumulates a loss, the asset's cost basis is actually "stepped down" to its FMV at the date of the decedent's death. As a result, the heirs lose the accumulated loss for tax purposes. Thus, if property is acquired by Dad for $200,000 (no improvements and no depreciation) and its FMV had dropped to $120,000 at Dad's death, the heir's basis is the FMV at the death date, i.e. $120,000, and the $80,000 loss is eliminated for tax purposes. A possible remedy if the death is predictable is for Dad to sell the property and realize a loss that can be offset against other capital gains that Dad had before his passing away.

Strangely enough, these rules do not apply when appreciated assets are given as gifts. In that case, the donor's basis is **carried over** to the donee, meaning that the donee's basis is equal to the donor's basis. If the donor's adjusted basis is greater than the FMV of the property at the time of the gift, the loss is not carried over and the basis is the fair market value of the property at the time the gift was made.

If the gift was subject to gift tax, the amount of that tax paid by the donor is added to the donee's basis in the asset. For example if Dad's basis in an asset is $50,000 and he gave it as a gift to Daughter when the FMV was $60,000, then (60,000−16,000=)$16,000 is free from gift tax and $44,000 is subject to Dad's gift tax (assuming Dad already exhausted the aggregate exemption of $11,060,000). If Dad paid $4,400 (10%) as gift tax, then Daughter's basis is ($50,000+$4,400=)$54,400. If she sells the asset later on for, say, $70,000 her taxable gain is $15,600. If she sells it for $45,000, she has a loss of $9,400. However, the carry over basis is on only if during Dad's holding time the asset made some gain. If Dad suffers a loss during his holding, then no carry over takes place but the asset's FMV, at the day the gift is made, which is the Daughter's basis. The reason is that in such a situation Mom prefers to sell the asset rather than give it as a gift, giving the proceeds as a gift and using the loss to offset other gains and save some taxes.

In addition, the estate and gift tax rates only seem progressive, but there are some doubts about it. First, since the tax is levied on the donor and the decedent and not on the recipients, no matter how many heirs and donee share the property, the same tax obligation is imposed, whether the property is shared by only one donee or heir or by higher numbers. If a property is worth $21,060,000 and $10,000,000 is the taxable gift or estate (21,060,000−11,060,000) the tax (10%) would be around $3,945,800 (table at p. 140). If it is divided to 20 heirs or donees, each receives (21,060,000−3,945,800= 17,114,200/20=)$855,710, whereas if there is only one heir or donee the same amount of tax ($3,945,800) is paid and the one fortunate heir or donee receives a net amount of $17,114,200. Since those taxes are actually shifted [p. 5] to the recipients, this means that these taxes do not follow the vertical equity attributes (42). Those who get only $855,710 bear a tax of almost 40%, the same rate borne by the one who got $17,114,200.

In addition, remember that the annual exemption from gift tax is $16,000 or $32,000 per year per each person. With a little imagination, good planning, a lot of patience, and devoted and committed friends (say 20), one can realize how Mom and Dad are able to give their son or daughter a significant amount of tax-free wealth from the moment of the children's birth till they reach, say, the age of fifty.

The big question is why Congress has developed this type of hybrid and complicated system, which is quite inefficient in terms of redistribution and equal opportunity, instead of eliminating Code § 102, and taxing the heirs and the donees according to their economic ability after receiving the gifts and the inheritance. Furthermore, if the estate or gift is an appreciated asset, the capital gain, which is realized when it is disposed by the donor/deceased, should be taxable as well. In other words, under a real and meaningful comprehensive income tax, a gift or inheritance of appreciated assets represent two tax events, i.e. the realization of the donor's gain, and the accretion to wealth of the donee.

Chapter Eleven

FEDERAL EXCISE AND DUTIES

The Federal government levies numerous mandatory payments, which are called Excise Taxes, on goods and services, such as gasoline, alcohol, tobacco, air travel and medical insurance and services, which may be classified as Pigovian taxes [pp. 13, 36]. Following the traditional classification, excise taxes are considered consumption taxes, levied either on a per-unit basis (e.g. the gasoline tax is levied per gallon) or as a percentage of value on services (e.g. the federal excise tax on air travel is based on the ticket's price). Generally, excise taxes are collected either at the pre-retail level, i.e. from producers or wholesalers, or on final sales where they are shifted to the final consumers.

According to the U.S. President's Office of Management and Budget (OMB), excise taxes raise around 3 percent of total federal revenue. OMB also indicates that 40% of the total excise taxes go to the general budget and 60% are earmarked and funneled to designated Federal special trust funds.

The purpose of most of the excise taxes is mainly to deal with negative externalities, i.e. to serve as Mandatory Pigovian Payments [pp. 13, 36]. Excise taxes on gasoline, diesel and other transportation fuels, heavy vehicles, tires, and air and sea transportation, are earmarked to Federal trust funds, e.g. the Highway Trust Fund and the Airport and Airway Trust Fund. Excise taxes on fuels, crude oil, and fishing equipment are directed to finance trust funds that deal with environment conservation and protection. Excise taxes on coal, vaccines, and other items are earmarked to trust funds that deal with health matters such as the Black Lung Disability Trust Fund and the Vaccine Injury Compensation Trust Fund. Yet the general impression is that no serious attempt is made to shift the **full** social economic cost of the negative externalities to the producers and their customers, including medical and health damages caused by the pollution created by the products and their production processes. For example, the tax rate on gasoline, which is significantly lower than in in other Western countries (which also impose, in addition to tax on gasoline, substantial costume duties, purchase tax and even property tax on the vehicle itself). Such a low rate indicates that, in the U.S., there is no sincere attempt to include within the excise tax the full social cost of the negative externalities caused by gasoline.

In addition, excise taxes imposed on tobacco and alcohol are not shifted to earmarked government funds nor to organizations such as **Alcoholics Anonymous** or **Narcotics Anonymous**, which deal directly with the harm the products produce to the direct and indirect (e.g. "passive smokers", victims of crimes and accidents) consumers.

Most of the studies dealing with these excise taxes refer to them as measures aimed to deter the consumers from consuming the "sinful" products, although it seems that such deterrence could be considered more as an illegal punishment, as is implied in the majority opinion of the *Sebelius* case [pp. 41, 53]. As suggested above, real Mandatory Pigovian Payments should be calculated in order to shift the full social cost of the sinful products to those who enjoy them—the producers and the consumers. If a careful calculation indicates that the overall revenue is higher than the total social harm and damages, the overlapping amount might be considered to be a penalty or unconstitutional tax, which might not withstand judicial review (70) [p. 40].

A final note regarding the inconsistency of the use of excise taxes in the U.S.: a special excise tax of $0.75 is levied on each active vaccine recommended by the U.S. Centers for Disease Control and Prevention. Such a tax is quite surprising and even frustrating. The total revenue of this excise tax is earmarked and provides funding for the National Vaccine Injury Compensation Program to compensate vaccine-related injury or death claims for covered vaccines administered on or after October 1, 1988. A reasonable assumption is that getting vaccinated entails positive externalities. Vaccines reduce the chances of illnesses and even prevent plagues. They advance the quality of life and the general welfare, and in terms of economic analysis, they improve human and social capital as factors of production. Hence, vaccines should be subsidized by the government, instead of being penalized by a special tax.

Chapter Twelve

INCOME TAX

1. WHY INCOME TAX

The major and most common personal tax system in the Western countries is income tax, although as we proceed, we realize that in reality it is a hybrid system.

Income is considered to be a good benchmark of economic ability [p. 51] and a benefit that taxpayers derive from the public goods and services, which are provided by the government [pp. 51, 71]. As is discussed, there are several approaches to defining the term Income: the narrow British Source system, the broadest economic definition, A Comprehensive Tax Base and a quasi-limited broad definition, which is used in the U.S. Income can be defined from its sources as well as from its usages. This chapter deals with the definition and attributes of income as the tax base in general, with reference to the U.S. Internal Revenue Code. The fifth part [p. 183] elaborates the income tax system in the U.S.

The current income tax is quite complicated. It could be much clearer and more understandable if the legislators, governments, powerful groups, and policymakers gave up their tendency to use income tax to promote some other economic and social goals, instead of using it as a pure tax designated only for one sole purpose—to finance government spending [pp. 21–29]. Nevertheless, the following is an analysis—though a bit artificial—of the income tax structure, which aims to allow a methodical study of the U.S. tax system: its sources, rationales and objectives, flaws and deficiencies, and the causes of those flaws and possible remedies.

2. METHODOLOGY: ON THE APPROPRIATE WAY TO DISCUSS THE GENERAL PRINCIPLES OF THE INCOME TAX CODE

A. Using an Analytical Structure

The structure we use here is a simple eleven stage model, which enables us to see how the various rules are connected to each other; how they evolve from the very basic starting point—the definition of income as the tax base—up to the most complicated rules and provisions. Such a structure provides us with a road map, which shows us where we came from and where we are heading for. The analysis we offer here begins with the basic Archimedes point, which is the rationale for the tax base and its definition.

B. Income as the Tax Base

The model's first stage deals with the tax base, its definition and its attributes, its rationales, and purposes. It deals with the study of the income tax base: why is income the major tax base in modern democracies?

As was concluded above [pp. 21, 71] the personal tax system should be based on the benefit the taxpayers derive from the public goods and services provided by the elected government, which can be measure by the taxpayer's economic ability [p. 51]. A further inquiry reveals that there are three possible alternatives to measuring economic ability: net wealth, income, and consumption. We study the pros and cons of each alternative and try to understand why income has been chosen [pp. 153–180]. Do we need to choose one of these bases exclusively? Alternatively, may we rather have a hybrid base, an income tax that contains some attributes of the consumption and net-wealth components?

Once we consider Income, we realize, as is discussed below [pp. 158–170], that there are both narrow and broad definitions of this term. In addition, it may be observed from two different points of view. One is from the sources side, i.e. where income comes from. The other one is from the usage side, i.e. where income goes to [pp. 157, 188]. From the uses side, income is used for current and future personal consumption. Future consumption is financed by current personal savings. Hence, Income = consumption + saving.

As we proceed, we see that there are some basic attributes of income for income tax purposes.

- There is no income without a gain, profit or accretion to wealth;
- there is no income without consumption or saving; income that is not consumed or saved—probably spent on the creation of further income—is not taxable income;
- any consumption, including imputed income (57) [p. 160] should be considered as income;
- The legality of the income is irrelevant unless the taxpayer remits the fruits of the illegal activity;
- Income must be realized, yet the full meaning of the realization requirement is not yet clear enough [pp. 163, 180], future or potential income is not within the tax base;
- A return of capital is not income;
- Income could be gained by money or money's worth—income in kind;
- A forced gain, (compensation by confiscation or unwilling sale) is still income for income tax purposes;
- Transfer payments (141) without a clear and definite source, such as grants, out of good fortune (lotteries, sweepstakes or prizes should be considered income. Note that in theory, transfer payments include received gifts and even welfare benefits, provided that taxation does not bring the taxpayer below dignified standard of living. As discussed above, gifts are excluded from the income tax base and are supposed to be taxed under the estate and gift tax [p. 141].

As is discussed below, those attributes help us to analyze some complicated tax issues.

C. Income Classification

The second stage of our model deals with the classification of income into several categories. It contains two major dimensions. The first one distinguishes between Capital Gains (consideration for **selling** factors of productions) and Current-Ordinary Income (consideration for **using** factors of production). The second dimension focuses on current-ordinary income and draws a distinction between active income (return/

consideration for using human capital; labor) and passive income (return/consideration for using real capital and other assets).

D. Taxation of International Activities and Investments

The next stage deals with international business, trade, commerce and economic activities and investments, which produce income. In order to decide which country should (or could) tax the profit of transnational income, there is a need to establish clear rules ("tax jurisdiction"), in order to ensure that neither double-taxation nor double non-taxation occur.

E. Income Quantification

Income is not always a simple quantitative and measurable concept. Income, whether as an accretion to wealth or as a return on factors of production, is not necessarily paid, earned, or accumulated in money. Sometimes income is paid with assets, goods and services ("Income in kind", "Notional income"). Other times it is earned as a self-consumption of the taxpayer's own assets, i.e. "Imputed income" (57) [p. 160]. In order to evaluate the size of the income for tax consideration, the fourth stage elaborates some basic and accepted measuring rules for quantification of **Gross Income.**

F. Adjusted Gross Income and Taxable Income

Income tax is levied on **Taxable Income**, i.e. Gross Income minus those expenses that produce it during the taxable period, the allowable losses, and other allowable deductions and exemptions. Under the U.S.'s system, the process of moving from Gross Income to Taxable Income involves an intermediary stage—the calculation of Adjusted Gross Income (AGI)—allowing unreimbursed business expenses that produce the gross income and some non-business outlays permitted specifically by the Code to be deducted. Some examples are provided: certain medical expenses, self-employment taxes, alimony paid to a former spouse, contributions to certain retirement accounts, and the deduction for tuition and fees, including students' interest loans. All these special deductions are called "above the line" deductions.

Once the AGI is calculated, the taxpayers are allowed some more deductions (called "below the line" deductions). The major ones are called Itemized deductions, which are elaborated specifically within the Code. Taxpayers are allowed to give up the itemized deduction and deduct a fixed amount of standard deduction, though the latter is available only for U.S. citizens and resident aliens. The standard deduction in 2022 is $12,950 for single filers and married filing separately, $25,900 for joint filers and $19,400 for heads of household. These amounts have been expanded significantly, beginning in 2018, while the personal exemptions have been suspended.

They represent the legislature's acknowledgment of the constitutional right of human dignity, including the right of a dignified standard of living. U.S. Before the personal exemptions were suspended, [p. 35] citizens and resident aliens were allowed to claim personal exemptions for their dependents as well. Since the purpose is to guarantee a minimum standard of living, personal exemptions were phased out (94) for taxpayers with a significant taxable income. The phase out mechanism does not apply to the expanded standard deduction.

G. Tax Accounting and the Taxable Period

The next step in our model deals with the professional language that translates the outcome of economic activities into numbers. The tax system deals mainly with profits, gains and losses. The discipline that deals with the evaluation of these figures is accounting (2). Generally speaking, financial accounting rules, standards, and principles are applied and integrated into the tax systems. They are followed and enforced by tax laws, regulations and the tax administration's instructions and rulings, as long as they do not negate or contradict the tax laws' essence and purpose. Yet, as mentioned above [p. 106] the purposes of financial accounting and taxation are different. Hence, numerous adjustments and modifications of the former to tax accounting are needed.

H. Taxable Year

Timing is also a significant factor. As a matter of convenience, the measurement of the taxpayer's income is done periodically. The taxable period is set, quite arbitrarily, on an annual basis. Unusual fluctuations of the taxpayer's income over the years might impose an additional unintentional tax burden, mainly due to the progressive tax rate [p. 280]. In order to ease this burden, an accumulated income may be "spread" over certain taxable years either by income averaging, or by carrying business losses forward or backward.

I. Tax Unit

The eighth stage focuses on the idea that Income Tax taxes not only firms [pp. 105, 249] and business activities, but also personal economic activities of households (47, 56) and individuals. There are several possible tax units: households, such as individuals, spouses, and families; and firms, such as partnerships, private and public corporations. Corporate Income Tax, together with income taxation of dividends and capital creates a possible double—or even triple—tax on corporate earnings [p. 215]. In addition, under a progressive tax system, (98) [pp. 24, 55, 101] the assignment of income between taxpayers who have common economic interests may be considered inappropriate tax planning. For example, Mom earns a significant amount of income, so her marginal tax rate is the highest. By assigning part of her income to Son, whose income is low and whose marginal tax rate is zero, the family can save a lot of tax. Mom takes a deduction with a significant tax saving (133) [pp. 4, 240], higher than the tax Son pays on the assigned income. As we proceed, we learn how the tax system and administration cope with this phenomenon by treating certain transactions as illegitimate sham transactions.

J. Tax Calculations

The ninth stage deals with the way the final tax amount the taxpayer owes to the IRS is calculated. After the taxpayer's taxable income is determined, the process continues by defining the tax unit, the amount of personal exemption entitled, if any, what the applicable tax rates are (whether progressive for individuals, or flat rates for corporation), and any income subject to different (lower) tax rates. By applying the statutory tax rates and summing up the result, we arrive only to an intermediate amount—the **tentative tax** owed. It is indeed tentative since it is subject to subtraction of the tax credit (125) that the taxpayer is allowed to claim. After the subtraction of all the tax credits available from the tentative tax, we arrive at the ultimate tax owed.

K. Tax Returns, Disputes, Legal Appeals, Compliances and Enforcement

To know what is the tax's amount that the taxpayers owe, they have to make the above calculations and complete the process. In an ideal and well-educated society, where all of us acknowledge that we gladly pay the price for living in a civilized society, the next step would be sending the owed amount to the IRS. Unfortunately, we are not there, yet. We do have police forces, prisons, criminal courts and prosecutors. Our society still has thieves, embezzlers, tax offenders and (greedy) free riders. In addition, the complexity of the tax laws produces some ambiguities.

Taxpayers are required to communicate with the tax authorities. There are two major types of tax returns. One is an information return. Most American corporations, employers, banks and brokers that pay any type of income or payments subject to the US tax system, are required to submit that payment information to the IRS by using formal forms. The most common forms are W-2 and 1099.

The other type of return is an official form that most American adults, whether citizens, residents or even non-resident-aliens who have income which is subject to the U.S. income tax with a certain minimum annual income are required to submit every year, which includes all the necessary information needed to compute the taxpayer's tax liability.

The idea that underlies the tax payment system is "Pay as you go" or "pay the tax as earned or received" during the taxable year. Employers must withhold the estimated tax from their employees every month and remit it to the IRS. There are other American entities that have to withhold taxes, such as certain corporations, banks and brokers who pay passive income to their customers, and US corporations who pay dividends to foreign shareholders. Other taxpayers have to pay an estimated tax to the IRS that they calculate every four months. Failure to do so invokes penalties and interest payments. The quarterly estimated tax payments are just an advance tax payment. The final tax is calculated at the end of the year, when the annual tax return is submitted.

When the annual tax return is submitted, it includes all the taxpayer's business and personal information, deductions, exemptions and credits and the final amount of tax owed. Due to the "pay as you go" mechanism, it might be that the total tax withheld or paid as an estimated tax is higher than the tax liability. In that case the taxpayer receives a tax refund from the government. If the tax liability under the tax return is higher than the total tax withheld, the taxpayers owe additional tax and must pay their balances due by the original due date of the return or be subject to interest and penalties.

Naturally, disputes between taxpayers and the Tax authority should be resolved. In some cases where the dispute is not solved by negotiation, the tax inspector issues a ruling against the taxpayer's position. In such a case any taxpayer has a legal right to bring the dispute before the judiciary. There are several court venues available for taxpayers seeking to overturn an unfavorable IRS ruling. The U.S. Tax Court is usually the first to receive an appeal, as long as the taxpayer does not pay the deficiency. Other venues are Federal district courts.

L. Enforcement Collection and Criminal Procedures

The final stage of our model deals with issues of legal enforcement beginning with collection measures and ending with criminal procedures. This final stage is not discussed in this book.

Part Four

CHOOSING THE APPROPRIATE PERSONAL TAX BASE, ITS DEFINITION, AND ITS ATTRIBUTES

INTRODUCTION

As mentioned above, a systematic analysis of the major personal tax systems should begin with basic premises, an Archimedes starting point from which our discussion stems from. The four canons of good tax are our starting point [pp. 9–16], not only as a referral point for decision makers, legislature, tax authorities, and social scientists, but also as a constitutional yardstick that enables us to appreciate whether the tax system is based on the public's consent. Furthermore, they should serve as a major criterion for the purpose of interpreting the current tax laws. Once we agree upon those canons, and after reviewing the various tax bases, we can begin a thorough examination of the preferred tax base; what kind of major tax system is the most suitable system for our goals.

A fair and equitable tax system requires using principles of vertical and horizontal equity [p. 14]. The conceivable and possible criteria for equality and differences between taxpayers are their benefit they receive from the public goods and services and their economic ability which, as argued already, [p. 71] do not contradict, but rather complement each other: those who have more economic ability benefit more from public goods and services; either as producers, who use more of the social capital available by the organized society, or as consumers of the major public goods and services, i.e. the recognition of private property and its protection. Hence the more wealth the taxpayer has, the greater benefit they derive from the government. Since the benefit and the ability are basically the same, and since economic ability is a concrete measurable criterion, a practical and reasonable conclusion is that we should use economic ability as the same complementary measures to the benefit, which is more elusive, a bit abstract, and difficult to measure from a legal point of view.

Once we agree upon that economic ability is the correct/adequate substitute for the benefit principle, and we can use it as practical criterion for differences and equality between taxpayers, we move on to consider the three possible measurements of economic ability: *Net Wealth, Income, and Consumption*. During the taxpayer's life span, those three indices almost overlap. We come into the world without any wealth or tangible property, and we perish the same way, unable to take any properties with us. Thus, whatever gain and profit come in during our lifetime is spent on our consumption—including the satisfaction we derive from distributing our property and wealth through gifts and bequests. This insight leads to a simple conclusion advocated by a German legal scholar, George von Schanz and later developed on by two American economists Robert M. Haig and Henry C. Simons in the 1920s and 1930s [p. 159], which may be summarized by saying that income is equal to consumption; present/current consumption and future consumption, which is saving. Hence, **Income = consumption + saving.**

The major difference between income and consumption is a matter of observation and timing: consumption and income are opposite sides of the same coin. Income from the **sources** side is equal to current and future consumption from the **usage** side [p. 157]. Furthermore, if indeed income = consumption + saving, then moving one item from one side of the equation to the other provides: **consumption = income − saving**. That means that for measuring consumption, it is enough to measure income and allow an immediate deduction of any outlay which is not consumption, whether current or capital, which leads us to a cash flow basis [pp. 117, 171]. A further inquiry presented below [p. 256] reveals that the economic meaning of immediate deduction of capital investment is equal to the tax exemption of the return—up to the market interest rate—of the capital investment. Such a conclusion leads to a surprising claim: consumption tax leaves income from capital investment, up to the market interest rate, free from tax, and thus fully taxes only the return from the other means of production—labor and return on capital above the market interest rate.

The relationship between income and net wealth stems from the way that property's worth is evaluated. The value of any asset is equal to the present value (97) of the stream of goods and services that the asset produces in the future (either we sell them for money or money's worth or consume them by ourselves; in both cases the goods and services are considered income). Accordingly, current and future income is equal to net wealth (86, 97), subject to one major (and crucial) difference—***timing***. As is discussed below, income, as a tax base, measures the actual (the present/current) earnings, gains and profits, which are already **materialized ("realized")** [p. 163], whereas net wealth refers to **future, potential income** (103).

The following discussion of the three possible tax bases—net wealth, consumption and income—allows us not only to understand their true meanings, but also to better see the correlation between them and to better understand the current personal tax system.

Chapter Thirteen

NET WEALTH = FUTURE INCOME

1. THE THEORETICAL MERITS

Theoretically, net wealth is the most obvious measurement for economic ability. It is the balance between the total value of the taxpayer's assets minus the total value of their liabilities. Since the value of an asset is determined in accordance with the capitalization of the stream of income the asset is expected to produce (97), the asset's value represents its future or potential income. Assume, for example, that we consider purchasing a capital asset in the beginning of the first year that will yield an annual income of $100 at the end of each year for 5 years, and at the end of the fifth year its value as scrap ("salvage value" (110)) is estimated to be zero. Assuming the interest rate is 10%, then the estimate of the asset's value when it is purchased at the beginning of the first year will be as follows: the present value of the expected annual income ($100), capitalized to the beginning of the year plus the present value of the second year's expected income ($100) capitalized for two years, plus the third amount ($100) capitalized for three years, plus the fourth amount capitalized for four years, and finally the fifth amount capitalized for five years. The formula is simple:

$$\frac{100}{1.1} + \frac{100}{1.1^2} + \frac{100}{1.1^3} + \frac{100}{1.1^4} + \frac{100}{1.1^5} = 379$$

Hence, the asset's value at the beginning of the first year is about $379. This leads to a simple conclusion: the practical definition of taxation of net wealth is taxation of expected/**future** income; taxation of **potential** income; taxation of the prospect of earning income in the future.

2. THE UNCERTAINTY

A simple conclusion, which is crucially relevant for the pursuit of the preferred tax base, is that the value of the taxpayer's net wealth is totally based on uncertainty; on estimations and **uncertain assumptions**: what will be the annual income stream that the asset will yield in reality? For how many years? What will the asset's *salvage value* be at the end of its useful life? What should be the interest rate used for capitalization? In short, too many uncertainties.

In addition, a comprehensive tax system would tax all the income produced by the taxpayer's factors of production, tangible and intangible, including human capital. What is the present value of an intangible? Will it decline or increase over the years? Does knowledge erode over the years? Or maybe increase? Special difficulties arise in the case of human capital. For example, football player earns $10,000,000 during the current year. Alas, it is not certain whether he will continue playing on the same team, in the same country, or with the same skill and physical shape, health, and attractiveness in future years. What if he is injured and can't play for 6 weeks? For the whole season? What if his team does not make it to the play-offs? What if his fans change their taste and turn their backs to him? What if the interest rate changes? No doubt, it would be extremely difficult to calculate his net wealth every year for charging him on his annual net wealth tax, which requires, as does any other tax base, certainty and lack of arbitrariness. [p. 9]

Thus, basing the major personal tax on net wealth involves too much uncertainty and violates the first canon of a good tax system

3. THE TAXPAYER'S CONVENIENCE AND EFFICIENCY

Since taxation of net wealth means taxation of potential/future income, it might create serious liquidity problems for the taxpayer. Furthermore, taxation of net wealth violates the second canon of a good tax—the "taxpayer's convenience".

The annual calculation of net wealth, and possible litigation about it, puts an additional cost on both the taxpayers and the tax administration. Those measurements require the taxpayers to spend too much effort, time, and energy on the annual evaluations, on behalf of the pure income production activity. In other words, net wealth as a tax base is also poor in terms of the third canon—efficiency.

4. TAX RATES

Assume a taxpayer has one factor of production, which lasts for the next five years, with zero salvage value. (110) This factor produces an annual taxable income of $100,000. The average income tax rate is 15% and the taxpayer pays a total income tax of $15,000 each year. If we switch to net wealth tax, we expect the taxpayer to pay the same amount of $15,000.

Now assume the interest rate is 5%. In that case, the value of the factor of production is

$$\frac{100{,}000}{1.05} + \frac{100{,}000}{1.05^2} + \frac{100{,}000}{1.05^3} + \frac{100{,}000}{1.05^4} + \frac{100{,}000}{1.05^5} = \$432{,}900$$

There are several ways to deal with the preferred tax rates. If indeed we expect to have an annual tax payment of $15,000, the net wealth tax rate in the first year should be 3.465%. In the second year the value of the asset decreases to $354,600 and the tax rate has to be raised to 4.23%. The asset's value in the third year goes to $272,300 and the tax rate goes up to 5.5%; in the fourth year—$185,900 with an 8.06% tax rate. In the last year the asset's value is $95,200 with 15.75% tax rate.

A more reasonable way is to set the tax rate to a constant 7.4%. Accordingly, the tax payment would be $32,034 in the first year and $7,044.8 in the last one. The latter approach better represents the taxpayer's annual ability. In the first year it is higher, and since the asset's value declines over the years, the tax liability declines as well.

5. NET WEALTH—CONCLUSION

The emerging conclusion is that net wealth is inappropriate as a tax base. It might score high in terms of equity and fairness, but it very poorly addresses the other three canons: certainty, taxpayer's convenience, and efficiency.

Chapter Fourteen

INCOME

Another possible measurement that can be used to evaluate a person's economic ability is personal income. There are several approaches to defining income. There is a narrow definition and a broad definition. Before considering them, we should mention again that income may be measured either from its sources—what comes in, or by the way it is spent or used—its usages.

1. THE DUAL DEFINITION OF INCOME: SOURCES V. USAGE

As mentioned throughout the book, income can be defined according to its sources or its usages. Gains, profits and transfer payments (141) come in during our lifetime, and they are spent on our consumption—current or future—through saving.

From the ***sources side***, taxable income means profit, gains, and/or accretion to wealth. Hence it should not include any component that does not represent such accretion. If the taxpayer receives an income but assigns it to a third party in order to purchase goods or services that are used in their income production process, it is no longer their income but that of the third party.

From the ***usage side***, income means the individual's ability that is currently consumed or saved for future consumption. Humans are interested in having income for one major reason—to facilitate their consumption according to the standard of living they aim for. Consumption includes the satisfaction derived from buying non-durable goods and services and consuming them individually, by using one's own durable assets, or by transferring one's accumulated property and assets to loved ones through gifts and bequests. Sometimes humans decide to postpone some of their accessible means and save them for future consumption. Hence the usage-side definition of the term income is: income = consumption + saving.

Such a usage-side definition is very important for two reasons. First, it helps us to appreciate whether the tax base is a comprehensive one, i.e. whether it includes all the income's components. When consumption is greater than taxable income, the examination of the tax based is required. In addition, it can serve as an auxiliary test to determine the deductible expenses that are allowed for income tax purposes. Any outlay for consumption and private saving should not be allowed as a deductible expense. In addition, any outlay designated/aimed to produce income in the future, i.e. investment which saves an annual business deduction in the future, should not be allowed as a current deduction but may be amortized over the relevant years in the future. On the other hand, those expenses that are spent on the annual income production are neither private consumption nor investment or savings and therefore are not part of the individual income, i.e. they should be allowed as deductions.

There is a lovely illustration that might illustrate this concept. Imagine Robinson Crusoe living on a stranded island and his only means of livelihood is coconuts. In order to measure his ability by means of income (expressed as aforementioned only by coconuts), he may be asked to report every given period (a year) the number of coconuts he brings home. Or, he may be required to report at the end of the period how many coconuts he consumed and how many he saved. Under both methods we arrive at the same result. In other words, total income always equals its total possible uses: consumption + savings & investment. Within the scope of consumption that brings about satisfaction, we also measure the gifts that Robinson Crusoe makes to his friends and relatives. If he gives coconuts to Friday in consideration for the daily work that Friday performs (picking coconuts and guarding them and the coconut trees), it is not a gift but rather an assignment of the income, or a compensation for the use of factors of production—Friday's labor. Therefore, it is neither consumption nor saving. The amount of coconuts that are given to Friday is not considered Robinson Crusoe's income (he will be able to deduct it as an *expense*; an income assigned to Friday).

If Robinson has also a beautiful house where he dwells, his consumption also includes the value of the dwelling services he consumes every year. Hence, his income should also include the imputed income (57) from his house. In addition, if he receives some coconuts from his friendly neighbors (or inherits them) and either consumes the coconuts or saves them, they should be added to his income.

Now back to a twenty-first century example. A taxpayer just graduated law school. She doesn't have any tangible property (besides her human capital), hence we assume that for tax law her net wealth is zero. During the first year she sells legal services for $40,000. She pays her secretary $15,000, pays $12,000 for rent and utilities, and buys a new computer for $3,000. The computer is supposed to be used in the taxpayer's law firm for three years. At the end of the first year its value decreased to $2,000. During this year she spent $10,000 on private consumption.

From the ***sources side*** her taxable income is equal to whatever came into her account: out of $40,000, $15,000+$12,000 went to a third party to produce her annual taxable income, hence they should not be taxed. $3,000 went to the computers dealer but only 1/3 was used-up during the taxable year, and 2/3 of the computer's value is added to the firm's assets; it is considered investment to be used in the following years. Hence her taxable income is 40,000–(15,000+12,000+3,000)+2,000=$12,000.

From the ***usages side***, her personal consumption is $10,000 and the rest of her investment is $2,000, which is the addition to the firm's assets at the end of the first year (the total cost of the computer minus the value of its annual use) = $2,000 and the total amount of her consumption and investment (10,000+2,000=) is $12,000.

As will be seen later on, such dual analysis helps us to better understand some complicated tax questions, such as defining capital gains and distinguishing them from current income, the deductibility of capital expenses and losses, business expenses and losses, depreciation and amortization (20, 21, 30).

2. NARROW V. BROAD

A. The British Source Doctrine

The first time that income tax was levied in modern times was in Britain by William Pitt in 1798. It taxed six exclusive schedules ("sources"). Any receipt not falling within those schedules was not taxed. The American economist Henry Simons, in his ***Personal Income Taxation: The Definition of Income As a Problem of Fiscal Policy***, concluded that the rationale of the British scheduler system derived from the idea that the aggregate personal income for income tax purposes was supposed to be equal to the national income. Transfer payments (134) are made without any corresponding production or expectations of production; they are not earned. Hence, they are not included within the national income. Consequently, transfer payments were not considered income under the British income tax system. In other words, under the narrow British scheduler approach, income from the sources side was the return of any use of factors of production. The selling of factors of production created a problem under this system. Gains from such disposition ("Capital Gain") was not part of the income tax base for a very long time.

It is worth noting that, according to one unconfirmed assumption, the British scheduler system was intended to maintain the social gaps in England: the upper class people reported their income to "common" assessment officers. In order to prevent the commons from receiving and accumulating too much information about the true magnitude of the upper class's wealth, the taxpayers reported to each assessment officer separately on income from one schedule. For the sake of privacy, the officers were forbidden to exchange information, and this achieved industrial and social tranquility. No wonder, then, that the American scholars and courts were very reluctant to endorse such an approach.

B. Departing from the British Doctrine

Indeed, in the very early stage of the U.S. income tax era, the Supreme Court followed—maybe unintentionally—the narrow British approach. In 1913 in *Stratton's Independence v. Howbert*, the Supreme Court stated:

> *"Income may be defined as the gain derived from capital, from labor, or from both combined."*

In 1920, in *Eisner v. Macomber*, [p. 164] the Supreme Court followed this formula but signaled a significant development by adding the following comment:

> *"provided it be understood to include profit gained through a sale or conversion of capital assets"*

American economists observed this narrow approach with certain degree of criticism. If the goal of income tax is to correspond to the taxpayers' benefit from the public goods and services which is measured by their economic ability, the origin of the ability is not substantially relevant. In 1921 the American economist Robert Murray Haig described income as "the money-value of the net accretion to one's economic position between two points of time". In 1938 Henry Calvert Simons, who is considered one of the founders of the Chicago School of Economics, provided the broadest and most comprehensive definition of income as a tax base:

> *Personal income may be defined as "the algebraic sum of (1) the market value of rights exercised in consumption and (2) the change in the value of the store of property rights between the beginning and end of the period in question.*

This definition, which is known as the Haig-Simons equation, found its way, with few modifications, to the Supreme Court decision in *C.I.R. v. Glenshaw Glass Co.* (1953), when the Court considered whether punitive damages should be included within the income tax base:

> *"Here we have instances of undeniable accessions to wealth, clearly realized, and over which the taxpayers have complete dominion".*

However, a real and meaningful comprehensive income tax base has never been adopted in the U.S. The consumption that the taxpayer enjoys from using their own assets i.e. imputed income (57) is totally ignored despite it being a part of *"the market value of rights exercised in consumption"*.

Another deviation from the pure Haig-Simons definition is the realization requirement, which was mentioned already in the *Glenshaw* case. In addition, the legislature undermines such a comprehensive approach by providing a significant number of statutory exemptions.

C. Broad but Not Entirely—Imputed Income

Every durable asset produces a stream of annual income, which gives the asset its economic value, i.e. the present value (97) of the future stream of income plus the asset's salvage value. A house produces income, i.e. a stream of dwelling services consumed by either a tenant or by its owner. In both cases, the owner has income. If they use the house themselves, they have notional income as an owner on the one hand, and notional consumption expenses as the user on the other hand. From an economic point of view, it does not matter if they use the house for their own dwelling or lease it for a fee, which finances the rent they need to pay for another place they rent for their own dwelling according to their needs and priorities. In both cases they have the same economic ability; income on the one hand and private-consumption expenses on the other hand. The income should be taxed [after deducting the allowed expenses like depreciation (30) and interest payment on a mortgage, but not the maintenance expenses since they are part of their consumption]. Yet the consumption expenses are not deductible, since, as mentioned, personal consumption is part of the definition of the term income from the usage side [p. 157].

Note that business' durable assets such as machineries also produce a stream of income. If a machine is used by the owner's business, they have notional income on the one hand, and notional expense on the other hand. The significant difference is that with the non-business assets case, the non-monetary-notional expense is for private consumption, whereas with business assets the expense is a business one and should be deductible. In such a case there is a wash, i.e. the notional expenses offsets the notional income, resulting in a zero taxable income.

The nonmonetary notional income person derive from their property was termed "imputed income" (57) in 1943 by Donald Marsh in his *[T]he taxation of imputed income* article. He defined the term as:

> *"a flow of satisfactions from durable goods owned and used by the taxpayer, or from goods and services arising out of the personal exertions of the taxpayer on his own behalf."*

Accordingly, he argued that the imputed rental value of owner-occupied housing should be included in taxable income. This analysis is not limited to real estate only. Any durable asset that produces a stream of income that is consumed by the owner's self-use should be included within the term income and be subject to income tax as imputed income, e.g., private jets, yachts, collectables, art collections and even expensive jewelry that no doubt produce stream of income and are consumed by their owners. Indeed, a careful implementation of the Haig-Simons definition (*"the market value of rights exercised in consumption"*) produces a tax event, which does not infringe upon the above two canons of a good tax—the canons of certainty and the taxpayer convenience [pp. 10–11].

One should also consider any other consumer-durable asset, though since the common ones are used by most of the household, excluding such imputed income from taxation does not violate the principle of horizontal equity (42). This is because their annual imputed income is usually equal to their asset's annual depreciation i.e., a complete wash, so the taxable income is zero.

Surprisingly, no serious attempt has been made to tax the imputed income of non-business assets that represent a meaningful personal consumption. This omission, which provides a significant advantage to property owners, might be explained by a dicta made by the Supreme Court in 1934 (!) in the *Helvering v. Independent Life Ins. Co. Case*:

> *If the statute lays taxes on the part of the building occupied by the owner or upon the rental value of that space, it cannot be sustained, for that would be to lay a direct tax requiring apportionment. Pollock v. Farmers' Loan & Trust Co.*

Furthermore, the Court indicated that the rental value of a building used by the owner does not constitute income within the meaning of the Sixteenth Amendment.

A bit earlier in the *Morris v. Commissioner* (1928) case, the Board of Tax Appeals ruled against the government and supported the taxpayer's claim that the crops produced on his farm for his personal benefit were not income to the farmer. It seems that the Court disregarded the claim that from an economic point of view, the imputed income analysis (57) is completely identical to a case where a Farmer raises some crop and sells it to a customer. Then he uses the proceeds to buy some food for his own family. The money received is income from trade or business and the money spent is for personal consumption. The fact that the professional farmer merged the two transactions—selling his crop and buying food in one,—does not change the Farmer's economic ability. In both cases he uses his own factors of production—land, machineries, and labor—to acquire personal consumption.

In conclusion, the most significant problem with the current situation is the non-taxation of imputed income from durable assets. Durable assets such as real estate, private jets, yachts etc., usually owned by high income earners and the non-inclusion of the imputed income in their gross income provides them with a most significant tax advantage.

One should also consider the possibility that mere wealth also produces "intangible imputed income", such as political power and social status. Practical considerations probably prevent an accurate calculation of such imputed income but may justify a surtax (116) on the very wealthy.

Naturally, taxpayers with the highest economic ability have more durable assets, and consequently enjoy the highest amount of imputed income. Refraining from taxing such a significant source of income contributes significantly to the rising social gaps.

It is quite clear that the taxation of imputed income is part of the comprehensive definition of income for income tax purposes. It may be that the current position—the non-taxation of imputed income derived from durable assets—is the outcome of manipulation by the strongest interest groups—the capital owners—who were able to direct this subtle trend. It is quite doubtful that the result in the *Morris* case and the dicta and conclusions of the *Independent Life Ins. Co.* case would be held by the Supreme Court of the twenty first century, especially after the legislation of Code sec. 7872 [p. 193].

It is worth adding the following comment: So far, we have emphasized that the bulk of the imputed income relates to income from durable personal assets. A careful scrutiny of the above Farmer example reveals that there are actually two categories of imputed income. One is from durable assets—land and machines. The other is from labor, which can be illustrated by the following example: consider a **professional** painter who paints his client's house for five hours and earns $500+expenses. After deducting his expenses, the $500 is considered taxable income. If the painter instead paints his own house, using the same five hours, he earns (and consumes) $500 imputed income. Assuming the painter's marginal tax rate is 20%, he ends up with $400 for consumption after tax if he paints his client's house, but with $500 for consumption if instead he performs the same services for his own family. One may argue that failing to tax the imputed income from non-professional self-services not only violates the principles of fairness and horizontal equity (42) but also undermines the efficiency requirement. Yet, as Henry Simon indicated some 75 years ago, a practical and reasonable concession should drive us to give up the taxation of the non-professional self-services most of us provide ourselves. Such a concession does not violate either horizontal equity (most taxpayers shave themselves) nor vertical equity since these services are common among lower income taxpayers, and not taxing them may be considered as part of the progressive system.

D. Income in Kind—Barter Transaction

The most notable attribute of imputed income (57) is that there is no transaction involved. The taxpayer uses their own assets and labor. A different way to describe it is that the taxpayers are doing business with themself and there is no monetary payment involved.

Barter transactions are different. Although they do not involve monetary payment, these are transactions between the taxpayer and other person (or more, either another taxpayer or a client) who exchange goods or services. In such a case the proceeds of the exchange are supposed to be taxed in a way similar to how monetary transaction is taxed. Suppose that Trader bought a stock-in-trade for $100. When its fair market value is $120, he exchanges it in return for legal services that Lawyer provides him. Both Trader and Lawyer have income in kind; a gross income (54) of $120. In addition, both have also expenses in kind. Trader pays $120 for legal services (not in cash but with the goods he provides) and Lawyer pays $120 for the goods she bought (not in cash but by providing her legal services). The question of whether those expenses are deductible is answered according to the prevailing rules of deduction, regardless of the lack of monetary payment.

There are some significant practical problems. One is that such barter transactions are quite elusive, and the tax authorities might have some difficulties in tracing them. The second is the evaluation difficulties. Yet, accounting rules can ease these difficulties. Record keeping of stock-in-trade provides traceable information. In the famous British case, *Sharkey v. Wernher* (1955) the court concluded that a person, carrying on the trade of farming or any other trade, who disposes of part of their stock-in-trade not by way of sale in the course of trade but for their own use, enjoyment, or recreation, must bring into their trading account for income tax purposes the market value of that stock-in-trade at the time of such disposition.

Bookkeeping can also provide solutions to the Lawyer's income in-kind. If she is required to maintain a list of customers together with the details of the services she provides to each, then the income could be traced. In that case, the evaluation of income becomes much easier.

Note that the taxation of professional services provided "free-of-charge" (either through a barter transaction, a gift to family members or friends, or even self-service to the professional themselves) is required, otherwise the professional might face serious problems regarding the deductibility of the expenses relating to the service free of charge. Assume Dad is the head and the owner of a law firm. His son needs some legal services and Dad gladly agrees to provide them free-of-charge. Yet the junior lawyers who work on the case still receive their salary from the firm. If those salaries do not produce income, then they are not deductible expenses—they did not create any taxable income. Another way to examine this event is to realize that the free legal services provided to son gives personal satisfaction to Dad. We have already indicated [p. 154] that such satisfaction should be regarded as Dad's private consumption, i.e. income and not deductible expenses. Hence the value of the "free" legal service should be considered as Dad's income, or at least Dad's cost of these services, including the prorated general and management expenses should not be allowed for Dad as business expenses. Since from a practical point of view the disallowance of the expenses seems more complicated than taxing the income in-kind, and the above analysis indicates that theoretically Dad used his factor of production, realized an income and gave his son a gift, then it seems that the latter approach should be preferred. The alternative, i.e. giving up taxation and yet allowing Dad to deduct the cost of the provided free legal services, violates both vertical and horizontal equity.

As indicated above, [p. 161] in 1928 the Board of Tax Appeal in the *Morris* case rejected such a comprehensive and sweeping approach. The Board did not tax the imputed income (57) the farmer realized, and there was no deliberation of disallowing part of his farm's expenses. Under those circumstances one should understand the rationales for the enactment of Code Sec. 482, which is based on accounting principles. The major one is the Arm's Length Transaction (12). This statutory provision allows the IRS to distribute, apportion, or allocate gross income, deductions, credits, or allowances between or among firms that are owned or controlled directly or indirectly by the same interests, in order to avoid tax evasion, or to clearly reflect the income of any such transaction. The major application of the section is with regard to transfer-pricing of international activity where related parties try to shift income to low tax jurisdictions. Indeed, Code Sec. 482 does not refer directly to individual household and inter-family transactions, yet once such transactions are carried on within a firm (47), whose object is to produce earnings in its ordinary course of business, the courts—or the Congress—should reconsider the Morris decision.

Another specific provision is Code Sec. 7872, which provides a statutory solution for a specific barter transaction—a free/low interest loan. This is discussed below [p. 193].

E. Broad but Not Entirely—the Realization Requirement

If a taxpayer possesses an asset whose value increased, the appreciation, which produces a gain and an accretion to wealth, should be taxed. Yet, due to the realization requirement (103), which is discussed below, the gain is not taxed as long as the owner does not dispose of the property. Consequently, the taxpayer enjoys a significant tax deferral. The taxation of the imputed income eases the deferral problem considerably. If the property appreciates, the annual imputed income goes up as well, although the latter is the cause of the former. The appreciation occurs because the expected stream of income increases. Regardless, the taxation of imputed income (57) causes the economic gain derived from the appreciation to be taxed, though not instantly, but instead over the asset's lifetime Note though, that the taxed appreciation is added to the basis—the cost of the asset. Hence, when the asset is sold, the profit (or loss) is computed accordingly.

Although law professor William Andrews referred to the realization requirement (103) as the "Achilles heel", its underlying rationales are understood. Without it, the income tax system moves quite significantly toward taxing uncertain income and infringing upon the taxpayer's convenience requirement [pp. 10–11]; two deficiencies that are quite similar to the ones of the net wealth tax base. The problem is that some of the U.S. courts' decisions extended the realization requirement a bit too far.

Assume a person invests in a corporation—a separate legal entity. The corporation makes a profit and the investor gets richer, which is embodied in two similar ways. One, the profits are accumulated in shareholder's "account in the company"; if and when the company decides to distribute the earnings as dividends, she receives her share. Second, the value of her stocks goes up. Now suppose the corporation provides the investor with a stock dividend, i.e. more stocks instead of cash dividend. One way to treat this chain of events is to consider it as one transaction; it begins with an enrichment and ends with receiving a paper certificate that represent the enrichment that is at the disposal of the taxpayer; she can do whatever she wants with them. The Supreme Court saw it differently. In 1920, the Supreme Court's majority in *Eisner v. Macomber* [p. 164], described this transaction as two separate stages, neither one of which created a tax event. The first one is an enrichment without a realization. The other one is a receipt of paper certificates without any enrichment. The majority further, explained:

> *Income is not a mere gain accruing to capital; not a growth or increment of value in the investment; but a gain, a profit, something of exchangeable value, proceeding from the property, severed from the capital, however invested or employed, and coming in, being "derived"—that is, received or drawn by the recipient (the taxpayer) for his separate use, benefit and disposal—that is income derived from property.*

In his dissenting opinion, Justice Brandeis, expressed some concerns regarding the majority opinion:

> *If stock dividends representing profits are held exempt from taxation under the Sixteenth Amendment, the owners of the most successful businesses in America will, as the facts in this case illustrate, be able to escape taxation on a large part of what is actually their income.*

Hence he offered a more economic analysis as follow: a stock dividend is really a cash dividend since it is really two-step event: a cash distribution that is then used to purchase additional shares by the exercise of stock subscription rights.

Later on, the severance requirement, which was offered by the majority, was eroded. In *Helvering v. Bruun* (1940), the taxpayer, a Landlord, rented a property for a long term lease. According to the lease agreement the lessee removed an old building from the property and built a new one according to his own needs and specifications. Later on the lessee decided to give up the lease and the Landlord repossessed the property. The Court agreed with the government that the value of the new building as of the date of repossession minus the Landlord's basis in the old building was the Landlord's realized gain when he repossessed. The Court concluded:

> *[t]he realization of gain need not be in cash derived from the sale of an asset. Gain may occur as a result of exchange of property, payment of the taxpayer's indebtedness, relief from a liability, or other profit realized from the completion of a transaction. The fact that the gain is a portion of the value of property received by the taxpayer in the transaction does not negative its realization. . . . the [taxpayer] received back his land with a new building on it, which added an ascertainable amount to its value. It is not necessary to recognition of taxable gain that he should be able to* ***sever*** *the improvement begetting the gain from his original capital.*

A more accurate way to approach this event reveals that the tax authorities were easy with the taxpayer. A substantial economic inquiry requires the use of the "in kind-barter transaction" analysis, and the original transaction should be construed as follows: Landlord has a property with an old building. Lessee is interested in renting it, provided that the old building is removed and a new one is built. Landlord does not have the money. Tenant offers to lease the property for a long period of time and to pay the rent in advance for the whole period. Landlord agrees, receives the money and finances the construction. Lessee gets the possession of the real estate with the new building. The fact that there was no transfer of payments between the lessee, the landlord and the builders does not change the analysis. Instead of the lessee paying the landlord and the landlord paying the builders, the lessee pays the builder, or even does the construction himself. The tax aspects are the same for all these three alternative transactions. For the landlord, the construction cost should be treated as part of the rent the lessee pays in advance. If the landlord uses the cash basis reporting method (118, 132), he is subject to income tax on the same year he received the rent in advance, in this example, the money worth—a new building. The landlord spent the advance rent to cover the cost of the construction. Such spending is the landlord's investment, a capital expense and may be deducted gradually over the years as amortization or depreciation (31). The conclusion is clear. If the taxpayer was taxed only when he repossessed the rented property, after the lessee gave up the lease, he enjoyed a significant tax deferral. In other words, in leasing transactions, in order to minimize the Achilles' Heel of the income tax law, the Court should have decided that realization takes place when the core of a leasing transaction takes place—when the possession of the asset is shifted to the lessee. If the rent is paid in advance, the owner should be taxed instantly to ensure that no "canon of a good tax" is violated [pp. 10–11]; the taxpayer does not have liquidity and uncertainty problems.

Another interesting question regarding the realization issue arises when a property owner of an appreciated property takes a loan with a mortgage. Suppose Taxpayer purchases an asset for $100. Immediately afterwards the asset's FMV goes up to $500. According to the traditional analysis, as long as the taxpayer does not sell or exchange the asset, the gain is unrealized, and no tax event occurs.

The *Woodsam Ass. Inc. v. Com.* (2nd Cir. 1952) decision is an example of a case where the court went too far with the realization requirement. The Court of Appeals decided that even the receipt of nonrecourse mortgage (88) that was taken on an appreciated building does not constitute a taxable event.

We beg to differ. Regardless of whether the mortgage is recourse or nonrecourse, any lent money received by the owner of an appreciated asset, up to the difference between the asset's cost and its appreciation, should be regarded as realized gain. It has the two elements required to establish a tax event. One, using the above example there is a gain, an enrichment, an accretion to wealth—the $400 in this scenario—the asset was bought for $100 and sold for $500. Second, the underling logic and rationales for the realization requirement are satisfied. As mentioned, taxation of unrealized gains or profits contradicts two canons of a good tax, namely certainty and the taxpayer's convenience [pp. 9–11]. Due to the money received from the lender, the taxpayer does not have liquidity and uncertainty problems. Instead, he has the money at his disposal. He can use it according to his own discretion, though he has an obligation to pay it back in the future.

Admittedly, an accurate analysis is more complicated. It depends on how the taxpayer uses the amount of the mortgage received by the taxpayer.

Assume the following scenarios, which are based on the above example:

A. The taxpayer gets a mortgage of $400 (an amount equals to the "unrealized" gain) and consumes the proceeds.

B. The taxpayer uses the amount received of the "first" mortgage for purchasing another asset and uses it either for his own personal use (case I), or as a business asset in his own business activity (case II), or rents it and collects passive income (rent; case III); or spends it as a current expense in his income producing activity (case IV).

According to the traditional conventions, there is no tax event in either scenario; there has not been sale or exchange of the asset. And yet, a careful and accurate reading of the Haig-Simons definition suggests otherwise, even if the realization requirement is acknowledged and accepted. In all these four cases the taxpayer had an economic gain, and since he got the mortgage amount in his disposal and available to be used, which should be subject to income tax (here we do not distinguish between current income and capital gain). The "only" issue here is the timing.

The starting point is that, once the taxpayer has a gain and he can use it, the traditional justification of the realization requirement no longer holds. The uncertainty is quite low, and the taxpayer's convenience and the issue of liquidation are insignificant: the taxpayer has the money in his possession and can use it according to his own discretion, i.e. either consume, invest, or save it. On the other hand, the taxpayer is indeed under the obligation to repay the $400 loan in the future and the repayments should be considered while measuring the taxpayer's ability to pay. Hence, we can offer the following analyses for the above scenarios.

Scenario A: Remember that income on the usage side is equal to consumption. In addition, such consumption is under the Haig-Simons definition ("*the market value of rights exercised in consumption*"). Hence, a practical and workable conclusion is that the consumption of the enrichment should be taxed during its occurrence. In other words, the mere consumption is the realization of the gain. The consumption turns potential future income into real economic power the taxpayer uses. On the other hand, the repayment of the loan (the $400) should be deductible against the taxpayer's annual income in the same taxable year of the repayment—from any sources—since it reduces his ability. No doubt, such approach integrates some aspects of consumption taxation with income tax and represents the idea that income tax is indeed a hybrid of tax bases.

Scenario B: The common ground for all four cases is that the new asset produces income that should be included within the income tax base.

In case I, the taxpayer uses the amount received to purchase his own house and uses it for this purpose, i.e. private consumption. There are two alternative ways to tax the gain. One is to tax the amount received of the loan by using the analysis used for Scenario A. The other way is to tax the annual imputed income (57), the same way we tax the income under cases II and III below.

In cases II and III, the income that the asset produces is an integral part of the taxpayer's business or passive investment and is taxed directly. The taxpayer is allowed to deduct all the expenses that produce this income, including the annual depreciation or the amortization of the asset's cost. The question is: should the amount received of the first loan be included within the new asset's purchase price? No doubt that if these amounts were taxed directly while received by the taxpayer, they should be included in the basis, the cost of the acquired asset, otherwise they are taxed twice. This double taxation should be prevented by adding the amount that was taxed already to the basis of the new asset so the annual depreciation will be calculated using the full amount. Alternatively, no direct and immediate taxation takes place when the taxpayer receives the first mortgage's amount, but the same amount is not included in the new asset's cost for tax purposes.

To illustrate the two alternatives, suppose the new asset was bought for $750 using $400 the amount of the previously appreciated asset mortgage (5% interest), $250 from a new mortgage (6% interest), and $100 from the taxpayer's own saving. Assume that the annual gross income that the new asset produces is $90. According to the conventional practice, the taxpayer is allowed to deduct the following: the depreciation of the total cost of the asset (basis) and the interest payments. If the $400 were taxed directly when received, then the full amount of the depreciation should be allowed. On the other hand, if the $400 first mortgage amount were not taxed directly, then the analysis is a bit different.

There is a rule of thumb in income tax law that a taxable gain or receipt that was not included in the taxpayer's tax accounts cannot be used for income tax purposes. The basis of such an amount for income tax purposes is zero. Accordingly, if the $400 gain was not taxed when the taxpayer used it, he should not be allowed to include it within the new asset's basis. In other words, no depreciation deduction of the $400 cost of the new asset should be allowed. The only depreciation, in this example, is calculated on only (750−400=)$350. If indeed the depreciation on the $400 is not allowed, this means that the gain of the appreciated first asset is indeed taxed, indirectly and during a long period of time, i.e. the depreciation period. Note that under this approach the repayment of the loan (the $400) should be deducted against the taxpayer's taxable income of the taxable year the amount is paid.

The same analysis should be used regarding the interest deduction. Yet the discussion of the deductibility of interest payments deserves deeper scrutiny and we discuss it below.

It is noteworthy that the major and meaningful difference between a regular loan, with a non-appreciated collateral mortgage, and a loan guaranteed with an appreciated asset is that with the former there is no element of enrichment, profit, or gain, whereas the most significant factor of the latter is the appreciation of the collateral. Thus, the above analyses apply only on loans with appreciated collateral. Without it, there is no gain. The loan itself does not produce gain. Against the proceeds of the loan there is the liability to repay the amount, which in its present value (97) is equal to the money received. In other words, the gain in the mortgage transaction relates to the appreciation of the collateral and not the transfer/receiving of the loan money.

F. A Caveat—Is the Above Discussion Worth the Efforts?

In addition to the complexities of the above discussion regarding the different uses of the amount received of the original mortgage, the above analysis ignores a significant factor which is related to the adjusted basis of the original asset (for the sake of simplicity we assume first that it is a non-depreciable asset). It seems that if the original asset was bought for $100, that amount remains the basis of the asset for tax purposes. But this is wrong. As a general rule, loans should be repaid, even when they are secured with non-recourse mortgage, unless the circumstances encourage the borrower to abandon the depreciated asset (31) [pp. 191–212, 260–263, 262, 263]. Hence, the immediate taxation of the receipt of a loan with an appreciated asset as a collateral raises some serious doubts. The loan repayments might nullify the income. Using the above example: a taxpayer purchases an asset for $100, which appreciates to $500. The appreciation enables him to take a $400 mortgage and consume it. The above analysis suggested that the proceeds of the $400 will be considered realized income. In addition to the interest payments, the principal is paid back over, say, 8 years with an annual amount of $50. How should the annual principal payment of $50 be treated?

If the eight annual principal repayments of the principal nullify the income the taxpayer received in the first year ($400), one may wonder why bother? In the long run, the first year's income from the mortgage of the appreciated asset ($400) phases-out over the loan period. The answer is of course **timing** [p. 106] (126) and the time value of money (140). The significant factors here are indeed timing and the interest rates. If the interest rate is zero, the analysis offered here does not provide any advantage to the taxpayer. Once the interest rate goes up, the immediate taxation of the original asset's appreciation in the first year, and the annual decrease of the taxpayer's taxable income over the eight years provide the taxpayer a higher disadvantage. If, on the other hand, the taxpayer is not taxed immediately, and the repayments were not deductible during the next eight years he enjoys a tax deferral, which means tax saved (126).

Another option is to insist on immediate taxation on the year the mortgage is granted, and to allow the annual $50 principal payment as a deduction against the taxpayer's other income during the eight years, or, if needed, to allow it as a carry backwards or forward losses. The other alternative is immediate taxation of the amount received, with no current deduction for the $50 annual payment but to add those payments to the original asset's cost ($100). Accordingly, the adjusted basis/cost of the original asset at the end of the first year would be (100+50=)$150, and not $100. At the end of the 2nd year—$200 and at the end of the 8th year—$500. If the taxpayer sells the asset at the end of the eighth year for $550 his taxable gain is only $50; and if he sells it for $450, he has a loss of $50 that can offset other taxable gains. Furthermore, if the asset is a depreciable one, the annual increase of its cost also increases the annual amount of the depreciation.

As long as the current law draws a distinction between capital gains and ordinary income, it seems that the third option should be adopted. It is more accurate, and its application is quite easy.

G. Broad but Not Entirely—the Double Deductibility of Interest

Investors and businesses use loans quite often to finance their income production activity. We are not interested here with the risks and benefits consideration of such financing, but focus only on the income tax aspects, and the way the deductibility of the interest payments contributes to the long and consistent process of narrowing the tax base and increasing social gaps.

Assume Taxpayer has to spend an amount of money for his income production activity. He does not have the necessary amount ($1,000). Hence in year 1 he takes a loan with a market interest rate (5%) for one year and pays the current expense (a salary for his business manager). In year 2 he pays the lender the principal + $50 interest, a total of $1,050.

The practical way to treat this is that in year 1 he is allowed to deduct the full payment to the employee—$1,000. In year 2 he is allowed to deduct the $50 interest paid to the lender. But something is wrong here. After all, the taxpayer does not take any money out of his own pocket in year 1, but only in year 2 when he repays the loan. When he pays the $1,000 in year 1, this amount represents the present value (97) of the amount he owes to the lender—$1,050—that is due to be paid in year 2. The present value is (1,050/1.05=)$1,000. So, if he deducts the amount of $1,000 in year 1, that amount already includes in year 2's interest payment. If in year 2 he takes the $50 interest deduction, he enjoys a double deduction of the interest. In order to prevent such double deduction of the interest, he should be allowed only one of the following options: either deduct the present value of the principal (1,000/1.05=)$952.3 in year 1 and the interest payment of $50 in year 2; or deduct the $1,000 in year 1 and deduct nothing of the interest paid in year 2; or deduct the amount of $1,050 in year 2. Since he does not pay any money from his own pocket in year 1, it seems that the last option is the preferred one. He should take the deduction only when he takes the money out of his own pocket. The most important point here is to realize the significant advantage the taxpayer enjoys if the current practice allows him indeed to take the double deduction of interest. Such double deduction reduces the taxpayer's tax payments, increases the after-tax rate of return, and might contribute to the growing social gaps. Such analysis might shed light on another explanation to the Modigliani and Miller theorem, which argues that in a world **with** an income tax system, there are advantages for corporations/firms to be levered, due to the deductibility of interest payments (as opposed to the non-deductible dividends).

The same logic should also be used when the loan is used for purchasing of capital assets (17), though the calculation of the annual interest and depreciation is significantly more complicated, since the present value of the principle increases over the years, which leads to a consequently growing amount of depreciation every year. One may consider a practical solution: the depreciation or amortization should be based on the asset's purchasing price including the loans and no deduction for interest payments should be allowed. Once again, the important issue here is to present the idea that the tax base is too narrow due to the double interest deduction.

H. Conclusion—Real and Meaningful Comprehensive Income Tax Base Vis a Vis Raising Tax Rates

As presented above, the growing poverty and social gaps has driven some scholars, like Thomas Piketty, to suggest some radical solutions like an 80% tax rate on annual income of five to ten million USD. Alas, there are some more moderate steps that should be taken before using the "Doomsday Weapon". First, we should reconsider the elimination of the inefficient taxes on transfer payments—gift, estate and generation skipping taxes, and tax those transfer payments directly; taxing the donor on the gain derived from transfer of appreciated assets, and the donee for having received property that increases the donee's ability to pay. Second, imputed income (57) should be included within the income tax base. Third, the far-reaching realization requirement should be modified according to its original rationales, which derived from two of the canons of a good tax—the taxpayer's convenience canon and the certainty requirement canon. Fourth, the double deduction of interest should be eliminated.

In addition, some existing problems that were initiated by the legislature should be reviewed. The prominent ones are the special low tax rates for passive income and capital gains that, with the variety of tax incentives and reliefs [p. 31], that have turned the US income tax system into a regressive tax system.

All these measures could improve the implementation of a true and sincere comprehensive income tax base which follows the four canons of a good tax. [p. 9]

A subtle conclusion might be advice to Piketty. Instead of considering tax rates that might not stand a constitutional judicial review (70), closing the social gaps might be achieved by taxing the real benefit from the public goods and services, which is measured by ability to pay through a true, sincere, and meaningful comprehensive income tax base.

Chapter Fifteen

CONSUMPTION

1. CONSUMPTION AS A PERSONAL TAX SYSTEM

A popular way to describe the differences between consumption tax and income tax is to present the former as a tax that essentially taxes the taxpayers when they spend money, whereas the latter taxes them when they earn their income from their own labor, or receive passive income such as interest, dividend, capital gains, and even transfer payments. Traditional consumption taxes are usually regressive (106) and indirect, such as sales tax, value added tax [p. 115] or excise tax that applies to specific types of goods [p. 145]. In contrast, the personal consumption tax is a direct tax. Each individual taxpayer need to send an annual tax return indicating their annual consumption. Personal consumption tax may be progressive, i.e. higher tax rates on higher amounts of consumption. Measuring private consumption is not as difficult as it may sound. If it is agreed that income is equal to its usages, namely consumption plus savings and investment, then a change in that equation results in the following: consumption equals income minus savings/investment. Hence, under a consumption tax we can measure income and allow for the deduction of savings and investment payments. An additional elaboration brought scholars to name consumption tax as income tax on a cash flow basis [e.g. Professor William Andrews], meaning that every type of income or receipts on the one hand, and any outflow of money or money's worth on the other hand, are taken in consideration. A simple example should explain this. Suppose Taxpayer receives the following during the taxable period: a salary of $100,000; interest on municipal bonds of $5,000; a loan from a bank of $250,000; a dividend from a public corporation of $8,000 and the sum of $37,000 for selling an asset with an original cost of $20,000. On the other hand, he invests a sum of $125,000 in publicly traded stock; he pays a $500 interest payment on the new loan; a $400 interest payment on an old loan and repays the old loan's principal amount of $30,000. In this case his total income includes all the above receipts, (100,000+5,000+250,000+8,000+37,000=)$400,000. Note that although the gain of the sold asset is only $17,000 the full amount of $37,000 is included in the tax base, since its original cost was fully deducted—under the cash flow system—as an investment, so for the consumption tax calculation the asset's basis is zero. In addition, the new loan received, is a negative savings or negative investment, as any other debt, and should be added to the "cash flow income".

Note that when a debt (negative savings) is repaid, both principal and interest will be deductible from the consumption tax base since they represent the opposite of negative savings, i.e. part of the taxpayer's savings. Accordingly, the $125,000 investment in the stocks, plus the repayment of the old loan of $30,000 plus the total interest payments of $900 should be considered as Taxpayers total investment/savings of $155,900. Hence, total income ($400,000) minus total investments of $155,900 is Taxpayer's consumption of $244,100.

One significant problem, which is discussed below [pp. 180, 256] is that due to the immediate deduction of any investment, consumption tax has a built-in mechanism that fully taxes any income from labor, but provides a significant exemption for income from capital. Though, the scholars who support consumption tax and prefer it over traditional income tax show that a real and efficient progressive "cash-flow consumption tax" or "postpaid consumption tax" provides an exemption only for the riskless rate of return and taxes any other return to capital above the riskless rate.

2. THE DEBATE REGARDING CONSUMPTION TAX

There is extensive literature that enthusiastically supports private consumption tax as the primary personal tax system that should replace income tax. The reasons and arguments for this claim vary, beginning with Thomas Hobbes's somewhat naïve justification, which identified two human patterns of social behavior. One is socially positive behavior, which produces income and results in a communal increase in wealth ("*adding to the general pot*"). The second one represents negative and selfish behavior by the community's members, namely personal consumption that reduces the total social wealth ("*taking from the general pot*"). Since tax is a must, and unfortunately hurts those who pay it, it has to hurt the positive behavior less and discourage the negative one, which means taxing consumption rather than income. Yet as John Maynard Keynes (121) indicated almost a century ago, a reduction in personal consumption and excessive saving might create serious economic problems, inducing unemployment, recession or even depression.

One may identify John S. Mill's argument against **double taxation on saving** as the original argument for consumption tax. In a naïve way the argument, which, under income tax, has its own flaws and doubts [p. 178], refers to the fact that savings originate from earned income from labor, which has been taxed already. Assume a taxpayer has an earning from labor of \$1,000; she pays an income tax of \$300, consumes \$450 and saves \$250. The after tax savings produces \$25 (10%) a year. If the yield of \$25 is taxed, the meaning is—according to this argument—double taxation on savings since the principal (\$250) has been taxed already. A more sophisticated way to present the above relies on **the consumption tax neutrality** argument, which is based on present value calculation. The above savings of \$250 produced \$25 at the end of the first year. The taxpayer's accumulated saving without income tax is \$275, which in present value terms is equal to 275/1.1=\$250. If a 30% income tax is levied on the yield (\$25), the taxpayer pays \$7.5 and ends up with only 250+17.5=\$267.5, of which its present value (97) capitalized for one year is only (267.5/1.1=)\$243.18, which is lower than the original principal of \$250. Note though that the underlying—yet doubtful—assumption here is that the interest rate used for the capitalization is before tax (10%) [p. 178].

On the other hand, consumption tax contains a built-in mechanism that leads to a heavier burden on income from labor and preferential treatment on capital income and capital gains, which eventually leads to widening social gaps. The explanation is as follows: as is demonstrated below [p. 256], if the taxpayer is allowed to deduct from her income capital expenses, such immediate deduction provides her a significant advantage. An immediate deduction of an investment is equal to an exemption of the income derived from the investment under the following three conditions: the taxpayer has income from other sources so the immediate deduction produces a real tax saving (133) [pp. 4, 240]; the taxpayer's tax rate remains the same over the relevant taxable years; and the proceeds of the tax savings are invested in an investment that yields the same rate of return. Under this claim, and while remembering that consumption tax means the immediate deduction of any kind of savings or investment, the emerging conclusion is quite clear: consumption tax taxes income from labor more heavily than income from real capital. The consumption tax's supporters argue that "only" the riskless interest return is exempted from consumption tax, in order to avoid the double taxation on saving. Alas, the double taxation argument has its own deficiencies which are discussed below [pp. 178–179]. In addition, the impression is that a consumption tax taxes a poor taxpayer and a most wealthy but miserly one equally, which suggests that for political reasons, the chances of converting progressive income tax into progressive consumption tax might be quite slim. Furthermore, one should note that the process of moving from the current income tax to consumption tax is quite complicated and requires a very long transition period.

Chapter Sixteen

CONSUMPTION VIS A VIS INCOME

As shown above [p. 154] the deficiencies of net wealth as a tax base—mainly the uncertainty and the taxpayer's inconvenience [pp. 10–11]—leaves the two other bases to be considered: income and consumption.

Theoretically, when comparing between those two options, consumption better addresses prominent problems that income tax faces. One such problem is the higher tax rates under the progressive income tax during the taxpayer's most productive years, compared to the neutrality of consumption tax in terms of consumption-saving decisions. A second problem is the claim that income tax on passive income is indeed double taxation up to a certain level [p. 172]. The third advantage of consumption as a tax basis is that the realization requirement, which is the Achilles heel of income tax, does not pose any serious problems in the "cash flow consumption tax" system.

1. HIGHER INCOME TAX RATES OVER A SHORT PERIOD OF TIME

The first problem above derives from the arbitrariness of the progressive income tax, which is based on annual calculations. This may lead to unfair over-taxation of some taxpayers, due to the fluctuation of income over the years. Assume two single writers. One produces and sells a book each year for $25,000 over five years. The other one is able to produce only one book during the five years and sells it during just one taxable year for $125,000. Assume that the progressive tax rates Michael (98) is as follows:

Annual Income	Marginal Tax Rate	Tax Marginal Income	Accumulated Income	Accumulated Tax
$0–$25,000	5%	$1,250	$25,000	$1,250
$25,001–$50,000	10%	$2,500	$50,000	$3,750
$50,001–$75,000	15%	$3,750	$75,000	$7,500
$75,000–$100,000	20%	$5,000	$100,000	$12,500
$100,000–$125,000	25%	$7,500	$125,000	$20,000

Under these tax brackets, the first author pays (25,000*0.05=)$1,250 each year, and over the five years a total of (1,250*5=)$6,250. The second author, who reports a total income of $125,000 owes the tax authorities almost three time more—(1,250+2,500+3,750+ 5,000+7,500=)$20,000—although both have the same amount of ability to pay during the aggregate period of five years. To solve this problem, the legislature has to intervene, either by introducing a special provision within the code, which will allow the latter taxpayer to average her income over five years and include in her five annual tax returns of $25,000 each year, or to allow her to carry backwards or forwards the loses she suffers during the four years that she did not sell any book.

Furthermore, by its nature, a person's income from labor is not linear. In general terms, as babies we can't produce or earn any income, but we do consume. At a certain age, when we begin to mature, we may produce some income. Over the years this ability evolves and increases up to a certain stage—around the age of retirement. After retiring we might try to earn some money with part-time jobs, but eventually our productivity stops at a certain point before we perish entirely. In order to maintain a reasonable standard of living during these years, some special arrangements should be taken.

This earning circle/pattern during the taxpayer's lifetime is roughly represented in the illustration below:

Figure 16.1:

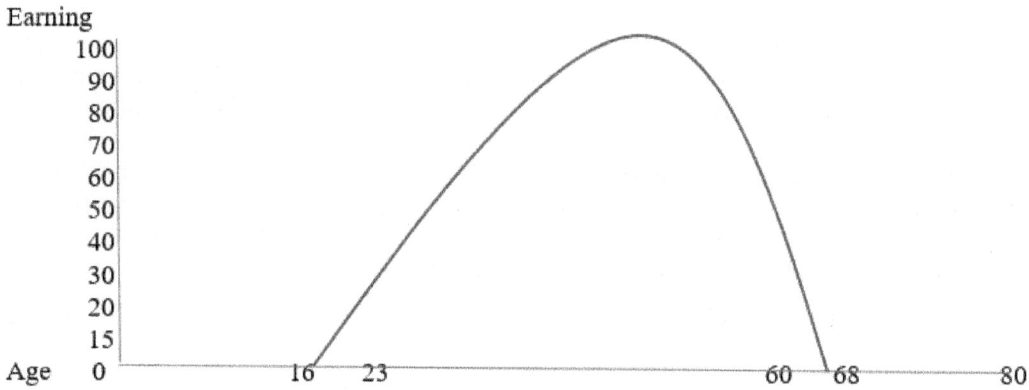

As we can see, until the age of 16 no earnings occur, and then our earning ability begins to climb to our peak around the age of 55 when we reach maximum earning ability. Then, unfortunately, the descent begins.

Once again, progressive income tax is heavier during our most productive time. As *Figure 2* shows below, when we earn significant income (in this illustration above $60,000 a year) we pay the highest income tax amount. When we earn little we pay less.

Figure 16.2:

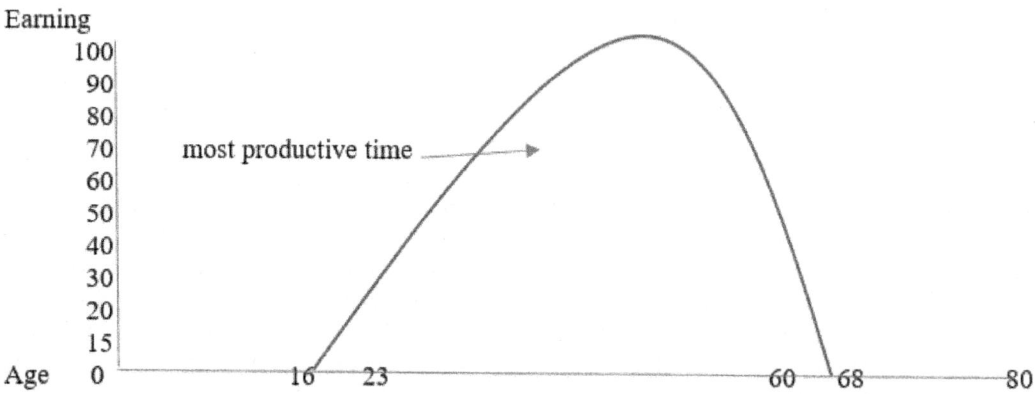

Once again we see that at the most productive time we run into higher tax rates. But somebody has to feed us as babies and children at the early stages of our life, and as elders at the end. Reasonable behavior might lead us to allocate some of our earnings during the peak years for our children's consumption, and some for our retirement. This idea may be roughly illustrated by the following *Figure 3*:

Figure 16.3:

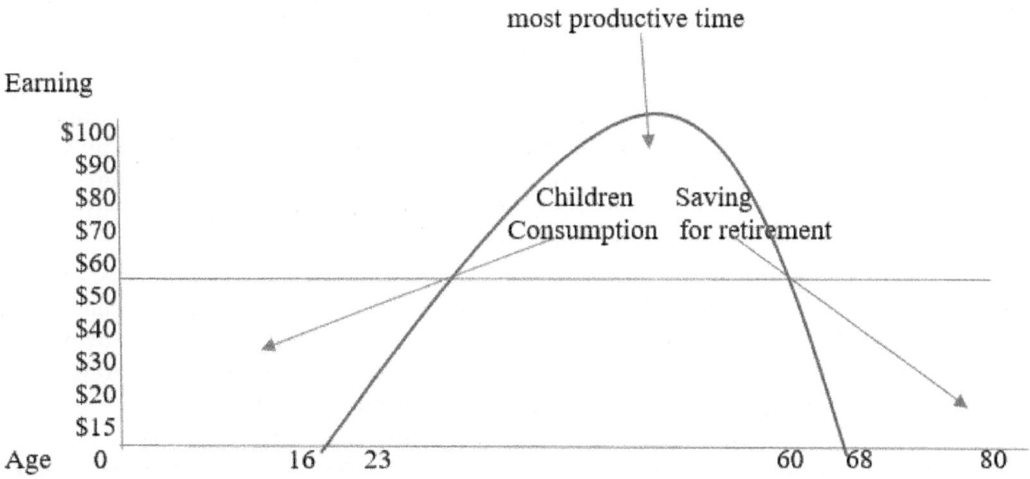

This illustration suggests that under such assumptions, a sensible taxpayer decides to set their standard of living at a constant rate of around $55,000 a year by spreading their aggregate income across 49 years (age 16 through 65) although they earn an average amount of around $85,000 a year during their working years and confine their annual standard of living to (85,000*49/80=)$52,000 by shifting the rest to pay the debts they accumulated between the ages 0 to around 16 (or by spending it on keeping up with their children's needs), and for consumption during retirement years. Hence, during every working year they move the amount needed for that purpose. The problem is that without intervention by the legislature, and due to the progressive income tax rate, they pay higher tax payments during their most productive time and won't have enough money to spread backwards and forwards, unless the legislature intervenes. The intervention might be conducted by allowing the taxpayers personal exemptions for their dependents—mostly children—and special deductions for contributions to pension plans like IRAs [pp. 253, 324].

Contrary to income tax, consumption tax is more considerate and liberal. Indeed, it has a built-in mechanism that solves the income fluctuation problem. It allows the taxpayer to determine the date of their tax liability according to their decisions as to the amount of their annual private consumption and its timing. Consumption tax allows the taxpayer to average their income over their lifetime according to their priorities, decisions and patterns of consumption. If we are totally reasonable decision-makers, consumption tax leads us to make the right decisions and average our consumption together with our annual consumption tax payments. One problem is that behavioral economic studies shed some doubts on whether we indeed take this direction. Do we have enough self-discipline to confine our spending when we have a lot of money and save it for a rainy day?

On the other hand, staying with income tax, which grants personal exemptions for dependents—including young children—and very attractive tax incentives for savings in designated pension plans, such as Investment Retirement Accounts (IRAs) might be more effective (especially if the penalties on early withdrawal are removed) in terms of spreading our life-time earnings and reducing the total tax payments during our most productive years.

Note that such exemptions and deductions for saving indirectly change the income tax system into a hybrid system that contains some of consumption tax's traits.

2. DOUBLE TAXATION ON CAPITAL INVESTMENT?

A second claim is that income tax on passive income is indeed inappropriate double taxation, up to a certain level [p. 172]. The validity of this claim is somehow blurry and doubtful. Remember that the goal is to tax the taxpayers according to their benefit, measured by their economic ability, regardless of its sources. Taxing the fruits of the taxpayer's labor is one component of their economic ability and taxing the return on their after-tax saving is another lair. For example: a young high-school graduate works very hard, make a nice income, pays her income tax and saves for a few years, earns interest up to a stage where she can pay, with her after tax saving, for her studies over seven years and becomes a lawyer. After graduation her income for her new profession is subject to income tax, although it should be considered as the return on her after-tax investment i.e. the cost of her studies. The conclusion is quite evident. As long as the education cost is deductible or depreciated, the supporters of the consumption tax face a real challenge: What is the difference between a saver who uses her savings on a financial investment and a saver who spends her savings by investing in her own human capital? As long as we are simply looking for the taxpayers' ability to pay, the origin of the ability is irrelevant.

As is shown below, there are some more serious doubts regarding the argument that consumption tax is indeed neutral.

3. IS CONSUMPTION TAX INDEED NEUTRAL?

A major argument is that income tax has a built-in incentive for early consumption whereas consumption tax is totally neutral; it does not encourage saving or consumption. This argument may be presented by the following illustration: Imagine two taxpayers: Sonya—a saver—and Carl—a consumer. Both are making an annual income of $1,000, which is received at the end of the first year.

In a world without taxes Carl consumes the amount of $1,000 at the end of the first year. Sonya decides to postpone her consumption for the second year and saves the $1,000, earns the market interest rate (10%) and ends up at the end of the second year with a consumption of $1,100, which is equal to the present value (97) of Carl's consumption, i.e. (1,100/1.1=)$1,000. (Note though, as is discussed below, that there are some doubts whether mere consumption should be capitalized for present value calculations).

Now assume the government enacted a 30% income tax. Carl pays $300 in income tax and consumes $700 at the end of the first year. Sonya pays $300 at the end of the first year as well, saves $700 and earns $70. Yet, since under income tax interest is taxed like any other income, she also pays a 30% tax of (70×0.3=)$21 on the interest she receives at the end of the first year and ends up with a total consumption at the end of the second year of [(700+(70×0.3)=]$749. In terms of present value it is seems that Carl is in a better situation: he was able to consume $700 at the end of the first year. Sonya, on the other hand, was able to consume $749, but only after waiting a full year. In present value's terms, compared to Carl, she consumes only (749/1.1=)$680.9. Hence, so goes the argument, under the income tax system the consumer has greater consumption, meaning there is an incentive to consume earlier and give up saving!

Now assume the government enacts a consumption tax instead, and intends to collect the same revenue. Carl still consumes the same amount ($700) at the end of the first year and pays $300 consumption tax (which is around a 42.8% rate). Yet the interest Sonya earns during the second year is not taxed (remember, no tax on income but only on consumption, i.e. income minus saving) and she is able to have $1,100, pay a consumption tax of $330 and consume $770, which is, in present value terms (770/1.1= $700), equal to Carl's consumption ($700) a year earlier. Hence consumption tax is neutral; there is no incentive for saving or consuming, and the decision of when to save and when to consume is left to the taxpayer's discretion and personal taste.

There are two significant doubts about the above neutrality argument, which we mentioned already. One is the interest rate used for present value calculation. The second one is a theoretical question—should consumption be capitalized at all?

With regard to the first question, the above calculations are based on the before-tax interest rate, i.e. 10%. Yet, under income tax system, both Sonya and Carl are subject to a 30% income tax rate, and one may wonder whether the interest rate that should be used for capitalization for a specific taxpayer is their ***net rate of return***, namely, under the example above, [10%−(0.3×10)=]7% interest for Carl and Sonya. In that case, we end up with the same amount of consumption in present value terms (97) for both Sonya and Carl even under income tax. Sonya's consumption of $749 in the second year, capitalized with 7% for one year produces the present value amount of (747/1.07=)$700, i.e. the same amount of Carl's consumption. Under this assumption income tax is neutral while consumption tax has a built-in incentive for saving. Under consumption tax Sonia has $1,100 in the second year, pays a consumption tax of $330 and consumes $770, which is, in present value terms (770/1.07=)$719.6, which is greater than Carl's consumption ($700) a year earlier.

4. PRESENT VALUE OF CONSUMPTION?

Regardless of the question of whether the interest rate that is used for present value calculations (97) should be before or after tax, a more general and essential doubt rises. Is it right to capitalize deferred consumption at all? After all, the taxpayer who earns the interest on her saving has an additional accretion to wealth; she is better-off than those taxpayers who did not save and did not earn such additional power to consume. Assume the cost of a round trip to Rome plus staying at a bed & breakfast is $2,500, whereas the same trip with three additional meals in a fine restaurant is $2,675. Both Carl and Sonia earned $3,571.50, and under income tax system paid 30% income tax and have a net amount of $2,500. Carl took the trip in the current year, whereas Sonia, for personal and professional reasons, decided to wait a year, made a deposit in her bank of the $2,500 and earned 10% ($250) interest, paid 30% income tax ($75), and took a better trip compared to the one Carl took in the previous year. Since she had additional disposable money ($125) she buys and enjoys the additional three meals. No doubt, she enjoyed her trip and consumed more than Carl (by $125), though it took place a year later. Indeed, in present value, under the traditional approach, she enjoyed (2,675/1.1=) $2,431.80, which is less than Carl's consumption ($2,500) (though, as illustrated above, if using the net interest rate—in this example 7% there are no differences between the two, even in terms of present value calculations) (97). But the mere idea of capitalizing a person's private consumption is quite strange. What if Sonia could not take the trip in year 1? What if Carl wanted to defer his trip to year 2, but could not take a leave from his office and reluctantly took it in year 1? It seems that when the issue is personal consumption there are too many variables that dictate the timing of the consumption, hence it is much more sensible to assume, in the above example, that the same pleasure Carl had in the first year's trip is equal to Sonia's pleasure from raising her baby during this year. What if instead of the extra three meals, Sonia was able to pay for the trip for her baby who joined her to Rome?

In short, when Sonia waited a year, saved the money from the first year, earned some interest that allowed her to spend more on her trip in the second year, she consumed more, and has a higher economic ability than Carl and should pay more tax.

5. REALIZATION IS NOT A REAL PROBLEM ALSO UNDER A SINCERE COMPREHENSIVE INCOME TAX BASE

As discussed above [p. 163], the traditional interpretation of the realization requirement poses some real challenges for the income tax system. Yet we saw already that those challenges may be solved quite easily by two kinds of solutions which derive from the Haig-Simons definition. One is the application of the idea of taxing the taxpayers' imputed income (57) [p. 160]. The second one is to treat any use of the appreciation of the taxpayers' asset as realization. A careful combination of these two measures can provide a satisfactory solution to the realization requirement, though with some administrative complications [p. 163].

6. TAXING LABOR ONLY?

A final comment about the relationship between the taxation of labor and capital and the overall tax burden: we saw that taxing consumption means taxing labor more heavily than capital income (e.g. Professor Alvin Warren). Taxing income means taxing both labor and capital. Yet in most of the countries, in addition to income tax, there are direct consumption taxes, such as VAT or sale taxes. Hence, when evaluating the domestic tax system and the balance between the tax on labor and on capital, the impact of the direct consumption tax should be taken into consideration as well. In other words, even under a completely balanced income tax—labor and capital are taxed equally with identical tax rates—the overall tax burden on labor is heavier than on capital due to the direct consumption taxes. Assume a family with an annual income of $25,000. It pays a 5% income tax of $1,250 and consumes the remaining $23,750 on basic consumption. If there is an additional direct consumption tax (sales tax, VAT, or GST)—(145) [p. 114] of 10%, the total burden of the family is (1,250+2,375=)$3,625, which is a (3,625/25,000=) 14.5% tax rate, almost three times the designated income tax rate for the family's income. If the income tax system offers some significant preferences to capital income, including lower tax rates for interest and capital gains and some tax deferral for certain non-realized capital gains, then the imbalance between the taxation of labor and capital is more severe. Such a system adds a significant dimension to the most worrying phenomenon of growing social gaps throughout the last centuries in the Western societies [pp. 72, 90]. Replacing a comprehensive income tax system with a consumption tax system will surely intensify this phenomenon.

7. CONSUMPTION V. INCOME—CONCLUSION

The debate about the more appropriate personal tax system has not yet been settled. The literature that supports consumption tax is growing. The variety of the proposals and their names are extensive: "X tax", "A Consumption-Type or Cash-Flow Personal

Income Tax"; "labor earnings tax" and lately "a postpaid consumption tax" which can be progressive and, under certain circumstances and careful design, be made to tax the yield to capital as the source of present consumption. Yet, as indicated above, some of the premises and assumptions used by the supporters of consumption tax are in doubt. In addition, as law professor Michael Graetz concluded some 40 years ago, the cost of moving from the current income tax system and replacing it with a general consumption tax—including a long generational transitional period—is not worth the benefit, if indeed there is a benefit. In addition, the chances that consumption taxes will intensify the growing gaps between capital and labor earners are quite high.

On the other hand, keeping the general income tax system with some modifications (special deductions for dependents and for pension plans; improving the method of income averaging over several years and reexamining the carry forward and backwards loses; updating the realization requirement and taxing imputed income) (57) might be a better choice.

The following flow chart presents the process of several stages that helps us to evaluate the qualities and attributes of the possible tax bases in terms of the four canons of good tax and according to the basic requirements for a good tax system. [p. 9]

Figure 16.4:

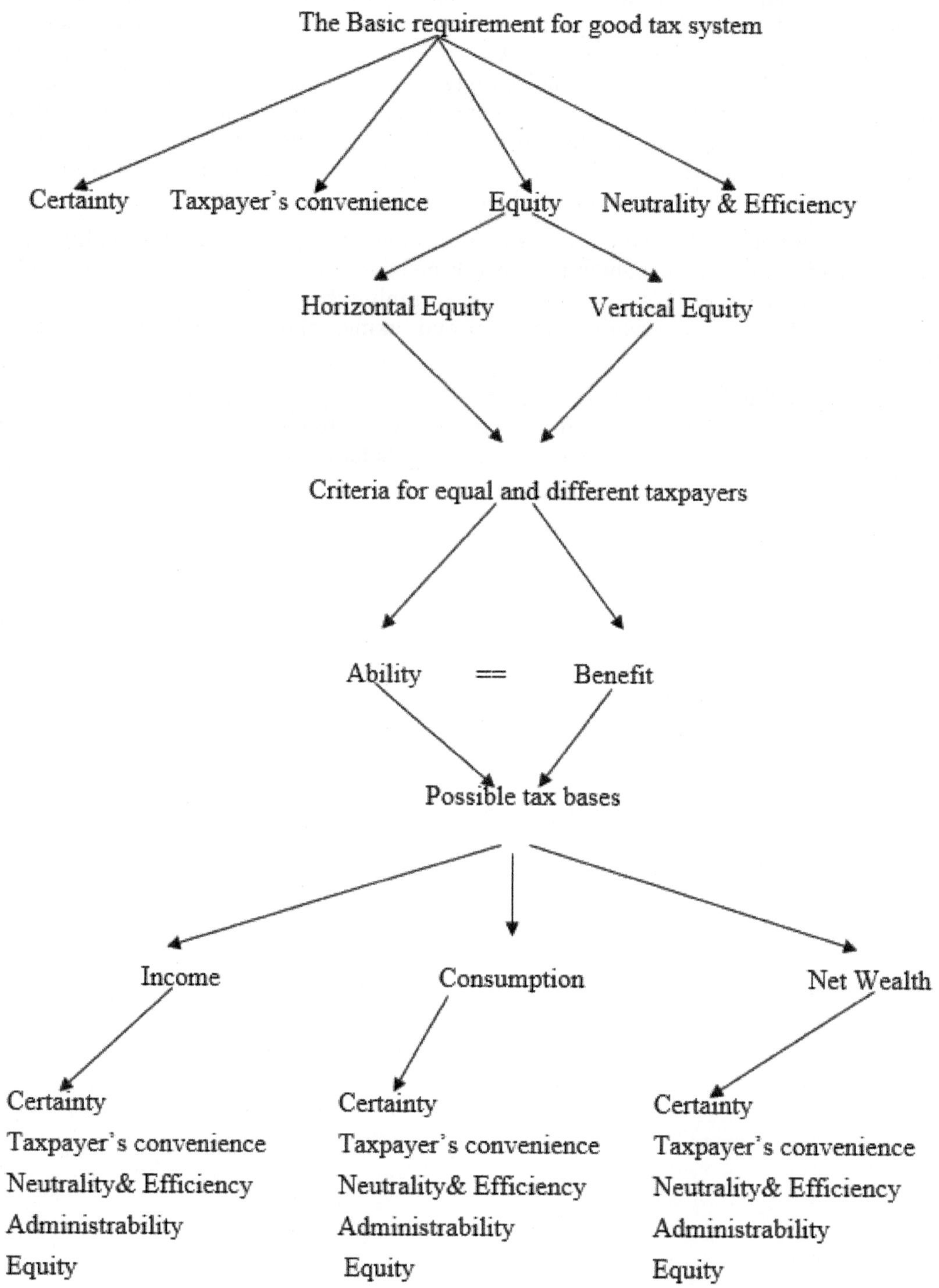
The Basic requirement for good tax system
Certainty
Taxpayer's convenience
Equity
Neutrality & Efficiency
Horizontal Equity
Vertical Equity
Criteria for equal and different taxpayers
Ability
==
Benefit
Possible tax bases
Income
Consumption
Net Wealth
Certainty
Taxpayer's convenience
Neutrality& Efficiency
Administrability
Equity
Certainty
Taxpayer's convenience
Neutrality& Efficiency
Administrability
Equity
Certainty
Taxpayer's convenience
Neutrality& Efficiency
Administrability
Equity

Part Five

ANALYZING THE U.S.A. INCOME TAX SYSTEM

BACKGROUND

Now that the foundation of the theory, the concepts, the principles and the goals of a good tax are laid, this part studies the American income tax system, its advantages and deficiencies.

1. A BRIEF HISTORY OF THE AMERICAN INCOME TAX

In 1862, in order to support the Civil War effort, the U.S. Congress enacted the nation's first income tax law, which was based on the principles of graduated or progressive taxation (98) and of withholding income tax (136) at the source. After the Civil War, in 1872, the Federal Income Tax was repealed. In 1894, a federal income tax was passed by the Congress. In the following year, the Supreme Court held that the tax was unconstitutional, due to the apportionment requirement. Consequently, the requirement was removed in 1913 by the 16th Amendment [p. 40]. In the same year, Congress passed the Revenue Act of 1913, imposing an income tax on both individuals and corporations. Initially, the tax was conceived as a "class tax" on the wealthy, since only the individuals with the very highest incomes paid it. It was noted that an average of 5.6 percent of the total population were covered by taxable returns in the period from1918 to 1932. During wartimes, World War I and particularly World War II, the income tax expanded dramatically to finance the war effort. In the midst of World War II the tax converted from a "class" to a "mass" tax. This change is also reflected by the top marginal individual tax rate that, upon the enactment of the tax, went from about 7% (1% normal tax and a 6% surtax) up to 90% at the end of the Second World War. While the top marginal tax rate was high for the next three decades, the code was filled with "loopholes", and a panoply of tax preferences and exclusions for fringe benefits and deductions. The Tax Reform Act of 1986, which is considered by many as the most extensive overhaul reform of the Federal tax system since the income tax was enacted, was intended to move away from a system that was used to achieve and accomplish goals other than the raising of revenue. Its purpose was to broaden the tax base by eliminating many tax reliefs and preferences, closing significant "loopholes", and simultaneously lowering the top effective marginal tax rate to 28%. In the years following the 1986 tax reform, many of the reform's achievements were eroded by the enactment of dozens of targeted tax breaks (122), (131), new and innovative "tax shelters", and aggressive tax planning. Currently, the dire need for a comprehensive tax reform seems apparent.

As for the revenue amounts, and some interesting data and estimations [pp. 93–95], according to the IRS, in 2019, taxpayers filed 148.3 million tax returns, reported earning nearly $11.9 trillion in adjusted gross income, and paid $1.6 trillion in individual income taxes. The Congressional Budget Office (CBO) estimates that the federal government received $370 billion in corporate tax revenue over the fiscal year 2021. Furthermore, we mentioned already [pp. 93–96] the incredible estimation regarding the average income tax rate of the wealthiest 400 billionaire families in America paid an average of just 8.2 percent of their income—including income from their wealth that goes largely untaxed.

2. THE STRUCTURE

The key issue, as we emphasize quite often, is the starting Archimedes point, the first stage, which is the definition of income as the tax base. First, we realize that there is an accurate and economic definition, namely the Haig-Simons equation. Yet the statutory starting point is "Gross Income", a concept that eventually led to a meaningful deviation from the economic definition. One may identify three major expressions of this deviation. The first is a long list of statutory exemptions (43) introduced by legislators to the definition. Second, the non-taxation of imputed income (57). The third one is the far reaching interpretation of the realization requirement (103). All of these have significantly eroded the U.S. income tax base.

A naïve assumption is that these three traits are the result of rational legal evolution. A more realistic assumption might be that these traits, which narrow the tax base, serve some specific interest groups, i.e. the wealthiest.

Once we finish with the tax base, we proceed and study the remaining components of the U.S. income tax system through the eleven stages model.

The following flow chart aims to enable us to see the whole picture and not to be lost in the complicated details of the system. It is the frame of our journey. It describes the eleven basic stages one should consider in order to reach the final tax payments of an individual taxpayer. As we proceed, we discover some more "stations" or "stops" that we use for getting to our final destination. Yet, the chart is just an auxiliary tool meant to help perceiving the whole picture. Nothing is sacred within it.

The U.S.A. Income Tax System in a Nutshell:

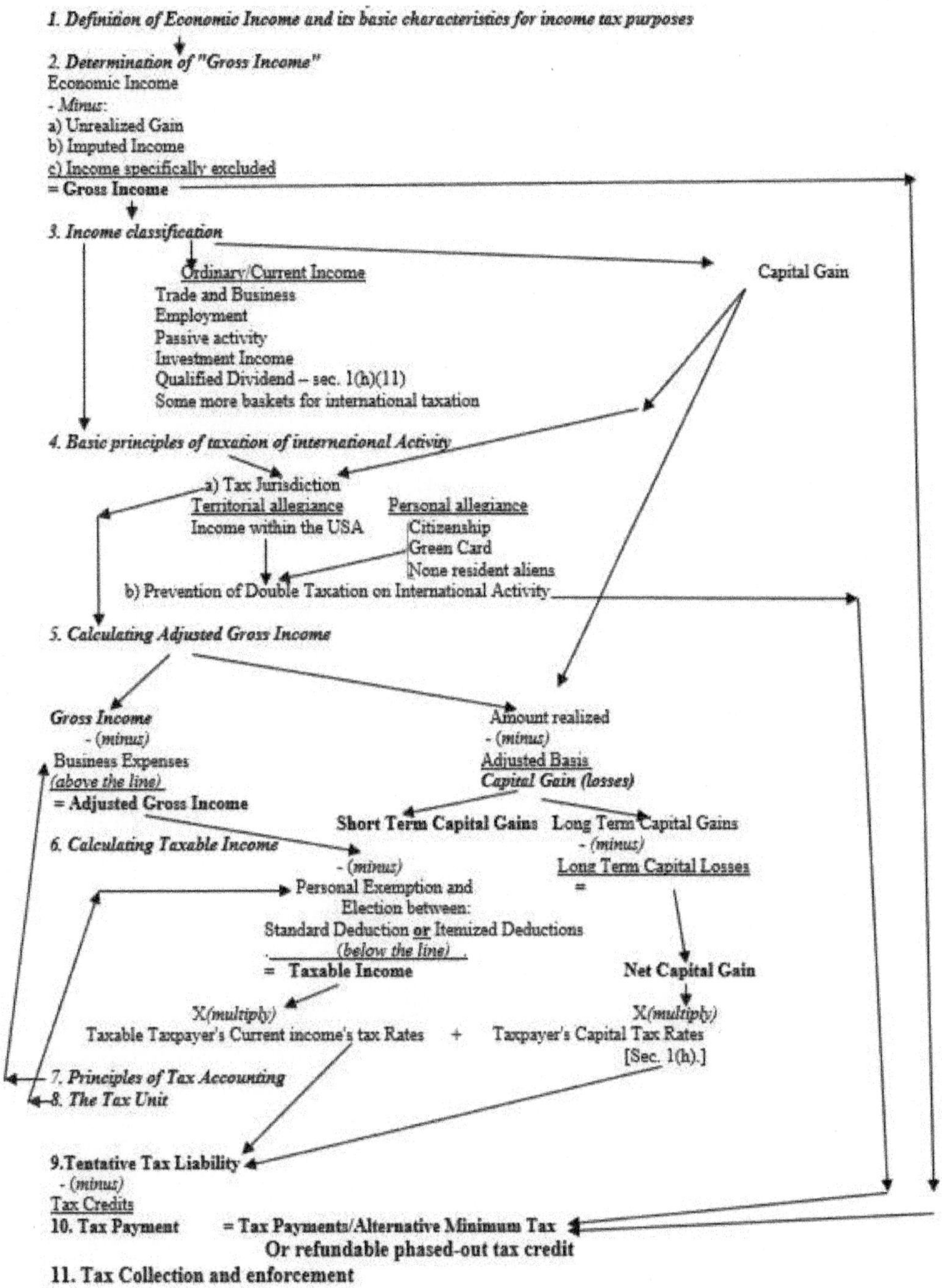

Chapter Seventeen

STAGE ONE—THE INCOME TAX BASE DEFINITION AND ITS ATTRIBUTES

1. THE TAX BASE—STATUTORY PROVISIONS

Since 1874, the **Internal Revenue Code** (hereafter the Code or IRC) is the main body of the domestic Federal statutory tax laws of the U.S.A. that deals with income tax, employment taxes, estate and gift taxes and various excise taxes. The current Internal Revenue Code of 1986 is published as Title 26 of the U.S.A. (USC).

Code Sec. 1 imposes the Federal income tax on the taxable income of U.S. citizens and residents, and on estates and trusts. Nonresident aliens are subject to federal income tax on their income earned within the U.S.A. [Sec. 871]. The corporate income tax is imposed by Code Sec. 11.

Code Sec. 61 further elaborates the definition of gross income: "Except as otherwise provided in this subtitle, gross income means all income from whatever **source** derived, including (but not limited to) 15 items".

As mentioned already [p. 157], the term income may be approached from two aspects—the sources side and the usage side.

A. Defining Income from the Sources Side

The resemblance of Code sec. 61 to the narrow British approach of defining the term income for income tax purposes [p. 158] is quite evident, probably because the first U.S. Revenue Act of 1892 was heavily inspired by the British income tax system.

As explained, [p. 158] the ***narrow approach*** puts its emphasis on the term *source* which is also used in IRC Sec. 61. According to this approach, which was developed by the British and their colonies, income for tax purposes includes only receipts that have a constant source; income, for purposes of income tax, must derive from a fixed "*source*" that yields revenue income. In the absence of a source, there is no "income" to be taxed. In early cases, the U.S. Supreme Court followed the major British trend and stated in 1913: *"Income may be defined as the gain derived from capital, from labor, or from both combined."* Seven years later the Court added an important proviso: *[the definition of income] include profit gained through a sale or conversion of capital assets*. It took another 33 years—probably due to significant pressure of scholastic literature [p. 159]—for the Court to signal the complete departure from the "Source doctrine" and to adopt a comprehensive definition: *"income means undeniable accessions to wealth, clearly realized, and over which the taxpayers have complete dominion* [p. 135]*"*. This famous quotation represents the Haig-Simons equation, a *Comprehensive Tax Base*. I.e. taxing the taxpayer according to their economic ability regardless of its sources. Alas, later developments brought some reservations to this new trend. Instead of using a sincere comprehensive tax base, the legislature chose to narrow the economic approach by introducing a legal concept, namely the term "**Gross Income**" as the tax base. That enabled the legislators, influential interest groups, and politicians, to erode the tax base by introducing various exclusions. The most significant one is the exclusion of accretion to wealth that is created by inheritances and gifts [pp. 135, 143]. In addition, the tax authority never made a sincere effort to include within the Gross Income imputed income (57) that the taxpayers consume enjoying their own property [p. 160]. Furthermore, the courts, as a general rule, provided a broad interpretation of the realization requirement (103), and hence further narrowed the income tax base [p. 160]. Consequently, what should have been an easy and simple chore—defining the income tax base in a straight, equal and democratic way—has turned out to be a complicated mission [pp. 147, 160], which requires some elaboration, guidelines and attributes in order to comprehend the full meaning of the term Gross Income for the U.S. income tax system.

B. Defining Income from the Uses Side

The above equation of income = consumption + saving [p. 157] is sustained only as long as the term income, from its sources side, is indeed comprehensive. Once we realize that under the American system the term Gross Income has been narrowed, the equation does not hold any longer. Assume a taxpayer plans to live very lavishly. During the taxable year he does not work. His aunt passed away and left him a bank account with one million dollars. His uncle left him a very nice house worth $800,000, with an annual fair market value rent of around $48,000 and annual depreciation of 2%. An old painting that he bought for $5 in a garage sale turned out to be an original work of art by a famous artist and is appraised to be worth $25,000. The taxpayer lives in the new house he now owns. He takes half of the million dollars and spends it on a three-month exclusive tour around the world. He keeps the rest of the money and invested it in tax-free municipal bonds and receives 5% interest.

He applies to get a $20,000 loan and the bank agrees, provided the appreciated work of art serves as a security. Once he gets the loaned money, he uses it for a travel to the FIFA World Cup in Qatar. Under the U.S. income tax system his Gross income is only $25,000, since the two inheritances are excluded from Gross Income, the appreciation of the work of art is considered an unrealized gain [p. 165], and the imputed income is not taxed in the U.S.A. [p. 160]. Nevertheless, on the usage side his consumption is (500,000 trip+48,000 dwelling+20,000 FIFA game=)$568,000. His saving is [500,000 bank account+(800,000 house−16,000 annual depreciation)+the reinvested interest of $25,000=]$1,309,000 and the total consumption and saving is $1,877,000.

The difference between the income from the sources side, under the current U.S. income tax system, and from the usage side is amazing: around $1,852,000! (Note that since the $25,000 municipal bonds' interest is tax exempted the difference between his economic income and taxable income is even larger).

If the U.S. tax system would follow the application of the Haig-Simonds definition that still acknowledges the realization requirement, but up to its reasonable application, the taxpayer's income from the sources side would be as follows:

The two inheritances=$1,800,000 Imputed income (57) [p. 197] from the house (48,000−16,000 depreciation)=$32,0000 [pp. 191, 212, 260–263].

Realized gain from the work of art's appreciation=$20,000 (though the total gain was $25,000 only the loan proceeds should be considered realized [pp. 160–168]).

Municipal bonds' interest=$25,000

Total income=$1,877,000.

In this case, income from the sources side (1,877,000) = Consumption + Saving (1,877,000) from the usage side. As indicated this is not the current U.S. income tax system's approach.

2. INCOME'S ATTRIBUTES/TRAITS

A. Income Represents Gain, Profit or Accretion

Whatever the definition adopted for the term income as a measurement for As indicated this is not the current U.S. income tax system's approach. Yet, one rule is clear: there is no income, unless there is a gain, enrichment, or accretion/addition to wealth. Receipt of money that does not represent gain, profit, or accretion is not considered income. Therefore, a receipt of a free-market interest loan is not considered income of the lender, since it does not signify accretion or addition to one's economic ability. The cash that the taxpayer receives is offset by their obligation to repay the loan. This can be demonstrated by the following simple example:

At the beginning of Year 1, B receives a loan of $100 for three years with an accrued-compound interest (64) rate of 10% per year (the market interest rate). Immediately after the loan is made, B's balance sheet is as follows:

	Cash	Liabilities	Liabilities' Present Value	Enrichment
Year 1	100	$133.1	$(133.1/1.1^3)$=$100	0

Therefore, so long as the taxpayer pays the loan's principal plus the market interest, the mere receipt of the cash does not enrich him and he does not have any taxable income.

However, if B receives a subsidized loan, for example, with an interest rate of 5%, while the market interest rate is 10%, then it is easy to see how the subsidized loan enriches him:

	Cash	Liabilities	Liabilities' Present Value	Enrichment
Year 1	100	$115.76	$(115.76/1.1^3)$=$86.97	$13.03

If the loan is given to him in consideration for the use of his factors of production, the enrichment ("the saved interest") is part of the compensation. If the loan was made between relatives or friends, the enrichment might be considered as a gift.

This simple example has a bonus: it demonstrates another trait of income, i.e. income does not have to be monetary, but rather can also be in kind, equivalent to money, money worth. The above amount of $13.03 was not given to the taxpayer in cash; the cash—the principal—he got was paid back. His income was the economic benefit derived from using somebody else's money for below market price.

Furthermore, suppose now that the lender waives the loan and the debt is canceled. In that case, once again, the borrower has accretion to his wealth:

	Cash	Liabilities	Liabilities' Present Value	Enrichment
Year 1	100	$0	$(0/1.1^3)$=$0	$100

Once we agree that if there is no profit, gain, or enrichment, we face the problem of defining real economic gain during inflationary times. Suppose an asset was bought some 30 years ago and had increased in value at the same rate as the increase in consumer prices. In real terms there is no gain. Hence, taxation of capital gain or even ordinary income should take this fact into account, since taxing these illusionary gains effectively becomes a confiscation of wealth and changes the tax basis.

There are two notable ways to cope with the inflation phenomenon for income tax purposes. With regard to capital gain, the solution is actually very simple. The purchase price of each asset is indexed to the official Consumer Price Index (CPI) published at the day of the purchase. When the asset is sold with a nominal gain the basis is adjusted to the inflation rate and only gain above the inflationary one should be considered as real taxable gain. Suppose a taxpayer purchases a capital asset on October 2000 for $1,000. The CPI was 135 point. She sells the asset on February 2010 for $2,500, when the CPI is 152. Under such assumptions her nominal gain of (2,500−1,000=)$1,500, is divided into two components: the inflationary gain is 1,000−(1,000*152/135)=$126 and the rest (1,500−126=)$1,124 is a real gain.

An interesting question is what happens in the opposite case, when a nominal profit is created for the taxpayer but a real term calculation results in an inflationary loss? For example, suppose the selling price in the above example is only $1,100. In that case the real economic loss is (1,126−1,100=)$116. To the best of our knowledge, the tax authorities known to us do not recognize such a loss for tax purposes.

The above indexing process for capital assets would be too complicated for current income, especially for stock in trade. A practical solution would be to ignore such calculations as long as the annual inflation rate is reasonable, and to adjust only the progressive tax rates for individuals to the annual inflation rate. Note though that by allowing such an adjustment we undermine the role of income tax as an automatic stabilizer [p. 82].

A final note regarding enrichment. A healthy person has the ability to produce a certain amount of money, and his economic value is measured accordingly. If he is hurt, his economic value goes down. He suffers a loss. In case he wins a tort suit (or receives money from his insurer) the loss is recovered. Hence the compensation does not cause any enrichment or accretion to wealth; recovery means he is back to his previous position. Therefore, the compensation (excluding punitive damages) should not be included within gross income to begin with. Surprisingly enough, the Court of Appeals of D.C. did not see it this way. In the *Murphy* case [pp. 41, 245] the final decision was that the taxpayer's compensation for emotional distress could be taxed under Article I, Section 8 of the Constitution even if the recovery was not classified as "income" under the Sixteenth Amendment and that gross income under IRC Section 61 includes compensatory damages for non-physical injuries, even if the award is not an "accession to wealth". As the court commented: "Principles of statutory interpretation could show § 61(a) includes Murphy's award in her gross income regardless whether it was an 'accession to wealth,' as Glenshaw Glass requires". No doubt, the *Murphy* case is very problematic, yet the Supreme Court declined to review it.

One explanation is that the Courts did not appreciate or believe that emotional distress could be a cause for a serious economic loss. Otherwise, the decision that might shed some doubts on the first trait of income i.e. that it represents a gain, profit or accretion to wealth.

B. Capital Recovery Is Not Income

Another trait of the term income for income tax purposes, which will help us understand the complex rules pertaining to depreciation and amortization deduction (20, 21, 30), is that a recovery of capital invested is not income. When a person invests money to purchase an asset that will produce future income ("capital asset"—17, 20), and the asset produces income, part of it constitutes a recovery ("refund") of the investment and does not represent profit, earning, or gain; it is neither accretion to wealth nor personal consumption. For instance, a capital asset is purchased for $379. In the first year, the asset produces $100. If we assume that by the end of the year the value of the asset decreases to $303.20, then, out of the proceeds of $100, the decline of the asset's value ($75.80) represents a capital recovery and only the balance of $24.20(100−75.80) is a gain that should be taxed as taxable income [p. 262].

Another way to reach the same result is by determining that the amount of the annual decrease in value, (in the example 379−303.20=$75.80), is the amount of *annual depreciation* (30, 31) that is deductible annually against gross income. In the above example, gross income of $100 minus the annual depreciation of $75.80 equals an adjusted taxable income [p. 248] of $24.20.

A good example of the need to identify the capital recovery is the taxation of annuity (11). Annuity is a financial product sold by financial institutions, usually insurance companies, which accept deposited funds from an individual and then, at a certain date, pay out to the beneficiaries a stream of continuing payments with a fixed total monthly or annual amounts. The calculation of the annual payments is based on a "**sinking fund**" method, meaning that the individual receives back all of their deposited principal plus interest. Accordingly, each payment contains two components: one is the return on the deposit, usually interest; the other is the recovery of the investment. In a way, annuity is similar to a "reversed" mortgage where the bank-lender loans the initial principal to the individual borrower, and the borrower pays back fixed monthly payments composed of the interest and the refund of the loan's principal.

There are several types of annuities. The two major ones are a fixed time annuity and a life annuity. A fixed time annuity is a terminating stream of fixed payments over a specified and limited period of time. A life annuity provides payments for the individual's lifetime. The taxation of the former should be quite straight forward; the interest is taxable, and the recovery of the principal is tax free since it does not represent any accretion to wealth, but rather a non-taxable "capital recovery".

1) Alternative Calculations for Extracting the Capital Recovery out of the Annuity Installment

For a simple example of a ***fixed annuity,*** assume that a beneficiary's initial investment is $100,000, the interest rate is 5% and on a certain date the beneficiary begins to receive a fixed payment of $1,056.25 a month for 10 years. In that case, the expected aggregate amount is equal to (1056.25*12*10=)$126,750, hence the total gain is $26,750. If the beneficiary received the amount of $126,750 in one installment, then the $100,000 represents capital recovery and the $26,750 represents taxable gain. Alas, since the annuity provides 120 monthly installments, the extraction of the interest or the capital recovery is more complicated.

One way to tax the interest is to wait the whole 10-year period and, at the end of the 120th month, the taxpayer should be taxed on the accumulated interest of $26,750. Such a method should not be considered seriously; it represents a significant tax deferral since part of the gain is realized already on the first installment.

Another way is to tax the first 25 installments in full (1056.25*25=)$26,406.25; out of the 26th installment, $443.75 is part of the taxable gain, and the rest of the payments are non-taxable capital recovery. This option is also not reasonable because it results in premature taxation of profits that have not yet been created or realized.

Both alternatives are wrong since the former represents tax deferral, whereas the latter represents premature taxation. The most accurate way is to identify both components—i.e. the capital recovery and the return-interest—in each of the 120 installments. According to the sinking fund method and the compound interest calculation, the first installments should contain higher interest amounts and smaller capital recovery. As time goes on, the ratio changes: the interest component declines and the capital recovery goes up. Since the financial institution bases its payments on such calculations it can provide the taxpayer an accurate report.

In a ***life annuity*** all the parties (the beneficiary, the paying institution and the IRS) do not know how many installments will be actually paid to the beneficiary. Though the institution bases its calculation on assumptions regarding the beneficiary's life expectancy, the chances are that the beneficiary might live longer or shorter than expected. In the former case the beneficiary gains more than expected and under the latter he gains less since he may not receive all his initial principal.

2) The Statutory Formula

Under the U.S. income tax system, the legislature provides a statutory solution, i.e. a statutory formula aimed to extract the capital recovery from each installment. The underlying assumption of the statutory solution is based on a concession; i.e. in some cases the taxpayer ends up paying too much in taxes while not being able to fully recover the initial investment, while in other cases—if the taxpayer lives longer than expected—they will be considered as receiving tax-exempt capital recovery in each installment although they already received back all their initial investment.

According to Code Sec. 72, the capital recovery component in an annuity is determined by a statutory formula. First, the "exclusion ratio" should be computed. It is equal to the investment in the annuity divided by the expected return; the expected return is the total amount the taxpayer expects to receive under the annuity contract. If payments are for a fixed period or a fixed amount, the total payments is the sum of the guaranteed payments. [Code § 72(c)(3)(B); Reg. § 1.72–5(c)]. If payments are to continue for life, the expected return is determined by multiplying the sum of one year's annuity payments by the statutory life expectancy, which is based on statutory actuarial tables prescribed by the Secretary of the Treasury [Code § 72(c)(3)(A); Reg. § 1.72–5(a)].

The second stage computes the capital recovery component ("Amount excluded from gross income") by multiplying the exclusion ratio and the annuity payment.

The amount excluded from taxable income represents the portion of the annuity payment that is considered a return of capital. The remaining portion of the payment represents the interest element and is taxable [I.R.C. § 61(a)(9)]. The annuity starting date is defined as the "first day of the first period for which an amount is received as an annuity" [Reg. § 1.72–4(b)].

3) A Numerical Calculation—a Fixed Annuity

Using the above example, suppose the initial investment is indeed $100,000 and each monthly installment is $1,056.25. The contract guarantees a fixed period (10 years) with no life expectancy involved. The amount excluded from taxable income is computed as follows:

First, the exclusion ratio is determined at the time annuity payments first begin ("the annuity starting date"):

$100,000 (Investment)

$126,750 (Expected Return)=0.789 (Exclusion Ratio)

The exclusion ratio is applied to each payment as follows: (Exclusion Ratio) 0.789*1,056.25 (monthly installment)=$834 (Amount Excluded from Taxable Income). Accordingly the taxable component is (1056.25−834=)$223.

4) A Numerical Calculation—a Life Annuity

Assume now that the taxpayer invests $100,000 and the institute agrees to pay $1,000 each month for the taxpayers' lifetime. Assume that the statutory life expectancy is 12 years (144 months). In that case the expected return is equal to (1,000*144=) $144,000; the exclusion ratio is (100,000/144,000=)0.694 and the amount excluded from taxable income is (1,000*0.694=)$694, whereas the $306 is taxable income.

With regard to other kinds of capital investment, the computation of the annual amount of the capital recovery is not a simple matter and it will be discussed below [p. 256].

C. Income in Kind—Non-Monetary Barter Transactions

1) Exchange of Good or Services "Free of Charge"

Assume that Janet, a property owner, has a big apartment building with several apartments, for which the annual market rent is $15,000 per year per apartment. Bob is a good and reliable handyman. Janet allows Bob to live in one of the apartments, free of monetary consideration, in exchange for Bob taking care of all the other apartments' maintenance during regular working hours.

First, we should analyze the above transaction economically [p. 162]. A reasonable assumption is that both parties have given valuable things and received in return a quid pro quo consideration, otherwise they would not conclude the deal. Janet gave Bob the right to live in one of her apartments and in return received maintenance services. Since we assume that both parties are reasonable people, they value the exchanged services as equal (if the rent is higher than the maintenance services, Janet would rent the apartment for its fair market price, pay Bob a lower salary and keep the balance for herself, and vis versa). Both have paid and received the same amounts. From an economic point of view, Bob uses his factor of production—human capital—and receives a salary of $15,000 and pays his rent not with money but with the maintenance services he provides to Janet. Janet uses her factor of production—a rental building—and receives the rent, not in money but with Bob's services, and pays him his salary, not in money but with dwelling services—"a free rent". Hence both taxpayers have income and expenses. That should be the legal result under the doctrine of arm's length transaction (12) and Code Sec. 242 [p. 162].

The question of whether such expenses in-kind are deductible for both taxpayers should be decided as if the payments are in monetary means instead of in-kind. Since Bob uses the apartment for his own dwelling, his payment in kind is for personal consumption, hence it should not be deductible; Janet paid in kind the building's maintenance fee, and she should be allowed to deduct it against the rent she receives for renting the other apartments. The logic applies to Bob. If his job requires a 24 hours service and he must be available "on call", then the free rent apartment is not considered a compensation for Bob's services, but as a matter of Janet's convenience. Hence might be exempt from income tax, as if he received the annual rent, and paid it back as an ordinary and necessary business expense.

In order to better understand the correct analysis above, we may introduce a third party to a barter transaction: assume Farmer John, a citrus grower, needs a worker to prune the trees in the citrus grove. He hires Henry for $1,000 to perform this job. In order to finance this expense, John decides to lease a corner of his field to a Nancy, a vegetable grower, for $1,000. After one month Henry quits and John offers Nancy the job. She agrees. John pays Nancy the amount of $1,000 for her pruning services. Nancy pays John the amount of $1,000 as rent, grows some vegetables therein, and sells them for $1,300. After a while they decide to save the deposits and withdrawals from their checking accounts. They agree upon a more efficient deal. She works for him free of charge and he allows her to use the field free of charge.

It is quite clear that all three variations of the transaction (first with Henry, then with Nancy and the cash payments and the last one with the "free exchange") are economically identical and should bear the same tax consequences. John still has income from the lease. Nancy is paying him not in money, but in kind with the performance of her pruning services. There is no doubt that John is also paying Nancy a salary, not in money, but in kind with the right to use the field. Similarly, Nancy's consideration for her work for John is not in money, but in kind with the right to use the field. She also pays rent, not in money but with her work. Hence, both John and Nancy have **non-monetary income and non-monetary expenses**. Such analysis is similar to the one used by Justice Brandeis in his minority opinion in the *Eisner v. Macomber* case [p. 164].

Once again, the question of whether the "non-monetary expenses" of the two will be allowed as deductions for income tax purposes is answered according to the nature of the expenses, regardless of whether they are paid in money or money's worth. Suffice it to say: if the expense paid in cash would be deductible, the fact that it is paid in rights, goods, or services should not change the result and the in-kind expense should be deductible as well.

Consider an insurance agent whose major business was selling property and casualty insurance policies. Since she was worried from losing her regular clients she agreed with some to sell them life insurance as well with a significant discount and waive her regular commissions on those life insurance policies from the insurer and indeed never got them. Her marketing efforts succeeded and none of her clients deserted her. A substance over form analysis [p. 107] suggests that the taxpayer (the insurance agent) got the premiums from the insurer for both the property and casualty insurance, as well as for the life insurance, and then spent the latter amount for keeping those fortunate clients for her major business. The tax consequences are simple: the taxpayer has a gross income of the amount received for selling both types of insurance, and business expenses—marketing—spent in order to maintain her major occupation.

The United States Court of Appeals for the 10th Circuit in *Mickey L. Worden v. Comm'r*, 2 F.3d 359 (1993), took a shortcut. The court concluded that under his contracts with the insurer, the taxpayer never had any right to the commissions for the life insurance, and therefore the "phantom income" from those transactions cannot be imputed to him.

The court added:

"It makes no difference, in our view, whether what petitioner did here was legal under state law. Illegal income is taxable; only illegal deductions are prohibited under I.R.C. Sec. 162(c). Here petitioner structured the transactions with his clients so that he never earned, had any entitlement to, nor received any sum representing the "basic commission" upon which respondent would have him pay taxes. If Federal Home Life Insurance Company changes its contract to make petitioner remit to it the whole and not the net premium, then we might have a different case. But we see no difference between the instant case and one in which a real estate broker cuts his normal agent's commission to make a sale of real property".

Now suppose that an identical insurance agent approaches a big company and reaches the following agreement with its CEO: The big company purchases property and casualty insurance, and in return the CEO purchases personal life insurance with a significant discount, which is equal to the life insurance commission the taxpayer waived. Now we see why the economic analysis is needed. The real economic situation is the notional assumption that the taxpayer receives the premium for the CEO's life insurance and spends it on an illegal payment—a bribery. According to the court's analysis there were neither gross income nor business expenses for the agent. As a result of the court's conclusion in the *Worden* case, a bribery payment was actually deducted, which is of course against the current law and its practice (Code Sec. 162(c)(2)).

2) Below Market Interest Loan

For another example, Dan works for Diane for an annual salary of $40,000. Dan wants to buy a new asset and intends to take a loan of $50,000 with a market interest rate of 5%. Hence he asks for an annual raise of $2,500 and agrees to work an additional 1 hour a week. Diane agrees. She has some money in her savings account. She receives interest from the bank and pays the additional salary of $2,500. Since both loans have transaction costs, Diane and Dan agree as follows: Diane withdraws $50,000 from her bank account and lends it to Dan without charging him any interest, in return for the 1 extra working hour.

These two examples (the Janet and Bob exchange and the free interest loan between Dan and Diane) are similar in essence; both describe a barter transaction that does not involve cash payments. Every economic analysis will reveal a clear result, identical to the previous analysis: in every barter transaction, each of the parties has "non-monetary" income and "non-monetary" expenses. Diane receives interest from Dan from his extra one hour of work a week, and she pays him his raise of $2,500 a year. Dan receives the raise of the same amount and pays Diane the market interest of 5%, i.e.

$2,500. As mentioned above, the calculation of the present value of Dan's obligation to pay back the loan to Diane leads to the same conclusion.

After a series of inaccurate and confusing court decisions, Congress embraced the above analysis and enacted Code sec. 7872 in 1984, which is applied specifically only to loans with below-market interest rates.

The general rule is straightforward. When a loan is below the market interest rate, the difference between the applicable Federal rate (prescribed in regulations) and the contractual rate i.e. "the forgone interest", shall be treated as "**(A)** transferred from the lender to the borrower, and **(B)** retransferred by the borrower to the lender as interest".

This rule applies both to income tax and gift tax as well, though for gift tax it does not apply when the aggregate outstanding amount of loans between individuals does not exceed $10,000.

The forgone interest in the case of a term loan is the amount loaned that exceeds the present value (97) of all payments due under the loan. In order to compute the present value [p. 105], the discount rate is the "applicable Federal rate", which is prescribed in regulations issued by the Secretary of the Treasury. Since with demand loans—which are payable in full at any time on the demand of the lender—there is no fixed date of the loan's repayment, the forgone interest is the actual interest that is payable on the loan at a rate less than the applicable Federal rate. In other words, the lender is treated as paying the borrower, on the last day of each year, an amount equal to the difference between the interest that was actually paid and the applicable Federal rate.

This statutory rule applies to the following loans:

a. Compensation-related loans directly or indirectly between an employer and an employee, or an independent contractor and a person for whom such independent contractor provides services.

b. Corporation-shareholder loans directly or indirectly between a corporation and any shareholder of such corporation.

c. Any loan to any qualified continuing care facility pursuant to a continuing care contract, provided that the lender (or the lender's spouse) did not attain the age of 65 before the close of the year, and that the aggregate outstanding amount of all the loans between the parties exceed $90,000.

The Code also provides two safety nets: one applies to any below-market loan whose purpose is the avoidance of any Federal tax. The second one applies to any below-market loan which is not specifically described in the Code, if the interest arrangements of such loan—which should be elaborated in regulations—have a significant effect on any Federal tax liability of the lender or the borrower.

Note that this statutory rule treats a husband and wife as one person, and all the amounts indicated within the section are adjusted for inflation.

3) Dividend In-Kind

Another type of income in kind is a free use of corporate property, like cars, boats or vacation homes, by shareholders without paying the fair price.

Suppose Corporation A owns a house it can rent for $24,000 a year. The corporation adds the rent to its earnings and distributes an amount of $24,000 to one of its shareholders. The shareholder uses the amount received to pay her rent on an apartment she rents. Now suppose that Corporation A allows the shareholder to use the house free of charge instead of renting it to a third party. The above analysis should be used in this case. The FMV of the rent—in this case the $24,000—should be considered as a dividend. Corporation A has income in kind of $24,000 and a non-deductible payment of dividend. Shareholder has a dividend-in-kind of $24,000 and consumption of non-deductible expenses. The only doubt is about the corporation's income-in-kind. One may argue that the shareholder did not pay any consideration to the corporation, hence it did not receive any taxable income. Note that the courts agreed that the rent-free use of corporate property by shareholders is a constructive dividend (e.g. *Ireland v. United States*, 621 F.2d 731) but apparently they did not consider the same amount as the corporation's income in kind.

There are two concepts that should be used to support the conclusion that the above economic analysis should apply in this case and that the corporation indeed has income in-kind. In 1935 the Supreme Court, in its *Gregory v. Helvering* decision, adopted two accounting concepts and applied them to tax law. The first one is the *business purpose doctrine*, which means that where an economic activity has no substantial business purpose other than the avoidance or reduction of tax, the tax law may disregard it. The other one is the concept of *substance over* form [p. 107], which means that the economic substance of a transaction, rather a strict but inaccurate legal analysis, should govern for tax purposes. It is true that Corporation A does not have any specific formal or legal obligation to distribute its earnings. From a legal point of view the corporation and its shareholders are considered separate legal entities. Yet, the economic reality indicates that the corporation is the shareholders' agent. It is supposed to make gains and profits for its shareholders. Indeed, the shareholders do not have a legal right to receive dividends, but they do have expectations. They can put pressure—both economic and legal—on the corporation to distribute its earnings. Hence, when the corporation allows its shareholder free use of its property, it receives in return a relief from the same shareholder's pressure to receive a dividend in cash. It receives rent in kind and distributes it to the same shareholder who uses the property free of charge. There is indeed a quid pro quo transaction. The shareholder gives up her economic demand for receiving dividends and receives the free use of the corporate property. The corporation allows the shareholder to use the property free of charge and receives the shareholder's waiver to receive cash. Moreover, we have seen above that the definition of the term "income" in the U.S. income tax system does not require the existence of a "source" [p. 158]. Hence, even if the shareholder does not appear to waive the pressure to receive a dividend as consideration for the free-rent house, it is still clear that the company rents out the house for FMV.

D. Imputed Income

As is discussed above [p. 160], imputed income (57) represents an accretion to wealth, a private form of consumption which is income and should be included in the taxpayer's gross income. Alas, under the current U.S. income tax system the IRS does not make any serious attempt to apply this concept.

In some cases the distinction between income in kind and imputed income is not that clear, especially in inter-family transactions. Suppose Mom owns a big house in city

A. Her son lives in city B. Mom leases her house for $24,000 a month and sends the money to her son. Son uses the money and rents a big apartment in city B for his own dwelling. Under real comprehensive income tax purposes Mom should include the received rent of $24,000 in her gross income, deduct the related expenses (depreciation, maintenance etc.) but not the gift she gave to Son, and pay income tax on her taxable income. Son should include the amount received from Mom as income—it increases his economic ability—and the rent he pays is private consumption and is not deductible. Under the current law, the $24,000 Son received is exempted from income tax but should be treated as a gift received for gift tax purposes [p. 141].

Now suppose that Son relocates and moves to city A. Mom allows him to use the house and stops sending him the $24,000. The tax consequences should remain the same. Mon has a gross income of $24,000 and no deduction for waiving the rent. Son has a gift of $24,000 and no deduction for the in kind rent he pays to Mom. Under a comprehensive tax base, it does not matter if there is an arrangement between Mom and Son. Mom has an imputed income when she uses the house for her own purposes [p. 160], whether she uses it herself or lets her son use it. Under the analysis of the income-in-kind barter transaction both parties receive income and have expenses. Mom receives affection and love bestowed upon her by Son and gives him back a gift, whereas Son receives accretion to wealth—private dwelling consumption—and pays back with affection and love.

Currently, the IRS does not attempt to tax both Mom and Son.

E. Income Must Be Realized

The fact that the Constitution followed by Congress, chooses income, rather than net wealth, as the major personal tax base, might suggest that the founding fathers followed the first two requirements of a good tax: the tax should be certain and should consider the taxpayer's convenience. This choice indicates that income tax is the antithesis of net wealth; it is not intended to tax potential/future uncertain income, which might cause the taxpayer significant liquidity problems and create a labyrinth of tax payments and tax refunds. Instead, its aim is to tax actual, real and certain income. I.e. *realized* income where the taxpayer has already used their factors of production and managed to turn the potentiality of producing income into reality. As presented above, the way the court interpreted the realization requirement caused a leading legal scholar to tag it as the Achilles heel of the income tax system [p. 163]. As indicated, the courts' interpretation of the realization requirement allows certain taxpayers—especially property owners—to enjoy either tax deferral or consume the enrichment without paying income tax. As suggested above, taxing the property's imputed income (57) or treating any kind of **use** of the property's appreciation (such as getting a mortgage and either consuming the proceeds or using it as an investment) as realized taxable income significantly eases the problem.

In some cases, the distinction between the realization requirement and issues of tax accounting is not totally clear. Receipt for services that are not yet performed, or for goods that are not yet sold, is not realized income, since the taxpayer has not yet used their factor of production. It is a consideration for services that will be performed in the future or for goods that will be delivered in the future' i.e. it represents a potential income. As long as the transaction is not done, the taxpayers are under liability to perform their duties, and if they fail they have to pay back whatever they received as advanced payment.

Suppose L, a lawyer, is requested in year 1 to commit herself to providing specific legal services during year 2, if some events occur. In order to assure she will provide the services, L receives an advance payment of $10,000. If the event takes place her compensation will be $15,000, and after the performance she will collect the additional amount of $5,000. If the event does not take place, she is required to return $3,000. A strict application of the realization requirement produces the following conclusion. Out of the $10,000, $7,000 should be regarded as realized income: L used her human capital, i.e. knowledge, goodwill, and time. This amount is at her disposal without any obligation. The other $3,000 is just an advancement and should be regarded as a loan. If it does not bear any interest, it should be treated as a below market loan, subject to Code Sec. 7872. On the other hand, if the full amount of $10,000 is under her control and she uses it, the certainty and the taxpayer's convenience rationales are not violated if she is taxed. She has the cash to pay the tax, hence there are no liquidity problems. In addition, the uncertainty is not significant; if she returns the $3,000 to her client and receives a refund for the overpaid tax, no serious harm occurs. Hence in such a case we may relax the realization requirement. In fact, in 1932 the Supreme Court applied a practical approach in *North American Oil Consolidated v. Burnet* known as the doctrine of "claim of right": "If a taxpayer receives earnings under a claim of right and without restriction as to its disposition, he has received income which he is required to return, even though it may still be claimed that he is not entitled to retain the money, and even though he may still be adjudged liable to restore its equivalent."

Under this doctrine a taxpayers have to include in their gross income any contingent receipt as income, even though they may still be obligated to restore it, as long as they have control over it, regardless whether they concluded the transaction—i.e. provided the goods or services. Congress reacted by enacting Code sec. 1341, which provides that once the taxpayers return the receipt they may deduct the returned amount against their taxable income, or even receive a tax credit equal to the tax that was paid previously.

The most common realization problems relate to appreciated assets. For example: a trader bought inventory (67) for $60, with a retail price of $100. At the end of the taxable year, the stock's retail price increased to $150. There is no doubt that the taxpayer is enriched, not only once but twice. When he purchased the inventory, he had an enrichment of $40 (for the sake of simplicity we ignore the other business expenses), and at the end of the year he had another gain of $50. However, as long as the inventory is not sold, the profit is only expected and is not certain. It is possible that by the time the inventory is sold, its value or quality has changed, or other changes may affect the amount of proceeds of the sale and may reduce the profit or even bring a loss. Hence the certainty and taxpayer's convenience requirements justify realization and the deferral of the tax payment until the inventory is sold.

Now assume that X cop is a firm whose expected future income is quite modest—10% rate of return of its equity—and its shares are traded in a stock market for $1 per share. At the end of year 1 the corporation reveals that it has been able to develop a revolutionary "know how" and its expected rate of return went up significantly—say to 30%. Since the value of an asset is equal to the present value of its expected stream of income in the future, the value of the X cop's shares goes up to $1.30. Assume that S.H. bought 1,000 (10%) of X cop's shares, at the beginning of year 1, for $1,000. At the end of the year she is happy to learn that the shares' value is $1,300. She has an impressive increase of her wealth, but this increase represents potential income in the future, either when she receives the actual dividend from X cop or disposes the shares. As long as she keeps them and no dividend is distributed, the increase of her wealth is just a guess; an estimation. There is no certainty that the expectation will ever materialize. There are various reasons that might cause X cop's shares to lose value, resulting in S.H. never enjoying the above temporary accretion. Hence if S.H. is an investor, the mere appreciation of her stocks is not taxed before she sells them, unless, as suggested above [p. 163], she provides the appreciated stock as a collateral and uses the proceeds according to her discretion. In that case, both rationales that are underlying the realization requirement—certainty and the taxpayer's convenience—are satisfied; the taxpayer has the cash to pay and since both she and the lender estimate the value of the property, the level of the uncertainty is minimized, hence the appreciation of $300 should be regarded as realized income.

If the taxpayer is an active securities trader, Code Sec 475 offers her an option: "Qualified securities dealers" who elect the accounting method of "mark to market" treatment shall recognize gain or loss as if the property was sold for its fair market value on the last business day of the year, and then repurchased at that value on the first business day of the following year. The section also provides that dealers in commodities can elect mark to market treatment for any kind of commodity (or their derivatives) which is actively traded in a known, organized and established market. Such election is permanent and can be revoked only with the IRS's consent.

There is no clear reason why not to expand the mark-to-market-technique as a mandatory way of calculating the annual capital gain (or loss) of all investors in traded securities as well. One may consider easing the possible liquidly problems in case of a gain by charging the taxpayers at the end of the taxable year, yet allowing the postponement of the tax payments until the taxpayer chooses to pay or sells the property, with the mandatory interest charges but without any penalties.

Note that there are some other special treatments for different types of securities and stock trades, which are not discussed in this book.

F. No Income if There Is No Consumption nor Savings

Since income on the sources side is equal to current consumption plus future consumption (savings) on the usage side, any income spent not for private consumption or savings should not be taxed as taxable income. And *vice versa*: income spent on consumption or saving should be considered as taxable income, i.e. such payments are not deductible expenses (30), unless there is a specific Code provision that allows it. Indeed, Section 262 of the Internal Revenue Code provides: "Except as otherwise expressly provided in this chapter, no deduction shall be allowed for personal, living, or family expenses."

Suppose G is a car dealer in the U.S.; VW is a foreign auto maker who is very interested in G distributing its cars in the U.S. G has some doubts. In order to remove them, VW invites G and his wife for a professional tour in its overseas plants and covers all their expenses. The question is whether G has any taxable income. From the sources side the question is whether G got any gross income. According to the narrow definition: did he receive any compensation for using his factor of production? Under the comprehensive tax base, is there any accretion to his wealth, or does he enjoy personal consumption? The latter question leads to the usages side of the definition of taxable income. The transaction may be analyzed in a different way, i.e. G got income in kind from VW (in return for donating his time to checking the possibility that he will distribute its cars) and spends the same amount as business expenses, so he has a complete offset—a wash, unless the creation of the new dealership is considered a capital asset and the expenses should be capitalized and are not fully deductible when they were spent.

The Court of Appeals for the 5th Circuit, in its decision in *United States v. Gotcher* (1968), drew a distinction between the amounts related to the taxpayer and the amounts related to his wife. Since she did not have any role in her husband's business and did not participate in any business activity during the tour, the trip was primarily a vacation. This being so, the primary benefit of the expense-paid trip for the wife went to Mr. Gotcher in that he was relieved of her expenses. He should therefore be taxed on the expenses attributable to his wife. Nor are the expenses deductible since the wife's presence served no bona fide business purpose for her husband. Under Section 274(m)(3) a deduction is allowed for travel expenses incurred with respect to a spouse only if the spouse is an employee of the taxpayer and the travel of the spouse is for a bona fide business purpose.

As for Mr. Gotcher, he took the trip not for his own personal pleasure but as a business trip. During the tour he actually worked, checking the possibilities, the cars' quality, and the producer's dependability. Therefore, there was no consumption—current or future—for him. The reason for VW to finance his visit in its plants was due to its attempt to expand its business in the U.S. The court emphasized that the concept of economic gain to the taxpayer is the key to the income tax system; that this concept contains two distinct requirements: there must be an economic gain, and this gain must primarily benefit the taxpayer personally. Based on Code Sec. 119, which excludes from gross income meals or lodging furnished to employee for the convenience of the employer, the court indicated that for expense-paid items that are received by the taxpayer, the value of these items will not be gross income even though the employee receives some incidental benefit, if the meals and lodging are primarily for the convenience of the employer. In some cases, where it was evident that the trip was awarded as compensation for past services, the cost of a free-paid-trip should be included in the recipient's gross income. Since in the *Gotcher* case there was no evidence in the record to indicate that the trip was an award for past services and that VW's primary purpose of the trip was to induce Mr. Gotcher to take out a VW dealership interest, there was no gross income for Mr. Gotcher.

It may be that a more accurate analysis should be used: Mr. Gotcher receives gross income and then deducts the trip expenses. In that case, one may consider the trip as an investment, the creation of a new dealership that will produce income in the future. In other words, G, under this approach, should be considered as if he received income and uses it as an investment. On the other hand, such expenses will be deductible as maintaining Mr. Gotcher's running business and not capital expenses (72, 30) [p. 269]. The court's approach, as Code sec 119, is of course much more practical.

Regarding Code sec. 119, the courts tend to be quite strict while applying this exclusion. All conditions within this section must be met.

The Court of Appeals for the Sixth Circuit found in *Com. v. Anderson* (1966) that although a manager was on call 24 hours a day, he did not perform a significant portion of his duties in his house and the house was not a significant place of business for the employer. The court referred to the three conditions for excluding the value of lodging and meals furnished to employees: (1) that such lodging be furnished for the convenience of the employer; (2) that it be located on the business premises of the employer; and (3) that the employee is required to accept such lodging as a condition of his employment. Since the house provided to Anderson was not on the business premises, the court did not allow the exclusion for meals, lodging, and other utilities and private services provided to him by the employer. However, in *Lindeman v. Comm.* (1973), an hotel manager who was on call 24 hours a day was provided with a house free-of-charge that was not in the hotel itself but within the perimeter of the hotel property. He performed a significant portion of his duties in the house. Under these facts and circumstances, the U.S. tax court allowed the exclusion for lodging.

The same approach was exercised by the U.S. Court of Claims in its decision in *Adams v. United States* (1978). In that case the president of a Tokyo-based Japanese corporation was furnished in a very expensive residence free of charge. The court held that the amount in excess of the U.S. Housing Element was excludable from taxpayer's gross income since the following conditions were met: (1) the residence was built and owned by the employer, (2) it was designed, in part, to accommodate the business activities of the employer, (3) the employee was required to live in the residence, (4) there were many business activities for the employee to perform after normal working hours in his home because of the extensive nature of the employer's business and the high-ranking status of the employee, (5) the employee did perform business activities in the residence, and (6) the residence served an important business function of the employer, therefore the residence in question was a part of the business premises of the employer. In other words, the taxpayer and his family's private consumption was taxed—as the U.S. Housing Element. Only the excess, which derived from the employer's convenience and requirements, was excluded.

The Supreme Court held, in *Commissioner v. Kowalski*, (1977), that "cash meal allowances" were not excludable under Section 119. In that case, the State instituted a cash meal allowance for its state police officers. Prior to that time, all troopers were provided with mid-shift meals in kind at various meal stations located throughout the State. A trooper unable to eat at an official meal station could, however, eat at a restaurant and obtain reimbursement. The meal-station system proved unsatisfactory to the State because it required troopers to leave their assigned areas of patrol unguarded for extended periods of time. As a result, the State closed its meal stations and instituted a cash-allowance system. Under this system, troopers remained on call in their assigned patrol areas during their mid-shift break. Otherwise, troopers were not required to eat lunch at any particular location as long as it was in the patrol area and, indeed, could eat at home if it was located within that area. The Supreme Court held that cash meal allowance payments were not excludable under Section 119, since they were funds over which the taxpayer had complete dominion and they were not meals "furnished by the employer". In *Silba v. Commissioner* (1980), The Ninth Circuit Court of Appeals used a much more liberal approach. The taxpayers, who were employed as firefighters by the Los Angeles Fire Department, attempted to deduct from their incomes their share of expenses from mandatory meals at firehouses where they worked 24-hour shifts. The Court of Appeals upheld the taxpayers' claim and decided that they had the choice to either deduct these expenses or exclude them from their gross income.

As mentioned above [p. 46], Code Sec. 107 and the surprising interpretation used by the Supreme Court (in the *WINN* Case) and the Court of Appeals for the Seventh Circuit in the "the *FFRF v. Lew* case" are quite unusual exceptions for the basic principle that required taxation of private consumption.

G. Earning from Illegal Activity Is Income

Income that is produced as a result of illegal activity is part of the offender's gross income. A common argument that has been raised by offenders is that, by taxing income created by an illegal activity, the public—through its elected agents and governmental agencies—become a partner, an accessory to the criminal activity. Such approach was rejected long ago by the Supreme Court in *James v. U.S.* (1961), but only after a series of confusing and conflicting previous decisions. The courts reached the conclusion that not only that taxation does not wash the criminal aspects of such activity, nor does it create a semi-partnership between the wrongdoer and the public, but avoiding taxing illegal income provides privileges to criminal activity or even an immunity that is unavailable for honest and law abiding taxpayers.

Note though that the rule is based on the definition of gross income. As long as, the offender acquires the income, he does not have a consensual obligation to repay it to anybody, or any restriction as to his disposition of the funds, he has gross income under the "claim of right" doctrine (23) [p. 199]. But what should the rule be if the offender repays the loot? If he does it during the same taxable year he committed the offense, or if there is clear evidence that he will pay back the full amount and the victim agrees, before the end of the taxable year, to treat the improper taking as a loan, then if the amount repaid is only the principal without interest, the illegal income is eliminated (there is no enrichment) and should not be included within the offender's gross income, but the applicable Federal rate should be added to the taxpayer's income as a free interest loan transaction (Code sec. 7872) [p. 195].

Furthermore, if the taxpayer pays the tax on such illegal activity and later on, in another taxable year, he returns the loot to his victim, he could deduct the returned amount against his taxable income in that taxable year. Moreover, he may even receive a tax credit under Code Sec. 1341, which significantly undermines the claim of rights doctrine (23) [p. 199]. If he does not have any gross income in that year and the foreseen following years (e.g. he is serving his criminal sentence in prison for several years; he is quite old and there is no chance he will be able to earn income) then he has a Net Operating Loss (NOL). In year 2 he commits an offence and steals $30,000 and loses his job. After three years, in year 5 he is caught and sent to jail. He should be taxed in year 2 on the illegal income of $30,000. In the same year (year 5) he repays the victim the entire amount of $30,0000+$472.85, which is the compound 5% interest (the market interest rate). No doubt he is not enriched. If he pays 20% income tax on the $30,000 illegal income ($6,000) he ends up with capital of $3,527.15, instead of his original and legitimate saving of $10,000. In other words, part of his equity was confiscated by the income tax due to the practical inability to use both Code Secs. 1341 and 301 only because he does not have any income in years 3, 4 and 5. In such a case, the tax is no longer income tax but rather a confiscation of property without due process (33). Furthermore, such situations lead to double punishment.

The above confiscation of offender's property and the double punishment should be avoided. Indeed it could be, by applying the constructive trust doctrine. A constructive trust is a legal concept, recognized by courts, which may declare that a person who has illegally acquired a property, in order to prevent an unjustified enrichment, has an equitable obligation to transfer it to whom it rightfully belongs.

Hence, once the offender is caught and returns the loot, the repayment eliminates the income in year 2, since the offender is considered not as the legal owner of the loot, but as if he had been an express trustee from the date of the unlawful holding of the loot and has the obligation to return it at that date. Hence, the offender did not have any income during the period of time since he committed the offence until he returned it to the legal owner.

To illustrate: Suppose a taxpayer stole $10,000 from his employer and used the money to buy an asset, which he held for 4 years, until he was caught. During these three years the asset's value went up to $50,000. Under the constructive trust concept, he is obligated to return the asset to his employer. Now suppose he has enough income in year 5 and he claims a deduction of $10,000, since the gain of $40,000 (the asset's appreciation) is not his own but of his employer. Now suppose that out of the stolen $10,000 he spent $2,000 on private consumption and bought the asset for $8,000. After he was caught he reached a settlement with his employer and transferred the asset while the asset was worth, say $50,000. Once again he can deduct only $8,000—the cost of the asset—since the appreciation of the asset belongs to the constructive trustee—the employer. In that case his taxable income is $2,000—which is equal to his consumption. The same tax consequence should be applied when he does not have any income during years 3, 4, and 5. The constructive trust concept eliminates the illegal income in year 2 and there is no need for any deduction, credit (Code Sec 1341) or carry backward losses. Once the repayment is done, the loot should be considered as non-taxable income, similar to a loan, regardless of whether the repayment took place in the year the offence was committed or in any later years. In other words, once paid, the repayment reassures, retroactively, the classification of the transaction. If the taxpayer reported the illegal income in year 2 and paid the income tax due in the same year, and in year 5 he repays the amount, he may claim credit under Code Sec. 1341, subject to the taxation of the forgone interest under Code Sec. 7872 [p. 195].

If the above employee does not repay his employer-victim any amount, he has an accretion to wealth, an income, whether consumed or saved. Another way to look at it is to realize that if the offender does not follow his legal obligation he defaults the constructive loan. In such circumstances the taxpayer has the benefit of a cancelation/discharge of indebtedness, which is also income under the I.R.C. sec. 61(a)(12).

In short, we should consider illegal income as a constructive trust with tax consequences similar to a loan. If there are no reasonable chances that the taxpayer will return the full amount (e.g. the victim gives up, or is unknown), he should be taxed in the year he commits the wrongdoing. If there is a reasonable chance for repayment at the time the taxpayer reports the money to the tax authority, the money received should be treated, for tax purposes, as a loan. Furthermore, once he returns the money to the victim, the mere payment reclassifies the income into a loan whether due to the constructive trust doctrine or any other legal concept that obligates the offender to return the loot to the victim. If the repayment is only partial, the balance between the original amount of the stolen money and the actual repayment should be considered as a discharge of indebtedness and taxed accordingly. In addition, if the repayment did not include any interest, the taxpayer should be taxed also on the forgone interest under Code Sec. 7872.

H. Enforced/Compulsory Earning and Profit Is Also Income

The fact that a taxpayer makes their income unintentionally or involuntarily, apart from their free will or because they were forced to earn it is often irrelevant. Income that is produced by a taxpayer as a result of activity that was forced upon them against their will is usually taxable. If a person is forced to sell his inventory by a governmental decree, although he prefers to wait until price increases, the gain he makes through the forced transaction is considered as income. Even if there is no force but the taxpayer earns income without expectation, e.g. from lottery or gambling profits or gains, the income is taxable.

However, in some cases involuntary disposition of property enjoys special reliefs. Code Sec. 1033 provides for non-recognition of gains (but not losses) in the following cases: if (1) the gain is realized on an involuntary conversion of property as a result of its destruction in whole or in part, theft, condemnation, sale under threat or imminence of condemnation, or other similar events and (2) the property is replaced within a prescribed period of time with other property that is "similar or related in service or use" or with stock representing control of a corporation owning such property. A similar rule applies under Code Sec. 1033(g) that deals with certain involuntarily condemned realty to be replaced by other real property of "like kind". Such involuntary replacement is not considered a tax event and the taxation is deferred until the replacement is sold. That is, the basis of the new asset will be the same as the basis of the original replaced asset, which was disposed of through the involuntary transaction [p. 247].

In addition, Code Sec. 337(a) provides that if a liquidating corporation makes a "sale or exchange" of "property" within twelve months after adopting a plan of liquidation and distributes all of its assets within this period, the resulting gains (or losses) will not be recognized at the corporate level. Note that the purpose of this is to prevent the possibility of a "double tax," since any gain realized by the shareholder on the distribution will be taxed.

3. THE STATUTORY "GROSS INCOME"

As indicated above [pp. 159–170, 184] the economic definition of income is very broad and comprehensive. Even though the courts have tended to accept it the legislature has departed from the pure and meaningful Comprehensive Tax Base. Part of the reason for giving up the CTB relates to a number of conceptual and practical difficulties, mainly the need to balance the various requirements of "a good tax system". Another reason represents some basic and blunt concessions the legislators provided to powerful groups and lobbyists. Hence, the first stage of the inquiry into the income tax system does not begin with a general term—income—which would allow the court to shape its meaning and interpretation, but rather with a special term—Gross Income—which is defined within the Internal Revenue Code.

The following chart demonstrates the way Gross Income is defined under the U.S. income tax system. (Note that not all the statutory items which are excluded are included within the chart).

Figure 17.1: From Economic Definition of Income to Gross Income:

Chapter Eighteen

STAGE TWO—CLASSIFICATION OF INCOME

1. DOES CLASSIFICATION MATTER?

A preliminary question is: do we really need to classify income into different categories? The answer has two dimensions: a practical one and a theoretical one. For practical reasons the answer is very simple. The Code treats different types of incomes in different ways; hence we have to identify those types.

On the theoretical and substantive level there are at least two approaches. The first is that the classification is needed since different types of income deserve different handling. The other approach is that there is no need, nor justification, for income classification.

A. Reasons for Classification

One example for the first-practical approach is the aforementioned British "scheduler" system [pp. 135, 158]. Under this system, the income classification is of the highest importance. Each income has only one source. According to this approach, classification is essential. If the income does not fit with one specific schedule it is simply not income for income tax purposes. Furthermore, different provisions apply to different schedules.

An example of the need for classification is Mill's "double taxation on saving" argument mentioned above [p. 172]. In order to prevent such double taxation—assuming such argument is valid—it is almost impossible to identify the accurate return on savings. Business income is usually a mixture of return on its investments (machineries, real property, human capital etc.). A professionals' income is also produced by a return of their investment in their own human capital. Since it is not easy to identify these components out of the total return, then those who accept the "double taxation on saving" argument suggest a "second best" solution: to tax the total return on capital—whether income from capital, i.e. passive income, or capital gains, with a lower tax rate while income from labor—earned income, active income—is taxed with "ordinary" tax rates. Another approach is to replace the income tax system with consumption tax. As mentioned above, such solutions may be a major contribution to the growing inequality and social gaps in the Western democracies throughout the last several decades. [pp. 72, 90, 180].

Another aspect of the practical approach is the accounting matching rules (76), that require expenses to be matched with the income they produce. This aspect is discussed below [pp. 252, 280].

B. Is Classification Redundant?

The opposite extreme approach is based on the notion that income is a measurement of economic ability in the current year, and its sources are irrelevant, so no classification is needed. Following the Comprehensive Tax Base approach, the U.S. tax system tends to follow this extreme approach. Yet for practical reasons we can detect some signals that the U.S. legislature appears to have succumbed/surrendered to pressure and is abandoning the CTB.

However, in some cases the legislature was driven to introduce classification of income into different categories, to prevent improper tax planning that harms the public coffers and national economic efficiency. Consider for example a successful professional, such as a lawyer/accountant/physician/actor who makes significant income and has to pay a considerable amount of tax. She enters into a partnership agreement that has, at the early stage, a large amount of accumulated expenses (mainly interest obligations/ liabilities on non-recourse mortgage and depreciation deductions) with very little income, which results in a Net Operating Loss [p. 283]. Without this deduction, the chances the professional would enter such an investment are quite slims. Yet under a tax system where the income classification is totally immaterial, the taxpayer's share in the partnership's loss may be allowed as a deduction against her income from her regular profession, trade, or business. Hence the decision to enter into the partnership is based only on tax considerations and not business ones. The implementation of the "substance over form" concept [p. 107] would lead to invalidating its consequences for income tax purposes. Congress' solution was to create three categories for sources of income [p. 225]—business activity, passive activity and passive income—and to disallow the deduction of the above loss from the passive activity against the business activity income.

A similar problem exists if capital losses are treated as an ordinary loss and are allowed as a deduction against any other income. This creates what are called "cherry picking" opportunities: the taxpayer will be able to choose a convenient date to dispose of a losing asset and realize a loss, which will offset regular taxable income, and keep holding appreciated assets; hence they defer their tax liability. Due to the realization requirement [p. 163], without the capital loss limitation, the taxpayer would be able to decrease their taxable income despite the fact that their total economic ability might even increase. Hence, the IRC draws a distinction between capital losses and ordinary losses, and forces investors to match their capital losses against their capital gains.

Another practical reason for income classification stems from the legislature's intent to provide some tax reliefs for different types of income [p. 31]. Most notably the distinction is between ordinary income and capital gain.

Once profit is classified as a capital gain, a sub-classification is needed: a distinction between business or investment-oriented capital gains and personal gains. The latter is benefits from special exemptions. The major one is the total exemption of gain from selling a principal residence (Code Sec. 121).

If the profit is classified as ordinary-current income, an additional categorization is the distinction between capital income (i.e. passive current income derived from capital assets, such as rent, interest and dividends) and earned income, from labor (mainly employment, trade and business, self-employed professional).

The practical need for income classification also relates to accounting requirements and the matching rules (76) requirement, i.e. the taxpayer is required to match their expenses with the income that was produced by the same expenses. Matching is achieved by a careful identification of the specific activity, its earning and its cost [p. 280].

Another area of tax law relates to taxation of international activity. In order to prevent double taxation of income that is subject to more than one jurisdiction, a foreign tax credit is granted in one country for income tax paid to another country provided some rules and limitations. The major limitation is that the credit should not exceed the taxpayer's U.S. income tax liability prorated for the percentage of foreign taxable income to taxable income from all sources worldwide. This general rule is applied by further limiting by income category or basket. The limitations are computed separately for certain categories or "baskets," of the foreign source income: there are several baskets which are based on the distinction between passive income and active income. The former one includes capital gains, dividends, interest, rents, and royalties, as long as they are not produced in ordinary trade or business activities. The latter category is a residual one, meaning any income that is not considered passive category income [p. 230].

The simple flow chart below presents the basic classification process of the different categories of income.

Figure 18.1:

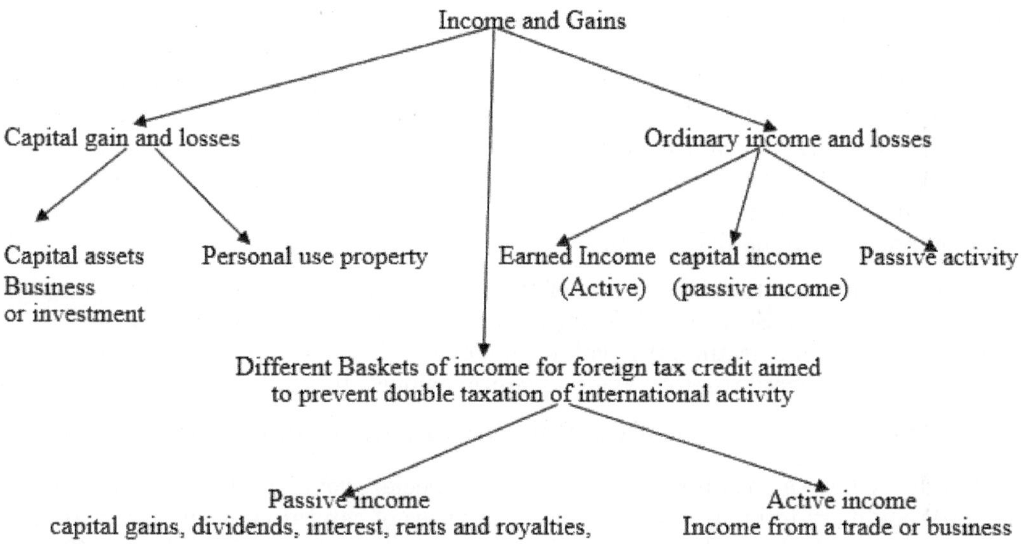

2. THE FIRST CLASSIFICATION—CAPITAL GAIN AND ORDINARY INCOME

The most meaningful classification is of capital gains and losses on the one hand and of ordinary income and losses on the other hand. One of the main reasons is very practical: under the current U.S. income tax system ordinary income tax rates are almost double the tax rate applicable to capital gains (in 2022, the maximum tax rate on long-term capital gain is 20%, while the top marginal tax rate on ordinary income is 37%). In some isolated cases (e.g. disposition of principal residence under certain conditions) the capital gain is totally exempted. On the other hand, as mentioned above, the Code provides severe limitations on the deductibility of capital losses.

The reasons for the lower tax rate on capital gains are various. One is John S. Mill's "double taxation of saving" argument [pp. 172, 207]. Second is that taxation of capital gain might create a "lock-in effect" that discourages renewal of capital assets, which will lead to economic inefficiency [p. 213]. Another argument refers to the fact that capital assets are held for a long period of time. This fact raises two other claims—the taxation of the imaginary gains generated during the inflation period and high tax rates due to the phenomenon of bunching. Both claims are discussed further below [pp. 210–211].

There are some serious doubts about the validity of those arguments. Although few of them have some validity, they can be dealt with and solved in better ways, discussed below. On the other hand, the lower tax rate for capital gains and other kinds of capital income may be considered as a pure privilege, which is granted to powerful interest groups, and provides a higher after-tax rate of return that eventually contributes to the phenomenon [pp. 96, 179, 183, 194, 213] regarding the average income tax rate of 8.4% that the wealthiest 400 billionaire families in America pay. Hence these lower tax rates for capital widen social gaps [p. 90] and reduce efficiency as well.

It should be noted though that the validity of the assumption that a lower tax rate available to **all taxpayers** who have capital gains is discriminatory is not so clear or obvious. One may argue that there is no discrimination at all if the lower tax rate is available to **all taxpayers**, poor or rich, domestic, or foreign who have capital gains or capital-passive income. This lower tax rate might meet the basic demand for equal treatment by "treating likes alike". On the other hand, most empirical findings indicate that only high-ability (wealthy) taxpayers have capital gains whereas lower-ability (poor) taxpayers have no capital to invest, hence, practically neither capital (passive) income nor capital gains are available for them. As a result, a lower tax on capital actually produces a ***regressive*** tax system (106), which violates the principles of horizontal and vertical equity [p. 14].

As mentioned, another dimension of the debate regarding the taxation of capital gains is based on John Stewart Mill's argument that any income tax on savings leads to double taxation. If this argument is valid, then even a lower tax rate on capital income and capital gain is discriminatory against capital owners. [p. 172].

A. The Characteristics of Capital Gain and the Required Adjustments

In order to have a good understanding of the special provisions dealing with capital gain, one should try to identify the special attributes of capital gain and compare it to ordinary income. The basic distinction, which was mentioned already and [pp. 148, 209] is discussed further below [p. 214], is that the former is produced through the **disposition** of a factor of production (a capital asset) whereas the latter is usually a current stream of income which is produced through **the use** of a factor of production. A known simile is that a capital asset is like a tree and ordinary income is like the fruits that grow on the tree. Sales of the fruits—which are the product of the factor of production—bring about ordinary income. The sale of the tree—which is the factor of production—usually brings about capital gain, unless it is reclassified by a statutory provision, such a recapture rule (105) [p. 212], as ordinary gains or losses. The primary and obvious characteristic of capital gain is that it is usually created and accumulated during some period, but the realization—the tax event—occurs at a single point in time. This trait raises a few problems.

1) Capital Gain and Inflation

The first is a problem in identifying *real* gain during a period of *inflation* (63). Due to inflation, the *nominal* original purchase price of the asset does not reflect its *real* purchase price. Therefore, it is possible that at the time of its sale, the price that the seller receives ("*amount realized*") is nominally higher than the original price, but the taxpayer does not gain **real** profit or gain; his power to consume has not increased. For example: an asset is purchased for $1,000 and after five years, during which the aggregate inflation is equal to 50%, the asset is sold for $1,300. From a real economic standpoint, not only did the taxpayer not earn a profit but he suffers a real loss; the taxpayer's power to consume decreased. In real terms, adjusting the asset's purchase price to the Consumers Index Price (CPI) indicates that the amount received actually equals, in real terms, (1,300*100/150=)$866.60 (assuming the CPI at the day of the purchase was 100 and at the selling day was 150). In other words, in order not to have a real economic loss the selling price should be (under the above assumptions) at least (1,000*150/100=)$1,500. If the amount realized is $1,600, the nominal gain equals $600, the adjusted purchase price is (1,000*150/100)=$1,500 and only $100 is real gain, while $500 is imaginary-inflationary gain.

The appropriate and practical solution (which has been adopted in several countries, but not in the U.S.) is to adjust the original purchase price (basis) of the asset to the inflation rate during the holding period. Such an adjustment can serve for capital gains purposes as well as for depreciation deduction.

2) Bunching and Averaging

The second problem derives from the said characteristic that due to the progressive tax rates, marginal tax rates are higher as a result of the fact that profit is accrued over several years but is realized at a single point in time. Assume that they are as follows:

Tax Rate Individual 2022

Taxable Income	Tax Rates	Tax Amount
0 to $10,275	10%	$1,027.50 plus 12% of the amount over $10,275
$10,276 to $41,775	12%	1,027.50 plus 12% of the amount over $41,775
$41,776 to $89,075	22%	4,807.50 plus 22% of the amount over $170,050
$89,076 to $170,050	24%	$15,213.50 plus 24% of the amount over $10,275
$170,051 to $215,950	32%	$34,647.50 plus 32% of the amount over $41,775
$215,951 to $539,900	35%	$49,335.50 plus 35% of the amount over $215,950
$539,901 or more	37%	$1162,718 plus 37% of the amount over $539,900

According to such a progressive structure, a person who earns an annual taxable income of $50,000 owes a tax of {4,807+[(50,000–41,775)*0.22]=}$6,616.50.

Suppose Asset A produces annual ordinary income of $50,000 for five years. Its owner's annual income tax payment is $6,616.50 and in total, over five years, is (6,616.50*5=)$33,082.50. (Note that for the sake of simplicity we ignore here the time value of money). If, on the other hand, the annual income of $50,000 is accumulated over five years and the total income of $250,00 is realized at the end of the fifth year, the amount of tax—in accordance with said table—is $46,565 i.e. $13,482.5 higher than if the gain was spread over the five years. This phenomenon is called bunching. The appropriate solution to this phenomenon is spreading or *averaging* the income over several years (in this example, five years), and the calculated annual tax is multiplied by five (with some minor adjustments in order to take into account the time value of money).

3) Purchase Price, Depreciation Deduction, and "Positive" and "Negative" Recapture

An additional characteristic of capital gain derives from the fact that the original price of the asset "changes" every year as a result of annual depreciation deductions that represent the capital recovery [p. 191]. Hence the purchase price should be adjusted accordingly. For example, a machinery purchase price ("basis") is $100,000 and the annual depreciation is 20%. After two years the adjusted purchase price is no longer $100,000 but (100,000−20,000−20,000=)$60,000. If it is sold after the second year for $70,000, there is a gain of $10,000; if it is sold for $55,000, there is a loss of $5,000.

Note that the depreciation deduction reduces the taxpayers "taxable income", hence producing tax savings (133) [pp. 4, 240], according to the taxpayer's marginal tax rate. Suppose the taxpayer's taxable income—before the depreciation deduction—is $500,000, hence her marginal tax rate is 35%. Taking a depreciation deduction of $20,000 provides her tax savings of ($^{35}/_{100}$*20,000=)$7,000. Suppose now, that the machine's market price at the end of the second year is indeed $70,000. The meaning is that the machine decreases in value less than anticipated by the statutory depreciation rate. The depreciation deduction (which is based on statutory estimation) should be only $30,000 over the two years, and if using a straight-line calculation, only $15,000 a year instead of $20,000. As a result the annual taxable income during these two years should be (500,000−15,000=)$485,000, and not (500,000−20,000=)$480,000. The taxpayer saves, due to the overgenerous depreciation deduction, a total tax amount of (10,000*0.35=) $3,500. When the taxpayer sells the asset with the (70,000−60,000=)$10,000 gain, the statutory estimation of the annual depreciation (20% over 5 years) is found wrong and at this time it should be amended by the taxpayer's refund to the government. The amount of the refund should be the same amount of the previous years' tax savings (133) [pp. 4, 240], to compensate the government for the saved income tax due to the previous over-deduction of the depreciation amounts. If the gain is treated as a capital gain, it will be subject to the lower preferred tax rate. In order to allow the refund such gain should be treated as ordinary income, subject to the taxpayer's marginal tax rate. In such way, the gain is ***recaptured* under Section 1245** (105) and is reclassified as ordinary income subject to the ordinary income tax rates.

The same logic should lead us also to ***negative recapture*** [pp. 212, 281]. Suppose the machine is sold at the end of the second year for only $55,000. The loss of (60,000−55,000=)$5,000 indicates that the total decrease of the machine's value during these two years is (100,000−55,000=)45,000 and not (2*20,000=)$40,000; which means that the annual depreciation deduction was too little: instead of $20,000 it should be (45,000/$_2$=) $22,500 every year. As a result of the 20% depreciation deduction that was taken by the taxpayer, the taxpayer's annual taxable income has been overstated; instead of $480,000 it should be only (500,000−22,500=)$477,500. As a result the annual over-taxation was [(480,000−477,500)*0.35=]$875 and for two years the taxpayer paid an additional tax payment of (875*2=)$1,750. When the asset is sold, the taxpayer should get a refund for the overpayment, hence the loss ($5,000) should be allowed as a deduction against the ordinary taxable income, which produces the same tax savings (133) [pp. 4, 240] of (5,000*0.35=)$1,750.

As can be seen, the recapture and the negative recapture provide a symmetric result (though not in present value (97) terms): in both cases the party that gains during the holding period is supposed to compensate the other party when the disposition of the asset takes place and the real capital recovery during the holding period is revealed.

4) Lock-In Effect and Non-Recognition Tax Deferral

The argument regarding the lock-in effect is simple: an old, unproductive, or low-return asset might be a burden on both the taxpayer and the national economy. It would be better to dispose of it and replace it with a newer/more productive/higher rate-of-return asset. Yet if the sale price produces a gain, and the gain is taxed, the tax is added to the transaction cost (143), so the rate of return of the new asset decreases. As a result, taxpayers who are subject to tax are reluctant to dispose of unproductive assets and to replace them with better ones. The economic stagnation caused by this effect—so goes the argument—reduces liquidity, deteriorates the mobility of capital, reduces beneficial replacement of old machinery, and causes significant fluctuation of prices in the financial and products markets.

Suppose a taxpayer owns a stock purchased at a price of $10, which has appreciated to a market value of $100 and yields an annual rate of return of 10%. The taxpayer has an opportunity to purchase a different investment with an expected annual yield of 12%. However, if the capital gains tax is 35% and the stock is sold for its FMV, the tax on the $90 gain is $31.50, and the taxpayer is left with only [$100−($90*0.65)=]$68.50 to invest in the prospective replacement investment. Since the return on the new investment is 12%, it produces a stream of income of only (68.5*0.12=)$8.22, and the taxpayer probably chooses not to replace his original stock (which produces an annual income of $10) with the more productive asset. Without the capital gain tax, the taxpayer probably invests $100 and receive $12 annual income.

Such an argument also applies to any other asset. In other words, the, "lock-in effect" may cause economic stagnation. Yet there some serious doubts regarding depreciable assets. They are related to the basic rules of annual depreciation [pp. 191–212, 260–263, 262, 263]. The total amount of the annual depreciation during the holding time could not exceed the original cost of the property. For example, suppose the taxpayer is at the top marginal tax rate of 35%. They use a depreciable asset, which was bought 5 years ago for $100. Assume further that the straight-line depreciation is 20% per annum, so the asset's basis for tax purposes at the end of the 5th year is (20×5=)$0. Beginning at the sixth year the taxpayer cannot deduct any amount of depreciation against their taxable income (137). If the fair market value of the asset—a machine, is $10, and it is sold for that price, the taxpayer is subject to a 20% capital gain tax of (10×0.2=)$2.

On the other hand, when the taxpayer buys a new productive machine for, say, $120 they enjoy the following tax savings (133) [pp. 4, 240]: an annual depreciation [pp. 191–212, 260–263, 262, 263] of (120×0.2=)$24 which is deductible and provides annual tax saving of (24×0.35=)$8.4, a total tax saving for 5 years—(8.4×5=)$42. As we can see from this simple example, the taxpayer's total tax savings in the 6th year, after paying the tax on the capital gain and deducting the new amount of depreciation of $8.4, his total tax saving, after paying the $2 capital gain on the old machine is (8.4–2=)$6.4. Under these simple assumptions, a reasonable taxpayer would prefer to dispose of the old less-productive machine and replace it with a new, more productive one, even if this transaction produces capital gain tax of $2.

Moreover, economists disagree about the real magnitude of the lock-in effect on our economy. Anyway, providing additional tax reliefs for capital gain, beside the lower tax rate, is quite difficult to justify. For example, the exemption from capital gain on death and "*step up basis*" [p. 143] i.e. when a person bequeaths a capital asset loaded with accumulated capital gain, there is no capital gain tax on death, yet the basis of the asset for the heir (Mom) is its fair market value at the date of the death. As a result, Mom holds an unproductive, yet appreciated asset, and the family waits until Son inherits it.

Another example: Code Sec. 1031 provides a tax deferral, i.e. no gain or loss is recognized on the exchange of property held for the productive use in a trade or a business or for investment if such property is exchanged solely for property of "like kind". This section allows the taxpayer to "exempt" the capital gain on an old machine if it is replaced by a new ("like kind") machine, provided the original cost ("basis") of the new machine is reduced by the amount equal to the exempted capital gain from the sale of the old asset. The full meaning of such a solution—which is called *"roll over basis"*—is not a real exemption but rather a non-recognition provision that "just" defers the tax payment [p. 247].

Supposed a taxpayer fully depreciated the full cost of a machine, sells it for $400, adds another $600 and buys a new machine for $1,000. The $400 is a capital gain but under Code Sec. 1031 is not recognized so the $400 gain is not taxed upon the machine's disposal. Yet the new machine's purchase price (basis) for tax purposes is only (1,000−400=)$600 for depreciation deduction purposes and for capital gain calculation when disposed as well. Under the lower capital gain tax rate, and the higher tax saving (133) [pp. 4, 240] from the annual depreciation, one may wonder whether using this tax deferral provides a real benefit.

It should be noted that Section 1031 also applies to exchange of certain investment property, such as real estate and personal property, but not to financial investments, such as stocks. However, under Code Sec. 1045 a similar tax deferral is available to taxpayers who realize a gain from the sale of a "qualified small business stock". Taxpayers may rollover tax-free such realized gain when the sale proceeds are reinvested in other qualified small business stock. The rationale for this provision is to encourage individuals to invest in emerging growth companies, and to encourage them to reinvest any profits once the original investments mature.

B. The Distinction Between Capital Gain and Ordinary Income

The importance of distinguishing between capital gain and current income stems from the low tax rates that apply to the former. There are two ways to draw the distinction between capital gains and ordinary income. The first is based on traditional approach, i.e. formulas developed by legal literature and case law. The second relies on an economic analysis based on the understanding the way capital gains (or losses) are created.

Before we discuss the distinction, we begin first with what we call "disguised capital gain".

1) Capital Gain in Disguise: The Causes for Capital Gains or Losses: Ex-Post v. Ex-Anta Profits

There are some cases where an asset produces annual income, yet the income is not separated from the asset but instead is added to the asset's value. Consider a grove that is sold a month prior to the fruit picking season, or a debenture which earns compound interest, (64) or a stock of shares of a company with significant undistributed profits. If all three assets are sold, the price the owners receive includes two types of consideration: one is for the ex-post retained earnings, and one is for future ex-anta earnings. The price of the ex-anta earnings is computed according to present value (97) of the future income. If there is a gain it usually represents a capital gain. On the other hand, the price, which is allocated to the fruits, to the compound interest and to the corporate retained earnings the ex-post gain, represents ordinary income: an inventory in the grove case, interest in the debenture issue, and a dividend in the case of the corporate's retained earnings.

A) Accumulated/Compound Interest Is Not Capital Gain

Assume a person purchases a debenture for $100 which carries the market interest rate of 10%. If the interest is paid at the end of the first year, it will be considered as ordinary income. If the interest is compounded and accumulated annually, we can assume that the value of the debenture will increase at the end of the first year to $110 (provided no other circumstances are changed during the holding period). If the taxpayer sells the debenture at the end of the first year for $110, is it possible that all the profit will be considered capital gain? One should argue that ordinary income does not change its character and turn into capital gain only as a result of a change in the form of its realization. The argument is clear and simple: realized ordinary income always remains ordinary whether it is paid periodically or accumulated and sold with the asset that produces it. As long as the income (such as interest, or even dividends as is discussed below), is realized, though not paid yet, it remains ordinary income. Suppose some market conditions have changed, the market interest rate goes down, or the economic stability of the debenture issuer has improved, and thus the debenture is sold for $112. The gain of (112−100=)$12 should be divided into two different parts. $10 represents an ex-post realized interest, an ordinary income, whereas the other $2 represents an ex-anta gain and should be treated as a capital gain.

B) Corporate's Retained Earnings Are Not Capital Gain

A similar analysis should also be used for stock of a corporation that accumulates profits. For example: suppose that during one year, John Doe invests $500,000 in C corporation, which is 5% of the company's stock. During that year, the company earns $20,000,000 and pays a corporate tax of 20%. The company's after-tax profits are consequently $16,000,000 and John's prorate gain is (16,000,000*0.05=)$800,000. Assuming that no other circumstances change (as economists like to use the *Ceteris paribus assumption*), at the beginning of the second year, John Doe sells his stock to Joanne for $1,150,000. Under current law, John Doe should report a capital gain of $800,000. Furthermore, suppose that a few weeks later, Joanne, the buyer, receives a $800,000 dividend from the company. Joanne must report the $800,000 dividend as taxable income. Under such a system, and with the special tax rates for capital gains and dividends, while assuming that John's tax rate on capital gain is 15% and Joanne's tax rate on the dividend is 20% [p. 316], the above corporate earnings of $20,000,000 are triple-taxed and the total revenues collected by the IRS are:

Corporate tax (20%*$20,000,000)	=	$4,000,000
(John's "share" (5%) is $200,000)		
John's capital gain tax (15%*$800,000)	=	$120,000
Joanne's tax on dividend (20%*$800,000)	=	$130,000
Total tax paid	=	$4,250,000

Since John and Joanne share 5% of the corporation's earnings of $20,000,000, which is $1,000,000 total, then the total tax on the 5% earning is (200,000+120,000+130,000=) $450,000 which is (450,000/800,000=) which is a 56.25% aggregate tax rate.

As we can see, John's share of the profit of (20,000,000*0.05=)$1,000,000, which was done at the corporate level, is taxed three times and the total tax burden on such a profit is 56.25%!

The significant difference between this example, and the previous one, which deals with compound interest, is that the interest payments are deductible expenses by the debenture's issuer while the dividend paid by the corporation is not deductible. The several alternative ways to deal with this issue are discussed below [pp. 312–314].

2) The Legal Distinction

The basic principle should be simple: a return, profit or gain derived from ***using*** a factor of production is ordinary/current income. A gain or profit derived from ***selling*** the factor of production is capital gain (or loss). Hence, the problem relates to the situation where property is sold: whether the sold property is a factor of production, i.e. assets that produce income such as machinery, corporate shares, real estate etc., or whether the sold asset or services are current assets such as inventory (67) or professional services. The sale of a capital asset brings about capital gain (or loss).

The Code makes this basic distinction a bit more complicated. Section 1222 provides that a capital gain or loss arises from the "sale or exchange of a capital asset". The term "capital asset" is defined by Section 1221 as all property, excluding eight listed exceptions, the most important of which are real or depreciable property used in a trade or business (e.g. machinery, a desk or a computer used by a lawyer, etc.).

If a property that is used in a trade or business is held for less than one year, any profit or loss from the disposition of the property is considered as ordinary income or loss. If such a property is held for more than one year, the sale of such property is governed by the special rules of Section 1231. Under these special rules, property used in trade or business for more than one year gets the "best of both worlds": any gain from the disposition of the asset is treated as a capital gain and any loss is treated as an ordinary loss. An additional consideration regarding this issue is discussed below [p. 270].

One major problem is that property cannot be always easily identified. Property gets its character as a capital asset or current one according to various circumstances: the taxpayer's profession and occupation; the frequency of transactions carried out by the taxpayer, etc. If a desk is built by a carpenter and is sold at a profit (or loss), it is considered ordinary income (or loss), since it is a product made by using the carpenter's human capital. When the same desk is sold by a lawyer who used it in her office, it is considered as a "property used in a trade or business". If the desk was held for less than a year, any gain or loss from the disposition of the desk is treated as an ordinary loss. If the desk was held for more than a year, any gain is treated as a capital gain (subject to the recapture rule under Section 1245 [p. 212]) and any loss from the disposition is treated as an ordinary loss. The same desk sold by an antiques collector may bring out another type of asset—a collectable. Stock of shares is considered a capital asset in the hands of an investor because it produces passive-ordinary income in the form of dividends, but in the case of a stock trader or dealer, the profit is considered ordinary income, since it is a product of the taxpayer who uses "know-how" and human capital. And yet, sometimes it is difficult to decide whether the taxpayer is a dealer or an investor.

In order to draw a distinction between capital gains and ordinary income it is important to decide if the sold property was held by the seller for passive investment purposes (hence it is a capital asset), or was used in a trade or business (hence it is a 1231 quasi-capital asset), or was held as an inventory (67) primarily for sale to customers in the ordinary course of a trade or business (hence it is subject to the ordinary income treatment).

3) Case Law

The courts have developed a series of tests in order to distinguish between capital gains and ordinary income. The seven factors that were mentioned most often are known as the seven pillars of capital gain treatment (e.g. *U.S. v. Winthrop*, (5th Cir. 1969)). The factors below indicate whether a transaction produces ordinary income or capital gains.

(1) The nature and purpose of the acquisition of the property and the duration of the ownership; a longer period indicates an investment motive and character and vice versa.

(2) The extent and nature of the taxpayer's efforts to sell the property; the harder and more intensive the efforts, the closer to an ordinary income transaction, and vice versa.

(3) The number, extent, continuity, and substantiality of the sales; the more frequent sales, the closer to ordinary transaction, and vice versa.

(4) The extent of subdividing, developing, and advertising to increase sales; a more extensive of such activities bring the transaction closer to an ordinary one.

(5) The use of a business office for the sale of the property is an indication of a business activity rather than an investment, i.e. ordinary income.

(6) The character and the degree of supervision or control exercised by the taxpayer over any representative selling the property; the higher degree the greater probability the transaction is a business one.

(7) The time and effort the taxpayer habitually devoted to the sales; the more extensive indicate business activity.

The common ground for all these seven pillars seems clear: the more active and knowledgeable the seller is, the more they use their human capital in order to increase the asset's value and produce a gain; hence, the gain is a product of **using** a factor of production—human capital—which is an **internal** factor of the taxpayer [p. 148]. The less active and knowledgeable the taxpayer is, the less they use their human capital and the more they rely on other factors of production, real and social capital. Therefore, the gain is created due to other **external** causes, i.e. changes over which the taxpayer does not have significant control of their causes. In other words, the more active the taxpayer is in the appreciation of the asset and its selling process, the closer the gain is to being classified as active income and vice versa.

4) The Causes for Capital Gains or Losses: Internal and External Causes for the Gain

The study of the causes of profit or loss that relate to property, together with the proposed rule here, whereby profit created by **using** factors of production is current income, whereas profit derived from **selling** factors of production is capital gain [p. 148], should lead to the formulation of a clearer and more accurate test for distinguishing between current income and capital gains. As is known, the gain (or loss) from the sale of assets relates to the change in a property's value during the period that begins at its purchase date and ends at the date of sale. As is discussed above [p. 105] the value of property is determined according to present value of the expected stream of income the property produces during its lifetime (plus its salvage value. Accordingly, the profit (or loss) is created due to a change in one or more components that are used in the capitalization process that determines the property's present value. Those components are: the annual stream of income expected from the asset; the number of the production years; the interest rate; and the residual value ("salvage value") at the end of the period.

Gain or loss from selling property are the results of a change in a property's value from the date of its purchase until the date of its sale. As discussed above [p. 105] the value of a property is determined by the capitalization of the expected stream of income the property is expected to produce during its lifetime (plus its salvage value (109)) i.e. the present value (97) [pp. 106, 155] of the expected stream of income = the property value. Hence, any change in one of the components used in the capitalization process directly affects the property value. The variables are the following: the estimated annual income; the number of years; the market demand and supply for the sold property, including unexpected changes in the public taste, the success of the competition, and the cost of the raw material; and the periodical interest rate. Each change in any of these variables changes the value of the property, which leads to a gain or to a loss. The crucial question is: who causes the change? If it was caused by the taxpayer's activity, knowledge, and resources, i.e. the taxpayer **uses** their factor of production of such labor, knowledge, skill, real capital and their efforts, then the gain is a product of a change they caused by **using** real and human capitals. Hence, the gain is ordinary income. It was created by a change that is **internal to the taxpayer**. As discussed above the internal causes are derived from the common ground of the above case law tests known as the seven pillars [p. 217].

If, on the other hand, the taxpayer does not have control or significant influence over the causes of the change—such as a change in the aggregate demand or supply; change to the annual interest rate; economic growth or recession; domestic currency devaluation or revaluation; then the role of the taxpayer on the changes is minor. The taxpayer did not use their factor of production, but rather sold it by deciding the timing of the sale. The change was caused by **factors external to the taxpayer, mainly by social capital**.

Indeed, in most cases the taxpayer controls the timing of the sale. If the timing was an extremely meaningful or crucial factor, and the taxpayer used their professional experience, knowledge, and loaned money, then, once again, they used their factor of production—mainly human capital—and the profit should be classified as ordinary income. The profit is caused by an **internal change**. One may conclude that profits derived from speculation of a non-professional dealer should be classified as ordinary income since the speculator uses their internal skill and efforts, their own human capital.

5) Royalties and Intellectual Property

There are several ways to compensate the creator of intellectual property (e.g. patents, literary works, works of art, "turn key" value, and goodwill). One way is for those creators to receive periodical royalties, with or without an advance payment. Another way is to set a fixed price which a publisher/user of a patent pays the creator.

Since intellectual property produces current income to its owner, one may argue that such property is a capital asset, hence selling it produces capital gain.

Yet the above tests that deal with external-internal causes, and what factor of production has been used and created the profit, should lead to a clear conclusion. If the seller is the creator, the gain is ordinary income, regardless the method of payment. The gain is a return to the creator for **using their own** human capital. When the creator begins their work, the value of their vision is probably insignificant. Due to their education, imagination, creativity, skills, know-how and understanding of the market, they turn an idea into a profitable asset.

If, on the other hand, the creator forwards their intellectual property to another person in a commercial transaction, the new owner has a capital property, unless they are not a dealer of such properties.

If the creator uses an intangible asset in their business for a while, the asset is turned into a capital asset. Though the idea of a self-transaction [p. 162] has not been applied in the U.S., it should be considered. A person uses their factor of production and creates an asset with market value. If they sell it to another firm, the profit should be regarded as ordinary income, very similar to a sale of inventory (67) (although intangible). Once they designate the "intangible inventory" into a capital asset that produces current income, tax law should regard them as selling that inventory to themself for its FMV. Hence, they should include the notional income (62) in their tax return for that year. Later on, they should regard that amount as the basis of the capital asset that generates income, whether to the creator of the intangible who turned the nature/characteristics of the asset into a capital asset (sale to himself) or to another taxpayer who purchased the asset from the creator.

The general rule seems to follow this analysis but not entirely. Section 1221(a)(3) denies capital asset status to "a copyright, a literary, musical, or artistic composition, a letter or memorandum, or similar property" if the property was created by the taxpayer's "personal efforts" (or for the taxpayer in some cases). Moreover, the disqualification also applies for gifts and to all persons in a chain of transfers (a series of gifts). Hence, if the property was sold to a third party, then the taint is removed and the property can qualify for capital gain treatment. However, Section 1235(a), which was enacted in 1954 created a tax incentive meant to encourage the development of inventions by individual inventors who, prior to 1954, often were subject to ordinary income tax rates upon the sale of their creation. Under this important exception, a sale of all substantial rights to a patent by any holder (including the creator) is considered the sale of a capital asset, regardless of whether payments in consideration of such transfer are payable periodically or contingent on the productivity or use of the patent.

6) Goodwill

For some reasons there is a tendency to classify business goodwill as a capital asset. Yet it seems that a more accurate analysis should lead to a different conclusion. Based on the above tests, a distinction should be made between business goodwill that the business develops by itself, and goodwill the business acquired from a third party. Once again, the former is created by a firm, a business, its employees/owners' efforts, skill, work and capital. Before it has been created, it had no commercial value. Due to the business input its value increases. The cause of the increase is internal, is the business using its factors of production. Hence, the proceeds from the sale of the created goodwill, according to the above external-internal test, should be classified as current income and not capital gain. This conclusion is supported by the argument that the cost of creating goodwill (and other intangibles, e.g. workforce in place, customer base, knowhow etc.), such as business, commercial, and advertisement expenses, are considered as ordinary deductible business expenses and should be deducted on the same taxable year they are spent [p. 272]. The deductibility of such expenses indicated, once again the causes of the gain are internal. On the other hand, the sold goodwill is a capital asset in the buyer's hand.

Treating the proceeds of self-created goodwill as capital gain and allowing the deductibility of the expenses of its creation as ordinary business expenses produces a significant distortion. Based on the notion that an immediate deduction of capital expense is equal to the exemption of the return of the investment up to the same rate of return [pp. 172, 256] tax law professor Calvin Johnson has shown that under the current (then) tax rates, the deductibility of the cost of the created goodwill against ordinary income, which is subject to a 35% income tax rate, and allowing a capital gain tax rate on it, increases the internal rate of return of the firm on such transactions by 2.5 times. The right solution, in order to prevent such distortion, is to allow the deduction of the goodwill creation as ordinary and necessary expenses on the one hand and treat the profit when it's sold as ordinary income.

Suppose a firm buys goodwill for $100,000 and takes the allowed annual amortization deduction (20, 21) of 6.6%. After 10 years the firm sells the goodwill. The price for the goodwill is estimated at $150,000. Since the firm deducted the cost of the goodwill as depreciation, the basis of the asset is no longer its original cost but is its adjusted basis, which is (100,000−66,666=)33,334, the total gain (150,000−33,334=) of $116,666 should be taxed, according to our analysis, as ordinary income, since it has been created by the firm, and according to the above "internal" test is a return on the business for using its factor of production. Note that even if the sale is considered as a capital asset, the amount of (100,000−66,666=)$33,334 should be recaptured (105) and is subject to the ordinary income tax rates. [p. 212] and the (150,000−100,000=)50,000 should be classified as ordinary income

7) Disposition of Business

The sale of a business is usually not treated as a sale of one asset. Instead, each of the businesses' assets are treated as being sold separately for determining the seller's tax liabilities. The assets are classified as capital assets, depreciable property used in the business, real property used in the business, or property held for sale to customers, such as inventory or stock in trade (67). The gain or loss of each asset is figured accordingly. The sale of capital assets results in capital gain or loss. The sale of inventory results in ordinary income or loss. The sale of real property or depreciable property used in the business and held longer than 1 year results in gain or loss from a Section 1231 transaction [p. 216]. An exception to this rule, which is not discussed here, relates to a partner who sells their partnership interest (Code Sec. 741).

C. Quasi Exemption, Tax Deferral, and Real Exemption from Capital Gain

Code Sec. 1222 defines capital gain as: "The gain from the sale or other disposition of property shall be the excess of the amount realized therefrom over the adjusted basis". Hence, in order to calculate the capital gain, the taxpayer must determine the value of two terms: "amount realized" and "basis" and then subtract the latter from the former.

The amount realized is the sum of any money received plus the fair market value of the property received. The adjusted basis is the original cost with some additions and subtractions. The additions include the purchase costs, cost of improvements, legal fees and selling costs (which were not allowed as current deductions). The subtractions include depreciation, or casualty losses (22) that were deductible in previous years.

These definitions shed some light on the two types of exemptions from capital gain. The first is a full and final exemption; i.e. the gain is totally exempted while the sale takes place and it is not taxed in the future. For example, Section 121 excludes from gross income the first \$250,000 (or \$500,000 in the case of married couples filing jointly) of capital gain realized on the sale of a principal residence. Another example is the "*step-up basis*" in the case of bequests [p. 214].

The second type is a disguised/quasi exemption. For example, Code Sec. 102 grants an "exemption" for capital gain when an appreciated asset is given as a gift. However, such an exemption is just a deferral; a quasi-exemption due to the requirement that the donee's adjusted basis should be equal to the donor's. Therefore, when the donee sells the asset later on in a taxable transaction, the whole gain that accumulated in the hands of the donor and the donee will be taxable to the donee. For example: suppose Grandma bought 100 shares for \$200. After a while, when the market value is \$350 she gives the stock to Mom. The capital gain of (350−200=)\$150 that is realized by the gift is "quasi-exempted". When the stock's market value goes up to \$500, Mom gives it to Grandchild. Once again the gain (500−350=)\$150 is not yet taxed. When Grandchild sells the stock in the market for \$750 her adjusted basis is \$200 and her taxable gain is not only (750−500=)\$250 but (750−200=)\$550. Due to the rollover basis the whole gain within the family is eventually taxed, though with a significant deferral.

Note that the rollover basis also applies for the annual depreciation deduction if the asset is depreciable, i.e. the annual depreciation deduction is reduced with the same amount of the "exempted" capital gain. In the above example if the said asset is a depreciable one, both Mom and Grandchild's annual depreciation would be calculated on the basis of the grandmother's original cost (\$200).

D. Tax Rates on the Net Capital Gain Under the Current Law

The Code draws a distinction between short-term capital gains (and losses) and long-term capital gain (and losses).

As mentioned, appreciated capital assets that are sold by individuals after being held less than one year (short-term capital gain) are taxed as ordinary income, which might be up to 37% [p. 306].

Until more than a decade ago, capital gains were considered as part of the taxpayer's taxable income subject to the ordinary tax rates. No longer. Congress enacted a special reduced tax rate for capital gains, gain for disposition of collectibles and certain small business stocks. The term "net capital gain", means the amount by which a net long-term capital gain for the year is higher than the net short-term capital loss for the taxable year. The term "net long-term capital gain" means long-term capital gains reduced by long-term capital losses including any unused long-term capital loss carried over from previous years [Code Sec. 1(h)(3)].

The lower tax rates on "net capital gain" is 0% if the taxpayers' taxable income is up to $40,000 [p. 316]. The tax rates for 2022 are as follows: [I.R.C. 1(h)(1)(A–F)]

Taxable (ordinary) income (individual)	Tax rate on net (long term) capital gain
0–40,000	0% rate for long term capital gain
40,000–445,850	15%
$445,851 and above	20%

Yet, there are a few other exceptions where capital gains may be taxed at rates greater than **20%**:

1. The taxable part of a gain from selling section 1202 qualified small business stock is taxed at a maximum **28%** rate.
2. Net capital gains from selling collectibles (such as coins or art) are taxed at a maximum **28%** rate. [I.R.C. 1(h)(4)]
3. The portion of any unrecaptured section 1250 gain from selling section 1250 real property is taxed at a maximum **25%** rate.

Capital gains by corporations do not receive preferential treatment, and are taxed at the ordinary corporate tax rate, i.e. a maximum rate of 21% [Code Sec. 11].

As mentioned, capital losses offset capital gains, yet if the losses exceed the gains, then up to $3,000 are deductible against current/ordinary income. A higher net capital loss (the unused part) can be carried over to the next years. A carried over loss remains long term or short term. A carried over long-term capital loss is offset against long-term capital gains before it reduces that year's short-term capital gains. The remaining capital loss may be "carried forward" to the next year and claimed as a capital loss against both capital gains and up to $3,000 against ordinary income on that year's tax return and so on until it is completely used up, or until the death of the individual who incurred the loss.

The lower tax rates for capital gains raises some serious questions.

It is a little surprise that tax planners as well as hedge funds and private equity industries have found the ways to exploit this regressive tax and have been able to structure their clients' income and their own funds so that most significant fractions of income are painted as capital gains and enjoy the lower tax rates.

The major problem is—as discussed above [p. 95]—that the low tax rate on long-term capital gains is a prominent and significant factor for the fact that the share of income going to the top 1 percent of earners has doubled since 1979, and the share going to the top 0.1 percent has almost tripled. Furthermore, the wealthiest 1 percent of Americans own about 40 percent of the nation's wealth. The meaning is quite straight forward. The lower tax rate on long term capital gains not only erodes the progressivity of the income tax system but actually turns the system into a regressive one. Such a system is not only problematic in terms of social justice and tax equity but also in terms of economic growth and efficiency. In his "Price of Inequality" Joseph Stiglitz claims that one of the major causes for the economic crisis in 2008 was the lack of progressivity of the U.S. tax system initiated by President Reagan's administration.

In one of the most influential op-eds in the New York Times (April 14, 2013), which was included later on in Stiglitz' 2016 book "The Great Divide: Unequal Societies and What We Can Do About Them"), Stiglitz commented:

> "*With such low effective tax rates—and, importantly, the low tax rate of 20 percent on income from capital gains—it's not a huge surprise that the share of income going to the top 1 percent has doubled since 1979, and that the share going to the top 0.1 percent has almost tripled, according to the economists Thomas Piketty and Emmanuel Saez. Recall that the wealthiest 1 percent of Americans own about 40 percent of the nation's wealth, and the picture becomes even more disturbing.*"

We also mentioned the IMF's Note by Ostry et al [pp. 90–95], which is based on solid empirical data, that claims that inequality can undermine progress in health and education, cause investment-reducing political and economic instability, and undercut the social consensus required to adjust in the face of shocks, and thus that it tends to reduce the pace and durability of sustainable economic growth.

3. THE SECOND CLASSIFICATION—CLASSIFYING ORDINARY INCOME AND LOSSES

A. The Basic Categories of an Ordinary Income

Reminiscent of its British origins, the U.S. Tax Code [Sec. 61(a)] elaborates on 15 types of gross income. Yet, the Code uses specific wording to indicate that the British Scheduler system has not been adopted in the U.S.A., and that the numerated list is not exclusive nor has any significance in term of classification: "Except as otherwise provided in this subtitle, gross income means all income from whatever source derived, including (**but not limited to**) the following items":

(1) Compensation for services, including fees, commissions, fringe benefits, and similar items;

(2) Gross income derived from business;

(3) Gains derived from dealings in property;

(4) Interest;

(5) Rents;

(6) Royalties;

(7) Dividends;

(8) Alimony and separate maintenance payments;

(9) Annuities;

(10) Income from life insurance and endowment contracts;

(11) Pensions;

(12) Income from discharge of indebtedness;

(13) Distributive share of partnership gross income;

(14) Income in respect of a decedent; and

(15) Income from an interest in an estate or trust.

In addition, the Code mentions alimony and separate maintenance payments.

We have already mentioned that under the U.S. tax system, the need and the tradition of classifying ordinary income and losses into different categories is quite limited, but its significance is growing, as demonstrated by the enactment of the Net Investment Income Tax in 2013. Under the current system, there are four main categories:

The first category is active income which is "earned income" derived mainly from labor i.e. human capital. It does not include passive income or portfolio (investment) income. The other categories are investment income, passive and trading income, and net gain.

B. Active Income; Trade or Business; Employees and Self-Employed

The main sub-category of active income is income from Trade or Business, which applies to firms [pp. 105, 249] (47)—every self-employed individual who run their own business, and to incorporated organizations. Though the Supreme Court concluded long ago that this class of income also applies to employees, more recent legislation in the area of the deductibility of unreimbursed employee expenses signals a new approach that draws a distinction between self-employed individuals and employees. Under this trend, there are some significant limitations on the deductibility of employees' business expenses [p. 293]. One explanation for these limitations is based on what we term the "dual capacity of the employee as a taxpayer" [p. 293]: on the one hand, an employee is a "member of a firm" (47) [pp. 105, 249] and their economic activity should be seen, observed and analyzed through the firm's interests; on the other hand, employees have their own professional interests that sometime differ from those of their employers; hence, they should be treated as having income from a trade or business.

A second category is income or loss from "Passive Activity", meaning income or loss derived from an investment that constitutes a trade or business but the pertinent taxpayer is not "materially participating" (actively engaged) in that business but has only a financial interest in it. [pp. 208, 293]

A third category is portfolio income, which is derived from investments and includes capital gains, interest, dividends, and royalties.

The two major practical reasons for distinguishing between the above categories are for tax rates and for expenses and losses deductions [pp. 281, 283].

As shown above, under the current law, passive income is subject to lower tax rates in many cases, but not always. For example, rental income—which is passive income—is subject to the ordinary income rate. Furthermore, beginning in 2013, a 3.8 percent Medicare contribution tax (also known as the "Net Investment Income Tax" (NIIT)) was imposed by Section 1411 on the net investment income of certain taxpayers whose income is over a specified threshold amount. Investment income includes both income from "passive activity" as defined by Section 469 and income from interest, dividends, annuities, royalties, and capital gains from portfolio. It also includes a specific type of income from trade or business, only from trading financial instruments or commodities. Other types of earned income are not subject to NIIT.

The classification is significant for certain matching rules [pp. 208, 279] that limit the deductibility of certain business expenses or losses. For example, business expenses of "passive activity" are only deductible against income from passive activity; passive losses cannot offset active income (e.g. wages or salaries) or "portfolio income" (e.g. dividends and interest). Expenses and losses within a trade or business, including employment (though unreimbursed employees' expenses are subject to certain limitations [p. 293]) are allowed against any type of income. In addition, under **Code Sec. 163(d)**, an individual taxpayer may only deduct "investment interest" (interest on debts incurred to acquire investments) against investment income. Under a similar rationale, Code Sec. 165(d) provides that losses from "wagering transactions shall be allowed only to the extent of the gains from such transactions." Similarly, Code Sec. 183 restricts deductions of expenses that are incurred in personal hobbies and other not-for-profit activities (private consumption), to the taxpayer's income from such activities.

C. The Basic Classification

As a general rule a business activity is quite easy to identify. Selling professional services or stock in trade produces income from trade or business. The same is true with passive income: renting real estate produces passive income. Yet the borderline is too broad, and the range of possibilities is immense. For example, suppose a taxpayer runs his own auto-repair business in his own property. The prices he charges for his services are probably calculated according to the compensation for the services he provides—based on his skill, knowledge, and working hours—but also on the return on the real property and other capital assets he uses, and the profit he makes when he sells and installs auto parts to his customers. Hence, theoretically, part of his income is active—the income from selling professional services, including his managerial skills, and from selling stock in trade. The other part of his income is passive—the return on his capital investment in his business. Note that if the cost of his background professional education is also considered as an investment, then part of the compensation for the services he performs should also be classified as a return on his invested capital.

Furthermore, suppose that after a certain period of time, the taxpayer decides to retire, and he rents his business as a "going concern" to a colleague. The classification of the rent that he collects depends on the essence of the deal he makes. If he receives a fixed amount of rent, which does not depend on the performance of the new owner's business, it seems that the rent should be classified as passive activity income, though part of it is a return on the goodwill that he was able to develop, hence it should be regarded as a return on his effort and activities in the past, i.e. active income from human capital [p. 220]. Now suppose that the rent he collects is a percentage of the business' turnover; or a percentage of the business' net profit; or suppose it is agreed that both parties are sharing the business' expenses and losses; or the old owner agrees that the new owner can still use the old owner's name—i.e. his goodwill—and even can consult with the old owner. From an economic point of view, each of these possibilities represent some degree of a business partnership where each party's income may be considered as income from trade or business.

A rule of thumb might ease the problem. The "trade or business" title is just a framework. The real classification should be based on the actual or factual test: does the taxpayer uses his own human capital to produce his income? Is his income **earned income** which is produced from work, time and knowledge? Though such a rule improves the test, the statutory "passive activity" test improves it further: even when income is classified as business income, if the taxpayer (a capital investor in a partnership, or even a goodwill) is not actively engaged in the income producing process, his income is not "earned income", and if the business suffers losses his losses are from "passive activity".

Yet both tests do not eliminate the problem. Another practical rule might help further: the Incidental should follow the tenet, the essence, the core of the matter. In order to avoid subtle and endless classifications and legal and factual disputes, classifications should be made according to the most prominent trait of income, and they should be based on the need and the purpose of the classifications. The income of the auto repairman who works in her own business should be classified as earned income, even though part of her income is a return on her investment in the business. The application of the substance over form principle also may provide guidelines helps in preventing the taxpayers from abusing classification in an artificial way. Consider an educated taxpayer who invested a significant amount in her education. After a while, she graduated and started working. Her income has two dimensions: compensation for her work including her time and performing services, and a return on her capital investment in her education. From an analytical point of view, the former should be classified as earned income and the latter as capital income. For practical reasons, tax law gives up such subtle classification and taxes the whole compensation as earned income compensation.

Chapter Nineteen

STAGE THREE—TAXATION OF TRANSNATIONAL ACTIVITY

1. BASIC CONSIDERATION AND PREMISES

The U.S. taxation of international activity system is composed of two separable aspects—i.e. tax jurisdiction and the prevention of double taxation, though another aspect: prevention of double non-taxation.

Tax jurisdiction deals with the question of which income, or whose income is subject to the domestic tax system. What are the considerations that should be taken into account in order to tax the income or the taxpayer?

In our global village, almost any international or transnational economic activity might lead to the problem of double taxation. A citizen of one country who is a permanent resident of another country produces their income—both passive and active—in one of those countries or in a third one. Which country is entitled to tax them? If all three, they might end up with an over 100% income tax. From an economic point of view such an outcome results in an economic inefficiency. The double/triple tax will certainly distort the local taxpayer's decision regarding how and where to produce income. In addition, if indeed they are subject to such a heavy tax burden, principles of vertical and horizontal equity are violated. Hence, there is a general understanding that double taxation should be prevented, as a matter of efficiency—tax neutrality—and as a matter of equity.

As indicated above and further discussed below [p. 232], for the last several decades there has been a new concern around the world. Due to the growing mobility of capital and human capital, aggressive tax competition among nations, and the flood of information that produces international transparency, the volume and the sizes of double non-taxation has become a major concern for both international organizations, such as the OECD, IMF and WTO, as well as the governments of the U.S.A. and the E.U. [p. 58]

A. Normative Consideration: Tax Jurisdiction and Its Justification

The normative consideration is mainly based on the question of the different states' entitlement [p. 63] to share the tax revenue derived from international activities. In modern times the first and most impressive attempt to present a comprehensive approach was made by a group of four scholars nominated by the League of Nations, who published their report in 1923. The report—which adopted committee member Professor Edwin Seligman's theories—presented a thorough analysis of the production and uses of wealth. The report considered several possibilities of ties and connections between states, taxpayers, and processes, such as political allegiance (citizenship, temporary residence, permanent residence or domicile), the location of wealth, and its use. Based on the ability to pay theory, the committee used the **economic allegiance** doctrine, [p. 69] which aims to allocate the tax revenue from international activities among the different states and governments. The factors that should be taken into account are the location of the taxpayer's economic interests and the states' contributions to the different processes that produce the taxpayers' wealth, and its recognition and use.

The interests that establish the economic allegiance are the following: the process of production; the process that forms the fruits of the production and turns it into recognized and usable wealth; and the process of using the wealth (current consumption and saving). Accordingly, all the states and governments that contribute to one of these processes are entitled to get their share. Hence the committee concluded that a state's jurisdiction to tax is justified by both basic economic allegiances: the source jurisdiction, i.e. the location of the production of income, and the residence jurisdiction—the location of the consumption or saving of income (where the taxpayer resides).

As suggested above [p. 71], the ability to pay and the benefit principles usually lead to similar conclusions. Indeed, British scholar John Tilley elaborates the underlying rationales for the dual criteria of tax jurisdiction:

> *"The [resident] is taxed because, whether he be a [domestic] subject or not, he enjoys the benefit of our laws for the protection of his property. The [non-resident]—because in respect of his property in the [state] he enjoys the benefit of our law for the protection of that property".*

Needless to say that the latter enjoys the benefit of the host country either as a producer or consumer of their income [p. 71]. As for the former, a country may reach the conclusion that the personal connection should be rather broad. If it considers its citizenship to be a valuable asset which provides significant benefits to its subjects, it may use citizenship in addition to domicile or permanent residence as the indication of personal allegiance.

Based on the above discussion, the first principle of taxation of international activity emerges: the **benefit principle**. According to this principle, the state is entitled to tax the taxpayer or their activities since it provides benefits to the production process or to the taxpayer by enabling them to operate, to consume or to save through its public goods and services. The taxpayer owes the state the price for using its public goods and services in all these three activities—producing wealth, consuming it, or saving it.

B. Efficiency Consideration: The Prevention of Double Taxation

It goes without saying that the above criteria and the benefit principle, which underlie the tax jurisdiction, may lead to double or even multi taxation. If every state that provides any type of benefit to the taxpayer's interest is entitled to tax, there may be more than one state that deserves tax revenue.

Long ago it was agreed that in order to promote economic efficiency, double taxation (and of course multi-taxation) should be avoided. In modern times economic efficiency calls for tax neutrality: in order to enhance the global, international and domestic welfare, the decision regarding the location of a given economic activity, including capital investment, should be tax neutral, i.e. not affected, or distorted, by tax considerations. The belief adopted by the U.S. Department of Treasury is that "Maximizing global welfare is probably the best way to maximize U.S. economic welfare. All nations are likely to do better over the long term by establishing international tax policies that encourage private investors to make the best use of resources".

At the first stage, two types of tax neutrality were discussed: Capital Import Neutrality (CIN) and Capital Export Neutrality (CEN).

CIN means that all the taxpayers operating in a certain state should be subject to the same tax regime in the source state. In other words, CIN calls for territorial taxation, i.e. taxation of all taxpayers—both residents and non-residents—only by the source state and exemption of the foreign source income. In that case, taxation has no effect on business competition and expansion opportunities within each state.

The common understanding of CEN is that it is best achieved when investors are taxed at a total tax rate, which equals the rate of their country of residence. In other words, CEN calls for a worldwide taxation of the state's residents, regardless whether the income is sourced within or outside that state.

During the last fifty years or so some, scholars have gone farther and suggested additional guidelines for tax neutrality: National Neutrality (NN, which focuses on the enhancement of domestic welfare instead of global); Capital Ownership Neutrality (CON, which requires that ownership patterns not be distorted by taxation); and National Ownership Neutrality (NON, which is based on the assumption that equally productive inbound foreign investments substitute for any outbound investment). Yet, the most fascinating development in that field is that there is no consensus regarding which one of the above concepts is the best. Furthermore, it is quite evident that CEN and CIN contradict each other, and complete tax neutrality is infeasible as long as a full unlimited foreign tax credit is not offered by any state. It is noteworthy that lately there has been a tendency to conclude that CIN, which requires a pure territorial system, may achieve the best result.

Whether we agree with such a conclusion or not, one important conclusion arises: to promote efficiency and greater global and domestic welfare, a **single tax**—no more and no less—should apply to any international (and domestic) transaction and income. Hence, Avi-Yonah has argued long ago, that a coherent international tax regime exists, which has been developed into customary international binding law embodied in both the tax treaty network and in domestic laws, and that it forms a significant part of international law. Such customary international law should prevent states from conducting harmful tax competition.

2. TAX JURISDICTION

There are two principal ways to determine whether a state has tax jurisdiction over the taxpayer or their income. The first way is what is known as the *territorial connection* between the **income** and the state. The second is the *personal connection* i.e. the connection between the **taxpayer** and the state.

A. The Territorial Connection: The Source State

The territorial connection is an acceptable factor in all income tax methods in the Western societies. In accordance with this connection, the state has the authority (and the power) to tax income that was produced *within* its territory (*the source state*). In order to determine whether the income is sourced within the U.S., the Code contains a list of source rules (Code Secs. 861–865). If the income is not sourced within the U.S. (income is *outside the U.S.A.*) then we turn to the personal connection.

B. The Personal Connection: The Residence State

Under the U.S. tax system there are three types of personal connections for individuals: non-residents who hold a U.S. "Green card", and resident aliens, who are determined according to the substantial presence test which requires a minimum number of presence days in the U.S.A.: 183 days over three consecutive years, which is calculated as follows: at least 31 days in the current year, 1/3 of the presence days in the first preceding year, and 1/6 of the presence days in the second preceding year. In addition, all the U.S. citizens are considered U.S. residents for income tax purposes. Note that there are only two other countries that use citizenship as a test for the determination of residency for tax purposes: Mexico and The Philippines.

As for corporations, the personal connection applies to domestic corporations. The general rule is very formal. A corporation is considered to be a domestic corporation if it is created or organized under the laws of the United States, any State, or the District of Columbia. No substantial test or criteria related to place of management can establish domestic corporation status. However, there are a few specific statutory provisions that consider certain foreign corporations as domestic, such as Code Sec. 269(B)(1), which applies to foreign corporations that are stapled to a domestic corporation. Some foreign subsidiaries of U.S. corporations (CFCs) which have passive income [Code Secs. 952 953(d)]; and foreign subsidiaries organized under the laws of a contiguous foreign country and maintained solely for the purpose of complying with the laws of such country, and are owned and control 100% by a domestic corporation, may, at the option of the domestic corporation, be treated as a domestic corporation [Code Sec. 1504(d)]. In addition, a foreign corporation shall be treated as a domestic corporation if such corporation would be a surrogate foreign corporation [Code Sec. 7874(b)].

C. The U.S.A. System: A Territorial or a Personal Connection Is Sufficient

Once one of the connections (the territorial or the personal) is established, the income or the taxpayer is taxable under the U.S. income tax. Furthermore, if a person maintains one of the above personal connections they are subject to the worldwide income tax and not only to the income within the U.S.A.

3. DOUBLE TAXATION AND WAYS OF PREVENTION

As already mentioned, transnational activity that extends over several states/ countries might be subject to more than one jurisdiction and bring about a situation of double taxation. In other words, a taxpayer will be subject to income tax on the same income in more than one country. Such situation undermines both the principles of equity and efficiency, and should be prevented.

Under the U.S. system, the two major ways to avoid or prevent double taxation are the unilateral *foreign tax credit* and bilateral tax treaties.

A. Unilateral Means: Foreign Tax Credit

The unilateral foreign tax credit method [p. 328] is quite simple at first glance: any income subject to U.S. income tax whose source is outside the U.S.A. is entitled to "foreign tax credit". The basic rule is that "the first bite (of the tax pie) goes to the source country". Yet the residence country provides a limited tax credit. As a rule of thumb the foreign tax credit is limited to the lower of the foreign tax amounts, or the tentative domestic tax amount.

There are several theoretical ways to set the limitations, such as "per country limitation" or "per type/category of income limitations" ("Baskets"). In general, the U.S. allows foreign tax credit for the foreign source income within the same type of income (income "basket"). The main income baskets are for passive income (primarily interest, dividends, royalties, rents, or annuities received by subsidiary), financial services income (income earned in banking, insurance, or finance), shipping income (income earned in international shipping activity), and general limitation income (primarily income earned abroad in the active conduct of a trade or business other than financial services, shipping, or income in the passive baskets). Income in each of these baskets is subject to a separate foreign tax credit limitation. Any excess foreign tax credits can be applied to offset the residual U.S. tax on foreign source income, of the same basket, earned during the previous two years or the following five years. If the credits cannot be used within that period, they are lost.

To demonstrate: Suppose Jim is an American-green-card-holder, who has some passive income from U.S. sources and works in the Netherlands for $30,000 a year. Assume this income is subject to the Dutch income tax of $6,000. The U.S. tentative tax payment on the same income from working in the Netherlands is $7,000. In that case, the Dutch government (the source state) gets the full amount of $6,000 and the U.S. government receives the residual amount of (7,000−6,000=)$1,000. On the other hand, if the Dutch tax payment is $8,500, the $1,500 is not refundable tax credit (37, 82, 125) against the U.S. tax on passive income. Instead, it may be carried backward for two years or forward for five years and offsets against U.S. tax on any foreign income from trade or business, including employment.

B. Bilateral Means: Tax Treaties

Notwithstanding the fact that all the treaties are bilateral for the time being, most of those treaties have some basic common ground. The differences between the various treaties are usually marginal.

There are three major models of tax treaties: the OECD's, the UN's and the U.S.A.'s. In every treaty there are detailed definitions of the main terms in the treaty, such as: "residence of a contracting state", "permanent establishment", "personal services" etc. The treaties were principally intended to divide the "tax pie" between the two contracting countries; provide tax relief for purposes of preventing double taxation; and arrange for the exchange of information between the tax authorities of the said countries. In all of the tax treaties, there is a provision that prohibits each of the contracting countries from discriminating against the citizens of the other country. However, every contracting country is entitled to grant its citizens or residents tax benefits or tax reliefs due to personal status.

Usually, the above-mentioned rule that the first bite goes to the source country is applied by tax treaties only to active income. The residence country gets the first bite of the passive income.

The treaties usually specify most of the types of income and determine which of the contracting countries has the right to impose the tax, and which of the countries waives its right. In certain circumstances, the treaties provide that the two countries both have the authority to tax certain income and the prevention of double taxation is determined either within the treaty or within domestic law. In some cases one country may tax a certain type of income with a lower tax while the other country provides a tax credit to that lower tax rate and collects the rest.

4. INTERNATIONAL TAX COMPETITION: DOUBLE TAXATION AND DOUBLE NON-TAXATION

As indicated above [p. 232], one of the most important questions in the "globalization era" relates to the effectiveness, wisdom, and legitimacy of tax competition among those countries/states, that try to attract foreign capital. Some scholars have termed this competition as a "race to the bottom" that may dismantle the welfare state: the reduction of the tax rates decreases the states' revenues, which undermines the state regulation, cuts welfare programs and other public goods and services, and which eventually increases social gaps and poverty, undermines social solidarity and government's responsibility, and eventually decreases social capital as well. Such tax competition, which usually leads to a sweeping tax reduction may lead, under certain circumstances to lower economic growth, especially during times of economic crisis and recession. It does undermine the single tax benefit and the benefit principles. The constitutional discussion [pp. 6–8, 36–56] provides an additional dimension to the debate regarding discriminatory lower tax rates to foreign and capital investments.

The international community has begun to express serious concern regarding aggressive international tax planning that causes a huge amount of revenue losses. The OECD has published its action plan for Base Erosion and Profit Shifting (BEPS), which elaborates several options, such as a multinational treaty and guidelines for sovereign states to amend their domestic laws in order to cope with such phenomena. In addition, laws known as the General Anti-Avoidance Rule (GAAR), which prohibit "aggressive tax avoidance" have been passed in several developed countries including the United States (2010) [p. 58].

5. TAXATION OF TRANSNATIONAL CYBER ACTIVITIES

All these rules and developments, which are presented here in a nutshell, are indeed fascinating and challenging. The digital/cyber era adds a new dimension to this area of law. If a Permanent Establishment is crucial for allocating income to a specific country, how can the PE be established for an activity that takes place over the internet? Where is the place of production of digital intangible assets, which are created by professionals who are located in several labs and offices around the globe, and who communicate and exchange ideas and knowledge over the internet? Where does the sale of any kind of intangible (such as software, intellectual creations and advertisements) take place? Does it matter if the transaction is between Business to Business, or Business to Consumer? These are some new basic questions that the new era poses to the international and domestic communities [pp. ix, 60].

The OECD's report on Base Erosion and Profits Shifting (BEPS) elaborates the challenges:

> *The spread of the digital economy poses challenges for international taxation. This report sets out an analysis of these tax challenges. It notes that because the digital economy is increasingly becoming the economy itself, it would not be feasible to ring-fence the digital economy from the rest of the economy for tax purposes. The report notes, however, that certain business models and key features of the digital economy may exacerbate BEPS risks, and shows the expected impact of measures developed across the BEPS Project on these risks. The report also describes rules and implementation mechanisms to enable*

efficient collection of value-added tax (VAT) in the country of the consumer in cross-border business-to-consumer transactions, which will help level the playing field between foreign and domestic suppliers. The report also discusses and analyses options to deal with the broader tax challenges raised by the digital economy, noting the need for monitoring developments in the digital economy over time.

Chapter Twenty

INCOME QUANTIFICATION

As mentioned above, income may be paid not only with in money but also in kind, in money's worth [pp. 160, 162, 197]. In addition, tax law also has to cope with situations where groups of related taxpayers, who have common business or economic interests, are engaged in a transaction where part of the profits or gains are transferred between the members of such a group. In such a case the price indicated within the transaction documentation does not represent the true economic consideration. A common example is when a group uses transfer pricing methods (142) in order to shift the bulk of the profits of such a group from high tax regimes to lower ones or between related individuals with different tax rates.

In such cases, the practical question is how much income has the taxpayer actually earned? How should it be quantified?

The general answer is that the value of the transaction for tax purposes ought to be based on the market value of the sold merchandize (goods or services); as if the transaction has been carried out in Arm's length (12) between the parties. Indeed, Reg. 1.61–2(d)(1) provides that if services are paid in kind, i.e. in money's worth, the fair market value of the consideration must be included in the taxpayer's income. If the services were rendered at a stipulated price, such price will be presumed to be the fair market value of the compensation received in the absence of evidence to the contrary. Obviously, in cases where the taxpayer shows that the lower price has been set due to a pure bad bargain/transaction or to an ordinary business discount that aimed to attract regular customers, the lower price would be used for tax purposes.

The rationales for the arm's length rule are now clearer. First, in order to discourage taxpayers from underreporting their gains and lowering their taxes, the law assumes that the parties are reasonable and their transactions are according to rational business behavior. Second, when a taxpayer sells goods or services to a relative or any other related person, for below the market price, the imputed income (57) analysis helps us to realize that from an economic point of view the seller receives the fair market value of the sold property and paid back the buyer the difference between the market value and the actual price paid. The notional back payment made by the seller should be regarded as income in kind; if it is a personal gift to a relative, it is probably not deductible as the seller's business expenses. On the other hand, if the buyer is an influential figure and the motive behind the low-price sale is a business promotion, then the notional/in kind income should be offset against the back payment as a business expense, unless it was an illegal payment such as bribery.

1. COMPENSATION IN KIND

Suppose taxpayers receive income in kind, such as corporate shares, options or stock in trade, or free professional services, as compensation for the performance of their duties. Such compensations are taxable and the only question is the quantitative one. The question has a dual dimension: What is the value of the goods or services that the taxpayer ought to include within her tax return? The other dimension is of the grossing-up mechanism. If the taxpayer is an employee subjected to the withholding system, a gross-up income mechanism (83) should be considered.

As for the first dimension, the general rule is that the amount of the income is the market value of the goods and services received. The concept of taxation of barter transactions is already familiar [pp. 193, 197]. Suppose a lawyer provides legal services to a furniture manufacturer. In return she receives some furniture "free of charge." In that case we assume the manufacturer sells the furniture in the market, receives the market price (and has taxable income) and pays the lawyer her compensation. The manufacturer has a gross income and if the legal services were given to the business he can deduct the same amount as a business expense. The lawyer has to include the market price of the furniture as her income. If the furniture is used at her home, there is no deduction for her. If she uses the furniture at her office, it should be considered as the price of a capital asset and may be deducted, according to some tests through depreciation or current expenses [pp. 252–256].

Yet we still have a dilemma. Which market price should be used here? A wholesale price—assuming the manufacturer sells his products to dealers and charges them a wholesale price; or maybe the retail price—the same price the lawyer would have paid if she bought the furniture in a regular store?

Generally speaking, the fair market value is the "arm's length" price (12), at which the property would change hands between a willing buyer and a willing seller, neither being under any pressure or compulsion to buy or sell and both having reasonable knowledge of relevant facts. Furthermore, if the manufacturer pays his suppliers with stock in trade, at a time when he could not reasonably have been expected to receive its usual selling price, the value of the furniture is not the usual selling price but is the amount for which the quantity of property contributed would have been sold by the donor at the time of the transaction. Assume that the manufacturer's cost is $75, his wholesale price is $100, and retail price is around $130. The supplier provides "free of charge" service to the manufacturer, and in return receives the said furniture. Here we have a unique situation: the manufacturer's market price is the wholesale price—$100—and his gain is $25. He also has a deductible business expense of $100, whereas the lawyer's income is $130. Something seems wrong. Indeed we should use the concept of a barter transaction and income in kind in order to resolve the issue. In a non-barter transaction, the lawyer provides legal services and receives her fee of $130. The manufacturer sells his furniture for $100, adds another $30 and pays the lawyer. If the legal services are for his business he has a deduction of $130. The lawyer has a gross income of $130 and the manufacturer has an income of (25+30=)$55 profit ($25 for his regular gain from the whole sale and another $30 as the value of the legal services he would have paid if the transaction was carried out with money payments. Hence, the lawyer has $130 of income and an expense of $130 from purchasing furniture that she can deduct immediately or depreciate (30, 31) [pp. 191–212, 260–263, 262, 263]. If it is for her personal use, she has only income of $130 and no deduction. Note though that the manufacturer finances the payment to the lawyer from two transactions. One is from providing the furniture to the lawyer. The other one is income from other sales to other buyers. If he is required to include $130 in his gross income from the lawyer transaction, he will be taxed twice on the $30. Hence the right way is for the manufacturer to report the barter transaction as a sale of its usual sale, i.e. $100 and the lawyer has to report the $130 from the services she provides to the manufacturer. This means both parties have to include in their gross income the fair market value of the goods and service each of them provides i.e. the manufacturer's gross income is the **retail** price.

Another problem is when an employee receives income in kind from their employer. Due to the withholding requirement (136) a gross-up procedure (83) should be considered. We begin with a simple and common assumption, shown in this example: an employer provides his employee with a salary of $1,000. Assume the employee's tax rate is 25% (ignoring the progressive tax structure for the sake of simplicity). The employer withholds the tax and pays the employee the net income of $750. The employee uses said that amount to buy a golden ring with a FMV of $750 for his own personal use. Assume now that the employer offers another employee—"employee 2"—with the same position, a fringe benefit instead of the cash salary. Employee 2 agrees, knowing that his earnings are equal to his colleagues'—employee 1. The employer allocates $1,000, buys the golden ring for $750 and sends the IRS the withheld tax of $250. In both cases both employees' gross income is $1,000 and their tax of $250 was withheld by the employer and sent to the IRS. In other words, the cost of the taxable fringe benefit is grossed-up. The technique is simple: since the employee has a net income of 75% and the marginal tax rate is 25%, the assumption is that the employer has the duty to withhold the tax and pay the employee 75% of the income, hence 75% is equal to $750 and 100% is equal to (750/0.75=)$1,000 or GI=NI/1−MTR, where GI is gross income; NI = net income and MTR = the employee's marginal tax rate; in this example (750/1−.025=)1,000.

Now assume that the employer decides to grant his employees with a bonus, a private car, which costs $15,000.

The bonus is taxable, and the employees' marginal tax rate is 30%. The tax that the employer has to send the IRS of the amount withheld should be calculated as follows: the gross-up income is calculated in a simple basic presentation: if 70% is equal to $15,000 then 100% is equal to 15,000/0.7=$21,428, which is the grossed-up income. Hence, 30% tax of $21,428 gross income is equal to (21,428*0.3=)$6,428. and not (15,000* 0.3=)$5,000. Bottom line: the taxable gross-up income is (15,000/0.7=)$21,428 and the tax is (21,428*0.3=)$6,428.

Assuming the taxpayers' tax rate is 30% (ignoring the progressive rates for the sake of simplicity) then when an employee receives a fringe benefit worth $130 that amount represents (100−30=)70% of their before-tax taxable income, and 100% of their taxable income, which is equal to (100*130/70; or 130/0.7=)$185 and after a 30% tax is withheld the net income is $130. Under this example, the IRS receives (185*0.3=)$55, the employee's net after-tax income is $130 and the employer has $185 of deductible expenses.

2. PRIZES AND LOTTERY GAINS

In some cases, taxpayers receive income in kind in a non-voluntary transaction. Suppose a married couple—the taxpayer—buys a charity lottery ticket and wins the first prize, or participates in a radio talk show, answers some questions and wins a pair of tickets for a luxury cruise (*Turner v. Commissioner*). The ticket's retail price was quite significant, but the taxpayer was able to persuade the court that they would never pay the retail price; that the value of the winning ticket for them was not equal to its retail cost. The taxpayer argued that the value of the ticket should be based on the taxpayer's subjective circumstances: the winning ticket was not transferable and not salable and there were other restrictions on its use, and in any case if the taxpayer would have tried to sell it they would have had to offer a substantial discount. The Court preferred to the subjective ticket's value over its retail price (though the final amount was higher than the taxpayer's report).

Hence the conclusion that we draw is as follows. When income in-kind is received, its evaluation should be focused on the usage side of income (61)—consumption and savings. Hence, the value of the income in kind should be based on the benefit the taxpayer enjoys from its consumption—currently or in the future. The price of goods or services that are consumed in a free-market economy is their purchase price. Their fair market value represents the benefit the purchaser enjoys from consuming them. Hence, for income tax purposes, income received in-kind should be based on its fair market value. Yet, in unusual cases, where the taxpayer is able to provide some solid evidence which indicates that their subjective enjoyment from the goods or services is lower than their FMV, and that they would never spend their resources on purchasing them at their FMV, the gross income should be set according to the subjective benefit. Yet, a clarifying word: the subjective evaluation of income in kind is required, more so, when the income is not received in a transaction between two parties when the taxpayer does not provide pre quo pro consideration to the other party. After all, the consideration that the radio station received from the couple was only a small fraction of the total consideration that the station received from all participants in the radio show's lottery. In other words, if the taxpayer had given the radio station full consideration for the prize he received, it is likely that their gross income would have been determined according to an objective FMV of the ticket.

Chapter Twenty-One

GROSS INCOME, ADJUSTED GROSS INCOME, AND TAXABLE INCOME

1. THE TAX BASE: TAXABLE INCOME

Income tax is levied on "Taxable Income" [Code Sec. 1]. The term "taxable income" means gross income minus the deductions allowed [Code Sec. 63(a)]. Gross income means all income from whatever source derived [Code Sec. 61(a)]. And, as the above flow chart indicates there is a list of items that are excluded from Gross Income [p. 206]. In order to move from Gross Income to Taxable Income, there is one additional stage which is termed **Adjusted Gross Income** (AGI). It is an interim stage. AGI means, in the case of an individual, gross income minus some enumerated deductions and exemptions [Code Sec. 62(a)].

Again, AGI is an interim stage. After the taxpayer's AGI is set, additional deductions are taken in order to determine the final tax base: "***Taxable Income***". Three types of deductions are used to move from AGI to Taxable Income: **Personal Exemptions, and either Itemized deductions** or **Standard deductions** [p. 287]. However, the special rules of the TCJA in place until 2026 have eliminated the personal exemption in lieu of a larger standard deduction. The common ground for those deductions, which is discussed below [pp. 287–288], is that they are a combination of personal consumption, nondiscretionary expenses, and indirect cost of the taxpayers' ability to produce earned income [p. 278]. Instead of the itemized deduction, taxpayers have the option to elect the standard deduction, a fixed amount of money, which releases the taxpayer from the tedious duty of keeping book records and elaborating actual expenses. In addition, AGI is used as a yardstick that sets some limitations on the amounts or percentages of some itemized deductions or other benefits to some taxpayers—usually low-income earners.

The deductions that are allowed from Gross Income in computing the AGI are called "above-the-line deductions". The deductions that are allowed from AGI in computing Taxable Income are called "**below-the-line deductions**".

The following simple formulas present the relationship between Gross income, Adjusted gross income and taxable income:

- Gross income = Economic income − (non-realized income + imputed income (57) + statutory exemptions/exclusions).
- Adjusted gross income (AGI) = Gross Income − Above the line Deductions.
- Taxable income = AGI − (Personal Exemptions + below the line Deductions).

We began our journey of defining taxable income with the broadest concept of Economic Income and narrowed it down to the statutory definition of Gross Income. Based on the discussion above [pp. 197–198] we concluded that there are three basic traits that narrow the economic definition of income and lead to the term Gross Income. The first two were developed by the courts: the realization requirement (103) and imputed income (57). The third one derived from a series of statutory provisions—"exemptions"—that specifically exempt certain types of income from being taxed.

Once the taxpayer's gross income is set, the next stage is narrow the tax base to the Taxable Income. For this purpose, there are three kinds of factors that eventually reduce—directly and indirectly—the taxpayer's gross income and enable computation of the taxable income: **Exemptions**, **Deductions** and **Offsetting of losses**. In addition, there is another factor that reduces the final tax payment, which is a tax credit (125).

2. THE SOCIAL AND ECONOMIC SIGNIFICANCE OF EXEMPTIONS, DEDUCTIONS, OFFSETTING LOSSES AND TAX CREDITS

A. The Tax Savings of Deductions, Exemptions and Offsetting Losses

As is discussed above [pp. 4, 31–36], under progressive tax rates, any deduction, exemption and offsetting losses that are not phased out (94) [p. 35] provide a higher tax savings (133) to those taxpayers with greater economic ability and a smaller tax saving to those taxpayers with lower income. Hence, using TRI (84, 127, 131) [pp. 3, 31] violates horizontal and vertical equity. On the other hand, one may argue that they promote efficiency. They encourage the taxpayer to increase their labor supply and income in order to gain higher tax savings. (133) [pp. 4, 240]

The use of tax incentives in order to achieve or promote economic, social, and demographic national goals is quite risky and involves deficiencies and problems. It creates constitutional problems—it may violate the constitutional principles of equality, property rights, and freedom of contract and occupation [p. 36]. It infringes on and endangers some basic principles of the democratic system, since, despite the publication of the tax expenditure budget, the general public is not aware of the full extent of the true meaning and costs of the incentives. In addition, the public's agents are exposed to political pressure from powerful interest groups. The use of tax incentives also creates economic inefficiency, *inter alia* due the low cost of capital which produces a "moral hazard" (79).

B. The Possible Relation Between the Employer's Tax Rate and the Level of the Employee's Compensation

Generally, wages and salaries, including taxable fringe benefits, which are paid by the employers to the employees are deductible as trade and business expenses (unless paid for the creation of capital assets, trading stock, or they are illegal). As mentioned already above [p. 101], lower tax rates on employers might lead to lower compensation, higher unemployment, and greater social gaps. The underlying rationale is that employers are looking for their highest after-tax earnings and are more reluctant to increase their out-of-pocket expenses. I.e. as the expense's tax saving (133) [pp. 4, 240] is higher, so is the willingness to spend more on expenses, and vice versa. This idea may be demonstrated by the following assumptions:

1. Corporations (whether shareholders or management and high paid officers) are looking for the highest net (after-tax) profits.
2. The corporation's activities maximize its profit. The free market sets its prices.
3. The corporation's income is X.

4. The corporation's expenses are *Y*.
5. The corporation's salaries and wages are a significant part of its expenses.
6. The corporate tax rate is *t*.
7. The corporation's after-tax earnings are *P*.

The after tax-earnings are the corporate income minus expenses times the after-tax rate.

Hence: $NP=(X-Y)*(1-t)$, and the derivative of the net earnings is

$$\frac{\partial P}{\partial Y} = 1-t$$

Since *t* is always smaller than 1, there is a negative correlation between NP and Y; once Y is increased, *NP* is decreased in the above ratio $1-t$. I.e. when an employer increases its expenses by 1 the net profits go down by $1*(1-t)$. In other words, in a given amount of expenses, the higher the payer's tax rate (and tax saving), the lower its net earnings and vice-versa.

For example, assume that an employee gets $3,000 a month and the employer's marginal tax rate is around 50% (Corporate tax + Tax on dividend). Due to the employers' tax saving (133) [pp. 4, 240] of the $3,000 deduction, $1,500 is paid by the treasury and $1,500 goes out of the employer's (shareholders') pockets. Assume now that the employer's tax rate goes down to 15%+10%. In that case, the employer's tax saving, as well as the treasury's share, goes down to (3,000*.25=)$750 and the employer's out of pocket share goes up to $2,250. Hence, whenever there is tax cut that reduces the employer's tax rate, greedy employers and shareholders will put in efforts to reduce the employees' aggregate compensation, either by salary reduction or workforce cuts. A superficial empirical examination indicates that when the tax rate was significantly reduced during the early eighties, the employees' compensation did not follow the inflation rate—i.e. a reduction in real terms—and as indicated above [pp. 90, 97, 101], the gaps between capital and labor rose. We suspect that if the corporate tax rate was reduced to 15%, this tendency would be enhanced, and the general direction of constant decrease of compensation for labor would continue [p. 285]. Moreover, if employees' compensation is reduced, the government's revenue will be reduced further and the national deficit might be greater than expected.

The emerging conclusion is evident. Tax cut for employers, especially for corporations, eventually leads to lower salaries or workforce cuts, or both. Such results might open a vicious circle: they causes lower government revenue, which leads to less public goods and services, lower income for labor and a higher rate of unemployment, higher net income (after tax) for corporations and capital owners, higher rates of social gaps, and in the long run, defective social and human capital and declining sustainable economic growth.

C. Are Tax Credits Better?

A popular argument is that providing tax incentives through tax credits (125), instead of exemptions or deductions is preferable, since tax credits provide the same tax savings (133) to all taxpayers. The validity of such an argument is doubtful. First, if the amount of the credit is higher than the taxpayer's tentative tax liability, such taxpayer does not enjoy the whole benefit of the credit, e.g. if a taxpayer's tax liability is $2,000 and the credit amount is $3,000, she only enjoys a tax saving (133) [pp. 4, 240] of $2,000 and $1,000 is lost, [p. 319] unless it is a negative/refundable tax credit (37, 93, 94, 125) [p. 325].

Second, since tax credits are not part of the net income concept but rather are a kind of TRI [pp. 3, 31] (84, 127, 131), their economic meaning is a government grant free of tax. If a taxpayer's tentative tax is $5,000 and she is granted a tax credit in the amount of $750, she actually receives a net grant of $750. In order to appreciate their full economic value in a society whose tax system is based on the principles of equality and tax equity, the tax credits should be grossed-up (83) [pp. 237, 319] according to the taxpayer's marginal tax bracket. For example, assume three taxpayers: A's marginal tax bracket is 0%, B's is 15% and C's is 50%. All three of them are entitled to a $1,000 tax credit (A receives a refundable credit). The grossed-up (83) government grant that A receives is (1,000/1=)$1,000; B's grant is (1,000/0.85=)$1,176.50, whereas C's amounts to (1,000/0.5=)$2,000. Hence, even the tax credit system provides a greater benefit to the higher income taxpayers, unless it is specifically phased-out [p. 35] or even refundable, like the Earned Income Tax Credit [p. 325].

D. Various Exemptions

As indicated already [pp. 4, 240], the effects of the exemptions on taxpayers is similar to those of deductions and offsets, i.e. they reduce the taxable income and provide different tax savings (133) [pp. 4, 240] for different taxpayers according to their tax rates: unless they are phased-out, they provide greater relief for those with the higher tax rates, smaller relief for those who are subject to lower rates, and no relief at all to those taxpayers whose tax rate is zero.

The exemptions may be classified into the following major categories, according to their purposes: exemptions that derive from the "net income concept" (84); exemptions that intend to serve as tax incentives; disguised exemptions which do not exempt income but just defer the tax event [p. 221]; exemptions that are aimed to allow the taxpayer a minimum and dignified standard of living (25) [pp. 50, 128, 149]; and exemptions that represent the legislature trading accuracy for the sake of simplicity and administrative efficiency.

1) Exemptions Derived from the "Net Income Concept"

In order to prevent taxation of items that do not represent real gains, profits or accretion to wealth, and to reduce the amount of unnecessary legal disputes and litigation, the Code elaborates special exemptions that remove the doubts and make it clear that such items are excluded from taxable income.

A) Meals or Lodging Furnished for the Convenience of the Employer

Code Sec. 119 excludes from gross income meals and lodging provided to employees, their spouses, and their dependents, pursuant to employment if such provisions are intended for the convenience of the employer and not as compensation for the employee's services. As is discussed above [p. 200], in order to determine whether the meals and lodging are indeed for the convenience of the employer, the Code elaborates two conditions: first, whether the meals and lodging are provided as a **Condition of Employment**. In the case of meals, meals are considered to be intended for the convenience of the employer if they are furnished on the employer's **Business Premises** (e.g. highways restaurants are not considered business premises for highway's patrol officers). In the case of lodging, lodging is considered to be intended for the convenience of the employer if the employee is required to accept such lodging on the business premises of their employer as a condition of their employment.

The "Employer's Business premises" has several aspects and tests:

a) the residence is owned by the employer,

b) it is designed, at least in part, to accommodate the business activities of the employer,

c) in case of lodging:

   1) the employee is required to live in the residence,

   2) there are significant business activities for the employee to perform after normal working hours in his home because of the extensive nature of the employer's business and the high-ranking status of the employee,

d) the employee actually performs business activities in the residence,

e) the residence served an important business function of the employer.

The "Condition of Employment" test means that the meals or lodging are provided "due to the nature of the employer's business"; there must be a direct connection between the lodging or meals furnished and the business interests of the employer served thereby. E.g. a certain type of residence for the employee is required and "it would not be reasonable to suppose that the employee would normally have available such housing for the use of his employer".

The lodging and meal exemption is not free from doubt. If we regard the lodging and meals from the usage side of the definition of income, then those benefits are part of the employee's personal consumption and should be included in the employee's taxable income. On the other hand it seems that those benefits are not compensation for the employee's services. It seems that the exemption is regarded as a practical compromise where litigation considerations on the one hand and sensible rules where trivial follows the substance on the other should lead to a comprehensive exemption. Indeed, it might be a better solution if the code exempts only those benefits whose value is insignificant (lodging and meal provided to a night guard; a quick lunch for customers, service staff etc.), and taxes those benefits that provide significant consumption to the employee and their relatives (e.g. a luxury mansion to the corporate executives). A more accurate rule would allocate part of the benefit to the employee's income and tax them accordingly.

Yet the current rule is that subordinate follows the essence, i.e. those benefits are totally exempted. The idea is that the employee has an obligation to perform their services and promote the employer's business interests; that the main reason for providing the lodging and meals is to serve the convenience of the employer and not to compensate the employee. The Code indeed ignores the benefit and the consumption the employee enjoys from the performance of their services. If we insist on taxing the benefits/enjoyment the employee derives from the performance of their duties, we might end up facing the dilemma that Henry Simon presented: how can the tax system draw a distinction between the two bodyguards of the opera-loving Kaiser who goes to an opera every night, wherein one of the bodyguards enjoys operas, and the other suffers from them?

While Section 119 exempts employees from including the cost of meals in their income, Congress was aware of the consumption element of the meals. Hence, Congress enacted Code Sec. 274(n) that deals with the **deductions** that are allowed for employers. This section limits many (if not even most) deductions for food, beverages and business entertainment up to 50% of their cost, based on the notion that: "some portion of business meal and entertainment expenses represent personal consumption (even if the expenses serve a legitimate business purpose). . . .[D]enial of some part of the deduction is appropriate as a proxy for income inclusion of the consumption element of the meal or entertainment."(HR Rep. No. 111, 103d Cong., 1st Sess. 645 (1993)). The expenses that are subject to the 50% limitation include, *inter alia,* the cost of the provision of food during office meetings and partner meetings; meals with clients, customers and vendors that will benefit the business; meals while on business travel status, and so on.

Note that in addition to Code Sec. 119, Code Sec 132 excludes some insignificant employee fringe benefit such as no-additional-cost services, qualified employee discounts, working condition fringe, de minimis fringe, and qualified transportation fringe, which represent the legislature giving priority to simplicity and administrative efficiency together with some aspects of tax incentives. As mentioned above, another similar exemption, which is designed for clergymen seems to violate the Establishment Clause and the constitutional principles of equality [p. 47].

B) Compensation for Personal Physical Injuries or Sickness

Code Sec. 104 excludes compensation for personal physical injuries or sickness from gross income. The Supreme Court (*Commissioner v. Schleier*) has decided that in order to qualify for the exclusion, a taxpayer must establish that prosecution or settlement of an underlying claim is based on tort or tort-type rights, and that the receipt of damages is on account of personal physical injuries or physical sickness. The underlying rationale of this exemption derives from the classical purpose of tort law i.e. to provide *full compensation* for proved harm; its very essence is restoration to the original state by rewarding the injured a sum of money which will put them in the same position as they would have been if they had not sustained the wrong for which they are getting the compensation or reparation. Therefore, such compensation does not represent any gain or profit, hence no taxable income. In order to avoid arguments and litigation such compensation is specifically excluded from gross income.

Note that prior to 1996, the Code excluded compensation for **personal** injuries. In that year, Congress amended Sec. 104 and replaced "personal" with "physical" injuries. Hence, damages or symptoms of emotional distress do not give rise to the exclusion. The amendment was a result of a growing and overwhelming number of claims and arguments for damages in lawsuits for mental injuries.

Following the above line of rationale—restoration to original state, no gain or profit—the Court of Appeals for the District of Columbia Circuit held in its first judgment in the *Murphy* case [pp. 41, 190] that damages awarded to compensate a taxpayer for emotional distress do not constitute "income" within the meaning of the Sixteenth Amendment and struck down the amendment. The court found that the taxpayer's award for emotional distress or loss of reputation is not taxable because her damages "were awarded to make [her] emotionally and reputationally 'whole' and not to compensate her for lost wages or taxable earnings of any kind." The court added that historical evidence indicated that "the framers of the Sixteenth Amendment would not have understood compensation for a personal injury—including a nonphysical injury—to be income." The award, in such situations, constituted only monies that "made the injured whole" and, in effect, are a return of her "human capital."

Yet the original three judges agreed to rehear the case and eventually overturned their own original decision. In its new ruling the Court ruled that gross income under Section 61 of the Internal Revenue Code does include compensatory damages for non-physical injuries, even if the award is not an "accession to wealth". The court then dismissed the non-constitutional arguments, by concluding that:

> *Principles of statutory interpretation could show § 61(a) includes Murphy's award in her gross income regardless whether it was an "accession to wealth," as Glenshaw Glass requires. For example, if § 61(a) were amended specifically to include in gross income "$100,000 in addition to all other gross income," then that additional sum would be a part of gross income under § 61 even though no actual gain was associated with it. In other words, although the "Congress cannot make a thing income which is not so in fact," Burk-Waggoner Oil Ass'n v. Hopkins, 269 U.S. 110, 114, 46 S.Ct. 48, 70 L.Ed. 183 (1925),* ***it can label a thing income and tax it, so long as it acts within its constitutional authority, which includes not only the Sixteenth Amendment but also Article I, Sections 8 and 9****. See Penn Mut. Indem. Co. v. Comm'r, 277 F.2d 16, 20 (3d Cir.1960) ("Congress has the power to impose taxes generally, and if the particular imposition does not run afoul of any constitutional restrictions then the tax is lawful, call it what you will") (footnote omitted). Accordingly, rather than ask whether Murphy's award was an accession to her wealth, we go to the heart of the matter, which is whether her award is properly included within the definition of gross income in § 61(a), to wit, "all income from whatever source derived."* (Emphasize added)

The Supreme Court denied review of this very unusual and problematic decision [pp. 41, 190].

2) Exemptions That Intend to Serve as Tax Incentives

The Code also provides some exclusions aimed to encourage or discourage certain activities or actions (127, 131), [pp. 3, 31] that may be considered as causing negative externalities which should be eliminated by Pigovian tax (131), [p. 36]. Such activities are, for example, employer contributions to employees' accident and health plans (Sec. 106) and qualified scholarships for students (Sec. 117).

A) Employer Contribution to Employee's Accident and Health Plan

The rationale underlying such exclusions is quite simple. As long as there is no comprehensive mandatory health care system in the U.S.A., any responsible government has to try to ensure that most of the population has a certain degree of health insurance. Due to the adverse-selection market failure (8), [p. 127] one way to achieve this goal is to encourage a large amount of individuals to join non-mandatory health insurance by reducing its cost. A general subsidy for any citizen may be too expensive and increases inefficiency. Mandatory medical insurance is a loaded issue in the U.S.A. The compromise is a limited subsidy provided only to employees and self-employed individuals.

Without the exclusion, if employers buy or provide medical insurance to their employees, the benefit would be considered as part of the employee's compensation subject to income tax, while the cost would be deductible for the employers. The exclusion eliminates the symmetry: the employers are still allowed to deduct the cost but the employees are exempted. The Code excludes from the employee's gross income any contributions which their employers make to an accident or health plan (not necessarily insurance) for compensation to the employees for personal injuries or sickness incurred by them and their relatives. The employer may contribute to such a plan either by paying the premium (or a portion of the premium) on a policy of accident or health insurance covering one or more of their employees, or by contributing to a separate trust or fund (including a fund referred to in Section 105(e)) which provides accident or health benefits directly or through insurance to one or more of their employees.

The cost of self-employed health insurance for medical and qualified long-term care is fully deductible if paid to a plan established under the taxpayer's business, and the business's income equals or exceeds the insurance amount. Yet this deduction is available only for the period the taxpayer or their spouse are not eligible to participate in an employer-subsidized health plan.

In addition, any taxpayer is entitled to deduct direct medical expenses subject to some limitations and restrictions.

One could argue that those exemptions (and deductions) should not be classified as tax incentives but rather as Congress' recognition that the tax base should indeed be based on the concept of discretionary economic power (25) [pp. 12, 291]. In other words, the underlying rationale is the constitutional principle of the assurance of dignity for every member of the society, which requires a right for a decent existence—to a minimum standard of nutrition, health care and other essentials of life [p. 50].

B) Qualified Scholarship for Students

Under Section 1.162–5 of the regulation, a taxpayer cannot deduct educational expenses. Indeed, the cost of college education is usually considered as a personal expense which is not deductible (*Carroll v. Commissioner*); the fact that the petitioner's education is helpful to him in the performance of his employment does not establish that its cost is deductible as a business expense. Yet, in some cases the taxpayer is allowed to deduct educational expenses where the expenses were incurred to maintain or improve skills that were required previously by the individual taxpayer in their employment [Regs Sec. 1.162–5(a)(1)]. This category includes refresher courses or courses dealing with current developments as well as academic or vocational courses that are aimed to improve or expand the taxpayer's expertise, e.g. a tax lawyer who studies for an LL.M degree in taxation. However, no deductions are allowed if the education is part of a program of study that will lead to qualifying the individual in a new trade or business, or if it is needed to meet the minimum education requirements for qualification of the taxpayer's employment [Treas. Regs. § 1.162–5(b)(3)(i)]. As is discussed below, a more accurate analysis of tuition fee deductibility is to ask whether they are current expenses or capital ones. Are they aimed at preserving the taxpayers' existing trade or business, or improving it? If the expense is one that ***maintains*** the current trade and does not improve it, it is fully deductible in the year it is incurred [pp. 259, 270].

As a general rule Code Sec. 102 excludes from gross income any gift which is granted out of pure generosity (and not as a return for goods and services). This exclusion does not apply to prizes and awards nor to scholarships and fellowship grants, probably since the motives behind such scholarships are varied and some are not out of pure generosity and may entail some obligations the recipient accepts in return. However, Code Sec. 117 specifically excludes any amount (including the value of contributed services and accommodations) paid or allowed to, or for the benefit of, an undergraduate or graduate student, to aid such individual in pursuing their studies. The excluded items include the cost of tuition, matriculation, and other fees which are furnished or remitted to the student, including room and board.

3) Disguised Exemptions

As discussed above [p. 221] the mere fact that some gains are exempted from gross income does not mean necessarily that they escape taxation. Though the Code (Sec. 102) excludes gifts; inheritances, bequests, and devices from gross income, in the case of gifts the exclusion just postpones the timing of the tax event but does not exempt it entirely. Though gifts are excluded from gross income, the economic gain that is accumulated during the aggregate holding period is eventually taxed through rollover of the adjusted basis of the property in the first disposition that is not exempted. Of course, such postponement is valuable since "deferred *tax* is a *tax saved*" [p. 105].

The Code (Sec. 1031) provides a similar disguised exclusion (hence the term used is "non-recognition" of gain instead of exclusion or exemption) for a gain (or loss) upon the disposition of property in a "like kind exchange: no gain or loss is recognized if property held for productive use in a trade or business or for investment is exchanged solely for property of a like kind to be held either for productive use in a trade or business or for investment [p. 205]." 1031(a)(1). In addition, the non-recognition provision applies when property held for a productive use in a trade or business and is exchanged for property held for investment and vice versa. Some properties are excluded from that section and are not entitled to this tax deferral (e.g. inventory (67), stocks (28), bonds, notes or any kind of debt, interests in a partnership or trust and chose in action). An exchange is not within the provisions of that section if, as part of the consideration, the taxpayer receives money for the above excluded property. Similarly, a transfer is not within the provisions of that section if, as part of the consideration, the other party to the exchange assumes a liability of the taxpayer (or acquires property from the taxpayer that is subject to a liability). Note though that a transfer of qualified property, which meets the above requirements, may be entitled to the provisions of that section, even though the taxpayer transfers not-in-kind property or money. However, the non-recognition treatment does not apply to that additional not-in-kind property. The words "like kind" have reference to the nature or character of the property and not to its grade or quality.

The non-recognition is indeed just a deferral measure: the basis of a property that was acquired on a "like-kind" exchange shall be the same as that of the property exchanged, decreased in the amount of any money received by the taxpayer, and increased in the amount of gain or decreased in the amount of loss to the taxpayer that was recognized on such exchange.

The Code provides some more non-recognition provisions such as for involuntary conversions (Sec 1033) [p. 205] and for gain from qualified small business stock to another qualified small business stock (Sec. 1045).

Note that the exemptions of inheritance are different. Here the Code truly excludes inheritance from income tax (as long as the current system has estate and gift taxes). Code Sec. 1022 offers—by a "step up" basis [p. 143]—the executor of an estate to allocate up to 1.3 million in basis for singles and 3 million for surviving spouses to the property of the estate. This will effectively give most recipients a tax basis in the property equal to the full market value at the date in which the inheritance takes place.

4) Simplicity and Administrative Efficiency

Sometime the required rule is simple and straightforward, yet its application is complicated and burdensome. It might create unnecessary complexity where the outcome is quite insignificant. In such cases the legislature prefers simplicity and administrative convenience over accuracy. Such is the case regarding employees' insignificant fringe benefits, e.g. no-additional-cost service, qualified employees' discounts, working condition fringe, de minimis fringe, and qualified transportation fringe. See Code Sec. 132. All these are mixed purpose benefits, and an allocation rule should be used. Yet a practical cost-benefit analysis suggests giving up the complicated chore of allocating these benefits and allowing such deductions in whole. Another example is the standard deduction (113) [p. 287] which is allowed to those taxpayers who are not ready or willing to handle their ledger or to collect and maintain receipts of small amounts that are spent for producing income; instead of itemizing their deduction, they claim the statutory fixed amount standard deductions.

3. ADJUSTED GROSS INCOME—GENERAL PRINCIPLES

AGI is the second crossroads/reference point on the map that leads us toward the taxpayer's tax base—"Taxable Income". It is the intermediary stage between Gross Income and Taxable Income.

AGI is defined, in the case of an individual, as gross income minus certain deductions, elaborated in the Code (Sec. 62). The most important and significant ones are trade and business expenses; certain trade and business deductions of employees (the code distinguishes between reimbursed and non-reimbursed employees' expenses); and expenses that are spent in order to produce other types of income. Those deductions from Gross income are called "above-the-line" deductions, as distinguished from "below-the-line" deductions which are subtracted from a taxpayer's AGI in order to arrive at the taxpayer's Taxable Income.

Above-the-line deductions are fully deducted whereas certain below-the-line deductions are phased-out (94) [p. 321] or subject to other kinds of limitations for high-income taxpayers (e.g. Code. Secs. 25B, 67, 68, 213). In addition, these deductions are available to all taxpayers regardless of if they prefer the standard deduction.

The idea of "above-the-line" and "below-the-line" deductions has a purpose: to draw the distinction between the former—pure income producing expenses (no private or investment expenses) that should be fully deducted without any limitations, and the latter which have either mixed expenses or even private consumption or saving, but the legislature decided to allow parts of them for various reasons (improving a sense of equity, TRI (127, 131) [pp. 3, 31] etc.). Alas, as we see below this distinction has been indistinct due to the legislature's inclusion of some expenses that do not meet the traditional requirements of business expenses within the above-the-line deductions.

The Code provides specific provisions describing in detail the "above-the-line" deductions. Most of them refer to ordinary and necessary expenses paid or incurred during the taxable year in carrying on any trade or business (Code Sec. 162). In addition, the Code specifically forbids private expenses (Code Sec. 262) and capital expenses (Code Sec. 263) from being deductible. Yet some expenses that should be considered private consumption are allowed by the legislature as above-the line-deductions.

A. Households' Private Saving and Firms' Business Investment

First, a brief introduction of two economic concepts should be presented: Households and firms. [p. 105]

1) Households

Roughly speaking, economic activity is aimed for one purpose: to satisfy our needs and desires. In modern life the most common vehicle to provide us with our needs and desires is wealth, or if you will, money. Note this is the purpose of ***economic activity***. It is not our contention that all our needs and desires can be satisfied or met by economic activities or wealth; just consider the story about the old Greek philosopher walking in Athens' markets and mumbling to himself: "so many goods I do not need". Nevertheless, from an economic point of view, we as human beings have a dual capacity; we have two types of ***economic entities*** (as opposed to legal entities that lawyers are so fond of using). On the one hand we are consumers; on the other hand, we are income producers.

As households (56) we consume over our lifetime everything we earn. At the very end of the process, one should realize that everything that came in during our lifetime eventually goes out, and will be spent by us, either by our own spending/consumption or by the satisfaction of forwarding our wealth to our heirs, or beneficiaries in case of philanthropic donations, for their own consumption. When managing our private non-business activity, we consume as individuals or ***households.*** When a household saves some money, it actually defers its current consumption to later days; i.e. private saving is future consumption.

Individuals as income earners may operate either through professional/ occupational activities (either self-employed or as employees) or as investors who invest in capital assets that produce income—either passive income or capital gains. Either way the following discussion regarding firms applies to all kinds of economic activity that produce income.

2) Firms

Firms (47), [p. 105] either corporations, partnerships, or self-employed individuals, by definition, do not consume. They are means/tools/ends whose purpose is to provide individuals with the wealth to enable their own private consumption. A firm's only purpose is the production of income.

A firm may use its earnings through one of the following three ways:

- Uses it in order to produce its annual income, e.g. pay rent, salaries, electricity and other bills, etc.
- Invests it for the purpose of producing income in the future or avoiding expenses in the future.

- Distributes it to its individual owners, enabling them an improvement in the quality of their life, i.e. private consumption.

3) Household's Saving and Firm's Investment

For a firm, its major purpose is to maximize its owners' profit: to increase its earning from the sources side and to distribute the earnings to the owners for their own consumption or saving.

When a firm is saving, it advances its future business spending. For example: suppose a new newspaper ("the firm") is trying to create its own goodwill and strives to have 300,000 new subscribers during the next 5 years. In order to accomplish that end it realizes that it has to spend $100,000 each year for the next five years on advertisements and marketing. Now suppose that an old newspaper is willing to let our firm use its customers list of 300,000 subscribers for an annual fee of $100,000, or for an advance payment in the amount of $416,900 for using the list for the next five years. Our firm is facing the following dilemma: whether it should spend a total of $500,000, payable in five installments of $100,000 each year during the next five years, or pay in advance—*invest*—the amount of $416,900, which is the present value of the $500,000 (97) [pp. 106, 155]. If it chooses the latter option, it pays the $100,000 for the first year and the rest of the money is meant to save the firm from spending an annual payment of $100,000 in the next four consecutive years. Another example: assume that a firm needs a computer. It can rent it for $200 a year or purchase it for $497. In both cases buying the assets means saving part of the future annual expenses in the first year. Such saving is indeed an ***investment***.

No doubt, households might be in a similar position. Suppose a family considers its dwelling needs. It has two options: to buy an apartment or to rent an identical one. Just for the sake of simplicity assume the apartments' lifetime is 15 years and the salvage value (110) is zero. The annual rent is $15,000, the interest rate is 10% and the transaction takes place at the beginning of year 1. The apartment's fair market value is the present value of these annual installments i.e. $15,000+15,000/1.1+15,000/1.1^2+...$ $15,000/1.1^{14}$=$121,905 (97) [pp. 106, 155]. The family faces the same dilemma as the above firm: whether to pay a certain amount each year, or save the next years' annual payments by making one prepayment.

Though the firm's ***investment*** and the ***family's*** prepayment for the apartment are similar in ***form***, they differ in ***substance***: the former is an advance payment of business or profit-seeking expenditures; the latter is a form of saving on future consumption's cost. Hence the former should eventually be allowed but not the latter. In other words the disallowance of the business investment is just a matter of ***timing***.

If the firm's investment is used to purchase an asset that loses its value over its useful lifetime—e.g. a machine, building, etc. which are usually termed depreciable assets (31)—the annual deduction is just a matter of ***allocation***. If the investment is for an asset that does not lose its value due to production process—such as a piece of land or a corporate stock—the deduction has to wait until the asset is disposed (unless there is a specific "mark to market" provision) [p. 200].

The allocation process is done by an annual depreciation, amortization (20, 21). or other matching rules (76). The significant difference between a fully current deduction of the firm's investment and a future deduction is a matter of timing and interest—the time value of money (126, 140). If the interest rate is zero, the tax system will be indifferent regarding whether to allow the taxpayer to take a full deduction immediately or to defer it pro rate over the investment's productive life.

Note that the family apartment is also losing its value each year, yet the loss represents the family's annual consumption—the dwelling services the family derives from the apartment—thus no deduction should be allowed.

B. Deductibility of Expenses from the Usage Side—Consumption Plus Saving

As was mentioned, the income tax base from its usage side (61) is equal to current consumption plus saving [p. 157]. Accordingly, households' consumption and saving should be taxed, i.e. not subtracted from the tax base: no deduction should be made for those payments. We may also assume that personal gifts are aimed to maintain personal consumption of both the donor—their personal satisfaction from helping their beloved ones—or of the donee. Hence such gifts and bequests should be included within the tax base [p. 137] and therefore should not decrease the tax base, i.e. not be deductible. Donations for non-profit organizations (87) might also be considered as part of the donors' satisfaction, hence part of their personal consumption. On the other hand, some believe that contribution to the "third sectors" promotes society's welfare and the government's general goals and reduces the government's expenses on public goods and services. In other words, by donating charitable contributions the taxpayer directly promotes the government's goals. If in addition they would be asked to fully pay their taxes, they might "double finance" the government's goals, i.e. double taxation [p. 14]. That might be one of the rationales underlying the code provision of a special tax deduction for charitable contributions (Code Sec. 170) [p. 289].

C. Deductibility of Expenses from the Source Side—the Cost of Income Production

When we observe spending from the sources side (60), outlays that are aimed to produce income are not part of private consumption. Income spent on financing the cost of the annual earnings represents no consumption nor gain, profit or accretion to wealth. It is not part of the tax base. It should be subtracted from the tax base—it should be ***deductible***. Such income may be spent on the cost of the current year's income production—"current expenses." Business investments are expenses that are aimed at producing income over a longer period of time—"Capital expenses."

Capital investments are spent during the taxable year but their impact lasts longer. They create assets with economic value that last over the current year. Hence, the money spent is not entirely wasted within one taxable year. Investments do not represent a decline in the taxpayer's economic ability. If a taxpayer spends $1,000 on purchasing a non-depreciable asset (31) (e.g. piece of land), her wealth has not decreased: instead of having a sum of $1,000, she has an asset worth $1,000. She just exchanges money for an asset. Since there is no real spending, no deduction should be made.

Capital investments that lose their income-producing faculty over their useful years due to the production process (e.g. machines, buildings) are called depreciable or amortized assets. The cost of such assets should be allocated to the period of those years. The part that is allocated to the current year's income producing process is not an investment but the cost of earning income in that taxable year, and should be deducted against the current year's taxable income. From the investment's balance, which declines over the asset's useful life, only the annual decrease should be deducted during the taxable year (138) [pp. 191–212, 260–263, 262, 263]. Suppose the asset—a machine which lasts five years—was bought for $1,000. Assuming that the annual decline is linear [p. 263], then at the end of the first year it loses only $200 (20%, or one-fifth of the original cost) and the rest ($800) is still part of the taxpayer's wealth. The $200 is wasted during the taxable year for income producing, not for private consumption. It represents the production cost of that year's taxable income, and therefore should be subtracted from the taxpayer's taxable income. The same is true at the end of the second, third, fourth and the fifth years. Such subtraction is done either through ***depreciation***, ***amortization*** (20, 21) or, in some rare cases, through common matching rules (76). Note that after the end of the fifth year the original expense is fully deducted, and the book value of the machine (its "basis") is zero.

Another way to look at the investment cost is through its alternative. The cost of the above investment should be equal to the present value (97) [pp. 106, 155] of five annual rent payments. Hence the investment is actually a prepayment of the annual rent for 5 years. By paying the investment cost the taxpayer saves the current and the next four years' rent payments. In other words, the annual depreciation is quite close to the annual rent if interest (64) is taken into account.

D. Deductible Expenses

The picture is getting clearer and quite simple: any way you look at it, "deductible expenses" are those types of outlays that should not be taxed. From the "sources side" they do not represent profits or gains. Once the taxpayer spends them for the annual income producing purposes, they are not part of his possession or wealth, and therefore are not part of the tax base. They are the cost of the earning. They are the ***cause*** for the gain; they produce it. From the "usage side" the income which is not funneled for neither consumption nor saving for future consumption, and once again, it is not part of or a component of the taxable income.

Furthermore, a solid reassurance for the basic rule for the deductibility of business or profit-seeking expenses should examine the non-deductibility of saving expenses from another dual point of view: a positive aspect and a negative one. From the sources side the ***positive*** rule indicates that those expenses that are spent in order to produce annual income are deductible. The ***negative*** rule implies that those expenses that are not for the production of annual income are not deductible. From the usages side we could use a similar dual approach, though in a reverse aspect: under the usages side the ***negative rule*** states that those expenses that **are** spent for consumption—current or future—or for investment are not deductible. The ***positive*** rule implies that the expenses which **are not** for private consumption or investments are deductible.

The basic rules and their rationales should be clear now: expenses for personal consumption (including personal saving) are not deductible unless the legislature provides a special provision to the contrary. Non-consumption, income-producing expenses are deductible over the years they produce income. Current expenses, i.e. expenses that produce income during the current year and do not extend past the taxable year, are fully deductible during the current year, unless the legislature specifically prohibits them. Investments ("capital expenses") are spread across multiple taxable years ("depreciated", "amortized" or otherwise matching the annual income producing process [pp. 191–212, 260–263, 262, 263]) and only their annual contribution to annual income is deductible. Hence, though both outlays for consumption and for capital investments are not deductible, the major and significant difference between them is clear: the former are not allowed. Regarding the latter, it is a matter of timing. They are allowed according to their annual decrease. These rules are subject to special statutory provisions instructing otherwise.

So far we have presented the pure rationales for the deductibility rules. Note though that there are some exceptions to those rules, mainly statutory ones that represent the legislatures' desire to achieve certain goals or improve principles of equity or efficiency. Such is the case when the legislature implemented the "nondiscretionary power to consume" as the tax base (25) [p. 12]. For example, though medical expenses are considered private, special, or outstanding medical expenses are considered "below-the-line" deductible expenses (Code Sec. 213) [p. 292]. In addition, some personal expenses might be considered as deductible since they represent a decrease of the taxpayer's wealth, such as casualty losses (22) [pp. 32, 50] (Sec. 165(h)). In addition, in order to encourage taxpayers to save part of their income for future consumption, the Code provides a special, yet limited, deductions for deposits in pension plans ("IRAs") (Code Sec 401), which are "above-the-line". Losses from gambling or wagering of recreational gamblers should be considered as if derived from private consumption, and yet they are deductible against the taxpayer's gains from wagering activities (Code Sec. 165(d)). On the other hand, even if such activities were conducted as a trade or business, as opposed to a hobby, the court concluded that such losses cannot be deducted against any other income from other sources including other business [*Valenti v. Comm.* (1994)].

On the other hand, some current expenses otherwise deductible are not allowed if they are for illegal purposes (bribes or any other kickback payments) or if they might violate the public order or public rule [Code Sec. 162(c)].

The following concise flow chart summarizes the general concepts. It will be followed by detailed examples, demonstrations and exceptions.

The emerging rules may be depicted with the following flow chart:

Figure 21.1:

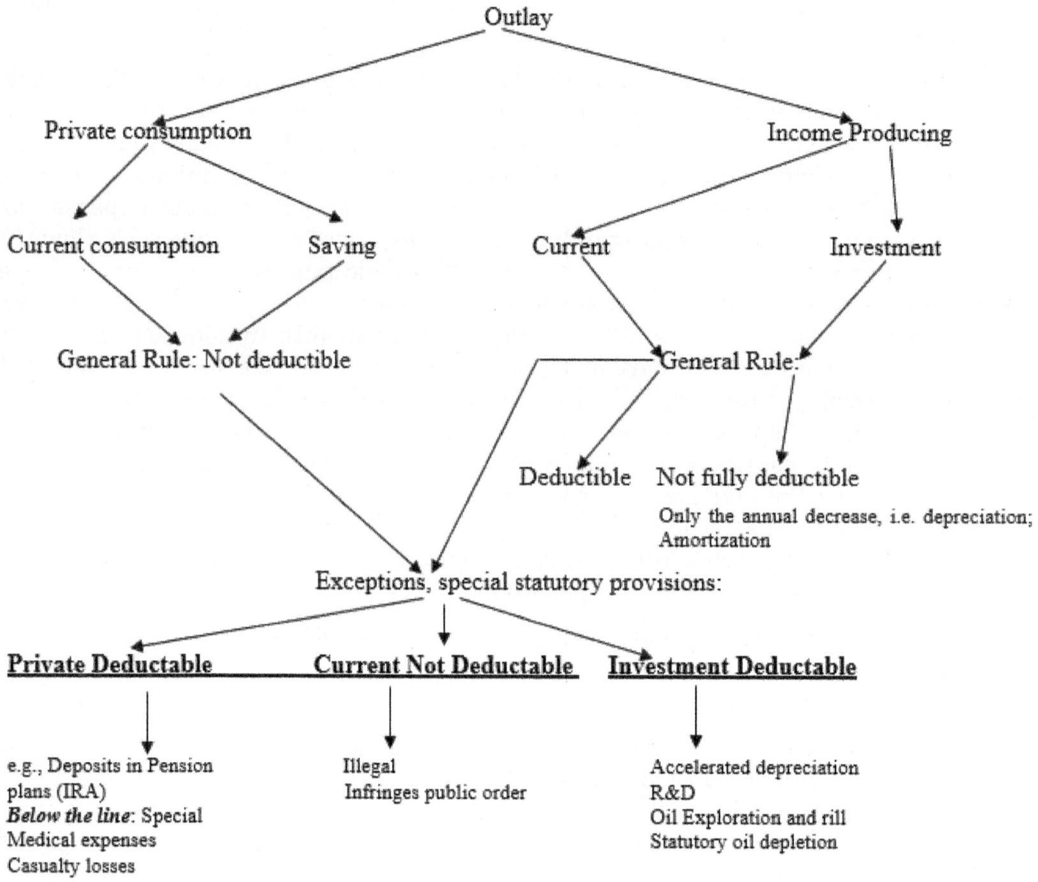

4. IMPLEMENTATION OF THE GENERAL PRINCIPLES

A. Expenses for Private Consumption

Though the concept of private consumption should be clear by now, the issue deserves some further discussion and reevaluation. There are many assumptions and presumptions that should be considered closely and maybe reconsidered.

1) Commuting to the Workplace

Code Reg. 1.262–1(b)(5) represents the traditional policy that: "the taxpayer's costs of commuting to his place of business or employment are personal expenses and do not qualify as deductible expenses. Similarly, Reg. 1.162–2(e) provides that "commuters' fares are not considered as business expenses and are not deductible." [*Commissioner v. Flowers* (1945)]. Yet, daily transportation expenses in going between the taxpayer's home and workplace may be deducted in some special circumstances e.g. where the work location is temporary and outside the metro area where the taxpayer lives and normally works [**Rev. Ruling 99–7, 1999–1 CB 36**]. In addition, under Code Sec.162(a) deductions for travel expenses while "away from home" in the pursuit of a trade or business are allowed. "Home", for that matter, is the entire city or general area where the taxpayer's main place of business or work is located, regardless of where the family home is. The typical travel expenses, while away from home, which are deductible are travel by airplane, train, bus, or car between home and business destinations. Deductible expenses while on a business trip include also meals and lodging, cleaning and laundry, business calls and other communication costs, other than amounts which are lavish or extravagant under the circumstances.

One may assume that in the old days, where people used to work close to their homes, the decision to move away from the workplace and commute was based on the taxpayer's sole discretion; a private decision to live in a different place. Hence, such travel expenses were considered private. Time has changed though. Travel expenses in modern days are almost non-discretionary in most cases, so they should be regarded as an involuntary cost for the production of income. Nevertheless, there might be one good reason for disallowing them, as long as they relate to private car travelling: Pigovian Mandatory Payment (PMP) (93) [pp. 13, 36] Riding a private car to the workplace creates significant negative externalities (44), mainly pollution, which entails higher medical expenses for the general public, and traffic jams that create unnecessary extra expenses (e.g. spending too much time on roads, being late to work and losing precious leisure time). In addition, the use of private cars requires additional use of real property, which increases the real estate prices. The disallowance of such private car expenses shifts the economic damage back from the general public to the private car owners and to the car manufacturers, who cause the damage. A sensible legislature should encourage taxpayers to instead use public transportation by allowing the deductibility of the purchase of public transportation for work and back.

2) Child Care

Another example of expenses that have traditionally been considered private are working parents' child-care expenses. The choice to have children is a private decision made in consideration of one's personal lifestyle. One may assume that in the Victorian era, young mothers did not leave their children for employment purposes. This is no longer the reality. The decision of having a child is indeed a private one. Yet, once a child is born, their parents have moral and legal obligations and duties to give up work and/or to spend a significant amount of money on taking care of the children. Part of such spending is indeed the parents' consumption. The other part is the parent's non-discretionary expenses that should be allowed. Congress copes with that problem by offering several means. Two are directed towards the parents and one to their employer.

A) Tax Credits for Children and Dependents

As is discussed below [p. 319], Code Sec. 21 provides the **Child and Dependent Care Tax Credit (CDCTC)**, which is a non-refundable tax credit (125), available for working families who pay expenses for the cost of childcare, adult dependents, or an incapacitated spouse.

In addition, Code Sec. 24 provides a phase-out refundable **Child Tax Credit** for families with AGI up to $130,000 for a qualified child (under the age of 17). The maximum amount of the credit is $1,000 per child. The phase-out starts at AGI of $110,000 at the rate of $50 for each additional AGI of $1,000, up to AGI of $130,000.

B) Employer Exclusion: Flexible Spending Accounts

Code Sec. 129 exempts from employees' gross income amounts paid or incurred by the employer to a separate written plan (Flexible Spending Account—FSA) for the exclusive benefit of their employees to provide them with dependent care assistance. The exemption also applies to the value of care in a daycare facility provided, operated or sponsored by an employer. The maximum amount exempted is $5,000, regardless of the number of children or dependents in the family. Unlike the CDCTC, which requires that both partners in a married couple work, only one parent must work in order to qualify for the FSA exclusion.

No deduction or credit is available to an employee under this clause for any amount excluded from the gross income of the employee by reason of the exemption under Code Sec. 129. Nevertheless, if a family has childcare expenses that exceed the amount set aside in a FSA, it may qualify for a CDCTC. For example, a family with two or more children is qualified for $6,000 of expenses for CDCTC. If the family excludes $5,000 from their salaries in order to pay for childcare expenses in an FSA, it may claim the difference between the two ($1,000) for a CDCTC.

B. Capital Expenses

1) The Economic Significance of Immediate Deduction of Capital Expenses

Assume a taxpayer in a 40% marginal tax bracket makes an investment of $100 in a non-depreciable/non-amortizable capital asset (20, 21, 31) which, at the end of the holding period, has increased in value to $400 i.e. a total rate of return of 300%. There are four income tax situations. In situation A, no deduction is allowed for the amount of the investment in advance, but rather only at the time of realization (103), at the end of the holding period, when the asset is sold for a gain of $300 and it is taxed at 40%—assuming that the capital gain tax rate is the same as on ordinary income. In situation B, the amount of the investment is deducted immediately when the asset is bought, against the taxpayer's income from other sources. Since the taxpayer's tax rate is 40%, it means that the investment produces a tax savings (133) of $40, hence the taxpayer's economic cost (out of her own pocket) of the asset is only $60; the other $40 were funded by the IRS. In situation C, no immediate deduction is allowed for the investment, but the gain is totally exempted from income tax. In situation D the taxpayer invests $167, which is immediately deductible, has the 300% rate of return, which produces (167*300%=)$501 gain, and sells the investment for (501+167=)$668. The meaning of the immediate deduction is that her economic cost—after the (167*0.4=)$67 tax saving—is $100.

These four situations are compared in the following table:

Table 21.1:

I	II	III	IV	V	VI	VII	VIII
Situation	Amount of Investment	Economic Cost After Tax Income	Gross Income	Amount of Income (IV–II)	Income Tax (40%)	Net Income After Tax	Rate of net return
A	$100	$100	$400	$300	$120	$180	180%
B	$100	$60	$400	$400[1]	$160	$180[2]	300%
C	$100	$100	$400	$300	0	$300	300%
D	$167	$100	$668	$668	$268	$300	300%

1. Since the amount of the investment was deducted when it was invested, its cost for tax purposes is zero (the "basis" for tax purposes), and, therefore, gross income upon receipt constitutes taxable income
2. The taxpayer's economic gain was derived from the fact that the economic cost of her investment was only $60 and not $100, since she was entitled to a deduction, and the tax savings of $40 brings her to a situation in which her real cost was only $60. The amount that she received when she realized the investment is $400 and, therefore, her economic gain is $400−$60=$340, and after tax of $160, the net gain of $180 is left.

As Prof. Andrews demonstrated some 46 years ago, this table shows that the rates of net-after-tax return (300%) in situations B and D, in which the investment was immediately deducted, equals the rate of net return in situation C (300%), in which the investment was not immediately deducted, but the gain is totally exempted immediate deduction of the investment's cost = tax exemption of the investment return.

Note though that for this conclusion there have to be three conditions: the taxpayer's tax rate remains constant; the taxpayer has income from other sources, so the deduction produces a real tax saving (133); and the proceeds of the tax saving are invested in an investment that yields the same rate of return.

There are some other convincing ways to demonstrate the claim that the immediate deduction provides a significant benefit to the taxpayer. Assuming the taxpayer, at a marginal tax rate of 35%, invests $10,000. Immediate deduction produces tax saving (133) [pp. 4, 240] of $3,500 so the economic cost of the investment is only (10,000−3,500=)$6,500. The gross rate of return is 10%. Any dollar produced from the investment is subject to 35% income tax (assuming the proceeds are considered ordinary income or are recaptured (105)). Assuming a 10% rate of return, the taxpayer is left with an after-tax net income of (100%−35%=)6.5% (which is 0.065) or $6,500, which is (6,500/10,000=) 65% (which is 0.65). The meaning is clear: the after-tax rate of return 6.5%/65%, or (0.065/0.65=) is 10%, i.e. like any other tax exempt investment.

Another, and even clearer way to present the argument is to compare two taxpayers. One identifies a $1,300 investment that produces a 10% tax-free return, whereas her neighbor is less fortunate and invests $2,000 in a taxable investment that produces a 10% taxable rate of return. Both taxpayers are subject to a 35% tax rate. If the neighbor is allowed to immediately deduct his investment, the economic cost ("out of his pocket") of his investment is only [2,000−(2,000*.35)=]$1,300. Yet the 10% return on the initial investment of $2,000 is $200 and 35% tax is $70. Accordingly, the neighbor's after-tax rate of return is (200−70=)$130, which is 10%, equal to the former investor who earns $130 tax free.

Needless to say, that if for any reason, in addition to the immediate deduction of the investment, the proceeds of the deducted investment are tax free, then we have a negative income tax. Furthermore, if the gain is subject to the preferred capital gain tax rate (15%), the after-tax rate of return is almost double due to the deduction [p. 272] The neighbor in the above example ends up with an after-tax income of [200=(200*.15)=]$170 and a net rate of return of 170/1,300=13% instead of 6.5% compared to taxable ordinary investment.

On the other hand, denying the deduction of an *entire* expense that was paid for a depreciable/amortizable asset (31) [pp. 191–212, 260–263, 262, 263] also creates distortions. It is clear that when only part of the expense constitutes an investment and the other part is of a current investment character, only the first part should not be deducted, otherwise the true meaning is that the tax base is changed indirectly. The same is true if the current component of the expense should not be deductible. In both cases the tax base is changed: if yearly depreciation could not be deducted, which is actually a pro rate capital recovery of the invested capital, then the tax would be levied on the taxpayer's own capital ("equity") instead on her income, i.e. instead of income tax we might change the tax base into a property tax or wealth tax. Consider the following simple example:

A taxpayer with other resources that finance her private consumption has a saving account with $2,500 in it. At the beginning of the tax year, she withdraws $1,000 and invests it in her business as follows:

$200—office rent

$300—the cost of a computer with a life expectancy of 3 years

$400—employees' salaries

$100—other ordinary expenses (mail, telephone, electricity, etc.).

During the same year she sells professional services for $1,000 and deposits this amount back into her saving account.

Since we assume that the computer lasts for three years (30, 31), and that the basic depreciation method (20, 21) is the straight-line [pp. 191, 263], then the computer's book value at the end of the first year is (2/3*300=)$200.

At the end of the year her savings account has (1,500+1,000=)$2,500. In addition, she has an asset—the computer with a book value of $200. Her wealth or economic ability grew by $200: (2,500 saving account+200 computer=)$2,700, i.e. she realizes an enrichment of $200.

If the tax law allows her to immediately deduct the full cost of the computer, she would end up with no taxable income (revenue 1,000−total outlay 1,000=)$0, even though she has been enriched with $200. On the other hand, if the law disallows the whole cost of the computer, assuming that her tax rate is 20%, her taxable income (with no deduction for the computer's cost) is (1,000−700=)$300. A 20% tax would be $60 for her, which would be withdrawn from her savings. Hence, her wealth is reduced from $2,500 to (2,500−60=)$2,440. In other words, the disallowance of the annual computer's cost changes the tax base from income to net wealth.

Allowing her to deduct the annual cost of the computer (capital recovery; 33.3% straight-line depreciation) of $100 leads to the taxation of her real enrichment: her total deductible expenses are equal to [200+⅓(300)+400+100=]$800, which should be subtracted from her gross income, which provides (1,000−800=)$200. A tax of 20% of $200 is $40. In that case she deposits her after-tax amount of (200−40=)$160 into her savings account, which is equal to her after tax economic enrichment.

The simple example above is only one way to explain the idea of the need to prorate the cost of a capital asset over its useful life. A more technical way is presented below [p. 260].

2) The Statutory Rule

The statutory rule reflects the above idea regarding the deductibility of capital expenses. Section 263 disallows a deduction for "any amount paid out for new building or for permanent improvements or betterments made to increase the value of any property or estate". The rationale is already understood. Capital expenses for income producing activities are not allowed since they produce not only the current year's income but also the future years' as well (they provide "significant future benefits"); the investment portion does not decrease the taxpayers' wealth. Only the portion that is allocated to the taxable year (through depreciation, amortization or in some rare cases through accounting matching rules) is deducted in that year. Furthermore, an expense is considered to be a capital expenditure not only when it finances the purchase of a capital asset, but also when the expense's purpose is to ***improve*** the useful life or ***upgrade*** an existing capital asset. If an expense is a capital expenditure, it needs to be capitalized; this requires the firm to spread the cost of the expenditure over the useful life of the asset [pp. 191–212, 260–263, 262, 263]. If, however, the expense is one that ***maintains*** the asset at its current condition and does not improve it, it is fully deductible in the year it is made.

The problem of course, is with intermediate cases: what about expenses a law firm pays for printing paper in the last month of a taxable year, which will last into the next year? What about fixing machinery? Continuing professional education? Commercial expenses aimed to introduce a new product to the market? As has been indicated above, according to the theoretical analysis any expenses whose impact lasts more than the taxable year should be regarded as capital expenses and should not be fully deductible.

There are some practical solutions. A basic rule of thumb waives the matching rule when the purchased goods or services are ordinary and the expense is incidental to the conduct of the ordinary business activity, and its impact lasts within the firm less than one calendar year (12 months), e.g. a membership annual fee that is paid at the end of the year is fully deductible in the taxable year, though from a pure theoretical and accounting point of view it should be prorated. Common sense dictates giving up the implementation of the strict theoretical rules. In some cases, this "rule of thumb" has even been codified. For example, Code Reg. 1.263(a)–4, provides that costs incurred to create or enhance various intangibles are not required to be capitalized if the rights arising from the expenditure extend less than one calendar year (generally, 12 months after the taxpayer first realizes the rights). Another example is found in Reg. 1.162–3T(c)(2), which allows the immediate deduction of amounts paid to acquire or produce incidental materials and supplies that are carried on hand under some conditions.

3) Statutory Exception

In some instances the legislature provides some statutory concessions as well. Code Sec. 195 allows a phase-out deduction for start-up expenditures. Code Sec. 179 provides small businesses with some incentives aimed to increase their investments. Those exceptions are briefly discussed below [p. 267]. As is mentioned above [p. 256], such immediate deduction of capital expenses provides—under certain conditions—an exemption to the investment yield. Furthermore, such deduction changes the tax base from an income tax to a consumption tax system [p. 172].

C. The Need to Prorate Capital/Investment Expenses

1) Balance Sheet Representing Accretion to Wealth

Another way to demonstrate the need for the annual deduction of the capital assets component that is expendable over the taxable year is through a semi-accounting technique. Suppose that, at the beginning of year 1 the firm—a farmer—has $2,000. The firm purchases a piece of land for $1,700 and a machine for $300. At the beginning of the year the firm's balance sheet looks like this:

Equity:	$2,000	Land:	$1,700
		Machine:	$300
	$2,000		$2,000

The firm uses both assets to raise grains and sell the annual crop. The land does not lose its value over the years. The machine, on the other hand, does, annually. For the sake of simplicity we assume the annual decline of the machine's value is about 20% of its original cost, i.e. (300*0.2=)$60. If we overlook the business activity's result (profit or gain from the selling of the farm products) at that stage, the firm's balance sheet at the end of the year looks as follows:

Equity:	$2,000	Land:	$1,700
Profit (loss)	($60)	Machine:	$240
	$1,940		$1,940

The machine's annual decline of $60 represents an economic loss; a decline in the firm's wealth.

Now assume that the firm was able to produce business proceeds of $100 during the first year, and deposits those proceeds in a bank account. The balance sheet now looks like this:

Equity:	$2,000	Land:	$1,700
Decline of machine	($60)	Machine:	$240
Business proceeds	$100	Bank account	$100
Business gain	$40		
	$2,040		$2,040

As can be seen, due to machine's decline, the firm's annual gain/accretion to wealth is only $40 and not $100. The deduction is equal to the annual straight-line depreciation of $60.

2) Capital Recovery

Another way to consider the firm's annual prorated deductions (through depreciation, amortization, or matching rules), is through the ***capital recovery*** concept [p. 191]: when the firm receives its annual receipts from its investment, only the gain should be treated as income for tax purposes. The annual capital recovery is not a gain and should be subtracted from the tax base. From a theoretical point of view, the annual depreciation or amortization equals the annual capital recovery. To use an example, if the firm uses its machine and land in order to produce its $100 gross income, only part of that income represents earning or profit; the other part is capital recovery. Assume for simplicity that the annual decline of the machine's value is $40 and the land does not lose its value. The $40 is the annual capital recovery; it does not represent a gain hence it should not be taxed. The way we exempt it from taxation is by allowing the deduction of the capital recovery component as annual depreciation or amortization. [pp. 191–212, 260–263, 262, 263].

3) Saving Future Expenses

As said above, firms' investment means saving ***future*** business expenses. When a firm decides to buy a machine for $250 that lasts for five years, it could rent a similar machine for an annual rent of around $66.50 (assuming the interest rate is 10%). In that case the firm would deduct the annual rent of the above amount—$66.50—each year for five years. Instead, the firm offers to pay the machine's manufacturer in advance an amount equal to the present value (97) [pp. 106, 155] of the above five annual installments, which equals approximately $250. Hence, the firm should be allowed to allocate the cost of $250 as a business expense over the next five years. Under the straight-line method, the firm's annual depreciation should be $50 for each of the five years for a total of $250—the machine's actual cost. Note that one may argue that purchasing and renting the same machine should produce the same annual deduction. I.e. $66.50. Yet, when taking into account the interest that underlies the prepayment of the purchase price, the picture becomes clearer. The interest, which should be regarded as non-monetary benefit income that the firm receives in the form of a discount for buying the machine, should be added to the firm's annual income and should reduce the amount of the "machine's annual rent". For example: using the above assumptions, the annual rent is $66.50. The cost for renting the same machine for producing the next year's income (hereinafter: year 2) is also $66.50, paid at the end of the year, and the same price is paid for years 3, 4, and 5. The firm is ready to pay in advance, at the beginning of the first year, the full rent for five years. Using the present value calculation, and assuming the interest rate is 10%, the total amount the firm is willing to pay is the following:

$$\frac{66.5}{1.1} + \frac{66.5}{1.1^2} + \frac{66.5}{1.1^3} + \frac{66.5}{1.1^4} + \frac{66.5}{1.1^5} = \$250$$

The meaning of such annual payment is that only part of it ($66.50) is for the cost of the first year's earning and should be considered as a deductible amount. The rest

(250−66.5=)$183.50 is savings for the next four years' expenses, i.e. a deposit/loan that the firm makes to the manufacturer, which produces $18.35 interest, which is part of the firm's income providing a net deduction of (66.5−18.35=)$47.15 a bit lower than $50. In the second year the principal amount, which is reduced by the second year's annual rent of $66.50, is only (183.5−66.5=)$117 and the interest earned by the firm is $11.70 which produces the second year's net deduction of (66.5−11.7=)$54.80, and so on until the fifth and final year where there is no deposit and the total annual rent of $66.50 should be deducted.

Assume now that instead of renting the machine for 5 years, the firm buys it and is ready to pay the same amount of $250. The salvage value of the machine at the end of year 5 is zero. Under the straight-line depreciation, the annual deduction should be $50, instead of the amount for the first year of $47.55. Hence, something seems wrong. As will be shown below, there are two possible explanations to this enigma: either the straight-line depreciation does not represent the real decrease in value, or the example is wrong and unrealistic; after all in real life there are not too many machines that produce a constant annual income in equal amounts and then "disappear" (with a salvage value of zero) at the end of their fifth year. Similarly, nobody is willing to pay the same annual rent for a new machine versus for a 5 year old machine. It is much more realistic to assume that the annual income (or annual rent) is higher in the first year and goes down year after year. Under a more realistic assumption, i.e. that the annual income produced by a new machine is higher than that of an old machine, we find that the straight-line depreciation is quite reasonable [p. 262]. Hence, one may conclude the any type of accelerated depreciation includes a tax relief. (122, 131).

D. Economic Depreciation

In theory we are looking for real economic capital recovery. [pp. 191, 212, 260, 263] Economists consider that the right depreciation should be based on the accurate decline of an asset's value during the time-unit, i.e. the taxable year. Yet it is quite difficult to estimate the *ex ante* decline. Furthermore, an accurate annual *ex post* depreciation is also not practical since it requires an expensive evaluation process. Instead, legislatures look for practical, statutory general assumptions to be used in order to represent the best and closet *ex ante* estimation that reflects an asset's annual cost recovery.

In his "Tax Deductibility of Economic Depreciation to Insure Invariant Valuations" (1964) Nobel laureate professor Paul Samuelson offered an algebraic formula for computing the accurate amount of depreciation in order to evaluate the phase of capital goods wearing out. His assumption was that "If, and only if, true loss of economic value is permitted as a tax-deductible depreciation expense will the present discounted value of a cash receipt stream be independent of the rate of tax". His comment regarding the various methods used by legislatures that turned out to be tax incentives is noteworthy:

> *"Finally this discussion reminds lawyers and accountants that the only sensible definition of depreciation relevant to measurement of true money income is putative decline in economic value. Fast depreciation gimmicks in the Swedish, Japanese, German, British and American tax codes are not a return to just recognition of economic obsolescence—as any dealer in used machines will privately tell you. They are competitive bribes and giveaway, designed to undertax money income (and perhaps obviate the bias against capital formation inherent in taxing income rather than consumption or wealth), in order to*

attract investment from other countries and to stimulate the total of domestic investment growth. If we call spades spades let's call bribes bribes."

E. Allocation of Capital Assets Cost: Methods of Depreciation

As explained above the purpose of the depreciation deduction is not necessarily to reflect the annual wearing out of the real economic value of capital assets but rather to identify the annual components of an asset's **cost recovery** [pp. 191, 212, 260, 263]. Indeed, it might be that in most cases these goals are supposed to lead to the same result. Yet the former is much more complicated and controversial, whereas the latter, if done properly with no "gimmicks or bribes", is much more practical, as long as the system sticks to its limited goal: annual capital recovery (20), which is not taxed through its deductibility [p. 191]. Alas, although leading tax scholars claim that the most accurate **concession** is the *straight-line* method, legislatures can't resist the temptation of integrating some tax incentives into the depreciation deductions.

1) The Starting Point: Straight-Line Depreciation

In order to base the claim that straight line depreciation or amortization is a sensible and realistic concession, which is aimed to estimate the annual cost recovery, we use the above example—a machine that lasts for 5 years and in that period produces a declining stream of income. The rationale, which was offered by law professor M. Chirelstein, is simple: a new asset is more productive than an old one, whether because it is more efficient and produces better, or because it requires less maintenance cost during its early years. The following example is based on such assumptions.

Suppose a taxpayer is interested in buying a machine which produces the following declining stream of income at the end of each of these following years: Year 1: \$113.70; Year 2: \$106.10; Year 3: \$98.50; Year 4: \$90.00; Year 5: \$83.30. Assuming the interest rate is 10%, the present value of those five annual incomes at the beginning of Year 1 is \$379, based on the following calculation:

$$\frac{113.7}{1.1} + \frac{106.1}{1.1^2} + \frac{98.5}{1.1^3} + \frac{90.9}{1.1^4} + \frac{83.3}{1.1^5} = \$379$$

This is the price the taxpayer offers for the machine. The taxpayer's profit is the difference between the machine's cost and the aggregated stream of income the machine produces. The profit might be 10%, or it might be higher (or lower) depending on the taxpayer's performance.

The following table demonstrates that, under the above assumptions, the annual straight line depreciation amount—(379/5)=\$75.80—is a reasonable and realistic estimate.

Table 21.2: Straight-Line Depreciation:

The beginning of year Present Value (PV) of each of the five amounts received at the end of the year						Investment's Pv	Annual decline depreciation	Gross income	AGI
Period	1	2	3	4	5				
Beginning of Year 1	103.3	87.7	70.0	62.1	51.7	379			
End year 1	113.7 earned	96.4	81.4	68.3	56.9	303.2	75.8	113.7	37.9
End year 2	-	106.1 earned	89.5	75.1	62.6	227.4	75.8	106.1	30.3
End year 3	-	-	98.5 earned	82.6	68.9	151.6	75.8	98.58	22.7
End year 4	-	-		90.9 earned	75.8	75.8	75.8	90.9	15.1
End year 5	-	-		-	83.3 earned	-	75.8	83.3	7.6
Total							379	492.6	113.6

Since the straight-line method is just an estimation, accountants have not given up their efforts to provide a variety of workable depreciation methods; some in a sincere belief that their suggested methods reflect as close as possible the actual annual cost recovery; some to serve as tax incentives.

2) Depreciable/Amortizable and Non-Depreciable/Amortizable Assets

Depreciable/amortizable assets (31) by their nature deteriorate over time, either physically (a machine), or because they have a predetermined artificial life (e.g. a patent or a copyright), or by obsolescence. The theoretical assumption is that the owner of a depreciable/amortizable asset is left with nothing at the end of the asset's life-time except for the proceeds that the asset has generated during its lifetime and its salvage value (i.e. its value when sold as scrap). The owner's cost of an asset is dissipated and its value is depleted; all that remains is what the asset has produced. Some non-depreciable/non-amortizable assets are deemed physically inexhaustible (raw land). Others have finite lives, but do not deteriorate over these lives (a non-sinking loan). Other depreciable/amortizable assets deteriorate in a strictly physical sense, but not over a reasonably determinable period (masterworks of art, collectables). Still others neither deteriorate nor even have a theoretically finite life [corporate shares; costs of establishing new business; perpetual annuity (11)]. The common characteristic of all non-depreciable/non-amortizable assets is that time does not deplete them; they do not represent capital recovery; their values may change, but the changes are not due to use or the mere passage of time but rather to changes in the economic environment [p. 191].

Code Sec. 167 provides a depreciation or amortization deduction for the exhaustion of property used in a trade or business or held for the production of income. In order to be eligible for amortization under Section 167, an intangible asset or benefit must have a limited useful life the length of which can be estimated with reasonable accuracy.

It is noteworthy that the IRS Publication 946 "How To Depreciate Property" (*Reviewed or Updated: 07-Mar-2022)* refers to depreciation as:.

> *"an annual income tax deduction that allows you to* ***recover the cost or other basis*** *of certain property over the time you use the property. It is an allowance* ***for the wear and tear, deterioration, or obsolescence*** *of the property".*

IRS Topic No. 704 Depreciation (*Last Reviewed or Updated: 19-May-2022*) uses similar language and elaborates on all the methods of appreciation allowed under the current law:

> *"You generally can't deduct in one year the entire cost of property you acquired, produced, or improved and placed in service for use either in your trade or business or income-producing activity if the property is a capital expenditure. Instead, you generally must depreciate such property. Depreciation is the recovery of the cost of the property over a number of years. You deduct a part of the cost every year until you fully recover its cost".*

3) The Modified Accelerated Cost Recovery System (MACRS) and the Alternative Depreciation System (ADS)

The current depreciation method in the U.S. is the Modified Accelerated Cost Recovery System (MACRS), which is applied for most tangible capital assets. Under this method, which is indeed an accelerated one that provides significant advantage to most taxpayers, assets are classified into various categories either by type of asset, or by business in which the asset is used. Where a general class based on the nature of the asset applies, that class takes precedence over the use category. As a general rule there are eight categories, which are based on the length of the assets' lives: three, five, seven, ten, fifteen, and twenty years. Another two classes are residential rental properties, which are classified into twenty-seven-and-a-half years, and commercial real properties, which are under the thirty-nine-year category. These two classes are not eligible for the accelerated system but only for the straight-line depreciation method. The shorter period for residential properties, compared to commercial real properties, reflects Congress' belief that a shorter depreciation period might decrease the rent prices for residential tenants.

Statutory shorter lifespans are provided for certain property, including computers and peripheral equipment, certain high technology equipment, special purpose agricultural structures, and certain other items. Certain property in regulated industries, as well as films, video tapes, sound recordings, and certain other items are excluded from MACRS. Additionally, leasehold improvements to real property are generally treated as real property under MACRS.

The Alternative Depreciation System (ADS) is based on the straight line method and is designated for specific assets with specified lengths of time. Usually it is a residual method that applies only at the taxpayer's election. Yet in some specific cases (such as any tangible property used predominantly outside the United States during the year, subject to certain exceptions) ADS is mandatory. It is also mandatory for taxpayers who are subject to the Alternative Minimum Tax (10) [p. 328]. ADS statutory lifespans are the same as regular depreciation lifespans for a few classes, but are generally somewhat longer than regular lifespans for most classes.

4) MACRS—the Major Traits

The basic rule of any depreciation system, including the MACRS, is that the total aggregate amount of the depreciation deduction cannot exceed 100% of the asset cost.

The starting point of the MACRS is the traditional straight-line depreciation, meaning that an asset's annual cost recovery is based on its original cost minus its estimated salvage value divided by the years of the asset's life. For example, assume an asset was bought for $50,000, is classified into the 5-year category, its salvage value is zero, and the annual rate of the straight-line depreciation is (100%/5=)20% or $10,000. Under the accelerated 200% declining balance the annual rate over the five years is doubled and is computed on the declining balance. Accordingly, the annual depreciation deduction under a consistent double system should be as follows:

Year	Balance	Depreciation rate	Amount	Aggregate depreciation	End year balance
1	50,000	40%	$20,000	$20,000	$30,000
2	30,000	40%	$12,000	$32,000	$18,000
3	18,000	40%	$7,200	$39,200	$10,800
4	10,800	40%	$4,320	$44,520	$5,480
5	$5,480	100%	$5,480	$50,000	0

There are two additional factors that should be considered. First, since the amounts of depreciation in the first years are higher than the amounts that would have been allowed under the straight-line method, at some point the annual deduction under the MACRS is lower than the amount which would be computed under the straight-line method. The second factor is the time the asset is placed into the taxpayer's use.

As can be seen from the table above, the annual amount of depreciation in the third, fourth and fifth years are lower than the amount if the taxpayer was using the straight-line method ($10,000 per those years). In order to prevent such a result and provide the taxpayer with the best of the two systems, the Code uses the "optimal point", when the taxpayer shifts from the declining method to the straight-line method in the year in which the latter produces a higher amount then the former. Hence the deduction on the third and the fourth years is $7,200 and for the fifth year the balance is $3,600.

As for the second factor, in most cases the newly bought asset is not placed in the taxpayer's business at the first day of the taxable year. Instead of computing the exact number of days in the year the asset was placed, some practical conventions are used. Tangible personal properties that are put to service during the year are treated as if they were placed in service in the middle of the tax year ("half-year convention"). Real property is considered placed in service in the middle of the month in which it was acquired ("mid-month convention"). Special rules apply for pro-rating deductions for short tax years and for the first year of business, or where more than 40% of tangible personal property additions are in the final quarter of the year. When the "half a year convention" is used, only half a year's depreciation is allowed in the year the asset was put in service, and the other half a year's depreciation is added after the last year of its service or after the end of its statutory life.

Using the optimal point and the half-year convention, the following table—which is taken from the above-mentioned IRS Publication 946—shows the annual depreciation deduction under a common MACRS method for a five year asset:

Table 21.3:

Year	Basis	Annual Depreciation Deduction	Accumulated Depreciation	Ending Book Value	
1	$50,000	$10,000	$10,000	$40,000	DB
2	$50,000	$16,000	$26,000	$24,000	DB
3	$50,000	$9,600	$35,600	$14,400	DB
4	$50,000	$5,760	$41,360	$8,640	SL
5	$50,000	$5,760	$47,120	$2,880	SL
6	$50,000	$2,880	$50,000	$0	SL

Explanation: the annual depreciation deduction under a straight-line method would be 100%/5=20%. Double rate is 40%, hence the deduction for the first full year would be (50,000*40%=)$20,000. Since the half year convention is applied, the depreciation deduction for the first year is only half of the full amount, i.e. (20,000/2=)$10,000. The declining balance method leads the asset's book value at the beginning of year 2 to be (50,000−10,000=)$40,000. The deduction for year 2 is (40,000*40%=)$16,000. In the third year, the declining balance produces a book value of $24,000 and the deduction amount is (24,000*40%=)$9,600. The balance for year 4 is [50,000−(10,000+16,000+9,600)=] 14,400, hence the deduction for the fourth year is (14,400*40%=)$5,760. At that "optimal point" the method is shifted to the straight line method, so the deduction for the fifth year is also $5,760. The balance for the (half) sixth year is (5,760/2=)$2,880, which is totally deducted.

The following table shows the declining balance rate for each property class and the first year for which the straight line method gives an equal or greater deduction.

Table 21.4:

Property Class	Declining Method	Balance Rate	Year
3-year	200% DB	66.667%	3rd
5-year	200% DB	40.0	4th
7-year	200% DB	28.571	5th
10-year	200% DB	20.0	7th
15-year	150% DB	10.0	7th
20-year	150% DB	7.5	9th

Source: Publication 946 (2021), How To Depreciate Property, (last review and revised 22 March 2022)

5) Special Rules for Immediate Deduction of Capital Expenses

Code Sec. 179 allows any trade or business to elect to deduct capital expenses that were spent to purchase various types of property—tangible, depreciable, personal property or even buildings bought by small business—as a current expense instead of capitalizing it and depreciating it over the years. The availability of such election is subject to some limitations. The deduction amount (total cost of the assets) is limited to $1,080,000 for the tax year of 2022, provided that the total amount the firm spent on Code Section 197 property during a single taxable year is up to $2,700,000 in that year. In such case, the amount of the deduction is phased-out dollar for dollar, e.g. if the total amount spent during the taxable year is $3,000,000 the allowed deduction would be only $780,000. An additional limitation is that, for any taxable year, this deduction may not exceed the taxpayer's aggregate income from the active conduct of trade or business for that year. Nevertheless, deductions that are not allowed during one taxable year because of this limitation can be carried over to the next year. Other depreciable properties that are not eligible for this deduction are subject to the above annual depreciation deductions.

For tax years beginning after 2017, the TCJA increased the maximum Section 179 expense deduction from $500,000 to $1 million. The phase-out limit increased from $2 million to $2.5 million. These amounts are indexed for inflation for tax years beginning after 2018.

A special arrangement was legislated in the Small Business Jobs Act (2010). The major aim of this arrangement was to encourage the formation of new businesses by providing them with an amortization deduction for eligible expenses which were spent before the opening of the business.

The IRS allows you to deduct $5,000 in business startup costs and $5,000 in organizational costs, but only if your total startup costs are $50,000 or less. If your startup costs in either area exceed $50,000, the amount of your allowable deduction will be reduced by the overage. And if your startup costs are more than $55,000, the deduction is eliminated.

For instance, if your startup costs were $53,000, you'd have to subtract $3,000 from the $5,000 deduction and would only be allowed to deduct the remaining $2,000. And if your startup costs were $56,000, you wouldn't qualify for the deduction at all. The costs remaining after your deduction should be amortized (paid off over a period of time) annually in equal portions over the next 15 years.

6) Depreciation of Intangible Assets

Tax authorities around the world tend to argue that the depreciation deduction depends entirely on the legislature's grace. If an asset is not classified by a statutory provision as a depreciable asset, then no depreciation is allowed. Such was the case with goodwill. The IRS Regulations indicated specifically: "No deduction for depreciation is allowable with respect to goodwill". Such an approach disregards the concept of capital recovery. Hence, the Supreme Court actually rejected the IRS' rigid approach (*Newark Morning Ledger v. U.S.*, 1993) and allowed the taxpayer to deduct the cost of an asset called "paid subscribers". The Court concluded that such an asset is depreciable when the taxpayer demonstrates that it is wasted over an ascertainable period of time. Furthermore, the Court indicated that it is more faithful to the purposes of the Code to allow the depreciation deduction for "the Code endeavors to match expenses with the revenues of the taxable period to which they are properly attributable, thereby resulting in a more accurate calculation of net income for tax purposes". Hence, if a taxpayer can prove with reasonable accuracy that an asset used in their trade or business or held for the production of income has a value that is wasted over an ascertainable period of time, that asset is depreciable under Code Sec. 167, regardless of the fact that its value is related to the expectancy of continued patronage.

Furthermore, the Court closely analyzed the application of the "mass asset rule", which relates to self-generating assets. The rule provides that certain kinds of intangible assets are properly grouped and considered as a single entity; even though their individual components may expire or terminate over time, they are replaced by new components, thereby causing only minimal fluctuations and no measurable loss in the value of the whole. The Court has found that the paid-subscribers-asset is not self-regenerating. It has a finite number of subscribers who are discontinued over a reasonably predictable period of time with no automatic replacements. Furthermore, the replacement—the new subscribers—were recruited only through the substantial efforts of the taxpayers. The asset consisted of identifiable subscriptions, each of which had a limited useful life that could be estimated with reasonable accuracy according to generally accepted statistical principles. Hence the asset should be amortized according to the statistical evidence the taxpayer provided.

7) The Congress Reaction: Code Sec. 197

The *Morning Ledger* decision was followed by the enactment of Code Sec. 197. Effectively, Section 197 allows the amortization of most types of goodwill and other intangibles that are purchased (but not created—"unless the taxpayer created them in acquiring assets that make up a trade or business or a substantial part of a trade or business") by the taxpayer. The taxpayer determines the amount of the deduction by amortizing an intangible's adjusted basis ratably—i.e. in a "straight line"—over a 15-year period beginning with the month that the taxpayer acquired the intangible. Accordingly, a taxpayer can amortize [pp. 191–212, 260–263, 262, 263] the following acquired assets using that 15-year straight line method: goodwill, going concern value, a patent, a copyright, workforce in place, a trademark, a covenant not to compete and other similar arrangements entered into in connection with the acquisition of a business; information bases (include any information base, including customer-related information bases); know-how such as any patent, copyright, formula, process, design, pattern, package design, computer software or interest in a film, sound recording, video tape, book, or other similar property, provided the interest is acquired as part of a purchase of a trade or business; customer-based intangibles; supplier-based intangibles; licenses, permits, and other rights granted by governmental units; franchises, trademarks, and trade names; contracts for the use of, and term interests in such intangibles, and other similar items.

On the other hand, Code Sec. 197(3) elaborates a list of intangibles that are specifically are excluded from the above list.

F. Capital Expenses: Preserving v. Improvement—Tangible Assets

1) Maintenance v. Upgrading and Improving an Asset

As was discussed above, the main trait of capital expenses is that they finance the acquisition of an asset that lasts more than one year, contrary to normal and ordinary repair costs, regular maintenance, or fixing a broken machine, which neither extend the expected original useful life of the asset nor upgrade its quality. Hence they are considered current expenses and are deducted in the year incurred. On the other hand, the cost of improvements or upgrading the firm's assets is a capital expense as long as it adds to the asset's current value, considerably lengthens the asset's useful life, or adapts it to a different use. The courts and the legal literature offer some idioms and tests for classifying an expense as a capital investment: does the expense provide a lasting benefit? Do the payments create a separate and distinct asset having a useful life extending substantially beyond the end of the taxable year? Do the costs give rise to a significant future benefit? If the answer to these questions is positive, the costs are considered capital investments and should be capitalized. Note that none of these tests are exclusive.

The problem of course is that there are some expenses that are related to capital assets, but should be treated as current-deductible expenses if they meet the following tests: does the expense maintain the **existing** income-producing property? Has the money been spent for the protection of an **existing** investment? Or for the continuation of an **existing** business, or the preservation of an **existing** business property from loss or diminution? If so, they are deductible expenses within the meaning of Rev. Code 162.

The crucial question then is what is "**existing**" property? The answer depends on the character and attribute of each type of trade, business and property.

2) Preserving the Existing: Depreciable Assets

The "existence" of depreciable property decreases every year. Hence, an expense that prevents the expected decrease is not a current expense but a capital one; it prolongs the asset's expected life. This claim may be illustrated by the following example: suppose a firm purchased a machine for $1,000 which lasts five years. Under the straight line depreciation [p. 263], the value of the machine during those five years is depicted as a negative slope e-g in *Figure 21.2* below:

Figure 21.2:

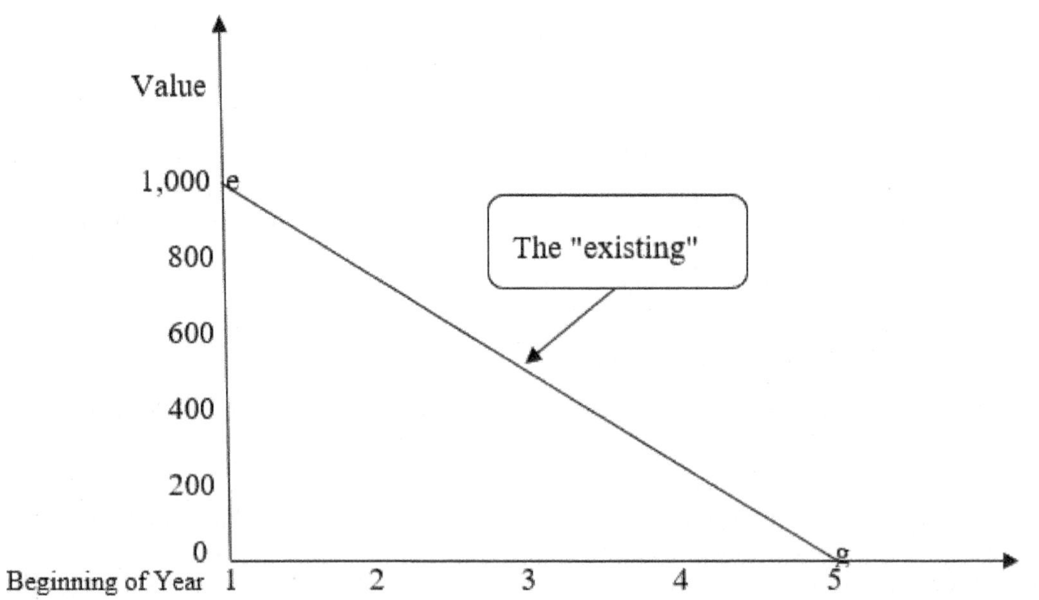

Slope ***e-g*** depicts the expected value of the property, i.e. the property's expected income production over five years. Any maintenance cost spent by the taxpayer is a current expense and should be deductible as long as it maintains slope ***e-g***. On the other hand, any expense that prolongs/extends the "existing" income production above and beyond the expected line is a capital expense.

Suppose the above property is a motor. In the beginning of the 3rd year the motor—with a book value of $600—has broken and needs to be completely overhauled for the price of $160. Without the overhaul, its value is zero (assuming no salvage value). After the overhaul has been done, the motor's fair market value goes up to $800, and its useful years is extended for another 2 years. The following illustration *Figure 21.3,* demonstrates this.

<u>Figure 21.3:</u>

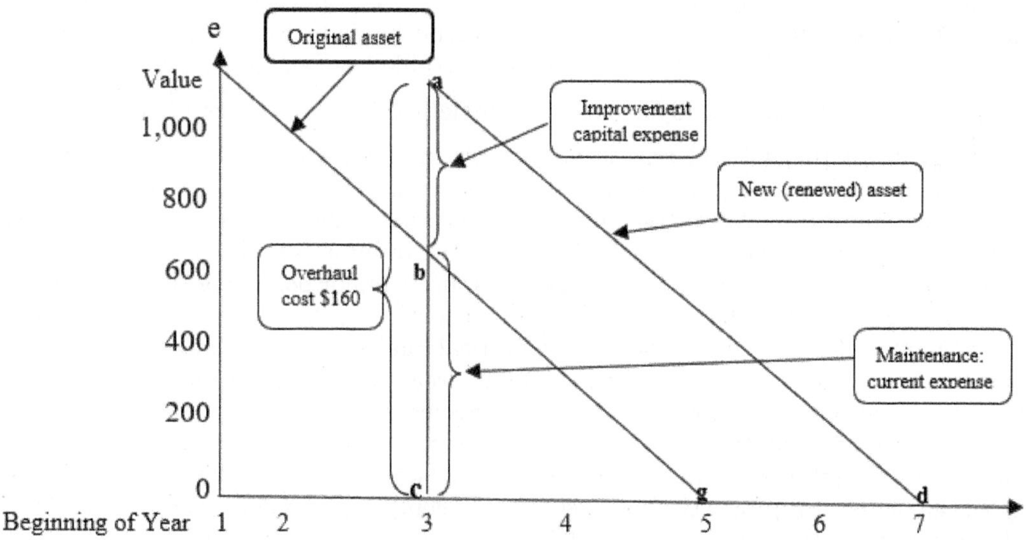

As can be seen, the $160 expense, which is depicted with slope ***a-c,*** extended the motor's productive lifespan beyond its original 5 years to 7 years (slope *a-d*). Therefore, it should be considered as a capital expense. On the other hand, without spending this $160, the motor's value would have been zero. Under an accurate analysis, the $160 overhaul expense should be treated in the following way: a relative part of the original expense of $160, which is depicted in the figure as ***b-c,*** is for the maintenance of the original "existing" asset. The ratio of the motor's book value when it was broken ($600) over its new value after the overhaul was performed ($800), should be multiplied by the amount spent, which equals (600/800*160=)$120. That amount represents the cost of preserving the existing motor and should be deducted. The other relative part, (160−120=)$40, which is depicted as ***b-a,*** represents the improvement of the motor, the extending of its original expected lifespan, and should be considered as a capital expense. It should not be deducted immediately, but rather be added to the renewed motor's basis and depreciated accordingly [pp. 191–212, 260–263, 262, 263].

Surprisingly, the logic of such theoretical analysis can also be found within the current law. Under Code Section 1231, a capital **loss** of a depreciable asset is treated as an ordinary loss under certain conditions. This provision, which we name "negative recapture" [pp. 212, 281], provides a lead for the same solution (by using a constructive disposition). If we assume that when the motor broke, the taxpayer disposes of it for its market value—zero—and purchases a second-hand motor for a fair market value of $800, then the loss of $600—***b-c***—is "negatively recaptured". As a net Section 1231 **loss,** it is fully deductible as an ***ordinary*** **loss**. The cost of the newly-bought second-hand renovated motor (the "basis") of $800 is a capital expense.

Following the above example, if the firm decides instead to spend $160 on the old motor's overhaul in order to bring it to a similar condition as the second-hand motor, this amount is a substitute for a "double action" phenomenon: 1) a constructive sale of the old motor, hence a current deduction of Sec. 1231 loss of $600, and 2) a constructive purchase of the renewed one, i.e. a capital expense of $800. While considering the actual cost of $160, the same ratio of the loss to the fair market value of the overhauled asset (in this example 600/800 or 3/4) should be used: 3/4 of the amount—$120—is spent in order to ***maintain the existing motor*** and should be deducted. 1/4 of the overhaul cost—$40—is for extending its value beyond the taxable year and should capitalized.

Note though that such analysis is not implemented by the IRS or the taxpayers.

The relevant [Regs 1.162 and 1.263(a)] "are intended to reduce controversy and provide clarity on how to determine whether an amount paid must be capitalized"; thus, they do not follow the above analysis. For example, assume that K owns a manufacturing building. K discovers several leaks in the roof of the building and hires a contractor to inspect and fix the roof. The contractor discovers that a major portion of the decking has rotted and recommends the replacement of the entire roof. K agrees and pays the required amount for the entire roof. Our theoretical analysis would lead to an allocation of the cost: part of the replacement cost should be treated as repair or maintenance (and thus immediately deducted) and part as an improvement (and thus capitalized). Instead, the regulation adopted the administratively practical "all or nothing" approach: a taxpayer must capitalize as an improvement a replacement of a part that comprises a major component of a property. Because the roof comprises a major component of the building structure, the regulation (§ 1.263(a)–3), example 14) treats the replacement as an improvement and K must capitalize all the cost. Notwithstanding this result, the regulation also includes a "**safe harbor for routine maintenance**" (*1.263(a)(i)*). Under this *safe harbor,* performing certain routine maintenance activities is not required to be capitalized as an improvement, even if otherwise such an activity would have been considered as an improvement.

G. Preserving the Existing: Intangible Assets

The study of the deductibility of expenses of intangible assets requires a distinction between a couple of questions. The main distinction is, once again, between the acquisition cost and the maintenance cost.

1) Intangible's Acquisition

A firm can acquire intangible assets either by buying them from their creator or by developing them. If the firm bought an intangible and it serves the firm for a long period of time in its income-producing process, its cost should be considered as a capital expense. If it has a limited lifespan, it could be depreciated or amortized [pp. 191–212, 260–263, 262, 263, 269].

If the intangibles are developed/created by the firm itself, one may wonder whether the cost of creating them should be immediately deductible as long as they are considered capital assets.

Law professor Calvin Johnson pointed out [p. 220] that, under the current law, which provides lower tax rates for capital gains, there is an asymmetry. The asymmetry is caused by the fact that the costs of creating goodwill and other intangible assets are immediately deducted as current expenses on the one hand, and the gain derived from their sale is taxed at preferred tax rates of capital gain on the other hand. This yields a negative tax, which leads to an increase of the internal rate of return, only due to the effect of the immediate deduction [p. 256], from 10% to 25%. In terms of economic efficiency and tax equity, these are undesirable results.

2) Intangible's "Maintenance"

The costs of developing and maintaining the firms' constant growth should be regarded as maintaining the ***existing*** **income-producing process** and should be deductible as ordinary and necessary expenses.

Most of the firm's intangibles, such as goodwill, customer-base, workforce and know-how, are graphically depicted as a positive slope. Their value grows in the ordinary course of business. According to an established insight in business and marketing management literature, "evolve, adapt, grow, or otherwise—perish".

The economic value (ability to produce income) of an experienced lawyer is greater than the economic value of a beginner. Goodwill and the customer base of a successful, well-based old firm is greater than the goodwill and the customer base that the same firm had in its earlier stages. The quality of an experienced labor force is higher than that of an inexperienced one, and so on. Businesses evolve, expand and adjust to new developments of the market-place; otherwise, they are doomed to disappear. The value of most firms'/business' intangibles, typically generated by the firms themselves, is usually increased in the ordinary and normal course of the business' operation. The expected ability of a trade or business to produce income is not constant and flat, but rather is rising. Thus, the businesses' expected income production—the "***existing***"—is indeed a positive slope. This claim is supported by business management research and insights. Several models introduce various stages or phases in the development of firms. As the economics professor Edith Penrose (with Christos Pitelis 4th revised ed, 2004) put in her, "The Theory of the Growth of the Firm" the basic claim is straightforward: "Growth is essentially an evolutionary process and based on the cumulative growth of collective knowledge and of evolution in the context of a purposive firm, which involves the accumulation of knowledge unique to the firm". Though, some argue that the concept of grow or perish applies to all businesses except small ones (e.g. family-owned or neighborhood small stores). Growth could occur as either an evolutionary or revolutionary process, but the growth itself is crucial.

The same concept is also found in marketing literature. Some, like Chris Stutzman in his *Adapt Or Perish: The Five Habits Of Highly Adaptive Marketers* (2010), have concluded "in the future, there will be two types of companies—those that are agile and adapt to consumers' changing media behavior and those that go out of business".

The above-mentioned claims are demonstrated by the following example: suppose a new firm has a goodwill which is worth zero in the beginning of the first year of its existence. Over the course of the next five years it evolves, grows and expands, so at the beginning of the fifth year the value of its goodwill goes up to $1,000.

This is depicted as a positive slope ***a-b*** in *Figure 21.4* (below):

Figure 21.4:

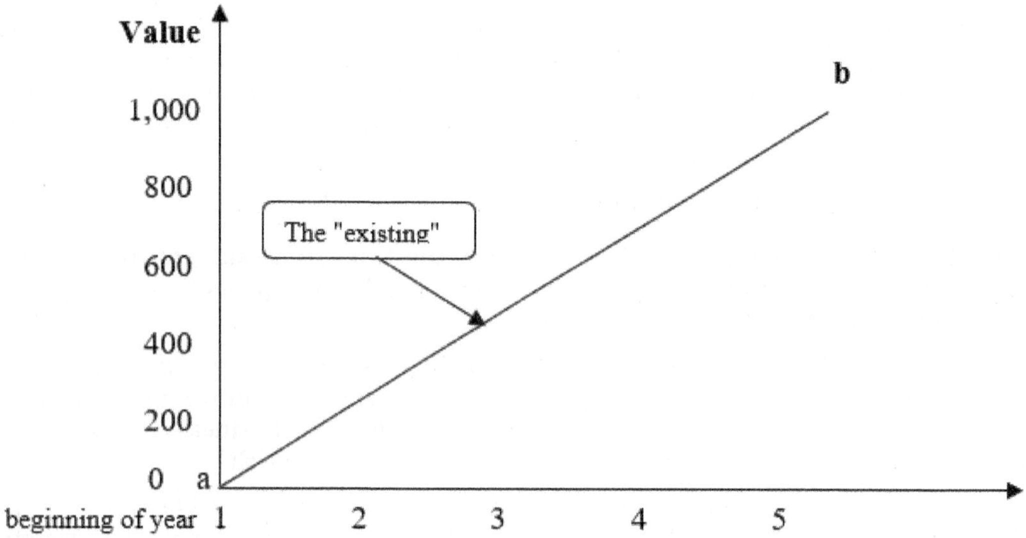

The cost of all the activities that enabled the firm to evolve, grow and expand according to expectations is the cost of ***maintaining the existing business; they are orderly and necessary expenses to the ongoing business***. Accordingly, any expenses spent by the firm for this purpose, including advertisement expenses, professional training expenses, salaries and bonuses paid to the workforce, as well as expenses involved with the expansion of the customer base, are current expenses. The expenses that maintain the firm's constant goodwill growth—slope *a-b*—are ordinary ones, like any other expenses, which maintain the trade and business' expected growth. Such expenses should be regarded as deductible ordinary and necessary current expenses and not be capitalized.

The economic value of a professional cardiologist (or a business's goodwill) increases constantly every year (positive slope ***c-d*** in the below illustration, *Figure 21.5*). Suppose that during the course of the third year, a new surgery technique is implemented (or a new business process or method), which the taxpayer has to acquire in order to maintain her professional (or its business) status in the market place. Consequently, the cardiologist enrolls in a special professional training program and pays the tuition. Even if the payment is significantly high and is not recurrent annually, its purpose is to maintain the existing human capital (or the business' goodwill) which is a rising slope and is indeed a deductible expense according to case law, as is depicted in *Figure 21.5* below.

Figure 21.5:

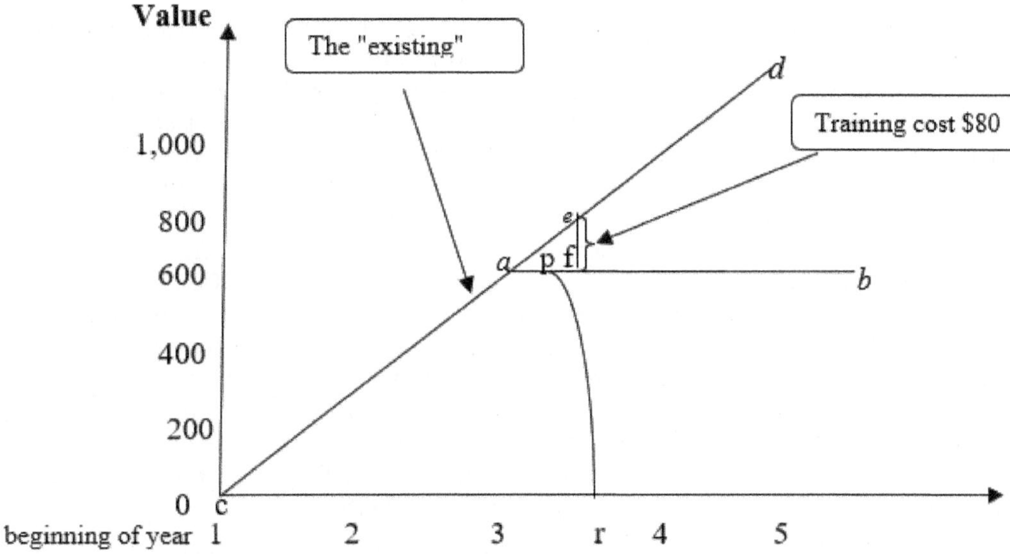

Suppose that at the beginning of the third year the economic value of the taxpayer's goodwill and know-how is estimated to be worth $600. At that point, when a new technique is available (for the cost of $80), the taxpayer faces a choice: if she does not acquire it, her professional know-how ceases to increase at the expected rate (depicted by rising slope ***c-d***) and stays constant (depicted by the constant flat line ***a-b***). In that case she may lose her business/professional status in the marketplace. (One may argue that without the training she will eventually perish professionally, which is depicted in vertical slope ***p-r***). If she participates in the training and pays its cost ($80) she restores her original "existing" professional ability to produce the expected growth of (taxable) income she is used to (slope ***c-d***). Hence, the amount paid ($80, depicted by ***f-e***) is to maintain her existing income producing ability, i.e. she keeps the business activity in an efficient operating condition, and the training cost is a deductible expense.

Such analysis has been adopted—though not completely—by case law. In *Colorado Springs National Bank v. U.S.*, *NCNB Corporation v. U.S.*, a bank was expected to grow and constantly adapt new banking techniques and procedures. When a new credit card system was introduced, the bank had to adopt that service and begin to use it. It spent significant amounts of money for this purpose. If it had not, it would have lost its position within the banking industry. It would have dropped from the above slope ***cd.*** and might reach slope ***pr.*** Spending the needed amounts brought the bank back to the existing ***cd***, hence the amount spent was considered by the Supreme Court to be ordinary and necessary deductible expenses. The new credit card operation was merely "a new method of operating an old business." The Court considered the business of a bank to include loaning money to customers and the new operation—the credit card—was simply a new way of doing so

On the other hand, if a bank takes over another financial institute, the cost of changing the corporate structure for the benefit of future operations is not an ordinary and necessary business expense; if the money is spent for creating a separate and distinct asset, which has a useful life extending substantially beyond the end of the taxable year, such cost is capital expense (**INDOPCO, Inc.**).

The rule may seem quite straightforward: if the expenditure creates or enhances "a separate and distinct asset", then that expenditure must be capitalized. Any costs that result in significant future benefits accruing to the taxpayer above and beyond the mere expected expansion are capital in nature and not immediately deductible. However, in practice it was claimed that the future benefit analysis requires looking at the special facts of each case and such an approach cannot provide "the certainty and clarity necessary for compliance with, and sound administration of, the law" [67 Fed. Reg. 7,701 (Dec. 19, 2002)]. In fact, this issue spawned many controversies. The Treasury responded by issuing a detailed regulation [**§ 1.263(a)–3**, called the "INDOPCO regulation"]. According to the IRS proposal, the primary purpose of which was to "reduce the burden on both taxpayers and IRS field personnel". The lengthy and highly detailed INDOPCO regulation provides some bright-line rules on whether specified types of expenditures must be capitalized or can be immediately deducted. These regulations are taxpayer-favorable, since they constrict the class of cases in which capitalization is required as compared with prior law. This result was justified by the Treasury on the grounds that it is consistent with the policy goal of reducing controversy.

The "future benefits" analysis also applies to human capital such as professional know-how.

Note that the symmetry which is discussed above is restored. The costs of creating the intangibles are current and immediately deducted on the one hand, and the gain (or loss) from selling them should be classified as ordinary gross income instead of capital gain [p. 218]. This conclusion solves Professor Johnson's asymmetric dilemma (19) [p. 220] and is justified since the creating of the said intangibles is done by the firm's use of its own factor of production, hence the gain is ordinary-current income (19) [pp. 148, 209, 217].

5. THE STATUTORY PROVISIONS: *ORDINARY AND NECESSARY EXPENSES*—ABOVE THE LINE DEDUCTIONS

We know already that taxable income represents gain, profits, or accretion of the taxpayer's wealth or economic ability. The gain and profit's costs should be deducted against the earning. They should be allowed as deductions to arrive to the taxpayer's AGI and eventually to their taxable income. Such costs are, *"all the ordinary and necessary expenses paid or incurred during the taxable year in carrying on any trade or business"* as provided in IRC Sec 162.

The basic requirements are two: the expenses should be ***ordinary*** and ***necessary***. The U.S. courts have tended to conclude that the meaning of the term ordinary [expenses] means current as opposed to capital expenses/investments, whereas necessary [expenses] means real cost of the earning and not a disguised personal consumption.

As mentioned already, Code Sec. 62 defines the term Adjusted Gross Income (AGI) through elaborating what is called "**above-the-line deductions**". It elaborates the general rule that pertains to allowable deductions in order to arrive to the individual taxpayers' AGIs. They are available to all individual taxpayers, both self-employed and employees. The prerequisites, conditions, and limitations of the deductibility of the payments, contributions and expenses are particularized within other Code sections referred to by Sec. 62. For example: Code Secs. 161–168, which deal with trade and business expenses; reimbursed expenses of employees; certain expenses of performing artists; certain expenses of officials; certain expenses of members of reserve components of the U.S. Armed Forces; trade and business losses, including losses from sale or exchange of business property; amounts paid to a financial institutions as penalty for premature withdrawal of funds from a time savings account, certificate of deposit, or similar class of deposit; certain payments attributable to rents and royalties; and certain deductions of life tenants and income beneficiaries of property. Other Code sections that are mentioned in Sec 62 are the following: § 194 (reforestation expenses); § 212 (relating to expenses for production of income); § 217 (moving expenses); § 219 (certain amounts contributed to retirement savings); § 220 (payments for Archer MSAs, which is a savings account for employees' healthcare services); § 221 (interest on education loans); § 223 (contributions for health savings accounts); § 404 (contributions for pension, profit-sharing, and annuity plans of self-employed individuals); and § 611 (relating to depletion of property held for the production of rents or royalties).

The "above-the-line deductions" must meet also the "negative" conditions of Code Sec 262, which specifically disallows a list of personal, living, or family expenses. Others disallowance provisions are found in other Code sections such as 162(c), which disallows illegal bribes, kickbacks, and other such payments or 274, which prevents the deduction of certain payments for entertainment, amusement, or recreation.

A. Interest Payments

Until more than half century ago, all interest (46) payments [p. 105] were deductible. Not any longer. The basic idea is quite clear. Under reasonable matching rules [pp. 279–281] interest payments (64) should be added to the cost of the goods or services that were bought by loaned money. If a taxpayer borrows money and spends it on private consumption, the interest payments are part of the consumption's cost, i.e. part of his taxable income (from the usages side—[pp. 157, 188]) and should not be deducted. Indeed, Code Sec. 163(h) specifically provides that personal nonbusiness interest is not deductible.

The rules pertaining to other types of interest payments are not that clear or concise. Interest payments on acquisition of a capital asset with loaned money should be added to the asset's cost; to its basis. Furthermore, we mentioned already that an immediate deduction to a business deduction that was financed with borrowed money and the additional deduction of the interest may result in double deduction of the interest payments [p. 169]. In addition, we saw that in some cases the current deductibility of interest produces double deduction [p. 169].

Nevertheless, Congress turned in a different direction. Code Sec. 163 signals the general rule: "There shall be allowed as a deduction all interest paid or accrued within the taxable year on indebtedness." The limitations, prerequisites and exceptions are provided in other Code sections. Hence interest paid on a loan that finances a depreciable asset is deductible annually and is not added to the asset's cost, as long as the asset is already used in the trade or business. On the other hand, prepayment of interest on acquiring—or creating—a capital asset before it becomes operational is capitalized and added to the asset's cost. Other interest payments on indebtedness, which are used for the operation of a trade or business, are considered the cost to the taxpayer of doing business and therefore are deductible like any other business expenses. As mentioned, Code Sec. 221 allows certain taxpayers to deduct interest above-the-line on education loans—up to a certain limit.

The code provides some matching rules (76) [pp. 279, 281] that are aimed to prevent tax abuse. For example, Code Sec. 163(d) provides that interest on money borrowed for a passive investment is only deductible to the extent of investment income. A similar section provides that interest paid on loans that finance **passive activity** [p. 281] should not be treated as an ordinary business expense but be added to the cost of the passive activity.

In addition, there are some personal interest payments (e.g. "*qualified home mortgages*" and "*home equity indebtedness*" up to a statutory ceiling) that are allowed as below-the-line deductions [p. 288]. As mentioned above, [p. 4] such a deduction creates a severe distortion to the housing market and increases social gaps.

B. Mixed Expenses: Business and Private Consumption

A practical problem arises pertaining to mixed-purpose expenditures where the payment has a dual purpose: producing income on the one hand and private consumption on the other hand, e.g. the above lodging and meals or away-from-home expenses [p. 254]. In such cases, the taxpayer should try to separate the expense into its components, prove the business portion, and deduct it. The problem is when the taxpayer is unable to clearly identify the non-private consumption components. An "all or nothing" approach creates serious difficulties. Disallowance of the business portion of the expense, on the one hand, or allowing the consumption portion on the other, indirectly changes the tax base, either into a wealth tax in the former option, or moves away from income and ability to pay criteria in the latter [p. 153].

There are several ways to avoid these two undesirable options. The simple way is to use a statutory reasonable allocation between the private and business components. Another statutory semi-allocation method is to allow the deduction of such expenses subject to a percentage or fixed amount limitation. The latter is found in the "below-the-line" itemized deductions [pp. 287, 288]. In addition, case law and Revenue Ruling serve as significant guidelines for the allowing or disallowing the mixed character expenses.

Code Sec. 274(n) is a major example of statutory rule. Only 50% of the amounts classified as *business meals and business entertainment* may be deductible, hence 50% of such expenses are regarded as taxable personal consumption. For a 35% income tax plus other mandatory payments such Social Security, Health Insurance, and state income tax, this means that around 75% of these expenses are not allowed to be deducted and they come of the taxpayer's pockets.

Another example is the statutory treatment of unreimbursed employee expenses. Such expenses are treated as "below-the-line" and subject to some limitations that are discussed below [p. 293].

The case law approach is less flexible, and the general tendency is the "winner takes all" approach. The courts look for the ***cause*** of the outlay. If the major cause is a business or profit-seeking one, the whole expenditure is deductible, even if it contains some personal-consumption aspects. If the court finds that the cause or the motive is a personal one, the outlay is not deductible even if it contains some business attributes.

C. Illegal, Immoral and Anti-Public-Policy Expenses

Statutory provisions prohibit the deduction of payments that are considered to be against the public order or public policy, such as fines for committing criminal offences (Code Sec. 162(f)); or portions of treble damage payments under antitrust laws (Code Sec. 162(g)); or illegal bribes or kickbacks (Code Sec. 162(C)), whether within the U.S.A. or even for foreign governments officials; or expenses related to illegal drug trafficking (280E). Note that these disallowances bring about a double taxation situation: the payees are taxable (as long as they are subject to U.S. income tax) and the payer is taxed as well due to the disallowance.

D. Tax Arbitrage

"Tax arbitrage" is a simple example of the taxpayers' attempts to reduce their tax bills. Suppose a taxpayer takes a loan with a 5% interest rate and purchases tax-exempted municipal bonds. In addition, she has a significant income from her business, which is subject to a 40% marginal tax rate. Her tax saving (133) [pp. 4, 240] from deducting the interest payments against her income from the municipal bond is zero, whereas if she deducts it against her business income the tax saving is 40%. The same problem arises if the investment is not tax-free but its return—dividend, capital gain [p. 316]—is subject to a lower tax rate of 20% compared to 35% on ordinary income. Note that the analysis offered above [p. 169] suggests that most interest payments create tax arbitrages. Furthermore, according to the **Modigliani and Miller theorem**, in a world without taxes and under an efficient market with no transaction costs, the value of a firm is unaffected by how that firm is financed. Yet in a world with corporate taxation, due to the interest deduction, there are advantages for corporations that finance their businesses with loans.

Another problem is when one of the taxpayer's businesses or investments results in a loss, i.e. the deductible expenses are higher than the income [p. 283]. Suppose **Business 1** is an ordinary business that the taxpayer is an active part of. **Business 2** is a business that the taxpayer is not actively engaged in—i.e. it is a "passive activity" [p. 281] that produces a loss in the short term. The **Investment** is a corporate stock. Once again, if the only concern is taxation of the taxpayer's ability, the loss, which reduces the overall taxpayer's ability, should offset both the business and the investment's profits. On the other hand, such result creates inefficient decisions, since the only reason for the taxpayer to invest in **Business 2** was the tax benefit. Without this benefit they will not participate in such business [p. 220]. Though reasonable matching rules can take care of such problems, the legislature has had to step in and provide several "anti-tax arbitrage" rules, which are discussed below.

E. Matching Rules, Depreciation, Recapture and Losses

1) Matching Rules in General

Economic behavior should be based on rational decisions. One prerequisite for such decision is information. When a firm conducts a business, engages in an occupation or any other activity that is intended to make gains or profits, or considers making certain investments, it has to be able to predict the business result of each activity; which activities result in a profit that justifies continuation as usual; which activities needs to be reconsidered and improved and which activities should be terminated. The basic tools that are supposed to provide such information are what is called in accounting the *matching rules* (76) [pp. 106, 299]. These rules match income and its costs. They provide a simple tool that helps business decision-makers to see the end result of each economic activity. *Horizontal* matching helps us match the expenses that were paid to produce certain income with the same income. The simple table below demonstrates the idea of the matching rule: during a certain period—a year—Business A's expenses should be deducted only against Business income. The same is true for Businesses B and C.

Business A		Business B		Business C	
Income	Expenses	Income	Expenses	Income	Expenses
Xxxxx	xxxxx	Xxxxx	xxxxx	xxxxx	xxxxx
Gain (loss): xxxx		Gain (loss): xxxx		Gain (loss): xxxxx	

In addition, an activity is examined over a certain period of time. Usually, the period of time that is chosen is one year. *Vertical* matching consists of matching rules limited to a certain period of time. The idea of vertical matching rules is demonstrated in the table below:

Year 1	Business A "square 1"		Business B "square 2"		Investment C "square 3"	
	Income XXXXX	Expenses XXXX	Income XXXX	Expenses XXXX	Income XXXX	Expenses XXXX
	Gain (loss):xxxx		Gain (loss): xxxx		Gain (loss): xxxx	
Year 2	Business A		Business B		Investment C	
	Income XXXXX		Expenses XXXX		Income XXXX	
	Gain (loss):xxxx		Gain (loss): xxxx		Gain (loss): xxxx	

Under a strict implementation of matching rules, each "square" is separated from the others, i.e. Business A's expenses in year 1 should be subtracted only against Business A's income in year 1, etc. Accordingly, a rigid implementation of the matching rules for income tax purposes would lead to the disallowing of the losses that occur in one year within one activity ("square") to offset against gains or profits of another year or another activity. In terms of the above tables, no loss in one square can shift and offset income produced in another square, neither horizontally nor vertically.

On the other hand, under a complete and comprehensive income tax system, i.e. all the different components of economic ability are added and the aggregate income is taxed according to the taxpayer's tax rates without any delay or tax deferral, and all types of income are subject to the same tax rates' schedule, there is no need for using these matching rules (76) for income tax purposes. Yet, we are not already there. Under the current tax system, there are different rules of realization (103) [pp. 163, 198] and there are a variety of tax rates for different kinds of income. Hence individual taxpayers might face significant temptation to abuse the system, mainly by subtracting expenses that were spent on activities that are tax-exempt or subject to lower tax rates against income that is subject to higher tax rates.

2) Statutory Matching Rules

The statutory matching rules (76) are intended primarily to prevent tax abuse or tax shelters. The most significant solution embraced by Congress is to create three different categories of income: **Active income** derives from activities in which the taxpayer materially participates; **Passive activity** (defined at Code Sec. 469), and **Portfolio income**, which is passive investment income such as interest, dividends, and capital gains which are derived from the sale of investment property.

The basic rule requires that losses in each category should offset only income in the same category. Code Sec. 165(c) provides the basic limitation to offset losses: the loss should be either incurred in a trade or business or from any **transaction** entered into for profit, though not connected with a trade or business. Code Sec 469(a) disallows any passive activity loss, or passive activity credit for the taxable year. Such accumulated losses and credits can be offset only when the taxpayer's interest in this activity is terminated in a qualified disposition.

Passive losses can only be deducted against passive income. Losses from at-risk investments can only be deducted against the income generated by that activity. At-risk limitation losses for that particular activity are restricted to the income (which does not include the recapture of previous losses), produced by that activity.

Another statutory matching rule is aimed to prevent "*Tax arbitrage*", [p. 279], i.e. when assets, which are acquired with debt, produce preferred income such as municipal bonds that produce exempted income. The interest payments on such a loan are disallowed under Code Sec. 265(a)(2).

Another example of a statutory matching rule that is designated to prevent tax shelters is the case where a capital asset is sold for a loss. The rule requires the taxpayer to match such a loss against gains derived from selling other capital assets, which are subject to preferred tax rates, and not against ordinary income. Code Secs. 1211 and 1212 limit the possibilities of offsetting capital losses. Losses are allowed to be offset only against capital gains (though individual taxpayers are entitled to offset capital losses against ordinary income up to a ceiling of $3,000 annually). Excess or unused capital loss in a given year can be carried forward to the following years without time limitation (corporations are limited to a "carry back" of 3 years and/or a "carry forward" of 5 years). The main purpose of this limitation is the prevention of "cherry-picking" [p. 208]: realization of capital losses in order to reduce taxes on ordinary income, while retaining assets that have unrealized capital gain.

Code Sec. 1341 is also a matching rule [pp. 199–204], which aims to ease the over-taxation caused by the claim of right (23) [p. 199].

Code Sec. 267(a)(1) prohibits, with some statutory limitations, conditions and definitions, the deduction of any loss from the sale or exchange of property, directly or indirectly, between related persons. Furthermore Sec. 267(a)(2) elaborates certain matching rules aimed to prevent an aggregate tax saving (133) [pp. 4, 240] or tax deferral resulting from transactions between related persons. It states that a deduction is allowed only in the same taxable year the payee includes the payment within their gross income. Related persons under this section are, *inter alia*: members of a family, as defined in subsection (c)(4); an individual and a corporation of which more than 50 percent in value of the outstanding stock is owned, directly or indirectly, by or for such individual; two corporations which are members of the same controlled group; and other related persons which are connected by various types of trusts.

Code Sec 404(d) disallows a trade or business any deduction of payments to independent contractors until the year the contractor includes the compensation in their gross income.

Code Sec. 83 limits any payer, including employers, the deductibility of the compensation for services that were paid by transfer of property only if its value is equal to the amount required to be included in the recipient's gross income.

3) Case Law

Code Sec. 274(e)(2) allows the deductibility of expenses for goods, services, and facilities, to the extent that the expenses are treated by the taxpayer, with respect to the recipient of these fringe benefits (entertainment, amusement, or recreation), as taxable compensation to an employee on the taxpayer's return of tax as wages to such employee and for purposes of tax withholding at source on wages.

In the *Sutherland* case (8th circuit ct. 2001), an employer provided certain fringe benefits (free use of its business jet for personal consumption) to its high-ranking officers. The officers were taxed on the value of the flights according to a known formula which is based on flights miles, and not on the actual cost to the employer, which was larger. The employer included within its business expenses all costs related to the maintenance and operation of its corporate jet, including those expenses that were connected to the officers' personal flights. Those expenses were larger than the amount that the officers reported as their taxable fringe benefits. The tax commissioner substantiated his decision to disallow the full amount of the corporation's expenses on Code Sec. 274(e)(2) and limited them to the amount that was included within the officers' taxable income. The 8th Circuit ruled in favor of the taxpayer and allowed it to include all the jet maintenance and operation costs, regardless of the smaller amount that was reported as the officers' income. This decision is rather strange. Instead, the basic matching rule and the basic rule of an equitable tax system should lead to a general conclusion that employers are not allowed to deduct compensation to their employee in any amount higher than the latter is paid. Any compensation paid to an employee is deductible by their employer as compensation paid for purchasing services for their trade or business. If an employer pays their employee a certain amount—say $100—but the employee include only $80 in his income, then the market value for the services he provided to them must be only $80—the cost of the professional services. The other $20 must be regarded as a gift, which is not deductible by the donor. If the $20 is not a bona fide gift, but rather disguised compensation, it should be included within the employee's gross income and only then should it be deductible by the employer.

The same analysis should be applied when an employer reimburses their employee his meals and entertainment expenses, which are subject to a 50% limitation under Code Sec. 274(n). The employer should be allowed to deduct the full reimbursed amount: 50% as the employer's trade or business expenses she spends through her employee, and the remaining 50% as the employee's compensation.

4) Depreciation, Recapture and "Negative Recapture" Rules

One may consider the depreciations and recapture (105) [pp. 212, 283] rules as mere matching rules as well: the underlying rationale of the recapture provision of Code Sec.

1245 is that it derives from the practical concession found in the depreciation system that the purpose of depreciation deductions is to keep the taxpayer's annual "capital recovery" untaxed. An accurate calculation of annual capital recovery involves a great deal of estimation; an *ex ante* anticipation in order to determine the asset's value at the beginning and end of each taxable year. Such estimation requires a tremendous administrative burden. The second-best solution is the statutory annual depreciation provisions [pp. 260, 263]. As such, the statutory depreciation amounts are supposed to be an optimal approximation to the real capital recovery. They are not accurate. Sometimes the annual deduction they provide is too high annual deduction, and sometimes it is too low. Yet the above discussion suggests that the current depreciation methods which are used by the U.S. legislature are clearly in favor of the asset owners.

The recapture rules (105) [p. 212] aim to take care of the "mistakes" caused by the inaccuracy of the annual statutory depreciation deductions that the taxpayer took during the previous years' holding period. Hence, when a depreciable capital asset is disposed of at a gain, in most of the cases the gain is the result of overly high depreciation deductions ("capital recovery") that were taken during the holding period, which consequently reduced the taxpayer's ordinary income during those taxable years. Instead of going back to the previous taxable years and changing the taxable income retroactively, the recapture rule indeed recaps (adds) the "missing" ordinary income to the taxable income, i.e. reclassifies the gain into ordinary income subject to the ordinary tax rates instead of the preferred ones.

Though not everybody acknowledges it, the same idea—the recapture of "inaccurate" depreciation—is used regarding capital losses. Code. Sec. 1231 reclassifies capital loss derived from selling depreciable assets as ordinary loss. What seems to be an unusual approach may be explained in two ways.

The first explanation is based on historical background facts: the origin of this approach—Sec. 117(j) of IRC 1939—was enacted in 1942 in order to support the U.S. shipping industry during the Second World War. Its announced goal was to provide favorable treatment to disposition of ships and other property used during the war. Yet it is hard to believe that this phenomenon would last for more than 80 years without a better and more updated explanation.

The other explanation (that applies only to depreciable assets) is based on principle of tax symmetry and embodies a mirror image of the recapture provision (105). We call it a "negative recapture rule". The same underlying rationale discussed above [p. 212] for the recapture rule (when a depreciable asset is sold for a gain which is reclassified as an ordinary income) should apply also when the asset is sold at a loss: the loss indicates that during the holding period the annual depreciation deductions were evidently too low, and consequently the annual taxable income was too high. When the asset is disposed of, it is time to correct the previous years' mistakes and to compensate the taxpayer for paying too much income tax. Allowing the taxpayer to offset the loss against ordinary income retrieves the previous years' over-taxation. In other words, the negative recapture is a reflection of the "reversed" "tax benefit rule" (121).

5) Net Operating Loss

A net operating loss (NOL) occurs when a taxpayer's business deductions for a taxable year are higher than their annual taxable income. Such a situation is created when deductions from a trade or business (including employees and self-employed individuals), and casualty and theft losses (22) completely wash the taxpayer's income and the balance is negative.

The general rule is that NOL may be carried backward for 2 taxable years preceding the taxable year of such loss, or carried over to each of the 20 taxable years following the taxable year of the loss. In certain circumstances the carry backward period is extended to 3 taxable years if the loss is an "**eligible loss**", i.e. if it occurred from losses of property arising from fire, storm, shipwreck, or other casualty including theft; or if the loss occurs to a small business or to trade or business of farming and it is attributable to presidentially-declared disasters [pp. 32, 50]. Furthermore, the carry backward is extended to 5 years if the taxpayer has a farming loss.

The taxpayer is entitled to decide whether to carry the NOL backwards or forwards. Yet, the entire amount of the NOL for any taxable year ("loss year") shall be carried to the earliest of the taxable years to which such loss may be carried. The portion of such loss which shall be carried to each of the other taxable years shall be the excess, if any, of the amount of such loss over the sum of the taxable income for each of the prior taxable years to which such loss may be carried. NOL is deducted "above-the-line" against the AGI.

F. Employee's Business Expenses

Under the U.S. income tax system, an employee's income is considered as income from trade or business. Hence, subject to certain limitations, employees should be able to deduct the business expenses they spend during their earning activities, the same way a self-employed taxpayer does. Yet, we mentioned already the unique position that employees hold, i.e. their "dual capacity as taxpayers" [pp. 224, 293]. Such a dual capacity leads to a conclusion that the deductibility of some of the employee's expenses should be determined through the employer's eyes. In order to draw a distinction between employee and self-employed deductions, we first briefly mention the common business expenses that are allowed to self-employed taxpayers as above-the-line deductions:

1) The general requirement is "ordinary and necessary" business expenses. I.e. a common and accepted expense that is helpful and appropriate for the taxpayer's trade or business;
2) Educational expenses that are for the maintenance or improvement of skill required by **current** trade or business;
3) Travel expenses if necessary to carry out the performance of the business;
4) Amounts expended for meals and lodging while away from the business-home in the pursuit of a trade or business, provided the amounts are not lavish or extravagant under the circumstances;
5) 50% of meals and entertainment expenses directly related the taxpayer's trade or business.

When employees spend those expenses, they are allowed to fully deduct them only if their employer reimburses them. If the employer does not, the employee may still deduct them but only as "itemized" ("below-the-line") deductions [p. 287], which are subject to some significant limitations elaborated below [p. 293].

G. The Correlation Between the Employers' Tax Rates and Their Inclination to Offer Fair Compensation to Their Employees

As is discussed above [p. 240], a low tax rate provides a smaller tax saving (133) [pp. 4, 240] from any deductible expenses, and vice versa. The most common expense that employers have direct control of is their employees' compensation. As is suggested above [pp. 101, 240], a tax cut for employers—both self-employed and corporations—might lead to wage cuts, unemployment, increased social gaps, decreased government revenue, smaller amounts of public goods and services, inferior human and social capital, a higher national deficit, and consequently a worse social and economic structure.

The following chart attempts to provide a good workable view of the structure of the process one should use when moving from "Gross Income" to "Adjusted Gross Income".

Figure 21.6:

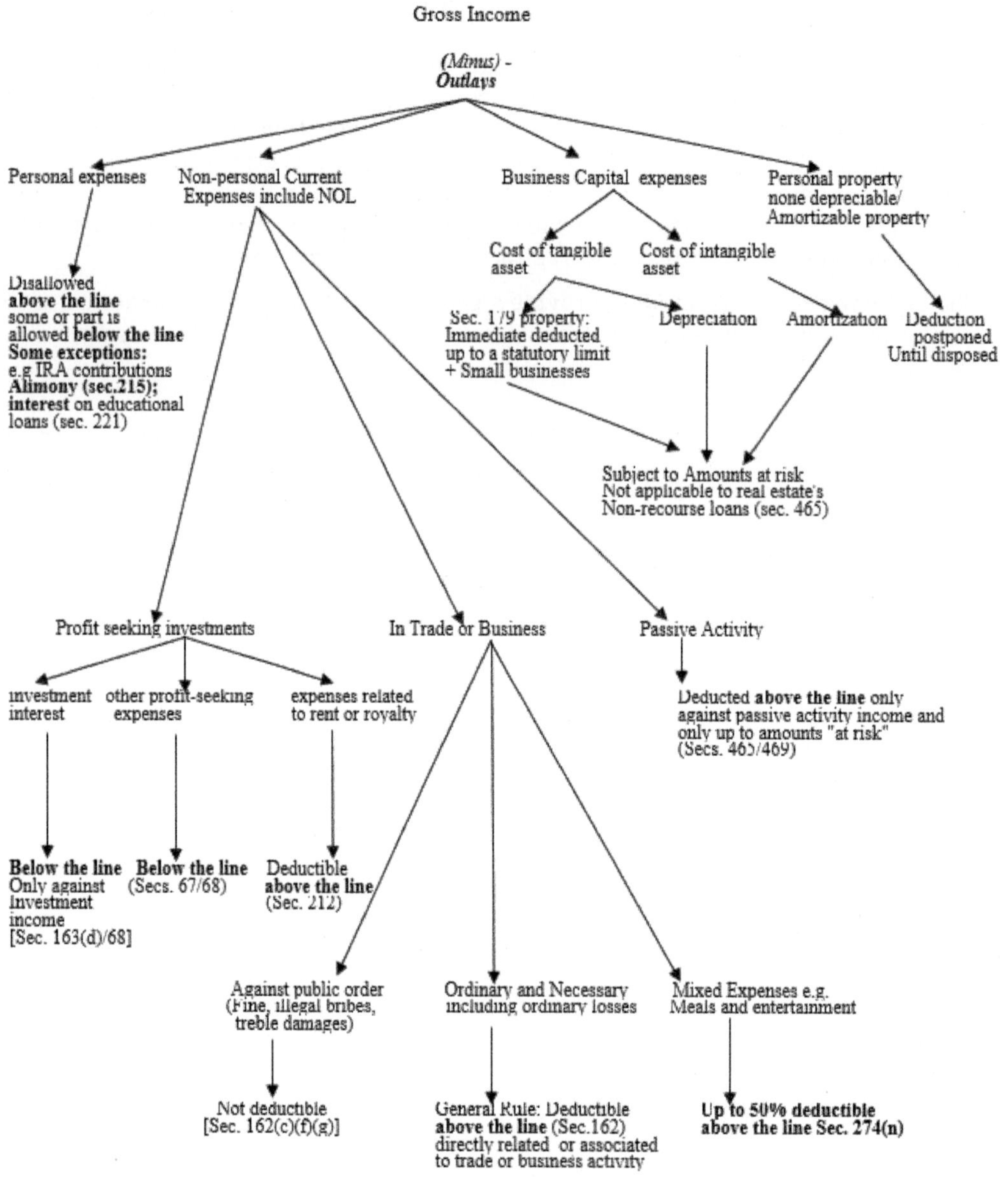
Gross Income
(Minus) -
Outlays
Personal expenses
Non-personal Current Expenses include NOL
Business Capital expenses
Personal property none depreciable/ Amortizable property
Disallowed above the line some or part is allowed below the line Some exceptions: e.g IRA contributions Alimony (sec.215); interest on educational loans (sec. 221)
Cost of tangible asset
Cost of intangible asset
Sec. 179 property: Immediate deducted up to a statutory limit + Small businesses
Depreciation
Amortization
Deduction postponed Until disposed
Subject to Amounts at risk Not applicable to real estate's Non-recourse loans (sec. 465)
Profit seeking investments
In Trade or Business
Passive Activity
investment interest
other profit-seeking expenses
expenses related to rent or royalty
Deducted above the line only against passive activity income and only up to amounts "at risk" (Secs. 465/469)
Below the line Only against Investment income [Sec. 163(d)/68]
Below the line (Secs. 67/68)
Deductible above the line (Sec. 212)
Against public order (Fine, illegal bribes, treble damages)
Ordinary and Necessary including ordinary losses
Mixed Expenses e.g. Meals and entertainment
Not deductible [Sec. 162(c)(f)(g)]
General Rule: Deductible above the line (Sec.162) directly related or associated to trade or business activity
Up to 50% deductible above the line Sec. 274(n)

Chapter Twenty-Two

STAGE SIX—TAXABLE INCOME: "BELOW THE LINE" DEDUCTIONS

1. IN GENERAL

Adjusted Gross Income—AGI—is indeed an interim stage. After the taxpayer's AGI is set, additional deductions are taken in order to determine the final tax base—the "***Taxable Income***". Three types of deductions are used to move from AGI to Taxable Income: **Personal Exemptions**, and either **Itemized deductions** or **Standard deductions**. Instead of the "itemized deduction", taxpayers have the option to elect the standard deduction, a fixed amount of money that releases the taxpayer from the tedious duty of keeping book records and elaborating actual expenses. Until the Tax Cuts and Jobs Act of 2017 sunsets in 2026, the Code's personal exemption is $0, and the standard deduction is significantly higher.

The common ground for those deductions, which are discussed below, is that they deviate from the pure and analytical tests for the cost of the income producing process discussed above. Instead, they represent a combination of personal consumption, nondiscretionary expenses, some social concessions, administrative efficiency, and indirect cost of the taxpayers' ability to produce earned income.

2. PERSONAL EXEMPTION

In order to ensure that the income tax does not push individuals below a dignified standard of living the Code offers a safety net which guarantees that income below a certain minimum is tax free. Code Sec. 151 provides any individual the right to claim a personal exemption for themselves and for any dependents they support who do not file their tax returns separately. Nonresident aliens are allowed only one exemption for themselves. The personal exemption amount is indexed annually for inflation and due to its social purpose, it is phased out (94) as the taxpayer's AGI reaches a certain amount. The Personal exemption amount for 2016 is $4,050. For single taxpayers it begins to phase out at AGI of $259,400 and is totally exhausted at $381,900. Currently, the temporary rules of the Tax Cuts and Jobs Act of 2017, set to sunset in 2026, have set the Personal Exemption amount at $0 (which is offset by an increase in the standard deduction).

3. STANDARD DEDUCTIONS

As one can imagine, bookkeeping of the itemized and miscellaneous deductions may be considered by most of households/families as a tedious and almost unbearable chore. Hence, for those taxpayers who share this feeling, Congress enacted Code Sec. 63(c), which offers taxpayers the choice of giving up "below the line" itemized deductions [p. 288] and taking instead a ***standard deduction*** (113) in order to arrive at their *taxable income*. The standard deduction is a fixed amount indexed to inflation, and it varies according to family size and marital status. The standard deduction disregards whether the taxpayer actually had any expenses. Not surprisingly, most high-income taxpayers prefer to itemize whereas most of those with lower incomes take the standard deductions. According to statistical data published by the IRC, "nearly two out of three taxpayers take the standard deduction rather than itemizing deductions, such as mortgage interest, charitable contributions, and state and local taxes"

The amounts of the standard deduction for the 2022 tax year, is $12,950 for individual, $25,900 for a couple and $19,400 for heads of household.

The standard deduction option is not available for non-resident aliens or for married taxpayers who file a separate tax return if one of them prefers itemized deductions. The standard deductions are not phased-out, which is understandable, since taxpayers with large incomes prefer to itemize their expenses.

4. ITEMIZED DEDUCTIONS

The optional itemized deductions are open to all U.S. individual taxpayers who are ready to give up the standard deductions and instead claim actual and documented expenses.

The purpose of the itemized deductions is mainly to promote social causes. Most of them should be considered as TRIs, meant to encourage individual taxpayers to acquire their own dwelling, or to assure a minimum standard of living through allowing certain non-discretionary personal expenses such as local taxes, casualty and theft losses, or high medical costs. Another deduction aims to encourage taxpayers to donate money to their favorite nonprofit organizations. A special kind of itemized deduction is offered to employees for expenses they spend during their own professional activities that are not reimbursed by the employer. Those deductions are subject to various limitations.

A. Interest on Home Mortgage

As was mentioned, no above-the-line deduction is allowed for any personal interest payments. Hence, credit cards interest on personal purchases, interest on car leasing or loans etc. are considered part of the cost of personal consumption and are disallowed [p. 277]. The most significant exception to this rule is the Code Sec. 163(h), which allows not only the deduction of interest paid by a taxpayer on their first mortgage ("*qualified home mortgage*") up to a cap of $750,000. The same limitation of $750,000 applies to the total amount of loans secured by the taxpayer's main home or second home which includes both first and second mortgages. Note that until 1987 there was no limit on the amount of the loan. After this year and until the end of 2017 the limit was set at $1,000,000 and in 2018 the limit dropped as stated to $750,000. Thus, if the loan was taken before 1987, or even if it has been refinanced, the $1,000,000 does not apply. The same logic applies to a loan taken before the beginning of 2018.

There are some serious doubts about the impact of these deductions on the market for small and inexpensive apartments. Since tax saving (133) [pp. 4, 240] increases with income, these deduction, which are part of the taxpayers' consumption, reduce the economic cost of big luxury apartments and houses for high income taxpayers, which in turn increases the demand for such housing, reduces the supply of inexpensive apartments, increasing their prices and thus leaving the low-income earners with less chance to fulfill the American dream. Furthermore, not only do low-income taxpayers enjoy lower tax savings from such deductions, but due to the limitations on itemized deductions discussed below, their chances to even enjoy these deductions at all are seriously in doubt.

In addition, the fact that such mortgages are used to finance private consumption is considered a very risky phenomenon for the national economy. Some scholars even argue that such deductions contributed to the world economic crisis of 2008.

Note that since these deductions are more valuable to high income taxpayers, Congress offers additional relief in order to assist lower-income individuals with owning a home. Code Sec. 25 provides a Mortgage Tax Credit to those taxpayers who are granted a Mortgage Credit Certificate (MCC) by a state or local government. The credit, which is discussed below [p. 320], is nonrefundable (82), limited to a certain amount ($2,000 a year) and subject to some preconditions. If the taxpayer itemizes deductions and claims a home mortgage interest deduction, the tax credit amount must be subtracted from that deduction.

B. Student Loan Interest Deduction

A common way for students or their families to finance their higher education is to receive "qualified student loans" which are repaid usually after graduation. These loans bear interest. Code Sec. 221 allows an individual to deduct in a taxable year an amount equal to the interest paid by the taxpayer during the taxable year on any qualified education loans. The deduction is limited to a maximum amount of $2,500 per year. It is subject to a phase-out (94), which begins at a Modified Adjusted Gross Income—MAGI (6) of $65,000 and is gradually reduced up to a MAGI of $80,000 for individuals. If the taxpayer's MAGI is larger than $80,000, the interest payments are no longer deductible. These amounts are doubled in case of couples filing joint returns.

C. Charitable Contributions

Code Sec. 170 allows individual taxpayers to deduct their charitable contributions made to non-profit organizations (87) whose goals are to promote or provide activities and services in the areas of education, religion, science, etc. The contribution must be characterized as a donation where the donee does not get any goods or services in return. As a general rule, the deduction amount is subject to 50% of the taxpayer's Adjusted Gross Income, though the contribution may be made in cash or in kind (but not by untaxed services). If the donation is made by appreciated property (but not stock in trade), the taxpayer enjoys the best of both worlds: the appreciation escapes capital gain tax and the amount allowed of the deduction is the market value and not the original cost of the property donated, subject to a limitation of "only" 30% of the taxpayer's AGI. As discussed above [p. 251] one of the explanations for the charitable contribution deduction is the idea that such donations directly promote the government's general goals and reduce its expenses on public goods and services. If such donations are not deductible there is a chance that the donor might pay twice to society [p. 14]. Yet, a realistic, maybe cynical observation may raise some doubts about the concept of providing tax breaks to charitable donations. It allows the taxpayers to earmark their tax payments and designate them to some public goods and services according to their own social, religious, and political inclinations. On the one hand it indeed allows some leeway in terms of the taxpayer-government relationships and puts some restrictions and limitations on the government's power. Yet one should remember the above "Coalition" claim regarding the allegiance between the government and capital owners [pp. 24, 75]. Low-income taxpayers who make sincere, yet small donations, probably are not concerned too much with the deduction. A taxpayer whose marginal tax rate is 15%, who donates $500 to her favorite charitable organization, saves a total of $75, if preferring itemized deductions over the standard deduction. She might be willing to contribute only $425 out of her pocket even without the deduction under Code Sec. 170. On the other hand, significant amounts of contributions are made mostly by higher income taxpayers, with a purpose of turning the NPOs into a funnel whose aim is to promote and achieve goals that the Coalition would face significant difficulties with if the politicians tried to accomplish them through transparent debates and deliberations open to the public's scrutiny. The simple and obvious examples are religious establishments that the government, due to the Establishment Clause, is prohibited from supporting directly, but those religious institutions enjoy indirectly a huge amount of Federal money through this deduction. The same is true for political organizations. As stated above [p. 34], the indirect support of the government for NPO actually indicates that the government fails to provide some of the public services it considers essential or at least desired, and the free market is unable to provide them due to market failure caused by adverse selection (8). Therefore, the government transfers those services not to the free market but to non-profit organizations, which are funded in part by the government's waiving of taxes through the said deduction. Such a process is in fact a privatization of the process of setting national priorities and goals, and entrusting of it to individuals—probably high-income earners—and to companies. An accurate and realistic analysis of this phenomenon leads to a difficult conclusion: such a process undermines the basis of the democratic concept.

The most fundamental rule of democracy is that each citizen has one vote. We all vote for a party or for a president as our agents and they, as a *representative government,* are supposed to serve the public according to their promises and agenda that the public approves through the national election. They are supposed to collect taxes and finance the public goods and services according to their own discretion and pledges made to the voters. The deduction of charity contributions undermines this concept. In terms of social-economic national decisions and redistribution of income, this deduction gives the donor more than one vote. Furthermore, it seems almost obvious that a democratic system with a representative government will not be able to function if any taxpayers can earmark their tax payments to a specific government project. A realistic observation concludes that this is exactly the case with the deduction of charitable contributions.

This problem was enhanced by the **Citizens United** Supreme Court decision (2010) when the Court concluded that the First Amendment protects political spending by corporations or unions to support or denounce individual political candidates in the elections process. Such a situation wherein tax-deductible donations are made by the wealthiest, who use their corporations to funnel unlimited amounts to non-profit-organizations, strengthen the ties between politicians and the wealthiest and enhance what is called crony capitalism. Eventually, this decision provides further political influence to the Coalition [p. 24] and increases the power of the wealthiest over the U.S. decision-making process.

Note that the argument here is not anti-NPO activities. It only doubts the extra power a donor receives by earmarking their tax payments and designating them to specific goals that did not receive the approval of the representative government. If a 35%-tax-rate-taxpayer is bona fide willing to donate one million dollars, to a non-profit organization, and the amount is tax deductible, it means that she donated a sum of $650,000 from her own pocket. Without the deduction she might donate "only" $650,000. In such a case the NPO loses an amount of $350,000 but this amount reaches the elected government, which is supposed to provide the services in accordance with the democratic process

D. Casualty and Theft Losses

Since gross income is mainly measured by accretion to wealth (though subject to the above three exceptions [pp. 160–163]) then if a taxpayer sustains an event that reduces their wealth, such reduction should be taken into account in order to quantify their annual accretion to wealth. A slightly different observation focuses on the definition of the tax base as discretionary economic power (25) [p. 12]. Since losses, caused by from fire, storm, shipwreck, or other casualty (22), or from theft ("casualty and theft losses") are not discretionary or part of the taxpayer's private consumption, they should not be taxed, i.e. they should be deductible.

Another explanation that was discussed above [pp. 32, 50–51] is that the tax deduction for casualty and theft losses might be understood as stemming from the failure of the government to provide the needed protection to taxpayers who suffer from such losses.

Under Code Sec. 165(c)(3), a taxpayer who sustains unreimbursed personal losses resulting from casualty or theft may deduct the amount of such loses as an itemized-below-the-line deduction.

Casualty loss can result from the damage, destruction, or loss of private property from any sudden, unexpected, or unusual event such as a flood, hurricane, tornado, fire, earthquake or even a personal accident, that the taxpayer had no control over and was unable to prevent with reasonable measures.

The amount of casualty losses is generally the adjusted basis of the property if the loss is a total one. If the property is a "personal-use" property or is not completely destroyed, the amount of the casualty loss is the lesser of:

- The adjusted basis of the property, or
- The decrease in fair market value of the property due to the casualty

Theft losses are a result of criminal intent actions of taking and removing money or property with the intent to deprive the owner of it. The amount of theft loss pertaining to property is generally its adjusted basis.

Code Sec. 165(h) introduces a limitation applied only for casualty and theft losses: any casualty and theft loss shall be allowed only to the extent that the amount of the loss to an individual arising from each casualty, or from each theft, exceeds $100. Furthermore, net casualty loss (the excess of personal casualty losses over the personal casualty gains for such taxable year) is allowed only to the extent where it exceeds 10 percent of AGI. "Personal casualty gain" means the recognized gain from any involuntary conversion of property not connected with a trade or business or a transaction entered into for profit, arising from fire, storm, shipwreck, or other casualty, or from theft.

E. Local and States Taxes

Code Sec. 164 allows taxpayers to deduct as itemized deductions those taxes which are paid as state and city income taxes, real estate taxes and other type of property taxes. Since such taxes are mandatory, they reduce the taxpayer's wealth and do not necessarily provide discretionary consumption (25) [p. 12] though part of the state and local government do provide personal consumption. I.e. the consumption of the public goods and services, which are provided by local government in return for the local taxes. That private consumption should be included in the taxpayer's taxable income, as any other private consumption. Under such analysis, which is supported by the "Tiebout Model" [p. 76], the Code Sec. 164 deduction is actually a Federal government subsidy to state and local governments.

F. Un-Reimbursed Medical Expenses

Another example of the idea that only discretionary power to consume should be included within the income tax base, and non-discretionary payment should be deducted, is the deduction for unreimbursed unusual medical expenses under Code Sec. 213. This deduction is for medical payments for the taxpayer, their spouses, and their dependents. Taxpayers are increasingly tempted to argue that lavish standard of living expenses are aimed to protect the taxpayer's family's health as the average standard of living cost increases. Country club membership fees, sending the kids to boarding schools so mom can rest and relax, in-house lifts, etc. are a few examples of the taxpayers' innovations. The general rule is more restricted. Allowable medical expenses include payments to physicians, dentists, surgeons, chiropractors, psychologists, counselors, physical therapists, osteopaths, podiatrists, home health care nurses, and cost of care for chronic cognitive impairment. The cost of medical insurance and premiums for qualifying long-term-care insurance (for certain ages) are also included, as are payments for prescription drugs and insulin, the cost for medical auxiliary devices such as crutches, wheelchairs, prescription eyeglasses, and hearing aids. Medical expenses also include the cost of travel to and from medical facilities. On the other hand, the following expenses are not deductible: over-the-counter medications, health and county club membership fees, ordinary cosmetic surgery, and other semi-medical expenses.

Code Sec. 213(a) limits the deductibility of the above unreimbursed medical expenses to amounts that exceed 7.5% of the taxpayer's AGI. Hence, a routine-check-ups usually won't make it. Only unusual or unexpected (non-discretionary) medical expenses are permitted. For example: suppose two taxpayers spend $5,000 on medical expenses. A has an AGI of $20,000 and B has an AGI of $200,000. A's deduction would be [5,000−(20,000*.075)=]$3500; B, on the other hand, won't be able to deduct any amount: (200,000*0.75=)$15,000. B will be able to deduct any amount spent on medical expenses only if the aggregate amount exceeds $15,000 a year.

5. MISCELLANEOUS ITEMIZED DEDUCTIONS

In addition to itemized deductions, the Code uses another vehicle for below-the-line deductions: "Miscellaneous Itemized Deductions" (Sec. 67). The only reason to classify such items in a different category is to subject some of them to a special 2% limitation discussed below.

The way to identify the miscellaneous itemized deductions is through an elimination process: The Code [sec. 67(b)] lists certain deductions that are not subject to the 2% floor limitation. Only those that are not included within this statutory list are indeed miscellaneous itemized deductions. IRS Reg. § 1.67–1T provides some examples for miscellaneous itemized deductions paid by employees ("unreimbursed") and cost of passive income.

A. Unreimbursed Employee's Business Expenses: The Dual Capacity of an Employee as a Taxpayer

As we noted earlier, one explanation for the special limitations on the deductibility of employees' unreimbursed expenses should be based on what we call the "dual capacity of the employee as a taxpayer" [p. 224]. On the one hand, an employee is a "member of a firm" (47) and their economic activity should be considered through the firm's interests; if the firm does not share the employee's expenses, one may regard it as an indication that the expenses are neither necessary to the employee's performance of their duties nor to the employer's business activity. On the other hand, employees have their own professional interests that sometime differ from those of the employer, such as their status in the labor market, their own professional knowledge, etc. Hence the fact that the employer does not participate in the employee's expenses should not have any effect on the deductibility of such expenses. This is the case for continued educational expenses.

Such an explanation should lead us to the following conclusions: those expenses that represent the employee's performance of services that promote the employer's interest should be allowed only if the employer reimburses their employee. If those expenses are not, no deduction should be allowed to the employee. Such expenses are, for example, employee's business travel expenses while performing their duties for the benefit of the employer. If the employer does not reimburse them, it is a good indication that they are not necessary or ordinary and the employee has spent them as a volunteer or for her own consumption. On the other hand, if the expenses are not directly connected to the employees' performance of their duties but rather relate to their professional status, which may be different from the employer's interest, such expenses should be allowed regardless of the employer's contribution. Such expenses are educational expenses: just assume that an employee wants to participate in a professional seminar. His professional interests are obvious: he wants to maintain his goodwill as a leading figure in his professional field, to get promotions or to open his own business. These kinds of reasons are exactly why employers are reluctant to support their employee's educational expenses and do not reimburse them. In such cases the rule should be straightforward: if a self-employed professional is allowed to deduct such educational expenses spent for maintaining her human capital, [p. 270] so should a professional employee regardless of whether the employer reimburses them.

Congress' approach is a bit different. It does not draw the above distinction between the motives or the purpose of the expense (i.e. whether for the interest of the employer or for the self-professional interest of the employee). As a general rule, there are no special limitations to the deductibility of employees' reimbursed expenses. They are subject to the same rules that are applied to self-employed taxpayers, and they are deductible above the line. As for unreimbursed expenses, the Code treats all employees' business expenses alike, and the rule is a sweeping one: all unreimbursed business expenses are treated as miscellaneous itemized deductions, though the courts on several occasions have used the fact that if an employer refrained from participating in an employee's expenses, this should be an indication that the expenses were personal consumption and not business deductible.

Under the current statutory rule of Code Sec. 68, an unreimbursed employee's expenses are subject to the following limitations:

a) The amount spent by the employee must exceed, in aggregate, 2% of the employee's ***adjusted gross income***;

b) If AGI exceeds the "applicable amount" [defined in Code Sec. 68(b)], the amount of the itemized deductions, [p. 288] otherwise allowable for the taxable year, shall be reduced by the lesser:

   (1) 3% of the excess of AGI over the applicable amount, or

   (2) 80% of the amount of the itemized deductions otherwise allowable for such taxable year.

The following are examples of employees' unreimbursed expenses that are classified as miscellaneous itemized deductions and are subject to the above limitations: depreciation of a computer or cellular phone required for use in work for the convenience of the employer; tools needed; work clothes and uniforms required by the employer, which are not suitable for ordinary daily use outside work; required protective clothing, such as hard hats, safety shoes, and glasses; union dues; membership fees paid to professional organizations and chambers of commerce; subscriptions to professional journals; work-related continued education and conferences expenses; job hunting expenses in the same professional field.

Note that some of these expenses may face a Constitutional challenge. Consider the last three examples above. If a self-employed taxpayer spends them, she could deduct their total cost, above the line, without special limitations. On the other hand, if an employee spends the same amount for the same own professional purpose and his employer does not reimburse the cost (the employer does not want strong competition in her office; or she might be afraid that the employee will be hired by a competitor, or will decide to establish his own firm, and so on) the employee is actually discriminated against only because of being an employee. After all, though the employee has a strong professional interest in maintaining his stature in the professional market, [p. 270] the employer does not have a serious business interest in these kinds of expenses.

On the other hand, one has to remember that employees have some privileges under the current system. For example, we mention some special exemptions, which are provided only to employees:

1) Under Code Sec. 119 [pp. 200, 201, 242] employees' meals and lodging are exempted if they are provided for the convenience of employer on the employer's premises and the employer requires the employee to accept lodging as condition for work; Code Sec. 107 provides a similar exemption for Ministers' lodging. [p. 46]

Although the above sections apply only to employees, for self-employed persons who perform similar services and are required by their client to receive similar conditions, it is quite unlikely that they will be taxed on any acceptance of these conditions. Moreover, if these conditions are reported as gross income, they will be able to deduct the value of the conditions as an ordinary and necessary expense.

2) Under Code Sec. 132 the following fringe benefits, which are provided by employers to their employees, are exempted:

   a) no additional cost service;

   b) qualified employee discount;

c) working conditions;

d) qualified transportation;

e) reimbursement of qualified moving expense;

f) qualified retirement planning services.

3) Code Sec. 105 exempts reimbursement of medical expenses, accident & health insurance which are provided by the employer;

4) Code Sec. 106 exempts the employer's contribution to employees' accident and health plans;

5) Another exemption is available under Code. Sec. 79 for group-term life insurance for employees.

Note that self-employed workers are allowed to deduct their own payments for most of the above purposes.

B. Passive Income Deductions

Under the current code provisions, most of the expenses that are attributed to passive income, i.e. passive investment or profit-seeking activities that do not constitute trade or business activity, are deducted below the line as miscellaneous itemized deductions. Hence, such deductions are subject to some limitations that do not apply to expenses spent on active income—income from trade or business. One explanation for such "discrimination" might be that, for producing active income, taxpayers have to leave home, use transportation and their own human capital, and incur other consumption-related expenses that are not allowed to be deducted from passive income, whereas taxpayers with passive income do not have such expenses. Hence the *discretionary power to consume* of taxpayers with active income is lower than that of those taxpayers with the same amount of passive income. In order to eliminate such differences, the Code is more generous with the former taxpayers.

C. Special Limitation on Miscellaneous Itemized Deductions

Under Code Sec. 67, Miscellaneous Itemized Deductions are allowed only when the total deduction exceeds 2% of the taxpayer's adjusted gross income. For example, if a taxpayer's AGI is $60,000, she can deduct only when the amount of her miscellaneous itemized deductions exceeds (60,000*0.02=)$1,200.

Note that the 2% limitation applies after the application of any other limitation. This means that any limitation or restriction placed on the amount of a miscellaneous itemized deduction shall apply prior to the application of the 2 percent floor. For example, in the case of an expense for food or beverages, only 50% percent of that expense is allowable as a deduction because of statutory limitations (Code Sec.274(n)) and the otherwise deductible 50 percent of the expense is treated as a miscellaneous itemized deduction and is subject to the 2 percent floor.

D. General Limitation/Reductions of Itemized Deductions

In addition to limitations under Code Sec. 67, (which applies only to *miscellaneous itemized deductions*), Code Sec. 213 (*medical expenses*) and Code Sec. 165(h) (*casualty and theft losses*) discussed above, Code Sec. 68 put another limitation on the deductibility of most of the *itemized deductions:* those deductions are reduced by a ceiling limitation set in Code Sec. 68. The idea was that taxpayers with a high AGI have enough discretionary power to consume, hence those deductions are not essential any longer. Under Code Secs 68(a) & 68(b)(1) an individual's itemized deductions are reduced by 3% of the amount by which their AGI exceeds a dollar threshold, which is $300,000 for a married couple filing a joint return, and $250,000 for an unmarried individual. However, the reduction may not exceed 80% of the **itemized deductions** otherwise allowable. The threshold amounts are adjusted for inflation.

For example, if a married couple's AGI is $500,000, and their total amount of itemized deductions is $50,000 the allowable amount is reduced by [(500,000−300,000)* 0.03=]$6,000 to the amount of $44,000. However, if the married couple had an AGI of $10 million, their total amount of itemized deductions would be reduced by 80%, from $50,000 to [50,000−(50,000*0.80)=]$10,000.

Note that this limitation does not apply to medical expenses—which are subject to the 7.5% limitation, nor to casualty loss—which is subject to the 10% limitation.

The below flow chart summarizes the below-the-line allowed deductions and their limitations.

Figure 22.1:

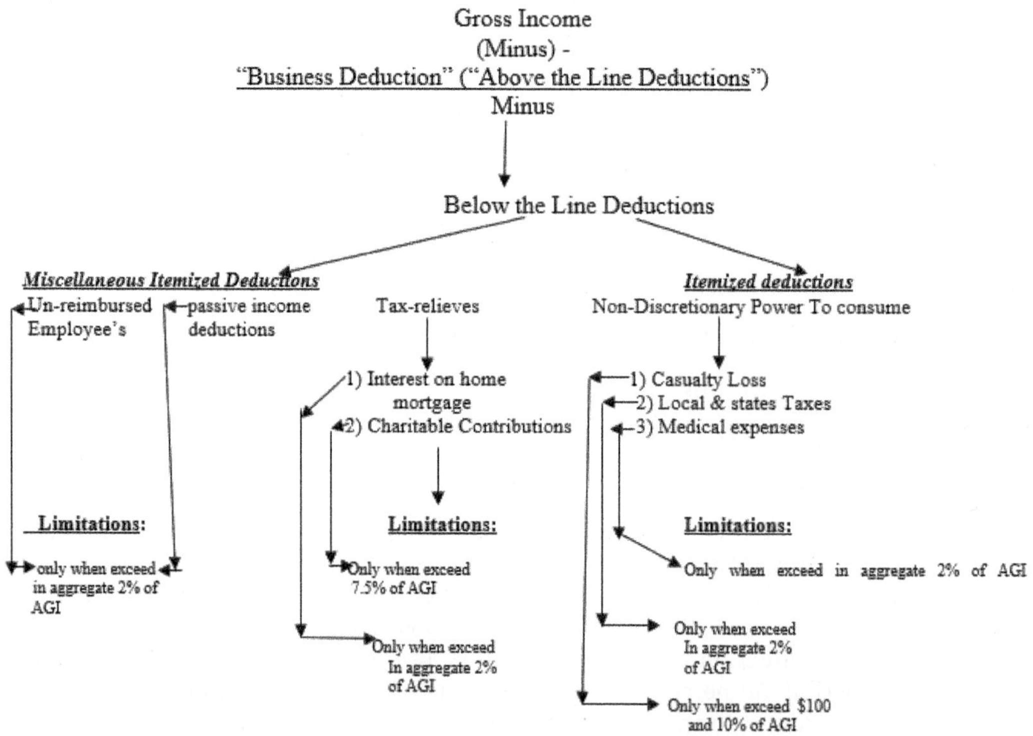

To summarize: there are three main types of statutory rules regarding the deduction of expenses. One—deduction of expenses helps in determining the tax base. Deductible expenses reflect the income tax base. I.e. expenses for private consumption are part of the tax base, since income = consumption + savings. Therefore, the business expenses allowed as a deduction are not expenses for consumption, nor for saving or investing. In any case, such expenses are those that are incurred for the purpose of generating income in that tax year; they are business expenses.

Another type of statutory provisions is intended to clarify the rules when the taxpayer spends a mixed expenditure, which has a business component as well as a private or investment one. In such a case, the need arises to demarcate the line between allowable and non-allowable expenses.

The third type of statutory provisions expresses the legislature's policy to allow the deduction of expenses that, according to the basic rule, should not have been allowed, but the legislature's decision, for various reasons, to allow their deduction.

Chapter Twenty-Three

STAGE SEVEN—TAX ACCOUNTING

1. IN GENERAL

Accounting (2) is primarily a most important tool designed to provide reliable reports of business and financial information to a firm's management and to interested external parties [p. 106]. It is a systematic and comprehensive recording method of financial transactions which refers to the process of measuring, summarizing, analyzing, and translating various economic and business transactions into an accepted language. As mentioned above there are several areas of accounting. The most relevant to our book are the basic principles of financial accounting and their adaptation to a special area which is termed tax accounting.

Financial accounting focuses on the reporting of an organization's financial information, including the preparation of financial statements, to external parties such as investors, creditors, and various regulators, including the IRS. The recording of financial transactions is called bookkeeping, and the basic acceptable bookkeeping method for big firms and those who have trade-in-stock in their trade or business is called a "double entry" system. This system requires that every entry to an account requires a corresponding and opposite entry to an additional account, e.g. a sale of an asset for a certain amount in cash requires the firm to write in its ledgers two entries: one, a debit to its cash account of that amount and two, a credit of the same amount to the revenue account. The logic of the double entry method is based on the elementary equation of net wealth: the firm's equity is equal to its sum of credit minus the debits. Hence, debit and credit entries must be equal, and the result reflects a negative or positive equity.

The accounting rules, standards and methods are supervised by approved or recognized accounting organizations, who make sure that the accounting methods comply with the Generally Accepted Accounting Principles (GAAP), which are set in the U.S. by the Financial Accounting Standards Board (FASB). Most Western countries—though not the U.S.—have adopted the new International Financial Reporting Standards (IFRS).

2. WHY TAX ACCOUNTING

Code Sec. 446(a) states the general rule for tax accounting: "taxable income shall be computed under the method of accounting on the basis of which the taxpayer regularly computes his income in keeping his books". Sec. 446(b) provides the exceptions: "If no method of accounting has been regularly used by the taxpayer, or if the method used does not clearly reflect income, the computation of taxable income shall be made under such method as, in the opinion of the Secretary, does clearly reflect income".

The rationale behind these provisions was explain by the Supreme Court in *Thor Power Tool Co. v. CIR*, (1979):

> *"The primary goal of financial accounting is to provide useful information to management, shareholders, creditors, and others properly interested; the major responsibility of the accountant is to protect these parties from being misled. The*

primary goal of the income tax system, in contrast, is the equitable collection of revenue; the major responsibility of the Internal Revenue Service is to protect the public fisc."

Hence, the method of accounting that is regularly used in keeping the taxpayers' books is usually used to compute taxable income as well, unless one of the above statutory exceptions applies or the principle of financial accounting leads to an unequitable collection of revenue.

A. Income Reporting

Pure accounting theory is quite reluctant to use the cash method. Yet, Congress has acknowledged it. Code Sec 446(a) states the general rule: taxable income shall be computed under the method of accounting on the basis of which the taxpayer regularly computes their income in keeping their books. Sec. 446(c) permits certain taxpayers to compute taxable income under any of the following methods of accounting:

(1) the cash receipts and disbursements method ("cash method");

(2) an accrual method;

(3) any other method permitted by this chapter; or

(4) any combination of the foregoing methods permitted under regulations prescribed by the Secretary.

Code Sec. 448 prohibits the following non-farming taxpayers to use the cash method if their average annual gross receipts for the 3-taxable-year period exceed $5,000,000: (1) C corporations, (2) partnerships which have a C corporation as a partner, or (3) tax shelters as defined in Code Sec. 461(i)(3).

B. Cash Method

The Cash method is used by individuals (both employees and self-employed), partnerships, and small corporations who provide professional services, even if they trade inventories, as long as the inventories are not substantial, e.g. gardeners, dentists. Under the cash method, income is not counted until cash (or money's worth—"in-kind") is actually received and expenses are not counted until they are actually paid. Note that the cash method should be distinguished from the "cash flow" system. The latter ignores the matching rules [p. 279] and takes into account a cash flow (paid or credited) whether it is for capital assets or ordinary-current purposes, e.g. the Value Added Tax system [p. 117]. The former does follow the matching rules and requires that expenses for capital investment should be prorated over the investment's expected life if it is a depreciable or amortized asset, or otherwise be counted only when the investment is disposed of. In addition, capital gains are distinguished from ordinary-current income [p. 214]. The claim of right doctrine (23), as well as Code Sec. 1341, are significant factors of the cash method [pp. 199–204].

Code Reg. 1.446–1(c)(1) indicates that under the cash method all items which constitute gross income (whether in the form of cash, property, or services) are to be included for the taxable year in which they were actually or constructively received. Likewise, expenditures are to be deducted for the taxable year in which they were actually made.

Under the constructive receipt doctrine—which was acknowledged by case law [*Davis v. Com.* (1978); *Hyland v. Com.* (1949)] and is elaborated in Reg. 1.451–2—in order to prevent tax deferral, a taxpayer is not allowed to postpone income which is available to the taxpayer without substantial limitations, by agreeing to defer its receipt or failing to collect it in the current taxable year. However, a prearranged deferred compensation agreement, under which an employer agrees to defer a portion of compensation until the taxpayer's retirement, is recognized by the IRS. In this case the taxpayer would be taxed only when receiving the deferred compensation. In addition, a mere promise to pay without a note or secured document is not regarded as a receipt of income under the cash method.

With regard to expenses, prepayments in advance for several years of current expenses, such as insurance, rent, or compensation are deductible on a prorated basis over the years to which the benefits relate, e.g. if a taxpayer pays rent in advance for three years, the payment is prorated—as with any other depreciable or amortized assets—over the pertaining three years, regardless of whether the income reporting method is a cash or accrual basis.

C. Accrual Basis

A full discussion of the accrual method and the inventory accounting systems are out of the focus of this book and only a few of their basic principles are mentioned (67).

Most of the taxpayers that are prohibited from using the cash method use the accrual method. In addition, any trading or manufacturing business with gross receipts over $1 million per year, which has an inventory that is designated to be sold to customers in its ordinary course of business, is required to use the accrual method as well.

Under the accrual method, income is counted when it is earned or realized [pp. 163, 198]. In other words, under the accrual method taxpayers are required to report amounts due when a service is completed, or goods are shipped, and the amounts due have been billed or invoiced. Expenses are counted when the obligation to pay is incurred; when all events occur that establish the taxpayer's legal obligation to pay, as long as the amount due can be computed with a reasonable accuracy. The actual cash payment is irrelevant.

For example, suppose that a lawyer enters into an agreement with a professional, according to which the latter will provide window cleaning services for the lawyer's office building for $1,000. On December 2015, the professional provides the cleaning services and the lawyer does not dispute his obligation to pay. On January 2016, the lawyer pays the agreed payment of $1,000 to the professional. If both the lawyer and the professional use the "cash method", the lawyer can deduct the cleaning cost (as a trade or business expenses) and the professional must include the income in 2016, when the cash was actually paid. If both of them use the "accrual method", the lawyer can deduct the cost and the professional must include the income in 2015, when the obligation was incurred and the income was earned and realized when the service was provided. If they use different methods, each of them is supposed to report the income or the expense according to their usual methods as long they are not related taxpayers.

D. Inventory

Inventory (67) includes any final goods as well as supplies/raw materials that will physically become part of an item intended for sale in the ordinary course of a trading or manufacturing businesses.

The computation of gains (or losses) from trading in inventory may be a complicated and tedious process, though the principle is quite straight forward. Like with any other asset, the gain (loss) is the difference between the asset's sale price and its cost. If the inventory includes only a few items that are easily identified, there should not be serious difficulties, i.e. the cost of the individual units are tracked and used as the units' basis ("Cost of Goods Sold"). The problems begin when the quantity of the inventory is significant, its components—raw materials—are numerous, and the prices are changed during the process.

In the following discussion we introduce very basic principles of tax accounting of inventory related to trading firms, though the same principles apply to manufacturing firms as well.

Since inventories are initially measured at cost, the computing process relies on several points of time: the date of sale; the date of acquiring the goods sold; and the date of the closing account of the taxable year. At each point there is a need to calculate the value of the goods, including the value of the closing account, which is identical to the opening inventory account of the subsequent year. Since the sale price is usually known to the firm, the key question is what the cost of goods sold is. The answer depends on the need to identify the items that are sold: were they those which were acquired earlier? Later? Or maybe the average price of all the items that were acquired during the taxable year?

The three major assumptions that are used in order to set the cost of goods sold are "First-in-First-out" (FIFO), which uses the assumption that the inventory items that were acquired first are sold first; "Last-in-First-out" (LIFO), which assumes the reverse, i.e. those items that were acquired last are sold first, and; "weighted average cost", which assumes that the cost of goods sold is based on the weighted average of all the inventory's acquisition costs. The following basic and simple example demonstrates the application and differences between these three assumptions/methods.

Suppose that, in the first half of a year, a trading firm purchases a number of items (say 300) at different dates and different prices. In January it bought 100 items for $10 per item; in March, another 100 items for $12 per item, and in May another 100 for $15 apiece. For the sake of simplicity, we assume that the firm sells the goods in the second half of the year for a fixed price of $20 apiece. Suppose it was able to sell only 80 items during the year. Is the firm's gain [(80*20)−(10*80)]=$800 under FIFO? Or only [(80*20)−(15*80)=]$400 under LIFO? Or maybe we use some kind of averaging calculation to set the cost of the sold goods to (10+12+15/3=)$12.3, hence the gain is [(80*20)−(12.3*80)=]$616? And what about the entire gain (or loss) the firm has during the year, which takes into account the potential gain on the appreciated (or depreciated/deflated) inventory? The answer depends on the value of the inventory the firm has at the closing inventory account at the beginning and end of the year. Should that value be estimated using the inventory's fair market value ($20)? Or on its cost? If the answer is the former, then the question is whether the unrealized gain should be taxed? If the answer is the latter, the answer depends on the above assumptions—FIFO, LIFO or the Weighted Average.

For income tax purposes, the three methods (FIFO, LIFO and the weighted average, though in rare cases the actual costs of individual units) are available for the taxpayers. Furthermore, taxpayers are allowed to switch from one method to another, but only if they meet the conditions and limitations of Code Sec. 263A and Code Reg 1.263A–7(c).

In times of rising prices, such under inflationary conditions, FIFO leads to higher income and higher tax payments, hence taxpayers prefer the LIFO method. In times of price reduction, they probably prefer FIFO.

In term of the closing inventory account, under the FIFO method the evaluation is based on the "cost or market—the lower." This means that, if the Fair Market price goes up, the closing inventory stays on the actual-original cost. If the prices go down, the closing inventory is based on the inventory's FMV. This means that the taxpayer suffers an unrealized loss, which may offsets the taxpayer's income [p. 283].

Chapter Twenty-Four

THE TAX UNIT

While describing the U.S. income tax system, we have focused on the principles of the **personal income tax**, its aims and rationales, i.e. the taxation of individuals and households according to their economic ability which finances their personal consumption in its broadest sense—current and future, through personal savings and inheritances. Legal entities cannot consume, only humans can. Legal entities only serve as a tool, a vehicle that enables humans to earn income and to fulfill their needs and wants. Although income tax is levied, with some significant modifications, on corporations, trusts and partnerships, our book does not deal with those entities in depth. This chapter deals mainly with the personal tax units: individuals, couples and the family.

With regards to corporate taxation, we briefly discuss the purpose of corporate taxation below [p. 310]; whether it should pursue only the taxation of corporations' individual owners, i.e. serve only as a tool or a funnel, or maybe there are some justifications for it to impose a separate and additional tax burden on corporations?

The taxation of partnerships is also outside of this book's discussion. It is sufficient to mention the basic principle: for income tax purposes the general rule is a "statutory lifting the veil" to reach the human partners. Though the legal and business worlds create complicated and sophisticated models of partnerships—including partnerships of individuals and corporations—those models deserve special tax treatment which is beyond the scope of this book.

Using legal trusts has become a prosperous industry for tax planners in the U.S. Trusts provide significant tax deferrals and in some aggressive cases can obviously increase social gaps in the U.S. This field deserves special and thorough research beyond the bounds of this book.

This chapter deals with the personal income tax units: individuals, couples, and families.

1. INDIVIDUALS

The major reason for discussing the issues of individuals as a "tax unit" is due to the progressive tax system. (98) Under a pure flat tax-rate system, there would be no serious reason to consider the individual source of income. If everybody is subject to, say, a 20% flat income tax rate, who cares if the income belongs to Mom, Dad, a child, a relative or a stranger? Under a progressive tax system, it is a totally different issue.

A. The Married Couple Dilemma

Suppose Mom's taxable income is one million dollars a year while Dad stays at home and takes care of their three children. Assuming that the current tax rates are as shown in Table I below, we can see a most significant difference between a case where only Mom reports her taxable income of one million dollars and a case where the family is allowed to split this amount between its five family members with a fifth of that amount as individuals. A third alternative is that the one million dollars are divided evenly between Mom and Dad. The following Table presents the progressive tax rate under the current U.S. system updated to 2022 with rounded numbers.

Note that the following computations are based only on the tax rates. The amount of personal exemptions, standard deduction and the fact that they are phased-out in different amounts was not taken into account. Those factors have some marginal impact on the whole picture.

Table 24.1:

Taxable Income	Marginal Tax Rate	Tentative Tax Due
0–$10,275	10%	10% of taxable income (TI)
$10,276–$41,775	12%	$1,027.50+12% of TI above $10,275
$41,776–$89,075	22%	$4,807.50+22% of TI above $41,775
$89,076–$170,050	24%	$15,213.50+24% of TI above $89,075
$170,051–$215,950	32%	$34,647.50+32% of TI above $170,050
$215,951–$539,900	35%	$49,335.50+35% of the TI above $$215,950
Above $539,900	37%	$162,718+37% of the TI above $539,900

If Mom reports the one million dollars taxable income as an individual, her tentative tax due (before taking care of any tax credits) is {162,718+[(1,000,000−539,900)*37%]=} $332,955 (“possibility 1”). If she can split the income between all the family members and each reports a taxable income of $200,000, each individual tax bill would be {$34,647.50+[(200,000−170,050)*32%]=}$44,231.5. In such a case the whole family’s tentative tax bill is (44,231.50*5=)$221,157.50 and the family would save (332,955−221,157.50=)$111,797.50 (“possibility 2”). If the taxable income is divided only between Mom and Dad, each of them reports a half a million dollar taxable income and their combined tentative tax amount is {[49,335.50+(500,000−215,950)*35%]*2=}$297,506 (“possible 3”), which still provides a significant reduction of the couple’s tax bill (332,955−297,506)=$35,449.

It is noteworthy that when dealing with such high personal income, one should take into consideration the fact that the standard deduction, personal expenses (while there are effective) and some other tax breaks, including child care credit, which were mentioned above [pp. 248, 255], are phased-out (94) and are not available to Mom.

Note that in order to be allowed to use “possibility 2”, Mom has to assign the income to the family’s members or look for a special statutory provision. Assuming that she does not hire any of them to help her with the professional services she provides to her clients, an assignment of income for income tax purposes is not permissible. The basic rule is that the fruit (income) belongs to the tree (factor of production). Yet the family is an economic unit; a household (56) that traditionally shares its resources and consumption according to its discretion. It would be sensible for the tax system to treat the family’s income according to that reality. Yet Congress took a different path and adopted a compromise between “possibility 1” and “possibility 3”: this couple is allowed to file a joint return and pay $299,758.

Indeed, the development of the taxation of families, focused mainly on married couples, is a fascinating story.

Upon the enactment of the income tax in 1913, there was no special treatment for married couples. Each taxpayer had to file their own tax return. Yet, under the civil and family laws of some states ("community property states"), all property accumulated by a husband and wife during their marriage becomes joint property, regardless of who earns it and who has the property's legal title. Not surprisingly, by the 1920s, some couples in community property states began to report their income on separate tax returns, where each spouse claimed half the couple's combined income. After a short legal battle, the Supreme Court ruled [*Poe v. Seaborn* (1930)] in favor of the taxpayers' claim and allowed couples in community property states to evenly split their aggregated income for Federal income tax purposes. Needless to say that many couples in common law states—with no community property rule—had the same amount of income, but one earner was paying a higher amount of income tax.

B. The Congress' Compromise

In order to unify the Federal income tax treatment of married couples, Congress introduced the joint return system in 1948, which evidently followed the concept of community property, but not entirely. This system—which was modified a few times and is described briefly below—created some problems. In some cases, it created a marriage penalty for certain couples but in other cases it provided marriage bonuses. The problem arose from the conflict between three accepted concepts: progressivity, horizontal equity between married couples, and marriage neutrality. Note that the validity (or strength) of the last concept has some doubts.

In his famous testimony before the House Committee on Ways and Means in 1972, tax law professor and then-Assistant Secretary for Tax Policy Edwin S. Cohen demonstrated that "*No algebraic equation, no matter how sophisticated, can solve this dilemma. Both ends of a seesaw cannot be up at the same time.*" The major question is: should two individuals that get married pay a greater amount of income tax than they paid before marriage, and be subject to a marriage penalty; or pay less than they paid before getting married, enjoy a marriage bonus? One reason for this dilemma is that non-discretionary personal consumption—especially dwelling expenses and grocery bills—of married couples is lower than that of two single taxpayers, hence the couple's discretionary economic ability is higher than two single taxpayers with the same combined income. If they pay the same amount of income tax, the vertical equity principle (42) is violated [p. 14].

The mathematical proof for this dilemma, which was presented by Professor Cohen, is as follows:

Assume there are four individuals, A, B, C, and D. Their taxable income is as follows: A and B each have $10,000, C has $0, and D has $20,000. Accordingly, their tax due (T) is T(A), T(B), T(C) and T(D). Assume the progressive tax rates are 10% on the first $10,000 and 15% on $20,000. Hence, A and B's tax due is (10,000*10%=)$1,000 each; the tax due on C is $0 and D's tax due is [($10,000*10%)+(10,000*15%)=]$2,500.

Under these assumptions we get equation one:

(I) **T(C)+T(D) > T(A)+T(B).**

Assume now that A and B, as well as C and D, get married. Both couples have the same aggregated income—$20,000.

Assuming that we do not want to have any marriage penalty or marriage bonuses (marriage neutrality), each couple should pay the same tax amount they paid before they got married. Hence couple AB should pay the same amount they pay before their marriage—(1,000+1,000=)$2,000—so the second equation looks like this:

(II) **T(AB)=T(A)+T(B).**

Under the requirement of marriage neutrality Couple CD should pay (0+2,500=)$2,500 and the third equation is therefore as follows:

(III) **T(CD)=T(C)+T(D).**

Yet both couples have the same combined taxable income, hence if couples are to be treated as a tax unit both couples have the same amount of taxable income—$20,000 and should pay the same amount of tax. This is shown in the fourth equation:

(IV) **T(CD)=T(AB).**

If T(A)+T(B) is equal to T(AB), and T(C)+T(D) is equal to T(CD) then we arrive at the following new equation five: **T(CD) > T(AB)**, which contradicts the above equation IV.

Note though that careful scrutiny may call into question "marriage neutrality". Two single taxpayers with $10,000 taxable income each, who maintain two separate households, need to spend more on their basic needs—rent, mortgage, insurances, food etc.—than two married taxpayers with a combined taxable income of $20,000. The couple is able to run their own one household in a more efficient way and with less non-discretionary expenses. Under these circumstances, equations B and C lose their merits.

The compromise that Congress adopted is represented in Code Sec. 1, which provides four different tax return filing statuses:

- **Married individuals filing joint returns and surviving spouses:** For married couples who combine their income on one tax return—Code Sec. 1(a).
- **Head of household:** Individuals who are considered single for filing purposes and provide more than half the support for a child and are able to claim that child as a dependent—Code Sec. 1(b).
- **Single:** Unmarried individuals (other than surviving spouses and heads of households) who file individual tax returns—Code Sec. 1(c).
- **Married individuals filing separate returns:** Each spouse files their own tax return—Code Sec. 1(d).

Now suppose that Mom and Dad have decided to share together the chores and the joy. Mom decreases her work supply and spends more time with the kids, and Dad starts to work. Mom's taxable income is now $650,000 and Dad's is $350,000. If they file a joint return, their combined tentative tax due is still $299,758. Instead, they consider submitting a Married Filing Separately tax return,

Now, Mom's tentative tax due is $207,775 while Dad's is $78,753. Since the combined tax due is $286,528, the family's first choice is to each file a single tax return, where their combined tentative tax due would be lower: Mom's tentative tax due under a single tax return would be $184,955; Dad's tentative tax due under a single tax return would be: $78,753 and the combined amount would be $263752, lower than under both joint return and married filing separately. Alas, the couple's first choice is not allowed as long as they stay married.

In *Druker v. C.I.R.* (1982) a couple argued the unconstitutionality of the so-called "marriage penalty". Their claim was that the income tax structure unfairly discriminates against working married couples, hence it violates the equal protection clause of the Fourteenth Amendment. The Court of Appeals of the 2nd Circuit disagreed. The court found that Congress' compromise is sensible. It indicated that the tax schedules were set so that a single person's tax liability under § 1(c) would never be more than 120% of that of a married couple with the same income filing jointly under § 1(a). The court also noted that

> *"Not all married couples are so 'penalized'. For the couple whose income is earned primarily or solely by one partner, marriage still offers significant tax savings. As a general rule of thumb, marriage will increase a couple's tax burden as compared with that of two single persons whenever the lesser-earning spouse earns 20% or more of the couple's total income and decreases its tax burden whenever the lesser-earning spouse earns less than 20%."*

There is an additional alternative that the couple may consider: divorce. In that case, one of them would file a single tax return and the other one would file a head of household tax return, which is subject to a special tax rates

Under these tax rates, if Mom's taxable income as the head of household is $650,000, her tentative tax due would be $201,950 Dad's tentative tax due as a single taxpayer would be: $78,753 and the combined amount would be $280,703. Hence, if the only concern is income tax, divorce might be a possibility.

As mentioned already, due to the phased-out mechanism the couple might conclude that Dad should be the Head of Household to enjoy parts of the tax breaks like (the suspended) personal exemption, and child-care credits.

C. Dependent Children

According to Code Sec. 152 a "dependent child" is a child who one or both parents claim as dependent for income tax purposes and who meets one of the following conditions: under age 19 at the end of the year; under age 24 at the end of the year and a full-time student; permanently disabled at any age.

Code Sec. 6012(a)(1) sets the general rule regarding the duty to submit an annual tax return: all individuals, regardless their age, are required to make returns of income if they have for the taxable year a gross income which equals or exceeds the exemption amount (usually the amount of $2,000, but currently $12,950, with ongoing inflation adjustments, until 2026).

A dependent child is exempted from submitting a tax return if they had less than $1,100 of annual unearned income. The reason is that such income is treated as income of the parent who claims the child as a dependent. In this case this unearned income is subject to the parent's tax rates, but only if the parent's rate is higher than the child's. Another exception is when a dependent child is a college student who spends more than half of their earned income for their personal support. In that case the unearned income is subject to the student's tax rates.

Unearned-passive income means interest, ordinary dividends, capital gains, rents, certain royalties, social security benefits, pension and annuity income, unemployment compensation, alimony, taxable scholarship and fellowship grants which are not compensation for a child labor's and income (other than earned income) received as a beneficiary of a trust.

A dependent child's earned income—active income from employment—is taxed under the child's name. The first $12,950 is actually exempted due to the standard deduction for a dependent child, which is the total earned income plus $400, up to a maximum of $12,950. In this case the dependent child does not have to file a tax return. Any additional earned income is subject to the applicable tax rates discussed above.

A child who has only unearned income must file a return if the total is more than $1,100.

Parents are eligible, under certain conditions and limitations, which are discussed in the following chapter, for both Child Care Tax Credits and for Child Tax Credits.

2. INDIVIDUAL TAX UNIT—CONCLUSION

The above discussion did not intend to introduce a full and detailed picture, or to serve as guidelines for married couples' tax planning. The purpose is to present general approach in the U.S. regarding the taxation of families, and to imply that this approach might rely too much on some traditional assumptions and concepts. It ignores modern phenomena of new concepts of marriages, co-habitation, and even new signals indicating that the current generation in Western society is relatively reluctant to make long-run social and personal commitments. Evidently, the Treasury and Congress have to reconsider the concept of the personal tax unit.

3. CORPORATIONS

As indicated already, the major focus of our book is on personal taxation: the taxation of individuals who enjoy public goods and services and have to pay for them. The personal aspect is embodied also in the definition of income from its usage side as personal consumption—present and future through saving [p. 188].

From an economic point of view, we draw a distinction between two economic term of art: firms (47), which produce income, and households (56), which consume it. Innovative legal minds have created legal entities that serve humans in their pursuit of wealth, i.e. a legal separation between households and firms that came with the tricky idea of limited liabilities, which enables individuals to function as an incorporated firm without taking too many economic risks and responsibilities. In modern times these legal entities, known as Corporations or Companies, produce and create wealth, but as virtual entities they are not able to consume it. They are just a tool, a vehicle, a means to create wealth for humans' consumption.

If indeed the purpose of personal taxation is to tax individuals, the most basic and simplest way to do so is to ignore the above legal separation—piercing the corporate veil—and tax individuals' shares in a company's income. Yet, there are certain legal problems with this: the major one is that a corporation's investors, i.e. the shareholders, are not eligible to receive their share in the earnings for a specific time, and due to the realization requirement (103) [pp. 163, 180, 198] the corporation's owners—the shareholder—are not taxed until the corporation's income is legally distributed and reaches the individual shareholders' possession. As a result, a significant tax deferral (126) may take place. The problem that the legislatures around the world face is how to overcome such a deferral. The solution is income tax on corporations—a Corporate tax. There are several models for corporate taxation, though discussion of them is beyond this book. Here we confine ourselves to presenting the basic traits of the U.S. model and some basic questions in this area.

A. Corporate Taxation in the U.S. in a Nutshell

As a general rule, U.S. corporations, i.e. corporations organized under the laws of one of the U.S. states, are subject to the Federal Corporate tax. Foreign corporations are also subject to that tax on any of their income that is produced within the U.S. The Corporate tax is a flat 21%. Corporations are also subject to the Alternative Minimum Tax [p. 328]. Corporations' taxable years are usually a calendar year, though for tax collection purposes, they are required to pay quarterly estimated tax payments. Special provisions allow controlled groups of corporations to file a consolidated tax return. Corporations' earnings may be retained or distributed to their shareholders as dividends, which are subject to reduced income tax rates according to the identity of the shareholders—individuals, U.S. corporations or foreign taxpayers. Special tax treatment is provided to some corporate transactions such as formations, mergers, acquisitions, reorganizations and liquidations.

The way the current U.S. tax system copes with the tax deferral problem is by using relatively high tax rates applied to corporations and lower rates for individual shareholders who receive the net—after corporate tax—earnings. To illustrate: when a high-income taxpayer, who is subject to the top marginal tax rate of 35%, uses a "regular" corporation to operate her high-income business, her tax deferral is quite insignificant, since, as is detailed below, the top corporate tax rate is 35%. Furthermore, when the net corporate earnings are distributed as dividends they will be subject to the maximum rate of 20% [p. 316]. The aggregated tax due on the business earnings (both the corporation's and the individual's) is [21%+(1−0.21%)*0.20%=]36.8%, which is (36.8−37=) only 0.2% lower than the top marginal tax bracket on individuals. Note that other mandatory payments were not taken into account, nor was the flexibility of running a business through corporation that allows the shareholder to withdraw earnings from "her" corporation in various ways such as compensation for services as the corporation's employee or self-employed worker, interest payments, and rent, all of which (but not dividends) are deductible by the corporation and are fully taxed when received by the individuals in accordance with their tax rate and personal deductions and credits).

This basic description embodies two underlying assumptions in the current U.S. system: one is that using a corporation does not allow a significant tax deferral. The other is that the two prominent privileges provided to shareholders for operating their businesses through corporations—limited liability and the economies of scale (40)—are public goods (101) offered by the government's legal system and its enforcement. Those who benefit them, i.e. the corporation's owners, should pay for them.

Further below we see that Congress and the IRS have not been consistent with this line of thought and have developed various ways for the shareholders to enjoy the benefit of more than two worlds.

The current law provides some very significant privileges to various categories of corporations. The most significant distinction that Congress has drawn is between small

Corporations—"S-Corporations"—and "regular non-small corporations—"C-corporations". In addition, the IRS has to cope with a unique legal entity, a Limited Liability Corporation (LLC), which is recognized by most states, and is discussed below [p. 313]. Both S-corporations and LLCs have the option to elect the way they are taxed: as a separate legal entity, i.e. a corporation, or as a transparent/look through company, where their shareholders are taxed directly according to their shares in the company. All three entities are discussed briefly below [p. 313].

B. Additional Tax Burden on Corporations?

The most fundamental question in this area is whether the corporate tax should be limited to the aggregated tax payments of its individual shareholders, i.e. as if the shareholders earned their income directly without the intermediate stage of the company, or whether the corporate tax burden should be heavier. As mentioned, one basic claim is that the shareholders enjoy two kinds of benefits: the privilege of limited liability and the economies of scale.

The concept of limited liability, which provides a kind of risk insurance, shifts some serious economic risks from the corporation's owners—the shareholders—to the public. Hence, limited liability, which is offered by the legislature, is a significant and valuable public good. It entails social costs, such as creditors' rights, supervising bankruptcies and regulating delicate economic, legal and welfare situations. Comparing between two individuals who operate in the same economic ways, the one who uses limited liability protection is in a better position. For this privilege, which comes with a social cost, they have to pay, as they would pay if they bought any other commercial insurance in the private market.

The corporate shareholders also enjoy a special economic privilege is the benefit of economies of scale (40) since corporations may raise unlimited amounts of shareholders and capital. This is a significant advantage, which is, once again, a public good offered by the government, and the shareholders who enjoy it have to pay for it.

C. Look Through—Transparent Corporations

Once the legal minds invented the concepts of separate entity and limited liability, and Congress decided to tax this creation—the Corporation—in order to prevent tax deferral and maybe to charge the investors for the two public goods mentioned above—limited liability and economies of scale—it was just a matter of time until someone decided to walk the extra mile for the benefit of the capital investors and provide them with the unique privilege of enjoying both worlds, i.e. enjoying the benefit of these public goods, especially limited liability, and at the same time being able to choose the applicable tax system, either as a corporation, a partnership, or as an individual. The first step was done by Federal tax legislation, which offered a unique tax unit termed Small Corporation (S-Corporation as opposed to a "regular" corporation—a C-corporation). The next step was taken by the states' legislatures by allowing the formation of the Limited Liability Corporation—LLC. Federal tax legislation did not directly react to this development. The tax administration, on the other hand, could not ignore this kind of states' creation and offered the investors a magic formula: to enjoy not only two options (C or S corporations) but various combinations through the "check the box" possibility, which allows U.S. companies, their subsidiaries and even certain types of foreign entities to choose for themselves how to be classified for tax purposes: as a C-corporation, as an S-corporation, or as an LLC, which opens a variety of hybrid tax planning options for individual taxpayers, small size corporations and even large corporations, which are permitted to use their own subsidiaries as LLCs, and eventually are able to keep an estimated two trillion dollars in earnings out of the reach of the U.S. government.

The following discussion briefly presents the basic concepts of S-Corporations, LLCs and C-Corporations.

1) Small Corporations

For some reason, the legislature reached the conclusion that although small size corporations provide the limited liability advantage, but not necessarily the benefit of economies of scale, they can be considered as transparent corporations for tax purposes. Under the U.S. tax system, relatively small corporations have the benefit of both worlds. On the one hand, their owners enjoy the protection of limited liability. On the other hand, for income tax purposes they have the option to be treated as if the veil of corporation is pierced, i.e. the legal entity is not treated as a tax unit, but rather its owners are taxed as they run their business as a partnership.

A) S-Corporation

Any U.S. corporation is eligible to be considered as an S-Corporation provided it meets the following basic preconditions: its shareholders must be individual U.S. Citizens and their number should not exceed 100. A corporation that meets these conditions has the right to elect to "pierce the corporate veil" and be treated—for income tax purposes—like a partnership. In such a way, an S-Corporation is not a tax unit. Instead, each of the shareholders is treated as a taxpayer with their own prorated share of the corporation's gross income, deductible expenses and the shareholders' own deductions and tax credits. Dividends, when paid, are not taxable again. In other words, an S-corporation is a transparent entity for income tax purposes.

One of the tax advantages of S-corporations relates to the fact that if a corporation chooses to be treated as a corporation and gives up transparency, an S-Corporation can hire its shareholders as employees and pay them "reasonable salaries" which would be subject to FICA taxes but any profits in excess of such "reasonable salaries" could be retained by the S-Corporation and enjoy the tax deferral or, if they are distributed, they would be treated as dividends not subject to FICA taxes.

B) Limited Liability Company (LLC)

A similar phenomenon called a Limited Liability Company (LLC) with slightly different—yet very significant—preconditions and traits is a recognized legal entity by most of the States.

Most states do not restrict the number of owners of an LLC—who are called members and not shareholders. There are no limitations on the members' number and identity—beside specifically non-qualified entities such as financial institutions like banks and insurance companies. LLC members may be individuals, corporations and their subsidiaries, other LLCs and even foreign entities.

The default treatment of a domestic LLC with at least two members is classified as a partnership for federal income tax purposes, unless it elects (by filling a simple form) to be treated as a corporation. The default treatment of an LLC with only one member is treated as a "disregarded entity", meaning that all its profits, deductions and losses pass through to its sole member. If an LLC is taxed as a partnership or a disregarded entity, its tax items are flowed-through to its members and the LLC is not required to pay any other income or corporate tax.

One significant disadvantage for LLC owners is that for LLCs that haven't requested to be treated as corporations, the tax rules for partnerships apply. In that case, LLC members cannot be hired by the LLC, hence their income is not considered as income from labor (employment income). Instead, all the company's profits are taxed as personal income to the members; each member is considered to have earned their own prorated share of the profits. Members' income from actively working for the LLC is treated as self-employment income.

LLCs are free to elect to be taxed either as S-Corporations or C-Corporations. If an LLC elects to be taxed as a C-corporation, it is subject to corporate taxation. It has to file a corporate income tax return and pay the corporate tax rates. Net—after corporate tax—earnings which are distributed as dividends, are subject to lower tax rate as described below [pp. 314–316].

C) S-Corporation v. LLC

A comparison between S-corporations and LLCs should make the picture a bit clearer.

There are some statutory limitations on S-corporations that are not applied to LLCs.

S-corps can have up to 100 shareholders whereas LLCs can have an unlimited number of members; S-corporations' shareholders must be U.S. citizens or residents aliens. LLC members can also be non-resident aliens, local and even foreign corporations; S-corporations' shareholders must be individuals, not legal entities like C-corporations, other S-corporation, LLCs, partnerships or any ordinary trusts. No such restrictions apply to LLCs. Both individuals and legal entities can be LLC members except for specific financial institutions.

D) C-Corporation

A C-Corporation is any other corporation that does not elect to be—or is not allowed to be treated as—an S-Corporation. It is a separate tax unit subject to corporate income tax regardless of the identity of its shareholders. Under the U.S. system, a C-corporation is considered a U.S. resident if it is organized under the laws of one of the U.S. states. Its earnings are subject to corporate tax and when they are distributed to its shareholders as dividends, they are taxed as the shareholders' income. Special rules deal with the taxation of dividends paid to corporate shareholders.

Without any specific legislation and under the assumption that each tax unit—corporations and individuals—is supposed to pay income tax according to the "regular" tax rates, there might be two major problems of over-taxation.

D. A Possible Triple Tax on Corporate Earnings

Assume a C-Corporation whose shareholders are only individuals. Assume John invests $100,000 (1%) in that C-Corporation. The C-Corporation does well and earns $20,000,000 annual taxable income. Assuming the corporate tax rate is 35% it pays corporate tax in the amount of $7,000,000, and the rest of the earnings (20,000,000−7,000,000=)$13,000,000 are retained, yet they are distributional profit, meaning a potential dividend. Assume, *Ceteris paribus* (other things constant), that the value of John's shares went up by (13,000,000*1%=)$130,000. John sells his shares to Ann for $230,000 and realizes a capital gain of $130,000. Assuming for the sake of the argument that the tax rate on capital gain is equal to the top marginal tax rate of 35%, John should pay $45,500. After 13 months Ann receives the corporate "distributable profits" as a **Qualified** dividend (104), [hereinafter "dividend"] of $130,000. Assuming Ann's marginal tax rate is 35% she would pay $45,500. The total corporate earnings of John's share (1%) is (20,000,000*1%=)$200,000; John's "share" in the corporate tax is (7,000,000*1%=)$70,000 and the total amount of tax of the three tax units—the corporation, John and Ann is (70,000+45,500+45,4500=)160,000 i.e. (160,00/200,000=) 80.5%!

There are several ways to avoid this triple tax. One is to exempt the retained earnings from double taxation, either from John's capital gains or from Ann's dividend. As is demonstrated below, basic rules of accounting principles and the corporation's ledger entries can provide the needed computation. Another way is tax all three tax units but allow Ann to offset the capital loss she suffers (if she sells the shares) against the dividend received. Assuming *Ceteris paribus*—no other changes in the market, corporate performance, and no additional retained earnings—Ann's loss occurs if she sells her shares immediately after receiving the divided for $100,000, assuming that the value of her shares after the distribution went back to (230,000−130,000=)$100,000.

Another way to eliminate or minimize the triple tax is to concentrate on the total/ aggregated tax burden on the three taxpayers—the corporation, the dividend receiver and the one who sells the stock with a gain—and set the desired aggregated tax rate, assuming the market will take care of allocation between all three of them. For example, if the desired tax is 35% it can be accomplished by the current corporate tax rate to the top marginal tax bracket on individuals—say 37% and exempting both the dividend and the capital gain up to the amount that represents John's share in the corporate distributable profits (in the above example—$130,000). A different way is to set the tax rate on the corporate, the dividend and the capital gain so the aggregate tax rate on all three tax events would be 37%. For example, suppose the corporate tax rate is 18%. C Corporation pays $3,600,000, and the rest of the distributable profits (20,000,000−3,600,000=)$16,400,000 are retained—distributable earnings. Assume, *Ceteris paribus* (other things constant), that the value of John's shares went up by (16,400,000*1%=) $164,000. John sells his shares to Ann for (100,000+164,000=)$254,000 and realizes a capital gain of $164,000. Assuming that the tax rate on capital gain is also 18%, John should pay (164,000*18%=)$29,520 and Ann's dividend is also $164,000. If the tax rate of the dividend that represents the corporate after tax is 4.24% the total aggregate tax payments on 1% of the corporate earning is (36,000+29,520+8,480=)74,000 which is 37%.

Referring to the current tax rates which are a flat corporate tax rate of 21%; and a progressive tax rate on dividends and capital gains, which are the same and depend on the taxpayer's annual taxable income as follows:

0% if the taxpayer's taxable income is below $40,041;

15% if taxable income is between $40,401 to 445,850; and

above $445,850 is 20%.

Assuming John and Ann's taxable income is below $445,850 and using the above example the aggregate tax rate on the 1% of the corporate earnings is as follows: 21% on the corporate earnings=200,000*21%=42,000+(200,000−42,000)*15%+(200,000−42,000)*15%=98,000 which is 98,000/200,000=48%.

If the legislature decides to eliminate this triple tax on the corporate "Distributable profits" and exempt either the tax on the dividend or on the capital gain, then the total tax is 42,000+23,700=65,700 and the aggregate tax rate is 65,700/200,000=32.85%. In both cases, identifying/isolating the corporate's distributable profits should be based on the corporate ledger and using following definition: "Distributable profits"—"the corporate profits accrued from the end of the tax year preceding the year of purchase of the share until the end of the tax year preceding its year of the stock's sale".

E. Distribution of C—Corporation Earnings

Once a C-Corporation makes its earnings it may retain them for any legitimate purpose, such as new investments, replacing old machineries, etc. It can also distribute all or part of its earnings to its shareholders. In order to avoid a full double tax, the Congress offers a reduced tax rate for "qualified dividends" paid to individual shareholders. **Qualified dividends**, as defined in Code Sec. 1(h)11) are dividends received during the taxable year, subject to certain holding periods (less than sixty days for common stocks or ninety days for preferred stock), from domestic corporations, and from "qualified foreign corporations" i.e. a foreign corporations from a country that maintains economic ties with the U.S., e.g. have a tax treaty with the U.S. Only qualified dividends are subject to the reduced tax rates which are shown in table VII below. In addition, under Code Sec. 1(h)(11) the individuals' tax rates on capital gain derived from dispossession of corporate stock are identical to the rates on for qualified dividends tax rates. Note that there are additional rates for different type of gains. Table VII shows the individuals' tax rates for gains derived from dispositions of three type of capital investment and for qualified dividends.

Table 24.2:

Ordinary tax rates for individuals	**Long-term capital gain tax rates**			**Tax Rate on Qualified Dividend**
	Collectibles and certain small business stock	Non-recaptured "Section 1250 gain"	Other investments including stocks	
10%	10%	10%	0%	0%
15%	15%	15%	0%	0%
25%	25%	25%	15%	15%
28%	28%	25%	15%	15%
33%	28%	25%	15%	15%
35%	28%	25%	15%	15%
39.6%	28%	25%	20%	20%

Going back to the example above, under these tax rates the total amount of tax paid by the Corporation, John, and Ann is much lower than 83.5%:

The Corporation indeed pays 35%, whereas but John and Ann are subject to significantly reduced tax rates: John's is 15% and Ann's is 20%. In that case, John's tax due is (130,000*15%=)$19,500 and Ann's is (130,000*20%=)$26,000. Thus, the total tax on the 10% of the Corporation's earnings (John's share in the corporation) is (70,000+ 19,500+26,000=)$115,500 which is (115,500/200,000=)57.75%. This is still higher than the maximum marginal tax rate for individuals. Such an aggregated tax rate might suggest that the Congress concluded that C-corporations' shareholders have to pay for the public goods they enjoy from the economies of scale and the limited liability. Though it is seems that with regard to S-Corporations, the Congress assumes that the limited amount of shareholders—up to 100 maximum—does not enjoy the economies of scale and therefore Congress does not insist on the benefit from the limited liability as a justification for an extra tax burden.

F. Multiply Tax on C Corporations

The above discussion pertains to C-Corporations that distribute their net after-tax earnings to individual taxpayers. Yet if the corporation's shareholders are other corporations, there is another chance for an almost infinite tax. Consider the following example: Corporation # 1 pays 21% corporate tax on its earnings and distributes them to Corporation # 2 who might pay a second 21% corporate tax and then distributes them again to a third corporation and so on. By the time the earnings get to the individual shareholders the aggregated tax could be extremely high!

Code Sec. 243's purpose is to prevent such a situation but not entirely. If Corporation # 2 receives dividends from Corporation #1, it can deduct either 50% or even 100% of these dividends depending on some circumstances.

G. What Is the Policy Behind All This

One has to admit that it is quite difficult to detect or identify a clear and consistent policy regarding the taxation of corporations. On the one hand, C-corporations and their shareholders are subject to a heavier tax burden; and in some cases—a multi-layer tax is due. On the other hand, the U.S. tax system allows small, medium-sized, and—under careful planning—even large corporations and their subsidiaries to elect the system they prefer to be taxed under and reduce their tax burden, or even to smuggle/sneak their income away from U.S. tax collectors by sophisticated tax planning. One guess is that the U.S. government is anxious to provide a lot of work to tax planners—lawyers accountants etc.—and by doing so increase the Gross Domestic Product (53) and the unemployment rate at the cost of widening social gaps. A more serious and grimmer guess is that the legislature was unable to cope with the above-mentioned Coalition. [p. 24]

Chapter Twenty-Five

TAX COMPUTATIONS

1. TAX RATES AND TENTATIVE TAX DUE

All the above tables present only the tentative tax due. Once the tentative tax is computed, the various tax credits further reduce the final tax liability.

2. TAX CREDITS

After the **tentative** tax payment due has been computed according to the relevant statutory tax rates, various tax credits (125) are subtracted and the final tax payment due is set. In other words, a tax credit is a dollar-for-dollar reduction of the tentative income tax due.

As mentioned already, Congress uses tax credits mainly as TRIs (122, 127) [p. 31]. Since the tax savings (133) from tax credits is higher than savings from a deduction or an exemption of the same amount [p. 240], tax credits sometimes serve as a safety net for low-income taxpayers. For these taxpayers, deductions or exemptions are of very limited use, if any, whereas the "dollar-for-dollar" credit provides better government economic assistance, especially where the credits are refundable, and phase out over time.

We mentioned already that the popular belief that tax credits are better for distributive justice purposes is flawed [p. 242]. A \$100 non-refundable tax credit which is granted to a zero bracket taxpayer is worth zero; Using grossing up mechanism (83), a tax credit of \$100 to a 20% marginal tax rate is worth (100/0.8=)\$125, and for a 37% taxpayer it is worth (100/0.65=)\$153.84.

In some cases, the amount of the tax credit is greater than the taxpayer's tentative tax due, hence the taxpayer is unable to enjoy the full relief. In order to ease this problem, Congress has devised a refundable tax credit (37, 82, 94), which means that that the IRS grants low-income taxpayers an amount which is equal to the unused credit. For example: if a taxpayer's tentative tax due is \$125 and he is entitled to a \$200 tax credit, with a refundable tax credit his final tax due will be zero and in addition he will receive a grant of \$75. Thus. the taxpayer enjoys the full amount of \$200.

Furthermore, in order to prevent a situation where wealthy taxpayers receive a tax credit that is aimed to support needy taxpayers, Congress has devised another solution—a phase-out [pp. 35, 248] tax credit (37, 93, 94), i.e. the tax credit amount begins to decrease once the taxpayer's AGI or MAGI (6) reaches a certain designated level, and is gradually eroded until the taxpayer's AGI/MAGI reaches a higher level, above which no credit is granted, as demonstrated in some examples below [p. 321].

Generally speaking, there are several categories of tax credits. One is designated to support households' personal and family matters, such as raising children and providing support for dependents, healthcare, dwelling, and education. This category, which might represent the concept of discretionary power to consume as the income tax base [p. 12], was provided in addition to the personal exemptions which were provided to the taxpayers themselves, their children and dependents [p. 287].

A second category is for environmental and other national goals, like providing economic assistance to residents who were affected by unique and unusual disasters, e.g. hurricanes.

A third category aims to ease the harsh circumstances that occur due to the following traits of the income tax system: the tax period of one year; the progressive tax rates; and the significant fluctuation of a human's ability to produce a constant stream of income over their lifetime. As demonstrated above [p. 175], one way to ease this harshness is to allow taxpayers to spread/average their income over their lifetime through averaging systems such as retirement plans.

The fourth category's aim is to support small businesses and their employees.

The fifth category, which is not a typical tax credit system but rather a Federal program, aims to help poor working families. Since the program is administered by the IRC it is called a "negative income tax" (NIT), though its formal title is Earned Income Tax Credit (EITC), and it provides refundable phased-out tax credits [p. 325] for working low-income taxpayers.

An additional type is a credit the U.S. Government provides to U.S. taxpayers for paying foreign tax payments on income that is also taxable by the U.S. [pp. 149, 230].

The following is a short description of the major tax credits offered to taxpayers under the current system.

A. Households' Tax Credits

1) Parent's Tax Credit

A) Tax Credits for Children and Dependents' Expenses

Code Sec. 21 provides a tax credit for low-income working individuals for their expenses on qualifying individuals, i.e. children under the age of 13, dependents and spouses who are physically or mentally incapable of caring for themselves, as long as they have the same principal place of abode as the taxpayer. The amount of allowed expenses incurred is up to $3,000 for one qualifying individual, and up to $6,000 for two or more qualifying individuals per year, provided these amounts do not exceed the taxpayer's earned income for such year. The credit is worth between 20 percent and 35 percent of these expenses, depending on the family's Adjusted Gross income. A family with an AGI of $15,000 or less is eligible for a tax credit equal to 35 percent of these expenses for a maximum amount of (6,000*0.35)=$2,100 if they have more than one child or dependent. The percentage is gradually reduced (but not below 20 percent) as the AGI increases by 1 percent for each $2,000. Hence, families with AGIs of $43,000 or more reach the lower rate of 20 percent, and they are entitled to the minimum credit amount of (6,000*0.2)=$1,200.

B) Child Care Credit

In addition to the credits for children and dependents' expenses, Code Sec. 24 provides a phase-out Child Tax Credit for families with a qualified child (under the age of 17). The maximum amount of the credit is $1,000 per child. The phase-out starts at MAGI (6) of $110,000 (for joint returns) at the rate of $50 for each additional MAGI of $1,000, up to MAGI of $130,000.

In rare and unique cases, a small portion of the credit is refundable for families with a small amount of earned income—above $3,000—whose tax due is below the credit's amount. In that case the refundable credit is equal to the unused portion of the child tax credit up to 15% of the taxpayer's earned income.

C) Adoption Expenses

Congress has provided two types of tax breaks to assist parents with qualified adoption expenses spent to adopt an eligible child. One is within Code Sec. 137, which excludes from an employee's gross income the amount that their employer covers of the adoption cost of the employee-adopters, up to a certain amount. The other provision is Code Sec. 23, which grants a non-refundable phased-out tax credit with the same limited amount. The taxpayer is not allowed both a credit and an exclusion for the same expenses. The allowable maximum amount for 2022 is $14,890 per child (there is no limit on the number of children), either for the exclusion or the credit. For example, if the total adoption cost of one child is $20,000, and assuming the employer covers the first $5,000, which are exempted, then the taxpayer is allowed a tax credit of (14,890−5,000=)$9,890. The credit is nonrefundable. However, any unused credit in one year may be carried forward for up to five years.

In the case of an adoption of a child with special needs, the qualified adoption costs are increased by an amount equal to the excess (if any) of $10,000 over the actual aggregate qualified adoption expenses subject to the maximum amount limitation. In other words, if the actual adoption costs are $4,000 for special needs adoptions the adopters are allowed the maximum credit of $14,890.

For both the credit and the exclusion, qualified adoption expenses (whether they are paid before an eligible child has been located/chosen or after the process is completed) include reasonable and necessary adoption fees such as legal costs, traveling expenses (including amounts spent for meals and lodging while away from home), and any other expenses that are directly connected to the adoption.

The credit (as the exclusion) is subject to limitations. The **income limit** is based on the adopters' MAGI (6). The credit/exemption begins to phase out at MAGI of $223,410, and it is reduced by 2.5% for each additional $1,000. Hence it is totally phased-out above MAGI of $263,410.

2) Credit for the Elderly and the Permanently and Totally Disabled

Code Sec. 22 provides a very modest nonrefundable tax credit for the elderly—over 65 years old—or those retired on permanent and total disability. The maximum credit available is $5,000 (single), but due to the various preconditions, the way it is computed and reduced by any type of income limitation, the actual amount is quite insignificant. Those taxpayers have to rely mainly on the refundable Earned Income Tax Credit [p. 325], the states' welfare systems, their pension plans, and social security allowances [p. 128].

3) Health Care

Though health care insurance is (still) not mandatory in the U.S. [pp. 130, 131] Congress provides significant tax incentives to extend such insurance. Code Sec. 106 exempts from the employees' gross income employer-provided coverage for an accident or health plan. As for self-employed taxpayers, Code Sec. 162(L) allows those taxpayers a deduction of the amount—up to the taxpayer's earned income—paid during the taxable year for insurance which constitutes medical care for the taxpayer and for their family and dependents.

In addition to these exemptions and deductions Congress offers various tax credits for health care. Code Sec. 45R provides a limited tax credit for employees' health insurance expenses for small employers.

Sec. 1401 of the Affordable Care Act (Obamacare) provides a refundable credit ("Premium tax credit"—PTC) to individuals and families who obtain healthcare insurance policies through a state or a federally-facilitated healthcare exchange, and whose income falls between 100% and 400% of the applicable federal poverty line. Other factors that are considered are the family size and age, and the state of residence. To be entitled to the refundable credit the taxpayers have to pay healthcare premiums up to a qualified percentage of their family income, which varies between 2 to 9.5%, depending on the family's income. The higher the income, the smaller the percentage. The refundable credit can be paid in advance directly to a healthcare insurer and the taxpayer makes up the remaining balance.

4) Dwelling

A) Tax Credits for New Home Ownership

In addition to the mortgage interest deduction mentioned above [p. 288], Code Sec. 25 provides a nonrefundable Mortgage Tax Credit to those no- or low-income taxpayers who are granted, by a state or a local government, a Mortgage Credit Certificate (MCC). The MCC program is designed to help homebuyers who take a new mortgage provided they meet the following preconditions: they did not own a home for the previous three years; they intend to use the purchased home as their own primary residence; their income and the home purchase price should meet certain guidelines; the interest is paid to an unrelated person.

The maximum amount of the credit is a percentage of the interest payment (set by the pertaining MCC program). If the certificate interest rate exceeds 20 percent, the maximum amount of the credit is $2,000 a year. The credit is available as long as the taxpayer actually lives in the home and pay the mortgage. If the credit for any taxable year exceeds the applicable tax limit for such taxable year, such excess is carried over, under certain limitations, to each of the 3 succeeding taxable years.

B) Tax Credits for Developers

Since the deductions for mortgage interest payments are not refundable, they are of no practical help for low- or no-income-taxpayers. Inevitably, some people are unable to purchase a home and, in order to avoid being homeless, have to try renting instead. Aiming to reduce homelessness, the Federal government cooperates with local governments to indirectly provide affordable housing for the neediest. Code Sec. 42 allows the U.S. Treasury Department to allocate Low Income Affordable Housing Tax Credits (LIHTCs) to each state that participates in such a program. These income tax credits, equal to a certain percentage of the cost incurred for development of low-income certified units, is granted for up to 10 years to each qualified taxpayer—developers and equity partners—who develop and maintain apartments as affordable units for low-income tenants.

The available credits are granted through competition among developers and investors. Naturally there are some preconditions and ceilings to apply for these credits. The major ones are the following: at least 20% or more of the residential units in the development project are both rent-restricted and occupied by individuals whose incomes are 50% or less of the area's median gross income; at least 40% or more of the residential units in the development are both rent-restricted and occupied by individuals whose incomes are 60% or less of the area's median gross income; the low- or no-income tenants can be charged a maximum rent of 30% of the maximum eligible income, which is 60% of the area's median income adjusted for household size as determined by the U.S. Department of Housing and Urban Development.

5) Education

A) American Opportunity Tax Credits (AOTC)

The modified Code Sec. 25A offers, since 2016, a unique partial phased-out refundable tax credit which aims to assist taxpayers (including their spouses or dependents) who participate in academic studies. The credit, worth up to $2,500 per student per year, is available for the students' qualified tuition and related expenses (i.e. fees and course materials required for the enrollment or attendance of the pertaining student), paid during the first four years of their studies. Since it aims to assist only relatively low-income taxpayers with low tax payments due, 40% of the credit ($1,000) may be refundable. On the other hand, the tax credit begins to phase out when the single taxpayers' Modified AGI (6) reaches $80,000, and it is totally eroded once the taxpayer's MAGI is over $90,000 (these amounts are doubled for joint returns).

There are some preconditions, such as: the type of degree the student pursues; the number of courses (at least ½ the normal full-time workload for the course of study the student is pursuing); and the amount of the qualified tuition and related expenses as mentioned above. As a general rule a lifetime amount limitation is applied, and the aggregate amount of the credits cannot exceed $15,000 for all taxable years.

In addition, the student must be free of any federal or state felony conviction for possessing or distributing a controlled substance (illegal drug) as of the end of the taxable year.

B) Lifetime Learning Credit

Code Sec. 25A(2) allows the taxpayer to elect, instead of the American Opportunity Tax Credit (AOTC), a lifetime learning nonrefundable credit of up to $2,000 for qualified education expenses paid to all eligible students. Under this election, the phase-out begins at a MAGI of $59,000 ($118,000 joint) and is totally eroded once MAGI reaches $69,000 ($138,000 joint). Though the AOTC, when available, provides better relief, the advantages of the lifetime learning credit are that it is available for all years of higher education and for courses meant to acquire or improve job skills, for an unlimited number of taxable years; students don't need to pursue a degree or other recognized education credential; the credit is available for one or more courses, and felony drug convictions don't make students ineligible.

6) Averaging Income Through Saving and Pension Plans

A) Contributions to Pension Plans

As mentioned above [p. 175], due to the progressive tax system and the fact that our productive periods are fluctuated, we saw that at our most productive time we run into higher tax rates while at the earliest and latest stages of our lives our earnings, especially from labor, are basically nil. Hence an averaging system is needed; a process that should allow two types of allocation of our earnings during our peak years for our children's consumption on the one hand, and for our own consumption during our retirement times on the other hand. The former allocation is taken care of through the aforementioned personal exemption for children and dependents [p. 287], and credit for child and dependent care expenses [p. 320]. The latter allocation is done by the tax benefits offered to both self-employed taxpayers and employees for their (and their employers') contributions to "Individual Retirement Arrangements ("IRAs") [pp. 177, 253]. There are several types of IRA plans. The most common ones are the Traditional IRA, the 401(k) plan, and the Roth 401(k) plan. The primary tax benefits for contributing to an IRA (up to a statutory ceiling) are the deductions and exemptions of the taxpayers' and their employers' contributions, the tax-deferred or tax-free growth on earnings while the funds are invested in plans **or** exemption of the amounts withdrawn at retirement in the case of the Roth 401(k) plan.

B) Retirement Savings Contributions Credit (Saver's Credit)

Since deductions and exemptions are usually meaningless for low- and even moderate-income taxpayers, Congress offers them an additional tax incentive for saving for retirement.

Code Sec. 25B allows any eligible individual (over the age of 18 who is not a dependent of another taxpayer and not a full time student) a nonrefundable phased-out tax credit equal to a percentage of qualified retirement savings contributions up to a maximum amount of $2,000, depending on the taxpayer's AGI. For a single taxpayer with an AGI up to $20,500, the tax credit is 50 percent of the contribution amount. For the taxable year of 2022, for taxpayers with an AGI between $20,501 and $22,000, the credit is 20 percent. For a single taxpayer with an AGI between $22,001and $34,000, the percentage goes down to 10 percent. No such credit is allowed to single taxpayers with an AGI over $34,000. For joint return taxpayers, the above amounts are doubled.

7) Other Tax Credits for Individuals, Households, Employers and Businesses

The purpose of the above short introduction of some of the major and the most common tax credits, which are offered directly and indirectly to individuals, households, employers, developers and equity partners of the Low Income Affordable Housing industry, and certain bondholders, is meant to reveal to the readers the basic concept of tax credits, the phase-out and refundable mechanisms, and their purposes. Another goal is to expose Congress' aims, purposes and rationales for using tax credits in order to promote its national goals. It is noteworthy to indicate that there is quite a long list of tax credits offered by the government in order to induce taxpayers to accomplish national goals which otherwise should be executed by the government. Among other goals are the promotion of new energy efficient homes, using cleaner gas in automobiles, investing in Research and Development, encouraging the preservation of "historical buildings", investing in renewable energy, producing renewable energy, and incentivizing employers to hire groups facing high rates of unemployment. All these programs are subject to limitations and preconditions. Note that Code Sec. 38(b) provides a long list of many types of tax credits.

B. Earned Income Tax Credit (EITC)

1) The Rationale and Its Development

The EITC is not a conventional tax credit. It is actually a government grant, which is probably given due to administrative efficiency considerations, or maybe it has something to do with the IRS' public relations ("we do not only take but also give". . .). One popular idea is that the government sets a certain amount of taxable income that might provide a reasonable standard of living. Those who have more taxable income than that amount should pay income tax. Those whose income is below that amount should get a governmental grant that brings the taxpayer's taxable income up to that amount.

The EITC is granted only to working individuals and families. The rationale behind this concept may be found in Arthur Okun's illustration that explains why a sensible legislature should provide economic assistance to deprived citizens in order to enable them to join—or rejoin—the workforce, so they can become self-supported and enjoy self-sufficiency. Suppose a person considers two work opportunities: one offers $8 per hour (which is hardly enough to maintain a minimum standard of living). The other one offers a starting wage of $6 per hour (which is below the minimum standard of living), yet after a certain period of training in this job the wage goes up to $14 per hour (an amount that provides a reasonable standard of living). The rational choice is quite clear. Those who are unable to wait and survive the training period will be forced to choose the first $8 per hour job and will eventually endure low income, life on the verge of poverty, and an insufficient contribution to the national economy. Those persons who can make up the lower pay of $6 per hour during the interim period until their pay goes up to $14 per hour will be able to reach a reasonable and dignified standard of living, and will eventually increase the national economic growth. Naturally, a poor and uneducated person faces a very serious obstacle in getting such intermediate financing (from a bank or any other lending institution). Such a situation calls for the intervention of the government. One of the major means for providing such intermediate financing is the Earned Income Tax Credit, which is known also as the Negative Income Tax.

In 1940. British politician and intellectual writer Juliet Rhys Williams was the first to officially propose—alas, unsuccessfully—the concept of a negative income tax in the U.K. The idea reached the U.S. and was introduced by economics professor and Nobel laureate Milton Friedman in his book Capitalism and Freedom (1962). Robert Lampman, professor of economics at the University of Wisconsin, embraced the idea and initiated several applied research studies. Between 1968 and 1979, several states conducted experiments in order to see whether the idea could be implemented.

In 1975, a modest version of the Earned Income Credit (EIC) was enacted and it has since been expanded into its current version.

2) The Current System in the U.S.

The current system in the U.S. offers refundable Earned Income Tax Credits (EITC) to the **working** poor with a minimum amount of earned income. This means that the

EITC does not provide grants to the unemployed. It purpose is to encourage labor. (37). Under Code Sec. 32, a taxpayer can claim a significant amount of refundable credit, i.e. "negative income tax" (82) as a percentage of their "earned income", up to a certain level. The EITC depends on a recipient's earned income. Specifically, the EITC phases in as a percentage of earned income (the "credit rate") until the credit amount reaches its maximum level. The EITC then remains at its maximum level over a subsequent short range of earned income, between the "earned income amount" and the "phaseout amount threshold." Finally, the credit gradually decreases to zero at a fixed rate (the "phaseout rate") for each additional dollar of adjusted gross income (AGI) (or earned income, whichever is greater) above the phaseout amount threshold. The following is a table which demonstrates the annual earing limitation, and the maximum amount of the credit depending on the taxpayers number of children:

Table 25.1:

Income Qualification Item	No Children	With 1 Child	With 2 Children	With 3+ Children
1. Max. 2022 Earned Income Tax Credit Amount	$560	$3,733	$6,164	$6,935
2. Earned Income Base Amount required to get maximum credit	$7,320	$10,980	$15,410	$15,410
3. Phaseout Threshold Amount Begins (for Single, or Head of household)	$9,160	$20,130	$20,130	$20,130
4. Income (AGI) Maximum When Credit Eligibility Ends (for Single, or household	$16,480	$43,492	$49,399	$53,057
5. Phaseout Threshold Amount Begins (for Married Filing Jointly)	$15,290	$26,260	$26,260	$26,260
6. Income (AGI) Maximum When Credit Eligibility Ends (for Married Filing Jointly)	$22,610	$49,622	$55,529	$59,187

By design, the credit only benefits working individuals and families. Families with children receive a much larger credit than workers without qualifying children. In 2022, taxpayers with no children were qualified to receive a maximum amount of $560, provided that their Earned Income Base Amount required to get maximum credit was $7,320; if they had 3 children they were entitled to receive $$6,935 if their required income was $15,410, and so on.

The phase out begins for 3-children taxpayers when the total earned income including the refundable credit is $6,935 and above, and it ends when the total income reaches the amount of $59,187 and above. Those taxpayers with total incomes over such amount are no longer eligible for the EITC.

In contrast to the substantial credit for workers with children, childless workers in 2022 [probably since they have more free time, which mean more potential working hours] can receive a maximum credit of only $560 after the expiration of the American Rescue Plan Act of 2021. Moreover, the credit for childless workers phases out at much lower incomes. Also, childless workers must be at least 25 and not older than 64 in order to qualify for the refundable credit. This limitation does not apply to workers with children.

The Tax Policy Center presents the following Figure which illustrates in a nutshell the most relevant factors that set the EITC amounts, for four types of eligible taxpayers—without children, with one child, with two children, and with three children. Note that at the time of writing, the Tax Policy Center has not released an update for 2022, and the 2021 chart includes increases in the EITC amounts for childless taxpayers due to the American Rescue Plan Act of 2021. The figure shows the following variables:

- The earned income amounts for getting the minimum amount of credits;
- At what level the credits amounts begin to grow and in what percentage;
- The maximum amounts of the credit, which remains at its maximum level over a subsequent short range of earned income.

When the phase out (credit declining) begins, and its percentage, until it is fully exhausted:

Figure 25.1:

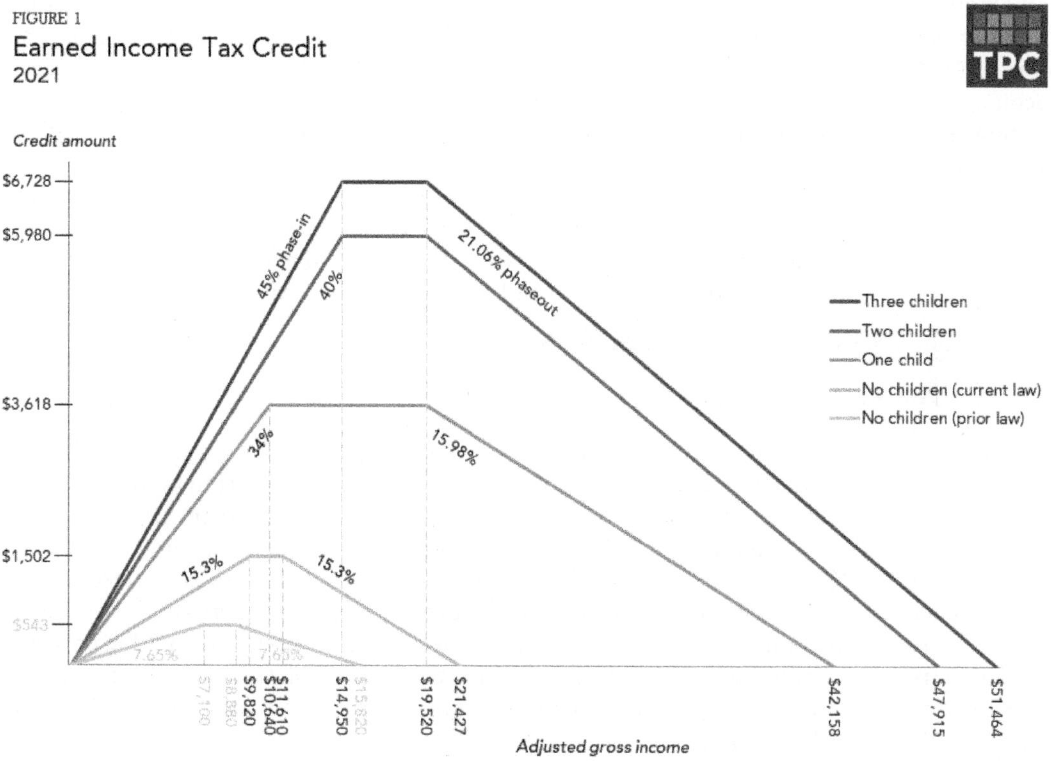

Source: Urban-Brookings Tax Policy Center (2021); Internal Revenue Procedure 2020-45, Internal Revenue Service; and H.R. 1319, "American Rescue Plan Act of 2021," 117th Cong. (2021.)
Notes: Assumes all income comes from earnings. Amounts are for taxpayers filing a single or head-of-household tax return. For married couples filing a joint tax return, the credit begins to phase out at income $5,940 higher than shown, or $5,950 if the couple has children.

C. Foreign Tax Credit

The last type of tax credit introduced here has nothing to do with TRI (127, 131) or social causes—it is a nonrefundable non-phased-out foreign tax credit. These credits are an integral component of the system of taxation of international activities, which was mentioned above [pp. 227, 230]. Its aim is to prevent double taxation of such income. In order to avoid tedious repetitions here, we very briefly mention the basic concept of the credit. As a general rule, there are two types of income from international activity that might be subject to double taxation: income of an American taxpayer (citizen or resident alien) whose source is outside the U.S., i.e. in a foreign source country, and income of a foreigner sourced within the U.S. In order to prevent double taxation there are two types of arrangements. The first one is based on domestic law (a unilateral arrangement). Here, the basic rule is that the source country gets the first bite of the tax pie and the residence country provides a foreign tax credit to its residents for taxes paid to the source country. The second type is based on tax treaties (134) where the first bite and the country that provides the foreign tax credit depend on the type of income—passive or active—and the treaty's provisions. In any case, the credit is subject to certain limitations. Generally, the foreign tax credit is limited to the lower of either the foreign tax amount, or the domestic tentative tax amount. The limitations in the U.S. are set by the "per baskets" concept. This means that the allowed foreign tax credit for foreign source income should be only for foreign taxes paid on the same type of income (i.e. an income "basket"). The main income baskets are passive income; financial services income; shipping income; and general limitation income, which includes income earned abroad in the active conduct of a trade or business other than within the previous mentioned baskets. Income in each of these baskets is subject to a separate foreign tax credit limitation. Any excess foreign tax credits can be applied to offset the residual U.S. tax on foreign source income, of the same basket, which is earned during the previous two years or the succeeding five years. Unused credits within that period are lost.

3. ALTERNATIVE MINIMUM TAX

A. The Basic Concept

As is discussed throughout of the book, the current system is quite far from a true Comprehensive Tax Base model. The first reason for this is that the courts and the IRS have distanced themselves from the economic concept of the term income as a measurement of the taxpayer's ability and have tended to provide a limited interpretation of the statutory term of Gross Income [pp. 160–169]. The source of the second reason is at the political level. The legislature (and the politicians) are evidently unable to resist the temptation of using their power to give away, from the general national treasury, some quasi-hidden benefits to their constituencies, or simply surrender to powerful groups and lobbyists by granting enormous amounts of TRI (83, 84, 122, 127, 131, 134) [p. 31].

The first version of Congress' attempt to prevent total erosion of the income tax base and to keep government revenue up to a non-dangerous level was done using the Tax Reform Act of 1969, when the Congress enacted an "add-on tax" on high-income taxpayers of 10% of the sum of tax preferences in excess of $30,000 in addition to the taxpayer's regular tax due. This concept—of creating an additional tax system instead of trying to cope directly with the problems of TRI (127, 131)—has been modified several times and has led to the current Alternative Minimum Tax ("AMT").

The concept of the current AMT (Code Secs. 55–59) is basically the same as the original legislation of 1969. It is quite unique. It is based on two parallel income tax systems; the "regular" one and the "alternative" one. The latter is indeed a kind of a safety net which aims to assure that individuals and legal entities that enjoy various TRI (131) should pay a minimum income or corporate taxes.

While corporations are also subject to the AMT, we focus on the individual taxpayers.

B. The Calculation

There are five steps in computing the AMT liability. The first one is the redetermination of the income tax base, by adding back into to the Gross Income and Taxable Income many TRIs—exemptions, deductions [Code Sec. 56–58] and even some tax credits [Code Secs. 55(c)(3) and 59]. Some adjustments and adaptions that should be made by the taxpayers in order to compute AMT relate to the following TRI: itemized deductions, like state and local income taxes, real and personal property taxes; the standard deduction and the personal exemptions—while they are valid; miscellaneous itemized deductions, more limited medical expenses, significant limitations on certain interest deductions, including home mortgage and investment interest [pp. 287–295]; straight line depreciation in various cases instead of any other accelerated depreciation [pp. 264, 282]; a limited percentage (10%) of mining exploration and development costs; some benefits which are usually provided to long-term contract expenses; and significant limitations on the deductibility of net operating loss [p. 283].

C. Exemption from the AMT Income

The second stage calculates the net amount of AMT income (AMTI). Once the AMTI is computed, the Code provides a special exemption from AMT, which is supposed to compensate taxpayers for losing their personal exemptions—while there are in effect—and standard deductions available under the regular income tax.

The Alternative Minimum Tax exemption amount for tax year 2022 is $75,900 and begins to phase out at $539,900 ($118,100 for married couples filing jointly for whom the exemption begins to phase out at $1,079,800).

In 2022, the 28 percent AMT rate applies to excess AMTI of $206,100 for all taxpayers ($103,050 for married couples filing separate returns). For single taxpayers the phase-out begins at AMTI of $539,900 and is completely diminished at the amount of $843,500. For joint returns it begins at $1,079,800 and ends at the amount of $1,552,200.

D. AMT's Rates

The third stage calculates the tax due under AMT. There are two rates. For individuals—both single and joint returns—AMTI up to $206,100 is subject to a flat rate of 26%. For any AMTI above this amount the AMT rate is 28%. For married couples who file separately, the 26% rate applies to AMTI up to $103,050, and is 28% for any AMTI above this amount.

Note though that taxpayers with significant qualified dividends and long-term capital gains might be subject to the AMT system, but the tax rates for those types of income are not affected by the AMT and are subject to the preferred rates [p. 316].

E. The Taxpayers' Final AMT Due

The fourth stage computes the taxpayers' final tax due. In order to verify that the taxpayers' tax payment does not go below a certain minimum, taxpayers have to perform two computations. One is based on the regular income tax, where the taxpayer has to follow all the Code's and the regulations' provisions including the permissible/available use of all TRI, which of course reduce the final tax due. The second computation is based on the AMT, which as mentioned above, is a process of adjustments and adaptions that bring back/restore (to) the regular computation of a long list of TRI. Once these two alternative computations provide two different amounts of tax due, Code Sec 55(a) states the final fifth stage—comparing between the AMT liability and the regular tax due. The taxpayers then have to pay the **larger** amount of the regular tax due or the AMT tax due.

F. Who Needs AMT?

The result emerging from the current income tax system alongside with the AMT is quite confusing, frustrating, and disappointing. On the one hand, Congress has surrendered to too many political pressures coming from conflicting sides [pp. 24, 32, 75], by offering a huge amount of TRI. On the other hand, the courts are very reluctant to review [pp. 40–55] those TRI, which *prima facie* violate or contradict constitutional principles and human rights [pp. 31, 36]. Thus, instead of coping directly with the problems created by these TRI (127, 131) and eliminating them directly, Congress undermines them indirectly in a sweeping and uncontrolled way which creates, in some instances, unjustifiable and unpredictable results. A realistic observation leads to the conclusion that in fact, rather than canceling the TRI distortions, Congress tries to cope with them by offering a counter-distortion, which is a complex, complicated and arbitrary solution.

Conclusion

The book has ended, but the story lingers on. The whole story is complicated and complex, mainly due to the many sides, source, aspects, and political forces that underlie the tax field.

Before we dived into the stormy waters of the U.S. tax system, we decided to present a number of theoretical insights dealing with tax justifications in the modern era. The first two parts deal with the General Theory of Taxation and the need for a comprehensive and interdisciplinary approach towards tax policy and tax law analyses. The rest of the book deals with current U.S. tax system.

The multiple sources of tax law and their optimal implementations are various and include, *inter alia,* social philosophy, macro-economics, public finance, accounting, finance, public law (constitutional and administrative), business law, international law, criminal law and what has manifested in recent centuries into a fascinating and unique interdisciplinary legal field—tax law.

Modern democracy in modern times, conceptualized in Europe and adopted and has developed by the American Founding Fathers, recognizes human dignity and rights including property, equality, and freedom of all kinds. Citizens are not required to maintain the private interest of the government and its members any longer.

Democratic ideas, the understanding that governments are elected to serve their constituents, seem clear to us today. Our governments do not possess or own anything. Anything they have is owned by the public and is intended for the public. Taxes are no longer compulsory payments; they are based on tacit consent measured by the benefit we receive from the public goods and services provided by our elected government, with a clear goal: to enhance the public wellbeing. Indeed, they are as mandatory as the money a customer owes to the grocery store after she takes merchandise and is obligated to pay for it. The collection process of taxes might be tougher than the collection of private debts, but this is only because the "free riders" phenomenon is more common in the public market. Since tax offenders cause a severe negative externality, they should be deterred by tougher means.

Our main justification for the tax owed by firms and households, is the benefit we all enjoy from the elected government. Regarding firms, we present the Joint Project doctrine, according to which the public, through the government, invests public-social capital in the wealth-creation-process and is entitled to receive a return. As a result we consider tax as a profit-sharing mechanism intended to share the firms' income to all investors of the three factors of production- real capital, human capital, and social capital. Households benefit from the consumption of the goods and services that the government provides, and they are required to pay the appropriate price for them. In other words, a good tax system is based on the taxpayers' consent.

Philosophers and ethicists paved the way to a new scientific field—the study of the general welfare, wellbeing and a just distribution of wealth. This field later evolved into the science of economics. Adam Smith's Wealth of Nations had developed, inter alia, the concept of taxes in democratic regimes, and characterized what should be regarded as an acceptable tax in such societies: the Four Canons of good tax. Under the concept of Social Contract, we buy social goods and services from the elected government, and pay taxes willingly to improve our lives in a civilized society. Consent took center stage and replaced the old rulers' tyranny and arbitrary payments. The best expression of this idea is the catchphrase that symbolizes the creation of the American nation: "no taxation without representation," which has substantial legal, constitutional, and even economic significance in modern times. That is to say, in a liberal society, no person is required to make any payment—including taxes—without consent Under the current U.S. constitutional and legal systems, the collective tacit consent is expressed through two democratic and constitutional institutions: the national election, and the public- elected agents' approval of the national fiscal policy and spending. Congress has been empowered to impose taxes for declared purposes—"to pay the Debts and provide for the Common Defense and General Welfare of the United States"(U.S. CONST. art. I, § 8, clause. 1). Accordingly, we proposed that the tax for constitutional interpretation is a **pure** tax, a tax whose sole purpose **is to raise revenue** for financing the expenses of the elected government. The purpose of other mandatory payments—regulatory taxes which are within the power of the Congress under the Commerce Clause of Article 1 Sec. 8 clause 3—is different. Their purpose is to restore free-market principles and rearrange the right economic price of a product in two different yet similar cases, which occur due to market failures, i.e. negative and positive externalities.

Considering this distinction, we recognize that although Congress has a few limitations regarding its power to levy pure tax, the Court has been demonstrated a most significant reluctance to use Judicial review (70) on pure taxes. Hence, we proposed that Judicial review of Pigovian taxes and tax reliefs would be tighter and stricter than of pure taxes.

The power to levy pure taxes is indeed constrained to the assumption that the taxpayers consent to pay. Such consent can be assumed only if the tax is justified as an acceptable, i.e. a good tax, which takes us back to the Adam Smith's "Four Canons of good tax": Certain and not arbitrary; Convenience for the contributor; Efficient; and Fair and Equitable. We conclude that the collective consent to pay the tax can be assumed only if the tax meets those criteria, adapted to the 21st century.

A notable analysis of optimal taxation concludes that almost every tax creates economic distortion—deadweight loss/excess burden—which means that the loss of welfare caused by the tax is greater than the government's revenues. Hence, in order for the tax to meet the efficiency requirement, the government has to assure that the benefit the public derives from the collected tax is higher than the welfare loss it creates. Admittedly, it is almost impossible—for the time being—to provide measurable tools to satisfy this requirement in the legal sense. Yet, if taxpayers are able to prove that the government has failed in providing them public goods or services on a specific occasion (such as national disasters, or any other extreme situations) then they are entitled to a discount—tax breaks—on their tax bill. In some other cases, if the government fails to maintain law and order, the taxpayer is allowed to take a deduction for casual and theft losses.

We have proposed a broad, wholistic, and precise meaning for Public Goods and Services—PGS, which includes, *inter alia* physical and intangible infrastructure, the right of property and its protection, law and order, freedom of contract and occupation, a stable and growing economy, good education, regulated banking and insurance industries, and even welfare services and other economic advantages. These PGS enable us to function, both as firm—while producing income—and households who consume such goods and service for achieving their desired standard of living. These PGS are commensurate with the taxpayers' economic ability. Therefore, taxpayers with a higher economic ability derive greater benefit from the PGS than those with a low economic ability. The benefit principle is the justification for pure taxes. The ability is a very practical, efficient, and workable criterion for the benefit we enjoy as a return on our tax payments. Eventually ability can be used for applying both horizontal and vertical equity.

The same reasonings provides a free-market justification for progressive taxation. Like in the private market, low-ability taxpayers are unable and unwilling to purchase PGS that higher-ability taxpayers consent to purchase at full price.

The three possible measures of economic ability are net wealth, consumption, and income. Their advantages and disadvantages are discussed at length.

The impact of the tax provisions on people's behavior is quite an enigma. We do not know yet how taxes increase or decrease work supply. Politicians, especially those who are supported by powerful groups, often preach that the effect is negative, while ignoring the "income effect" of taxes. Further, who bears the tax burden remains elusive. This is because it can be shifted from the taxpayer to their employees, suppliers, or customers, according to the supply and demand for the provided good and services' elasticity.

Once we laid down the theoretical aspects of interdisciplinary field of tax law, we begun to present the current tax system in detail.

First we offer description and analysis of the major tax bases and other mandatory payments. Since Value Added Tax (VAT) has become part of tax systems around the world, any international transaction must consider its implications, its concepts, and its major traits. The VAT system is introduced, here, even though it has not (yet) been integrated into the Federal tax system in the U.S.

The concept of property taxes and their relation to income tax is mentioned briefly. Though the national Social Security and Health Insurance programs deserve much deeper consideration, they are presented here concisely, since they are financed by mandatory payments, which are provided due to market failure caused by the adverse selection phenom. We do not discuss the various states' sale taxes.

We deal with the taxation of Wealth Transfer—Estate, Gift, and Generation Skipping Transfer Taxes. Should transfer payments be taxed at all? What is the basis for the argument that such a tax is actually double taxation? Does that argument have any merit? Alternatively, would it be more sensible to cancel this tax with all its loopholes and generous exemptions, and integrate it efficiently with income tax?

We discuss the major alternatives for personal tax bases that can measure the taxpayer's ability: Net wealth, Consumption, and Income; their advantages, and disadvantages. We realize that the major differences between these bases is mainly a matter of timing. Since the value of an asset is measured by the present value of the future income it produces, net wealth tax, as is true for any other property tax, is on the taxpayer's future or potential income. Since income from its sources side is equal to its uses, i.e. current and future consumption i.e. current saving, then consumption can be measured as income minus saving. A consumption tax has some real advantages over income tax, but those advantages can also be achieved by some modifications to income tax. Furthermore, the personal tax may in fact be a hybrid system composed of some combined income tax and consumption tax traits.

Most countries, including the U.S., choose income as the personal tax base.

The U.S. courts rejected the British narrow-schedular system but also refrained from adopting the Comprehensive Tax Base, which followed the Haig-Simons formula, i.e. income equal to its uses: consumption + savings. The courts disapproved of the IRS's attempts to include imputed income (57) within the definition of income. Thus, the case law definition for Income has been formulated by the Supreme Court as follows: [u]ndeniable accessions to wealth, clearly realized, and over which the taxpayers have complete dominion". Furthermore, the courts gave the realization requirement (103) a broad interpretation, which allows the consumption of gains from appreciated assets to be free of tax. In addition, the legislature has provided numerous exemptions from "Gross income", including gifts, estates and inheritances, and significant amounts of Tax Relieves and Incentives (TRI)—exemptions, deductions, and tax credits—which are elaborated on throughout the book.

The discussion of the U.S. income tax system is conducted in two stages. The first discusses the economic definition of the term Income as signifies economic ability. Accordingly, we see that personal consumption—current and future trough current saving—and business saving—i.e. investment—should be included within the income tax base. This allows us to better understand some of the complex problems with the current income tax system.

The second stage presents the methodological model we developed for use in analysing the U.S. tax system. The model has 11 steps, starting with the U.S. definition of income and ending with various some aspects of tax collection.

A Summary of the model:

1) We examine the differences between the economic definition of the term income with the IRC definition of "Gross Income.

2) We sort the major categories of gross income utilizing the traditional factors of production: real capital and human capital. The first classification draws the distinction between capital gain or losses, which is a product of disposition of factor of production, and the current income which is produced by using of the factors of production. To refine the distinction, we offer an accurate analysis that presents the causes of the formation of capital gains or losses resulting from a change in the capitalization of the future stream of income that the property is expected to generate in the future. The other major classification relates to the various categories of ordinary income: active-earned income of firms—businesses and household, whether employees or self-employed; passive income such as interest, rent, dividend and any other type of earning that does not require taxpayers to significantly use their human capital and the unique category—passive activity income. This classification enables us to understand the rationale for significant amounts of provisions and rules that apply in different ways to different categories of income.

3) We introduce the U.S. taxation of transnational transaction. Two major issues are dealt with: tax jurisdiction and the prevention of double taxation and double non-taxation.

4) We discuss income quantification. This stage is required mainly when the taxpayer receives compensation in kind instead of money, or when a transaction is between related parties or when it is tainted as a sham or an artificial one.

5) We move on to the determination of the Adjusted Gross Income—AGI—i.e. subtracting allowable deductions and exemptions, by statutory provisions—"Above the Line Deductions"—that mainly describe ordinary and necessary expenses, including net operating losses.

6) AGI is an interim stage. Additional deductions are taken to determine the final tax base—the "Taxable Income". Three types of deductions are used while moving from AGI to Taxable Income: Itemized deductions or Standard deductions and the suspended personal exemption. We noted that the common ground for those deductions, is that they deviate from the pure and analytical tests for the cost of the income producing process. Instead, they represent a combination of personal consumption, nondiscretionary expenses, social concessions, administrative efficiency, and indirect cost of the taxpayers' ability to produce earned income. In addition, most of the expenses that are attributed to passive income, are deducted Below the Line as miscellaneous itemized deductions.

7) We briefly discuss the basic rules of tax accounting—including Income Reporting, cash, and accrual methods of reporting, and special rule regarding inventory.

8) We describe the various type of tax units, including several types of corporations and partnerships. We focuses on individual, married couple, head of household and the way the tax code relates to the taxpayers' dependents.

9) We explain tax Computations: The statutory progressive tax rates that relate to the taxpayer's taxable income presents only the tentative tax due. Various tax credits, which are subtracted from the statutory rates further reduce the final tax liability. Tax credit is a dollar-for-dollar reduction of the tentative income tax due. We discuss three type of tax credits: A "simple", a "Phased-out" and a "negative tax (EITC)" credits. In addition, we discuss the Alternative Minimum Tax, its concept, goals, and rates.

10) and 11) The last two stages deal with tax payments, tax collection and criminal offences. We believe that they are too technical and practical and exceed the scope of this book. Though very important and meaningful we should not bother the readers of our book.

Final Words

This is where our journey ends.

Ultimately the book evolved to include two dimensions, a professional-educational one and social one.

In the professional-educational dimension we presented a comprehensive analysis of the current tax system. We introduced the various theories, justifications and multiple sources of the interdisciplinary field that make up tax law. For this purpose, we laid a solid foundation designed to impart an inclusive, wholistic, and comprehensive knowledge and understanding of tax laws, to students, lawyers, accountants, judges, social scientists, policymakers and other interested readers. We elaborated upon the sources of the tax laws, their logic and purposes, the proper ways of analysis and interpretation of tax legislation.

Our major justification for taxation is based on the following assumptions.

a) Pure tax is based on the taxpayers' **consent** and the **benefit** principle.

b) Public Goods and Services (PGS) provided by the government include recognition of legal and constitution rights, and their protection, basic liberties such property rights, as freedom of movement, contract and occupation, law and order, regulated banking and insurance industries, supervised education etc.

c) Household and firm benefit from the same PGS.

   Households—by consuming such services.

   Firm—by using those services for their income production. Just to illustrate: a good education system and welfare services provide skillful labor and capable customers prevents delinquency, criminal activity and violence, and ensures that economic activity is not interrupted.

d) The Joint Project approach suggests that the wealth creation process consists of using three factors of production: real capital, human capital, and social-public capital. The public, through the government, invests in social-public capital (tangible and intangible) and is entitled to receive a return on its investment—the tax that the firms pay to their investors. Accordingly, tax is a profit-sharing mechanism between the income producers and the government.

The distinction between "pure" taxes and regulatory taxes is intended to facilitate judicial review of legislation that grants tax reliefs or imposes Pigovian taxes. These two measures, which sometimes violate constitutional rules, are aimed to regulate the appropriate prices of private GS according to free market principles, in cases where certain activities or production create positive and negative externalities.

As we researched and studied the professional dimension, the social dimension was gradually revealed. We asked whether the current tax system follow the Constitutional authorization to levy taxes "*to pay the Debts and provide for the common Defense and general Welfare of the United States*".

A grim story unfolds: Over the years, the U.S. tax system deviated from the basic cannons of good tax. It has become a complex, complicated, non-transparent system to the point of violating the public's right to know and is often incomprehensible to the taxpayers. The process did not develop on its own. Powerful factors have deliberately complicated the tax system. Itis a product of a "Coalition" of interested greedy groups, comprised of the wealthiest members of society together with anxious and ambitious politicians that are consistently dependent on fundraising. Such a coalition finds the means to provide considerable tax reliefs that are economically worth billions. Alarmingly if they were granted directly by the government, these benefits would not stand up to public scrutiny and would not receive the approval of the public representatives in the legislative bodies. The contribution of these tax benefits (including a narrow tax base, an ineffective tax on wealth transfer, generous tax reliefs and incentives) to the devastating phenomenon of unimaginable social gaps is quite obvious. A phenomenon that is not only non-ethical and morally wrong, it also undermines economic efficiency, and sustainable economic growth, , and the very concepts that the U.S. had strived to achieve from its original inception.

If President Clinton was right when he used the phrase "It's the Economy, stupid", then maybe we should have title our book "It's the Taxes, s. . .". Indeed, the tax system reflects the current state of the democratic system. It is not transparent; it is deceptive; it ignores the constitutional right of freedom of information and avoids an accurate and thorough analysis of the scope and substance of the property rights. It overlooks the fact that it is not possible to produce wealth, accumulate it and protect it without the contribution of the PGS. Further, the current tax system does not serve its major intended purpose. Rather than achieving the stated constitutional purpose of tax, i.e. financing the elected governments' expenses spent on the public's wellbeing and interest, it has been turned into a regulatory system. Its seems that the legislature and administrations have completely forgotten the basic idea of modern democracy—that taxes should be paid with the taxpayers' consent and in accordance with the benefit principle, which eventually also justifies progressive tax system. We followed the claim, that the benefit and the economic ability are not in contradiction but rather complement each other. Accordingly, the ability to pay is a practical yardstick for the benefit that firms and households derive from the existence of a democratic government.

The current U.S. tax system has turned into complete chaos. It contains a large-scale collection of provisions designed to regulate social, commercial, and economic activities through Pigovian taxes and tax reliefs and incentives, which is often far from the "four canons of good tax" criteria. Paradoxically, rather than being based on principles of equity and fairness, which eventually lead to sustainable economic growth, it erodes progressivity and has become a regressive system, with lower tax rates applied to capital, and higher rates applied for labor. The stated purpose of Tax Reliefs and Incentives are aimed at assisting deprived families, but in reality most of those reliefs are not available to the lower class. Such a regressive system enhances social gaps and hurts social solidarity and economic growth [pp. 90–95]. Indeed, it seems that the tax legislators are often detached from their voters and their true public missions.

Admittedly, the tax system is inseparable from the modern democratic system, with its flaws and deficiencies becoming clearer and more evident as the data accrues.

A valiant observation of this process would lead to the conclusion that there is no chance for any U.S. politician to be elected if they do not have tremendous economic resources. Either a candidate is exceptionally wealthy or can raise the needed funding from those who have the means. Consequently, one may wonder whether the candidates finds themselves obliged to serve the public or, rather the donor's goals and interests. To paraphrase G. Stigler and, more recently, J. Tirolle: the public hardly has a chance. Those who should be held accountable for economic crises find ways, with the government's support, to dodge responsibility. Thus, the public pays the price by additional tax burdens on the middle classes, or through a failing austerity policy. Under such a system, the cornerstone of democracy and free market, i.e. meritocracy, is eroded; social solidarity is lost, exploitation of human rights rise, and genuine economic efficiency is lost.

At its current state, the original purposes and rationales of U.S. political human rights have been forgotten, or worse, are being abused. We are trained to worry about personal property rights, while ignoring the fact, which has been identified by economics professor Joseph Stiglitz and other leading scholars, that a small amount of people (1%?) covets the public's property. The right to privacy has turned into a shield for villains. False freedom provides an opportunity for powerful groups to exploit weak segments of society and enables huge social gaps. The interpretation of the political and artistic freedom of expression have grown to an unacceptable constitutional permission for brainwashing and twisting the genuine consumers' will, as predicted by various scholars: Canadian scholar Marshall McLuhan, American economists Thorstein Weblen and John Kenneth Galbraith, and others. This has also been recently demonstrated by Akerlof and Shiller. Indeed, we tend to ignore the fact that when Adam Smith conceived the invisible hand, commercial advertising, marketing, and branding industries hardly existed, compared to the monstrous dimension in our era.

The original purpose of constitutional rights was to protect the weak individuals and minority groups, who are generally the natural target of oppression and abuse by the majority. In reality, two and a half centuries later, we are witnessing a destructive process of distortion, perversion and twisting of these rights: the right to private property has become a permission for capital owners and powerful groups to covet public property; the citizens' right to freedom of speech and the public's right to know have become a license for advertisers to brainwash the public and manipulate its will and desires; the personal right to privacy also received a commercial and economic dimension in modern days, which enables it to serve as the shield of the villains. Indeed, the justified concept of constitutional protection of the individual from a possible majoritarian tyranny has developed into a sociological phenomenon of individualism, which has gradually turned into selfishness.

Globally, the ethical aspects of Adam Smith's Wealth of Nations and the famous Lockean provisos have been thrown out, abandoned, or simply ignored. Especially in the U.S., modern economics have drawn away from the "worldly philosophers" and instead now concentrate on profit maximization. The concepts and advantages of commonwealth, solidarity, mutual responsibility, and collectivism have been deserted. Greed and economic success have taken the center stage.

How did the American society, founded on social values of solidarity and "commonwealth", come to a state of dangerous polarization? We aim to detect the prominent causes for the phenomenon in which a significant number of American academics, politicians and various parts of the public turned their backs on the very principles that served as inspirational upon the birth of the American nation. Among other factors we should realize that something bad has happened to economics in American academia. Instead of dealing with the general welfare, the American economic academy, with the generous support of research foundations with overt or hidden interests, began to study the economy of profit maximization. Evidently, academics and researchers from departments of economics, mathematics and exact sciences, were tempted and indeed were drawn by graduate schools of business administration.

Public education was marginalized; it had been assigned in many states to the lower classes. The other classes prefer an expensive private education while enjoying some tax advantages—a process that undoubtedly increases social gaps.

The ethical principles, social solidarity, Commonwealth, collective well-being and the right to pursuit happiness of each and every person, and other original and sincere concepts of free market and competition are the cornerstone of the American nation. Yet, when scrutinized, a different image emerges: a harsh, cruel, and selfish capitalism grew in the U.S. It distorted and twisted the principles of the invisible hand into a system where the government provides in various ways substantial privileges through three events in the late history of the country.

The last resort of human rights, namely the Judicial Branch operates slowly, at high costs, to the extent that it may discourage those without the means to reach its gates. The courts have become almost inaccessible to those who most need the protection of their rights, despite the blessed Pro Bono work and the legal aid clinics in most law schools. Even worse, the process of appointing judges and Justices, which was originally entrusted to elected public servants—the President and the Senate—is in fact uprooted. Powerful organizations, such as the Federalist Society, and individuals who were never elected by the public, now play a leading role in determining the political orientation of the courts in general and the Supreme Court in particular.

Even noble goals of encouraging sincere philanthropic activity are thwarted and abused by improper use. It enables wealthy taxpayers to gain significant influences on our public life—backed by the Supreme Court with its decision in the Citizens United case—under the guise of tax-deductible contributions. The concept of the free market and free competition, which recognizes market failures that a responsible government is supposed to address, has been replaced by a harsh and cruel capitalist concept according to which the government grants privileges to the capital and its owners.

These are some major symptoms. The interesting question is what are their sources? We identified a few:

In the early 1940s, commercial television burst into our lives. The wizards of branding, marketing and sales have made us, as described clearly by John Galbraith and others, desire and crave public and private goods and services that we do not want and certainly may not need.

Later, during the "Healing Revivals" of the 1950s, Protestant Christian and Evangelist churches—originating from the Calvinist movement—spread the quasi belief that materialistic and financial successes indicate divine affection; that the God's "chosen", measured according to material success and wealth, and will inherit heaven!

The third devastating occurrence took place during the term of President Ronald Reagan. His anti-social activity and the tremendous growth of social gaps during his era are well known. His tax policy was based on two quasi-scientific, populist, and eye-catching beliefs: the Laffer curve, which suggests that high tax rates reduce the state revenues, and the Trickle-Down argument that offers the idea that it is appropriate to encourage the creation and accumulation of wealth because the wealth leaks down and eventually reach the weaker strata. Both concepts have long been disproved and refuted. Rather, as Stiglitz demonstrated, wealth trickles up. Nevertheless, the impact of these two beliefs on the influential decisions-makers still predominates.

A paramount expression of this trend may be found in the academic studies of economics. In most textbooks in public finance courses, their scholarly authors are satisfied with presenting simple proof for the conclusion that almost any type of tax results in an excess burden/deadweight, which means that the tax amounts collected by the government are lower than the loss of the aggregate welfare of all taxpayers. Yet, some of those books neglect to mention that in return the taxpayers receive valuable goods and services; that the simple yet major requirement of a good tax system is that a tax ought to be efficient and ought to increase the total wellbeing of the community's members, not to decrease it; that the value of the public goods and services that the elected government provides must be higher than the deadweight loss. And so, every year, tens of thousands of Economics graduates enter the job market with their brains washed by the simplistic and shallow idea that tax is evil.

The major traits of democracy are general elections where any citizen has basic human rights, rule of law, equal protection, and the right to vote. There is no doubt that the democratic system these days is not at its peak. We may refer to one of the cleverest scholars in the history of humankind—Plato. The Greek mathematician, physicist, and philosopher described the four stages of the collapse of the democratic system. Perhaps we did not pay enough attention to the fact that Western society passed the tyrant juncture and moved—alas for a short period—to the "philosopher-king" era, and then entered the oligarchy stage. Maybe we took for granted that anybody has the right to be elected, no matter the candidates' motives, ambitions, commitments, and abilities. We wisely put a limit on the duration of the president's term, but we forgot to put a similar boundary on the members of the House of Representatives and the Senate.

The last centuries have enabled us to recognize the important concepts of human dignity, genuine freedom, and the need to protect the sole individual and the minority from various forms of oppression. We should not give up those rights. However, we should reconsider the election system, adapt it to the new reality and pursue a system that will assure that the elected government will be obliged to its only goal—to serve the public's interests; to be free from any type of pressure, both of self-interest as well as of powerful groups. In order to reach this desired state a severe and thorough revision ought to be performed regarding the current tax policy and fiscal legislation.

If Professor Jeffrey Sachs is right with his prediction regarding the growing social gaps due to the technological revolution, then the solution might be a new **fiscal policy**. One growing idea might be a Universal/Unconditional Basic Income (UBI), which is emerging lately as a realistic policy, not only in Northern Europe but also in the Netherlands, Scotland, and India. The idea, which was conceived in the 16th century by Thomas More in his book "Utopia", is quite simple: the government grants every citizen/resident an unconditional monthly fixed amount of money, which is aimed to ensure that every member of society has sufficient income to meet their basic needs and to provide human dignity. The grant should be taxed. For those whose grant is their only income, they would be below the taxable income due to the personal exemptions or standard deductions. The others would pay income tax according to their level of economic ability and the progressive tax rates. Preliminary findings indicate that such a universal grant has an insignificant impact on work supply, if any.

These are some basic examples of the growing urge to deal with the greatest danger to the Western democracies in their current form: the unbelievable increase in social gaps.

When the policymakers stop ignoring this danger and the political and moral leaders succeed in assimilating the social, moral, and economic distortion inherent in unlimited greed, it will also be possible to offer efficient measures and tools to improve our social and economic life.

Appendix A

PRESENT AND FUTURE VALUE TABLES

TABLE A1: PRESENT VALUE OF A SINGLE PAYMENT

The table presents the present value (for today) of 1 U.S. Dollar that will be received in the future (the table presents periods of 1 to 15 years; the left column indicates the numbers of the years; the upper row indicates the various interest rates ranging between 0.5% to 10%). For example, if we need to know the present value of \$100 received at the end of the fifth year, where the "discount/interest rate" is 6%, we find that it equals \$74.70 (the mathematical computation is $100/1.06^5$). If the interest rate is only 0.5% the present value would be \$97.50.

From a reverse point of view, if we invest the amount of \$74.70 today with 6% interest, we'll receive at the end of the fifth year the amount of \$100. The math formula is as follows:

$$PV = FV * \left[\frac{1}{(1+i)^n}\right]$$

Where PV = Present Value

FV = Future Value (1 in this case)

i = Interest Rate

n = Years

Rate Year	0.5%	0.75%	1%	1.5%	2%	3%	4%	5%	6%	7%	8%	9%	10%
1	0.995	0.993	0.990	0.985	0.980	0.971	0.962	0.952	0.943	0.935	0.926	0.917	0.909
2	0.990	0.985	0.980	0.971	0.961	0.943	0.925	0.907	0.890	0.873	0.857	0.842	0.826
3	0.985	0.978	0.971	0.956	0.942	0.915	0.889	0.864	0.840	0.816	0.794	0.772	0.751
4	0.980	0.971	0.961	0.942	0.924	0.888	0.855	0.823	0.792	0.763	0.735	0.708	0.683
5	0.975	0.963	0.951	0.928	0.906	0.863	0.822	0.784	0.747	0.713	0.681	0.650	0.621
6	0.971	0.956	0.942	0.915	0.888	0.837	0.790	0.746	0.705	0.666	0.630	0.596	0.564
7	0.966	0.949	0.933	0.901	0.871	0.813	0.760	0.711	0.665	0.623	0.583	0.547	0.513
8	0.961	0.942	0.923	0.888	0.853	0.789	0.731	0.677	0.627	0.582	0.540	0.502	0.467
9	0.956	0.935	0.914	0.875	0.837	0.766	0.703	0.645	0.592	0.544	0.500	0.460	0.424
10	0.951	0.928	0.905	0.862	0.820	0.744	0.676	0.614	0.558	0.508	0.463	0.422	0.386
11	0.947	0.921	0.896	0.849	0.804	0.722	0.650	0.585	0.527	0.475	0.429	0.388	0.350
12	0.942	0.914	0.887	0.836	0.788	0.701	0.625	0.557	0.497	0.444	0.397	0.356	0.319
13	0.937	0.907	0.879	0.824	0.773	0.681	0.601	0.530	0.469	0.415	0.368	0.326	0.290
14	0.933	0.901	0.870	0.812	0.758	0.661	0.577	0.505	0.442	0.388	0.340	0.299	0.263
15	0.928	0.894	0.861	0.800	0.743	0.642	0.555	0.481	0.417	0.362	0.315	0.275	0.239

TABLE A2: ACCUMULATED PRESENT VALUE OF A SERIES OF EQUAL PAYMENTS RECEIVED IN THE FUTURE

This table represents the accumulated present value of a series of equal payments received in the future during a number of years ranging between 1 and 15 years; the upper row indicates the various interest rates used for capitalization, ranging between 0.5% to 10%. For example if an asset is estimated to produce a constant annual amount of \$100 for 5 years with zero salvage value after the fifth year, and the interest rate is 10%, then the asset's value at the first year is equal to \$379.10. If the interest rate is only 0.75% the asset's value goes up to \$488.90. The math computation is as follows:

$\frac{100}{1.1} + \frac{100}{1.1^2} + \frac{100}{1.1^3} + \frac{100}{1.1^4} + \frac{100}{1.1^5} = 379.1$, and: $\frac{100}{1.075} + \frac{100}{1.075^2} + \frac{100}{1.075^3} + \frac{100}{1.074^4} + \frac{100}{1.075^5} = \$488.9$

Where PV = Present Value

C = Cash flow per period (1 in this case)

n = Years

i = Interest Rate

Rate Year	0.5%	0.75%	1%	1.5%	2%	3%	4%	5%	6%	7%	8%	9%	10%
1	0.995	0.993	0.990	0.985	0.980	0.971	0.962	0.952	0.943	0.935	0.926	0.917	0.909
2	1.985	1.978	1.970	1.956	1.942	1.913	1.886	1.859	1.833	1.808	1.783	1.759	1.736
3	2.970	2.956	2.941	2.912	2.884	2.829	2.775	2.723	2.673	2.624	2.577	2.531	2.487
4	3.950	3.926	3.902	3.854	3.808	3.717	3.630	3.546	3.465	3.387	3.312	3.240	3.170
5	4.926	4.889	4.853	4.783	4.713	4.580	4.452	4.329	4.212	4.100	3.993	3.890	3.791
6	5.896	5.846	5.795	5.697	5.601	5.417	5.242	5.076	4.917	4.767	4.623	4.486	4.355
7	6.862	6.795	6.728	6.598	6.472	6.230	6.002	5.786	5.582	5.389	5.206	5.033	4.868
8	7.823	7.737	7.652	7.486	7.325	7.020	6.733	6.463	6.210	5.971	5.747	5.535	5.335
9	8.779	8.672	8.566	8.361	8.162	7.786	7.435	7.108	6.802	6.515	6.247	5.995	5.759
10	9.730	9.600	9.471	9.222	8.983	8.530	8.111	7.722	7.360	7.024	6.710	6.418	6.145
11	10.677	10.521	10.368	10.071	9.787	9.253	8.760	8.306	7.887	7.499	7.139	6.805	6.495
12	11.619	11.435	11.255	10.908	10.575	9.954	9.385	8.863	8.384	7.943	7.536	7.161	6.814
13	12.556	12.342	12.134	11.732	11.348	10.635	9.986	9.394	8.853	8.358	7.904	7.487	7.103
14	13.489	13.243	13.004	12.543	12.106	11.296	10.563	9.899	9.295	8.745	8.244	7.786	7.367
15	14.417	14.137	13.865	13.343	12.849	11.938	11.118	10.380	9.712	9.108	8.559	8.061	7.606

Appendix B

TABLES OF FUTURE VALUE

TABLE B1: FUTURE INCOME OF A SINGLE PAYMENT

This table presents the future value of 1 USD that is invested for a certain period (between 1 and 15 years) for a different rate of return (0.5 to 10% interest). The left column indicates the numbers of years; the upper row indicates the various interest rates. For example: If \$100 is invested today for 8% compound interest, the amount received after 8 years is \$185.10. With 1% compound interest return, the amount received will be \$108.30.

The math computation is $100*1.08^8=185.093$; and $100*1.01^8=230.45$.

The math formula is as follows: $FV=PV*(1+i)^n$

Where FV = Future Value (1 in this case)

PV = Present Value

i = Interest Rate

n = Years

Rate Year	0.5%	0.75%	1%	1.5%	2%	3%	4%	5%	6%	7%	8%	9%	10%
1	1.005	1.008	1.01	1.015	1.02	1.03	1.04	1.05	1.06	1.07	1.08	1.09	1.1
2	1.010	1.015	1.020	1.030	1.040	1.061	1.082	1.103	1.124	1.145	1.166	1.188	1.210
3	1.015	1.023	1.030	1.046	1.061	1.093	1.125	1.158	1.191	1.225	1.260	1.295	1.331
4	1.020	1.030	1.041	1.061	1.082	1.126	1.170	1.216	1.262	1.311	1.360	1.412	1.464
5	1.025	1.038	1.051	1.077	1.104	1.159	1.217	1.276	1.338	1.403	1.469	1.539	1.611
6	1.030	1.046	1.062	1.093	1.126	1.194	1.265	1.340	1.419	1.501	1.587	1.677	1.772
7	1.036	1.054	1.072	1.110	1.149	1.230	1.316	1.407	1.504	1.606	1.714	1.828	1.949
8	1.041	1.062	1.083	1.126	1.172	1.267	1.369	1.477	1.594	1.718	1.851	1.993	2.144
9	1.046	1.070	1.094	1.143	1.195	1.305	1.423	1.551	1.689	1.838	1.999	2.172	2.358
10	1.051	1.078	1.105	1.161	1.219	1.344	1.480	1.629	1.791	1.967	2.159	2.367	2.594
11	1.056	1.086	1.116	1.178	1.243	1.384	1.539	1.710	1.898	2.105	2.332	2.580	2.853
12	1.062	1.094	1.127	1.196	1.268	1.426	1.601	1.796	2.012	2.252	2.518	2.813	3.138
13	1.067	1.102	1.138	1.214	1.294	1.469	1.665	1.886	2.133	2.410	2.720	3.066	3.452
14	1.072	1.110	1.149	1.232	1.319	1.513	1.732	1.980	2.261	2.579	2.937	3.342	3.797
15	1.078	1.119	1.161	1.250	1.346	1.558	1.801	2.079	2.397	2.759	3.172	3.642	4.177

TABLE B2: FUTURE VALUE OF ACCUMULATED SERIES OF PAYMENTS RECEIVED IN THE FUTURE

This table presents the future value of an accumulated series of amounts invested each year during a certain period (1 to 15 years) where the interest rate ranges between 0.5%–10%.

For example: if we invest an annual amount of $1,000 every year for 12 years and rate of return is 6%, we receive at the end of the twelfth year $16,870. If the rate is 0.75%, the total amount after the 12th year will be $20,141.

The computation is:

1,000+(1,000*1.06)+(1,000*106$^{2)}$)+(1,000*106^{3}). . .+(1,000*1.06^{11})=16,870;

1,000+(1,000*1.0075)+(1,000*1.0075^{2}) . . . .=$1,250.80

The math formula is as follows:

$$FV = C * \left[\frac{(1+i)^n - 1}{i}\right]$$

Where FV = Future Value

C = Cash flow per period (1 in this case)

n = Year

i = Interest Rate

Rate Year	0.5%	0.75%	1.0%	1.5%	2%	3%	4%	5%	6%	7%	8%	9%	10%
1	1	1	1	1	1	1	1	1	1	1	1	1	1
2	2.005	2.008	2.01	2.015	2.02	2.03	2.04	2.05	2.06	2.07	2.08	2.09	2.1
3	3.015	3.023	3.030	3.045	3.060	3.091	3.122	3.153	3.184	3.215	3.246	3.278	3.310
4	4.030	4.045	4.060	4.091	4.122	4.184	4.246	4.310	4.375	4.440	4.506	4.573	4.641
5	5.050	5.076	5.101	5.152	5.204	5.309	5.416	5.526	5.637	5.751	5.867	5.985	6.105
6	6.076	6.114	6.152	6.230	6.308	6.468	6.633	6.802	6.975	7.153	7.336	7.523	7.716
7	7.106	7.159	7.214	7.323	7.434	7.662	7.898	8.142	8.394	8.654	8.923	9.200	9.487
8	8.141	8.213	8.286	8.433	8.583	8.892	9.214	9.549	9.897	10.260	10.637	11.028	11.436
9	9.182	9.275	9.369	9.559	9.755	10.159	10.583	11.027	11.491	11.978	12.488	13.021	13.579
10	10.228	10.344	10.462	10.703	10.950	11.464	12.006	12.578	13.181	13.816	14.487	15.193	15.937
11	11.279	11.422	11.567	11.863	12.169	12.808	13.486	14.207	14.972	15.784	16.645	17.560	18.531
12	12.336	12.508	12.683	13.041	13.412	14.192	15.026	15.917	16.870	17.888	18.977	20.141	21.384
13	13.397	13.601	13.809	14.237	14.680	15.618	16.627	17.713	18.882	20.141	21.495	22.953	24.523
14	14.464	14.703	14.947	15.450	15.974	17.086	18.292	19.599	21.015	22.550	24.215	26.019	27.975
15	15.537	15.814	16.097	16.682	17.293	18.599	20.024	21.579	23.276	25.129	27.152	29.361	31.772

Lexicon: Initial Explanations and Definitions

By an alphabetical order

	The Term	Explanation and Definition	Pages
1.	***Ability to Pay; Economic Ability***	A possible criterion for measuring equality between taxpayers is the taxpayer's economic ability to contribute their fair share to the public cost of goods and services. Another common and accepted criterion is the benefit the taxpayers enjoy from the public goods and services which are provided by the government (14). As discussed in the book these two criteria are not in contradiction but rather complement each other. The more ability taxpayers have, the greater benefit they receive from the public goods and services provided by the government. Hence, economic ability is an adequate and more practical measure of the said benefit. Economic ability can be measured through income (38), (58), consumption (25), or savings (111).	
2.	***Accounting: Financial; Management and Tax Accounting***	A set of professional rules and regulations aimed to provide financial information and interpretation about an organization's business and financial activities. **Financial accounting** is one branch of accounting involving processes by which financial information about a ***firm*** (47) is recorded, classified, interpreted, and communicated. It is an important tool for public use like shareholders, financial institutions, government agencies, and any other bodies that need to receive reliable information about a firm. **Management** accounting is used within an organization to provide the needed information to the managerial level. **Tax accounting** is a set of special accounting rules, based on financial accounting and adapted to the tax system (118).	
3.	***Admissible Bookkeeping Records***	A set of accounting records adapted to the tax system that are part of the tax accounting rules. They follow the ***Tax Commissioner*** (123) regulations approved by the tax inspectors or by the district courts. Once the taxpayers' bookkeeping is "***admissible***", the burden of proof to justify the ***tax assessment*** (119) is upon the ***tax assessing officer*** (15).	
4.	***Administrative Law***	An area of public law that governs the activities of administrative agencies of local and central governments. A common definition is that	

administrative law is based on four components: (1) it defines the authority and structure of administrative agencies; (2) it specifies the procedural formalities employed by agencies; (3) it determines the validity of agency decisions; and (4) it defines the role of courts and other governmental entities' review in relation to administrative agencies. The administration's actions and decisions are subjects to Judicial review (70), both in issues of its authority and jurisdiction to act ("What"), and its discretion in exercising its powers and authorities ("How").

5.	***(Asset) Adjusted Basis***	The original basis (purchase price, cost or fair market value when possessed by the taxpayer) of an asset plus any increases for improvements and any decreases for depreciation or amortization (20, 21) deductions taken by the taxpayer during the holding period.
6.	***Adjusted Gross Income (AGI); Modified Adjusted Gross Income (MAGI)***	AGI is calculated by subtracting from the individual's Gross Income (54) the income tax code's enumerated deductions (30). AGI serves as a benchmark that determines certain other allowable deductions or tax credits (125). Modified Adjusted Gross Income is computed by adding back certain deductions to the AGI.
7.	***Advance Tax Payments***	In addition to the general system of tax withholding (136), self-employed taxpayers and corporations are also subject to an advance tax payment system during the taxable year. The advance tax payments are usually calculated as a percentage of the periodical turnover of the business minus tax withheld. During the taxable year self-employed taxpayers have to pay ten advance payments and corporations have to pay four. Failure to pay those payments on time may result in civil and criminal procedure and interest charges. At the end of the taxable year the taxpayers submit their tax returns and if the total advance tax prepayments are higher than the final tax liability, the taxpayer receives a tax refund.
8.	***Adverse Selection***	The tendency for insurance to be purchased only by those who are most likely to need it, raising its cost and reducing its benefits. Asymmetric information (75), especially in health and social insurance, creates a market failure (75). In a free market (49), health and social insurers may lose their customers if trying to set their premiums regardless of the

potential costumers' personal conditions and information, which the insurer does not possess, while the insured does. Healthy candidates avoid insurance and fewer customers buy it. Consequently, the premium goes up, hence more healthy people find the new premium too high and refrain from buying it and give it up; a new price increase occurs, and the vicious circle leads to the collapse of the program. As a result, most Western societies provide a national compulsory health and social insurance.

9. ***Alternative Minimum Tax—AMT*** An alternative to the general income tax system. Since the general system provides various Tax Reliefs and Incentives (TRI) (84), which significantly reduce the taxpayer's tax liability, the alternative minimum tax (AMT) is a sort of safety net, which aims to prevent the total erosion of the "regular" income tax base, especially by high income taxpayers, who use significant amounts of TRIs. The computation of AMT is done by adding significant deductions and some tax credits back into the taxpayer's AMT. In fact, taxpayers have to compute both their regular taxable income and the AMT, apply the applicable tax rates and pay the larger amount of tax.

10. ***National Annual Budget*** Funds for federal government programs for the following year must be authorized by legislation. The long process of such legislation begins with the president's budget request to Congress, which then delivers it to an "authorized committee". The request includes spending and revenue proposals, along with policy programs that contain budgetary aspects. The budget resolution serves as a guideline for the actual appropriation and provides Congress with some control over the process. All new discretionary spending requires authority through enactment of annual "appropriation bills" or "continuing resolutions". In case a resolution is not passed for a certain year, the previous year's resolution remains in force, thus no new programs can be funded. If Congress fails to pass all of the appropriations bills before the start of the fiscal year, it could pass a "continuing resolution", which will provide temporary funding of government operations. Failure to appropriate funds results in a partial "government shutdown".

11. ***Annuity*** A financial product sold by financial institutions, including insurance companies, that accept

deposited funds from an individual and then, at a certain date, the institution pays out to the depositors a stream of continuing payments with a fixed total annual amount or an amount that increases at a fixed percentage each year. Annuities are primarily used as a means of securing a steady cash flow during the depositor's retirement. The calculation of the annual payments is based on a "**sinking fund**" method, meaning that at the end of the annuity period, the depositor receives back all of the deposit (one may regard annuity as a "reversed mortgage"). Any payment received by the depositors contains two components: one is the accumulated interest on the initial deposit and the other one is the initial investment recovery. For income tax purposes the former is taxable whereas the latter is tax free since it is capital recovery (20) that does not represent any accretion to wealth. There are several types of annuities. The two major ones are a fixed time annuity, which is a terminating stream of fixed payments over a specified period of time, and a Life annuity, which provides payments for a person's lifetime.

12. ***Arm's Length Transaction*** — A transaction in which the buyers and sellers of a good or service act independently and have no relationship with each other so the transaction is based on the good or service's fair market price. The concept is used in income tax law in order to determine the true taxable income of a controlled taxpayer, owned or controlled directly or indirectly by the same interests.

13. ***Artificial Transaction; Sham Transaction; Aggressive Tax Planning*** — When a business transaction or plan does not have earning a profit as its objective but is performed merely for tax motives. It is a transaction without a real and sincere economic substance, except for tax consideration. In such a case the tax authorities have a special power to disregard the legal/formal aspects of the transaction and tax it according to its economic substance, i.e. to analyze the transaction by preferring **Substance over Form**. In addition, artificial/sham transactions may result in civil and criminal tax procedures. Furthermore when a taxpayer schemes certain measures that may result in aggressive tax planning they have to notify the tax authority and provide full disclosure of the device.

14. ***Benefit Principle*** — A possible criterion for measuring equality and differences between taxpayers is the benefit that

taxpayers enjoy the public goods and services that the government provides. As noted, **Ability to pay** (1), is a good indication for the said benefit, and it is more practical measure for the benefit principle

15. ***Bookkeeping; Book Records*** Any firm conducting business has to follow the tax commissioner's regulations regarding bookkeeping, which aims to enable tax-must officers to easily inspect the business income/expenses records. The regulations are suited to several categories of business activities. It is the taxpayer's responsibility to find the most suitable category and follow the regulations requirements. Simple businesses can use ***single-entry bookkeeping*** records (16), whereas the standard for most businesses is the ***Double Entry system***. Failure to maintain appropriate sets of ***admissible bookkeeping*** (3) may result in civil and criminal procedures.

16. ***Bookkeeping Accounting Double/Single*** Most businesses maintain a record of all transactions based on the double-entry bookkeeping system. This system is the basis of the standard system used by businesses and other organizations to record financial transactions. Each transaction results in at least two entries: one account/column being debited, and one account/column being credited, with the total debits of the transaction equal to the total credits. Small and simple businesses maintain only a single-entry system that records the "bottom line" activity; income received, expenses, cost of assets, etc.

17. ***Capital Asset*** Property that generates more property, usually ordinary income (91); a factor of production. It is recorded on the ***firm***'s (47) balance sheet as capital. ***Capital assets*** include machinery, real property, financial assets, and other kinds of property whose productive power lasts more than one year. The cost of a capital asset is called a capital expense (30, 21) and a gain/loss stemming from selling such an asset is usually a capital gain/loss (18). Capital assets can be either tangible or intangible, depreciable (31) or non-depreciable.

18. ***Capital Gain/Loss*** Gain stemming from selling a capital asset (17), contrary to ordinary income (91) which is a product of using such an asset. Note that ***Capital Gain/ Loss*** should be distinguished from ***Capital Income***, since the latter is ordinary "passive" income which stems from using capital assets,

whereas income that stems from using human capital is active-earned income (36). Generally speaking capital gain (loss) is the difference between the amounts received—in cash or money's worth, which is usually the fair market value—and the adjusted basis (5) of the asset sold): its original cost adjusted to some changes that took place during the holding period. There is an ongoing debate whether ***capital gain*** should be taxed as ***ordinary income***. For the last decade or so, the general, yet questionable tendency has been to use significantly reduced rates for ***capital gain***. ***Capital Loss*** is usually offset against ***Capital Gains*** and not ***Ordinary income***. In certain cases ***Capital losses*** offset against ***passive income*** (36), which is subject to a reduced tax rate as well.

19. ***Capital Gain and Ordinary Income Distinguishing*** — One of the most bothersome and sometimes complicated tax problems is the distinction between capital gains and ordinary income (91) when the profit/loss is created from selling a property not within business activity. In contrast to the traditional case law definition, we offer a more accurate approach: capital gain (or loss) is the difference between the present value (97) of the total future stream of income expected to be generated by the asset, as determined at the time of purchase, and the present value of the total future stream of income expected to be generated by the asset, as determined at the time of sale. Furthermore, ordinary income is created by internal activity, i.e. it is created by the taxpayer's use of factors of production (financial or human capital) (45), whereas capital gain stems from activity external to the taxpayer, created by market forces; it is a result of **selling** factors of production instead of **using** them.

20. ***Capital Recovery, Depreciation; Amortization*** — A component of revenue that represents the recovery of the initial principal/investment, contrary to the current profit an asset produces. In other words, when an investment is made and it begins to produce a stream of revenue/income there is a need to identify the profit and repayment of the initial investment (11). The difference between the value of the investment at the beginning of the year and at the end—the annual decline—represents the annual ***capital recovery***. It is not part of the taxpayer's profit. The allocation between the profit and the capital recovery is extremely important for

income tax purposes since only the profit is taxable. Note that when a taxpayer makes an investment—a capital expense (21), its cost is part of the taxpayer's income from the usage side (61), hence it is not immediately deducted; only the annual decline should be. The annual decline is the cost of the income production process. It reduces the amount of the taxpayer's initial wealth; hence it should not be taxed. Typical examples are an annuity (11) or an investment in a machine that loses its original value during the income production process. The periodical receipts for those investments have two components: recovery of the initial investment and a profit, a taxable income. The former is capital recovery which should not be taxed under the income tax system. It does not represent a gain. Hence it is deductible as **Amortization**—usually for intangible assets, or **depreciation** for tangible assets (21). Both terms represent the same concept of capital recovery. Note that there are types of investments whose income production process is not connected with a constant and periodical decrease in value such as land or corporate shares. In such a case there is no ***capital recovery***, and no ***depreciation*** or ***amortization*** allowed; in case such assets lose their value and are sold at a loss, which can be offset against other capital gains.

21. ***Capital Expense; Depreciation; Amortization; Spreading Prepayments***

Accounting rules require ***matching*** (76) the income to those expenses spent in order to produce it. When a ***firm*** (47) purchases a ***capital asset*** (17), or prepays expenses for several years in advance (i.e. ***capital expense***), part of the payment is an investment (or saving some future payments), hence it is not fully deductible immediately in the same ***taxable year*** (138). Yet part of the outlay is for an income producing purpose for that year and should be allowed. The common way to allocate capital expense to each taxable year is by "spreading" it out over the years it serves to produce income. Usually such spreading is done by statutory regulations that set the annual ***depreciation/ amortization*** (20) deductions, which represent the annual ***capital/cost recovery*** (20), which are based on the estimation of the asset's productive lifetime. A straight-line depreciation is the accepted method. When the legislature's aim is to provide tax incentives it offers "***Accelerated depreciation***" so the capital expense is deducted at a higher rate across a shorter period. As for human capital, one may argue that the annual payments for pension plans are sort of human capital depreciation; Most income tax systems provide various deductions for pension plans' deposits, or tax exemptions for the pension payments.

22. ***Casualty and Theft Losses*** — A special deduction, allowed by a statutory provision, for a loss that arises "from fire, storm, shipwreck or other casualty, or from theft". The courts have often restricted the term "other casualty" to extraordinary, nonrecurring losses that go beyond the average or usual losses incurred by most taxpayers in day-to-day living.

23. ***Claim of Right*** — A doctrine which was developed by the judicial branch: it states that income received by a taxpayer under a claim of right and without restriction should be included within their Gross Income even if they have to return it in the future or are not entitled to retain it, or are still to be adjudged liable to restore its equivalent. The doctrine has lost significant force over the years, mainly due to some new legislation.

24. ***Constitutional Law; Human Rights, Constitutional Interests*** — ***Constitutional law*** is the study of the Constitution, which is the framework for the government's authorities, powers, activities and limitations. Its major purpose is to limit or define the authority and procedure of political bodies, including the legislatures—both Federal and local. The Constitution sets the country institutions such as the legislative, the executive, and the judicial branches, their jurisdiction, authorities, limitations, the way they are elected or nominated, etc. The Constitution, through its various Amendments, elaborates the recognized ***Human/ civil rights***, which are aimed to protect individuals and minorities from the oppressive power of the majority. The courts have the power to review—"judicial review" (70) any piece of legislation or governments' actions in light of a court's interpretation and discretion and void them if they violate the Constitution.

25. ***Consumption, Discretionary Power to Consume*** — From an economic point of view, we work, earn, give up our leisure time, spend and save in order to reach and maintain our desired standard of living; to satisfy our wants to consume now or in the future, be it by purchasing goods and services and

32. ***Discount Rate*** Interest usually is paid at the end of a time period. Yet it can be calculated at the beginning of the period; a process called discounting, which is a process of finding the present value (97) of an amount of cash at some future date.

33. ***Due Process*** A Constitutional requirement (the Fifth Amendment) that the government must respect all of the legal rights that are owed to a person according to the law of the land. It gives individuals a varying ability to enforce their rights against alleged violations by governments and their agents. Due process has served as a significant means for Judicial Review (70), as placing limitations on laws and legal proceedings, in order to define and guarantee fundamental, sometimes procedural fairness, justice, and liberty. The origin of the concept is British and it is found within the fifth and fourteen Amendments of the U.S. Constitution.

34. ***Double/Single Bookkeeping Accounting*** Most businesses maintain a record of all transactions based on the double-entry bookkeeping system. This system is the basis of the standard system used by businesses and other organizations to record financial transactions. Each transaction should have at least two entries: one account being debited and one account being credited, where the total debits must equal the total credits. Small and simple businesses maintain only a single-entry system that records the "bottom line" activity; income received, expenses, cost of assets etc.

35. ***Double Taxation on International Activity; Relief from Double Taxation; Foreign Tax Credit*** There is no unified income tax system around the globe. Hence, due to the different ***tax Jurisdictions*** (130), rules adopted by different states, the same income of the same taxpayer might be subject to tax in more than one jurisdiction. Based on principles of equity and efficiency, a common conclusion is that such double taxation is undesirable and tax systems have developed several ways to prevent it.

36. ***Earned/Active Income; Capital/Passive Income*** Income is usually classified into two major categories, according to the factor of production (45) used. ***Earned income*** uses human capital (labor, personal services). When real/physical capital is used it produces ***Capital/passive income***, such as rent, dividends, and interest (86). The distinction is not clear and sharp. Actually, most incomes are of a mixed character and when needed the income is classified according to its major attributes. For

example: when a self-employed auto mechanic provides services her income is a combination of using human capital (labor) but also a return of her real capital investment in the business: physical structure, machinery and stock in trade. Yet her income is most likely considered as earned income.

37. ***Earned Income Tax Credit (EITC) (Negative Income Tax) Refundable Credit*** A Federal government subsidy for low-income **working** individuals and couples with children in the form of a tax credit (125), which aims to provide incentives to work. Usually tax credits only reduce the tax amounts owed. Yet the EITC, which is also called "negative income tax" is refundable; meaning that the eligible taxpayers receive funds from the government. For very low income earners, the EITC increasingly phases in and then stays flat at a given amount that is supposed to provide a dignified standard of living. As the recipients' income continues to grow, the subsidy decreases gradually and eventually phases-out (82).

38. ***Economic Income; Income as a Tax Base*** There are several dimensions to the definition of economic income. The basic and most common is "any accession to the taxpayer's ability during the time period". As is discussed throughout the book [pp. 147, 157–170, 187–205], there are several concepts and approaches to defining the term Income for Income tax purposes in light of the four canons of good tax system (34).

39. ***Economic Policy*** The government's policy, which should be reflected by overall actions that the central government takes in the national economic systems. The major components of economic policy are monetary policy (77) e.g. setting interest rates (64) or regulate the amount of money in the domestic market. Fiscal policy (48) e.g. the volume of the national budget (and its deficit); Social policy; Tax policy; and the Labor market and the unemployment rate. Such policies are influenced by political concepts and beliefs. Conservative economists believe that the role of the government should be minimal and limited only to national security, recognition of property rights, freedom of contracts, and their enforcement; economic stability and economic growth; and the provision of public goods and services (101) when the private-free market (48) fails (49, 75) to provide them in an efficient way. Others believe that the government should deal with social policy issues as well, such as distributive justice and concepts of a welfare state, national

health insurance and education. No wonder the former believe in small governments and lower taxes and the latter believe in bigger governments and higher taxes.

40. ***Economies of Scale*** Benefits, advantages and efficiencies that a firm possesses due to their large size.

41. ***Elasticity*** **Income elasticity of demand** measures the responsiveness of the demand for goods and services to a change in the income of the people demanding the good, ceteris paribus. It is calculated as the ratio of the percentage change in demand to the percentage change in income. For example, if, in response to a 10% increase in income, the demand for a good increased by 20%, the income elasticity of demand would be 20%/10%=2. **Cross-elasticity of demand** or **cross-price elasticity of demand** measures the responsiveness of the demand for goods or services to a change in the price of other alternative goods or services. **Price elasticity of supply (PES** or **Es)** is a measure that is used to represent the responsiveness, or elasticity, of the quantity supplied of goods or services to a change in their price.

42. ***Equity; Vertical Equity; Horizontal Equity*** One of the prominent requirements for a good tax system is that the tax should be fair. The common criteria for fairness in taxation are principles of equity, which, contrary to multidimensional concepts such as justice, is a measurable uni-dimensional concept. Under Vertical equity different taxpayers should pay different tax payments; under Horizontal equity equal taxpayers should pay equal tax payments. Needless to say the determination of who are equal taxpayers and who are different is not simple. Based on our major premises the yardstick is the benefit the taxpayers enjoy from the government's provision of public good and services which is in accordance with their economic ability.

43. ***Exemption*** A tax provision which excludes the item exempted from taxation. Exemptions are subtracted from the taxpayer's Gross Income (54) in computing their Adjusted Gross Income (6), which eventually reduces the final tax owed. Exemption—as a ***deduction*** (30)—produces a ***tax saving*** (133) equal to the amount of the exemption multiplied by the ***Marginal Tax Rate*** (74).

44. ***Externalities*** Externality is an impact (positive or negative) on any third party not involved directly in a given economic transaction or activity. Participants in an economic activity do not necessarily bear all of the costs or enjoy all of the benefits of the activity. In a free market economy (49), this means that too much or too little of a good may be produced and consumed in terms of total cost or benefit to society e.g. a behavior of one person which affects the welfare of others that they do not pay the full market price for. For example: negative externality occurs when manufacturers who create air pollution compel costs or bad health on others while making use of public air. A Positive externality takes place, for example, when a certain manufacturer sets up a factory in a remote area and as a result all local residents benefit from the declined unemployment and the increased economic and social opportunities in the area. Pigovian taxes (93) are one possible solution that is meant to shift the cost of the negative externality to the manufacturers or to the user of the products that creates the negative externalities. On the other hand TRI (127, 131) might be considered as the public sharing the price of positive externalities caused by a taxpayer.

45. ***Factors/Means of Production: Real, Human And Social Capital*** The income or wealth production process involves factors/means of production. In our time we refer to three factors: Real Capital (money, real property-land); Human Capital (Labor, time, private knowledge, skills and abilities); and Social Capital (national physical infrastructure; law and order, rule of law, recognition of property and its protection, efficient economic markets, civilized society, social solidarity, good research and educational systems, skillful labor force etc.).

46. ***Fee, Duty, Toll*** As opposed to general taxes, these are payments which are paid to public agencies for a direct consideration: specific public goods and services provided by the administration. Although their rates are set by the administration (usually by by-laws or regulations) they are supposed to reflect as much as possible their market price and should not serve as disguised taxes.

47. ***Firm*** Any economic agency or body (regardless of its legal structure and entity, such as individual, partnership, corporation etc.). It is also referred to as the nexus of contracts, an economic organization which aims to produce income for its "members".

The firm produces income and distributes it to its members: salaries and wages to the employees; dividends and profits to the owners of its equity; interest to lenders; rent, royalties etc. to other property owners. Contrary to households (56), firms as such do not consume but produce income; they do not save but invest. In rare cases firms produce income and let their members consume it.

48. ***Fiscal Policy*** **Fiscal policy** refers to the government's social, economic and national security policies, usually reflected in the annual national budget, and its goals and means. Fiscal policy attempts to influence the national economic systems through changes in government spending and revenue (taxes).

49. ***Free Market; Free Economy*** A **free market** (as contrasted with controlled or centralized) is an economy in which prices of goods and services are set by an "invisible hand" (a term offered by A. Smith) based on the mutual free consent of sellers ("supply") and buyers ("demand"). In a free market buyers and sellers do not coerce or mislead each other nor are they coerced by a third party [government's regulation or monopoly power (79)]. In a free-market economy prices play the major role in quantifying the value of the goods and services. Due to competition between the various suppliers, prices tend to decrease, and quality tends to increase for the benefit and the welfare of the consumers and eventually the whole community. The underlying assumption is that humans act in order to improve their quality of life and their welfare; to increase their satisfaction. Individuals know better than anybody (including the government) what their best interests are. They know that the most prominent attribute to our life is a chronic shortage of goods and limited resources that we must to compete over in order to get. This competition is done through the pricing process and using alternative prices for each good. Every purchase comes with the recognition that we give up other goods. Our individual decisions—such as to work or enjoy leisure, what to purchase and for what price—provide higher welfare than the ones provided by a central governmental decision. Firms (45)—the private sector—are supposed to provide us goods in order to satisfy our needs and to set up the prices according to our demand and their ability. There is a general consensus that in reality there is no pure free market due to Market Failures

(75). The major causes for market failure are, *inter alia*, lack of symmetric information; the preference of the interests of pressure groups and large organizations over the public interest and its benefit; the lack of competition resulting from cartel agreements between large entities that allows them to control significant parts of the market and to set prices in a monopolistic manner (78); and, generally speaking, absence of coerced transactions or conditions on transactions.

50. ***Free Rider*** The definition of public goods and services (101) demonstrates the Free Riders problem. Most of us tend to consume the highest amount of goods and services for the lowest cost we can. Since the benefit to one individual from public goods or services is non-excludable, they may be tempted to enjoy it without paying its cost. Since the goods or services are also non-rival, not too many neighbors would notice or care. Essentially, a society with no free riders does not need any tax system at all. Everyone pays for what they "buy" from the government and consume it. Alas, there is no such country. We need to have taxes due to the free riders among us. As long as there is only a small number of free riders, society can survive. The problem begins when rational (yet short-sighted) members realize they can get along easily without sharing the public burden, and their number grows. If society allows free riders to evade their duty of paying their contribution to the public goods and services' cost, it won't be able to provide them, or the obedient members will be required to pay a much higher price. Life experience tells us that one of the most efficient tools to prevent or reduce the phenomenon of free riders (besides education) is to charge the public mandatory payments i.e. taxes alongside assertive collection enforcement.

51. ***Future Value*** The reversed calculation/process of **present value** (97): when we calculate the value of a present cash amount for the end of the period in the future, invested in a given interest rate (64). E.g. $300 today is worth $330 after 1 year, or 363 after 2 years, if the compound interest rate (64) is 10% [300*(1.1^2)].

52. ***Goodwill*** There is no single definition, clear, conclusive, and acceptable to the term business goodwill. It might be regarded as the business' reputation. The common approach is quite technical: the portion of

the market value of a business which is not directly attributable to its tangible assets and liabilities; the difference between the market value of a firm and the sum of the fair value of its net tangible assets. Another approach emphasizes the client's attraction attribute: goodwill is the value of the business asset that makes clients revisit the business. A more accurate analysis draws a distinction between goodwill and some other intangible assets that contributes to the firm's fair market value such as "turnkey" value, the quality of the firm's work force, and its customer base.

53. ***Gross Domestic Product (GDP)*** The total value of all goods and services produced within a country, regardless of the nationality of the firms. It is one of the ways of measuring the size of domestic economic activity in a given period (usually a year). It is also considered the total Value Added at every stage of production of all final goods and services produced within the country. One of the basic ways to measure GDP is by using the expenditure method: GDP = Private Consumption + Firms' Investment + Government spending + the balance of exports-imports. Another way is to add up all the goods and services produced within the country during a year. One problem with measuring GDP is the underground/unreported economy which is usually used for tax evasion or money laundering purposes. Lately, a significant number of scholars doubt whether GDP is a good indication for economic growth, let alone that it implies the quality of the economic wellbeing of the country's citizens and residents.

54. ***Gross Income*** As opposed to the economic definition of income (38) Gross Income is a term of art, which is defined in the IRC (65) that refers to income from all different sources (such as trade or business, employment, interest, capital gains, income from retirement accounts, alimony etc.) minus the statutory exemptions (43). It is the first step of the process that establishes the taxpayer's income tax liability. The next step is computing the taxpayers' "Adjusted Gross Income"—AGI (6), which is adjusted downward by various deductions (30) towards the taxpayers' Taxable Income (137).

55. ***Gross National Product (GNP)*** GNP is one of the ways of measuring the size of national economic activity. It is defined as the total market value of all final goods and services produced by the local firms (regardless of where the

production takes place, within or outside of the country) in a given period (usually a year). It is also considered the total Value Added at every stage of production of all final goods and services produced within by the domestic firms. The tendency today is to use GDP (53) instead.

56. ***Household*** An economic and not a legal term. Personal economic activity may be classified into two major categories: income **production**, and current and future **consumption**. As a general rule the income producing process is done by Firms (47), and the personal consumption (and personal saving) is allocated to Households, individuals and families.

57. ***Imputed Income*** A term of art which refers to ***income in kind*** (62) where there is no transaction with another party. Instead, the owner of a durable asset consumes the income that the asset produces through the annual self-use of the asset. E.g. we consume dwelling services while using our own apartment. From an economic point of view the apartment produces annual income. When we rent it out, we receive income. When we use it for our own accommodation we receive "imputed income". Under the current law imputed income is not part of Gross Income (54), hence it is not taxable. Note that in an exchange transaction with another party the income-in-kind is subject to income tax.

58. ***Income*** The most common tax base in Western societies is personal income, which is supposed to serve as a good measure for the taxpayer's economic ability. As was mentioned [pp. 147, 157–170, 187–205], there are several approaches for defining income for tax purposes (38).

59. ***Income Assignment; Assets Transfer; Expenses Attribution*** Under a progressive tax system (98) there is a significant incentive to assign income from taxpayers or activities that is subject to higher tax rates than taxpayers or activities that are subject to a lower tax rate, especially if they share common interest. Mom, who has a high income, will be happy to assign part of her income to her daughter, a student whose income is small and whose marginal tax rate (74) is low. The same result may be achieved if she transfers her daughter an income-producing asset. In the business world related firms are anxious to forward income of a gaining firm to a losing firm. The tax law contains provisions that

eliminates or limits the effects of such assignments and transfers (13).

60. ***Income from the Sources Side*** One simple way to measure a taxpayer's income is to take into account the return/proceeds from using factors of production (45) or selling them with a gain. In the U.S. income also includes transfer payments (141) unless they are specifically exempted.

61. ***Income from the Usage Side*** Income can be measured also from the usage side. Income can be used mainly for three purposes: For current consumption (42); for future consumption i.e. saving and investing; and for income producing activities. Hence Annual "Taxable income" (137) equals Consumption + Saving & Investment. This simple equation helps us analyze and understand complicated income tax problems such as ***business expenses*** (30), depreciation (20, 21), and tax accounting issues (118).

62. ***Income in Kind; Notional Income; Notional Expenses*** The return/compensation the taxpayer receives in an exchange transaction where no money changes hands. E.g. a worker is ready to provide personal services to a farmer, in return for renting a piece of land "for free". Each party uses its factors of production and receives a return. Both have income in kind. Furthermore, each of them also pays for the goods (land) and services (labor) they acquire. Farmer pays by providing the worker the right to use her land, while she buys labor services from the Worker. Worker buys these rights and pays for them with the labor services he provides. Both have income in kind and expenses in kind, in money's worth.

63. ***Inflation; Inflation Linkage; Inflationary Differential and Adjustments*** A phenomenon when there is a general increase in the price of goods and services over a period of time. Traditionally it is caused in times when the quantities of the goods and services remain unchanged, and the monetary means (money supply) grows. More money competes over a given amount of goods and the prices go up. Inflation is measured as the percentage rate of change of the Consumer price index, (CPI) which measures nominal consumer prices. In some countries all debts and financial assets are "linked" to the inflation rate. As a result, a lender receives from a debtor not only interest (64) but "linkage differentials" as well. The same occurs when the debt is linked to a foreign currency. The linkage

difference is nominal, yet it is an illusionary gain, not a real one, since such nominal gain does not increase the consumption power of the taxpayer. The same conceptual problem arises when an asset is sold during a time of inflation. E.g. an asset was bought for $1,000 and sold after a certain period of time for $1,250. If during the holding period there has been inflation of 15%, the nominal gain should be classified into two categories: $150 is inflationary/unreal gain and only $100 is considered real economic gain. The tax systems have developed several ways to cope with such phenomena. In the U.S. most of the amounts elaborated in the Code are adjusted to inflation.

64. ***Interest; Compound Interest Linkage Differential***

(simple) Interest is a fee paid by a debtor to a creditor for using the latter's money. Interest can also be thought of as "rent on money". The interest is calculated as a percent of the principal amount during a time period (daily, monthly, or annual). The interest rate reflects the price for using the money, and the risk the creditor takes by lending the money to the specific borrower. The higher the risk, the higher the rate. In addition, interest also reflects the anticipated inflation (63).

Compound interest is the method of adding accumulated interest during the agreed period of time (daily, weekly, monthly semi-annual or a year) back to the principal, so that new interest is earned on interest that was already accumulated/added to the initial principal, so the next period the interest is earned on the aggregate new principal. For example: assuming the interest rate is 10% and the principal is $100 per year, then at the end of the first year the principal and the interest amounts adds up to $110. If the loan is for 3 years and the interest is paid at the end of every year the interest annual payment is $10. If the interest is compounded and paid at the end of the 3rd year the creditor should receive 100+10+11+12.1=$133.1. The math equation is simple [FV=PV(1+i)n; where FV = future value, PV = present value, i = interest rate, and n = amount of time periods]. For practical reasons we tend to use time value and present value tables which can be found as Appendix A and B [pp. 343–347]. The "market interest rate" is used for present value (97) and future value calculations.

65. ***Internal Revenue Code;***

The **Internal Revenue Code—IRC**; more formally, the **Internal Revenue Code of 1986, as**

	Income Tax Regulations; Revenue Rulings	**amended** is the main body of the U.S. Federal statutory tax law organized topically, including Income Tax, Payroll Tax, Gift, Estate and Excise Taxes. The Internal Revenue Code is published as Title 26 of the United States Code (USC). **Treasury Regulations** are the tax regulations issued by the United States Internal Revenue Service (IRS) (66). These regulations are the Treasury Department's official interpretations of the IRC and are one source of U.S. Federal Income Tax law. Code Sec. 7805 gives the United States Secretary of the Treasury the power to create the necessary rules and regulations for enforcing the IRC. The regulations are organized according to the IRC sections that regulations interpret and explain. **Revenue Rulings** are public administrative rulings by the IRS that apply the law to particular factual situations. A revenue ruling can be relied upon as precedent by all taxpayers. Revenue rulings are published in the Internal Revenue Bulletin (Rev. Bull). They are part of second tier authorities and generally do not prevail over legislative regulations, courts' decisions and tax treaties.
66.	***Internal Revenue Service—IRS***	The *IRS* is a *U.S.* government agency; a bureau of the Department of the Treasury that is responsible for tax collection, tax law enforcement and the administration of the IRC (65). The head of the agency is the IRS's Tax Commissioner (123).
67.	***Inventory (Stock in Trade)***	A list of final goods or raw materials held available in stock by a business—a trader or a manufacturer—designated to be sold to customers [p. 302]. Cost of inventory, including cost of production, is not deducted when purchased or paid but only when sold. There are several methods to calculate profit from inventory sold. The most common method is to calculate the value of the goods sold minus the "cost of goods sold". This is simple where the cost of the goods is constant. Where it varies, there is a need for evaluation, especially for merchandise that cannot be traced individually. The most common accounting methods are FIFO (first in-first out) and LIFO (last in-first out). FIFO regards the first unit that arrived in inventory as the first one sold, whereas LIFO refers to the last unit arrived as first one sold. The gain from inventory is calculated as follows: beginning/ opening inventory (at the first day of the year) plus

purchase and production (during the year) minus closing inventory (value of the inventory within the business at the last day of the year). If the closing inventory decreases for any reason, the business suffers a loss which is deductible (72) even though no realization took place. On the other hand, if the closing inventory went up, and there is an economic gain, it is not taxed until it is sold in the future, since it is unrealized gain.

68. ***Itemized Deduction*** The amount paid by individual taxpayers which is allowed in arriving from the AGI (6) to "Taxable Income" (137), such as home mortgage interest expenses, some medical expenses, property taxes, and charitable contributions. Itemized deductions which require record keeping, receipts and other proofs that they are actually paid, are "below the line" (of AGI). Taxpayers have the option to claim instead the Standard deduction (113).

69. ***Joint and Separate Tax Returns*** Each U.S. taxpayer must submit an annual tax return to the IRS (66) As a general rule each individual who has taxable income is a separate taxpayer. Under the U.S. system, legally married couples are free to decide whether to file a ***joint return***, which in general terms combines both incomes and, roughly speaking enjoys lower tax rates. Yet in some cases the system causes a marriage penalty to certain couples and in some other cases it provides "marriage bonuses" to others, depending on the couple's earning circumstances [p. 305]. In addition, there are two more tax returns for **head of household** and **for unmarried Singles**. The statutory tax rates for each type of tax returns are different.

70. ***Judicial Review*** Whenever there is Constitutional or administrative disputes (24) and a possible infringement of human rights, there is a need for an independent judicial body to examine the alleged violation, in order to decide whether a violation occurs and if it is justified. Such an examination is a legal decision, and accordingly should be made by a court of law. Hence the term indicates the court's jurisdiction to examine these acts, including Federal or State legislation and may declare them void when it finds that the violation is not justified.

71. ***Law; Statute*** The term "Law" has many faces. Usually, for our purposes, it refers to any legally binding norm. A legal norm may be set by the legislature (primary

legislation), by the administration (secondary legislation through regulations or orders), by courts of law, and sometimes in certain systems by customs and even practices. An act of the legislature is known as "statute". Courts make law by interpreting statutes, or by developing the legal system or by filling gaps ("lacuna") found within a statute.

72. ***Losses; Ordinary Losses; Net Operating Loss; Capital Losses*** A loss occurs when the expenses are higher than the revenues. For income tax purposes, a net operating loss (NOL) occurs when the taxpayer's business deductions (30) for a taxable year are higher than their annual taxable income. NOL may be offset by other types of income, subject to some statutory limitations, and be carried forwards and two years backwards. Hence NOL provides a ***tax saving*** (133) and in some instances may be regarded as an asset. An important distinction is between current loss and Capital Loss, which occurs when an asset's selling price is lower than its adjusted basis (18). The former may offset ***Ordinary Income*** (91); the latter is limited only against ***Capital gains*** (18).

73. ***Mandatory Payments*** We use this phrase while drawing distinction between "pure" Tax (117) and other mandatory/compulsory payments. The latter are established by authorized government agencies, in order to finance specific goods or services, and are usually paid by a designated taxpayers. Some are PMP (93), others are TRI (131), Mandatory payments (73) should be subject to a more careful and strict judicial review (70) than pure taxes [pp. 19–27, 39–55, 71].

74. ***Marginal Tax Rate; Average Tax Rate*** Under a progressive tax system (54) a ***marginal tax rate*** (in percent of the tax base) is the tax bracket that applies to the last dollar of the tax base ["taxable income" (137) in case of income tax]. Marginal tax rate rises when the taxpayer's income increases and falls when taxable income decreases. An ***average tax rate*** is the ratio of the amount of taxes paid to the "taxable income". To demonstrate: if the progressive tax rate are 10% for the first $1,000 and 20% for the income between $1,001–$2,500 and if the taxable income is $2,000 the total amount of tax is $300 [(1,000*10%)+(1,000*20%)], the marginal tax rate is 20% but the average tax rate is only 15% (300/2,000). If the taxable income is $2,500, the total amount of tax is $400 [(1,000*0.1)+(1,500*0.2)]; the marginal rate is still 20% and the average rate is a bit higher: 16% (400/2,500).

Thus, in a progressive tax system ***Marginal tax rate*** is usually higher than the ***Average tax rate***.

75. ***Market Failure Asymmetric Information, Monopoly; Oligopoly*** Market failure prevents a free market economy from functioning efficiently. The market does not allocate resources in an efficient way and prices are not set in the best way. Hence the general welfare decreases. Since a free market is based on competition all the transaction's parties must possess full information. Asymmetric information is one of the most prominent market failures (8) which create some distortions, like **adverse selection** (8). Other causes for market failure are **Monopoly and Oligopoly** (78), and **Externality** (44). A general and accepted idea is that when market failure occurs a governmental intervention is needed.

76. ***Matching Rules*** Matching rules are accounting rules (2) that require the taxpayer to match between the cost of the activity/investment and the income that activity produces. There are horizontal matching rules, that attribute the cost to the income of different activities during the same taxable year; there are also Vertical matching rules that attribute the cost and the activities during different years. Tax provisions that deal with ***offsetting losses*** (72) are modifications of matching rules.

77. ***Monetary Policy*** The government and the Central-National Bank policies, which attempt to stabilize the economy by controlling interest rates (64) and the supply of money, the exchange rate of the local currency and the annual rate of inflation (63).

78. ***Monopoly*** A firm that is big enough to control its product's market and is able to eliminate its competition or to enter the market and dictate its products' prices. It creates a market failure (75) and there is a need for government intervention in order to maintain free competition. An oligopoly is a situation where a few firms dominate the market and bring about highly concentrated economic power to its members, creating a similar inefficiency as created by a monopoly.

79. ***Moral Hazard*** A market failure (75) caused by the natural tendency to consume more when we do not pay the full price, i.e.; an insured person may behave in a more risky way than they would have without insurance. The same behavior may occur with public goods (101) provided by the government without a direct tag price attached.

80. ***Mutual Funds*** A mutual fund is a company that brings together money from many interested investors, and invests it, on their behalf, in stocks, bonds or other assets. The combined holdings of stocks, bonds or other assets the fund owns are known as its portfolio. Each investor in the fund owns shares, which represent a part of these assets' holdings. There are a variety of types of mutual funds: **Equity funds**, which invest in stocks and are designed to achieve high profit, yet with higher risk. **Money market funds** that invest in short-term fixed income securities, which are considered a safer investment, but with lower return; **Fixed income funds**, that buy investments that pay a fixed rate of return; **Balanced funds** invest in a mix of equities and fixed income securities; **Index funds**, that aim to track the performance of a specific index (such as S&P 500, Dow Jones Industrial average and others); **Specialty funds**, that focus on specialized mandates such as real estate, commodities or socially responsible investing. The latter may refrain from investing in companies involved in ecological hazards, alcohol, tobacco, gambling, weapons, etc.; and **Fund-of-funds** are those funds that invest in other funds.

81. ***National Income*** A general term aimed at estimating the value of goods and services produced in an economy. This is calculated using a system of national accounts or national accounting, but there is no single accepted method to do that. Today the most common one is GDP (53).

82. ***Negative Tax; Refundable Tax Relief; Phase-Out*** This happens when a taxpayer can't enjoy the tax relief (127) since their tax liability is lower than the relief, such as a tax credit, usually due to a small amount of income, e.g. when the taxpayer's tax saving (133) from tax credit is 0. Yet in order to assist the poor a possible solution is to grant a ***Refundable tax credit***, which is actually a negative income tax (37). In order to encourage the taxpayer to improve their economic situation and be able to earn enough income from labor (36) the grant diminishes gradually; it is **phased out** (94).

83. ***Net/After Tax Income; Gross-Up Income*** A significant amount of personal income is withheld at the source, usually employers who withhold the estimated income tax from their employees' salaries (136). The income received by the taxpayer after this withholding is considered net/after tax income (85). In order to calculate the before-tax taxable

income a Gross Up process should be followed. The mathematical formula is quite simple: received income divided by 1-taxpayer's marginal tax rate. E.g. A taxpayer receives $1,600 net income. Assuming her marginal tax rate is 20% her taxable income is 1,600/1−0.2→1,600/8=$2,000. Yet due to the progressive tax system this formula is not always applicable accurately.

84. ***Net Income Concept*** According to the ***Net Income Concept***, in determining ***taxable income*** (137) taxpayers are allowed to deduct only the expenses that produce their income and not TRI (131); not those spent on personal consumption or on saving or investment. Yet, tax codes are loaded with TRI (131).

85. ***Net/Disposable Income; After-Tax Income*** The amount of the income left after the tax is paid, which is disposable for consumption or saving.

86. ***Net Wealth*** A possible tax base (120) that measures the economic ability of the taxpayer as the assessed value of the total amount of assets (intangible property, investments and future stream of income) minus the taxpayer's liabilities. The principal difficulty is that such a base contains too many uncertainties. Since the value of an asset is the present value (97) of the future stream of income we need a significant amount of information which is based only on evaluations (e.g. future income, interest rate, the longevity of the asset as an income producer and its salvage value (110) at the end of its productive life). In addition, intangible property and human capital also should be taken into account, though there are a lot of practical problems with their evaluation process [p. 154].

87. ***Non-Profit; Charitable Organization*** These organizations comprise the "third sector"; nongovernmental organizations that aim to serve the public with a "no profits motive". A NPO enjoys two major tax reliefs: its income is exempt (43, 30) and contributions received are deductible (69), or provide tax credit (125), to the donor. It is a good question whether these tax reliefs are justified.

88. ***Nonrecourse Mortgage*** A loan secured by real estate, where the borrower is not personally liable to repay the amounts borrowed in case of default. The lender's remedy is that it can possess the property. In case the property value declines and is below the debt value, the borrower might abandon the property and is discharged from their liability, i.e. the lender suffers the loss.

89. ***OECD—Organization for Economic Co-Operation and Development*** An international organization established by a convention signed by 20 countries in 1964. In 2022, 38 countries compose this forum which is committed to democracy and the market economy. Its major goals are to enhance sustainable economic growth and development, employment, and standard of living in Member countries, while maintaining financial stability, in order to encourage the development of the world economy and the expansion of world trade on a multilateral, nondiscriminatory basis in accordance with international obligations. The OECD provides a setting to compare policy experiences, seek answers to common problems, strive to identify good practices, and co-ordinate domestic and international policies. It deals with economic, environmental, and social issues and aims to improve policy and implement "soft law"—non-binding guidelines and recommendations that can lead to binding treaties. It initiates a very broad array of research, which is published—mostly free of charge—on its useful and impressive internet site [https://www.oecd.org]. Collaboration at the OECD regarding taxation has produced the growth of a global network of bilateral tax treaties. In the last few years it researched and published a significant amount of recommendations which aim to prevent double taxation as well as double-non-taxation and to cope with Profit Shifting and Base Erosion and aggressive tax planning by multi-national firms, including corporations whose major business is done through the new cyber world.

90. ***Optimal Taxation, Deadweight Loss, Excess Burden*** This is a theory which is a branch of Public Finance that considers how taxes should be structured in the most efficient/least destructive distorted way with the least social costs, or to give the best outcomes in terms of social welfare. In tax policy the assumption is that any tax (beside poll tax) distorts the taxpayers' behavior thus reduces their welfare. **Deadweight loss/excess burden** is the difference between the reduction of welfare created by the imposition of a tax and the amount of the government revenue the tax produces. This theory concentrates, for some reasons, on the welfare lost and not on the benefits the government provides due to the tax it collects.

91.	***Ordinary Income; Current Income***	Gain or profit stemming from **using** (but not from selling/disposing) factors of production (45). E.g. gains from renting property, dividends (28), and compensation for personal services. A common metaphor is of the "fruit and trees": income is the fruit of a tree, while the tree is the factor of production, the taxpayer's capital/asset (17) (share, human capital, rented property etc. (18)).
92.	***Pareto Efficient; Pareto Optimum***	An economic term that implies a condition where no individual can be made better off without another being made worse off. It is commonly accepted that outcomes that are not Pareto efficient are to be avoided. An allocation is ***Pareto efficient*** or ***Pareto optimal*** when no further Pareto improvements can be made. If economic allocation/ distribution is not Pareto efficient, there is theoretical potential for a Pareto improvement—an increase in Pareto efficiency, i.e. improvements to at least one member's welfare can be made without reducing any other members' welfare. Pareto optimal relates to the **fundamental theorems of welfare economics** (146).
93.	***Pigovian Tax; Pigovian Mandatory Payment (PMP) Coase Theorem***	Named after the British economist Arthur C. Pigou, this is not really a tax since its aim is not to raise government revenue but rather to restore the true economic price of products or actions that create negative externalities (44), which are transferred to a community or its members by undesired and un-internalized behavior or activities. PMP has a dual goal: first, to internalize behavior consequences by increasing the price of the undesired product or action, in order to shift their full social-economic cost to the producers and the consumers. The other goal is to allocate its revenue to fix the damage caused to the public by the negative outcomes. Note that it should not be considered as a penalty, but rather a means to restore the real free market price of a product by shifting the un-internalized social cost. For example, consider a mandatory payment on cigarettes or alcohol (a "sin tax"), or on polluting production process. We refer to them as Pigovian Mandatory Payments or PMP. Under the "Couse theorem" (named after law and economics professor Ronald Coase), Pigovian taxes are redundant. A trade in an externality (44) should be allowed instead. I.e. the polluting producers should be able to buy the right to pollute the environment from the

neighboring population, and the free market economy (49) can take care of the problem [p. 13].

94. ***Phase out TRI*** Various statutory provisions offer TRI (131), such as deductions, credits, or exemptions, to low-income taxpayers for social reasons. Hence, once the taxpayer's income increases, the benefit is no longer justified. In that case the amount of the benefit decreases gradually up to a point that it is totally gone; it is phased out.

95. ***Poll Tax*** A **head tax**, or **capitation** levied on each individual in a uniform, fixed amount "per head". It does not depend on any behavior or activity nor on income or consumption. It is considered allegedly as an efficient tax, from an economic point of view, since it supposedly does not distort any economic behavior and is not connected to any deadweight loss (90). Yet it is considered an unethical/ inequitable levy since it totally ignores the economic ability of the taxpayers. In the U.S.A. it was used to disqualify indigents from participating in the political process. The last time such a tax was enacted in the West was during the 1990's, by Margaret Thatcher's government in the U.K. It caused some real riots and it is believed that the tax contributed to the downfall of her government.

96. ***Positive-Active and Negative-Passive Human Rights*** Traditionally, positive or active human rights indicate the government's duty or obligation to actively provide its subjects with the basic economic and social means, which guarantee a dignified survival ("Second generation human rights"). Negative-Passive human rights represent the more traditional duty or obligation to refrain from violating and infringing human rights ("First generation human rights").

97. ***Present Value, Discounting, Capitalization*** An asset's value is commonly determined based on the expected yield of future income, the estimated value of the asset as scrap at the end of its expected useful life ("salvage value") (110) and the estimated interest rate—the **Discount Rate** (32) used to capitalize future income to its present value. The determination is done by reducing each future payment/periodical yield by the appropriate interest/***<u>discount rate</u>*** for each unit of time between the date when the payment is to be valued and the date when the cash is actually paid/ received. For example: assume we have to pay $100 at the beginning of the year. Once we postpone the

payment to the end of the year with no charge, the postponement is worth around \$7.40 if the interest/ **discount rate** is 8%, since the present value of \$100 under these assumptions is around (100/ 1.08=)\$92.60. Suppose now we want to rent an office for \$200 a year paid at the end of the year. We agree to rent it for 5 years and pay the rent in advance. The total **present value** of the cash flow of 5 installments of \$200 each is \$798.60, which is calculated as follows:

$$(100/1.08+100/1.08^{2}+100/1.08^{3}+100/1.08^{4}+100/1/08^{5})=798.6$$

Or, we can use the present value's tables [p. 343].

98. ***Progressive Taxation; Declining/ Diminishing Marginal Utility of Money and Other Justifications***

Progressive taxation is when personal (income as well as consumption) tax is levied in a system when the effective marginal tax rate (74) increases as the amount of taxable income/consumption increases. The major justifications for progressive taxation are three: the old one, but not scientifically proven, is based on the assumption that the marginal utility of money decreases (one who has \$10,000 a year enjoys much better an additional \$1,000 then the one who has \$200,000 and gets the same amount). Thus, in order to achieve "equal sacrifice" those who have more have to pay a higher tax rate/percent than those who have less. The second justification is based on the assumption that the personal tax system has to improve a society's social justice and the progressive structure of the tax system reflects on society's sense of social justice. The third justification is based on the taxpayers' consent to pay taxes according to their benefit from the goods and services provided by the government. Those with low economic ability do not enjoy public goods and services (101)(such as freedom of contracts, the right to property and its protection, law and order and functional markets) to the same extent that those with high economic ability enjoy them. The former are not interested in "purchasing" these "commodities", and are neither willing nor able to pay for them, while for the latter the value of these products is high and they benefit more from them, hence they are willing to pay for them. Therefore, according to the free market principles (49), low-ability persons' demand for public goods and services is smaller and they are only willing to purchase a small amount, while those with high ability enjoy a larger amount of these products, and their demand is higher and they consent to pay for them. In other words, those with low ability benefit less from the set of goods and services and consent to pay low tax rates, while those with high ability benefit more from these products and consent to pay higher tax rates.

99. ***Proportional Tax; Flat Tax Rate*** A tax system where the tax rate is fixed regardless of the amount to which the rate is applied; A system in which all levels of the tax base (income, consumption, or property) are taxed at the same rate; a flat rate.

100. ***Public Choice*** An academic discipline within the borderline between political science and economics, which studies the behavior of voters (referring mainly to the "median voter" theory), politicians, and government agents and their interactions in the social system under given rules of political/ constitutional systems. The economic tools used in this area are, *inter alia*, measurements of utility maximization, and game and decision theories.

101. ***Public Goods*** Economists believe that the free market (49) contains a built-in mechanism that can provide the goods and services needed to humans the best and most efficient way, through a pricing process that is set by free supply and demand. Yet there are some **market failures** (75) that prevent the free markets and the pricing process from fully functioning since uncoordinated markets are unable to provide these goods and services in desired quantities. **Free riders** (50) try to avoid payment as long as they can enjoy the benefit of goods and services that are provided to the whole public anyway. As opposed to private goods and services, there are some goods and services for which the most efficient distribution is that they will be provided by the governments, by government agencies or by NPO (87) as public goods and services. The most prominent attributes to such goods and services are that they are provided to the whole public; that they are non-rival and non-excludable. Non-rival means that consumption of the good by one individual does not reduce the amount of the goods available for consumption by others; non-excludable means that no one can be effectively excluded from using that good. For example, enjoying national security does not significantly reduce the amount of national security available to other members of our community, nor can residents be effectively excluded from "using"/enjoying it. There is not one

accepted classification/definition for public goods and services. Hence different societies may approach the issue differently. In some societies health services or education may be considered private services whereas in others they may be considered public ones.

102. ***Purchase Price; Adjusted Purchase Price*** ***Capital Gain/loss*** (17, 18) is the difference between the price the seller receives and the "cost basis"—the original **purchase price**, adjusted for several (negative or positive) changes that took place during the holding period, such as non-deductible improvements or investments, certain fees, and depreciation (20, 21).

103. ***Realized Income; Income Realization*** Since the value of an asset equals the present value (26) of the future stream of income, the difference between current income and the value of the asset that produces it is due to timing. I.e. in both cases there is income; one is the current income and the other is the future, a ***potential*** income; an income that the taxpayer has the power or the possibility to earn, e.g. a lawyer that has not yet provided her professional services but she possess the skills, talent and the qualifications to provide them for compensation. Her potential is an unrealized income. Once she provides the service, she turns a potential income into a realized one. She realized her income. Realized income is real, materialized and certain. Contrary to future/potential income it is a sure thing. It does not depend on any other factors. Her clients have a real liability, a debt, to pay her income. As long as she does not perform her services, she does not realize the income. On the other hand, a tax on net wealth (86) is a tax on unrealized/future/potential income, whereas tax on income is by definition a tax on realized, current income. Note though that we should not confused between issues of **realization** and issues of **tax accounting** (132).

104. ***Qualified Dividends*** Are dividends received during the taxable year, subject to certain holding periods (less than sixty days for common stocks or ninety days for preferred stock), from domestic corporations, and from "qualified foreign corporations" i.e. foreign corporations from countries that maintain economic ties with the U.S., e.g. have a tax treaty with the U.S.

105. ***Recapture; Negative Recapture*** — ***Capital gains*** (18) are subject to significantly lower tax rates (74) compared to ordinary income (58, 74). When a ***Depreciable Asset*** (31) is disposed of at a gain, we may conclude that during the holding period the taxpayer deducted too much ***depreciation/amortization/capital recovery*** (20, 21, 30) and consequently reduced their ***Ordinary Taxable Income*** (91, 137) too much during those taxable years. Instead of going back to the previous tax years and changing the ***taxable income*** retroactively, we ***recapture*** (add back) the "missing" ordinary income to the taxable income in the year of disposal by classifying the capital gain which is attributed to the "over depreciation" as ***ordinary income*** (and subject to ordinary tax rates) instead of capital gain (and the preferred tax rates). A ***negative recapture*** is needed when the sale produces a loss due to too little depreciation deductions that were taken during the holding period. In such a case the loss should be classified as an ordinary loss—NOL (72) and reduce ordinary taxable income instead of being treated as a ***capital loss*** (18).

106. ***Regressive Tax Rates*** — A system where the tax rate decreases as the economic ability increases. As a result, the average tax rates decrease with increases in individuals' income/consumption brackets. For example: a VAT that is levied in one flat rate on household consumption should be considered as a regressive tax: a family with $10,000 income per year spends all of it on personal consumption and is subject to, say, a 10% VAT for a total of $1,000 (10% of their economic ability), whereas a family with $100,000 of income spends only $50,000 on consumption and is subject to $5,000 VAT, which is only 5% out of their economic ability.

107. ***Rent-Seeking*** — In modern times (the original term goes back to the Middle Ages era) the term refers to actions aimed to obtain income or wealth by manipulating the social or political structure in which economic activities occur, instead of creating an economic surplus. It implies extraction of uncompensated value from others without increasing meaningful economic activity and productivity. A modern example is a powerful body spending wealth on political lobbying to enhance its own influence on the government in order to increase its share of existing wealth without contributing to its creation. Thus, the

impacts of rent-seeking are quite negative: a reduction of economic efficiency through inefficient allocation of resources; a reduction in wealth creation; loss of government revenue; increased income inequality and prevention of economic growth.

108. ***Research and Development Expenses*** Expenses spent by a firm while developing new products or intellectual property. Such expenses are ***Capital expenses*** (72, 30) and as such are supposed to be deductible only when the products are produced, sold and create realized (103) Gross income (137, 54). Yet there are very good reasons to encourage ***Research and Development (R&D)*** activity and indeed most tax systems around the world allow immediate ***R&D*** deductions. Such acceleration provides significant ***TRI*** (126, 131).

109. ***Royalties*** Income paid to the owner of intellectual property/intangible assets, such as a patent, trademark, musical and literary work, etc. by the users of those assets. If the owner is the creator, the income should be classified as earned income (36). Otherwise, the income is considered passive income or even capital gain.

110. ***Salvage Value*** The actual or estimated value of a capital asset at the end of its useful life; the asset value when sold as scrap.

111. ***Saving*** It is one possible way to use income. There are periods during our lifetime that we are unable to work and produce income; too young, too old, health problems, etc. that cause inevitable fluctuation in our annual current income. Since we want to keep our standard of living relatively constant, we have to save some of our income during our productive times for rainy days. We try to average our income so it will enable us to have reasonable consumption during our lifetime. Hence saving is actually future consumption.

112. ***Source Rules*** Taxation of international activity and prevention of double taxation (and double non-taxation as well), require accurate identification of the location of the income production process. Those ***source rules*** are usually statutory and may be found in a domestic law as well as within ***tax treaties***.

113. ***Standard Deduction*** Taxable income (137) is, *inter alia*, gross income (54) minus current deductible expenses (30). Taxpayers have the option to itemize their actual expenses (68), which requires strict record keeping.

Instead, they may choose to waive their actual expenses and claim the Standard deduction, i.e. a fixed dollar amount (For the 2022 tax year, the standard deduction is $12,950 for single filers and married filing separately, $25,900 for joint filers and $19,400 for heads of household.), which does not require any bookkeeping or proofs. There are additional amounts of standard deduction for age, blindness, or both.

114. ***Standing; Locus Standi*** — A legal term of art, which refers to the ability of a party to convince the court that they should be heard by a court of law since they have sufficient connection to a legal suit or petition that will be dealt with by the court.

115. ***Surplus Consumers Surplus; Producers Surplus*** — **Consumers' surplus** (27) is the economic gain derived by consumers while they are able to purchase a product for a price that is lower than the highest price that they would be willing to pay. **Producers' surplus** is the amount that producers gain when selling a product at a market price that is higher than the least that they would be willing to sell for.

116. ***Surtax*** — A special tax bracket—usually income tax—levied on incomes that exceeds a certain amount; on top of marginal tax rate (74). It can be calculated as a percentage of a certain amount, or it can be a flat dollar amount. In some cases, it is designed to fund a specific government program, or to raise instant revenue in an emergency situation, from the top income earners.

117. ***Tax*** — The common definition of tax is "unrequited compulsory/mandatory payments collected primarily by the central government". Our approach is a bit different. According to our approach [pp. 19–27, 39–55, 71], the term "pure" tax should be used only for those payments paid by the general public to the elected government in order to **finance its public goods and services** (101). Furthermore, Pure Tax, provides a fair and sensible "***quid pro quo***" consideration via ***public goods and services*** (101), though it is almost impossible to provide solid legal evidence regarding the direct and immediate connection between the tax and the benefits that the taxpayers derive from the public goods and services they consume. Hence, the underlying assumption is that tax is based on consent, and is considered mandatory as any other debt in the

private market [p. 76]. Accordingly, a "good tax" has two prominent traits. One refers to the income production process. From this aspect, tax is a profit sharing mechanism between those who possess factors of production (45) (e.g. real capital, human capital and social capital) and are entitled to a return on their input. The Government, as the public's agent and the social capital manager, is entitled also, as an owner of a factor of production, to get its share of the income and wealth [p. 70] produced by firms (47). The other traits refers to the consumption aspect of the taxpayers. Tax, in that respect, is the price the government charges for the public goods and services (101) it provides to households (56). Other Mandatory Payments (73) are not taxes. Their aim is to set the real market price of products or activities that create negative externalities.

118. ***Tax Accounting*** Accounting (2) rules and regulations for tax purposes issued by government regulations, tax authorities, and court decisions. They include ***Admissible Bookkeeping Records*** (3). ***Tax Accounting*** is based on ***Financial Accounting*** (2) with some differences, adjustments and modifications. Tax Accounting also provides rules regarding reporting methods (132) and the type of business bookkeeping (15), for each type of business activity.

119. ***Tax Assessment*** An official individual order issued by the IRS's (66) officials to a taxpayer indicating the taxable income and the tax owed. The order may be based on the tax return or on the officer's estimations, evaluations, and information. Taxpayers have the right to protest the assessment to the district ***assessing officer*** and if rejected may appeal to the district court or to the tax court.

120. ***Tax Base*** The index or criterion the tax is levied upon. In modern times taxes are levied on economic activity or assets. The most common tax bases are ***Income*** (58), ***Consumption*** (26), and ***Net wealth*** (86). Note that there are several definitions and implications to each of these terms.

121. ***Tax Benefit Rule*** Under this rule, if a taxpayer enjoys a tax benefit in a prior year because of a deduction and in a subsequent year it was found that it should not be taken, the amount must be counted as income in that second year regardless the tax year which was

applied in both years. The same accounting rule applies in a reverse situation: If in a previous year the taxpayer, due to the claim of right (23), included a taxable item in their tax return which was found in the subsequent year that they shouldn't have included, they should deduct the same amount in that second year, regardless of any change in the tax rates. I.e. "sometime you lose sometime you gain".

122. ***Tax Break*** — This is a common term referring to any item which reduces the taxpayer's tax liability, such as exemptions, deductions, or tax credits. In this book we refer to this term as a neutral term that does not distinguish between tax incentives, tax reliefs (131) or any provision that is part of the net income concept. (84).

123. ***Tax Commissioner; Tax Commission Internal Revenue Service*** — The Governmental agency that is in charge of the activity of the tax administration. The Tax Commissioner is appointed by the Government for a given period of time and is supposed to be totally independent with their professional decisions and actions. They are the head of the Tax Commission, a part of the department of finance, and are legally responsible for supervising the ***assessing officers'*** professional activities (66).

124. ***Tax Competition*** — An economic competition among countries and nations who try to attract foreign capital and investment by offering significant tax incentives (131) such as lower tax rates, generous exemptions and deductions. Some scholars express sincere apprehension that such competition may lead to a "race to the bottom" and the elimination of the welfare state. The OECD, the World Trade Organization and the EU have joined the general effort in fighting this competition.

125. ***Tax Credit*** — An amount that reduces the amount of the Tax due (as opposed to deductions or exemptions that reduce ***Taxable Income*** (137)). The process is as follows: Once we arrive at the ***taxable income***, we apply the applicable tax rates and arrive at the tentative tax payment. Then we subtract the total tax credits the taxpayer is entitled to, and arrive at the final tax amount the taxpayer owes the government. The credit's ***tax saving*** (133) is equal to the credit amount—"Dollar For Dollar". A refundable tax credit not only reduces the tax owed to zero but also provides a monetary grant—a negative tax. Note

though that the economic value of the credit is also higher to taxpayers with a higher tax rate.

126. ***Tax Deferral*** When a ***taxpayer***'s (89) economic activity ends in profits and they have a legitimate way to postpone the tax payment, the postponement provides tax profit, due to the **time value of money** (140). The postponement may be achieved by either actual delay in income reporting or by accelerating the deduction of business expenses (21) in advance or ahead of time. Note that tax deferral is not always a benefit, e.g. when the taxpayer's **marginal tax rate** (74) in the current year is lower than the coming years.

127. ***Tax Expenditure Budget*** A concept developed in the U.S. Any tax relief which is not in accordance with the ***Net Income Concept*** (84), is actually a government grant and should be included in the ***annual budget*** (10) as a government expense. In that way the public is supposed to be informed about any deviation from ***tax equity*** (42). Experience suggests that the tax expenditure budget has not achieved its goals—to reduce the amounts and the volumes of the TRI (131) and to better inform the public.

128. ***Tax Haven*** There is no one clear legal definition of this term. In general, it is a country, state, or territory that attracts foreign individuals and legal entities by offering little or no tax liability. The U.S. Government Accountability Office elaborated its major traits: no or very low tax rates; lack of effective exchange of tax information with foreign tax authorities; lack of transparency in the operation of legislative, legal or administrative provisions; no requirement for a substantive local presence; and self-promotion as an offshore financial center (OFCs). A tax haven government's idea is to offer foreigners a tax environment that enables them to avoid paying taxes in their home countries. Tax havens do not require actual residency or business operation within their territories in order to benefit from its tax policies. Switzerland, St. Marino, Lichtenstein, Monaco, the Channel Islands, Panama, Andorra, the Bahamas, Belize, Bermuda, the British Virgin Islands, the Cayman Islands, the Cook Islands, Hong Kong, the Isle of Man, Mauritius, and St. Kitts and Nevis are famous tax havens. Some argue that the U.K. also serves as tax haven for individuals who reside in the U.K. for up to 7 years (which can be expanded by

paying a certain amount), but are not domiciled there ("non-doms"). A Non-Domiciled resident is not liable to pay U.K. tax on their foreign (non-U.K.) source income, capital gains, and inheritance as long as those amounts are not brought into the U.K. International organizations such the OECD, WTO, the EU and even the U.S. Government, have begun to fight against the growing use—and abuse—of too many multi-national corporations and wealthy individuals taking advantage of those tax havens and engaging in aggressive tax planning to avoid paying any tax anywhere.

129. ***Tax Incidence; Tax Shifting*** Economic theory suggests that the economic effect of tax does not necessarily fall on those who legally owe it or pay it but rather on those who actually bear the burden. E.g. a corporate tax might be borne by the corporation's shareholders, its employees or customers or its managers, depending on the elasticity (41) of the demand for its products. In a free market economy (49) the greatest share of the tax burden tends to fall on the most inelastic party involved—the one who is affected least by a change in prices.

130. ***Tax Jurisdiction; Territorial Source; Personal Allegiance*** The taxation rules of international activities. According to the source base, income is taxed by the state in which the income is created within its territory ("***Territorial connection/allegiance***"). According to the personal base, income is taxed by the state that maintains ***personal connections/allegiance*** with the taxpayer who produces the income, such as residence or citizenship.

131. ***Tax Relieves and Incentives —TRI*** Though the optimal tax system has to be based on the ***net income concept*** (84), in the real world tax systems are loaded with provisions that reduce the tax burden on special activities or certain taxpayers. If the purpose of those tax reliefs—exemption (43), deduction (30) or tax credit (125)—is to favor certain activities or taxpayers, they are called ***Tax Incentives***. Those provisions are included within the ***tax expenditure budget*** (127). Some of these reliefs are not necessarily incentives but instead aim to compensate taxpayers for spending money and creating positive ***externalities*** (44).

132. ***Tax Reporting; Cash Basis; Accrual Basis*** Once income is ***realized*** (103), the taxpayers face the issue of timing of tax reporting. In general terms, and leaving aside special taxpayers like

contractors with unique systems of accounting, there are two major systems for the most firms: The ***Cash Basis*** and the ***Accrual Basis***. The former is a simple practice of recording sales and expenses only when cash is actually received or paid out; it ignores promises to pay or expectations to receive money or service in the future, such as payables and receivables. The latter method is considered more accurate and is most commonly used by businesses [especially those who have inventory (67)] which report income when earned and expenses when incurred regardless of whether cash or any other method of payments are actually transferred/ exchanged hand.

133. ***Tax Saving*** The practical question the taxpayers are occupied with at the end of the day is how much tax they save from an exemption (43), deduction (30) or tax credit (125), a loss (72), or any TRI (131). As for the tax credit, the net tax saving is indeed the amount of the credit, regardless of the taxpayer's marginal tax rate—"Dollar for Dollar", unless the credit is refundable (125). The tax saving of exemption, deduction or offsetting a loss is indeed equal to the amount of these measures multiplied by the ***Marginal Tax Rate*** (74). E.g. assume three taxpayers. A's marginal tax rate is 0%, B's is 25% and C's is 50%. Exemption/deduction or loss of $1,000 produces 0 tax saving to A, $250 to B, and $500 to C. If the tax relief is a tax credit of $200 it produces the same nominal amount of tax saving to all three of them, but A won't be able to enjoy it as long as her tentative tax payment is indeed 0, unless the credit is refundable. Note though that the economic value of the credit is higher to taxpayers in the higher tax rates.

134. ***Tax Treaties*** Usually there are bi-literal international treaties between two states aimed at preventing double taxation of income, capital gains and any other direct taxes on international activities and providing exchange of information between the two states' tax authorities. For indirect taxes, such as customs, tariffs and excises there are also free trade agreements (FTAs) that eliminate tariffs on most goods traded between the contracting countries, and some multinational tax treaties such as North American Free Trade Agreement (NAFTA), and the General Agreement on Tariffs and Trade (GATT) that was replace by the World Trade Organization

agreement governments have signed already), which contain some limitation of tax competition. The OECD in its recommendations also suggests some general guidelines for multilateral agreements aimed at fighting Profit Shifting and Base Erosion phenomena.

135. ***Tax Unit*** An economic and legal unit that can be treated as a separate entity for tax purposes. A tax unit may be an individual, a married couple, a partnership or corporation.

136. ***Tax Withholding*** In order to improve the tax collection process there is a duty on employers to withhold federal income tax, Social Security and Medicare fees from their employees' wages. Failure to withhold taxes or to forward them to the tax authorities is subject to civil and criminal procedures. The tax withheld is based on estimation which is done by the information the employee provides and the size of the salary. The final tax due is computed according to the taxpayer's annual tax return. If the tax due is smaller than the tax withheld the taxpayer gets a refund. In the opposite case the taxpayer has to make up the difference. In addition, U.S. firms who pay foreign taxpayers gross income such as compensation for services, interest, dividends, rents, royalties, and annuities, have to withhold 30% of the gross amount of the payment, subject to the provisions within the pertaining tax treaty (134). In some unusual cases there is a duty to withhold taxes from passive income at a flat rate if there is a chance that the payee does not provide the payer identification means or if the IRS requests it specifically.

137. ***Taxable Income*** A term of art, which refers to the income actually subject to the tax rates. Generally, taxable income is calculated by subtracting from gross income (54) whatever deductions (30) are allowed by the IRC or Regulations (65), including business expenses, specific deductions, and itemized deductions (68) that are subtracted from AGI (6).

138. ***Taxable Year*** For practical and administrative reasons, the taxable period for individuals is a full calendar year, beginning on January 1st. Each taxable year is a separate taxable period, and the taxpayer is not allowed to transfer income, deductions, or credits from one year to another unless it is specifically allowed [e.g. NOL (72)]. All the accounting

procedures, reports, and a firm's ledgers/ bookkeeping are aimed to reflect the Annual Income.

139. ***Taxpayer*** Any ***Tax Unit*** (135) who is subject to the duty to file a tax return and to tax payment.

140. ***Time Value of Money*** "Time is money" as long as the interest rate is a positive one. Any deferral of cash payment (without charging interest) provides the debtor an economic advantage, hence: "Tax deferral is tax saved". The method to calculate the amount of the advantage is based on the concept of "present value" or "future value" (97).

141. ***Transfer Payments*** Payments in money or money's worth where the payee does not provide any consideration in economic return. ("Moving wealth from pocket to pocket"). Examples of transfer payments include gifts, inheritance, interfamily support, welfare allowance, public support for students, including scholarships and financial aid, etc.

142. ***Transfer Pricing*** A term of art, which refers to a process of setting the price for goods and services sold between related entities. Usually, it refers to transnational transactions between related corporations (parents and subsidiaries). A basic and common example is when a subsidiary company sells goods or services to a parent company (or vice versa or between subsidiaries of the same parent). Transfer pricing can be used as a means of aggressive tax planning where the major profits of the related entities is shifted to a low tax regime [probably to tax havens (128)] and their costs and expenses to higher tax regimes. Suppose Parent is a registered company in Country A, which has very low tax rates. Its Subsidiary's plant is located in Country B, which has a high tax rate. Subsidiary sells its products (either tangible, intangible, or even services) for a very low price to Parent, which sells them for their market prices. In that case such transfer pricing allocates the profits of Subsidiary to Country A. As a result the common interest of Parent and Subsidiary is achieved, unless B's tax authority intervenes and applies the doctrine of Arm's length (12). There are several ways to set the Arm's length price, which are based mainly on accounting rules.

143. ***Transaction Cost*** The price spent by a transaction's parties in making an economic exchange. There are three types. 1) Search and information costs, which are spent in

determining that the required good or service is available, which one has the lowest price and the right quality, etc.; 2) Bargaining costs that the parties spend in order to reach an acceptable agreement; 3) Policing and enforcement costs spent by the parties to make sure the other party sticks to the terms and the conditions of the agreement.

144. ***Trickle-Down Economics; Trickle-Up Economics*** A theory that claims that the rich are the job creators: once they are encouraged by the government and receive money and other benefits, including tax incentives, there will be more jobs. "If you just legislate to make the well-to-do prosperous, their prosperity will leak through on those below." A counterargument is **trickle-up** economics, i.e. "if you legislate to make the masses prosperous, their prosperity will find its way up and through every class that rests upon them". I.e. all—even those at the top—could benefit by giving more to those at the bottom. (Both quotations are from Nebraska Congressman William Jennings Bryan during the Democratic National Convention in 1896.)

145. ***Value Added*** The additional value created at a particular stage of production. It refers to the contribution of factors of production (45). The value-added method is used to avoid double counting, i.e. the counting of the same input twice. The sum of the value added in each of the different stages of production equals the value of the final product.

146. ***Welfare Economics; Fundamental Theorems of Welfare Economics*** A branch of economics that uses traditional tools and economic insights in order to integrate economic disciplines with questions of income distribution and social justice. It analyzes social welfare in terms of economic activities. Under this discipline the individuals' welfare/wellbeing/ happiness is the center of economic activities and the purpose for the aggregate community's social welfare. Until lately, some argued that there is a trade-off between efficiency and equality. The latest research suggests otherwise, that minimizing social gaps enhances sustainable economic growth. There are two known fundamental theorems of welfare economics. The first one, which is derived from Adam Smith's invisible hand metaphor, states that a competitive equilibrium leads to a Pareto efficient (92) allocation of resources under certain conditions. The second one states that an efficient allocation can be attained by a competitive equilibrium, given the market mechanisms leading

to redistribution; though, due to selfishness and free riders, at least an initial wealth distribution should be designed by the government, and then the market takes over, provided it follow the basic guidelines of such initial design.

Table of Cases

Adams v. United States, 202
Anderson, Commissioner v., 201
Arizona Christian School Tuition Organization v. WINN et al., 43
Arizona v. Winn, 48
Brushaber v. Union Pacific Railroad Co., 55
Bruun, Helvering v., 164
Burk-Waggoner Oil Ass'n v. Hopkins, 245
Butler, United States v., 8, 39
Calder v. Bull, 52
Carroll v. Commissioner, 246
Chevron U.S.A. Inc. v. Natural Resources Defense Council, Inc., 57
Cohen v. California, 12
Colorado Springs National Bank v. United States, 275
Darusmont, United States v., 52
Davis v. Commissioner, 301
Droz v. Commissioner, 49
Druker v. Commissioner, 309
Eisner v. Macomber, 159, 164, 194
Flast v. Cohen, 46
Flowers, Commissioner v., 254
Freedom From Religion Foundation v. Lew, 43
Frothingham and Massachusetts v. Mellon, 45
Furman v. Georgia, 12
Glenshaw Glass Co., Commissioner v., 135, 159
Gotcher, United States v., 201
Gregory v. Helvering, 197
Hatcher v. Commissioner, 49
Hyland v. Commissioner, 301
Independent Life Ins. Co., Helvering v., 161
Ireland v. United States, 197
James v. United States, 203
Kowalski, Commissioner v., 202
Leathers v. Medlock, 48
Lemon v. Kurtzman, 46
Lindeman v. Commissioner, 202
Mayo Found. for Med. Educ. & Research v. United States, 57
Mickey L. Worden v. Commissioner, 195
Morris v. Commissioner, 161
Murphy v. IRS, 41
National Federation of Independent Business v. Sebelius, 26
NCNB Corporation v. United States, 275
Newark Morning Ledger v. United States, 268
Nichols v. Coolidge, 52
North American Oil Consolidated v. Burnet, 199
Penn Mut. Indem. Co. v. Commissioner, 245
Poe v. Seaborn, 307
Pollock v. Farmers' Loan & Trust Company, 40, 161
Sanchez, United States v., 26
Schleier, Commissioner v., 244
Sharkey v. Wernher, 162
Silba v. Commissioner, 202
Steward Machine Company v. Davis, 128
Stratton's Independence v. Howbert, 159
Templeton v. Commissioner, 49
Texas Monthly, Inc. v. Bullock, 46
Thor Power Tool Co. v. Commissioner, 299
Turner v. Commissioner, 11, 103, 237
Valenti v. Commissioner, 253
Welch v. Henry, et al., 26, 52, 53
West Coast Hotel Co. v. Parrish, 43
Winthrop, United States v., 217
Woodsam Ass. Inc. v. Commissioner, 165

Index

References are to Pages

ABOVE-THE-LINE DEDUCTIONS
Income and Income Tax, this index

ACCOUNTING
Economics, this index
Tax Accounting, this index

ADJUSTED GROSS INCOME
Income and Income Tax, this index

ADMINISTRATIVE LAW
Generally, 56–58
Interface with constitutional law, 56
IRS powers, 57
Judicial review, 57–58
Regulations, interpretive and legislative, 57
Statute of limitations, 58
Taxpayer Bill of Rights, 58

ADOPTION EXPENSES
Tax credits, 321

AFFORDABLE CARE ACT (OBAMACARE)
Generally, 41–43, 131–132

AFFORDABLE HOUSING
Tax credits, 322–333

ALTERNATIVE MINIMUM TAX
Generally, 328–330
Basic concept, 328
Calculation, 329
Exemption from AMT income, 329
Final AMT due, 329
Tax rates, 329

BELOW-THE-LINE DEDUCTIONS
Income and Income Tax, this index

BILL OF RIGHTS
Taxpayer Bill of Rights, 58

CAPITAL EXPENSES
Income and Income Tax, this index

CAPITAL GAIN AND ORDINARY INCOME
Income, this index

CHARITABLE CONTRIBUTIONS
Deductions, 289–291

CHILD CARE
Deductible expenses, 255–256
Tax credits, 320–321

CLASSIFICATION OF INCOME
Income and Income Tax, this index

CONSENT TO PAY
Constitutional right not to pay without consent, 48–50
Welfare economics and progressive taxation, 100, 102–103

CONSTITUTIONAL LAW
Generally, 6
Administrative law, interface with, 56
Equality, constitutional right to, 51–52
Establishment Clause, 46–48
First Amendment, tax laws and, 45–48
Punitive taxes, 53–54
Quality of tax laws and adjustment to constitutional principles, 8–9
Retroactive taxes, 52–53
Tax Legislation, Constitutional Law and Threats to Human Rights, this index

CONSUMPTION TAX
Generally, 171–173
Consumption *vs.* income, 180–181
Debate regarding consumption tax, 172–173
Double taxation on capital investment, 178
Higher tax rates over short period of time, 175–178
Income, consumption vis a vis
Generally, 175–181
Consumption *vs.* income, 180–181
Double taxation on capital investment, 178
Higher tax rates over short period of time, 175–178
Neutrality of consumption tax, 178–179
Present value of consumption, 179–180
Realization, 180
Taxing labor only, 180
Neutrality of consumption tax, 178–179
Personal tax system, consumption as, 171–172
Present value of consumption, 179–180
Realization, 180
Taxing labor only, 180

CORPORATIONS
Capital gain and ordinary income, corporate retained earnings, 215–216
Global agreement on corporate taxation, 60–61
Tax Unit, this index

CREDITS
Tax Credits, this index

CRIMINAL LAW
Generally, 61

DEDUCTIONS
Income and Income Tax, this index

DEFINITIONS
Generally, 21–26
Benefit justifications, 25
Free riders, 25
Legal definition, 26–27

Public goods and services, taxes as price for, 24–26
Pure tax, basic characteristics, 24–26
Pure taxes and regulatory mandatory payments distinguished
Generally, 21–24
Judicial review, 22
Negative and positive externalities, 21–22
Neutral definition, 23
Progressive taxation, 24

DEPRECIATION DEDUCTION
Income and Income Tax, this index

DISABLED PERSONS
Tax credits, 321

DIVIDENDS
In-kind dividends, 196–197
Qualified dividends, 316–317

EARNED INCOME TAX CREDIT
Tax Credits, this index

ECONOMICS
Generally, 73–108
Accounting
Generally, 106–108
Financial accounting, 106–108
Tax accounting, 108
Automatic stabilizers, taxes as, 82
Economic growth and taxes, 81–82
Economic growth, social gaps, redistribution and taxes
Generally, 90–98
Causes of growing inequality, 95–96
Equality and efficiency trade-off, 90–91
Inequality and economic efficiency, theory and empirical findings, 91–95
Taxes and inequality, 97–98
Efficiency of multi-bases tax system *vs.* single tax, 88
Finance theories
Generally, 104–106
Firms and households, 104–105
Interest and timing, 105–106
Firms and households, finance theories, 104–105
Gross domestic product and other alternative indicators, 79–81
Inequality. Economic growth, social gaps, redistribution and taxes, above
Interest and timing, finance theories, 105–106
Laffer curve, 89–90
Macroeconomics, public economics and
Generally, 78–82
Automatic stabilizers, taxes as, 82
Economic growth and taxes, 81–82
Gross domestic product and other alternative indicators, 79–81
Microeconomics and pricing process
Generally, 73–78
Decision to purchase, 74–76
Price of product, 76–77
Public goods and services, purchase price, 73–78
Reporting, payment and collection, 77–78
Tax justification, 73–78
Tiebout Model, 76
Optimal taxation. Public finance, optimal taxation and, below
Pricing process. Microeconomics, above
Progressive taxation. Welfare economics and progressive taxation, below
Public economics. Macroeconomics, above
Public finance, generally, 82–83
Public finance, optimal taxation and
Generally, 83–98
Deadweight loss, optimal taxation and, 85–88
Economic growth, social gaps, redistribution and taxes, above
Efficiency of multi-bases tax system *vs.* single tax, 88
Laffer curve, 89–90
Ramsey's optimal tax rule, 88–89
Work supply, optimal taxation and, 83–84
Public goods and services, purchase price, 73–78
Ramsey's optimal tax rule, 88–89
Social justice, worldly philosophers and welfare economics, 72–73
Sustainable economic growth, tax rates and, 103–104
Welfare economics and progressive taxation
Generally, 98–104
Justification for progressive tax system, consent to pay and benefit principle, 100, 102–103
Low tax, simple tax, flat tax (Hall and Rabushka), 102
Mirrlee's zero tax rate on high income, 100–101
Progressive tax system and reasons for, 98–100
Social justice, worldly philosophers and welfare economics, 72–73
Sustainable economic growth, tax rates and, 103–104
Zero tax rate, 100–101

ELDERLY AND DISABLED PERSONS
Tax credits, 321

EQUALITY AND INEQUALITY
Constitutional right to equality, 51–52
Inequality. Economics, this index

ESTABLISHMENT CLAUSE
Generally, 46–48

ESTATE, GIFT AND GENERATION SKIPPING TRANSFER TAXES
Generally, 135–144
Federal estate tax, 139–141
Federal gift tax, 141–142
Generation skipping transfer tax, 142–143
Preferred way to tax wealth transfers, 137–138
Taxation of wealth transfer in U.S., 138–143
Transfer tax or tax-free wealth transfer, 143–144
Whether transfer payments should be taxed, 135
Whether wealth transfer should be taxed, 136–137

EXCISE TAXES AND DUTIES
Generally, 145–146

FINANCE THEORIES
Economics, this index

FIRST AMENDMENT
Tax laws and, 45–48

FREE RIDERS
Criminal law, 61
Definitions, 25

FREEDOM OF THE PRESS
Discriminatory taxes and, 48

GENERATION SKIPPING TRANSFER TAX
Generally, 142–143

GIFT TAX
Generally, 141–142

GOALS OF TAX SYSTEM
Generally, 27–31
Narrow approach, rationales and reasons, 29–31
Role of government, differing approaches, 28–29
Size of government, free market, and capitalism, 27–29

GOODWILL
Income and Income Tax, this index

HEALTH INSURANCE
Social Security and Health Insurance, this index

HUMAN RIGHTS
Tax Legislation, Constitutional Law and Threats to Human Rights, this index

IN-KIND INCOME
Income and Income Tax, this index

INCENTIVES AND RELIEFS
Tax Incentives and Other Reliefs, this index

INCOME AND INCOME TAX
Generally, 147–151
Above-the-line deductions
Generally, 276–285
Employee's business expenses, 284
Employers' tax rates and fair compensation to employees, correlation between, 285
Illegal, immoral and anti-public policy expenses, 279
Interest payments, 277–278
Matching rules
Generally, 279–284
Case law, 282
Depreciation, recapture, and negative recapture rules, 282–283
Net operating loss, 283–284
Statutory rules, 281–282
Mixed expenses, business and private consumption, 278
Tax arbitrage, 279
Accumulated/compound interest, 215
Active income, 224–225
Adjusted gross income
Generally, 149, 248–254
Capital expenses, below
Consumption plus saving, 251
Cost of income production, 251–252
Deductible expenses, below
Depreciation deduction, below
Firms' business investment, 249–251
Households' private saving, 249–251
Usage and source sides, deductibility of expenses from, 251–252
Alternative Minimum Tax, this index
Analytical structure, 147
Annuity installment, extracting capital recovery, 191–193
Appeals, 151
Attributes/traits of income
Generally, 189–205
Capital recovery not income, 191–193
Enforced/compulsory earnings and profit, 205
Gain, profit or accretion, 189–190
Illegal activity, earnings from, 203–204
Imputed income, 197–198
In-kind income (non-monetary barter transactions), below
No income if no consumption or savings, 200–202
Realization requirement, 198–200
Barter transactions
Generally, 162–163
In-kind income, below
Below-the-line deductions
Generally, 282
Casualty and theft losses, 291
Charitable contributions, 289–291
Employee's business expenses, unreimbursed, 293–295
Home mortgage interest, 288–289
Itemized deductions
Generally, 288–297
Casualty and theft losses, 291
Charitable contributions, 289–291
Employee's business expenses, unreimbursed, 293–295
General limitation/reduction of itemized deductions, 295–297
Home mortgage interest, 288–289
Local and state taxes, 291–292
Medical expenses, unreimbursed, 292
Miscellaneous itemized deductions, 292–297
Passive income deductions, 295
Special limitation on miscellaneous deductions, 295
Student loan interest, 289
Local and state taxes, 291–292
Medical expenses, unreimbursed, 292
Miscellaneous itemized deductions, 292–297
Passive income deductions, 295
Personal exemption, 287
Standard deductions, 287–288
Student loan interest, 289
British doctrine, 158–160
Capital expenses
Generally, 256–260
Depreciation deduction, below
Immediate deduction, 256–259, 267–268

Pro rating capital/investment expenses
Generally, 260–262
Balance sheet representing accretion to wealth, 260–261
Capital recovery, 261
Saving future expenses, 261–262
Statutory rule and exception, 259–260
Capital gain and ordinary income
Generally, 209–223
Accumulated/compound interest, 215
Bunching and averaging, 211–212
Case law, 217–218
Causes for gains or losses, 215–216, 218–219
Characteristics of capital gain and required adjustments, 210–214
Corporate retained earnings, 215–216
Depreciation deduction, 212–213
Disposition of business, 220–221
Distinction between, 214–221
Ex-post *vs.* ex-anta profits, 215–216
Goodwill, 220
Inflation, capital gain and, 210–211
Intellectual property, 219–220
Internal and external causes for gain, 218–219
Legal distinction, 216–217
Lock-in effect, 213–214
Net capital gain, tax rates under current law, 222–223
Non-recognition tax deferral, 213–214
Purchase price, 212–213
Quasi-exemption, tax deferral, and real exemption for capital gain, 221
Recapture, positive and negative, 212–213
Royalties, 219–220
Seven pillars of capital gain treatment, 217–218
Capital recovery not income, 191–193
Casualty and theft losses, 32–33, 291
Charitable contributions, itemized deductions, 289–291
Child care, deductible expenses, 255–256
Classification of income
Generally, 148–149, 207–226
Capital gain and ordinary income, above
Losses. Ordinary income and losses, below
Ordinary income and losses, below
Reasons for classification, 207
Redundancy, 207–209
Commuting to workplace, deductible expenses, 254–255
Compensation in kind, 235–237
Compliance, 151
Computations. Tax Computations, this index
Consumption vis a vis income. Consumption Tax, this index
Corporate retained earnings, 215–216
Credits. Tax Credits, this index
Deductible expenses
Generally, 252–254
Capital expenses, above
Child care, 255–256
Commuting to workplace, 254–255
Flexible spending accounts, employer exclusion, 256
Ordinary and necessary expenses. Above-the-line deductions, above
Private consumption, expenses for, 254–256
Deductions
Above-the-line deductions, above
Below-the-line deductions, above
Deductible expenses, above
Depreciation deduction, below
Ordinary and necessary expenses. Above-the-line deductions, above
Depreciation deduction
Generally, 263–269
Capital gain and ordinary income, 212–213
Depreciable/amortizable and non-depreciable/amortizable assets, 264–265
Economic depreciation, 262
Goodwill and other intangible assets, 268–269
Immediate deduction of capital expenses, special rules, 267–268
Intangible assets
Generally, 268–269
Acquisition and maintenance, 272–276
Preserving existing assets, 272–276
Methods of depreciation, 263–269
Modified accelerated cost recovery system (MACRS) and alternative system, 265–267
Straight line depreciation, 263–264
Tangible assets
Generally, 269–272
Maintenance *vs.* upgrading and improving assets, 269–270
Preserving existing assets, 270–272
Disputes, 151
Dividend in-kind, 196–197
Double deductibility of interest, 169
Dual definition, sources *vs.* usage, 157–158
Employee's business expenses, 284, 293–295
Employees and self-employed, 224–225
Employers' tax rate and employee compensation, correlation between, 240–241, 285
Enforced/compulsory earnings and profit, 205
Enforcement, 151
Exemptions. Tax Exemptions, this index
Flexible spending accounts, employer exclusion, 256
Gain, profit or accretion, 189–190
Goodwill
Capital gain and ordinary income, 220
Depreciation deduction, 268–269
Gross income
Adjusted gross income, 149
Statutory gross income, 205–206
Historical background, 183
Home mortgage interest, 288–289
Illegal activity, earnings from, 203–204
Illegal, immoral and anti-public policy expenses, 279
Imputed income, 160–162, 197–198

In-kind income (non-monetary barter transactions)
Generally, 162–163, 193–197
Below market interest loan, 195–196
Dividend in-kind, 196–197
Exchange of goods or services free of charge, 193–195
Quantification of compensation in kind, 235–237
Income quantification, 149
Interest
Above-the-line deductions, 277–278
Double deductibility, 169
Home mortgages, 288–289
Interest loan, below market, 195–196
International activities and investments, taxation of, 149
Itemized deductions. Below-the-line deductions, above
Local and state taxes, itemized deductions, 291–292
Losses. Ordinary income and losses, below
Lottery gains, quantification of income, 237–238
Matching rules. Above-the-line deductions, above
Medical expenses, unreimbursed, itemized deductions, 292
Methodology, 147–151
Miscellaneous itemized deductions, 292–297
Narrow *vs.* broad
Generally, 158–170
Barter transactions, 162–163
British doctrine, 158–160
Double deductibility of interest, 169
Imputed income, 160–162
In-kind income, 162–163
Realization requirement, 163–168
Net wealth = future income
Generally, 155–156
Tax rates, 156
Taxpayer's convenience and efficiency, 156
Theoretical merits, 155
Uncertainty, 155–156
No income if no consumption or savings, 200–202
Ordinary and necessary expenses. Above-the-line deductions, above
Ordinary income and capital gain. Capital gain and ordinary income, above
Ordinary income and losses
Generally, 223–226
Active income, 224–225
Basic categories of ordinary income, 223–224
Employees and self-employed, 224–225
Trade or business, 224–226
Passive income deductions, 295
Personal exemption, 287
Prizes, quantification of income, 237–238
Quantification of income
Generally, 235–238
Compensation in kind, 235–237
Prizes and lottery gains, 237–238
Realization requirement, 163–168, 198–200
Returns, 151
Social and economic significance of exemptions, deductions, offsetting losses and tax credits, 240–242
Statutory gross income, 205–206
Structure of tax system, 184–185
Student loan interest, 289
Tax accounting and taxable period, 150
Tax arbitrage, 279
Tax base
Generally, 147–148, 187–206
Attributes/traits of income. Income, this index
Sources side, defining income from, 187–188
Statutory provisions, 187
Taxable income, 239–240
Uses side, defining income from, 188–189
Tax Unit, this index
Taxable income, 149
Taxable year, 150
Trade or business, 224–226
Transnational Activity, this index

INCOME AVERAGING
Saving and pension plans, 324

INJURIES OR SICKNESS
Tax exemptions, 244–245

INTEREST
Accumulated/compound interest, 215
Below market interest loan, 195–196
Double deductibility, 169
Finance theories, interest and timing, 105–106

INTERNATIONAL LAW
Generally, 58–61
Bilateral tax treaties, 59, 231
Corporate taxation, global agreement, 60–61
Double non-taxation, eliminating, 60
Foreign money, hiding by American taxpayers, 59
Transnational Activity, this index

INVENTORY
Tax accounting, 301–303

JUDICIAL REVIEW
Administrative actions, 57–58
Tax Legislation, Constitutional Law and Threats to Human Rights, this index

LEGAL SOURCES
Generally, 39–61
Administrative Law, this index
Criminal law, 61
International Law, this index
Other branches of law, 61
Tax law, 61
Tax Legislation, Constitutional Law and Threats to Human Rights, this index

LEGISLATION
Tax Legislation, Constitutional Law and Threats to Human Rights, this index
Tax reliefs, legislation of, 34

LEVYING TAXES
Power to Levy Taxes, this index

LOCAL AND STATE TAXES
Itemized deductions, 291–292

LOTTERY GAINS
Quantification of income, 237–238

MEALS OR LODGING
Furnished for convenience of employer, 242–244

MEDICARE AND MEDICAID
Generally, 131

NET WEALTH
Income, this index

NON-LEGAL SOURCES
Generally, 63–108
Economics, this index
Philosophy, this index

OCCUPATIONS
Freedom of occupation and tax legislation, 54–55

OLD AGE, SURVIVORS, AND DISABILITY INSURANCE (OASDI)
Generally, 129

OPTIMAL TAXATION
Economics, this index
One tax base *vs.* multiple bases, optimal taxation and equity, 115
Power to levy taxes, 13–14

ORDINARY INCOME
Income and Income Tax, this index

PENSION PLANS
Averaging income through saving and pension plans, 324

PHILOSOPHY
Generally, 63–73
Benefit principle
Ability to pay, 71–72
Joint project doctrine, role of tax and benefit principle, 68
Distributive justice, 71
Economic allegiance, concept of, 69
Human, real and social capitals, modern synergies, 68–69
Joint project doctrine
Labor justification, 65–67
Public property, concept of, 69–70
Role of tax and benefit principle, 68
Labor justification and joint project concept, 65–67
Labor justification for property (John Locke), 64–65
Profit-sharing mechanism, tax as, 70
Property rights, laws, and taxes, 63–64
Public property, concept of, and joint project doctrine, 69–70
Social justice, worldly philosophers and welfare economics, 72–73
Tax justification—forced labor, confiscation, consent and entitlement, 63

POWER TO LEVY TAXES
Generally, 7–17
Certainty requirement
Generally, 9–11
Non-arbitrary, 10
Realization requirement, certainty and, 10
Retroactive taxes, 9–10
Simplicity, 10–11
Convenience of contributor
Generally, 11–12
Discretionary power to consume and personal exemptions, 12
Human dignity, 12
Timing and tax payments, 11–12
Discretionary power to consume and personal exemptions, 12
Efficiency of tax administration, 12
Equality and efficiency, 15
Fairness and equality, 14
Good tax, requirements of, 9
No taxation without representation, 7–8
Non-arbitrary, 10
Optimal taxation, 13–14
Public consent, 7–8
Quality of tax laws and adjustment to constitutional principles, 8–9
Realization requirement, certainty and, 10
Retroactive taxes, 9–10
Road map, 15–17
Simplicity, 10–11
Timing and tax payments, 11–12

PRICING PROCESS
Microeconomics and pricing process. Economics, this index

PRIZES
Quantification of income, 237–238

PROGRESSIVE TAXATION
Welfare economics. Economics, this index

PROPERTY AND REAL ESTATE TAX
Generally, 125–126

PROPERTY RIGHTS
Generally, 55–56, 63–64

PUBLIC FINANCE
Economics, this index

PUNITIVE TAXES
Constitution and, 53–54

REAL ESTATE TAX
Generally, 125–126

REGULATIONS
Administrative Law, this index

RELIEF FROM TAXES
Tax Incentives and Other Reliefs, this index

RELIGION
Establishment Clause, taxes and, 46–48

RETIREMENT
Saver's credit, 324

RETROACTIVE TAXES
Constitution and, 52–53
Power to levy taxes, 9–10

SCHOLARSHIPS
Tax exemptions, qualified scholarships for students, 246–247

SOCIAL SECURITY AND HEALTH INSURANCE
Generally, 127–133
Adverse selection, 127–128
Affordable Care Act (Obamacare), 41–43, 131–132
Federal medical insurance, 130–131
Mandatory programs, need for, 127–128
Medicare and Medicaid, 131
Old Age, Survivors, and Disability Insurance (OASDI), 129
Social security in U.S., 128–133
Supplemental Security Income (SSI), 129–130
Tax credits, 321–322
Unemployment insurance, 129–130

SOURCES
Legal Sources, this index
Non-Legal Sources, this index

STANDARD OF LIVING
Dignified minimum standard of living, tax and right to, 50–51

STANDING
Taxpayer standing, 45

STATUTE OF LIMITATIONS
IRS, special statute, 58

STUDENT LOANS
Interest deduction, 289

SUPPLEMENTAL SECURITY INCOME (SSI)
Generally, 129–130

TAX ACCOUNTING
Generally, 108, 299–303
Accrual basis, 301
Cash method, 300–301
Income reporting, 300
Inventory, 301–303
Taxable period, 150

TAX BASE
Income and Income Tax, this index
One tax base *vs.* multiple bases, optimal taxation and equity, 115

TAX COMPUTATIONS
Generally, 150, 319–330
Alternative Minimum Tax, this index
Credits. Tax Credits, this index
Tax rates and tentative tax due, 319

TAX CREDITS
Generally, 319–328
Adoption expenses, 321
Affordable housing developers, 322–333
American Opportunity Tax Credits, 323
Averaging income through saving and pension plans, 324
Child care credit, 320–321
Children and dependents, 255–256, 320
Earned income tax credit
Generally, 325–327
Current system, 325–327
Rationale and its development, 325
Educational benefits, 323
Elderly and permanently and totally disabled persons, 321
Exemptions or deductions compared, 241–242
Foreign tax credits, 230–231, 328
Health care, 321–322
Lifetime learning credit, 323
New home ownership, 322
Parents
Generally, 320–321
Adoption expenses, 321
Child care credit, 320–321
Expenses of children and dependents, 320
Retirement saver's credit, 324

TAX DEDUCTIONS
Income and Income Tax, this index

TAX EXEMPTIONS
Generally, 242–248
Accident and health plan, employer contributions, 245–246
Disguised exemptions, 247–248
Employer's tax rate and level of employee's compensation, possible relation between, 240–241
Meals or lodging furnished for convenience of employer, 242–244
Net income concept, exemptions derived from, 242–245
Personal physical injuries or sickness, compensation for, 244–245
Qualified scholarships for students, 246–247
Scholarships for students, 246–247
Simplicity and administrative efficiency, 248
Social and economic significance, 240
Tax credits compared, 241–242
Tax incentives, exemptions intended to serve as
Generally, 242–247
Accident and health plan, employer contributions, 245–246
Qualified scholarships for students, 246–247
Tax savings, 240

TAX INCENTIVES AND OTHER RELIEFS (TRI)
Generally, 31–35
Casualty and theft losses, 32–33, 291
Economic activity benefiting the public, 33
Efficiency considerations, 35
Encouraging performance of activities or behaviors, 33
Exemptions intended to serve as incentives, 245–247
Government goals, executing and promoting, 33
Importance of and distinction between tax, TRIs and PMPs, 36–38

Legislation of tax reliefs, 34
Minimum income requirement, 31
Negative tax reliefs, 36
Phase-out of tax reliefs, 35–36
Pigovian tax payments (PMPs), 36–38
Privatization of government responsibilities, 34–35
Risky use of, 3–5
Selective discriminatory TRI, 35
Special personal needs and circumstances, 31–32
Who bears the burden and who enjoys, 5–6

TAX LEGISLATION, CONSTITUTIONAL LAW AND THREATS TO HUMAN RIGHTS
Generally, 39–56
Confiscatory nature of payments, 55–56
Consent, constitutional right not to pay without, 48–50
Defining income, 40–41
Dignified minimum standard of living, tax and right to, 50–51
Equality, constitutional right to, 51–52
Establishment Clause, taxes and, 46–48
First Amendment, tax laws and, 45–48
Freedom of the press, discriminatory taxes and, 48
Judicial review. Substantive judicial review of tax legislation, below
Lochner era cases, 43–44
Obamacare and required minimum essential coverage, 41–43
Occupation, freedom of, and tax legislation, 54–55
Power to lay taxes, constitutional provisions, 39–40
Property right, taxes and, 55–56
Punitive taxes, Constitution and, 53–54
Quality and substance of tax legislation, 40–44
Reluctance of courts to review fiscal legislation, 42–44
Retroactive taxes, Constitution and, 52–53
Standing as taxpayer, 45
Substantive judicial review of tax legislation
Generally, 44–55
Consent, constitutional right not to pay without, 48–50
Dignified minimum standard of living, tax and right to, 50–51
Equality, constitutional right to, 51–52
Establishment Clause, taxes and, 46–48
First Amendment, tax laws and, 45–48
Freedom of the press, discriminatory taxes and, 48
Occupation, freedom of, and tax legislation, 54–55
Power to tax, limitations on, 44–45
Punitive taxes, Constitution and, 53–54
Retroactive taxes, Constitution and, 52–53
Standing as taxpayer, 45
Takings Clause and confiscatory nature of payments, 55–56

TAX UNIT
Generally, 150, 305–317
C corporations
Generally, 314
Distribution of earnings, 316–317
Possible triple tax, 314–316
Corporations
Generally, 310–312
C corporations, above
Possible triple tax, 314–316
S corporations and LLCs, 313–314
Dependent children, 309–310
Individuals
Generally, 305–310
Dependent children, 309–310
Married couple dilemma, 305–309
Married couple dilemma, 305–309
S corporations and LLCs, 313–314
VAT, firms as tax unit, 117–118

TRANSNATIONAL ACTIVITY
Generally, 227–233
Benefit principle, 228
Cyber activities, taxation of, 232–233
Double taxation, prevention of
Generally, 228–229
Foreign tax credits, 230–231
Tax treaties, 231
Unilateral and bilateral means, 230–231
Efficiency consideration, 227–229
Foreign tax credits, 230–231
International tax competition, double taxation and double non-taxation, 232
Normative consideration, 227–228
Tax jurisdiction
Justification, 227–228
Territorial and personal connection, 229–230

TREATIES
Bilateral tax treaties, 59, 231

UNEMPLOYMENT INSURANCE
Generally, 129–130

VALUE ADDED TAX
Generally, 114, 117–123
Basic principles, 117–120
Canceled transaction and refund taxes, 122–123
Destination principle, 119
E-commerce transactions, 119–120
Final tax burden on consumers, 117
Firms as tax unit, 117–118
Illustration, 121–122
Invoice-tax credit, 118
Method of calculation, 118
Non-profit organizations and financial institutions, VAT on, 123
Operation, 120–121
Payments or refunds (third stage), 121
Self-administration, 118
Tax base, consumption-cash flow, 117
Tax exemption and zero tax rate, 119
Tax neutrality and prevention of double taxation, 118
Taxing imports and exempting exports, 119
Tentative tax, calculating (first step), 120

Total invoice tax, summing up (second stage), 120–121

VARIETY OF TAXES AND OTHER MANDATORY PAYMENTS
Generally, 113–115
One tax base *vs.* multiple bases, optimal taxation and equity, 115
Value Added Tax, this index

WEALTH TRANSFER
Estate, Gift and Generation Skipping Transfer Taxes, this index

WELFARE ECONOMICS
Economics, this index

ZERO TAX RATE
VAT, tax exemption and zero tax rate, 119
Welfare economics and progressive taxation, 100–101